RICHARD II

RICHARD II

Nigel Saul

YALE UNIVERSITY PRESS
NEW HAVEN AND LONDON

Set in New Baskerville by Best-set Typesetter Ltd, Hong Kong
Printed in Great Britain by St Edmundsbury Press

Library of Congress Cataloging-in-Publication Data

Saul, Nigel.
    Richard II/Nigel Saul.
    Includes bibliographical references and index.
    ISBN 0–300–07003–9 (hbk.)
    ISBN 0–300–07875–7 (pbk.)
    1. Richard II. King of England, 1367–1400.   2. Great Britain—
History—Richard II. 1377–1399.   3. Great Britain—Kings and
rulers—Biography.   4. Civilization, Medieval—14th century.
I. Title.
DA235.S26   1997
942.03′8′092—dc20
[B]   96–36062
                                                                                               CIP

A catalogue record for this book is available from the British Library.

3 5 7 9 10 8 6 4

For Jane, Dominic and Louise

CONTENTS

ILLUSTRATIONS

PLATES

MAPS

PREFACE

Richard II's career encompasses all the elements of a tragedy. At the end, there is the terrible denouement: the king's departure for Ireland, his cousin's return from France, Richard's inexorable loss of power, his deposition by the estates and his miserable death in prison. Further back, there are the disappointments and misfortunes of his private life: the premature loss of his beloved wife Anne, his subsequent search for companionship, his marriage to the child-bride Isabel and his failure to sire an heir. In his youth he had suffered the premature death of his father, the experience of a lonely upbringing and the destruction of his friends by his Appellant opponents. It seems that hardly ever in his life was the darker side absent. Even his greatest moment – the meeting with the rebels at Smithfield in 1381 – raised problems for him in that it came too soon: all his life he lived under its shadow.

Richard's career has long been a source of fascination to novelists and playwrights. Strangely, this century it has received relatively little attention from academic historians. It is over fifty years since a serious full-length biography of the king was published. The last one, Anthony Steel's *Richard II*, appeared in 1941. It is a book with many admirable qualities. It shook off the legacy of Stubbsian 'constitutionalism', and it offered the reader a vivid, and vigorously argued, view of the king. But today it comes across as curiously dated. Steel confined himself to use of the published sources – chiefly the chronicles but also, among the record sources, the chancery enrolments. Oddly for one who had worked so extensively on the exchequer rolls, he never drew on the documentary sources – the issue rolls, wardrobe books and inventories, all of which contain valuable material on the king. A second weakness of the book was that it was built around a political narrative. There was little or no discussion of Richard's piety, the role and character of his court, and the artistic and cultural achievements of the reign. These are significant lacunae. A modern academic biography of Richard needs to discuss these issues and to incorporate them into the general picture. Some of the most important recent advances in understanding the king have been made by scholars working in the fields of literary and art history.

My work on the present biography has absorbed me for the better part of ten years. In the course of this time I have incurred a good many debts. The first is to my college, Royal Holloway and Bedford New College, in the University of London. The college has not only provided me with an agreeable academic environment in which to work; it has also generously supported me in many ways, notably in the granting of sabbatical leave. Within the college, I owe an especial debt to my colleagues in the history department, and in particular to two successive heads of department, Jonathan Riley-Smith and Francis Robinson, for the support and encouragement which they have given. Grants over the years from the departmental research fund have allowed me to visit archives and attend conferences abroad. For much of my time at Royal Holloway I have been engaged in the teaching of a special subject on 'England in the Reign of Richard II', and it is a pleasure to acknowledge the stimulus which teaching of the subject has provided. It is often observed that heavyweight history books are a by-product of special subject teaching, and this one, I suppose, bears out the truth of the remark. May I take the opportunity, in particular, to thank four students who have supplied me with references or who have assisted with bibliographical searches – Shelagh Mitchell, Anna Gane, Pat Hawkins and Janet Randall. I realize, however, that there is an unconscious but genuine debt to all who have taken the course.

A book of this kind is in many ways a co-operative venture. Precisely for that reason my greatest debt is to all the other scholars working on Richard II's reign who have given me assistance over the years. In particular, may I thank Chris Given-Wilson, George Stow, Anthony Goodman, Simon Walker, Michael Bennett, Caroline Barron, Anthony Gross, Richard Schneider, Kay Staniland, Alistair Minnis, Dillian Gordon and Carole Rawcliffe, who have all, at various times, commented on my ideas or supplied me with references. I am also grateful to Jeremy Catto, Ralph Griffiths, Dorothy Johnston and David Morgan for reading drafts of chapters. Anthony Tuck kindly undertook the burden of reading a draft of the entire book in typescript. I owe particular thanks to Geoffrey Martin for allowing me access to the proofs of his edition of Knighton's chronicle in advance of publication.

Over a period of some eight or nine years many of us with interests in the later fourteenth century have had the opportunity to meet and converse at the sessions on Richard II and his age at the International Medieval Congress at Kalamazoo, Michigan. The Kalamazoo Congress has become a focal point for Richard II studies. A great deal of the credit for this goes to the convenor of the sessions, Professor Jim Gillespie, formerly of Notre Dame College of Ohio. Jim Gillespie's unique blend of geniality, impish humour and negotiating skill has made him the ideal conference organizer, and it is thanks to his initiative that the visit to Carlos Murphy's Irish-Mexican restaurant has become the much looked forward to high point of the conferences.

In its later stages this book has benefited greatly from the guidance of
Professor Jack Scarisbrick of Warwick University, the general editor of
the series. Jack Scarisbrick's ruthless, and entirely justified, use of the
pruning knife has made the book both sharper and more exciting to
read.

To conclude, I wish to record two more tokens of appreciation. The
first is to the Dean and Chapter of Westminster Abbey for permission
to consult, and quote from, the abbey archives. The second is to the
British Academy for the grant of a term's leave which allowed me to
complete this book. The dedication is to those who have had to endure
the presence of Richard II in their lives for so long.

ABBREVIATED REFERENCES

The following abbreviations are used in the footnotes. Generally, the full title is given only for the first reference, and thereafter short titles are used. These are fully extended in the bibliography.

All manuscript references are to documents in the Public Record Office, London, unless otherwise stated.

Annales	*Annales Ricardi Secundi et Henrici Quarti*, in J. de Trokelowe et Anon., *Chronica et Annales*, ed. H.T. Riley (Rolls series, 1866)
Anon.	*The Anonimalle Chronicle 1333–81*, ed. V.H. Galbraith (Manchester, 1927)
Arch. Cant.	*Archaeologia Cantiana*
BIHR	*Bulletin of the Institute of Historical Research*
BJRL	*Bulletin of the John Rylands Library*
BL	British Library
BRUC	A.B. Emden, *A Biographical Register of the University of Cambridge to 1500* (Cambridge, 1963)
BRUO	A.B. Emden, *A Biographical Register of the University of Oxford to AD 1500* (3 vols, Oxford, 1957–9)
Brut	*The Brut, or The Chronicles of England*, ii, ed. F.W.D. Brie (Early English Text Society, original series, cxxxvi, 1908)
CA	*Chronicon Angliae 1328–1388*, ed. E.M. Thompson (Rolls series, 1874)
CCR	*Calendar of Close Rolls*
CFR	*Calendar of Fine Rolls*
Chrons. Revolution	*Chronicles of the Revolution, 1397–1400*, ed. C. Given-Wilson (Manchester, 1993)
CP	*The Complete Peerage*, ed. G.E. Cokayne *et al.* (12 vols in 13, London, 1910–57)
CPR	*Calendar of Patent Rolls*
Creton	*A Metrical History of the Deposition of Richard II* attributed to Jean Creton, ed. J. Webb, *Archaeologia*, xx (1814)
CRSD	*Chronique du Religieux de Saint-Denys*, ed. M. Bellaguet (6 vols, Paris, 1839–52)
DC	*Diplomatic Correspondence of Richard II*, ed. E. Perroy (Camden Society 3rd series, xlviii, 1933)
DNB	*Dictionary of National Biography* (63 vols, London, 1885–1900)
EcHR	*Economic History Review*

EETS	Early English Text Society
EHR	*English Historical Review*
Eulogium	*Eulogium Historiarum sive Temporis*, ed. F.S. Haydon (3 vols, Rolls series, 1858–63), iii
Feud. Aids	*Feudal Aids* (6 vols, London, 1899–1920)
Foed.	T. Rymer, *Foedera, Conventiones, Litterae etc.*, ed. G. Holmes (20 vols, London, 1704–35)
Froissart	J. Froissart, *Chronicles*, ed. T. Johnes (2 vols, London, 1862)
HA	T. Walsingham, *Historia Anglicana*, ed. H.T. Riley (2 vols, Rolls series, 1863–4)
HKW	*History of the King's Works*, ed. R.A. Brown, H.M. Colvin, A.J. Taylor (3 vols, London, 1963)
House of Commons	*The History of Parliament. The House of Commons 1386–1421*, ed. J.S. Roskell, L. Clark, C. Rawcliffe (4 vols, Stroud, 1992)
HR	*Historical Research* (formerly *Bulletin of the Institute of Historical Research*)
HT	*History Today*
HVR	*Historia Vitae et Regni Ricardi Secundi*, ed. G.B. Stow (Philadelphia, 1977)
JBS	*Journal of British Studies*
JEH	*Journal of Ecclesiastical History*
JMH	*Journal of Medieval History*
KC	*Knighton's Chronicle 1337–1396*, ed. G.H. Martin (Oxford, 1995)
P&P	*Past and Present*
PH	*Parliamentary History*
PPC	*Proceedings and Ordinances of the Privy Council of England*, ed. N.H. Nicolas (7 vols, London, 1834–7)
Rot. Scot.	*Rotuli Scotiae* (2 vols, London, 1814–19)
RP	*Rotuli Parliamentorum* (6 vols, London, 1767–77)
SR	*Statutes of the Realm* (11 vols, London, 1810–28)
Traison et Mort	*Chronique de la traison et mort de Richart II*, ed. B. Williams (London, 1846)
TRHS	*Transactions of the Royal Historical Society*
Usk	*Chronicon Adae de Usk*, ed. E.M. Thompson (London, 1904)
WAM	Westminster Abbey Muniments
WC	*The Westminster Chronicle 1381–1394*, ed. L.C. Hector and B.F. Harvey (Oxford, 1982)
WHR	*Welsh History Review*
YAJ	*Yorkshire Archaeological Journal*

Chapter 1

RICHARD II AND SHAKESPEARE

Richard II is one of the most powerful of Shakespeare's history plays. It not only contains some of Shakespeare's most impressive poetry; its lyrical pathos and aesthetic unity give it a compelling force which its author rarely subsequently surpassed.

The theme of the play is provided by the events of Richard's last years – his exile of his cousin Bolingbroke, Bolingbroke's return, the king's downfall and deposition. The outcome of events is never in doubt: Richard's hubris, we know, is going to be followed by his nemesis. What attracts our attention is Richard's response to his plight. At the beginning, Richard is shown as a foppish, irresponsible young man, suspicious and cruel: his judgement is poor and his character ill-matched to his office. But later, in Acts III–V, as his material fortunes decline and the reality of power slips from his grasp, so he grows in stature: he becomes the reflective, philosophic king, bowing to circumstance. The play assumes the nature of a Passion.

Richard II was conceived as the first episode in an historical tetralogy. Roughly three or four years before, Shakespeare had written the 'Wars of the Roses' cycle: the three parts of *Henry VI* and *Richard III*. Encouraged by the success of these plays he turned to the earlier period: *Richard II*, written in 1595, was followed by the two parts of *Henry IV* and *Henry V*. In both tetralogies dramatic unity is provided by a single underlying idea: the terrible consequences for a realm of usurpation. The theme is announced in the bishop of Carlisle's speech in the deposition scene of *Richard*:

> My Lord of Herford here, whom you call king,
> Is a foul traitor to proud Herford's king,
> And if you crown him, let me prophesy –
> The blood of English shall manure the ground,
> And future ages groan for this foul act,
> Peace shall go sleep with Turks and infidels,
> And, in this seat of peace, tumultuous wars
> Shall kin with kin, and kind with kind, confound.
> Disorder, horror, fear, and mutiny,
> Shall here inhabit, and this land be call'd
> The field of Golgotha and dead men's skulls –

1

O, if you raise this house against this house,
It will the woefullest division prove
That ever fell upon this cursed earth.
Prevent it, resist it, let it not be so,
Lest child, child's children, cry against you woe.[1]

To Shakespeare and his contemporaries the history of fifteenth-century England was a commentary on the bishop's prophetic utterance. All the ills that were to afflict the realm – the rivalry between the dynasties, the factionalism and the bloodshed – flowed from Hereford's (Bolingbroke's) rebellion against Richard. Hereford was a perjurer and a usurper.[2] Because of the breach of his oath to his sovereign he had brought a curse on his dynasty. Every generation of his line was in some way to suffer for this. Henry himself was cursed with an 'unquiet' reign punctuated by rebellion.[3] Henry V, his successor, appeared to escape the hand of fate: his wisdom and prowess brought him mighty achievements in war against the French. It was in the reign of his son Henry VI that the full horror of the curse was to be realized. The kingship of Lancaster fell apart, and the country was dragged into civil war. Amid scenes of turmoil and strife, Henry VI was displaced by the Yorkist challenger, Edward IV. Edward, like Henry IV before him, brought many qualities to the exercise of government, but, again like Henry IV, he had committed the sin of perjury. Accordingly, punishment was visited on his dynasty by the murder of his sons and the rise of Richard of Gloucester. But by this time a saviour was waiting in the wings, in the person of Henry Tudor. Returning from exile, Henry triumphed over Richard at Bosworth and providentially healed the divisions by marrying Elizabeth of York. In the union that he effected between the two roses the greatness of the Elizabethan age was born:

We will unite the white rose and the red:
... England hath long been mad and scarr'd herself;
The brother blindly shed the brother's blood.[4]

Underlying Shakespeare's preoccupation with civil strife was a deeper concern for the social order. In the Elizabethans' world view civil discord imperilled the very existence of society.[5] This was essentially

---

[1] W. Shakespeare, *King Richard II*, ed. P. Ure (London, 5th edn, 1961), IV, i, 134–49.
[2] E.M.W. Tillyard, *Shakespeare's History Plays* (London, 1946), 59–61, offers a useful discussion of the history cycle. See also *King Richard II*, ed. J. Dover Wilson (Cambridge, 1939), xxxv–xxxviii.
[3] *King Richard II*, Act V, scene vi, 38–52.
[4] *King Richard III*, Act V, scene iv, 32–7.
[5] Tillyard, *Shakespeare's History Plays*, 10–17.

the medieval view of the world. Everyone and everything was held to have its allotted place. From the bottom of society to the top, people were linked in a 'great chain of being', which duplicated the order in heaven. The constituent parts of this order had to be nourished and protected. As Ulysses said in *Troilus and Cressida*:

Take but degree away, untune that string;
And hark what discord follows.[6]

If the polity fell apart, the universal principle of degree would be upset and the very existence of society endangered.

Ulysses's view was one that was widely held, and people would have seen it as a theme of *Richard II*. But there is evidence that there was another way in which the play was interpreted – as a political allegory. Lambarde tells a famous story of Queen Elizabeth coming from the play saying 'I am Richard II; know ye not that'.[7] Evidently, in Shakespeare's picture of a vain ruler encouraging flatterers and permitting unjust taxation she saw herself. But to a number of her subjects there were more striking resemblances between her favourite, the earl of Essex, and the usurper Bolingbroke. Essex, like Bolingbroke, courted the favour of the crowds; and Essex, like Bolingbroke, risked rebelling against his anointed sovereign. In February 1601, shortly before the earl's ill-fated putsch, a group of his followers procured a performance of *Richard II* at the Globe – doubtless in expectation of putting the audience in an appropriate frame of mind.[8] That the play had contemporary resonances was apparent to the censors in the chamberlain's office. When the first edition – the Quarto edition – was published in 1597, the chamberlain insisted on deleting the central deposition scene in Act IV, scene i; and the scene was omitted in the two subsequent editions that appeared in Elizabeth's lifetime.[9] In the uncertain conditions of the late 1590s, references to the uncrowning of a monarch could be misinterpreted.

It is doubtful if Shakespeare himself intended his play to be read in such directly political terms. It was never his practice to write topical plays as such. For the most part, his treatment of Richard appears to have been determined by his sources. The most important of these was Holinshed's *Chronicles of England, Scotland and Ireland* (1586–7), a compilation which provided him with the basic subject matter of his play. Other works that he drew on were Samuel Daniel's *The First Fowre Bookes*

---

[6] *Troilus and Cressida*, Act I, scene iii, 109–10.
[7] Lambarde's report is printed in Shakespeare, *King Richard II*, ed. P. Ure, lix.
[8] E.K. Chambers, *William Shakespeare. A Study of the Facts and Problems* (2 vols, Oxford, 1930), i, 354.
[9] *King Richard II*, ed. Ure, lvii.

of the civile warres (1595), Edward Hall's *The union of the two noble and illustre famelies of Lancastre & Yorke* (1548), and the anonymous play *Woodstock*; very likely *Woodstock* provided him with the inspiration for his portrayal of Gaunt.[10] Most, perhaps all, of these writers drew directly or indirectly on chroniclers who had written at the time. Holinshed, for example, drew heavily on the critical account of Thomas Walsingham of St Albans. Others, such as Daniel, drew on the more sympathetic French accounts of Jean Creton and the author of the *Traison et Mort.* The mixture of styles that we see in Shakespeare's treatment of Richard derives in large part from the differing emphases in the sources he was drawing on. Thus the anti-Ricardian tone of Acts I and II reflects his reliance on Holinshed, while the more sympathetic treatment in the later Acts was heavily indebted to sources of French origin.

Shakespeare's portrayal of the king, an amalgam of conflicting sources and the contrivance of literary artifice, has been heavily criticized by historians. R.H. Jones has denounced it as 'historically distorted', while Steel thought it over-dramatized.[11] Certainly, there are elements in it that are unhistorical. The real Richard was never put on trial in parliament; nor did he possess a horse called Roan Barbary. But the playwright's portrayal of the king, particularly in his fallen state, brings us remarkably close to the historical figure. The historical Richard was highly self-conscious in his kingship, just as Shakespeare's Richard is; he was also prone to changes of temperament, no less than the Richard of Shakespeare's creation. Certainly criticism can be made of the play. But that criticism should centre less on the liberties that Shakespeare took than on his rather striking omissions. Shakespeare ignored everything that happened between the king's coronation and 1397.[12] The Peasants' Revolt, the Appellant crisis, the pacification of Ireland and the making of peace with France: these are all omitted.[13] The reason, as Margaret Aston has pointed out, is that they had no relevance to his dramatic purpose. Shakespeare began with the Mowbray–Bolingbroke dispute because, for him, that was where the

---

[10] The fullest discussion of the sources of the play is ibid., xxx–lvii. In *Woodstock* the role of patriotic counsellor was taken by Thomas of Woodstock, duke of Gloucester, hero of the play and the king's youngest uncle. Shakespeare transferred the role to John of Gaunt.

[11] R.H. Jones, *The Royal Policy of Richard II: Absolutism in the Later Middle Ages* (Oxford, 1968), 113; A. Steel, *Richard II* (Cambridge, 1941), 2–3.

[12] A point forcefully made by H.F. Hutchison, 'Shakespeare and Richard II', *HT,* xi (April 1961), 236–44.

[13] The Appellant crisis refers to the takeover of government in 1387 by five lords (the duke of Gloucester, and the earls of Arundel, Warwick, Derby and Nottingham) who, in the parliament of February 1388 'appealed' or prosecuted the king's favourites. For discussion of the crisis, see below, Chapter 9.

chain of events culminating in the deposition began.[14] But if a proper perspective is to be gained on the reign, it is necessary to go further back, to Richard's early years as king. The starting point for our story is to be found in the political background to Richard's accession, and the government of England in the 1370s.

[14] M. Aston, 'Richard II and the Wars of the Roses', *The Reign of Richard II. Essays in Honour of May McKisack*, ed. F.R.H. Du Boulay and C.M. Barron (London, 1971), 286.

Chapter 2

BACKGROUND AND UPBRINGING,
1367–77

When Richard was born in 1367, England was the foremost military power in western Europe. Her armies had won spectacular victories in the field over the French and the Scots. Her navy assured her of superiority in the narrow seas; and commanders of English origin were active in theatres of war as far afield as the Baltic and the Mediterranean. No other power of significance could match England in the quality and effectiveness of her fighting men.

The scale of the English achievement was remarkable for a nation so relatively small. When Richard became king the population of England was probably no more than 2–3 million. A couple of generations earlier the figure had been nearer 6–7 million, but the Black Death in 1348–9 had reduced it by almost half. The population of France in the same period was probably in the region of 5–7 million.

The majority of England's people lived in the south, the south-east and the midlands. These were among the richest parts of the country. The soil was fertile and there was a well-established agrarian economy. On a typical southern manor a three- or four-course crop rotation was operated in large open fields divided into strips. Wheat was the most popular cash crop, while oats were grown for fodder and barley for malt. In the hillier areas of the north and the west there was a stronger pastoral emphasis. Here, sheep rearing and cattle grazing were the main sources of livelihood. The clips from the great sheep flocks, particularly those of the Cotswolds, provided England with her most valuable export. Over 40,000 sacks of wool were exported annually when the trade was at its peak in the first decade of the century; over 30,000 were still being exported sixty years later. The taxes levied on these exports, at the rate of 40s a sack, provided the English crown with one of its most lucrative sources of revenue. In the 1370s the yield from these was running at no less than £70,000 annually.[1]

England's administrative system matched the sophistication of its economy. The focal point was the central government at Westminster.

---

[1] W.M. Ormrod, *The Reign of Edward III. Crown and Political Society in England 1327–1377* (New Haven and London, 1990), 207. Ormrod gives figures for the customs revenues as a whole, but the largest element in these was the wool levy.

Broadly speaking, there were two categories of department there, the secretarial and the financial. The main secretarial office was the chancery, whose head, the chancellor, had custody of the great seal. Great seal letters could be issued on orders from the king under the privy seal or the signet, or simply by royal word of mouth; the letters would then be dispatched 'patent' (open) or 'close', as appropriate. On the financial side the main office was the exchequer, which audited the sheriffs' accounts and collected the bulk of the king's income. In Edward I's time a challenge to exchequer supremacy had come from the wardrobe, a household department, but by Richard's reign the wardrobe had declined in importance, and the only other major financial office was the chamber, a kind of royal privy purse. A link between the Westminster-based bureaucracy and the wider realm was provided by the local office-holders of the shires. The key official at this level was the sheriff, whose duties included serving and returning writs, collecting the county farms (revenues) and apprehending malefactors. As a result of the increase in his workload in the thirteenth century, the sheriff was joined by new officials, among them the escheator, who collected the crown's feudal revenues, and later the justices of the peace. Unlike the clerks in the central offices, these local officials were not full-time. They were members of the country gentry who served largely out of self-interest. Their execution of their duties was often patchy; none the less, England was by medieval standards a much governed country.

The power and efficiency of the English state were amply tested in the lengthy wars of the later middle ages. For nearly a century and three-quarters from the 1290s England was engaged in a series of conflicts either in the British Isles or on the continent. The period opened with Edward I's attempts to subdue the Welsh and the Scots. The Welsh were quelled in two fairly brisk campaigns in 1277 and 1282, but the Scots proved harder to overcome. A series of expeditions against them was mounted in the early fourteenth century, but their heavy cost nearly bankrupted the exchequer, and from the end of the 1330s the struggle was gradually abandoned. In the next generation the focus of attention turned to the continent. For more than half a century there had been growing differences with the French over the status of Aquitaine, the English-held duchy in the south-west of France: the point at issue being the terms on which the king of England held the duchy. There had been wars with the French over Aquitaine in 1294 and 1324. In 1337 yet another war broke out, but this time the outcome was different. Edward III, to circumvent the old feudal arguments, claimed the French crown himself. His mother Isabelle, Edward II's queen, had been sister of the last Capetian king, Charles IV, who had died in 1328: Philip IV, who had succeeded to the crown, being Charles's cousin. Philip responded by rejecting Edward's claim, but the

latter pressed his case and found support in the kingdom. In 1338 he
crossed to Flanders. The long struggle known as the Hundred Years
War had begun.

Edward's fortunes in the early stages of the war were mixed. In 1339
he launched an invasion of France from the north-east, but after failing
to take Cambrai, and in danger of running out of money, he had to
retreat. In the following year, despite a naval victory at Sluys, he
achieved little more. In September he agreed to a truce with the
French, and two months later he returned to England. In the following
decade he changed his tactics. Instead of putting a single army in the
field he deployed several simultaneously, with the object of diverting
and distracting the French. The strategy turned out to be remarkably
successful. In 1346 he scored a major victory over the French at Crécy
and twelve months later he took Calais. In the 1350s, after the interruption of the war caused by the Black Death, there were further English
successes. In September 1356 the Black Prince inflicted a surprise
defeat on the French at Poitiers, capturing King John himself. Edward
now felt that he had the crown within his grasp. In 1359 he launched a
massive campaign to deliver the knock-out blow. The campaign, however, faltered and he was obliged to negotiate, but the settlement
agreed at Brétigny (1359–60) conceded one of his key demands –
possession of Aquitaine in full sovereignty. Edward died in 1377 with
the respect and approbation of his subjects.[2]

The reasons for the English successes were several. One of the most
important was the internal disunity of France. By the 1340s there was
growing resentment among the nobility at the centralizing policies of
the Capetians, and many nobles in the north and the west looked to
Edward to champion their grievances. By allying with these lords,
Edward provided himself with bases on the French mainland. A second
reason for Edward's success was that he showed himself a master of
logistical planning. He understood the needs of his men and ensured
that they were met. Sir George Wrottesley commented that the army of
1346 was probably the best equipped to leave England before the
Egyptian expedition of 1882, and the evidence of the exchequer
accounts goes a long way to bear him out.[3] A third factor was Edward's
success in the management of men. The king knew how to enthuse all
those in his service. The leading magnates readily enlisted in his armies.
Henry of Lancaster, his cousin, for example, fought in southern France
in the 1340s and in Brittany and Scotland in the 1350s. The earls of
Northampton and Warwick saw almost continuous service in the cam-

[2] For Walsingham's obituary, see *HA*, i, 327.
[3] M. Prestwich, *The Three Edwards. War and State in England 1272–1377* (London,
1980), 195.

paigns of the 1340s and were at the king's side in 1359. The lesser
nobility and gentry were also active. Probably half of the entire English
nobility and knighthood were present at the siege of Calais in 1347.
These men fought partly for profit, because there were ample pickings
to be made in France, but in part too because of the glamour and
excitement of war: they wanted the opportunity to win fame and
perform brave deeds. Edward knew instinctively how to harness their
enthusiasm to his cause. He frequently organized, and participated in,
tournaments and round tables. He revived and built on his grandfather's cult of King Arthur, and he made the English court a centre of
companionship and honour. His identification of his cause with chivalry lay at the heart of his military success. More than any other European monarch or prince he embodied that vague quality, the spirit of
the age. In England, in the mid- to late fourteenth century, only one
other figure of consequence could match him in fame, honour and
distinction. That was his eldest son, Richard II's father, Edward of
Woodstock, prince of Wales – better known to history by the sobriquet
the 'Black Prince'.

Richard was always to pay conventional homage to the memory of his
father. He punctiliously observed the anniversary of his death each
June, and he commissioned the erection of a magnificent tomb in
his honour in Canterbury Cathedral.[4] None the less, father and son
were men of very different temper and outlook. The prince was a
soldier through and through; his son was of a less warlike disposition.
The prince was a man of vaguely puritanical religion; his son became
almost ostentatiously orthodox. Perhaps only a certain hauteur marked
them as sprung from the same stock. The prince, of course, was essentially a man in the mould of his father and great-grandfather. He was
above all a 'strenuous' knight, a great captain-in-arms.[5] For many of
his contemporaries he was the personification of chivalric courtesy.
To Chandos Herald, his biographer, he was 'the perfect root of
all honour and nobleness, of wisdom, valour and largesse'.[6] To the
chronicler Froissart, another admirer, he was 'the flower of English
knighthood'.[7] Scarcely any contemporary writer on warfare voiced

---

[4] The prince's tomb can be dated on stylistic grounds to the mid-1380s. The
obvious analogy is with the tomb of Edward III at Westminster, which was in hand
in 1386 (*CPR 1385–9*, 127).

[5] For the career of the prince see R. Barber, *Edward, Prince of Wales and Aquitaine*
(London, 1978).

[6] *Life of the Black Prince by the Herald of Sir John Chandos*, ed. M.K. Pope and E.C.
Lodge (Oxford, 1910), 2.

[7] Froissart, i, 508.

criticism of the prince. He was the paragon of virtue, the brave knight *sans reproche.*

The 'Black Prince's' career in arms had begun in 1346, when he was sixteen. In the summer of that year he accompanied his father on the expedition that was to culminate in the battle of Crécy. The king entrusted his son with command of the English van in the engagement. According to Froissart, the aspirant tiro acquitted himself with exceptional distinction. At one point he was completely surrounded by the French and his comrades appealed to his father for help but the latter, refusing, said it was better to let him win his spurs: which by nightfall he had done.[8] Success in a series of later engagements added to his fame: in a skirmish at Calais in 1349 he succeeded in rescuing his father from encirclement and put the enemy to flight; and in a naval engagement in the following year he fought off a large Spanish ship as his own went down. The first major independent command that he was given came in the following decade. In 1355 his father appointed him to the lieutenancy of Aquitaine, in anticipation that he would open a front in the south, while Lancaster opened one in the north. In the early months of his command he was engaged mainly in intermittent plundering and skirmishing. But in the following year, at Poitiers, he scored his most celebrated victory. Overcoming a French host half as large again as his own he cleared the field and took the French king himself prisoner. His reputation was now at its height. The following decade was to bring him further triumphs. In 1367 he launched an invasion of Castile in support of his ally Pedro 'the Cruel', who had been driven from his throne by his half-brother Henry of Trastamara. The English and Castilian armies met at Najera on 3 April, and there the prince won the last of his great victories. In the 1370s he suffered a number of disappointments. While lingering in Spain he contracted dysentery, and it seems that he never properly recovered from it. He went into action again in September 1370, when he besieged and sacked the city of Limoges, but by this time he had become an invalid. His military career was effectively over, and in 1371 he returned to England. In his final bedridden years he had only the memory of his past achievements to sustain him.

Richard's mother, Joan, princess of Wales, was a product of much the same social and cultural milieu as her husband.[9] She was of the blood royal, her father being Edmund of Woodstock, earl of Kent and sixth son of Edward I; and, like her husband-to-be, she was brought up at

---

[8] Ibid., 167.
[9] Little has been published on Joan. There are outlines of her career in *CP*, vii, 150–4, and *DNB*, xxix, 392–3.

court: according to Froissart, after her father's execution for alleged treason it was Queen Philippa who had taken charge of her. Joan grew up to be much admired for her beauty: Froissart described her as 'in her time the most beautiful lady in England, and by far the most amorous'.[10] Not surprisingly, in her teens she became the object of the competing attentions of several of the most celebrated knights of the day. The young William Montagu, second earl of Salisbury, and his steward of the household, Sir Thomas Holand, both wanted to marry her, but it was Holand whom she preferred. It seems that Thomas and Joan lived together for some years under a pre-contract of matrimony, but when the former went on campaign Salisbury married her, almost certainly against her wishes, and Holand had to reassert his rights. In May 1347 he petitioned the pope for her return, and Cardinal Adhémar was instructed to look into the case. He found Sir Thomas's claim to be valid, and in November 1349 a bull dissolving the marriage with Salisbury was issued. Three years after the ending of the dispute, on the death of her brother John, Joan became countess of Kent in her own right; and in 1360 her husband assumed the style earl of Kent by courtesy of England.

Her engagement to Edward, prince of Wales took place in the summer of 1361 after Holand's death. The marriage was by all accounts a love match and was arranged without the prior approval of the king. Since the two were related in the third degree, a papal dispensation had to be obtained and only after this was issued were the espousals solemnized. The wedding ceremony was conducted on 6 October at Lambeth by Archbishop Islip and attended by the whole royal family. The couple spent their first twelve months together at the prince's castles or manor houses at Berkhamstead, Bushey and Kennington. But in June 1363, after the prince had been invested with the duchy of Aquitaine, they left England for Bordeaux. From now on the prince was separated for lengthy periods from his wife, but he kept in touch with her by letter: one letter, in which he gave her news of the battle of Najera, opens: 'My dearest and truest sweetheart and well beloved companion . . .'.[11] In the years of the prince's decline, and more particularly in the wake of his death, Joan appears to have acted as a steadying influence in English politics, sorting out difficulties and reconciling enemies. In February

---

[10] J. Froissart, *Oeuvres*, ed. Kervyn de Lettenhove (Brussels, 26 vols, 1867–77), ii, 243. This passage is omitted in the edition in English by Thomas Johnes. There is a portrait of Joan of Kent in the St Albans book of benefactors (BL, Cotton MS Nero D.vii, fo.7ʳ) (plate 2). It is probably a conventional rather than an authentic likeness.

[11] 'Trescher et tressentier coer, bien ame compaigne': A.E. Prince, 'A Letter of Edward the Black Prince Describing the Battle of Najera in 1367', *EHR*, xli (1926), 418.

1377 she was instrumental in reconciling the Londoners to John of Gaunt, the leading figure at court, and in 1385 she mediated between Gaunt and her son.[12] What made her attractive as a mediator was the fact that she was in a sense above politics: while associated with the court, she was not of it; she enjoyed the trust of all sides. However, according to Walsingham, it was her failure in one attempted mediation that caused her death. John Holand, her second son by her first marriage, had murdered Sir Ralph Stafford, a close friend of the king.[13] She tried to reconcile the king to his half-brother, but failed. Overcome by grief, in August 1385 she died.

Richard was Joan's second son by the Black Prince. An earlier child, Edward of Angoulême, had been born in 1365, but had died at the age of six. The future king was born on 6 January 1367 at the abbey of St Andrew, Bordeaux. His baptism was an occasion of some note. Among his godparents were two aspirant kings who were visiting the prince's court at the time. The senior of these, and the chief sponsor, was Jaime IV, titular king of Majorca, while his main supporter was Richard, king of Armenia. It seems likely that Pedro, the deposed king of Castile, attended the ceremony too, as he was in exile at Bordeaux at the time.[14] The presence of three kings at the prince's court, coupled with the coincidence of the infant's birth on the Twelfth Day, later gave rise to the story that three kings came bearing gifts for him. A possible allusion to the story is found in the Wilton Diptych, painted in the 1390s, in the left-hand panel of which three saints, two of them kings, are shown presenting Richard to the Virgin and Child, opposite.[15]

Only a few details are preserved of Richard's early childhood. It is known that he had a wet-nurse, Mundina Danos, to whom he later

[12] See below, 21, 133.

[13] *HA*, ii, 130; and see below, 120.

[14] Thorne says that Richard was baptized in the presence of three 'magi' whom he names as the kings of Spain, Navarre and Portugal: *William Thorne's Chronicle of St Augustine's Abbey, Canterbury*, ed. A.H. Davis (Oxford, 1934), 591. The king of Spain is clearly Pedro, at this stage an exile; it seems that by the king of Navarre is meant Jaime of Majorca, another exile. The presence of the king of Portugal is problematical: see Barber, *Edward, Prince of Wales*, 193.

[15] For the Diptych, see below, 304–5. There is a possible allusion to the story too in Chancellor Houghton's opening address to the parliament of January 1377 at which Richard, as prince of Wales, presided. The chancellor urged his listeners to honour the prince as the three kings of Cologne had honoured the Son of God by bringing him gifts of gold, frankincense and myrrh (*RP*, ii, 362). The names 'Jasper, Melcheser, Balteser' were engraved on a ewer in the king's ownership at the time of his deposition: *The Ancient Kalendars and Inventories of the Treasury of His Majesty's Exchequer*, ed. F. Palgrave (3 vols, London, 1836), iii, 329.

granted a pension and who was to marry his tailor, Walter Rauf.[16] There is evidence too that he was provided with a 'rocker' to rock his cradle: one Eliona de France, whom he later rewarded, was employed in this capacity.[17] Both Mundina and Eliona were of French – that is to say, of Aquitanian – extraction. Mundina, indeed, was specifically said to be 'of Aquitaine'. It is reasonable to infer from this evidence that the language of the nursery was French and not English. Very likely in that case Richard's first tongue was French. There can scarcely be any doubt that he would have learned English in boyhood, for all of the aristocracy were English-speakers by this period, and by the 1380s a polite litera-ture for the court was appearing in that language. But Richard was always to retain his fluency in French: in 1395 on a visit to England Froissart gave him a book of poems in French because 'he spoke and read French very well'.[18]

At the beginning of 1371 Richard was taken to England. The prince, his father, was by now an invalid and could travel only with difficulty; and the loss of his elder son a few months earlier seems to have affected him deeply. In the previous year he had been in touch with the king: almost certainly he had requested permission to resign the duchy into his hands. In late January he, the princess his wife, Richard and a large retinue set sail from Bordeaux for Plymouth. The journey proved a difficult one. By the time that the ships dropped anchor at Plymouth, the prince was exhausted and had to spend several weeks at Plympton recovering his strength before he could complete the journey to London. From this time on his movements and activities are ill documented. In June 1373 he presided at a council at Westminster at which a papal demand for taxation was discussed, and on a few subsequent occasions he is found in consultation with his council.[19] It seems that he travelled very little. For most of the time he stayed at either Berkhampstead or Kennington, his two favourite residences: he had had extensive works carried out at Kennington in the 1350s.[20] It is likely that Richard generally lived in the same residences as his parents. In his last year before becoming king letters of his were issued at Kennington betweeen 15 and 28 February and at Berkhampstead on 25 March and again in May.[21] Richard was at Kennington in June when he learned that he had become king.

---

[16] *CPR 1377–81*, 120, 609.

[17] *CPR 1391–6*, 505.

[18] Froissart, ii, 577.

[19] Barber, *Edward, Prince of Wales*, 227–32; for the date of the council, see J.I. Catto, 'An Alleged Great Council of 1374', *EHR*, lxxxii (1967), 764–71.

[20] *HKW*, ii, 967–9.

[21] Kennington: *CPR 1377–81*, 157, 161, 169, 171, 190, 413; Berkhamstead: ibid., 17, 27, 155, 208.

Richard's upbringing in his years of boyhood or 'pueritia' would probably have followed the pattern usual among the aristocracy.[22] At the age of six or seven he would have been assigned a resident tutor or 'master' to oversee his instruction. The master's task would have been to advise him on most aspects of growing up: what to wear, how to behave in chapel and at table, how to speak properly and behave correctly with other people. And what the master himself could not teach he would have had plenty of experts to help him with: among them, chaplains, minstrels, huntsmen, and men who could teach reading and grammar. The master's regimen would probably have been informally structured. Almost certainly it had to be so, because in a household – unlike a school – there was no clear distinction between learning and everyday life. The emphasis would have been very much on the teaching of practical skills, the most important of these being riding, singing, dancing, hunting and – essential for a prince – letters. The teaching of letters probably began quite early, at the age of six or seven, although in some households it may have begun well before that. The pupil would have been given an introduction to the Latin alphabet by letters written on a board or in a little pamphlet. Then he would be taught to recognize words, to pronounce them and perhaps to sing them to the rules of plainsong. In the educationalists' view the language in which he was instructed should have been Latin; but Richard, who was never destined for the cloth, would probably have been instructed mostly in French or English. By his early teens he would also have been given his first taste of music. From Edward IV's instructions for the teaching of his children it is clear that music regularly formed part of young aristocrats' upbringing. The pupils were taught to harp, pipe and to sing; they may even have been taught rudimentary composition. There are signs that Richard developed some expertise in music. Certainly, the interest he was later to show in his chapel royal suggests an appreciation of its role in liturgy and in the projection of a regal image.[23]

In addition to learning the peaceful arts Richard would have been trained in physical skills. By the age of seven or eight, and certainly no later than ten, he would have been taught to ride. Horse-riding was a skill which was valued in its own right, because it encouraged coordination and developed the limbs; but it was also the prerequisite for learning the further exercises of hunting and tourneying. It is not known what aptitude Richard showed for tourneying, because later in

---

[22] For this and the following paragraph, see N. Orme, *From Childhood to Chivalry. The Education of the English Kings and Aristocracy, 1066–1530* (London, 1984), in particular Chs 5 and 6.

[23] See below, 320, 340.

life he is rarely found practising the sport: it was always his preference to watch over, rather than participate in, the lists. But it is clear that he was an avid huntsman. Every summer as king he repaired to the forests of Woodstock, Rockingham or the New Forest, and his love of the chase is attested by his purchase from a London goldsmith in 1386 of a knife to be used in the woods and a hunting horn of gold, embellished with green tassels of silk.[24] Richard may never have become a great warrior figure in his father's image; but he yielded nothing to him in his love of the sport of kings.

The masters who had charge of this regime of training needed the trust and affection of those committed to their care. Hence it was usual for them to be drawn from the ranks of their charges' parents' friends or closest servants. Richard is known to have been served by three masters at least: Sir Richard Abberbury, Sir Guichard d'Angle and Sir Simon Burley. Sir Richard Abberbury probably served only briefly. He was a scion of a Berkshire and Oxfordshire gentry family who had risen rapidly in service and had fought under the Black Prince in Aquitaine and Castile; but he was never one of the prince's inner circle.[25] Some time in the 1370s Abberbury was replaced by the second master, Sir Guichard d'Angle, an elderly Poitevin who, in his youth, had served with the king of France but had been captured at Poitiers and subsequently gave his allegiance to the English. In the 1360s Guichard became a close associate of the Black Prince, and he came to England to settle in the year after the prince's return. Richard obviously had some affection for him, for he created him earl of Huntingdon at his coronation.[26] Probably the ablest and certainly the most influential of the three 'magistri', however, was the last, Sir Simon Burley. Burley was a long-standing associate of the prince, whom he had served in both England and Aquitaine. The evidence suggests that he was appointed to take Guichard's place after the latter's capture by the French at the naval battle of La Rochelle in 1372,[27] and by the time of the prince's

---

[24] *Issues of the Exchequer, Henry III–Henry VI*, ed. F. Devon (London, 1847), 231.

[25] S. Walker, 'Sir Richard Abberbury (*c.*1330–1399) and his Kinsmen: the Rise and Fall of a Gentry Family', *Nottingham Medieval Studies*, xxxiv (1990), 119–20. Abberbury was the builder of Donnington Castle (Berkshire), for which the licence to crenellate was granted in 1386: M. Wood, *Donnington Castle* (London, 1964), 5, 21. In the account roll of the prince's receiver in 1377 Abberbury is described as steward of the prince's lands; he is nowhere referred to as 'magister': E101/398/8.

[26] *CP*, vi, 650–3; T.F. Tout, *Chapters in the Administrative History of Medieval England* (6 vols, Manchester, 1920–33), iii, 325–6.

[27] Guichard probably served as 'magister' again after his release: as R.F. Green, *Poets and Princepleasers. Literature and the English Court in the Late Middle Ages* (Toronto, 1980), 73–5, suggests, it may have been the practice to employ two tutors simultaneously.

death he had completely won the confidence of his young charge. After
Richard's accession, while very likely continuing as 'magister', he added
to his power by acquiring the office of vice-chamberlain of the household. His opponents, who were many, regarded his influence over the
king as excessive and undesirable, and he quickly became unpopular.
In 1387, when the Appellants took over, he was arrested and in the
following year tried in parliament and executed. There can be little
doubt that Burley was a major influence on Richard in his early years.
R.H. Jones has suggested that it was Burley who instructed him in the
exalted ideas of regality which he was later to articulate.[28] The main
evidence for this is his possession of a copy of Giles of Rome's *De
Regimine Principum*, a tract which stressed the role of the king's will in
government.[29] It is likely that Burley had read the work and had
absorbed its contents; and it is noticeable that in the 1390s Richard was
to pursue policies which had a great deal in common with Giles's own.[30]
However, there is a difficulty in isolating Burley as the sole source of the
king's knowledge of Giles. The *De Regimine* enjoyed a wide circulation in
England, particularly among the laity, and there were many others at
court who could have read it. Michael de la Pole, for example, a
chancellor in the mid-1380s, was clearly familiar with Giles's notion of
obedience; and so too was a successor of his in the 1390s, Edmund
Stafford. It is possible that Richard could have picked up his knowledge
of Giles's ideas from either, or both, of these men. However, while the
exact extent of Burley's influence on the development of Richard's
ideas of kingship remains debatable, there is no denying his influence
on the future king more generally. Richard looked to him as a father
figure and confidant. Burley guided Richard at his coronation, and
later he was the chief negotiator of his marriage.[31] Richard's lofty ideas
on courtly behaviour probably owed something to him: during his years
with his father at Bordeaux Burley had become familiar with the latter's
autocratic style and his insistence on etiquette. In his capacity as master
he would have passed on his knowledge of all this to his son. Richard's
own style in adulthood was to show a considerable affinity with his
father's, in particular in its high degree of formality.[32] Richard himself
would have had little direct knowledge of his father's court: he would
have been too young to remember it. But a picture of it – partial and
impressionistic, though still vivid – may well have been picked up from
his servants.

[28] Jones, *The Royal Policy of Richard II*, 144.
[29] M.V. Clarke, 'Forfeitures and Treason in 1388', *Fourteenth Century Studies*, ed.
L.S. Sutherland and M. McKisack (Oxford, 1937, repr. 1968), 120 and n.
[30] See below, 250, 385–6.
[31] See below, 87.
[32] See below, 344–5.

The background to Richard's upbringing was provided by the increasing likelihood of his early succession to the throne. His grandfather, who had become king in 1327, was by the 1370s over sixty and declining fast, and his father was seriously ill. It was clear that neither had long to live. The prince made his last, and rather pathetic, gesture in politics in 1376, in the so-called Good Parliament. Walsingham's chronicle is our source for the episode. Sir Richard Lyons – a royal creditor who was under investigation for corruption – had, so the chronicler relates, sent the prince a barrel of gold in the hope of winning his favour; but the prince refused to receive it, saying that the contents of the barrel were ill-gotten gains, 'for which reason he would not accept such a present nor help the donor nor favour his misdeeds'.[33] It is possible that earlier in the session the commons had been looking to him for support in their campaign against the courtiers, but by this time he was too weak to intervene to any effect. At the beginning of June he was moved from Kennington to Westminster. Here he distributed gifts to his servants and took leave of the king. He then summoned his son to his presence and bound him to stand by the gifts that he had made. Shortly afterwards there was a strange episode when Sir Richard Stury, one of the king's chamber knights, came to seek his pardon; allegedly, Stury had been appointed to liaise between the king and parliament but had falsely reported that the commons intended to depose the king, 'as they had deposed his father'. The prince reproached him for his evil deeds. Then his strength failed him. On Wednesday, 8 June – Trinity Sunday, as he had wished – he died.[34]

The prince's death left Richard as heir to the throne. Almost immediately there was pressure from the parliamentary commons for the boy to be recognized as the new prince of Wales. Something that lent urgency to the request was the commons' fear – which was almost certainly unjustified – that the boy's uncle, John of Gaunt, duke of Lancaster, had designs on the crown himself. In the second or third week of June a petition was submitted for Richard to be brought into their presence. This was done on 25 June. The archbishop of Canterbury, Simon Sudbury, made an eloquent speech to the effect that, though the prince was dead, he was still with them, for he had left behind a fair son, his very image, as heir apparent. The commons then asked that the king should at once make Richard prince of Wales. In reply the chancellor said that this was no business of the lords or the commons and that the king would be advised to take this step in the fullness of time.[35] Richard was finally invested with his father's titles five months later, on 20 November.

[33] CA, 79–80.
[34] Ibid., 87–90.
[35] RP, ii, 330.

For at least a century it had been usual for heirs to the throne to be given their own separate households, even if they were still under the supervision of their parents or a master. Richard may have been given such a household by the mid-1370s, but it was only on his creation as prince of Wales that he was allowed an establishment that did justice to his rank. The survival of an account roll of his receiver, John Fordham, a former secretary of his father, allows us to say a little about its structure and personnel.[36] The main departments were the privy seal office, the receiver-general's office and the chamber. The first two were both under the control of Fordham, while Burley, as chamberlain, headed the third. In addition, there was a great wardrobe, as there was at court, which provided the prince with his clothes. Superintending the whole was a council. In the period covered by the account – the first six months of 1377 – Fordham disposed of an income of £2,573 2s 4d, derived for the most part from the prince's estates but also including money from the confiscated temporalities of the bishop of Winchester and a donation from the citizens of London.[37] Since Richard was a minor, the greater part of the receipts went to his mother's treasurer, William Packington, 'for the expenses of his household'. Over the same six months the account records expenditure amounting to £2,165 4s 6d. There were payments to Guichard d'Angle, 'sent to Paris on the prince's secret business', to a munitions maker at Calais for guns and ammunition for the prince's castles in Wales, and to a mercer in Candlewick Street for red-ray cloth for his bargemen. Expenses were also incurred in supporting the other young noblemen who were brought up alongside the prince in his household. The most notable of these were John Arundel, the son of Sir John Arundel, and Henry of Derby, John of Gaunt's son and heir. Henry of Derby was also to be in Richard's company in the Tower during the Great Revolt. It is ironical that the playmate of his youth should, much later, have become his opponent and supplanter on the throne.

In the early months of 1377 a great many hopes were being entertained of the young Richard. People were looking to him, once he had acceded to the throne, to reverse the accelerating decline in the realm's fortunes. The chancellor, Bishop Houghton, caught the national mood of anticipation in an address to parliament in January: Richard, he said, had been sent to England by God in the same way that God had sent his only Son into the world for the redemption of his people.[38] The suggestion in the chancellor's remarks was that Richard would be continuing

---

[36] E101/398/8. For discussion, see Tout, *Chapters*, iv, 190–1.

[37] In late 1376 or early 1377 William of Wykeham, the bishop of Winchester, was charged with corrupt practices while chancellor and suffered temporary loss of his estates.

[38] *RP*, ii, 362.

the work of his predecessor; but to his audience it must have seemed more appropriate to think in terms of a new beginning. Since the reopening of the war by the French eight years earlier the tide of fortune had turned against the English. One by one the lands ceded to Edward III at Brétigny had been whittled away, until by the end of 1375 only the town of Calais and its marches and the Gascon coastal strip south of Bordeaux were left. In 1372 Pembroke had been given command of a major expedition to relieve Gascony, but on the way his fleet had been attacked off La Rochelle and he himself captured. In the following year Gaunt had marched across France from Calais to Bordeaux, but his retinue had suffered badly from dysentery and in the end the strategic gain to the English had been slight. Only Gregory XI's initiative in brokering a truce in 1375 had prevented the French from inflicting yet more humiliations on the English.

At home the state of affairs was hardly more encouraging. As Edward III declined into senility there was a leadership vacuum at court. The Black Prince was on his deathbed and Gaunt, the next most senior brother, was distrusted. Power was increasingly gathered into the hands of Alice Perrers, the king's unscrupulous mistress, and those who enjoyed her favour – chief among them William Windsor, her husband, and William Latimer, from 1371 the court chamberlain. The nobility, and in particular the military commanders, were almost completely excluded. In May 1376 popular discontent with the government boiled over in a crisis in the Good Parliament.[39] The chancellor and his colleagues had approached the commons for a grant of taxation to pay for an expedition against the French on the expiry of the truce. The response to their request was not what they had anticipated. When the commons deliberated among themselves, first one knight said that the king should 'live of his own' – that is, on his hereditary revenues; another complained about the removal of the wool staple from Calais; and a third called for the appointment of a joint committee with the lords.[40] The mood was more hostile to the government than it had been for thirty years. When the commons' Speaker, Sir Peter de la Mare, came back with a reply to the chancellor's request, he stepped up the pressure on the crown. The commons, he said, could not proceed with the 'business of parliament' until certain matters had been investigated: allegations had been made that Sir William Latimer had made improper profits out of the campaign in Brittany and that he had been responsible for the loss of two fortresses. It was further alleged that he and the financier Lyons had deprived the king of revenue by selling licences for evasion of the staple, had charged extortionate interest on

[39] For this parliament see G. Holmes, *The Good Parliament* (Oxford, 1975).
[40] *Anon.*, 80–1.

a loan to the king, and had engaged in the brokering of royal debts to their, and not the king's, profit. These were serious charges, he said, and the commons wished to maintain them as a body: in other words, they would use the procedure later to be known as impeachment. Gaunt was astonished at the commons' presumption. Walsingham, admittedly a hostile witness, reports him as saying, 'Do they think that they are kings and princes in this land? Have they forgotten how powerful I am?'[41] For a couple of weeks the duke held out against the commons' demands, but towards the end of the month he gave in. Latimer was temporarily imprisoned; Lyons was sentenced to forfeiture and imprisonment; and lesser associates of the two were dismissed from office at court. The duke's climb-down represented a remarkable triumph for the commons. For the first time in nearly forty years the combination of faction and popular discontent had brought the court to its knees.

But no parliament or popular assembly in the middle ages, however substantial its achievements, could impress its will on a reluctant government for long. The latter could simply ignore the commons' decisions or verdicts; alternatively it could seek to reverse them. In the wake of the Good Parliament Gaunt, who was the *de facto* leader of the court, did both. Over the summer he set about undoing the parliament's work. Latimer and Lyons were released from imprisonment and Alice Perrers was reinstated at court. Sir Peter de la Mare was arrested and imprisoned in Nottingham castle; and an attack was mounted on William Wykeham, bishop of Winchester, who had lent his support to the commons in parliament. Later, in December, summonses were issued for a parliament to meet in the New Year to overturn the judgements of its predecessor. Walsingham alleged that the elections were manipulated by Gaunt to secure the return of MPs who would be favourable to him.[42] It is hard to say whether this was true, but certainly a smaller than usual proportion of members who had sat in the previous parliament were re-elected to this one, and it may be significant that the commons chose as their Speaker Sir Thomas Hungerford, an MP for Wiltshire, who was Gaunt's steward in the southern parts. The assembly was not wholly subservient to the duke: it is noteworthy that a petition was submitted calling for the release of de la Mare from imprisonment. But the duke had little difficulty securing ratification of the measures he had taken since June. The sentences on Lyons, Perrers and the others were reversed; and at the end of the session a generous grant of taxation – in the form of a poll tax – was made to remedy the crown's shortage of money.

[41] *CA*, 74.
[42] Ibid., 112.

Inevitably, there was resistance in some quarters to the firmness with which Gaunt had reasserted royal authority. The fiercest opposition to the duke's policies was to be found in the capital. During the January session of parliament Gaunt had done little to endear himself to the citizenry. On 19 February he had pushed his way into St Paul's to rescue his protégé, the radical clerk John Wyclif, from the clutches of the bishop of London and his clerical accusers; and in parliament on the same day he had proposed that his ally Henry Percy, the marshal, should exercise the jurisdiction of his office in the city. The mob reacted to the duke's disregard for their feelings with fury. On 20 February they launched an assault on his palace of the Savoy; and from there they went to the house of Sir John Ypres, where they heard that he was dining, obliging the duke to take to his heels and seek refuge across the river at the princess of Wales's house at Kennington. The princess, perhaps at the duke's entreaty, used her good offices to promote reconciliation. Walsingham tells how she sent three of her knights, Burley, Sir Aubrey de Vere and Sir Lewis Clifford, to London to beg the citizens, out of love for her, to make peace with Gaunt: their answer being that they would do what she requested, but subject to conditions.[43] A meeting with the king was then arranged and a reconciliation of sorts effected. After this there appears to have been an easing of tension.

Gaunt was aware of his deep unpopularity in the country and was anxious to promote the young heir as a symbol of unity. The latter, as a result, was called upon to open parliament in January: the official record says that he 'sat in the king's place' as his grandfather's representative;[44] and it is clear from the silence of the sources that Gaunt kept himself well in the background. Very possibly the duke was responding to the mood of popular enthusiasm felt for the prince. On 25 January the Londoners, who held him in especially high regard, laid on a great entertainment in his honour. A company of 130 vizored mummers paraded through the streets of the city and rode out over the bridge to Kennington. They were dressed fancifully as knights, esquires, an emperor and pope with their retinues, cardinals and papal legates; the legates were cast as the villains of the piece, with horrible masks. As darkness was falling, they lit up the sky with their blazing torches. When the company reached Kennington, the prince and princess, Gaunt and his two brothers, the earls of Warwick and Suffolk and other lords came out to meet them. The mummers presented Richard with a set of loaded dice, with which he then won three gold objects from them. The prince responded by ordering wine to be brought and the company

---

[43] Ibid., 126.
[44] *RP*, ii, 361.

drank joyfully. Then he called on the minstrels to play, and they performed on trumpets, nakers and pipes. He and the lords danced on one
side and the mummers on the other.[45]

There was a political dimension to this play-acting, as there was to all
civic ritual, for the Londoners were bidding for the favour of their
future monarch. Richard, though only ten, was by virtue of his proximity to the throne a force to be reckoned with. Evidently the council
was no less aware of this than the Londoners. By early to mid-spring
measures were being set in hand to accord greater recognition to his
status. In a ceremony at Windsor on 23 April his grandfather dubbed
him a knight and admitted him to the Order of the Garter.[46] Shortly
afterwards, as the truce negotiated with the French in 1375 drew to a
close, preparations were made for a naval expedition in which he was to
take part. Ships were gathered in London in June and contracts were
made for the service of 3,940 troops. The leaders of the retinues were
to be the prince (at least nominally), John of Gaunt and the duke of
Brittany. On 17 and 20 June payments were made at the exchequer
for the retinues' wages.[47] But on Sunday, 21 June it was learned that
the king had died at Sheen. Preparations for the expedition were
suspended; and Richard's opportunity to win early fame duly passed.

According to Walsingham, the old king died virtually deserted, with
just a single priest at his bedside. The story may well be true, for in his
last weeks the king was attended only by his privy household. But his
final journey to Westminster for burial was a splendid, if solemn, affair.
A wooden funerary effigy was made to go on the carriage.[48] Over it was
erected a canopy fringed with silk. A pillow of gold cloth, lined with
fustian, was placed beneath the king's head, while a cloth of red satin
was draped over the hearse. The cortège proceeded slowly on its way
and there were overnight stops at Wandsworth, where Richard gave
offerings to the church, and at Southwark. For the final stage, from
Southwark to Westminster, the hearse was given extra coverings, of
golden cloth with cyprus baldachins. The coffin was put on display for
a few days on a catafalque in St Paul's Cathedral, where it was draped in
black cloth and buckram. From St Paul's it was moved to Westminster
Hall for a ceremonial lying-in-state. On the day of the funeral 400
esquires were in attendance at the bier, all dressed in black and carrying

[45] *Anon.*, 102–3.

[46] Ibid., 106. For expenses incurred in connection with the ceremony, see E101/
398/8.

[47] A. Goodman, *John of Gaunt. The Exercise of Princely Power in Fourteenth-Century
Europe* (London, 1992), 64.

[48] The head would have been based on the death mask which still survives. On
this subject see R.P. Howgrave-Graham, 'The Earlier Royal Funeral Effigies',
Archaeologia, xcviii (1969), 159–69. For the procession: E159/154, Brevia Directa
Baronibus, Easter term.

torches, while the hall itself was given a sombre air by the hanging of a black dorser behind the throne and black cloths along the walls. The funeral was held at Westminster Abbey on 5 July.[49] Among the many mourners who attended were the new king, the lords secular and ecclesiastical, and the knights and esquires of the household. Before the king's body was lowered into the ground, it was given a new wrapping of red samite (unornamented silk), and a cross of white silk was placed over it; when it was interred, another cross of white silk was placed on the coffin. A knight was employed to bear the king's standard and coat of arms.

With the funeral over, the old reign drew symbolically to a close. A new one had already begun.

[49] *Anon.*, 106.

Chapter 3

ACCESSION AND MINORITY, 1377–81

Richard's coronation took place in Westminster Abbey just eleven days after his grandfather's funeral, on Thursday, 16 July. It was the first coronation for half a century, and there was enormous popular interest. People travelled from virtually every part of the realm either to attend or to watch the ceremonies. Adam Peshale of Peshale, a Staffordshire esquire, travelled over a hundred miles from near Newcastle under Lyme. The journey was not one that he was to recall with any pleasure: he was attacked and robbed on the way.[1]

As in the past, the round of festivities began on the eve of the coronation, when the king rode in procession from the Tower to Westminster. The procession was a grand one. The men of Bayeux as usual led the way. After them came the representatives of the London wards, a corps of German mercenaries, a delegation of Gascons and the earls, barons and knights, all in due order, and robed in white in honour of the new king.[2] Richard himself followed behind, accompanied by Burley, who held his sword, and Nicholas Bonde, a knight of the chamber, who guided the reins of his horse. The route they took was along Cheapside, Fleet Street and the Strand. The streets were all packed, and a path had to be cut by the duke of Lancaster, now showing greater respect for the Londoners' feelings than he had a year earlier. Along the way all sorts of diversions caught the eye. In Cheapside the conduit flowed with wine for the duration of the procession – for three hours. Further west in the same thoroughfare a mock castle was built. In its turrets were positioned girls of the king's own age, dressed in white, who showered him with gilt scrolls as he approached and then descended to offer him wine in gilt cups.[3] It was a spectacle the like of which was not to be seen again until the procession marking Richard's reconciliation with the Londoners fifteen years later.[4]

The coronation on the next day provided the setting for pageantry of

---

[1] His assailant was his enemy Sir Hugh Wrottesley: SC8/146/7271. Adam probably attended the coronation as a retainer of his lord Hugh, earl of Stafford. For his background and connections, see *House of Commons*, iv, 61.
[2] White being the symbol of purity and childlike innocence.
[3] For descriptions of the procession, see *Anon.*, 107–8; *CA*, 153–6.
[4] See below, 343.

a more formal kind. It began in the morning with the procession from the palace to the abbey. The king was met at his seat in the palace hall by the archbishops and clergy and conducted thence to a stage in the centre of the church where his throne was placed. The choir then sang the anthem 'Firmetur manus tua', the psalm 'Misericordias domine in eternum' and a repeat of the anthem. Meanwhile, the archbishop vested himself for mass, and by the time the anthem had ended he was ready to lead the king to the altar. There Richard made his first offering, which took the by now traditional form of a pound of gold and a splendid altar frontal. Next the king knelt down, on cushions provided for the purpose, while prayers were said. Then he was raised up and led to a chair facing the altar where the archbishop administered the oath. Richard swore on the sacrament to uphold the laws and customs of his ancestors, to protect the Church and clergy, to do justice to all and, finally, to uphold the laws which the people would 'justly and reasonably' choose. In essence, the oath was the same as that which his grandfather had sworn in 1327 and his great-grandfather twenty years before that. The first three clauses were of considerable antiquity and were hallowed by long usage; but the fourth had been introduced in 1307, probably to ensure that Edward II would not go back on future promises as his father had gone back on those that he had made in 1297. It was a precautionary measure, conceived in an emergency, but preserved on Edward III's coronation, when the monarchy was still weak. By 1377 it was acquiring an air of permanence, a prospect not at all to the liking of Richard's advisers. The latter would have preferred to jettison it altogether, but in the circumstances that was hardly feasible. The most they could hope to do was to blunt its effect. Thus in the official record the words 'juste et rationabiliter' were added, to qualify the laws which the people would choose, and in the otherwise accurate account in the *Anonimalle Chronicle* the offending words were omitted.[5] The influence of Richard's officers and advisers betrayed itself too in a further change that was made to the traditional *ordo*, and that was the timing of the oath. Whereas previously the king had taken his oath only after he had been presented to the congregation for their acclamation, in 1377 Richard took it before: a rearrangement which served to emphasize the people's allegiance to a king who was already their ruler *de jure*. The remainder of the service followed the traditional form. After the congregation had voiced their assent, Richard was led back to the high altar; and while the archbishop began the prayer 'Veni Creator' he knelt down once more. Two choristers began the litany, and the archbishop and bishops sang the seven penitential psalms. After this came the most solemn part of the rite: the ceremony of consecration.

---

[5] *Foed.*, vii, 159; *Anon.*, 109–10.

Screened from view by a golden cloth, Richard was divested of his shirt and touched on the hands, chest, shoulders and head with holy oil. From this moment he was set apart from other mortals. He was God's anointed. He was not, as early medieval monarchs had considered themselves to be, the equivalent of a priest; but he was nevertheless endowed by the Almighty with special powers, the nature of which was made clear in the next part of the service when he was invested with the insignia of dominion. He was given the sword for the protection of the kingdom, the sceptre, 'the rod of the kingdom' and instrument for the correction of error, and the ring, 'the seal of holy faith' and symbol of his pastoral responsibilities. The boy king was then solemnly crowned, the crown being held by the archbishop on one side and the earl of March on the other. The long service was at last moving to its conclusion. What remained was the celebration of mass and the performance of homage by the leading barons. Sir John Dymock, the king's champion, appeared, as custom demanded, at the abbey door, but was persuaded to postpone his challenge until the evening. At the end, the procession left the abbey for Westminster Hall. The king, the Westminster writer disapprovingly noted, was carried shoulder high from the church by Simon Burley and in the commotion lost one of his shoes.[6]

How much impact, if any, the ritual of the coronation service had on the mind of the young king is virtually impossible to say. Much later Richard was to attach high importance to the fact of his anointing,[7] but at this stage he is likely to have been more impressed by the overall grandeur and magnificence of the occasion than by the significance of its individual parts. A coronation was the most solemn of medieval inauguration rituals: it was a ceremony that turned an ordinary young mortal into a monarch answerable only to God. In Richard's case, the coronation marked the accession of a prince who was already heir apparent. Its symbolism may have been a matter of less significance to those involved than was to be the case in 1399 when a usurper was crowned. All the same, every stage of the ceremony was replete with meaning, and Richard's advisers were careful to ensure that that meaning was not misunderstood. Hence the reversal in order of the oath and the archbishop's question to the people, which reduced the element of election to little more than an act of recognition. The point was reinforced a month or two later, in the first parliament of the reign, when the archbishop of Canterbury reminded his audience that Richard was

---

[6] *WC*, 414–16; and see below, 310.

[7] In 1388, in letters confirming the gift of a gold ring to the Confessor's shrine, he recalled that it was in the Confessor's church that he had received his royal anointing (WAM 9473).

king 'not by election, nor by any such path, but by lawful right of succession'.[8]

If the responsibility for this shift of emphasis lay with anyone, it lay with the king's uncle, John of Gaunt, duke of Lancaster. As steward of England the duke officiated at the coronation, and when it was over he took care to have its order of proceedings officially recorded.[9] From earliest manhood the duke had shown himself an unyielding defender of the prerogative: he had stood by the crown in the difficult earlier years of the decade and in 1376 had organized the defence of the court against the commons. But, for all the evidence of his record, he was suspected in some quarters of harbouring designs on the crown himself. A smear campaign was whipped up against him;[10] and after the coronation he decided that it would have to be challenged and answered. When parliament met on 13 October he asked if he could draw the king's attention to the terrible slanders that he had heard repeated against himself. What had been imputed, he declared, amounted to a charge of treason. Considering that he was a son of a king, and one of the greatest men in the realm, it was obvious that he had too much to lose by turning traitor. His ancestors on both sides, he continued, had been good and loyal men, and it would be strange indeed if he were to stray from their path. The speech had the immediate, and desired, effect of producing a display of solidarity. The prelates and lords rose to their feet and with one accord asked the duke to put a stop to such talk: no one, they said, would wish to hear such things said about him. Even the commons, his erstwhile enemies, sprang to his defence, and proclaimed him free from all blame or dishonour. Gaunt was reassured by these professions, but repeated his view that due punishment should be meted out to those who were the sowers of discord. Once that was done, he said, he would be prepared to forgive and forget.[11]

If the duke looked ill at ease in the role of an injured innocent, it was because he felt less confident of his position in the new reign than in the old. The new king, Richard, was a mere ten years old. Only once before since the Conquest had a child succeeded to the throne. That was in October 1216, when Henry III had become king. On that occasion a regency had been instituted, and a candidate to fill it had been found in William Marshal, a man trusted by royalists and barons alike. In 1377, however, no agreed candidate was available. Gaunt, the man

<hr/>

[8] *RP*, iii, 3.

[9] *CCR 1377-81*, 1-5.

[10] Every tale and every lie of which was eagerly lapped up by Walsingham: see, for example, *CA*, 163-4, 169, 195-6.

[11] *RP*, iii, 5.

with the strongest claim, was too unpopular, and the idea of a regency, if it was ever floated, was soon dropped. Instead, the pretence was maintained that Richard was fully competent to govern. He was allowed full use of the great seal to authenticate documents; government business was carried on in his name; and in the formal sense he was held as fully responsible for the conduct of affairs as his grandfather had been. But to suppose that this arrangement was more than a pretence would be naive. From 1377 to 1380 the day-to-day business of running the country was carried on in the king's name by a series of 'continual councils'. The first such council was nominated by the magnates at a meeting held on the morrow of the coronation. Its members were intended to be representative of the principal orders of landed society – two each being drawn from the prelates, the earls, the barons and the bannerets, and four from the knights.[12] At the same time, cutting across the principle of social representation were political affiliations which revealed how far the balance of power at court had changed since the death of the old king. Most striking was the omission of John of Gaunt; and hardly less so was that of the old king's two other surviving sons, Edmund earl of Cambridge and Thomas earl of Buckingham. It is possible that their membership was assumed, for they were given a general supervisory role by parliament; but, even if this were the case, it hardly made up for the membership proper which they might have expected as a consequence of their rank. The most senior figures appointed were the two earls – March and Arundel, the former a past adversary of Gaunt, and the latter a newcomer to the scene. The two bishops were also men of weight – Courtenay of London and Erghum of Salisbury, the former (the younger brother of the earl of Devon) another opponent of the duke, and the latter his chancellor and probably on this occasion a stalking horse for his master. Of the remaining members – eight in all – four were connected with King Edward's court and another four (Cobham, Stafford, Devereux and Segrave) with the Black Prince and thus with his son the king. It is clear that, as John of Gaunt's power receded, that of the Black Prince's former dependants advanced. Several more of the prince's men stepped into the leading offices of household and state: Sir Simon Burley became vice-chamberlain, and the clerks William Packington and John Fordham, keeper of the wardrobe and keeper of the privy seal respectively. A little later they were joined by another clerk, Alan Stokes, who became keeper of the great wardrobe, and Sir Hugh Segrave, one of the prince's executors,

---

[12] A precedent for this structure was afforded by the council nominated in the Good Parliament in 1376 (Holmes, *Good Parliament*, 105). For the 'continual councils' in general, see Tout, *Chapters*, iii, 326–47; N.B. Lewis, 'The "Continual Council" in the Early Years of Richard II', *EHR*, xli (1926), 246–51.

who took over as steward of the household.[13] Few of these men had caught the public eye before, but on Richard's accession they at last entered into their own.[14] As the dependants of one of the most successful and charismatic figures of the age they enjoyed a collective identity which gave the governments of the minority a character appreciably different from that of the conciliar governments of Edward III's last years. Their individual attitudes and beliefs are, of course, almost impossible to establish. The prince himself was believed, on somewhat elusive grounds, to have sympathized with the commons in their quarrel with the court in 1376; and Stafford, his retainer, was certainly regarded favourably enough by them to be nominated to the committee that liaised with the lords. But it is doubtful if they were perceived as being closely identified with either of the two parties that had opposed one another in the struggles of that year. That was one of their strengths. They were able to promote peace and reconciliation. The princess herself had mediated between Gaunt and the Londoners back in February.[15] Shortly after his accession her son built on these foundations by sending Latimer, Burley and two other of his knights to the capital to begin the work of establishing a lasting accord between them. He (or his advisers) also took the initiative in effecting a reconciliation between the duke and his old adversary, the bishop of Winchester.[16] The duke by all accounts co-operated with the regime, and co-operated willingly. He saw which way the wind was blowing, and there is nothing to suggest that he resisted it.[17] Walsingham's story that he left the court in umbrage, having taken offence at being asked to surrender Hertford castle, is no more than another instance of that chronicler's vilification of the duke.[18] The duke did indeed withdraw to the north. But it was not so much out of pique as out of necessity, for the deteriorating situation there required the attention of a senior figure. Earlier in the summer an English raiding force under Sir Thomas Musgrave, the keeper of

[13] For these men, see Lewis, 'The "Continual Council"'; and Tout, *Chapters*, iii, 328, 332; iv, 391, 397. Segrave also had connections with Gaunt: Goodman, *John of Gaunt*, 72. Goodman generally places greater emphasis than allowed here on the continued presence of Gaunt's men in government (ibid., 72–3). It is true, as Goodman states, that from 1377 the office of chancellor was filled by two of the duke's men in succession: Adam Houghton, bishop of St David's, and Richard, Lord Scrope, but the evidence of the rise of the prince's men following Richard's accession is too clear to be ignored; and it grew stronger with time: see below, 31.

[14] The main exception was Stafford, who had been nominated a member of the council during the Good Parliament of 1376 (Holmes, *The Good Parliament*, 102, 105n).

[15] See above, 21.

[16] *CA*, 148–50.

[17] In early 1378 he even went so far as to appoint his old adversary Bishop Courtenay one of his attorneys during his absence on active service (C76/62 m.1).

[18] *CA*, 163.

Berwick, had been intercepted and defeated by the Scots, Musgrave himself being captured and held to ransom.[19] Measures were urgently needed to stabilize the situation, particularly since a truce was still supposed to be operative. Gaunt was sent to the border with instructions to arrange a March Day (meeting) with the earl of Carrick, the Scottish king's son.[20] The settlement which they reached did not resolve any of the underlying issues in dispute, but at least the political temperature was lowered. By March the duke was on his way south again and in April he attended a meeting of the council.[21]

The council which Gaunt attended in April was rather different in membership from that which he had left in the previous summer. The body nominated in July had held office for only three months. In mid-October, during the first parliament of the reign, a successor to it was named. This was a similarly constituted but smaller body, drawn from a narrower political base. Among the prelates Courtenay and Erghum were reappointed, and a third prelate, Appleby of Carlisle, joined them. Among the earls March too was reappointed, but Arundel's place was taken by Stafford. Among the bannerets and knights Sir Richard Stafford, Sir John Devereux and Sir Hugh Segrave all retained their places, but a sizeable number including Lords Latimer and Cobham, Sir Roger Beauchamp, Sir John Knyvet and Sir Ralph Ferrers were dropped – their places being taken by Sir Henry Scrope.[22] The reason for this series of changes was almost certainly a desire to make a break with the past. Latimer, Beauchamp and the others who lost their places had all been associated with the discredited court faction of 1376. They were given a place on the July council for continuity's sake, but by October they were regarded as dispensable. The second council held office for almost exactly a year. The third and last of the councils took over in October 1378, during the Gloucester parliament. Again significant changes were made. Arundel and Suffolk succeeded to the places of March and Stafford as the earls, and Wykeham of Winchester and Harewell of Wells to those of the three previous bishops. Sir Robert Hales and Sir Roger Beauchamp came on as the two bannerets and Sir Aubrey de Vere and Sir Robert Rous as the knights bachelor.[23] Sir Ralph

[19] Ibid., 165–6. The raid had been provoked by the Scots' assault on English-held Roxburgh. For discussion, see A.F. Alexander, 'The War with France in 1377' (University of London Ph.D. thesis, 1934), 122–4.

[20] Rotuli Scotie in Turri Londoniensi . . . asservati, ed. D. Macpherson et al. (London, 2 vols, 1814–19), ii, 3; E403/466, 7 Jan. 1378.

[21] Goodman, John of Gaunt, 73.

[22] Lewis, 'The "Continual Council"', 248.

[23] Ibid., 250. Hales was the ill-fated prior of the Hospitallers who was to be

Stafford, Sir Henry Scrope and Sir John Knyvet (who appears to have continued as a councillor from the previous year) were dropped. The probable aim of these changes was to effect a still cleaner break with the past. Stafford, Scrope and Knyvet had all been closely associated with the government in Edward III's last years, and very likely there was pressure from the commons to have them removed.[24] The new appointees were chiefly men whose earlier careers had been with the Black Prince. Bishop Harewell and Aubrey de Vere had been employed in the prince's service, while Wykeham and the earl of Suffolk had been loosely identified with his cause during the Good Parliament. The changes of November 1378 merely reinforced the already clear dominance of the prince's men at the new king's court.

The three 'continual councils' formed the effective government of the country for the first three years of the reign, from 1377 to January 1380. The issues which had a claim on their attention were wide-ranging. As always, matters of patronage, finance and public order were in the forefront. But the most serious issue in 1377 was the renewal of the French war. On 24 June, just three days into the reign, the truce which had been negotiated at Bruges in 1375 came to an end. This was an event that the governments on both sides of the Channel had been preparing for. The French council had been particularly active. At the Clos des Galées, the naval base at Rouen established at the end of the thirteenth century, they had given their backing to a shipbuilding programme that brought the French navy to the peak of its medieval strength. By the end of the 1370s the French commanders probably had some 40–50 vessels at their disposal, perhaps 25 of them galleys (powered, that is, by oars as well as sails);[25] and to these were added each campaigning season the five to eight galleys assured by the French alliance with Castile. On the English side preparations had been less intense. For the duration of the truce the council had been hampered by an embarrassing shortage of money. The commons had made no grant of the levy on moveables since 1373, and the wool customs which were still collected would only cover the standing charges of defence. As a result, there was little or no cash in the exchequer to pay for forward preparations against the French. The government's embarrassment was ended in the parliament of January 1377, when the commons made a grant of a poll tax of 4d a head for the specific purpose of paying for the

murdered by the rebels in 1381. Sir Roger Beauchamp, a retainer of Gaunt's, had been Edward III's chamberlain in 1376. Sir Aubrey de Vere, a former retainer of the Black Prince, was uncle of Richard's future favourite.

[24] C. Given–Wilson, 'Royal Charter Witness Lists 1327–1399', *Medieval Prosopography*, xii, ii (1991), 57–8.

[25] C.F. Richmond, 'The War at Sea', *The Hundred Years War*, ed. K. Fowler (London, 1971), 105.

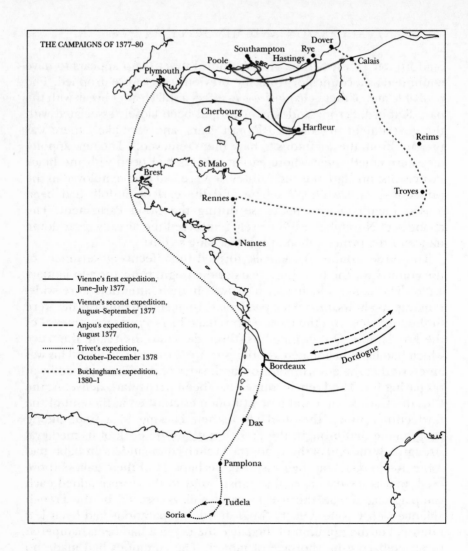

THE CAMPAIGNS OF 1377–80

Legend:
— Vienne's first expedition, June–July 1377
— Vienne's second expedition, August–September 1377
--- Anjou's expedition, August 1377
········ Trivet's expedition, October–December 1378
·-·-· Buckingham's expedition, 1380–1

organization of an expedition to serve at sea. Work on the expedition, which was to be under Richard's nominal command, began in the early spring; but with the old king's death on 21 June it had to be postponed until the autumn.[26] It was a singular misfortune that at the time when the truce was due to expire the council was entirely without forces to field against the enemy. It was a further misfortune that over the previous few years the country's naval strength had been run down. The king's own ships – the permanent element in any force put to sea – had dwindled from twenty-seven in 1369 to no more than five in 1378; and the

---

[26] See above, 22.

number of vessels available for impressment had undergone a similar and equally catastrophic decline.[27]

The extent of English weakness was shown in the series of hostilities that erupted in the second half of the year. The moment that the truce ended the French opened a co-ordinated offensive on no fewer than three major fronts – the English south coast, Calais and Aquitaine.[28] The fiercest assault was mounted on the first of these. In the fortnight beginning 29 June a powerful Franco-Castilian fleet under the French admiral Jean de Vienne swept through the Channel ports, looting and destroying as it went. Vienne's men landed at Rye and set fire to the defences; heading west, they handed out similar treatment to Rottingdean, Weymouth, Dartmouth and Plymouth. After a brief return to Harfleur to refit they set out on a second offensive, in the course of which they landed in the Isle of Wight and extracted a ransom of 1,000 marks (£666) from the populace. After launching assaults on Southampton and Poole and attempting a landing at Folkestone, they headed back across the Channel to join in the second thrust of the offensive, a combined land and sea assault on Calais. The French commanders' plan appears to have been to cut Calais off by land and sea. Vienne and his fleet blockaded the town on the seaward side, while the duke of Burgundy and his forces took up position on the landward. Burgundy enjoyed considerable success in reducing two of the forts which constituted the town's outermost line of defence: on 7 September Ardres, the south-eastern fort, surrendered, and a week later Audruicq followed suit. With the fall of these forts Calais itself lay open to attack. But then, quite unexpectedly, the threat was lifted. The French abandoned the siege and turned back. According to the chroniclers, they were deterred by the marshy terrain which the recent heavy rain had rendered impassable. Shortly afterwards the English commander, Sir Hugh Calveley, was confident enough to carry the war into the enemy's camp. Raiding the nearby town of Étaples, he plundered the market, held the merchants to ransom and carried away all the wine.[29] In the meantime, to coincide with their offensive in the north, the French had opened up a front in the south. In August the duke of Anjou and his forces swept down the Dordogne valley, taking the towns of Condat, Bergerac and Castillon. In an engagement at Eymet on 1 September his men captured the seneschal of Aquitaine, Sir Thomas Felton. By mid-September it seemed likely that Bordeaux itself was

[27] J. Sherborne, 'The English Navy: Shipping and Manpower, 1369–89', *P&P*, xxxvii (1967), repr. in his *War, Politics and Culture in Fourteenth-Century England*, ed. A. Tuck (London, 1994), 31–2.
[28] For a full discussion of the war, see Alexander, 'The War with France'.
[29] *CA*, 192–3.

going to be encircled and besieged. But a few weeks later, in early
October, Anjou turned back. According to the chroniclers, the defection of the lords of Duras and Rauzan posed a threat to his rear.
Whether or not this was the case, the danger to Bordeaux was lifted. In
the months that followed the English administration were able to start
rebuilding the duchy's defences. But the territory now left to them
amounted to little more than the coastal littoral.

The scale and ferocity of the French offensives made a speedy
response by the English council essential. In mid-August plans were
agreed for reviving the naval expedition deferred in June. On 13 and
17 August orders were given for the arrest of vessels and impressment
of mariners, and on 8 September the mayor of London was ordered to
proclaim that all the commanders participating in the force should
assemble their retinues in the capital by the 27th.[30] The fleet, numbering nearly 100 vessels, sailed under Buckingham's command on 1
November.[31] Its objectives appear to have been twofold – to attack a
large Franco-Castilian fleet moored off Sluys, and to relieve the English
garrison under siege at Brest. In the event, only the second objective
was achieved. A week or ten days after it set sail the fleet was dispersed
by a storm in the Channel and had to return to port. When it put to sea
again after refitting, probably in mid-December, it ran into fresh
trouble: this time there was a mutiny in Lord FitzWalter's squadron. But
it lived at least partly up to expectations. Sir Thomas Percy succeeded in
routing a fleet of Spanish merchantmen; and in January Buckingham
took possession of the castle at Brest.[32]

By the end of 1377 the worst of the French offensive was over, and in
the following year the council was able to begin planning offensive
measures of its own. In the first parliament of the reign, in October, the
commons had made a generous grant of a double fifteenth and tenth
(the tax on moveable property), and by the time this had been collected the exchequer was £100,000 the richer. Simultaneously, a shipbuilding programme had been initiated which, it was hoped, would
provide a fleet of some thirty or more balingers by the following
March.[33] With these resources at its disposal the government could
match the French for the first time in the scale of its military planning,
and the opportunity was seized to mount an expedition as ambitious as
any in the recent past. Its objective was nowhere openly stated. The

[30] Alexander, 'The War with France', 207–9.
[31] Anon., 116–17. The month's delay was caused by difficulties in assembling the
shipping. For the size and composition of the force, see Sherborne, 'The English
Navy: Shipping and Manpower', 36.
[32] Anon., 117; CA, 171–2, 191–2.
[33] For the shipbuilding programme, see Alexander, 'The War with France', 205–
6; Sherborne, 'The English Navy: Shipping and Manpower', 33–4.

recovery of Gascony was one possibility, but it is likely that a more modest objective was preferred – perhaps the ending of enemy dominance of the Channel or the establishment of a bastion on the Breton coastline. Overall command was entrusted to Lancaster, but the earls of Arundel and Salisbury were also given major responsibilities. The first indentures were sealed at the end of January, and protections were enrolled from mid-February.[34] But then nothing happened. February turned into March, and March into April. Lancaster still lingered on the south coast and finally on, or shortly after, 7 April Arundel and Salisbury sailed without him. The earls' achievements were insubstantial. They arrived off Harfleur, hoping to force the Risle estuary; but local levies repulsed their attack and, after withdrawing, they headed west to Cherbourg, where according to French sources they suffered in another engagement.[35] In the meantime, according to Walsingham, Lancaster was cavorting at home with Katherine Swynford, his mistress.[36] The duke did not embark until around 25 July, although his brother Buckingham had probably departed some four weeks earlier. The delay left the duke painfully exposed to Walsingham's ridicule. But the reason for it lay not so much in his attachment to his mistress as in the more matter-of-fact business of shortage of vessels. The construction programme initiated in the winter had not lived up to expectation, and the council was obliged to resort to impressment. In May and June royal sergeants-at-arms were sent to a host of ports to seize vessels for the duke's fleet. But by the time they had all been assembled, his mariners – by now tired of waiting – were deserting in droves.[37] The duke finally set sail in July, any advantage of surprise, let alone of co-ordination with other commanders, having by now been lost. He headed for the Norman coast in the hope of engaging the enemy; but the latter, forewarned of his coming, simply retreated up the Seine and placed themselves beyond his reach. He could not pursue them as he did not have any mounts. Thwarted of his objective, he took to the seas once more, and sailed westwards to St Malo. His intention here, it appears, was to capture the town – then garrisoned by the French – and to turn it into an English bastion on the lines of Brest. But once again

---

[34] E101/68/7/159-67; C76/62 mm.18, 21, 24.

[35] The Evesham writer says that they returned on 6 June without inflicting damage on the French (*HVR*, 50). Two of their commanders, Sir Philip and Sir Peter Courtenay, were worsted in an engagement with a Spanish vessel, Sir Peter and his men being taken prisoner (SC8/100/4990).

[36] *CA*, 195-7.

[37] Ibid., 195-6. On 30 November 1377 a number of towns were ordered to build a total of 25 balingers, each of 40-50 oars, these to be delivered by 1 March next (*CCR 1377-81*, 32-3). But it seems that in practice they simply failed to act on the order. I am grateful to Dr I. Friel for advice on this point. Orders for the arrest of vessels are to be found in E403/468, 28 May, 12 June; C76/62 mm.9, 10.

his plans misfired. The outcome of the siege depended almost entirely
on the miners' success in bringing down the walls. So vital was these
men's work that the earl of Arundel, who had by now joined the army,
was appointed to watch over it by day and night. One evening, however,
the earl and his men allowed their guard to drop, and the French
sallied forth and brought the mine down. A council of war was held and
it was decided to abandon the siege forthwith.[38]

The duke returned to England to face the inevitable accusations of
cowardice and incompetence. Over the years he had grown used to
these, and to some extent could live with them. Far harder to bear was
the charge of complicity in a crime committed during his absence
which had major implications for foreign policy. The crime was the
killing in August of an esquire by the name of Robert Hawley, while
resisting arrest, in Westminster Abbey. Hawley and his comrade-in-arms
John Shakell had taken refuge in the abbey to escape the clutches of a
government anxious to gain possession of a prisoner whom they had in
their custody. The outrage that followed – perpetrated in gross violation of the abbey's sanctuary – was the result largely of a miscalculation
on the part of the royal officer sent to arrest them. It was a dénouement
neither desired nor willed by the government. But it became a contemporary *cause célèbre*, and the chroniclers were unanimous in holding
Gaunt and the government morally, if not directly, responsible.
    The background to the story lay in the Black Prince's campaigns in
the Spanish peninsula a decade before. At the battle of Najera in 1367,
at which the prince had triumphed over the Castilians, the esquires had
captured a major Spanish grandee and cadet of the royal house of
Aragon, the count of Denia.[39] Understandably in view of the count's
rank, the ransom they demanded was a high one – 60,000 crowns; and
an arrangement was made whereby the count was released in exchange
for his son, so that he could return home to collect it. Finding the
money proved difficult, however, and the count asked his kinsman the
king of Aragon to intercede with the English council to secure a moderation of the esquires' demands. The council, concerned to improve
relations with the Aragonese, duly obliged, but all their intercessions
proved useless, and the esquires insisted on payment of the ransom in
full. Faced with this conflict between private interest and public need,
the council had little hesitation in giving priority to the latter. In
October 1377 it committed the esquires to the Tower, where they

[38] Froissart, i, 551–2; *CA*, 205.
[39] E. Perroy, 'Gras profits et rançons pendant la guerre de cent ans; l'affaire du
comte de Denia', *Mélanges d'histoire du moyen âge dédiés à la mémoire de Louis Halphen*
(Paris, 1951), 573–80, repr. in his *Études d'histoire médiévale* (Paris, 1979).

languished for several months. But in the following August they made a dramatic escape, and took sanctuary in the abbey. On instructions from the council the constable of the Tower, Sir Alan Buxhill, went after them. Backed up by a force of some fifty men, he managed to winkle Shakell out of the church, but Hawley slipped his grasp and ran back inside. In despair he ordered his men to drag him out. They tracked him down in the choir, where mass was being celebrated, and a scuffle broke out. A sacristan who tried to fend off the attackers was cut down, and Hawley himself dispatched on the steps of the high altar.

The Hawley–Shakell affair was more than a minor flash in the political pan. It reopened old wounds in the body politic and had repercussions on several areas of policy. First and foremost, it led to a renewal of the feud between John of Gaunt and the bishop of London, William Courtenay. Courtenay, an aggressive defender of ecclesiastical liberties, had crossed swords with Gaunt on several occasions before. In 1376 he had championed William Wykeham when the latter was being victimized by Gaunt, and in the following year he had been the prime instigator of proceedings against Gaunt's propagandist and pamphleteer John Wyclif. The proceedings against Wyclif had broken up in disorder in Courtenay's own cathedral on 19 February 1377, when Gaunt threatened to drag the bishop out by the hair of his head. Since then relations between the two men had improved. The reconciliation between Gaunt and the Londoners had owed much to Courtenay's mediation, and in the summer of 1378 the duke had sufficient trust in the bishop to appoint him one of his attorneys.[40]

In the wake of the violation of sanctuary all this good work was undone. Courtenay pronounced sentence of excommunication on Buxhill and everyone else involved in the deed with the specific and very pointed exceptions of the king, the princess of Wales and Lancaster – as if to imply that he suspected their involvement, but was prevented by lack of evidence from condemning them for it.[41] In the following month he infuriated the duke still further by refusing to attend a council meeting at Windsor, to which he had been invited.[42] The duke was only dissuaded with difficulty from going to fetch him in person. The inevitable result of this trading of insults was that the duke was dragged into a dispute to which he had not originally been party. But under his leadership – or, at least, with his co-operation – the court soon began to fight back against its ecclesiastical assailants. It changed the venue of the November parliament from its traditional meeting place within yards of where the sacrilege had occurred to Gloucester, a

[40] C76/62 m.1.
[41] CA, 210.
[42] Ibid.

hundred miles away. And, more substantially, it proposed constructing a justification for the breach of the abbey's sanctuary by saying that the right of sanctuary did not exist in cases of debt or account; or, if such a right had mistakenly been conceded in the past, this was 'not a privilege but a depravity' revocable by the king.[43] Among the lords and commons there was a substantial body of opinion willing to go along with this line; and it may have been for this reason that the abbot of Westminster travelled in person to Gloucester to counter it. Along with many of his peers, he feared that abolition of sanctuary was the thin end of the wedge; and that, unless prevented, it would be followed by proposals, like those heard a few years before, for the confiscation of the Church's wealth to pay for the wars. The abbot appeared before the commons, and by all accounts spoke well: so well, in fact, that the court now decided to bring along speakers of its own. A couple of days later the commons were addressed by John Wyclif and an unnamed doctor of laws: the two were men so persuasive, the *Anonimalle* writer says, that there was no clerk who could counter them.[44] The arguments which Wyclif used were ones that were later to appear in his writings: that the right of sanctuary was not open to debtors, and that in time of war the king could lay claim to the property of the 'possessioners' – that is the great landowners of the Church. What impact Wyclif had on his audience is not known. After parliament was dissolved, somewhat precipitately, on 16 November, the uproar abated. But the court did not forget the issue. It was after all not Lancaster – or not Lancaster alone – who had brought Wyclif along, but two courtiers, Sir Simon Burley and Sir Thomas Percy.[45] As far as these men were concerned, a satisfactory outcome had to be found; and this was finally achieved in the next parliament, held in the spring of 1379, when the right of protection to fraudulent debtors was successfully withdrawn.[46]

It is apparent from the acrimony in the Gloucester parliament that the Hawley–Shakell affair had major repercussions in internal ecclesiastical politics. But the repercussions in foreign policy were equally, and perhaps more, important. The effect of the release of the count's son, however unorthodox the manner in which it had been achieved, was to pave the way for a rapid improvement in Anglo-Aragonese relations. England's involvement in Iberian, and specifically Aragonese, affairs had its origins in her need to neutralize the danger posed by the

---

[43] *RP*, iii, 37. The quotation 'non privilegium sed pravilegium' is from *Eulogium*, 346. The play on words is lost in English.

[44] *Anon.*, 123.

[45] Ibid.

[46] *CA*, 223; *SR*, ii, 12.

Castilian navy. Since 1369, when Henry of Trastamara had won the crown with French backing, Castile had become little more than a satellite of her northern neighbour. Her galleys were regularly used by the French to attack English shipping and harry the English coastline. But her distance from England placed her beyond reach of reprisal. Gaunt's idea of leading an expedition to the peninsula as yet attracted little support, and diplomacy offered the only realistic way of counter-ing the Castilian menace.[47] Accordingly, in 1377 the council decided on an initiative to seek an alliance with Aragon, her eastern neighbour. The timing certainly favoured such a proposal, because Aragon was herself under threat from the French. Two years before, the duke of Anjou had claimed the Aragonese island of Majorca, demanding that the Aragonese king, Peter, surrender it and threatening force if the demand was refused. King Peter had no intention of complying, but nonetheless felt vulnerable enough to respond favourably to the over-tures then being made to him by the English. In October 1377 the chamber knight Sir John Roches and a Gascon clerk, Gerald de Menta, journeyed to Barcelona with instructions to discuss an alliance. The negotiations proceeded slowly; and even when the envoys returned in the following March, bringing with them a draft treaty, they did not feel entirely sure of the Aragonese king's intentions. Peter was by nature a cautious man, and so long as his kinsman's son remained captive in London, he would not commit himself in a hurry. In August 1378, however, the hostage problem was suddenly, if unexpectedly, resolved. Matters could now move more speedily. Roches was given new instruc-tions to convey to the Aragonese and set off immediately for Plymouth. But there he was held up by the shortage of vessels; and by the time he finally put to sea, the situation in the Iberian peninsula had dramati-cally changed.[48]

The event that had precipitated the sudden change was a Castilian assault on the independence of the small Pyrenean state of Navarre. Three months earlier Henry of Trastamara's troops had marched into, and occupied, the southern provinces of Navarre. The event was not altogether unexpected. Charles II, 'the Bad', the Navarrese ruler, had been living dangerously for some time. His dual role as both a king in his own right and a vassal of his neighbour the king of France presented him with a series of insoluble dilemmas which he could gloss over only by ambiguity and deceit. The dilemmas were similar in character to those that the king of England had long faced in his capacity as duke of

---

[47] For Gaunt's Iberian policy, see below, 95–6, 149.

[48] Alexander, 'The War with France', 243–9; P.E. Russell, *The English Intervention in Spain and Portugal in the Time of Edward III and Richard II* (Oxford, 1955), 249–61. Russell says that Roches was held up by the weather. But the real problem was that Gaunt had taken all the vessels.

Aquitaine. But in the king of Navarre's case they were aggravated by his country's smaller size and precarious location. Flanked on the north by France and on the south by Castile, Navarre survived by courtesy of its neighbours; and the only way that its ruler could avoid being reduced to satellite status was by seeking protection from such potentially sympathetic powers as England or Aragon. But it was precisely in his ability to conduct an independent foreign policy that he was likely to find himself circumscribed by his obligations to the king of France. An unwise or an untimely choice of allies, an over-daring move on the diplomatic front, and he could find himself being toppled. Charles knew only too well the risks he was running. He had turned against the Valois more than once before and had lived to tell the tale. But in 1378 it seemed as if his well of luck was running dry. In the spring of that year two of his envoys had been arrested in France, and the papers found on them were said to prove not only that their master was in communication with the English but also that he was plotting to poison the French king.[49] The latter took his namesake's guilt to be self-evident, and acted swiftly to forestall the possibility of sympathetic action on his behalf by the English. He ordered the confiscation of the Navarrese castles in Normandy, and within weeks these had been occupied by French troops. Charles the Bad's response was to speed up the negotiations that he had opened with the English. He dispatched an envoy to the English court to advise them of what had happened and, on hearing that his case had been sympathetically received, crossed the Channel himself, probably in June. He landed in Cornwall and rode to Windsor where, according to Froissart, he was warmly welcomed by Richard and his councillors.[50] The purpose of Charles's visit was to obtain military support for his kingdom; but his bargaining hand was weak, and the English government took advantage of it to extract an important concession in return. Charles was offered the services of 1,000 troops for four months 'for a campaign . . . inside the confines of Navarre or outside it', but only on condition that he ceded possession of the port of Cherbourg. He agreed; and on 27 June Cherbourg was formally taken over by an English garrison.[51]

Unfortunately for the Navarrese ruler the English troops arrived too late to be of immediate help. They were held up at Plymouth by a shortage of vessels and by the time that they disembarked in Gascony the kingdom was already being overrun. The invading force, as it

---

[49] R. Delachenal, *Histoire de Charles V* (5 vols, Paris, 1909–31), v, 184–94. The two agents also made confessions which the king was able to use. By the treaty of Vernon, 1371, Charles of Navarre was required to do homage to the French king for the barony of Montpellier.

[50] Froissart, i, 540–1.

[51] Initially on the basis of a three-year lease, later renewed (*Foed.*, vii, 201).

happened, was not French but Castilian. Henry of Castile harboured ambitions of his own in the Pyrenees and was only too happy to act as his ally's proxy. His army crossed the border at the end of June, and by October had occupied most of the southern half of the kingdom. But a total victory eluded him. Pamplona, the capital, though surrounded, refused to surrender so long as there remained hope of relief by the English; and when after three months it was learned in the Castilian camp that the English were on their way, a decision was taken to withdraw. By the time of their arrival the English were thus in a somewhat embarrassing position. They had made the effort to cross the Pyrenees; but, having done so, they found that there was little for them to do. Trivet, their commander, contented himself with leading an expedition against the Castilian town of Soria. Bad weather prevented him from storming the place, but he and his men returned laden with booty, and their raid had exposed the vulnerability of the Castilian countryside.[52] Trivet's services in the Pyrenees earned him a personal welcome from Charles on his return, but outward cordiality was no guide to that monarch's real intentions, and already he was thinking of suing for peace. Negotiations were opened with the French, and on 31 March a treaty was signed at Briones which brought the hostilities to an end.[53]

The decision to intervene in Navarre was of questionable merit for the English, for the costs were high and the prizes few. But the episode resulted in one strategic gain: the acquisition of Cherbourg. Possession of this Cotentin port fitted neatly into the evolving strategy of acquiring a ring of fortresses on the perimeter of France. Bordeaux and Bayonne had been English-held since the twelfth century; two centuries later Calais and Brest had been gained; and now there was Cherbourg. The justification for acquiring the fortresses was essentially twofold: firstly, they constituted a forward line of defence, shielding the south coast from attack and providing bases for operations at sea; and secondly, they could be used as invasion routes into France. The main argument against them was that they were expensive to maintain. The cost of Calais, on the government's own admission, came to £24,000 a year, and that of Brest to at least £8,000.[54] At the Gloucester parliament of

---

[52] For these events, see Froissart, i, 555–60; Russell, *English Intervention*, 264–73.

[53] Russell, *English Intervention*, 275–6.

[54] *RP*, iii, 34. Scrope's figure for Calais was probably fairly accurate: between 1378 and 1381 the town cost the exchequer annually £23,500: J. Sherborne, 'The Cost of English Warfare with France in the Later Fourteenth Century', *BIHR*, i (1977), repr. in his *War, Politics and Culture in Fourteenth-Century England*, 67. After 1389, when a truce came into effect, the cost of the town fell appreciably: see below, 256.

1378 the government's spokesman, Richard, Lord Scrope, cited the cost of maintenance as one of the grounds for seeking a grant of the moveables levy from the commons. His argument was that the barbicans, as they were called, were 'good and noble ports and entries for mounting attacks on the enemy'. The commons, however, were less persuaded of their virtues. In the commons' view the barbicans represented charges which the king should meet himself and which should not constitute a burden on the subject. Scrope's reply was that the barbicans contributed to the defence of the realm and the safeguarding of the seas and that without them the country would never enjoy peace.[55] He failed to convince his audience. At the end of the session the commons, resisting his blandishments, declined to offer a grant of the moveables levy and merely renewed the wool duties at existing rates, with a 'novel increase' of 13s 4d on each sack of wool to be taken until Easter.[56] The commons' position was a logical one and consistent with precedent. In the past, continuing charges like garrisons had always been met from the crown's own resources, and only a 'necessity' – a threat to the very existence of the realm – had justified recourse to public taxation. If, by its attempt to finance the barbicans from taxation, the government was seeking to extend the traditional grounds for such imposts, it did not succeed. However, only weeks after the Gloucester session a change in the military situation occurred which greatly assisted the government in its dealings with the commons. In December a crisis erupted in Brittany; and in the following spring the government made a renewed, and on this occasion a more successful, appeal to the assembly's generosity.

The background to the crisis in Brittany lay in a set of circumstances not dissimilar to those in Navarre. The duke of Brittany, John IV, like his Navarrese counterpart, lived in the shadow of his mighty neighbour the king of France, whose vassal he was; and, again like the Navarrese king, he sought to safeguard his independence by playing the French king off against his other neighbour, in this case the king of England. Balancing the two involved him in some delicate diplomacy. He could manage the task adequately enough in time of peace, but in war it became more difficult. With the resumption of hostilities in 1369 his position became all but untenable and in 1372 he declared openly for Edward III and fled to England. The French moved swiftly to occupy the duchy, and for the next six years Brest was the only town of any

Scrope's figure for Brest, however, seems a little on the high side. Between 1378 and 1381 the average annual cost of maintaining the garrison was roughly £5,500: Sherborne, 'The Cost of English Warfare', 67; M. Jones, *Ducal Brittany, 1364–1399* (Oxford, 1970), Appendix E.

[55] *RP*, iii, 36.

[56] Ibid., 37–8.

importance that held out against them. Resistance to the occupation was minimal; and the prospects for John's early return would have been bleak, had not Charles uncharacteristically overreached himself. In December 1378, encouraged by the expropriation of the Navarrese estates, he announced that he was annexing the duchy. On this occasion, however, he miscalculated. He offended the particularist feelings of the Bretons; and he paid for his insensitivity when in the following spring they invited Duke John to return.[57]

Their ruler's initial response to the invitation was surprisingly unenthusiastic. Possibly he wanted time to weigh the sincerity of his subjects' desire for reconciliation. But more likely he was conscious of his lack of money. During his stay in England he had become heavily dependent on income from the exchequer, and in the spring of 1379, when he received the call, the exchequer had hardly any spare cash to allow him. No subsidy on moveables had been granted in the Gloucester parliament, and the receipts from the wool and wine customs were already spoken for. To make ends meet, recourse was had to borrowing. In March and April nearly £14,000 was raised in sums, mostly small, lent by individuals and corporations – a figure which was a not inconsiderable tribute to the government's creditworthiness, but which nevertheless fell short of what was required.[58] It quickly became clear that a new parliament would have to be summoned, even though it was less than six months since the last one had ended. Accordingly writs were issued for the estates to assemble at Westminster on 25 April. Scrope once again pleaded the government's case, this time in his new capacity as chancellor. He described how he and his fellow ministers had coped since the previous December, and how a 'great council' of peers and prelates had met in February to sanction the raising of loans; however, he continued, the perils facing the realm were such that it had proved impossible to ordain remedy without making a new charge on the commons – hence the decision to summon the present parliament.[59] This time Lord Scrope received a more sympathetic hearing. The commons responded by granting the second of the poll taxes, this one graduated according to rank to forestall complaints of unfairness. With the prospect of money again flowing into the exchequer, the government could resume its military planning, and in July an agreement was made with Duke John promising him a force of 2,000 men-at-arms and as many archers for four and a half months to serve from 1 August.[60] The duke was in more buoyant mood now, and whatever reservations

[57] Jones, *Ducal Brittany*, 60–86.
[58] A list of lenders and of the sums lent is in *CPR 1377–81*, 635–8.
[59] *RP*, iii, 55–6.
[60] J.H. Ramsay, *The Genesis of Lancaster, 1307–1399* (2 vols, Oxford, 1913), ii, 130–1.

he had once had he laid aside. On 3 August he crossed the Channel
with a small escort and landed at St Malo.[61] An enormous crowd assembled on the beach to greet him. Walsingham describes how people
waded out up to their knees when his ship entered the harbour, and his
disembarkation turned into a triumphal progress.[62] The local political
tide appeared to be moving in his favour. Within a couple of days he
had received the allegiance of most of the Breton nobility, and the
French did not dare to oppose him. But at this crucial moment in
Anglo-Breton relations planning on the other side of the Channel was
running into difficulties. The yield from the poll tax was proving much
lower than expected, and when collection was complete no more than
£22,000 had been received.[63] The wage bill to which the government
was committed amounted to something in the order of £50,000. Clearly
plans would have to be scaled down. The force of 2,000 men-at-arms
and as many archers optimistically envisaged in July was reduced to one
of no more than 650 men-at-arms and as many archers. Command of
this smaller force was entrusted to Sir John Arundel, the marshal of
England and a soldier of repute. From the beginning, however, the
force was dogged by misfortune. Westerly winds kept it at Plymouth for
several weeks, and the men whiled away the time, so Walsingham says,
ravaging the surrounding countryside and assaulting the nuns in a
nearby convent. After such carnal self-indulgence, the men could
hardly expect the Almighty's support, and retribution was not long in
coming. The fleet finally set sail around 6 December, but within 24
hours it was caught up in a terrible storm and swept down-channel.
Nineteen vessels transporting horses were wrecked in Mount's Bay, and
others were blown into the Irish Sea. Arundel's flagship ran aground off
Ireland, and he himself was drowned. Not a man reached the shore of
Brittany.[64]

   The storm in the western approaches was soon followed by a storm in
parliament, which also claimed some notable casualties. The commons
were furious at the news of the débâcle, and their first demand was for
the dismissal of the 'continual councillors'. Sir John Gildesburgh, the
Speaker, said that the councillors had served the king for long enough

[61] *CA*, 234. The duke's first letters on landing were dated at the tower of Solidor,
St Malo, on 3 August (*Recueil des Actes de Jean IV, Duc de Bretagne, I, 1357–1382*, ed.
M. Jones, Institut Armoricain de Recherches Economiques et Humaines, xxviii,
1980, 63).

[62] *CA*, 234.

[63] *RP*, iii, 73. This was Scrope's figure and includes the proceeds of the clerical
tenth. E.B. Fryde, *The Great Revolt of 1381* (London, 1981), 11, gives only £19,000,
presumably referring only to payments by the laity.

[64] *CA*, 247–53: an example of Walsingham's reportage at its most brilliant. The
Westminster Abbey Liber Niger gives the date of Arundel's drowning as 16 December: WAM, Book 1, fo.87[r].

and at sufficient cost: no more should be appointed. The king was of good discretion and of fair stature; he was almost as old as his grandfather Edward III had been at the time of his coronation, and Edward had had no other councillors than his five principal officers. In the commons' view the present king's five equivalent officers should form the core of a new council: the officers should be chosen now from the ranks of the 'most sufficient' in the realm, and they should remain in office until the next parliament.[65] Speaker Gildesburgh's assault produced an immediate response from the ministers. The members of the 'continual council' were dismissed, and no successors were named in their place. Simultaneously the effective head of the administration, the chancellor Richard, Lord Scrope stood down, to be replaced by Archbishop Sudbury. These were the most radical changes in the personnel of government since Richard's accession.[66] The vigour with which they were pressed bore witness to the extent to which the king's ministers had forfeited support.

The truth of the matter, however, was that the members of the 'continual council' were being cast in the role of scapegoats. In characteristic English fashion they were blamed even for the weather. In the previous month a major disaster had befallen the English forces at sea. Richard himself could not be blamed for this because he was too young; so the 'continual councillors' had to be blamed in his stead. The manner of their dismissal came as a sorry ending to their two and a half years in office. Although they had few substantial achievements to show, their record as a whole had been a not unreasonable one. They had contributed to the restoration of domestic stability after a period of upheaval, and they had brought honesty and prudence to the management of the crown's financial resources. Moreover, they had performed their duties without succumbing to the corruption that had discredited their predecessors. These may have been modest enough achievements; but in the circumstances they were probably the most that could be hoped for. A conciliar regime by its very nature was unlikely to excel in either clarity of vision or efficiency of policy-making. Its strength lay in the opportunity that it afforded to achieve harmony through consensus. To a kingdom weakened by internal discord, as England was in

[65] *RP*, iii, 73. The implication of Gildesburgh's remarks was that the commons considered the king old enough to govern. But Richard was still only thirteen. It is possible that what they were thinking of was his passage from 'pueritia' to 'adolescentia'; but that was judged to occur at fourteen rather than thirteen: Orme, *From Childhood to Chivalry*, 6; and see below, 108.

[66] The treasurer and the keeper of the privy seal, however, remained in office. The commons also pressed for the appointment of a committee to investigate royal income and expenditure (*RP*, iii, 73–4). Such a committee was appointed, but it is doubtful if it ever met: Tout, *Chapters*, iii, 351–2; A. Tuck, *Richard II and the English Nobility* (London, 1973), 45.

1377, the councils offered the prospect of a broadly based government that embraced all the main political factions and estates of society. Figures of every background and affiliation were represented. Though increasingly it was the former dependants of the Black Prince who took the lead, on each of the councils there were men whose principal ties were with either Lancaster or the deceased king; while through the principle of representation by estate men were brought on who had no obvious affiliation with anyone.[67] By engaging the services of men of such diverse background the councils managed to avoid the narrow cliquishness that had characterized the governing elites of Edward's last years.

The cause of reconciliation was also served by the measures that the councils took to consult widely before taking major decisions. The councils of Edward's last years had consulted very little, and had made themselves unpopular as a result. The 'continual councils' avoided the predecessors' error; they regularly canvassed opinion at sessions that were known as 'great councils'. 'Great councils' were larger than usual gatherings, to which most of the lords were invited. In 1379 meetings of the body were held every few weeks, and thereafter as often as occasion demanded.[68] The meetings discussed a wide variety of business, ranging from matters of state, like the Hawley–Shakell affair, through disputes involving members of the nobility, to the rubber-stamping of decisions made elsewhere.[69] In membership the councils defy precise definition. They appear to have included the prelates and a fair scattering of the secular nobility, but not, it seems, any representatives of the commons. It was the absence of the latter which distinguished the councils from sessions of parliament and which limited the functions that they could perform – for only in an assembly attended by the commons could the government obtain consent to taxation. It is highly likely that the government had a preference for doing business with a council; in so doing, it could avoid the embarrassment to which the summoning of the larger assembly could sometimes lead. But, as Richard, Lord Scrope confessed when addressing the commons in May 1379, there were some remedies which only a parliament could ordain. He recalled how the parliament of October 1378 had declined to make a grant of the levy on moveables, allowing only a renewal of the wool and leather duties. The government had found this to be inadequate, and accord-

---

[67] Among the associates of Lancaster were Bishop Erghum and Sir Roger Beauchamp, the latter also a one-time chamberlain of Edward III. Among those without obvious affiliation who were on two or more of the councils were Bishops Wykeham and Appleby, the earls of Arundel and Suffolk and, a member of the third council only, Sir Robert Hales.

[68] Tout, *Chapters*, iii, 336 & n.

[69] *CCR 1377–81*, 85; *CA*, 210; E403/468, 12 Aug.

ingly had resolved to summon a great council 'of all the great lords of the realm, prelates and others', to meet on 20 January 1379. But one after another the lords had excused themselves from attendance, saying either that they were too busy or that they had only just returned from Gloucester, and a postponement had to be arranged. The meeting was rescheduled for 7 February, and this time there was a better response. The government sought, and gained, authorization for the raising of loans 'to ordain an army on the sea'; but it was recognized on all sides that resort to borrowing could only delay, not prevent, the evil day, and that 'if the mischief was to be remedied, a charge would have to be laid upon the commons'. So it was agreed, with some reluctance, that another parliament would have to be summoned.[70]

Scrope's narrative gives a revealing insight into the process of decision-making in the minority. It was a lengthy, cumbersome and sometimes frustrating business, frequently punctuated by appeals to parliament. Parliaments needed managing; and the ease with which they responded to that management varied from session to session. Sometimes, as in 1378, they could prove intractable. But more often, as in January 1380, it was possible to persuade them.[71] Certainly they were neither as obstinate nor as unrealistic as is sometimes supposed. All but one of the six parliaments summoned between January 1377 and November 1380 made a grant of direct taxation, either in the form of a poll tax or a levy on moveable property. This was a record of generosity almost without equal in the middle ages. On only one occasion – in 1379 – had the government been obliged to scale down its planning because of a shortage of money, and over the period as a whole it had been able to balance its books.[72] The result of this continuing supply of funds was almost an excess of military activity. Naval expeditions were launched virtually every year; retinues were equipped for service in theatres as far apart as Brittany and Navarre; enemy assaults on Calais and Aquitaine were checked and ultimately repulsed. And both in the English Channel and on land French ambitions had been contained. Yet overall there was an uneasy feeling among contemporaries that the English achievement amounted to less than the sum of its parts. Walsingham, for example, rebuked the nobility for their failure to attend to the nation's defence. He put into the mouth of the London merchant John Philpot a forceful speech condemning them for their idleness and reluctance to take up arms.[73] But the criticism, although understandable, was in fact misplaced. The nobility were not idle. Far

---

[70] RP, iii, 55–6.
[71] After the ministerial changes a grant of one and a half fifteenths and tenths was made.
[72] Sherborne, 'The Cost of English Warfare'.
[73] CA, 200.

from it: they were heavily represented in all the expeditions organized in these years. The real problem was that their efforts were inadequately co-ordinated. In 1378, for example, months of preparation were vitiated by a shortage of ships and by a failure to make effective use of those that were available: in April and May, when it was becoming clear that there were insufficient vessels to go round, there was an unseemly scramble in which Gaunt, at first the loser, ended up scooping the lot; Neville and Trivet, who were waiting to set out for Gascony, were obliged to hire ships in Zealand, and Sir John Arundel, the captain of Cherbourg, had to rely on impressment to provide himself with the transports that he needed for his horses.[74] The situation was never again to be as chaotic as it had been in 1378, but embarrassments still occasionally arose. In 1379 the opportunity to take advantage of Charles of Navarre's discomfiture was allowed to let slip by the late arrival in the kingdom of Trivet's men;[75] and in 1381 the earl of Buckingham was left high and dry because of a failure to alert him to his ally's imminent defection.[76]

When the full extent of military activity in these years is reviewed, it is difficult not to agree with the commons that the return on the money invested was disappointingly low. Since 1377 over £250,000 had been spent on the war.[77] Yet there were no victories at sea or in the field, and no territorial gains, to show for it. If the immediate cause of this underperformance was to be found in poor co-ordination of resources, this in its turn was but a symptom of a larger problem – the absence of effective royal leadership. In any kingdom or state fighting a war in the middle ages the personal leadership of the king was a vital element in the efficient mobilization of resources. In England's case this was even truer, given the kind of strategy that her commanders had evolved in the previous quarter-century. The essence of that strategy was the simultaneous deployment of two or more armies to divide and distract the enemy until one or the other could inflict a defeat. For such a strategy to be successful there had to be effective co-ordination of the constituent parts – and between those parts and the administration at home. In the middle years of his reign Edward III had provided such co-ordination to perfection. In the later years, however, when his grasp weakened, problems began to appear: for example, in the run-up to the negotiations at Bruges there was a mismatch between military operations and the conduct of diplomacy. In 1377 with the accession of a minor the problems could only get worse. No regent had been

---

[74] E403/466, payments by William Walworth and John Philpot, the treasurers of war; E403/468, 'exitus guerre', 28 May; *Anon.*, 189.

[75] See above, 39.

[76] See below, 55.

[77] Sherborne, 'The Cost of English Warfare', 66–9.

appointed who could act in the office of a king, and the uncertain relation between the councils and the royal uncles did not help.

This weakness on the English side was all the more unfortunate for coming at a time when there was a revival in the quality of leadership in France. Charles V, who had succeeded his father in 1364, was to show himself one of the ablest and most effective of France's later medieval monarchs. He was a man deeply conscious of the exalted nature of his office, who fostered a more ceremonious style to bolster the prestige of the Valois line.[78] At the same time, by skilful management he was able to broaden the base of his monarchy's support. He secured the backing of the magnates in the north and the west whom his father had alienated;[79] and he built up the Valois interest in the dependent duchies of Gascony and Brittany. On the external front he sealed a valuable alliance with Castile, which allowed him the use of that kingdom's navy. As a result of Charles V's achievements the French monarchy was in a far stronger position *vis-à-vis* the English than it had been thirty years earlier in the wake of Crécy. The transformation was evident in the French successes in the 1370s. Over a period of five or six years the gains which the English had made at Brétigny were gradually whittled away until little was left to them beyond the Gascon coastal strip from Bordeaux to Bayonne. But despite the intense pressure to which their forces were subjected, the English were never completely expelled, and the principal reason for this was Charles's reluctance to face his enemy in battle. Charles's formative years had been spent in the aftermath of Crécy and Poitiers and his recollection of these disasters was too vivid to allow him to risk all in a single engagement. Instead, he placed his trust in a Fabian strategy that aimed to wear down his opponent's resistance without exposing his own men to the hazard of battle. It was a strategy that brought him some remarkable successes; but it was also one that suffered from serious, even fatal, weaknesses. It laid the French countryside open to devastation by the enemy, and it deprived Charles himself of the chance to make the breakthrough which only a victory in battle could bring. In a word it produced stalemate; and the consequences of this were unsettling on both sides of the Channel. Among the populace of both England and France there was resentment at the continuing burden of taxation, and in England particularly there was frustration at the failure to find a solution to the military deadlock.

It was this current of unease that lay beneath the political and social tensions so evident in both kingdoms in the late 1370s and early 1380s. In England it was very largely this unease which accounted for the

[78] For Charles's style of monarchy and its influence on Richard later, see below, 350–3.

[79] J.B. Henneman, 'The Military Class and the French Monarchy in the Late Middle Ages', *American Historical Review*, lxxxiii (1978), 946–58.

parliamentary crisis of January 1380. Over the previous twelve to eighteen months the commons had become increasingly unhappy at the councillors' handling of the war, and with the news of the loss of Arundel's fleet their patience finally snapped. Resignations were called for and obtained: the members of the third 'continual council' left office *en bloc*, and the chancellor, Lord Scrope, went with them. These were events of wide political significance. The councillors' departure brought to an end a period when a measure of openness had been restored to decision-making in government and when reconciliation had been promoted at court. From this time on, and particularly from 1381, the process of decision-making was to become less open, and the background of the king's councillors was to be much narrower. The resignation of Chancellor Scrope had consequences of a different kind. Most obviously, there was a loss of drive at the heart of government. This arose partly from the fact that Scrope had been replaced by the ineffective Archbishop Sudbury but, much more, because Scrope himself, in his two and a half years in office, had shown considerable flair in his work as chancellor.[80] Something of the quality of the man can be sensed from the speeches that he delivered to the commons in parliament. These were models of their kind. They combined firmness with flexibility, and frankness with the occasional but necessary half-truth. Scrope always treated the commons as equals. He engaged them as partners in government and expected them to accept a share of responsibility for it. On the other hand, he always took a stand on the prerogatives of his office. At Gloucester in 1378, when he saw that he would have to give way to their request for a copy of the accounts, he took care not to let it become a precedent: he acceded to their demand, but said that he was doing so 'at the king's will and not at their request'.[81] He was clearly much the best publicist in the king's service in these years, and his talents were recognized in the regularity with which he presented the ministerial case to parliament.[82] But this does not necessarily mean that he was the architect of the policies that he expounded. As has been suggested, it is possible that he owed his position to John of Gaunt.[83] He had been a prominent retainer of the duke's since 1367, and he appears to have been a close ally of his in government in the 1370s. But,

---

[80] The assessment which follows differs from Tout's in *Chapters*, iii, 353. For Sudbury, see W.L. Warren, 'A Re-appraisal of Simon Sudbury, Bishop of London (1361–1375) and Archbishop of Canterbury (1375–1381)', *JEH*, x (1959), 139–52.

[81] *RP*, iii, 36.

[82] When he addressed the Gloucester parliament, he did so as steward of the household – before he became chancellor.

[83] Holmes, *Good Parliament*, 64–5; B. Vale, 'The Scropes of Bolton and Masham, c.1300–c.1450. A Study of a Northern Noble Family' (University of York D.Phil. thesis, 1987), 83.

however close his relations with the duke, it is doubtful if he simply took orders from him. Over the years he had accumulated connections with other lords. He was the recipient of bequests from John, Lord Neville and the earls of Arundel and Suffolk; and he served as executor or supervisor of the wills of these two earls, the earl of March and Ralph, Lord Basset of Drayton.[84] He was clearly someone who was widely trusted – and trusted not only by the lords but also, until his downfall, by the commons. In 1376, during the Good Parliament, the commons had appealed to him to give evidence bearing on his term of office as treasurer, and he had said that he would willingly do so and would spare no one in his concern for the truth.[85] His evident honesty in 1376 coupled with his acceptability to both Gaunt and the Black Prince's men marked him out for promotion early in the next reign, and after Richard's coronation he was appointed steward of the household. It was this office that he left fourteen months later when he became chancellor. If anyone has a claim to be considered leader of the government in Richard's early years, particularly in 1378 and 1379, it is probably he. But the area within which he could exercise such leadership was emphatically limited. Medieval politics centred on households, and there were at least two households of importance that had an existence largely independent of the ministers and council. One was, of course, the king's. This was loosely linked with the council through the presence on the latter, after 1378, of courtier knights like Aubrey de Vere and Robert Rous, but its relative detachment is attested by the absence of its most important official, the vice-chamberlain Simon Burley. The other was that of the princess of Wales. In the wake of her husband's death the princess had emerged as an important political figure in her own right, and the lowering of the political temperature that immediately preceded Richard's accession owed much to her mediatory work. In the minority years she took a keen interest in everything that affected the upbringing of her son, and all discussions concerning his marriage had to be conducted through her. The Navarrese agents who visited London to offer the hand of one of King Charles's daughters recognised this when they reported to their master that the proposal enjoyed the support not only of the council but of the princess too.[86] The envoys' optimism proved somewhat premature, as the idea fell victim to the collapse of Anglo-Navarrese relations that occurred in 1379. But a couple of years later, when King Wenzel stepped in with an offer of his sister's hand, negotiations were again conducted with due deference to the princess's wishes.

[84] S. Walker, *The Lancastrian Affinity, 1361–1399* (Oxford, 1990), 281; *The Scrope and Grosvenor Controversy*, ed. N.H. Nicolas (2 vols, London, 1832), ii, 25–6.
[85] *Anon.*, 87–9.
[86] Delachenal, *Histoire de Charles V*, v, 189.

With the resignation of Scrope and the ending of the system of 'continual councils' a turning point was reached in the politics of the minority. From this time the processes of government were to become less transparent; and simultaneously the influence of the household officials, notably of Burley, appears to have increased. The issues that confronted the officers and councillors, however, remained much the same. A response had to be found to the challenge presented by French power to English commercial interests, while the position of Duke John in Brittany needed to be buttressed against that of his rivals. It was the difficulties facing Duke John that received the government's attention first. At some stage in the parliament of January 1380 a proposal was tabled before the commons for an expedition to be dispatched to the duchy under the earl of Buckingham's command. Thanks to the skilful advocacy of the commons' Speaker Sir John Gildesburgh, a retainer of Buckingham's, the proposal was accepted.[87] The commons, before approving the necessary finance, sought assurances from the government that economy would be practised in the household; but once these had been given they responded generously with one and a half fifteenths and tenths. In March orders were given for the arrest of vessels and in summer the impressment of mariners began. By June the expedition was almost ready.

The leadership of the force was impressive. Among the captains were Lords Basset of Drayton, Bourchier, FitzWalter and Latimer and the renowned knights Hugh Calveley, Robert Knolles and John Harleston. In all, approximately 5,200 men were mustered.[88] The original plan appears to have been for the earl to make a direct crossing from Devon to Brittany. Yet again, however, a shortage of shipping compelled a change of plan, and it was decided instead to ferry the army across the shorter passage from Dover to Calais. It is possible that Buckingham welcomed the change because it gave him the chance to lead a great *chevauchée* across France in the tradition of Knolles's in 1370 and Gaunt's in 1373. The crossing was undertaken in stages in mid-July and on the 24th the great host set out.[89] Their route took them south-eastwards from Calais, past Thérouanne and Arras, towards the Somme at Cléry. From Cléry they struck more sharply eastwards in the direction of Rheims, and then headed due south again towards Troyes. At Troyes the duke of Burgundy awaited them with a large army, and Buckingham indicated a readiness to do battle; but in the event there was no engagement. Charles V was insistent that Burgundy avoid giving battle; and in deference to these instructions the latter withdrew and Buckingham

[87] For Gildesburgh, see *House of Commons*, iii, 185–7
[88] A. Goodman, *The Loyal Conspiracy. The Lords Appellant under Richard II* (London, 1971), 124.
[89] For accounts of the expedition see *CA*, 266–7; Froissart, i, 604–7, 608–20.

was able to press on. The earl cut a wide arc south of Paris, and headed westwards into the plains of Beauce. Ahead of him lay a countryside denuded of supplies, and behind, just out of reach, a great French host, constantly dogging his footsteps, yet declining to engage him. Only when he and his men prepared to cross the river Sarthe, in Maine, did it seem that the French might try to block their passage. But in the event they again held back. Two days previously, on 16 September, Charles V had died, and Burgundy and the other magnates returned to Paris. Buckingham was able to complete the remaining stages of his march unopposed, and a fortnight after arriving in Brittany he met Duke John at Rennes.

The meeting, when it came, was not an easy one. The death of Charles V had removed the principal obstacle to peace between the duke and the French court, and the presence in the duchy of English troops threatened to imperil the Breton's chances of negotiating an accord. The duke's main interest now was in getting Buckingham and his men out of the way as quickly as possible, and he proposed to do this by dispatching them to besiege the southern port of Nantes, which was notoriously pro-Valois in its sympathies. Buckingham was not averse to the idea because he intended over-wintering in the duchy in any case. But he could not undertake lengthy siege operations, least of all against a town as strong and as well provisoned as Nantes, without incurring expenses far in excess of what either he could afford or the duke could provide. An appeal to England for more money was all but inevitable.

From the government's point of view the fact that the appeal was not altogether unexpected did not make it any the more welcome. Buckingham had already spent the fruits of one parliamentary subsidy, and his needs could only be met by the granting of another. Yet back in January, when he had been awarded that subsidy, an undertaking had been given that another parliament would not be convened for at least eighteen months.[90] The hapless ministers were caught on the horns of a dilemma: either they called another parliament and risked incurring the commons' wrath or they acquiesced in the disintegration of Buckingham's army. Neither possibility was attractive, but the latter was somewhat less so than the former. Accordingly they went back on their promise and issued summonses for the estates to convene at Northampton – to suit Lancaster's convenience – on 5 November.[91] On Thursday, 8 November, Archbishop Sudbury began pleading the government's case. He made much of the many burdens that they had to bear, in Ireland as well as in Brittany, and of the heavy cost of supporting garrisons in Calais, Cherbourg and Brest; and he drew his

[90] *RP*, iii, 75.
[91] *CA*, 280.

audience's attention to the shortfall in customs receipts brought about by the disturbances in Flanders.[92] When asked to say how much money might be needed, he came up with the huge figure of £160,000. The commons' reaction was initially one of disbelief. Gildesburgh, who was again their Speaker, denounced the figure as 'outrageous and intolerable'. He said that he did not know how such a sum could possibly be raised and asked for permission to seek advice from the lords. The lords 'communed by themselves on the matter' and suggested a number of ways of meeting the chancellor's needs. These were a poll tax, a sales tax, and a subsidy on moveable property of the traditional kind; of these they made clear that they favoured the poll tax. The commons considered the advice and said that on reflection they would be prepared to make a grant to the government provided that the clergy did too. They thought the sum of £100,000 a reasonable one for the populace to bear, and offered to meet two-thirds of it by the levying of a poll tax on the laity, on condition that the clergy met the remaining third from a clerical tenth.[93] In this rather haphazard way was born the third and last of the poll taxes – the one that was to issue six months later in the outbreak of the Great Revolt.

From the start it was an ill-conceived impost. Indeed, had the lords and commons subjected the chancellor's figures to even moderately rigorous scrutiny, they would have discovered their inherent implausibility.[94] The biggest source of expenditure was of course the cost of keeping Buckingham's army in the field during the winter and possibly for as long as the full twelve months stated in the indentures. Undoubtedly this was going to be substantial, but it had already been met in part out of the proceeds of the one and a half fifteenths and tenths which the commons had granted in January. By October approximately £59,000 had been paid out in wages for the first five months of service, leaving £60,000–£70,000 to be found for the remaining seven.[95] As it

[92] *RP*, iii, 88.

[93] Ibid., 89–90. The clergy, of course, did not like the element of constraint implied here. For their protest to the king, see ibid., 90. The lengthy discussions that preceded the granting of the poll tax cast doubt on the *Anonimalle* writer's statement that the tax was 'lightly granted' (*Anon.*, 134). The problem of bias in the *Anonimalle* writer's work is discussed below, 65–6. A further point worth noting is that it was the lords and not, as so often supposed, the commons who were the chief advocates of the tax. The commons went along with the scheme; but it was not of their making.

[94] It is not clear how sure an understanding the commons had of the scale of royal income and expenditure. When attempting an assessment of royal revenue in negotiations with the council earlier in the reign, they greatly exaggerated income: M. Prestwich, 'An Estimate by the Commons of Royal Revenue in England under Richard II', *PH*, iii (1984), 147–55. It is possible that they were again led astray in the parliament at Northampton.

[95] E403/478, 'Exitus guerre', 21, 22, 29 May, 10 Sept. In the event, the expedition

happened, Buckingham and his army were to return early; but the government were not to know that, and in the meantime they had to budget on the assumption that they were committed to further heavy expenditure. Among the further claims on the exchequer was the cost of maintaining the barbicans. Calais, on Scrope's admission, cost £24,000 a year, and Brest roughly £5,500. Cherbourg may be assumed to have cost roughly the same amount as Brest. The barbicans, therefore, claimed some £35,000 of taxpayers' money. Ireland, to which Sudbury referred, claimed another £7,000. The cost of the Scottish border is more difficult to assess, but a figure of £4,000 may not be too erroneous.[96] In their entirety, then, the outstanding commitments came to about £110,000. To justify a claim for £50,000 more than this Sudbury must have had in mind additional commitments which he did not disclose. There can be little doubt that these were to be found in Portugal or Castile. On 15 July England had signed a treaty with Portugal which envisaged the provision of English military aid to that kingdom.[97] Gaunt considered support for the Portuguese a stepping-stone to the pursuit of his own claim to the crown of Castile. It was Gaunt's Iberian ambitions which formed the hidden agenda in Sudbury's fiscal arithmetic.

As soon as the issues of the poll tax started to flow into the exchequer (albeit more slowly than expected), preparations were made to send reinforcements to Buckingham, and the earl began to muse on his plans for an invasion of France in the next season. But he counted without his ally the duke of Brittany, who unknown to him was already planning to pull out of the struggle. In late 1380 the duke opened negotiations with the French and by 15 January a draft settlement had been agreed between them. The English council was taken completely by surprise, and Buckingham himself was humiliated. He had no alternative but to withdraw. The duke came to offer his farewells, but he refused to meet him. On 28 April he embarked for home and four days later, after a bad crossing, dropped anchor at Falmouth. He was arriving in a country on the brink of insurrection.

cost a total of £93,000 in wages and £8,000 in transport (Sherborne, 'The Cost of English Warfare', 68).

[96] The figures are taken from *RP*, iii, 34; and Sherborne, 'The Cost of English Warfare', 66–9.

[97] *Foed.*, vii, 262–5.

Chapter 4

THE GREAT REVOLT, 1381

The Revolt of 1381 was the largest and most serious outbreak of popular unrest in England in the middle ages. In the past, there had been many small or localized rural disturbances:[1] in the 1330s, for example, the villagers of Darnhall in Cheshire had fought a long and bitter struggle against the abbot of Vale Royal's efforts to reduce them to servility; and only four years before the Revolt the inhabitants of no fewer than forty villages in southern England had combined to fight for the privileges of 'ancient demesne' status under the crown.[2] Disputes between lords and tenants over the performance of obligations had long been common,[3] but never before 1381 had there been a general rebellion against the king's government. What happened in 1381 was altogether unique.

The immediate cause of the uprising is clear: the government's insistence on levying the third poll tax, which had been granted in November. The tax was bitterly resented in the country. Not only did it follow hard on a conventional levy of the fifteenths and tenths, but it was a manifestly unfair and inequitable imposition. The previous poll tax – of 1379 – had been carefully graduated according to the status and means of the payers; this one was not. It was levied at a flat rate, and a very high rate at that: 3 groats (one shilling) per person as opposed to one groat in 1377. In the schedule of the tax the better-off were enjoined to help the poor;[4] but no mechanism was provided for enforcement. Unsurprisingly the poor found themselves carrying the bulk of the burden, and they resented it. They resorted in large number to evasion. Commonly taxpayers concealed the existence of unmarried female dependants, widowed mothers, aunts, sisters and so on. Thus an

---

[1] The point is strongly made by R.H. Hilton, *Bond Men Made Free. Medieval Peasant Movements and the English Rising of 1381* (London, 1973).

[2] R.H. Hilton, 'Peasant Movements in England before 1381', *Essays in Economic History*, ii, ed. E.M. Carus-Wilson (London, 1962), 83–4. R. Faith, 'The "Great Rumour" of 1377 and Peasant Ideology', *The English Rising of 1381*, ed. R.H. Hilton and T.H. Aston (Cambridge, 1984), 43–73.

[3] R.H. Hilton, 'Freedom and Villeinage in England', *P&P*, xxxi (1965), reprinted in *Peasants, Knights and Heretics*, ed. R.H. Hilton (Cambridge, 1973), 174–91; idem, 'Peasant Movements in England before 1381', 73–90.

[4] *RP*, iii, 90.

unlikely male preponderance appeared in villages' populations. Naturally the exchequer officials were well aware of the deceit that was being practised upon them. Something like 450,000 taxpayers had 'disappeared' from the rolls since the levying of the 1377 tax.[5] In January the sheriffs and escheators were ordered to mount independent enquiries into the number of persons liable to the levy and to notify their findings to the exchequer.[6] A month later, on 20 February, the collectors themselves were told that, as the amounts they had collected were smaller than the exchequer had anticipated, they must speed up collection of the balances. When the collectors' attorneys appeared at Westminster in the course of February and March for the preliminary views of their accounts, they produced figures that demonstrated widespread fraud and evasion. Almost certainly they were told to discover and assess the missing persons. To oversee their activties, from 16 March fresh sets of commissions were appointed.[7] The new overseers were to search out all those liable to the tax, inspect the collectors' indentures and certify to the exchequer the number and names of the taxable. At the same time the deadline for final payments by the collectors was brought forward from 2 June to 21 April. In the late spring there was a flurry of activity in the shires. In the eastern counties the new commissioners seem to have set about their work with particular thoroughness and over 20,000 new taxpayers were uncovered.[8] Similar successes attended the work of the commissioners elsewhere. But the mood of calm in the country was deceptive. In April the sheriffs of London declined to collect the tax for fear of provoking unrest in the city.[9] Barely a month after that the final explosion came. On 30 May at Brentwood in Essex John Bampton, one of the new commissioners, was set upon by the villagers of Fobbing, Corringham and Stanford-le-Hope. According to the *Anonimalle* writer, the villagers said that they would not pay a penny more than they had already contributed.[10] Bampton ordered one of his sergeants to arrest the villagers' spokesmen, but the latter resisted and Bampton fled back to London. The government's response was to send Sir Robert Belknap, the chief justice of Common Pleas, on a commission of trailbaston to the county. Belknap attempted to open a hearing at Brentwood but, again according to the *Anonimalle* writer, he was set upon by a multitude

[5] C. Oman, *The Great Revolt of 1381* (Oxford, 2nd edn, 1969), 27–8 and Appendix II.
[6] *CPR 1377–81*, 627–8.
[7] *CFR 1377–83*, 250.
[8] Fryde, *The Great Revolt of 1381*, 15.
[9] Tout, *Chapters*, iii, 364.
[10] *The Peasants' Revolt of 1381*, ed. R.B. Dobson (London, 2nd edn 1983), 124. References to the chronicle accounts of the Revolt will be to the translations in this volume.

and sent packing. Afterwards, 'and before Whit Sunday', as the chronicler says, '50,000 of the commons gathered . . . and went abroad, throwing buildings to the ground and setting them ablaze'.[11] The torch of rebellion had been lit.

The levying of the poll tax was, of course, a major blunder by the government. Not only was the tax manifestly unfair and inequitable; the government's insistence on collecting it showed how seriously out of touch it was with the mood in the country. The taxpaying classes, and in particular the peasantry, were growing ever more resistant to taxation by the 1380s. Since the end of the previous reign three and a half fifteenths and tenths and two poll taxes had been levied. Yet in terms of benefit to the common good there was little to show for them. The English conquests in France had been whittled away; the seas were as dangerous as ever; and the coasts were exposed to French or Castilian raids. The general belief was that the king had been ill-advised by his ministers and councillors. The two most senior of his ministers, Sudbury and Hales, were relative newcomers to the political scene. Sudbury had been appointed chancellor only in January 1380, and Hales had taken up his office a year later. Sudbury was a competent and experienced diocesan, but a political lightweight; Hales at least had served for a brief while as a councillor in 1379 and had some military experience. Sudbury and Hales were both extremely unpopular in the country – but more for what they represented than for what they had done. Hales suffered from his association with the Hospitallers, the wealthy crusading order of which he was prior, while Sudbury was perceived as the personification of the 'Caesarean' clergy, the clerics who mingled the affairs of Church and realm. In addition to the chancellor and treasurer there were others around the king who were viewed with hostility or distaste. Foremost among these was John of Gaunt. Gaunt was disliked for his haughty demeanour and disdain for popular opinion. As a figure long influential behind the scenes, he made a convenient scapegoat for the accumulated failures and errors of policy in the 1370s and early 1380s. Understandably, in the course of the Revolt there were many attacks on his property: his palace of the Savoy

---

[11] The *Anonimalle* writer's account is the fullest surviving of the events leading to the outbreak of the Revolt. However, its witness may not always be reliable. As Dr A. Prescott has pointed out, there is no record of a commission being issued to Belknap. Belknap was holding routine sessions of assize in Essex and Hertfordshire in the last days of May, but his movements do not correspond to those given by the *Anonimalle* writer. On 30 May, the day that Bampton was assaulted at Brentwood, he was holding sessions in Essex, but at Stratford Longthorne. From that place he moved to Barnet (Herts.); but there is no sign that he was chased out of the county: A.J. Prescott, 'Judicial Records of the Rising of 1381' (University of London Ph.D. thesis, 1984), 128–9. For other points at which the *Anonimalle* narrative needs to be treated with care, see below, 65–6, 68.

in the western suburbs of London was burned down, and his castle of Horston (Derbyshire) pillaged.[12] There were also attacks on his dependants: his esquire Greenfield and physician William Appleton were among the rebels' victims in London.[13] Gaunt himself was in the north when the trouble began, for in May he had been commissioned by the council to negotiate a renewal of the truce on the Marches. When he first heard of the trouble, he sought refuge with the earl of Northumberland, but the earl refused him admission to his castles and in desperation the duke had to flee across the border to Scotland. If he had fallen into rebel hands, there can be little doubt that he would have suffered the same grisly fate as his retainers and the king's ministers.[14]

Though in many ways highly political in character, the Revolt also drew on deep underlying social and economic causes. The thirty or more years that had elapsed since the Black Death of 1349 had seen rapid change in the pattern of life in the countryside. As a result of the Black Death and the visitations that had followed it there had been a massive fall in population – from perhaps 6–7 million in the 1330s to barely 3 million fifty years later. Wages, as a result, had risen sharply: a ploughman or a skilled labourer who had earlier settled for a stipend of 10s a year could now command 20–30s in the market.[15] The government had responded to these changes by passing first the Ordinance (1349) and then the Statute of Labourers (1351). The effect of these measures had been to peg wages at their pre-Black Death levels. Juries brought many prosecutions under the laws, but even so wages had continued to rise. In a stream of petitions to parliament landowners and employers bemoaned their plight and asked for further restrictions on the movement of unfree labour.[16] Their grumblings may give a misleading impression of the movement of their real incomes. In the twenty or so years since the coming of the plague landowners had little

[12] *Peasants' Revolt*, ed. Dobson, 156, 183–4; D. Crook, 'Derbyshire and the English Rising of 1381', *HR*, lx (1987), 9–23.

[13] Goodman, *John of Gaunt*, 79; *Peasants' Revolt*, ed. Dobson, 162.

[14] For the duke's misfortunes see *Anon.*, 152–3; *KC*, 142–8. It is possible that letters were issued for the duke's arrest following Richard's acquiesence in the demand made by the rebels at Mile End for the punishment of the 'traitors': see S.K. Walker, 'Letters to the Dukes of Lancaster in 1381 and 1399', *EHR*, cvi (1991), 68–79. The view that Gaunt provided a focus for popular opposition is argued in E. Searle and R. Burghart, 'The Defence of England and the Peasants' Revolt', *Viator*, iii (1972), 381–2, 386.

[15] For evidence of wage rates from prosecutions under the Statute of Labourers see N. Ritchie, 'Labour Conditions in Essex in the Reign of Richard II', *Essays in Economic History*, ii, ed. E.M. Carus-Wilson (London, 1962), 91–111. There are examples of farm labourers' wages in J.E. Thorold Rogers, *A History of Agriculture and Prices in England* (7 vols, Oxford, 1866–1902), ii, 329–34.

[16] *RP*, ii, 278–9, 279, 296, 307, 312, 319, 320, 340–1.

difficulty in maintaining their standing relative to that of the other
ranks of society. One reason for this was that prices in the 1350s and
1360s had been consistently high: a quarter of wheat in the 1360s cost
roughly 6–8s, not far below the levels of half a century before. Lords
were able to enjoy receipts from market production that allowed them
more than to meet their outgoings.[17] A second reason for the lords'
success was that they were able to bring their ample jurisdictional power
to bear on their tenantry. A good many frequently invoked the
machinery of the manorial courts. Cases were brought against officials
who were suspected of slackness or corruption and against villeins –
unfree tenants – who tried to escape bondage by acquiring free land. At
Crondon in Essex, for example, a manor of the bishops of London, a
villein who had acquired a free tenement had it seized because 'he
never gave to the lord an increment of rent, nor rendered the said land
to the lord as he ought'.[18] There is also evidence of the lords' vigilance
in exacting the range of villein dues and, in particular, labour obligations. Cases are recorded of tenants being forced to stay on the manor,
to work on the manorial demesne or to take up tenements that had
fallen vacant. There are signs that pressure was sometimes exerted on
relatives to bring back errant tenants. At Drinkstone in Suffolk one
Robert atte Chirch was fined for failing to produce his two sons, 'which
he did not do, but refused'.[19] Professor Dyer has suggested that a kind
of second serfdom was emerging at this time. Evidence for this is to be
found in agreements which were sometimes made with villeins when
they were allowed to leave the manor. At Aldham in Suffolk in 1368 an
emigrant was required to return each year 'in the autumn to help the
lord': in other words, with the harvest. An unfree girl of Windridge in
Hertfordshire was allowed to leave provided that she should be 'ready
[to serve] the lord when he pleased to have her'.[20] From these cases
we can see that lords were using all the powers at their disposal to
strengthen their hold over their tenants. In effect they were maintaining their living standards at the expense of those beneath them in
the hierarchy.

Not surprisingly, the peasants bitterly resented the lords' policies. On
a number of estates there was resistance to manorial authority. At
Beddingham in Sussex in the 1370s tenants refused to perform labour
services on Sir William de Etchingham's demesne. At Otford and

[17] G.A. Holmes, *The Estates of the Higher Nobility in Fourteenth Century England* (Cambridge, 1957), 114; A.R. Bridbury, 'The Black Death', *EcHR*, 2nd series, xxvi
(1973), 577–92.
[18] C. Dyer, 'The Social and Economic Background to the Rural Revolt of 1381',
The English Rising of 1381, ed. R.H. Hilton and T.H. Aston (Cambridge, 1984), 24.
[19] Ibid.
[20] Ibid., 25.

Wingham in Kent, manors of the archbishops of Canterbury, there was a widespread withdrawal of services in the 1350s and again in the 1380s.[21] On many manors there was intermittent opposition to the exaction of labour services. In a sense, the Revolt of 1381 can be seen as an intensification of these localized episodes of unrest. It is striking how many of those who were involved had a record of earlier conflict with authority. John Cok of Prittlewell in Essex had been in arrears with his rent. John Cok of Moze also in Essex was amerced for failing to repair a building. Edmund Gerneys and Thomas Gardiner of Little Barton, Suffolk and Robert Wright of Foxearth, Essex were all amerced for allowing their animals to trespass on the lord's demesne.[22] These men were not down-and-outs. Many were among the most successful proprietors in their villages. Some were adding considerably to their holdings. John Fillol and John Geffrey of Hanningfield and James atte Ford of Takeley, three Essex rebels, were acquiring land in 1380. Geffrey, who had recently moved to Hanningfield from Suffolk, had bought a smallholding, and had obtained the reversion of a further 15 acres. Robert Wright of Foxearth, another Essex rebel, was increasing the number of animals that he owned, and his wife was the chief brewer in the village.[23] A high proportion of the rebels had held office in the manor as well. John Geffrey of Hanningfield was his lord's bailiff. Three-quarters of the known rebels from Essex, Suffolk and Kent are known to have served as reeves, pledges, bailiffs, jurors, aletasters, constables or in other positions of local responsibility.[24] These were men who knew how to lead and to command, and they had ample experience of organizing. Clearly the Revolt of 1381 was not a movement of the poor and the downtrodden; it was a movement of the more ambitious and assertive in society. What infuriated these proprietors was the impediments that were being placed in their way by the lords. The anger that they felt was exacerbated when the government unwisely insisted on levying the third poll tax. Through the carelessness of its actions the government had shown itself to be as unsympathetic to their aspirations as the lords. Denied any outlet for the expression of their grievances, the peasants were driven to take matters into their own hands. At the end of May they rose in rebellion.

[21] N.E. Saul, *Scenes From Provincial Life. Knightly Families in Sussex 1280–1400* (Oxford, 1986), 121 n.94; R.H. Hilton, *The Decline of Serfdom in Medieval England* (London, 1969), 40.

[22] Dyer, 'The Social and Economic Background', 35–6.

[23] Ibid. The affluence of some of the rebels was stressed by Hilton, *Bond Men Made Free*, 180. Hilton cited the case of Thomas Sampson, a Suffolk man, who owned some 300 sheep and 100 head of stock and had 137 acres under crop. The source here is the escheators' inquisitions *post mortem*, some of which were printed by E. Powell, *The Rising in East Anglia* (Cambridge, 1896).

[24] Dyer, 'The Social and Economic Background', 17.

The energy and initiative which the rebels had shown in initially taking matters into their own hands quickly became apparent as the disaffection spread. Within days of the attack on Bampton at Brentwood acts of disobedience occurred all over Essex. On 2 June a meeting took place at Bocking at which rebels swore to be of one mind 'to destroy divers lieges of the king and to have no law in England except only those which they themselves moved to be ordained'.[25] Men from Bocking were present at the fracas at Brentwood, and it seems likely that the spread of the insurrection had been planned in the wake of the earlier incident. Four days after making the oath the Bocking men and their allies launched an assault on John Sewale, the sheriff of Essex, and one Robert de Segynton, an exchequer clerk, at Coggeshall. By the 10th a larger group had massed at Cressing Temple, in the centre of the county, where they attacked and destroyed the preceptory of the Hospitallers, the order of which Hales was prior.[26] Even at this early stage of the Revolt, the rebels were extremely careful in their selection of targets. They did not indulge in indiscriminate looting or pillaging. They singled out for destruction the property of local office-holders, poll tax collectors and gentry connected with the central government. It is hard not to conclude that a considerable measure of central control was asserted over the progress of the Revolt.

By the early days of June there are signs that the men of Essex were linking up with fellow dissidents in Kent. The first trouble in Kent occurred on 2 June, the very day of the meeting at Bocking. It is reported that on that date Abel Ker led a band of men from Erith to Lesnes Abbey, where he forced the abbot to swear to be of their company. Ker crossed to Essex for reinforcements, and thereafter the movements of the Kent rebels closely mirrored those of the Essex host.[27] By 10 June both groups had organized themselves to advance on London, and by the 12th they had reached the city's suburbs. Credit for the remarkable co-ordination of the two bands should be given in part to the infamous Wat Tyler, who had by this time emerged as the Kentish leader and who may have had Essex origins.[28] But Tyler, able and

---

[25] KB145/3/6/1. For discussion of this see Prescott, 'Judicial Records of the Rising', 134–5; N. Brooks, 'The Organization and Achievements of the Peasants of Kent and Essex in 1381', *Studies in Medieval History Presented to R.H.C. Davis*, ed. H. Mayr-Harting and R.I. Moore (London, 1985), 252 also has valuable comments.

[26] Brooks, 'Organization of the Peasants', 255, 263.

[27] Ibid., 252–61.

[28] According to the *Anonimalle* writer, it was after the attack on Rochester castle that the insurgents chose Wat Tyler 'of Maidstone' as their leader (*Peasants' Revolt*, ed. Dobson, 127). Partial confirmation of the story is provided by the indictments of the jury of Maidstone hundred which say that Wat Tyler, John Abel and others were the 'first malefactors and maintainers of the malefactors and disturbers of the peace'. The jurors, however, said that Tyler was 'of Colchester'; and jurors from east

charismatic as he was, would have been powerless without the support that he received from the leading members of the individual rebel contingents. The rebel leadership as a whole was coherent, determined and tightly knit, and the men showed a single-mindedness in their pursuit of objectives.

The government's response to the disaffection was halting and slow. No effort was made to raise a force to disperse the rebels, presumably because it was thought that the loyalty of such a force would be uncertain. While the rebels were massing in the south-eastern counties, Richard and his friends were moving between Windsor and Henley-on-the-Heath in the Thames valley.[29] On Tuesday, 11 June the king and a few intimates moved to the security of the Tower. There they were joined by Sudbury and Hales, the earls of Arundel, Oxford, Warwick and Salisbury and the young Henry Bolingbroke.[30] On the same day communications were opened with the rebels in Kent.[31] An envoy was sent to the rebel leaders enquiring of their purpose. The Kentish leaders replied that they had risen 'to save the king and to destroy the traitors to him and the kingdom'. Richard asked the rebels to delay further action until he had the chance to speak to them; the rebels agreed, and a meeting was arranged for Thursday, 13 June, at Blackheath. By this stage of the Revolt, roughly a fortnight after the initial irruption, the rebel host had swelled to several thousands, and a direct encounter with them posed dangers to the king's person.[32] The council therefore decided that Richard should make his way out to the rebels by water. The king took a barge from the Tower in the morning, accompanied by the chancellor, the earls of Warwick, Salisbury and Oxford and others, and sailed to a point between Rotherhithe and Greenwich; there he began parleying. The *Anonimalle* writer says that, when he asked the rebels their demands they called for the heads of John of Gaunt and fifteen other traitors – among them those of the chancellor, the treasurer and the chief justice. Naturally, the king would not assent to this; nor, on the chancellor's advice, would he put ashore to negotiate. The exchanges quickly came to an end, and by noon or thereabouts the king was back in the capital.[33]

Kent refer to Tyler as 'of Essex' (Brooks, 'Organisation of the Peasants', 258, and references given there). It is possible that Tyler was an Essex man who had moved to Kent, this being a time of high mobility in English society.

[29] For the king's itinerary see Appendix.

[30] *Peasants' Revolt*, ed. Dobson, 129. Bolingbroke's presence is recorded by Knighton (ibid., 182).

[31] Ibid., 128–9.

[32] Froissart says that there were 10,000 at Blackheath, but the number must be regarded in some measure as an exaggeration (*Peasants' Revolt*, ed. Dobson, 144).

[33] Ibid., 129–30. Froissart too is valuable for this meeting: ibid., 144.

The sequel to the abortive encounter near Rotherhithe was the rebels' dramatic entry into London. The rebels had little choice but to resort to force once the parleying had failed, for their supplies were short and they needed a swift capitulation by the authorities if their movement was not to falter. Already some of the rebels had ridden westwards to Southwark and the environs of London Bridge. At Southwark they had made for the Marshalsea prisons, where they released the inmates and burned down the house of Richard Imworth, the keeper of the Marshalsea of King's Bench. Afterwards a smaller detachment had gone on to Lambeth to pillage the archbishop's palace.[34] By the afternoon of Thursday the rebels were poised to make an entry into London itself. On the mayor's orders the city's gates had been closed, and the drawbridge over the river had been pulled up; but there was confusion in the city, and some at least of the citizenry favoured letting the rebels in. A keeper in Bridge Ward – exactly who is not clear – lowered the drawbridge. The rebels then poured in, and for two days the city lay at their mercy.[35]

The government was faced with a situation that was both dangerous and volatile. The rebels had regained the initiative, and events were rapidly moving out of control. There was widespread pillaging and plundering in the city, and properties were being burned and destroyed. From London Bridge one rebel contingent moved westwards into the suburbs. They broke into the Fleet prison, released the prisoners, and then swept on to the lawyers' abode of the Temple, where they prised open the chests and burned the charters and records: hatred of the lawyers was to be a major characteristic of the Revolt. Further along the Strand they forced their way into Gaunt's palace of the Savoy and razed it to the ground. The Lancastrian chronicler Knighton says that they drank the wine in the cellars and cast the duke's plate into the river.[36] Another rebel contingent, operating in the east,

---

[34] Ibid., 155, 199–200.

[35] Ibid., 156, 168–9, 188. Two aldermen, John Horn and Walter Sibil, were indicted in November 1382 for admitting the Kent rebels over London Bridge; and another, William Tonge, was indicted for opening Aldgate to the men of Essex. The two indictments, however, were partisan statements. The incriminated aldermen were all victuallers and members of the same faction as the mayor, William Walworth; the accusations against them were made by their enemies, the followers of John Northampton, who had been elected to the mayoralty in October 1381. It is doubtful if a great deal of truth can be attached to them. For discussion see R. Bird, *The Turbulent London of Richard II* (London, 1949), 52–62; C.M. Barron, *Revolt in London: 11th to 15th June 1381* (London, 1981), 3; and, more generally, Hilton, *Bond Men Made Free*, 189–90.

[36] *Peasants' Revolt*, ed. Dobson, 183–4. The *Anonimalle* writer reports a rumour that the commons of London burned the Savoy before the 'commons of the country' arrived. It was doubtless all but impossible to tell which groups of people were responsible for which acts of destruction.

broke into Newgate and released the prisoners. From Newgate they went to St Martin-le-Grand where they seized Roger Leget, a 'questmonger', and dragged him to 'Goter Lane ende' in Cheapside to be beheaded. Further north, yet another group destroyed the Hospitallers' preceptory at Clerkenwell. The king and his councillors, trapped in the Tower, could only gaze over the scene in fright. The *Anonimalle* writer, who was an eyewitness to events, describes how the king reacted. Richard, he says, climbed to the top of a turret and looked out over the fires: he saw the Savoy, Clerkenwell hospital, John Butterwick's house and the houses of Simon Hosteler near Newgate all in flames. Later, he climbed another turret, on the eastern side facing St Katherine's where a host from Essex had gathered. The king gazed out, anxious and disconsolate.[37]

It was the task of the magnates and councillors attending the king in the Tower to find a way of restoring peace to the capital. On Thursday and Friday they held a number of meetings, one at least of them with the king, but unfortunately these meetings are ill documented. It cannot even be established for sure who was involved in them. The *Anonimalle* writer says that the earls of Buckingham, Kent, Warwick and Oxford, Sir Thomas Percy and Sir Robert Knolles and the mayor of London were with Richard on the Friday. Froissart also mentions the earl of Salisbury and various French or Low Country knights, from whom he obtained information; and there may well have been others.[38] The *Anonimalle* writer was in a better position than most authorities to know what was going on in the Tower, for almost certainly he was there at the time, but his account of events at this point is highly partisan.[39] The writer was

---

[37] *Peasants' Revolt*, ed. Dobson, 158, 159. The Evesham writer comments on the king's 'fear of the rebels' before he went to Rotherhithe (*HVR*, 63).

[38] *Peasants' Revolt*, ed. Dobson, 161, 191.

[39] The authorship of the *Anonimalle* chronicle has prompted a vigorous debate. A.F. Pollard, 'The Authorship and Value of the *Anonimalle Chronicle*', *EHR*, liii (1938), 577–605, argued the case for John de Scardeburgh, a chancery clerk who had connections with Yorkshire, where the chronicle was compiled. V.H. Galbraith, 'Thoughts about the Peasants' Revolt', *The Reign of Richard II. Essays in Honour of May McKisack*, ed. F.R.H. Du Boulay and C.M. Barron (London 1971), 46–57, suggested William Packington, the keeper of the wardrobe, on the grounds that John Leland, the Tudor antiquary, claimed to have seen a French chronicle which Packington had written. J. Taylor, *English Historical Writing in the Fourteenth Century* (Oxford, 1987), 277–84, offers reasons for doubting Packington's association with the chronicle. While declining to put forward a candidate of his own, Taylor concedes that the *Anonimalle* writer may have been 'a chancery clerk, or a clerk of the privy seal, located not too far from the person of the king', and 'almost certainly an eyewitness of the events which he describes' (ibid., 319, 318). H.M. Hansen, 'The Peasants' Revolt of 1381 and the Chronicles', *JMH*, vi (1980), 393–415, attempts to cast doubt on the value of the *Anonimalle* as an original source for the Revolt. But her argument, which is over-schematic, fails to convince.

contemptuous of the ministers and the lords and his lack of sympathy with them shows through in his account of their dealings with the king. He says that, when the king asked them for counsel, 'none of them could or would offer him counsel'. And later he says that 'they did not know how to advise him and were surprisingly abashed'.[40] In the *Anonimalle* writer's view all the important initiatives were taken by Richard himself: Richard, he says, ordered the mayor to proclaim that the rebels should assemble at Mile End; Richard arranged for the general pardon to be offered to the rebels at St Katherine's. The lords did little but tamely acquiesce. Such a relationship between the king and the lords is highly improbable. Richard was after all only fourteen at the time; and, while he undoubtedly showed courage in the crisis, he also suffered from lack of confidence and it is unlikely that he would have taken crucial decisions without advice. The natural assumption must be that the major decisions were taken by the king and lords together. There is strong evidence that this was the case in two of the main chronicle accounts of the Revolt. The first of these – the Evesham Abbey chronicle – is very brief, and says merely that the king took counsel ('Qui inito consilio').[41] The other – Jean Froissart's *Chroniques* – is more detailed. Froissart's witness has sometimes been called into question because of the writer's tendency to confuse events and to seek after rhetorical effect. But it is evident from his narrative that Froissart was well informed about events. He was an avid seeker-out of information, and it is likely that he numbered among his informants two men who were present with Richard in the Tower, Sir Robert Namur and the earl of Salisbury.[42] After the *Anonimalle* writer, Froissart was probably the best placed of the chroniclers to know what was going on. In any attempt to reconstruct the chain of events in the Tower his narrative deserves the closest attention.

Froissart offers a story of two meetings in the Tower: one on the Thursday and the second on the day after.[43] At the first of these, which was attended by the lords, Sir William Walworth, the mayor, proposed a night-time sally against the besiegers: the garrison in the Tower, he

---

[40] *Peasants' Revolt*, ed. Dobson, 159, 160.

[41] *HVR*, 64. The Evesham writer in general offers a notably unheroic view of the king's behaviour in the Revolt. He says that he fled to the Tower 'propter metum eorum' (on account of fear of the rebels), and notes that he rode out to Mile End 'valde timidus' (ibid., 63, 64).

[42] Sir Robert Namur was a patron of Froissart: G.T. Diller, 'Froissart: Patrons and Texts', *Froissart: Historian*, ed. J.J.N. Palmer (Woodbridge, 1981), 148. J. Sherborne, 'Charles VI and Richard II', ibid., 53, is critical of Froissart's treatment of the Revolt, but his strictures seem severe.

[43] *Peasants' Revolt*, ed. Dobson, 189–90. My reconstruction of events in the Tower follows the analysis of B. Wilkinson, 'The Peasants' Revolt of 1381', *Speculum*, xv (1940), 20–4.

argued, could begin the attack, and the force at the command of Sir
Robert Knolles, in his lodgings, could finish it off. The earl of Salisbury,
however, the most experienced soldier present, counselled against such
an idea and urged conciliation; and it was his arguments which were
eventually accepted. On the following day, Froissart says, there was
another discussion. The chronicler knew little of its course, but he was
quite clear about the outcome: the decision was made to arrange a
meeting with the rebels at Mile End.

If Froissart's reporting is correct, it appears there were two main
bodies of opinion on the council. On the one side were those who
favoured dispersing the rebels by force. Froissart implies that the principal spokesman of this party was Mayor Walworth; he does not say who
else was of the same opinion, but adds that the mayor received backing
from 'diverse notable and rich burgesses'. On the opposite side were
those, like Salisbury and Chancellor Sudbury, who favoured the opening of negotiations. At the first meeting, held on Thursday afternoon,
those advocating conciliation won the argument, and the use of force
was ruled out. Almost certainly it was as a consequence of this decision
that Richard shortly afterwards offered a general pardon to the rebels.
According to the *Anonimalle* writer a couple of knights were sent out
to make the proclamation, one of them standing on a chair in order
to be heard; but the rebels bellowed the knights down and called
for beheadings.[44] It was apparent from this débâcle that lengthier
negotiations would be needed to persuade the rebels to disperse. A
second meeting of councillors was held in the early hours of Friday
morning, with probably only the king and his leading officers – Sudbury
and Hales – in attendance. Froissart knew little about this meeting
but said that its outcome was the decision to summon the rebels to
Mile End.

There can be little doubt, given Froissart's evidence, that by Thursday
the 13th the council had formulated a policy, and that that policy was
one of conciliation. Historians in the past have been inclined to condemn the councillors' line as weak. Anthony Steel said that the councillors displayed 'a complete lack of leadership. . . . One and all they were
paralysed with fright.'[45] Steel's judgement is almost certainly too harsh.
Wilkinson has shown that conciliation was the only realistic policy that
the councillors could have followed in the circumstances.[46] The council
had little coercive power at its disposal – insufficient certainly to be sure
of dispersing the rebels by force; and a maladroit move, such as a sortie
from the Tower, could easily have provoked the very bloodbath which

[44] *Peasants' Revolt*, ed. Dobson, 160.
[45] Steel, *Richard II*, 78–9.
[46] Wilkinson, 'The Peasants' Revolt', 20–4.

it was the councillors' wish to avoid. The only sensible course was to persuade the rebels to withdraw from the city voluntarily. The council's aim was to attain this end by arranging the meeting at Mile End: the rebels' departure for the meeting would clear the streets of the mob; and the chance would also be given to the ministers trapped in the Tower to escape. One problem which it appears that the government never resolved was whether or not the negotiations with the rebels should be undertaken in good faith. The king and his ministers probably held different views on this, and it is unlikely that a clear line was agreed on in the Tower. But this issue apart, there was broad agreement on the general direction of policy: negotiations should be opened with the rebels, and the use of force deferred. Almost certainly the *Anonimalle* writer was aware of what had been decided. The reason for his silence was that he disagreed with it.

Early in the next morning, Friday, 14 June, it appears the king rode out for his meeting with the rebels. According to the *Anonimalle* writer, he was accompanied by his mother and half-brothers, several of the magnates, the mayor and other Londoners.[47] The journey to Mile End was an eventful one. *En route* the king was accosted by Thomas Farringdon, a London goldsmith, who had a vendetta against Hales and demanded restitution of his property. Diplomatically Richard promised him justice.[48] A little later the bridle of Nicholas Brembre's horse was grabbed by another Londoner, William Trewman, who complained of the injustices that he had suffered when Brembre was mayor. Probably at this point the princess and some of the knights turned back. Richard pressed on along the road with a smaller retinue. When eventually he reached Mile End, he found several hundred rebels assembled to meet him. Most of them came from Essex, but their spokesman remains unknown.[49] The rebels greeted the king courteously. They made two main requests of him. The first was that they should be able to deal with those whom they called the 'traitors'. Richard replied, again diplomatically, that they could have the heads of such traitors as had been judged by law. Secondly, they asked for the abolition of serfdom and for a standard rent for land of 4d an acre. According to Knighton, they complained to the king 'of their intolerable servitude and heavy oppressions';[50] and Richard, whether genuinely or otherwise, gave way to their demands. There at Mile End he had it proclaimed that 'he would confirm and grant that they should be free'; as a result

[47] *Peasants' Revolt*, ed. Dobson, 161.

[48] Farringdon's action is known from an indictment brought against him in King's Bench: *Peasants' Revolt*, ed. Dobson, 219.

[49] There is no clear evidence that Wat Tyler was at Mile End; the *Anonimalle* writer appears at fault on this point (*Peasants' Revolt*, ed. Dobson, 161 and n).

[50] Ibid., 183.

of his order charters of manumission were drawn up and issued. Walsingham included a copy of one such charter in his narrative at St Albans.[51]

In the eyes of some at least of the rebels Richard's concessions amounted to a signal to do whatever they liked with the traitors. Either while the king was at Mile End or shortly afterwards one medium-sized splinter group made straight for the Tower to seek some of the 'traitors' out. It was known that Sudbury and Hales were still in the precincts, for the two of them had already made an abortive attempt to escape. According to Walsingham, the rebel horde rushed up to the main gate, and the garrison, terrified by the noise, granted them admission.[52] Once inside, the rebels plundered and pillaged freely. In the privy wardrobe they took away coats of mail, helmets and standards bearing the royal arms and those of St George. In the royal living quarters they sat on the beds, poked at everything 'with their filthy sticks' and joked familiarly with the soldiers. A number of rebels tried kissing the king's mother. A few others tracked down young Henry of Derby, Gaunt's son, and would have killed him but for the intervention of one John Ferrour. Archbishop Sudbury and Sir Robert Hales were discovered in hiding in the chapel of St John in the White Tower. Both were beaten and dragged out to Tower Hill, where they were beheaded. According to Walsingham's account, no fewer than eight blows were needed to sever the archbishop's head.[53]

In the light of these events the king and his ministers were obliged to reconsider their strategy. The concessions at Mile End had probably satisfied a good many of the rebels, but there were many more who were still roaming the streets and thirsting for blood. Part of the problem was that it was difficult for both the king and the rebel leaders to enforce any agreement, for a great many bands were operating, many of them in isolation from one another. Probably there was no alternative to arranging another meeting. A messenger – who may have been Sir John Newton, the constable of Rochester[54] – was sent to the rebel leaders, and it was agreed that Richard would convene with them the next day at Smithfield. In the meantime the looting and killing continued. There were attacks on the London Guildhall and on the property of the Hospitallers at Highbury: at Highbury Hales's manor house was burned to the ground. Worse still, there was a general assault on the aliens. Between 150 and 160 foreigners are said to have been killed in various parts of the city. Among the victims were no fewer than

---

[51] *CA*, 298–9.
[52] *Peasants' Revolt*, ed. Dobson, 171–5. Walsingham, characteristically, offers the most colourful account of the rebels in the Tower.
[53] Ibid., 174.
[54] So says Walsingham: ibid., 177.

thirty-five Flemings who were dragged from the church of St Martin
in Vintry and beheaded on the same block.[55] Tyler himself is said to
have sought out a Fleming of particular ill-repute, the financier Sir
Richard Lyons.[56]

Richard prepared for his second encounter with the rebels by seeking
the intercession of his patron, St Edward. Early on Saturday afternoon,
in the company of a large bodyguard, he went to the saint's shrine at
Westminster Abbey. He spent what the abbey's chronicler called 'some
time' at the shrine and left an offering on the altar.[57] Afterwards,
according to the *Anonimalle* writer, he had a meeting with the anchorite
attached to the abbey and confessed to him.[58] Thus encouraged and
fortified, he rode out to Smithfield. The composition of his retinue is
not known, but it seems that he was accompanied by at least a couple of
hundred men-at-arms. According to most of the narratives, the king's
party drew themselves up on the east side of the field, near the priory,
while the rebels, led by Tyler, kept to the west. The mid-space was clear.
Richard ordered Mayor Walworth to summon Tyler to come to him.[59]
Tyler rode to the king on a little horse, dismounted, half bent his knees
and then shook the king familiarly by the hand, calling him 'brother'.
When the king asked why he and his fellows would not return home,
Tyler swore, and demanded a charter embodying some new concessions. He called, in addition to the abolition of serfdom, for an end to
outlawry, the disendowment of the Church and equality among all
men below the king. Richard conceded these demands saving only
the regality of the crown. There was then a pause, and no one said
anything. At this point events appear to have become confused. The
well-informed *Anonimalle* writer offers one account of what happened.[60]
Tyler, he says, demanded a jug of water because it was so hot. After
downing it, he demanded a flagon of ale as well and, after downing that,
clambered on to his horse. At this point an esquire of the king's caught
sight of the rebel and denounced him as the most notorious thief in the
county. Tyler rounded on the esquire, and Walworth retaliated by
trying to arrest him. Tyler lunged at the mayor with his dagger but
missed, and the mayor in turn struck out, injuring him on the shoulder.

---

[55] Ibid., 162.

[56] Ibid., 189. For Lyons, an associate of Alice Perrers who had been impeached in
the Good Parliament of 1376, see above, 19–20; and A.R. Myers, 'The Wealth of Sir
Richard Lyons', *Essays in Medieval History Presented to Bertie Wilkinson*, ed. T.A.
Sandquist and M.R. Powicke (Toronto, 1969), 301–29.

[57] *Peasants' Revolt*, ed. Dobson, 163, 202–3. For Richard's devotion to the cult of St
Edward the Confessor see below, 311–13.

[58] *Peasants' Revolt*, ed. Dobson, 163.

[59] So says the *Anonimalle* writer; Walsingham ascribes the role to Sir John Newton
(*Peasants' Revolt*, ed. Dobson, 164, 177). For Newton, see above, 69.

[60] *Peasants' Revolt*, ed. Dobson, 163–6.

Bleeding badly, Tyler rode part of the way across the square, then collapsed to the ground within sight of his men. The account of the *Anonimalle* writer finds support in its essentials in a number of other sources. Walsingham, Froissart and Knighton all agree on the central role of Walworth, but differ from the *Anonimalle* and from each other on how the scuffle broke out. According to Knighton, Wat Tyler was holding a dagger during his interview, fingering it 'like a boy'; and when he looked ready to use it against the king Walworth struck at him.[61] Froissart suggests that Tyler provoked an incident. In his account, the rebel demanded a dagger held by one of the king's esquires and, when the latter refused to hand it over, became threatening. Walworth came forward with some of the guards and rounded on him. He knocked him to the ground and an esquire, Ralph Standish, finished him off.[62] Walsingham and the Evesham writer also have the rebel leader killed by several sword thrusts in the body.[63]

Interpretations of these accounts vary as much as the accounts themselves do. Wilkinson, in his study of the sources, argued that Tyler himself provoked the fatal confrontation.[64] The essence of his argument is that the rebel behaved arrogantly and persisted with his demands even when they had been all but conceded by the king. Kriehn, on the other hand, supposed that the king and his men had laid a plot: it was their aim, he argued – an aim successfully accomplished – to ensnare Tyler and in this way to render his men leaderless.[65] Oman, avoiding the extremes of these views, implied that the scuffle may have broken out accidentally.[66] It is certainly not easy to establish the truth, given the inadequacy and inconsistency of the sources; but there are a number of grounds for endorsing Kriehn's view that the councillors had planned the scuffle. In the first place, and most tellingly, there is a comment of Walsingham's. Walsingham says that the moment Tyler fell the king's men surrounded him.[67] It is evident that they had come well prepared. They knew exactly what to do: the rebel leader had to be seized, and his followers on the other side of the square had to be prevented from catching sight of his body. In the second place, there is the scarcely less striking fact of the Londoners' preparedness for his death. All the chroniclers are agreed on this.[68] When Tyler was killed, they tell us, the

---

[61] Ibid., 185–6.

[62] Ibid., 194–6. Froissart calls him John Standish, but his real name was Ralph.

[63] Ibid., 178; *HVR*, 66.

[64] Wilkinson, 'The Peasants' Revolt', 24–9.

[65] G. Kriehn, 'Studies in the Sources of the Social Revolt in 1381', *American Historical Review*, vii (1901–2), 475–7.

[66] Oman, *The Great Revolt*, 74–6.

[67] *Peasants' Revolt*, ed. Dobson, 178.

[68] Ibid., 166, 179, 197, 204: the comments of the *Anonimalle* writer, Walsingham, Froissart, and the Monk of Westminster respectively.

Londoners were quickly on hand to act. Walworth rode 'hastily to the city'; word was put around as to what had happened, and in no time well-armed levies from the wards were pouring out. As the *Anonimalle* writer graphically put it, the rebels were enveloped 'like sheep in a pen'.[69] The signs are that a well-organized strategy was put into effect. If a guess were to be made as to the authors of the plan, the likeliest candidates would be Mayor Walworth and Sir Robert Knolles; the former had long advocated tough action, while the latter was a soldier of repute and experience. Significantly, Froissart says that Knolles brought his own retinue on to the field with him and was so keen to tear into the rebels that Richard himself had to restrain him.[70]

Richard's own role in the unfolding of this drama is, of course, well attested. As both Froissart and Walsingham stress, when Tyler was slain, the king spurred his horse and rode out into the rebel midst. Waving his arm, he cried, 'You shall have no captain but me. Just follow me to the fields without, and then you can have what you want.'[71] He pushed his way through the mêlée and, when the panic had subsided, the crowd started moving. Walsingham, Froissart and the others were keen to stress Richard's role in the triumph. As a result it is often easy to forget that it formed part of a larger strategy. The king's object was to get the rebels moving as quickly as possible away from the centre of London. To achieve this, he sent an order to them to reassemble in his company at Clerkenwell. Contrary to what is often implied, he did not ride with them there himself; the *Anonimalle* says that he made his way by a different route.[72] Nor does it seem that he made the journey unprotected: he was accompanied by Walworth, who had returned from the city, and a retinue of knights. When the rebels reassembled, Richard probably said a few conciliatory words to them. According to Walsingham, he confirmed the terms that had been agreed at Mile End; the *Anonimalle*, more briefly, says that he offered them mercy.[73] Shortly afterwards the process of dispersing the rebel host was set in motion. Many of the rebels, shaken by the death of their leader, were already taking to flight. According to the *Anonimalle* writer, Richard detached a couple of knights from his retinue to lead the Kentishmen away: the knights took them through London and then out over the bridge, 'so that each might go peacefully to his home'.[74]

Tyler's death at Smithfield was the turning point in the history of the

[69] Ibid., 167.

[70] Ibid., 197–8.

[71] Ibid., 179, 196.

[72] The rebels were 'to come to him' at Clerkenwell, not to follow him there: ibid., 166.

[73] Ibid., 167, 180.

[74] Ibid., 167.

Revolt. The rebels, deprived of their greatest and most charismatic leader, were left spiritless and broken. In London, certainly, the rebellion was over. The royal authorities had regained the initiative, and the threat to public order was effectively ended. It is true that groups of rebels were still active in parts of East Anglia, Hertfordshire, Yorkshire and elsewhere but, once the news of events in London spread, the energy went out of these movements. By July, in almost every part of England, the authorities had regained control.

With the immediate crisis over, the council turned to restoring order in the realm. Preliminary measures were taken on the very day of Wat Tyler's death. An *ad hoc* commission was given to Knolles, Walworth, Brembre and two other Londoners to take action to restore order in London and prevent further disturbances; and an oyer and terminer commission was granted to the same men in association with Chief Justice Belknap to initiate judicial proceedings against the rebels.[75] Further commissions were issued in the next few days which do not appear to have been enrolled. On 18 June letters were sent to the sheriffs ordering them to proclaim the enforcement of the peace and to take whatever measures were necessary to crush the rebels.[76] Powers of a similar sort were given on 20 June to the earl of Buckingham and Chief Justice Tresilian throughout England and to the constable of Dover and the sheriff of Hampshire in their own bailiwicks.[77] Three days later commissions granting military and judicial powers were issued to the magnates and leading gentry in most of the counties of southern England.[78] The letters authorized the commissioners to deal with the rebels 'according to the law and custom of England', and most of the commissioners appear to have acted in accordance with their instructions. It seems that few summary executions were carried out. In London Mayor Walworth executed a number of leading rebels: among his victims was John Starling, who was reputed to have beheaded Sudbury.[79] Elsewhere in England, however, only Bishop Despenser of Norwich, who was active in suppressing the rebellion in Norfolk, appears to have followed his example. A possible reason for this moderation is the fact that there was considerable doubt as to the legal status of the crimes committed by the rebels. The Statute of Treasons of 1352 had defined treason in deliberately narrow terms and had not made specific reference to popular insurrection. The crown's

[75] C66/310 m.4d; *CPR 1381–5*, 18, 23. For a full account of the judicial proceedings that followed the revolt see Prescott, 'Judicial Records of the Rising', esp. 36–58.
[76] *CA*, 314–15; *HA*, ii, 16–17.
[77] *CPR 1381–5*, 23.
[78] Ibid., 69–71.
[79] *Peasants' Revolt*, ed. Dobson, 308–9.

policy – at least, to judge from the terms of the commissions it issued – appears to have been to encourage a view of the insurgents as traitors. But local commissioners were not always – indeed, not often – of the same opinion. In many cases they preferred to define offences as felony. As a result many of the most prominent rebels escaped lightly. Farringdon, Horn and Sibil in London, and Thomas Sampson in Ipswich, all got away with periods of imprisonment, while many lesser rebels obtained pardons.[80]

Only one county offered active resistance to the council, and that was Essex. Richard had resolved to make a personal visit to Essex to oversee the pacification. He left the capital on 22 June with a sizeable retinue, and on the following day he reached Waltham.[81] There a deputation of Essex rebels came to see him. Lacking nothing in audacity, they began bargaining with the king. First, they demanded confirmation of the privileges granted at Mile End; and then they asked for exemption from attending the king's courts, save for the annual view of frank-pledge. Richard, according to Walsingham, rounded on them. 'You wretches,' he said, 'detestable on land and sea: you who seek equality with lords are unworthy to live. Give this message to your colleagues: rustics you were, and rustics you are still; you will remain in bondage, not as before, but incomparably harsher. For as long as we live we will strive to suppress you, and your misery will be an example in the eyes of posterity. However, we will spare your lives if you remain faithful and loyal. Choose now which course you want to follow.'[82] With this rebuke ringing in their ears the envoys were sent packing. The rebel leaders, to whom they reported, however, were in no mood to give in. Dispatching summonses all over the county, they quickly mobilized a force at Great Baddow and Rettenden near Chelmsford. On or around 27 June they advanced to the Billericay area. There they occupied a strong position on the edge of a wood, covering their flanks with ditches and rows of carts chained together. By now a force under the command of the earl of Buckingham and Sir Thomas Percy was being sent against them. The advance guard met the rebels on Saturday, 28 June. There was a skirmish – it could hardly be called a battle – and the rebels fled. The militants headed for Colchester and later for Sudbury in Suffolk, where

---

[80] C. Petit-Dutaillis, 'Causes and General Characteristics of the Rising of 1381', C. Petit-Dutaillis and G. Lefebvre, *Studies and Notes Supplementary to Stubbs' Constitutional History*, ii (Manchester, 1915), 300–2. For the offences – or alleged offences – of Farringdon, Horn and Sibil see above, 68 and 64; and for Sampson, see above 61 n.

[81] I.e. Waltham Forest. For Richard's itinerary at this time see Appendix, which is here based on W.H.B. Bird, 'The Peasant Rising of 1381: the King's Itinerary', *EHR*, xxxi (1916), 124–6, and W.M. Ormrod, 'The Peasants' Revolt and the Government of England', *JBS*, xxix (1990), 1–30, in particular 20–1.

[82] *Peasants' Revolt*, ed. Dobson , 310–11.

they hoped to find support. Northern Essex and Suffolk, however, had already been pacified and, instead of receiving assistance, the rebels found themselves under attack from a force under Lord FitzWalter. Once again they were routed, and many more prisoners were taken.[83] By this time the revolt in Essex was all but over. To discipline the rebels the council appointed a commission of oyer and terminer under the new chief justice, Sir Robert Tresilian.[84] Tresilian appears to have set about his task with severity. According to Walsingham, he pressurized juries into divulging the names of rebels and, wherever possible, he construed offences as treasons rather than felonies. In the course of his hearings some nineteen rebels were executed by hanging and another dozen by hanging and drawing. Walsingham naturally approved of the policy. Whereas other justices, he said, 'had simply beheaded the rustics', Tresilian visited upon them the penalties for the most heinous offence of all.[85] Not surprisingly the judge's sessions acquired the reputation of a 'bloody assize'.

Richard had been staying in Essex for much of the time that Tresilian was holding court and he may have attended some of the hearings. In Walsingham's view the king fully supported the chief justice's policy. Walsingham stressed the feelings of contempt that the king showed for the rebels at this time and noted that he personally gave the chief justice his commission.[86] Certainly it is unlikely that Richard felt any mystical sympathy for the rebels: all his adult life he was to lay emphasis on the subject's obligation of obedience. Nevertheless, there are grounds for thinking that his attitude to the rebels' treatment was more complex than Walsingham – and, indeed, historians subsequently have – supposed. Barely a month before, in London, Richard had been closely involved in the policy of conciliation and concession. The proclamation which had been issued offering the rebels pardon and asking them to return home had been sealed with the king's signet, his

---

[83] Ibid., 311–12.

[84] *CPR 1381–5*, 73. His predecessor, Sir John Cavendish, had been executed by the rebels near Mildenhall.

[85] *Peasants' Revolt*, ed. Dobson, 312–13. Unfortunately the plea roll for Tresilian's hearings does not survive, and it is impossible to provide verification of Walsingham's report of the justice's tactics. Walsingham's account, however, is broadly supported by Knighton and the Westminster writer (ibid., 314; *WC*, 14); the latter says 'The royal judges were now everywhere in session. . . . Gibbets rose where none had been seen before, since the existing ones were too few for the bodies of the condemned.' For some indictments to Tresilian's commission see KB9/166/2. These are printed in translation in J.A. Sparvel Bayly, 'Essex in Insurrection, 1381', *Transactions of the Essex Archaeological Society*, new series i (1878), 216–19. A few Essex cases also crop up in King's Bench: these are printed ibid., 214–16.

[86] *Peasants' Revolt*, ed. Dobson, 312.

personal seal.[87] It is possible, even probable, that Richard believed he had negotiated with the rebels in good faith: Walsingham himself says that at Smithfield he confirmed to them the charters granted at Mile End.[88] Long after the quelling of the Revolt Richard continued to show an interest in manumitting the villeins. In the November parliament of 1381 the chancellor said that he would willingly free the villeins if parliament authorized him to do so.[89] As late as the beginning of July the rebels themselves were still placing their faith in him. On the 2nd of that month the men of Somerset had draft letters of manumission drawn up for submission to him for sealing.[90] These are scattered and perhaps, in isolation, unimportant pointers to the king's attitude, and it is hard to know what to make of them. It may be unwise to attach excessive significance to the rebels' view of the king, for throughout the insurrection they had seen him as a potential ally awaiting release from his councillors' thrall. Perhaps more instructive is the evidence of Richard's own authenticated statements and deeds at this time. On a couple of occasions Richard voiced his feelings about the rebels 'with his own mouth'; and each time, interestingly, he showed himself unsympathetic. On 23 June at Waltham, as we have seen, he had personally ('in persona propria') rebuked the envoys of the rebels of Essex and condemned them to servitude. A couple of days later, on 26 June, according to a note on the exchequer memoranda rolls, he 'by word of mouth' ordered Sir Peter le Veel and Sir Robert Passelewe to go to Wiltshire and Hampshire to suppress all signs of revolt there.[91] Between them these pieces of evidence show Richard actively involved in the policy of concerting repression. Yet alongside them has to be set the fact that the revocation of the charters of manumission was delayed until 2 July, a full seventeen days after the triumph at Smithfield. It is difficult to account for this simply on grounds of political expediency, for the action could have been taken much earlier. The possibility has to be considered that Richard himself was responsible for the delay. At the back of his mind he may have had doubts about reneging on an agreement that he had entered into in good faith. As late as the autumn he was evidently still having reservations about the decision – hence the offer which the chancellor made on his behalf in parliament to free his villeins if the lords would theirs.[92] It is worth remembering that the king

[87] Ibid., 275.
[88] Ibid., 180; and see above, 70. It is fair to add that Walsingham says that he did this only because he knew that Essex was not yet pacified (ibid.).
[89] RP, iii, 99.
[90] B.F. Harvey, 'Draft Letters Patent of Manumission and Pardon for the Men of Somerset in 1381', EHR, lxxx (1965), 89–91.
[91] Peasants' Revolt, ed. Dobson, 310–11, and above, 74; G.O. Sayles, 'Richard II in 1381 and 1399', EHR, xciv (1979), 820–2.
[92] RP, iii, 99.

was only fourteen when the rising erupted, and in the tense and confused atmosphere of the time it would be surprising if he had reached a clear and considered view of all the issues involved.[93]

Richard's infirmity of purpose contrasted sharply with the incisiveness and determination which the council showed at this time. In the wake of the triumph at Smithfield ministers and council had lost little time in switching to a policy of repression. The architect of this policy was probably William Courtenay, Sudbury's successor at Canterbury and, from August, the chancellor.[94] Courtenay was a figure of a very different stamp from his predecessor. Vigorous, active and purposeful, he was a leader rather than a manager of men. In political terms he was a conservative, and he had little sympathy with notions of conciliation.[95] Under his influence the council was quickly won over to a much tougher policy. The centrepiece of the strategy was the royal visitation to Essex. The visitation's purpose was to overawe the rebel heartland with the majesty of royal authority. Richard was provided with a massive armed bodyguard, and he took with him the administrative departments and the staff of the two seals. While travelling with the king the chancellor raised levies in other parts of the realm. In Walsingham's words, 'messengers were sent into the country asking all those who loved the king and honoured the realm to hurry to London well-armed and on horseback'.[96] It is unclear how many responded to the king's appeal. The figure of 40,000 given by Walsingham is unsupported, but a sizeable force is suggested by the payment to the keeper of the wardrobe of 2,000 marks for the wages of 'men-at-arms and archers going . . . by the king's order for the salvation of the realm'.[97] As in an expedition in war, the operations against the rebels were centred on the king's household. Richard's retinue in Essex was a household force, and elsewhere in the realm it was the household's financial office, the wardrobe, which co-ordinated the magnates' work of repression.

---

[93] In particular, he may not have appreciated the concept of property rights in serfs until reminded of this by the November parliament (for which see below, 79–81).

[94] After Sudbury's murder the great seal had been given to the earl of Arundel 'for the day' (*Anon.*, 146; *Peasants' Revolt*, ed. Dobson, 162). On 16 June Arundel was replaced by Sir Hugh Segrave, the steward of the household, who was to hold office 'until the king could more conveniently provide himself with another chancellor'. Courtenay was Segrave's successor (Tout, *Chapters*, iii, 375–6; vi, 16).

[95] For Courtenay's career as a churchman see J. Dahmus, *William Courtenay, Archbishop of Canterbury, 1381–1396* (Philadelphia, 1966). Dahmus unfortunately says little of Courtenay's political career, but the tenor of his outlook is suggested by his vigorous opposition to heresy. For his letters to diocesans condemning heresy see M. Aston, 'Lollardy and Sedition, 1381–1431', *P&P*, xvii (1960), repr. in *Peasants, Knights and Heretics*, ed. R.H. Hilton (Cambridge, 1973), 278.

[96] *HA*, ii, 14.

[97] E403/484, 25 June.

Payments from the wardrobe were made to the earls of Buckingham, Kent, Salisbury, Warwick, Derby and Suffolk to cover military expenses: Buckingham is known to have been active in suppressing dissent at Gloucester after leaving Essex, and Warwick, according to Walsingham, was sent to the midlands.[98] Once the immediate task of restoring order had been completed, the repressive policy was extended to the enforcement of villein labour obligations. Royal assistance was offered to several landowners and employers who were experiencing difficulty in reasserting their rights over disobedient villeins;[99] and a useful precedent was provided for the reimposition of seigneurial demands by an order in July that tenants on the royal manor of Langley in Buckinghamshire should perform their full customary services.[100] Overall there was an obvious confidence and sense of purpose in the council's handling of policy: the objectives were clearly defined and the measures needed to achieve them boldly executed.

But reactions to the council's policy were mixed. In the shires in particular people were unhappy. The gentry – who were the traditional leaders of the county communities and who filled all the main local offices – were highly suspicious of what they saw as the heavy-handed intervention of the government. In their view the likely effect of such intervention would be to challenge the well-being and harmony of the local communities. If the fabric of society were to be restored, and the lower orders recalled to obedience, the wisest policy, they believed, would be to grant commissions to those who actually knew and understood the workings of local society: that is, to the gentry. In the wake of the Revolt the leaders of several of the county communities went to the king to voice their unease. Among the first to do so were the gentry and nobility of Kent. In July Richard had announced a visitation of Kent, having heard rumours of a renewal of discontent there. The 'magnates and notables' of the county interceded with him, pointing out, as Walsingham said, 'the evils which such persecution would inflict on all members of an ignorant people'.[101] They offered to stand surety for the local commons; the offer was accepted and royal intervention averted. A couple of weeks later a similar initiative was taken by the gentry of Hertfordshire. Chief Justice Tresilian and his fellows, having completed their hearings in Essex, were about to move to St Albans to conduct enquiries into the insurgency there, and it was feared that widespread

[98] E101/400/11; R. Holt, 'Thomas of Woodstock and Events at Gloucester in 1381', *BIHR*, lviii (1985), 237–41; *HA*, ii, 28. Sir Richard Poynings was given authority against the rebels in Sussex: E159/161, Brevia Directa Baronibus, Michaelmas m.32.

[99] *CPR 1381–5*, 73; *CCR 1381–5*, 74–5.

[100] *CCR 1381–5*, 2.

[101] *HA*, ii, 14.

damage and destruction to the locality would result. A local office-holder, Sir Walter atte Lee, approached the king and asked for a commission to be granted to him and two other knights to take appropriate action against the insurgents. As he was subsequently to explain, it was better for the matter to be dealt with by local men, 'friends and neighbours' of the malefactors, than by strangers or outsiders. The king accepted his plea and, according to Walsingham, a commission was then issued.[102]

The initiatives of these two groups of gentry highlighted the growing alarm in the country at the council's policy. There was a belief, particularly widespread among the gentry, that the campaign of repression was being pushed too far. While there was agreement that exemplary punishments were needed to restore order and to deter future rebellion, a 'bloody assize', like Tresilian's, risked dividing local societies and provoking the renewal of discontent. What the gentry wanted was for a recognition of the need for reform to be set alongside the measures of repression. Hitherto the king and his ministers had given little attention to the case for reform. Since mid-1377 they had enjoyed the strong support of the parliamentary commons, and so in a sense they had hardly needed to. However, in the wake of the Revolt, when the policies of earlier years were suddenly called into question, the position was very different: the issue could no longer be avoided. When parliament assembled in November for the first time since the Revolt, the council faced a commons angrier and more critical than at any time since the Good Parliament. The consensual approach of the past had gone.

The object of summoning parliament had been the usual one of remedying the king's lack of money.[103] But from the very outset proceedings were dominated by the Revolt and its aftermath. The first matter to be considered was the row between John of Gaunt and the earl of Northumberland over the latter's refusal to admit Gaunt to his

---

[102] *HA*, ii, 22–6. Atte Lee resided at the manor of Albury. He had already served four times as knight of the shire for Hertfordshire and was to serve again for another six; he also served three times as a member for Essex. In county administration he had been a JP, and in 1389–90 he was to be sheriff. For his career see *House of Commons*, iii, 577–9. No record is found on the patent roll of the issue of a commission to atte Lee, but that does not mean that Walsingham's account is at fault: as A. Prescott has shown, in the confused aftermath of the Revolt a number of important judicial commissions were not copied on to the roll ('Judicial Records of the Rising', 41, 43–4).

[103] The council was planning a major expedition to France led by the king. Since income from the third poll tax had been some 20 per cent below expectation, negotiations had been opened with the merchant community for a loan, and it was hoped that security for this loan would be provided by a grant of taxation. The outcome was a modest renewal of the wool subsidy: see below, 81.

castles in June.[104] The duke demanded a formal apology from the earl; the latter initially resisted, but later submitted, and on the fifth day of the session the two exchanged a kiss of peace.[105] A second issue considered early on was that of the terms on which the rebels were to be pardoned. Richard had wanted to grant a general amnesty, from which only certain important leaders and notable malefactors were excepted; the commons, however, wanted to exclude the burgesses of Bury St Edmunds, Cambridge, Canterbury and other towns where there had been rioting. In the end the commons gave way, and a general amnesty was issued.

In the second week, after this initial business had been settled, the matter of the pacification of the realm was considered. The commons, to judge from the official roll, wanted the lords to take up the issue on their behalf. The lords, however, refused to do so on the grounds that this would be contrary to 'the custom and form of parliament'.[106] The commons themselves then cast restraint to the wind, and their Speaker, Sir Richard Waldegrave, made a dramatic plea for reform.[107] The country was suffering grievous oppression, he said, 'because of the outrageous multitude of embracers of quarrels and maintenance, who act like kings, so that justice and law are scarcely administered by anyone'. The commons of the realm were 'pillaged and destroyed' by purveyors for the king's household, who gave nothing for the goods that they took, by the subsidies and tallages that had been incessantly levied, and by the oppressions committed by the king's ministers. These many 'outrages' made the 'mean' commons feel so oppressed that they had risen up and committed 'the mischiefs which they had in the revolt'. Further trouble could be expected from them unless 'proper remedy was provided in time for the aforementioned oppressions and mischiefs'. Turning at this point to suggestions for remedies, the Speaker asked for the existing ministers to be dismissed from office,

[104] See above, 59.

[105] Anon., 155–6; WC, 20–2; RP, iii, 98. For discussion see Goodman, John of Gaunt, 89–91.

[106] RP, iii, 100.

[107] Ibid., 100–1. It is unclear to what extent Waldegrave was speaking for himself or for the commons as a whole. According to the roll, he was speaking for the commons, but his position hitherto had been insecure. On 18 November, over a fortnight into the session, he made a request to be relieved of his office as Speaker. When ordered by Chancellor Scrope to continue, he demanded a restatement of the council's programme for the session on the grounds that the commons were disputing what it was. The chancellor, recapitulating the commons' 'charge', told him to pay special attention to the manumission of the peasants (ibid., 100). It is possible that the commons simply wanted clarification of the agenda; but equally they could have been uneasy with the line on policy that the Speaker was taking (J.S. Roskell, The Commons and their Speakers in English Parliaments, 1376–1523 (Manchester, 1965), 127–9).

and 'virtuous and more sufficient' men to be put in their place. Speaker Waldegrave's dramatic discourse produced an immediate response from the council. In the first place, the chancellor, Archbishop Courtenay, was removed from his office. Courtenay had only been appointed in August, but he no longer commanded the confidence of the commons, and his place was taken by Richard, Lord Scrope, a veteran administrator who had earned the plaudits of the commons in 1376.[108] Secondly, a commission was appointed to survey and reform the king's household. It was a distinguished body: Gaunt and the two archbishops were the leading members; the remaining members were the bishops of Winchester, Ely, Exeter and Rochester, the earls of Arundel, Warwick, Suffolk, Stafford and Salisbury, the chancellor, five bannerets 'and others'.[109] At the same time it was agreed that two senior lords be appointed to reside perpetually in the household 'to counsel and govern' the king; these men were the earl of Arundel, who was emerging as a leading critic of the government, and Sir Michael de la Pole, a banneret of Lancaster's.[110] Early in the New Year, after the king's marriage, when a second session of the parliament was held, further concessions were made to the commons. A series of measures was approved for streamlining the exchequer: the process of accounting was speeded up, and communications between internal departments improved. Perhaps more importantly to the commons, limits were placed on the fees charged by exchequer clerks.[111] In recognition of these several concessions the commons agreed to renew the subsidy on wool exports for a further year.[112]

The commons continued to press for reform in the next three or four parliaments. Twice in 1382 they returned to the issues which Speaker Waldegrave had raised in November. In May they urged the king to ease the burden on his subjects by retaining feudal escheats in his hand; and in November they pressed for 'wise' officers and 'honest and discreet' councillors to be appointed – the names of the former to be announced before the end of the session. To each of these requests the king returned an equivocal answer.[113] Subsequently they concentrated on two issues of more immediate concern to them: the lords' distribution of badges and the corrupt behaviour of officials. In 1383 and 1384 they

---

[108] See above, 50–1.
[109] *RP*, iii, 101.
[110] Ibid., 104
[111] These measures were not enrolled on the statute roll until after the May parliament of 1382, but they clearly relate to petitions which the commons had submitted some time between November and February. For the petitions see *RP*, iii, 118–19, and for the statutes, *SR*, ii, 21–3.
[112] *RP*, iii, 104–5.
[113] Ibid., 139, 147.

secured concessions on the latter issue: the king granted petitions for observance of the Statute of Purveyors and for curbs on the assize justices' receipt of fees and robes.[114] On the matter of the distribution of badges, however, they ran into fierce opposition from the lords. A request at the Salisbury parliament of 1384 for wide-ranging curbs on the lords' freedom to grant these devices was met with a firm rebuff from Gaunt: the duke said that the magnates were perfectly capable of disciplining their dependants themselves.[115] The duke and his allies in the nobility apparently had little sympathy with the commons' campaign for reform. Their sympathies, it seems, lay much more with the ministers and council. They were anxious to preserve their freedom of action and disliked any proposals that seemed to threaten their ability to defend their own interests. Like Archbishop Courtenay – and like Chancellor de la Pole later – they wanted priority to be given to performance of obedience; reform could be left until later.

The lords and the parliamentary commons thus drew sharply contrasting conclusions from the crisis of the uprising and its aftermath.[116] The commons, fearful of a renewal of discontent, urged the case for comprehensive reform. They put forward a powerful and internally consistent set of arguments. The king's subjects, they said, were groaning under the burden of misgovernment. To ease their plight, the king should appoint 'wise' and 'discreet' councillors and seek to live within his means. At the same time he should reawaken in his subjects a sense of their obligations: he should ensure the honest performance of their duties by his officials and curb the activities of the maintainers and embracers of law suits. There were certainly parts of this analysis with which the nobility could agree, for they, like the commons, were sensitive to the dangers of advice by 'evil councillors'; and they, like the commons, were concerned at the size and cost of the household. But in general they found themselves siding with the officers and the crown. A sharp difference of view thus emerged between the main elements of the political community. It was a difference which was to diminish in significance only when Richard's own management of affairs gave rise to fresh areas of concern in the mid-1380s.

[114] Ibid., 146, 158–9, 200; SR, ii, 30, 33, 36. The commons wanted assize justices to be prohibited from receiving fees from lords in the areas where they were hearing cases.

[115] WC, 80–2. For further discussion of the badges issue, see below, 200–1, 263–4.

[116] See on this, A.Tuck, 'Nobles, Commons and the Great Revolt of 1381', The English Rising of 1381, ed. R.H. Hilton and T.H. Aston (Cambridge, 1984), 194–212.

Chapter 5

MARRIAGE AND DIPLOMACY, 1381–3

At the end of the 1370s Richard was probably Europe's most eligible bachelor. He was young, personable and handsome. He was heir to an ancient and distinguished lineage. And he had at his disposal the resources of a kingdom fabled for its wealth.

The task of advising the king on a possible bride was essentially that of his mother – the Princess Joan – his chief officers and the council. Generally in the middle ages royal marriages were arranged so as to further the ends of national diplomacy, and Richard's councillors and advisers would have wanted to use his marriage in this fashion. Given Richard's eligibility, no shortage of offers could be expected from prospective fathers-in-law. It would be the councillors' task to weigh the various offers and to alight on the one most favourable to English interests.

The first offer to be received was from the Holy Roman Emperor, Charles IV. In a letter to the council sent shortly after Richard's accession the emperor extended the hand of his eleven-year-old daughter Anne. Early in 1378 two other offers followed: an offer from King Charles V of France of the hand of his daughter Marie, and a rival bid from his enemy Charles of Navarre of a match with one of his own daughters. Charles IV's offer was rejected almost immediately, probably because it held out insufficient prospect of diplomatic gain.[1] The other two were viewed more sympathetically. Richard's mother was said to favour the Navarrese proposal, on the grounds that King Charles was a man of good lineage and that an alliance with him would serve as a focus for anti-French sentiment. Negotiations with the king proceeded smoothly for a couple of months, but in April they were effectively halted by Charles V's confiscation of his namesake's French properties. The Navarrese king lost his attractiveness as an ally, and the proposal for a match was set aside.[2] Negotiations with the French broke down shortly afterwards. These had never enjoyed more than a marginal chance of success. The English saw them mainly as a vehicle for extracting concessions from the French, while the French themselves showed

---

[1] E. Perroy, *L'Angleterre et le grand Schisme d'Occident* (Paris, 1933), 136.
[2] Ibid., 136–7.

little or no interest in making the necessary territorial concessions. At whose behest the talks were broken off is not clear, but broken off they were, by May at the latest.[3] Attention then focused on two other possibilities. One was the idea of a match with a daughter of King Robert II of Scotland; this, however, raised little enthusiasm in London because of the long-standing English dislike of the Scots.[4] The other, a more promising starter, was that of an alliance with the Visconti dukes of Milan. Relations between England and Milan had been close since Lionel of Antwerp, Edward III's second son, had been betrothed to Violante Visconti in 1368.[5] In the late 1370s they had been cemented by the presence in Lombardy of the English mercenary Sir John Hawkwood, who formed a close association with the Visconti family. It was through Hawkwood's good offices that Milanese interest in a match was first communicated to England. The possibility was discussed by the council in April or May 1378, and two envoys (one of them Chaucer) were sent to the duchy to test the ground and report back. The reception they received was cordial, and on their return to England they were accompanied by a party of Milanese councillors.[6] Discussions continued over the winter of 1378–9, and by March 1379 were sufficiently advanced for a second embassy, composed of Michael de la Pole, John Burley and George Felbrigg, to be dispatched with full powers to discuss the terms of a treaty of marriage. But then it appears that negotiations drew sharply to a halt. Felbrigg returned to London, while his fellow envoys went on to Rome. No agreement was reached, and Catherine, Richard's intended bride, was later married to Duke Bernabo's nephew Giangaleazzo.[7] The change of plan was as sudden as it was unexpected.

What appears to have happened was that the negotiations had been overtaken by events at Rome. In 1378 a double election to the papacy had plunged the Church into schism. In April 1378, following the death of Gregory XI, Bartholomeo Prignano, archbishop of Bari, had been elected pope as Urban VI in deference to the wishes of those who wanted Gregory's successor to be an Italian. Five months later, following the defection of all but three of the cardinals involved in the earlier election, a rival candidate was chosen in the person of Robert of Geneva, who took the title Clement VII. The issues separating the two

[3] Ibid., 142 and n.

[4] Ibid., 72; Walker, 'Letters to the Dukes of Lancaster', 73–4.

[5] Lionel had died only a matter of months after the betrothal on 17 October 1368 in Piedmont (CP, iii, 258).

[6] Perroy, L'Angleterre et le grand Schisme, 137–8.

[7] Ibid., 137–9, for the details of these embassies. De la Pole, Burley and Felbrigg received wages from 26 March 1379 (E364/14 m.4).

men were as much personal as political, but undoubtedly elements of national rivalry made a contribution to the débâcle. Urban's backing came chiefly from the Italians, English and Germans, and Clement's from the French and their allies, the Scots and the Castilians. Allegiance to the two popes was in large measure a reflection of the lines of diplomatic demarcation that cut across Europe. The overlap of secular with ecclesiastical politics helps to explain why the schism lasted for so long: it could not be settled until the larger dispute between England and France had been settled. For all the manoeuvring to find a solution by some of the most gifted men of the age, it was to be forty years before the faithful of Europe were again to be united in obedience to a single pontiff.

The earliest years of the schism saw the two popes moving rapidly to consolidate their respective positions. Urban had the edge over his rival in being in physical possession of the Holy See and its shrines, but this was an advantage to some extent neutralized by Clement's control of the bureaucracy at Avignon. Clement was also fortunate in having a relatively compact and cohesive power base in the French-dominated world. Urban's support was spread more thinly around Europe: the principal rulers who gave him their backing – the kings of England and of the Romans and the various Italian princes – lived far apart and had relatively few interests in common. If Urban were to consolidate his position, it was essential for him to draw his supporters into a firmer alliance. Richard's search for a bride, when it became known, gave him the perfect opportunity to do this. Over the winter a scheme was hatched by the Curial diplomats for a match between Richard and a princess of the imperial house of Luxemburg. In essence the scheme was a revised version of Charles IV's proposals of a year before. Its principal sponsor appears to have been Pileo de Prata, archbishop of Ravenna, one of Urban's closest advisers and a man of wide diplomatic experience. As the special emissary of Gregory XI Pileo had been instrumental in both negotiating the truce between England and France at Bruges in 1375 and in promoting negotiations between the two powers following its expiry two years later.[8] His knowledge of the courts and chanceries of Europe was probably without equal in Rome. If anyone could pull off a diplomatic coup for the pope, it was assuredly he.

Measures to implement the scheme were taken almost immediately. Some time during the winter the English envoys to Milan were summoned to Rome and the proposal for an Anglo-imperial alliance was

[8] 'The Anglo-French Negotiations at Bruges, 1374–1377', ed. E. Perroy (Camden Miscellany, xix, Camden 3rd series, lxxx, 1952), v–vi.

put to them. In December, even before their response was known, Pileo
began a mission to Germany to win the support of the new king of the
Romans, Charles's son Wenzel. He arrived in Prague in March and
quickly gained an ascendancy over the impressionable eighteen-year-
old ruler. The two had a series of meetings over the summer, and at the
end of them Wenzel wrote a letter to Richard, which his visitor must
virtually have dictated, dwelling on the evils of the schism and urging an
alliance between the two rulers to unite Christendom in obedience to
the one true pontiff. The English were more responsive to Wenzel's
initiative than they had been to Charles's of a year earlier. It is possible
that they had already been in contact with the king through the agency
of envoys at the imperial diet at Frankfurt.[9] On receipt of the letter they
sent new instructions to de la Pole and Burley in Italy, ordering them to
go north to Prague to seek out Wenzel and discuss his ideas with him.
The change of heart on the English side was attributable to a number
of factors. In the first place, there were fewer prospective brides to
choose from in mid-1379 than there had been a year or two earlier, as
one possibility after another fell by the wayside. Secondly, the idea of
marriage to the daughter of an emperor exerted a growing appeal:
Charles IV, the most successful of the Luxemburg rulers, had been
crowned in Rome by the pope in 1355, and at this stage there was every
likelihood that his son and successor would receive the same honour.
Thirdly, and most importantly, there was the prospect of using an
alliance with the Luxemburgs as a means of bringing pressure to bear
on the French. Charles IV (1346–78) in his early years had been
strongly francophile in outlook. His father, John the blind, had been
killed fighting for the French at Crécy. He himself had been brought up
at the French court; his first wife Blanche was a sister of Philip VI, and
his sister Bonne had been Charles V's first wife. But with the passage of
time his ties with the French had begun to weaken. His second, third
and fourth wives were from within the empire, and his own interests
came to focus on the building up of a power base for his dynasty
in Bohemia.[10] His line in foreign policy became steadily more independent. In 1378, for example, he did not follow the French in recognizing Clement VII; he offered his allegiance to Urban. Clearly there
were openings and opportunities that the English could exploit. If they
could contract a marriage alliance with the Luxemburgs, the process of
detaching them from the French could be accelerated. The latter
would be deprived of an ally and would begin to look more isolated in

[9] A. Tuck, 'Richard II and the House of Luxemburg', *Richard II. Power and
Prerogative*, ed. A. Goodman (Oxford, 1998).
[10] For Charles's dynastic policy see B. Jarrett, *The Emperor Charles IV* (London,
1935); V. Dvoráková and others, *Gothic Mural Painting in Bohemia and Moravia,
1300–1378* (Oxford, 1964), 41–50.

Europe; and their readiness to seek peace on English terms might to that extent be greater. While there was little prospect that the Luxemburgs would be willing to take military action against their former allies, there seemed no other – and certainly no better – way of increasing the pressure on France to submit.

De la Pole and Burley, the two English envoys to Italy, left Rome for Germany probably towards the end of September.[11] They had meetings in Germany with both Wenzel and the legate and reported the outcome, which was evidently favourable, to the council in London. Shortly afterwards, they began the journey home. *En route*, however, they had the misfortune to fall into the hands of bandits, who detained them until heavy ransoms were paid for their release – £933 in de la Pole's case and 500 marks in Burley's.[12] It was not until 20 May 1380 that they finally returned to London. A fortnight later a council meeting was held to discuss their report, and a decision was taken to dispatch a new embassy to negotiate terms for a treaty of marriage.[13] The commission was entrusted to men close to the king – Robert Braybrooke, his secretary and a kinsman of his mother; Sir Simon Burley, his tutor; and Sir Bernard van Zetles, a Bohemian-born knight of the Black Prince.[14] The envoys left England almost immediately, on 18 June, and made their way to Bohemia, where discussions proceeded smoothly. It was agreed that final negotiations should open early in the New Year in Flanders, each side being equipped with full powers to conclude an alliance. John Gilbert, bishop of Hereford, the earl of Kent, Sir Hugh Segrave, steward of the household, Sir Richard Abberbury and Walter Skirlaw, all of them men in the princess's trust, were named on 26 December to treat in the king's name. The party crossed to Bruges on 2 January, and when the imperial envoys led by the duke of Teschen arrived a few weeks later, the final stage of the negotiations began. By March most of the remaining details had been settled, and the two sides decided to make the crossing to London. On arrival they were lavishly received by John of Gaunt, who dined them at the Savoy on 3 April; and on 2 May, in the presence of the king and an assembly of prelates and magnates, the final treaty was sealed.[15] The first clauses of this document addressed the formal arrangements for the marriage. Anne was to be brought to Calais towards the end of September at Wenzel's expense

---

[11] Unless otherwise stated, the details of the embassies to Prague are taken from Perroy, *L'Angleterre et le grand Schisme*, 140–1, 145–51.

[12] E403/499, 9 Nov. 1383; 9 Jan. 1384.

[13] This is probably the council in connection with which letters of summons were sent to John of Gaunt, the prelates, magnates and others on 12 May (E403/478, 12 May).

[14] Perroy, *L'Angleterre et le grand Schisme*, 145.

[15] *Foed.*, vii, 290–5.

and provided with a dowry, the size of which was to be settled later; Richard was to bring her from Calais to England, to marry her, and to have her crowned immediately afterwards. The later clauses of the treaty dealt with the broader issues of Anglo-imperial co-operation and were more equivocal. A perpetual alliance was pledged between the two kings and their subjects, and a solemn union was proclaimed against all schismatics and those who opposed the one legitimate pope. However, no mention was made of the possibility of offensive military action, and the English reserved to themselves the right to make truces and to conclude treaties with their adversaries even if the latter were schismatics. In English eyes the treaty was chiefly a means of bringing pressure to bear on the Valois; it was never conceived as the preliminary to an Urbanist crusade.[16] To that extent it fell short of the highest hopes that had been placed on it by the pope and his energetic envoy.

The ceremony of sealing the treaty was accompanied by a lavish distribution of annuities to the duke of Teschen and his fellow envoys. The duke himself was given 500 marks, Peter de Wartemburg and Conrad Creyer, two of Wenzel's court officials, 250 marks each, and lesser luminaries either 500 or 200 florins.[17] Then on 13 May Simon Burley, Walter Skirlaw and George Felbrigg set off for Prague in the company of the Bohemians to secure ratification of the treaty and to complete arrangements for Anne's passage to London.[18] They met Wenzel in August, and the treaty was ratified on 1 September. A messenger returned quickly from Prague with the news, and the government began to make preparations for the queen's coming. On 3 and 20 September letters were sent to the knights of the royal household ordering them to assemble in London in readiness for a crossing to Calais.[19] But then a lengthy period of waiting ensued. Anne had barely set out from Germany by September; and even when she did, probably no earlier than the end of the month, her progress was slow. According to Froissart, she stayed for a month at Brussels as the guest of her aunt the duchess of Brabant. The duchess would not allow her to proceed further so long as the French privateers who were operating in the Channel threatened her passage to England. Thanks to mediation by the duke, however, a safe-conduct was obtained, and it was deemed safe for her to travel. She went on via Ghent to Bruges, where she was welcomed by the count of Flanders. From there she travelled to the Flemish border town of Gravelines, where the earls of Devon and Salisbury received her with a guard of 500 men-at-arms. The Brabantine

[16] Perroy, L'Angleterre et le grand Schisme, 152.

[17] CPR 1381–5, 4. The duke of Teschen was the Emperor Charles IV's cousin. He had been brought up at the emperor's court.

[18] E364/14 m.6d; E364/15 mm.7, 10d.

[19] E403/ 484, 3 Sept., 20 Sept.

escort took its leave, and in the company of the English lords she made the short journey to Calais.[20]

At Westminster by this time the two houses of parliament were in session, discussing a royal request for taxation. On 13 December proceedings were adjourned until the New Year to allow the members to join in the forthcoming festivities. Five days later, on 18 December, Anne and her escorts made the crossing from Calais to Dover.[21] She and a few attendants sailed in one ship, the horses and the rest of the retinue in the others. Her disembarkation at Dover was marked by an incident which Walsingham, ever watchful for omens, took as a sign of ill times to come. As the result of a heavy groundswell, the ships in the harbour were set crashing against one another, and the vessel from which Anne had alighted was broken to pieces.[22] Whether or not this incident interfered with the formal ceremonies of welcome Walsingham does not say. On the third day after her landing Anne was conducted to Canterbury and thence to Leeds castle, where she spent Christmas.[23] The council probably hoped to bring her to London early in the New Year, but it was not until the middle of January that she finally made her entry into the capital.

The moment of her arrival in England found the council embarrassed and unprepared. In the first place, a dispute had broken out over who should officiate at the coming ceremonies. By rights the honour should have gone to the new archbishop of Canterbury, William Courtenay; but Courtenay had not yet received the pallium, and a rival claim was made by Robert Braybrooke, by now bishop of London, and a man who had been heavily involved in the negotiations leading to the marriage. A settlement had to be negotiated between the two, and it was eventually decided that Courtenay should officiate at the coronation and Braybrooke at the wedding.[24] The second difficulty was that the crown was facing a cash-flow crisis. By January the exchequer's coffers were almost empty, and the councillors had to resort to emergency borrowing to ease their problems. All the regular lenders were approached and asked to dig into their pockets. The abbot of Westmin-

---

[20] Froissart, i, 681.

[21] She was accompanied by a retinue of bannerets and royal household knights: E364/160, Trinity term, m.14.

[22] HA, ii, 46.

[23] WC, 22.

[24] Ibid., 22–4. Braybrooke, who was related to Richard's mother, may have been appointed specifically to perform the wedding. The formalities of his appointment to London were rushed through in haste. He was given livery of his temporalities on 27 December; he was consecrated at Lambeth on 5 January; and he was granted his spiritualities on the day after that: L.H. Butler, 'Robert Braybrooke, Bishop of London (1381–1404), and his Kinsmen' (University of Oxford D.Phil. thesis, 1952), 68–9.

ster, the bishop of Winchester and Nicholas Brembre, the London grocer, were among those who responded generously.[25] By the middle of the month there was evidently enough cash in the treasury to allow the government to proceed. On 18 January, after a formal welcome by the Londoners at Blackheath, Anne was led triumphantly into the capital.[26] On 20 January she and Richard were married in Westminster Abbey, and two days later in the same church she was crowned.[27]

Anne's arrival seems to have aroused little interest in England. None of the chroniclers bothered to give detailed accounts of the celebrations in London, as they did of Richard's coronation in 1377, and most contented themselves with a few lines noting her arrival and subsequent marriage in the abbey. Such comments as were offered were for the most part mildly critical. Walsingham complained of the cost of the whole business, and said that the king would have done better to marry Bernabo Visconti's daughter.[28] The Monk of Westminster, with unusual sourness, said that Anne's coming seemed more in the nature of a purchase than a gift, given the amount that the king had had to lay out to secure 'this little scrap of humanity'.[29] At the root of this criticism lay dissatisfaction with the financial arrangements for the match. These had the appearance of being wholly favourable to Wenzel. When the treaty had been negotiated it was informally agreed that the precise size of the dowry that Anne would bring would be settled at a later date between the two parties. The matter was presumably raised by Burley and Skirlaw when they met Wenzel in August, but by that stage it must have become apparent that no dowry at all would be forthcoming because Wenzel could not afford one. Only a few months earlier, indeed, he had been reduced to begging his future brother-in-law for

[25] E403/487, 9 Dec. (Brembre); E403/493, 11 Nov. (Wykeham); WAM 12216 (an undated request to the abbot of Westminster, which on internal evidence may be dated to the turn of 1381–2).
[26] For the Londoners' reception see Brut, 338–9; G. Kipling, 'Richard II's "Sumptuous Pageants" and the Idea of the Civic Triumph', Pageantry in the Shakespearean Theatre, ed. D.M. Bergeron (Athens, Georgia., 1986), 88.
[27] As in 1377, people travelled from all parts of the realm to attend. The West Country knight Sir John Dinham came up from Devon (Cornwall Record Office, AR37/41/1). I am grateful to Hannes Kleineke for this reference. It is possible – though the arguments are far from conclusive – that the coronation ordo known as the Liber Regalis (WAM 38) may have been commissioned in connection with Anne's coronation.
[28] CA, 331.
[29] WC, 24. There was even some open hostility to the match: in London malefactors tore down the arms of the king and the emperor which had been hung on the fountain in honour of Anne and her husband as they processed through the city: Calendar of Select Plea and Memoranda Rolls of the City of London, 1381–1412, ed. A.H. Thomas (Cambridge, 1932), 3.

subsidies. By the terms of an agreement made at the same time as the treaty Richard committed himself to lending the German the sum of 80,000 florins – roughly £12,000.[30] An initial payment of £3,000 was made there and then. Further instalments followed in December and January, and by the time the last payment was made, in August, some £7,500 had been handed over.[31]

Though Wenzel has often been judged an improvident and self-indulgent ruler, his difficulties were not entirely of his own making. To a large extent he was paying the price for his father's mistakes in his last years. In 1373 Charles had embarked on the process of dividing up his dominions among his kin. He had granted Brandenburg and Görlitz to his sons Sigismund and John respectively, and Moravia to his nephews Jost and Prokop. Only Bohemia went to Wenzel.[32] Charles's purpose had been the usual well-intentioned one of medieval rulers: to ensure that as many as possible of his kin were provided for. But its inevitable consequence was to deprive Wenzel of the wide territorial base that he needed in order to make his rule over Germany effective. Bohemia was admittedly the jewel in the crown, the largest and most important of the lands that Charles had ruled. It was probably also the richest. But in the late fourteenth century it was no longer as productive of revenue as it had once been. The silver mines, which had been the foundation of the Caroline prosperity and which had paid for the rebuilding of Prague, were operating at a reduced level of activity, and the tax revenues they yielded were much lower than before.[33] Wenzel, to a greater degree than his father, was forced into reliance on the traditional revenues of the German king-emperors – taxes levied on the towns, the profits of justice and the various dues collected from villages and towns in recognition of rights of lordship. These were barely sufficient to meet the peacetime costs of government, and by the early 1380s Wenzel was slipping into debt. Projects to which he was committed, such as seeking coronation by the pope in Rome, were being postponed, and cutbacks were being made in the building programmes in Prague. One possible solution to the problem was to seek consent to the levying of public taxation, but this was more easily said than done. There was no tradition of public taxation in Bohemia, and consent would have been difficult to obtain. In the short term there was probably little alternative to seeking

---

[30] *Foed.*, vii, 296–7; 301–2. Though the transfer was termed a loan, there was no realistic possibility that the money would be repaid.

[31] *WC*, 24 n.2; Perroy, *L'Angleterre et le grand Schisme*, 152 n.2.

[32] Jarrett, *Charles IV*, 236.

[33] *Cambridge Economic History of Europe*, ii, ed. M.M. Postan and E. Miller (2nd edn, Cambridge, 1987), 722–3; for the financial resources of German kingship in general, see F.R.H. Du Boulay, *Germany in the Later Middle Ages* (London, 1983), 24–7.

subsidies from foreign rulers, humiliating though this was. The approach to the king of England appears to have been made towards the end of 1380. The Bohemians peddled the argument that the loan was needed for the 'urgent business of the empire and Church', but there could be little doubt as to what was really involved: the elimina-tion of imperial debt.

If Wenzel's appetite for money is easy enough to understand, the readiness of the English government to satisfy it is more puzzling. With the exchequer almost empty and collection of the poll tax abandoned, the council were in no position to be lavish with their bounty. Yet not only did they offer no resistance to Wenzel's demands; over a period of some fifteen months they made every effort to meet them. There appear to be two main explanations for their pliability. In the first place, it seems that they were anxious to wean Wenzel from his family's long-standing ties with the French, and dangling a financial carrot was probably a useful way of tempting him to move in their direction. In the second place, Richard himself appears to have been in favour of payment. His commitment to the marriage alliance was certainly well known at the time. According to Walsingham, 'he chose Anne as his bride above all others', and did so in full awareness that a Milanese match would have been more beneficial to the exchequer.[34] By agreeing to the subvention Richard was probably demonstrating his personal commitment to the alliance and his affection for the young bride who personified it.[35]

While the subvention to Wenzel attracted attention by its sheer size, it was by no means the only item of expenditure to which the marriage alliance gave rise. Most obviously, there were the gifts in money and in kind lavished on the Bohemian envoys to England. Annuities of several hundred marks were granted to the duke of Teschen and six others in May 1381, when the treaty was signed, and rewards of a smaller but still significant order were offered to the attendants and retainers who came over with Anne in December.[36] In addition, there was the cost of the

[34] CA, 331.

[35] This commitment to Anne's kin continued into the 1390s. In a striking gesture, in 1393 he ordered a requiem mass to be celebrated in St Paul's for the soul of Elizabeth of Pomerania, the queen's mother (WC, 516).

[36] For annuities granted to Bohemians at the time of the treaty see CPR 1381-5, 4; and for the grant of a tenement in London to a Bohemian household knight of the king, Roger Siglem, ibid., 581. The Westminster writer commented critically on Richard's policy of 'marrying some of the queen's countrywomen to men of rank at royal expense' (WC, 160-2). It is unclear how many such marriages were arranged, but at least a few were. A well-known example is the marriage of Margaret, the duke of Teschen's daughter, to the king's knight Sir Simon Felbrigg, for the two are commemorated by a fine brass at Felbrigg, Norfolk (plate 19). There are also instances of the reverse arrangement: of English wives being found for Bohemian

lavish hospitality offered to the visiting Bohemians. The more senior of the party were encouraged to stay on at court long after the wedding in January. A number of them were still in England in the summer, and the duke of Teschen himself did not leave until August or September.[37] This extraordinary generosity to the Bohemians was not prompted by reckless extravagance on Richard's part. In the delicate business of medieval diplomacy a large element of game-play was involved. Embassies had to be grand enough to carry weight in the courts that they were visiting, and hospitality had to be lavish enough to attest the wealth and magnificence of the ruler offering it. There was little room for economy in the battle to sway opinion by appearances. This was as true of the negotiations in 1380 and 1381 as of any others in the middle ages. Wenzel wanted to affirm his status as an aspirant to the imperial crown, while Richard wanted to establish parity of esteem with Wenzel who, although impoverished, was the son of an emperor. In this unreal, slightly fantastical, world of gesture politics outward show counted for nearly as much as reality.

Richard, of course, would have been the first to recognize the importance of protocol and form in politics. Both were central to his own sense of being. He was never a person given to profound thought or to probing beneath the surface of things; his concern was always to impress by appearances. He revelled in the extravagant and the theatrical – indeed, in almost every aspect of the showier side of politics. Even as a boy he had had a strongly developed sense of occasion. He knew to an uncanny degree how to attract attention to himself, as his spirited performance in meeting the rebels at Smithfield showed. With the passage of time his preoccupation with form became so strong that it consumed his whole being, stifling every other feeling or emotion. But in these early years of adolescence it was still tempered by an immaturity and spontaneity which enabled him to reach out and awaken a response in others. It is noteworthy how easily he was able to develop an affective relationship with the young Anne. The bond that was

knights. One Bohemian for whom an English bride was found was 'Here Sigle', presumably Roger Siglem, to whom Richard gave the present of a gilt cup in 1387 'in die de desponsacione suo' (E403/518, 12 Oct.). There are also a few instances of English prebends and benefices being granted to Bohemian clerks. In 1383 the prebend of Selsey, in Chichester Cathedral, was granted to Bernard Lobdewe, a clerk of the duke of Teschen (*CPR 1381–5*, 365). In a similar vein, in July 1385 custody of Montacute priory was granted to Nicholas Hornyk, the queen's confessor (*CFR 1383–91*, 108, 130). For further discussion of the presence and role of Bohemians in England, see A. Simpson, *The Connections between English and Bohemian Painting during the Second Half of the Fourteenth Century* (New York, 1984), ch. 1.

[37] Perroy, *L'Angleterre et le grand Schisme*, 162. Some of the Bohemians were still in England several years later. Sir Otes Berge did not obtain a writ of passage to leave the kingdom until 8 October 1383 (C81/1340/16).

established between them was one of remarkable strength and intimacy for an arranged marriage at this level of society in the middle ages. Richard was as conspicuously loyal to her as she was to him. He had no mistresses, nor she, as far as is known, any lovers. There is no record of illegitimate royal progeny for the twenty years of the reign. The king's grief on her death in 1394 is well attested. So distraught was he that he ordered the manor house at Sheen, where she had breathed her last, to be destroyed.[38] There can be no more dramatic demonstration of marital commitment than that.

It is clear that at the level of personal relations Richard's marriage to Anne was a success. In terms of delivering the hoped-for diplomatic and military gains, however, it was an almost complete failure. The responsibility for this failure lay in large measure with the king of the Romans. Despite the obligations that he was under, Wenzel would never commit himself to any course that conflicted with his own interests. When pressed by the English to sever his ties with the French, he fell back on one excuse after another. To begin with, he argued that severance would be incompatible with the treaties that his father had signed with the French. Later on, he said that he saw his role as that of a mediator between his brother-in-law and the king of France.[39] What he was really trying to do was to play for time. In the first half of the 1380s he still entertained the ambition of making the journey to Rome to be crowned. However he was concerned that, if he left after severing relations with the French, he would risk retaliation in his absence. Accordingly his intention was to keep open the channels of communication with Paris while fobbing off the English with excuses. The English were not so innocent as to be taken in by the king's evasions; they were well aware what his game was. For that reason they tried to increase the pressure on him by making an approach to the pope – who, if anyone, could be presumed to have an interest in seeing the terms of the treaty honoured in spirit as much as in the letter. But to their obvious disappointment they gained no more satisfaction from him than they did from Wenzel. Urban was worried that the French duke, Louis of Anjou, was about to mount an invasion of Italy in support of his claim to the kingdom of Naples. He was therefore anxious to retain the favour of Wenzel, on whose assistance he thought he might need to call. His one gesture of goodwill to the English was to publish bulls declaring null and void any alliance that Wenzel or his father might have made with schismatics – thus undermining Wenzel's argument that he could not act because of his father's alliance with the French.[40] The value of

[38] *HVR*, 134.
[39] Perroy, *L'Angleterre et le grand Schisme*, 160.
[40] Ibid., 161–3; *CCR 1381–5*, 147–8.

the bulls was much reduced by their failure to name France as a schismatic power, but they had their use as bargaining counters, and on 20 August 1382 another embassy was dispatched to Prague to negotiate an offensive league against all schismatic rulers – in particular against the king of France and his allies, the kings of Scotland and Castile. The embassy's chances of success were never high to begin with, and they were reduced by the departure of the papal legate from Prague in December. For some four months the envoys laboured at their task, but in the end they gave up. Early in the New Year a fresh treaty was negotiated which placed no firm obligations on Wenzel. Perpetual friendship was pledged between the two kings and their subjects, but no commitment was made to an offensive alliance against any schismatic powers.[41] By the end of 1382 it was apparent that the treaty of London was to all intents and purposes a dead letter. It had failed to pressurize the French into offering concessions, and it had done nothing to bring an early end to the schism. Its legacy was a marriage of which the king approved, but of which his subjects were suspicious. In political terms its significance was slight.

When the royal wedding and coronation were over, the parliament which had assembled before Christmas resumed its deliberations on the affairs of the realm. Decisions were needed on a number of matters, chief among them the future direction of foreign policy. Since the collapse of the Breton alliance and the return of Buckingham's expedition, English policy had drifted. Few initiatives of importance had been undertaken on either the diplomatic or the military front. To an extent, the cause of the malaise was to be found in the financial constraints which had limited the scope of English activity abroad. However, there were also some genuine differences of opinion on the council. One faction, led by the duke of Lancaster, favoured attacking France from the south-west by opening up a front in Spain, while the other preferred a more conventional strategy of attacking from the north, perhaps through the Low Countries. It was a choice, as the chancellor was later to represent it, between the 'way of Spain' ('chemin d'Espaigne') and the 'way of Flanders' ('chemin de Flandres'). In 1381 the advocates of the former route had triumphed, and an expedition had been sent to Portugal under the command of Edmund of Langley, earl of Cambridge.[42] That expedition had quickly run into difficulties, however, and pleas were sent back to England for assistance. Considerable argument followed as to whether such assistance should be offered or a

[41] Perroy, L'Angleterre et le grand Schisme, 163.
[42] For discussion, see above, 55, and below, 96-9.

fresh initiative undertaken in defence of English interests in Flanders. It was not until the year's end that a consensus of sorts emerged.

English interest in Spanish affairs had been aroused back in the early 1370s. In 1371, following the seizure of the Castilian throne by Henry of Trastamara, Lancaster had married Constance, daughter of the deposed Pedro, and laid claim to the throne in her right.[43] In the following year he secured recognition of his title from his father and began constructing the alliances essential for a successful descent on the kingdom. The obvious countries to approach were Castile's neighbours, Aragon and Portugal. Aragon under Peter III blew hot and cold, and in the end refused to make any definite commitment. Portugal under Fernando, however, proved more responsive. An embassy to Lisbon on Gaunt's behalf led by the Galician exile, Juan Fernandez de Andeiro, resulted in the making of an alliance between the two rulers in July 1372, and a couple of months later hostilities with Castile were begun. For the Portuguese these turned out to be little short of disastrous. The border defences were breached, and the city of Viseu captured. The English could not volunteer any assistance, because they were themselves under strain in Gascony, and on 19 March 1373 Fernando had to submit to humiliating terms with Henry. Though he maintained a friendly relationship with the English for the rest of the decade, there was little that he could do actively to assist their cause.[44]

In 1379 a fresh opportunity for intervention arose following the death of Henry of Trastamara. Henry's successor, his twenty-year-old son Juan I, was a less vigorous man than his father. Morbid and introspective, he was irresolute and lacking in determination. Fernando saw his chance to assert his independence again. Encouraged by de Andeiro, he reactivated the alliance between himself and the Lancastrian pretender. Terms were agreed on 15 July 1380. An English force of 1,000 men-at-arms and 1,000 archers under the command of Edmund of Langley was to be dispatched to Portugal to make war on Castile. Once on Portuguese soil the force was to be supplied with Portuguese mounts; Fernando himself was to make war on Castile in common cause with Earl Edmund with the aim of putting Duke John on the throne; and as an earnest of the friendship between the two sides a marriage was agreed between Earl Edmund's six-year-old son Edward and Fernando's daughter and heiress Beatriz, aged ten. By this alliance the prospect was held out of Edward becoming joint ruler of Portugal after Fernando's death.[45]

Finance for the proposed expedition was sought at the ill-fated

---

[43] For Castile's entry into the French orbit after Henry's accession, see above, 39.

[44] Russell, *English Intervention*, 186–201; A. Goodman, 'John of Gaunt, Portugal's Kingmaker', *HT*, xxxvi (June 1986), 17–18.

[45] Russell, *English Intervention*, 296–9.

Northampton parliament of November 1380, though the official record of the assembly nowhere actually admits as much. The government chose to be secretive about its intentions, and with good reason. Lancaster's unpopularity and the commons' suspicion of the viability of the 'way of Spain' made it highly unlikely that a request for fiscal support for an expedition to Iberia would be endorsed. The only way in which the government could obtain the money was by subterfuge: hence the curiously roundabout tactics which Chancellor Sudbury used in this parliament. In his opening address to the commons, Sudbury asked for a grant of £160,000 but only gave details of commitments amounting to two-thirds of that sum. The commons, strangely taking his figures on trust, granted him his request; and as a result he was left with some £40,000–£50,000 in hand for use in Iberia. This was enough to pay not only for Earl Edmund's expedition but for a possible second expedition as well. From a strategic point of view there was a good deal to be said for fielding two expeditions. A single army would have stood little chance of triumphing over an enemy army on the latter's home ground; two armies could divide and distract the enemy, allowing one or other to deliver a knockout blow. Against this advantage, however, had to be set the danger that the government could easily find itself over-committed. In budgeting to spend so much, it was already straining popular tolerance to the limits. It had succeeded – rather surprisingly – in carrying parliament with it, but there was no assurance that it would be able to carry public opinion as a whole. Low returns from the 1379 poll tax had already indicated growing resentment at the level of taxation and the attempt to enforce collection of the third poll tax two years later completed the disillusionment. In the wake of the mighty Revolt of 1381, collection of the tax had to be abandoned, and plans for overseas military intervention accordingly scaled down. When Earl Edmund and his retinue sailed for Portugal, it was without the assurance that a second expedition would eventually support them.

The earl's departure, originally planned for the spring, was itself held up by the Revolt. He was told to delay sailing for as long as his troops might be needed to restore peace. In the end, he left Plymouth towards the end of June, and dropped anchor in the Tagus in mid-July.[46] Elaborate ceremonies were laid on by the Portuguese to welcome their allies. Fernando himself went aboard Cambridge's flagship to greet the earl, his wife and the young Edward. When the time came for the English to disembark, the countess of Cambridge walked on the king's arm at the head of a solemn procession through Lisbon to the cathedral, where mass was said. Banquets and festivities followed, and after Fernando (previously Clementist in obedience) had given his

---

[46] Ibid., 311.

obedience to Urban VI, the betrothal of young Beatriz and Edward was celebrated. With their elders watching, the two paraded down the aisle, arm in arm. In the evening, after prayers had been said, they retired to bed, and a blessing was pronounced on their union by the archbishop of Lisbon.[47]

When the civilities were over, the two sides turned their attention to the planning of military operations. The first problem to be overcome was the lack of mounts. In the treaty it had been laid down that mounts would be supplied by the Portuguese, but the latter had so far failed to come up with any. Orders were urgently dispatched to the king's vassals to send their best animals to Lisbon for the army's use, and Edmund himself was shortly supplied with no fewer than twelve. His followers, however, found their needs satisfied more slowly. Largely as a result of this problem no military activity was undertaken in the summer, and it was not until December (by which time indiscipline was rife) that the force finally made a move from Lisbon towards the border. Earl Edmund in an attempt to maintain good relations with his hosts forbade looting and raiding, even in enemy territory. But his troops, whose wages were by now substantially in arrears, often had no other way of supporting themselves. With supplies running low, the earl decided by the year's end to send home for help. In the parliament of January 1382 a proposal was submitted on his behalf by his brother of Lancaster for a second expedition to be sent to the peninsula. Few can have been greatly surprised by the initiative. Knowledge of the duke's ambition to open a second front must by now have been fairly widespread, and interest centred largely on the terms and conditions that he would propose. In a verbal 'proffer' he offered to lead a force of 2,000 men-at-arms and 2,000 archers to Portugal or Spain for six months if the realm would lend him £60,000 to cover his men's wages.[48] There was a lengthy debate on the proposal, but in the end it was rejected. So Cambridge was left to soldier on alone. For another five months he waited in frustration while his allies and hosts bickered among themselves. His force became ever more demoralized, and his authority was challenged in a mutiny. By July, however, a resolution of affairs appeared to be at hand. News reached the camp of a Castilian advance on the town of Elvas, a mile or two west of the border. The Anglo-Portuguese army moved forwards, and near Badajoz the two sides selected a site for the armed engagement which seemed inevitable. But there then followed an almost comical anticlimax. The Castilians withdrew, and the Portuguese made no attempt to follow them. Unbeknown to the earl, a deal had been done between the two sides behind

---

[47] Goodman, 'John of Gaunt, Portugal's Kingmaker', 18.
[48] *RP*, iii, 114.

his back. Juan agreed to evacuate Portuguese territory, and Fernando to betroth Beatriz to Juan's second son, also called Fernando. Beatriz's betrothal to Edward of Cambridge was by implication to be dissolved. Earl Edmund, of course, was furious. Not only had his campaign ended in failure; he himself had been subjected to personal humiliation. There was nothing for him to do but pack his bags and return home.[49]

The news of the débâcle in Portugal did nothing to shake Lancaster's confidence in the ultimate viability of the 'way of Spain'. On the contrary, it increased his determination to see it pursued with the backing of adequate financial and military resources. Lancaster had never conceived of the Portuguese venture in isolation. All the time he had seen it as part of a larger strategy involving an attack on Castile from two fronts. In successive parliaments in 1382 he strove to get a second front opened. His first attempt, in January, had faltered because the price that he had demanded was considered too high. The second, made in October, seemed more likely to succeed because the price had dropped from £60,000 to £43,000. The lords, when asked to express an opinion on the duke's terms, offered their support – though adding the rider that, if an army were sent, it should be one that was large enough. The commons were much less enthusiastic: Earl Edmund's failure in Portugal, news of which arrived in the course of the parliament, had brought the 'way of Spain' into disrepute, and there was widespread distrust of the duke's apparently self-interested approach to foreign policy. As late as 20 November, a month after the end of parliament, Gaunt was still anticipating official approval, for he was writing to his retainers to summon them for service in Spain; but in reality by the end of the year his cause was lost.[50] Opinion gradually coalesced in favour of the other route which the chancellor said that the Lord God had opened – the 'way of Flanders'.

The consideration that gave the advocates of the latter route the edge in the argument was the greater importance of Flanders than Spain to the English economy. Flanders was unquestionably England's most important trading partner. The greater part of the English wool clip was sent there each year to be made into cloth, and a high proportion of it came back in the form of tapestries and luxury clothing for the well-to-do. The regular supply of wool was vital to the economic well-being of both countries. If it was interrupted, the looms would come to a halt in Flanders, and the livelihood of the English exporters and growers would be undermined. A harmonious relationship between the two countries was therefore of the highest importance to them both. It was

---

[49] Russell, *English Intervention*, 314–37. Cambridge was back in England by about 24 Nov. 1382 (*WC*, 29 n.8).

[50] *RP*, iii, 133, 136–7; *John of Gaunt's Register, 1379–83*, ed. E.C. Lodge and R. Somerville (2 vols, Camden 3rd series, lvi–lvii, 1937), ii, no. 775.

precisely that relationship which was threatened by developments in
the county from 1379.

The source of the problem lay in the tensions that beset Flemish
political and economic life in the later fourteenth century. The count
of Flanders, Louis of Mâle, had to share the exercise of power in his
domains with the great cities that were the material foundation of his
prosperity – Ypres, Bruges and, above all, Ghent; and the interests of
the two parties did not always coincide. The count, a vassal of the king
of France, looked to the French for protection and leadership, whereas
the cities, ever watchful of their economic interests, looked more to the
English. Coupled with this problem was the often uneasy state of relations within and between the cities. In several of the cities, as in others
in Europe, the urban proletariat, composed mainly of weavers and
fullers, found themselves locked in conflict with the ruling patriciates.
At Ypres they seized control and organized a reign of terror between
1359 and 1361. At Bruges there were disturbances in 1351, 1367 and
1369. The patriciates sought to guard against the growth of insecurity
by establishing control over the cities' hinterlands and fending off
competition from other towns. This policy made co-operation between
them very difficult. The Ghentois, in particular, were sensitive to the
pretensions of the Brugeois, whom they suspected, rightly, of enjoying
greater favour with Count Louis. When therefore in 1379 Louis permitted the Brugeois to build a canal from their city to the river Lys,
threatening the Ghentois' control of that river's traffic, the latter
reacted with vigour. They rose in revolt, assassinated the local officer of
the count and burned down Louis's newly built castle at Wondelgem,
on the outskirts of the city.[51] The civil war thus provoked, which lasted
for six years, did enormous damage to the Flemish economy and turned
the county into another battleground in the long-running struggle
between England and France.

The interruption to the flow of wool caused by the Flemish crisis was
a major factor in swinging English mercantile opinion behind the 'way
of Flanders' in autumn 1382. It was also instrumental in shifting the
position of the government, for a decline in wool exports was felt in
a decline in tax receipts and thus in a shrinkage in income at the
exchequer. But it was not only economic considerations that weighed
on the government's mind. There was also a political factor of major
importance to be taken into account: the matter of the succession to
the county. Louis of Mâle had no male issue. His heir was his daughter

---

[51] For developments in the Low Countries in this period, see F. Quicke, *Les Pays-
Bas à la veille de la période bourguignonne, 1356–1384* (Brussels, 1947); R. Vaughan,
Philip the Bold. The Formation of the Burgundian State (London, 1962), 16–38; A.P.R.
Coulborn, 'The Economic and Social Preliminaries of the Crusade of 1383', *BIHR*,
x (1932–3), 40–4.

Margaret, and whoever married her would inherit the county on her father's death. In the early 1360s Edward III had almost succeeded in securing the girl's hand for his son Edmund of Langley. The terms of the alliance had been settled, and the date of the marriage fixed. But at the last moment the pope, under pressure from Charles V, refused to grant the necessary dispensation from consanguinity. The way was thus paved for a rival bid from France, and five years later in 1369 a French prince, Philip the Bold, duke of Burgundy, a brother of Charles V, walked off with the prize. As a result of this coup Flanders was set fair to pass into the French orbit. From the English point of view the implications were disastrous. Not only would the French be able to bring greater pressure to bear on the English economy; they would be able to threaten the country from some of the finest harbours between the Atlantic and the Baltic.[52]

But then, in the early 1380s, came the uprising in Ghent and the opportunity that it offered for English intervention. Initially the English were slow to react. In 1379 and 1380 they had other external commitments on their hands.[53] In 1381 the Great Revolt had a paralysing effect on the processes of government; and in the first half of 1382 there remained the nagging fear that further taxation to pay for the war would provoke fresh unrest. However, on 3 May 1382 a remarkable victory which the Ghentois scored over Count Louis at Beverhoutsveld at last overcame their hesitations. Ghent's position in Flanders was seen as more secure, and it was deemed possible to open negotiations with her. On 27 May two merchants, Edmund Halstead and Richard Wodhall, were dispatched to meet the leader of Ghent, Philip van Artevelde, son of Jacques van Artevelde, who had led the city in an earlier revolt against the French in 1340. The envoys came back to give their report in mid-June, and then returned on 22 June in the company of two more experienced diplomats, Thomas Stanley and George Felbrigg.[54] Further embassies went back and forth over the summer, but it was not until October that the Ghentois finally disclosed the terms on which their master would conclude an alliance. These were pitched high. First, the English were to repay the sum of 200,000 crowns which

---

[52] J.J.N. Palmer and A.P. Wells, 'Ecclesiastical Reform and the Politics of the Hundred Years War during the Pontificate of Urban V (1362-70)', *War, Literature and Politics in the Late Middle Ages*, ed. C.T. Allmand (Liverpool, 1976), 169-89. Palmer, *England, France and Christendom, 1377-99* (London, 1972), 20-2, argues strongly that it was the political rather than the economic factors that led to English intervention in Flanders. While this was probably so, it was the economic factors that were responsible for swinging opinion in the commons behind the policy.

[53] See above, 38-44.

[54] For the progress of the negotiations, see Perroy, *L'Angleterre et le grand Schisme*, 174-5; E364/16 m.4; E403/490, 15 July, 18 Aug. Wodhall was bailiff of Guines (*CPR 1381-5*, 402).

van Artevelde alleged his father had lent Edward III to enable him to undertake the siege of Tournai in 1340; and secondly, they were to move the wool staple from Calais to Bruges for a transitional period of three years, at the end of which it would be moved to another town of Ghent's choosing.[55] Froissart portrays the English lords, led by Lancaster, as reacting to these demands by asking for time to consult the king, and then collapsing into laughter as soon as the Ghentois had left the room.[56] No English government could possibly have allowed its policy on a matter as important as the wool staple to be dictated to it in the way that van Artevelde had proposed. The Ghentois had made a major miscalculation. The English may have been keen to contract an alliance with them, but they were not prepared to do so at any price. For a while there was deadlock, and it seemed that the 'way of Flanders' might be abandoned in favour of its rival, the 'way of Spain': Chancellor Braybrooke certainly hinted as much in October, when he urged the commons to give their backing to the latter scheme. What saved the day for the Flemings was the timely intervention of a man who had so far contributed little to the discussions – Henry Despenser, bishop of Norwich.

Bishop Despenser, younger brother of the Garter knight Sir Edward Despenser of Tewkesbury, Gloucestershire, was one of the most colourful figures of the age. A proud, arrogant man, vigorous and martial in temperament, he was almost wholly unsuited to the cloth. Not for nothing was he known to contemporaries as the 'warlike bishop'. In his youth he had taken part in the crusade which Urban V had proclaimed against Bernabo V in Lombardy, and in 1381 he had been active in crushing the rebels in an engagement at North Walsham in his diocese.[57] The proposal that he now made, in the parliament of October 1382, was wholly in keeping with his character. It was to turn what had hitherto been seen as a wholly secular enterprise into a crusade. With the outbreak of the schism, and the division of Christendom into two competing obediences, this was a perfectly workable proposition. Louis of Mâle, like his overlord the king of France, had committed himself for Pope Clement VII. An expedition led against him in the name of Urban VI would thus automatically qualify for that pope's approval, and those participating in it for the privileges conferred by the crusading indulgence. The scheme suffered from one major disadvantage: namely that, while Louis was Clementist, his subjects were Urbanist, and it would be difficult to fight the one without injuring the other. This was a difficulty for which the bishop and his supporters spared little thought, however,

---

[55] Perroy, *L'Angleterre et Le Grand Scisme*, 175.

[56] Froissart, i, 716–17.

[57] For his career, see *DNB*, v, 860–2.

for it was more than outweighed by one corresponding advantage – that the expedition could be financed in part by the sale of crusading indulgences, thus lessening the burden on the taxpayer. To a political class terrified by the fear of provoking further unrest through the resumption of heavy taxation, this was an irresistible attraction. Accordingly, at the end of the October parliament the commons submitted a petition endorsing the bishop's proposal; and as a further earnest of their support they made a grant of a single fifteenth and tenth which, although ostensibly to be spent by the council, was clearly intended for episcopal use.[58] Assured of the financial backing he needed, the bishop pressed ahead with his plans. Not even the news, which he received in late November, of the Ghentois' defeat by the French at Roosebeke dented his enthusiasm. On 21 December he took crusading vows in a ceremony in St Paul's Cathedral and had a cross erected at the entrance to the choir to serve as a rallying point for his supporters.[59] People quickly came rushing in to enrol. The challenge for the bishop was to decide how best to channel their energies into mounting an effective and coherent military challenge to the French in Flanders.

The quality of the bishop's organization was exemplary. According to a set of regulations preserved in Knighton's chronicle, in each diocese he appointed a set of commissioners who in turn would recruit preachers and confessors from the mendicant friars. These friars would tour the parishes accompanied by receivers. Anyone who wanted to go on crusade in person would be granted absolution once he had sworn to present himself to the bishop and agreed to an indenture of service for one year. Anyone who wanted to send a soldier to fight in his place would have to swear, again before receiving absolution, that his recruit would be an 'able and adequate fighter'.[60] Precautions of this sort were essential if the bishop were to be assured of a professional and disciplined force. The response to his call was so enthusiastic that he was in serious danger of ending up with a sprawling and ill-disciplined rabble. Walsingham with pardonable exaggeration tells us that there was scarcely anyone in England who did not either enlist in person or give money.[61] His statement is borne out by the lengthy lists of protections issued by the crown in the early months of 1383: they include the names of saddlers, carpenters, drapers, apprentices and shoemakers.[62] Almost every trade and occupation was represented.

---

[58] *RP*, iii, 134, 140.

[59] *WC*, 32.

[60] *KC*, 330–2; N. Housley, 'The Bishop of Norwich's Crusade, May 1383', *HT*, xxxiii (May 1983), 15–20.

[61] *HA*, ii, 85.

[62] C76/67 mm.16–18. Protections were sometimes sought out by those who had no intention of going but wished to take advantage of the immunity from litigation

When it contemplated the composition of the army, the council must have had grave reservations as to its likely effectiveness. Although they had given permission to Despenser on 6 December to recruit men for his force, it is significant that two months later they were still withholding full approval. A minority on the body, led by Lancaster, were passionately opposed to the bishop's plans and did everything in their power to block them. When the proposal for an expedition to Spain fell by the wayside, they latched on to another idea which had been floated in the previous year – for an expedition led by the king himself. This exercised a certain fascination over those who wanted to see Richard take the field as soon as possible and emulate the achievements of his father and grandfather. But in the circumstances of early 1383 it suffered from two major disadvantages. Firstly, it would have required the dispatch of a far larger army than the exchequer could afford; and secondly, there was little evidence of interest on the part of the king himself.[63] As late as January 1383, when a great council was held at Westminster, the pretence was maintained that a royal expedition was official policy.[64] But by the end of February, when parliament again met, it had evidently been dropped. The bishop gave a detailed presentation of his proposals, and this time they were accepted without demur. The advocates of the 'way of Flanders' had triumphed.

The size of the bishop's army is difficult to gauge. In his original submission the bishop had said that he would take 3,000 men-at-arms and as many archers, but at a later stage he scaled down the numbers to 2,500 men-at-arms and the same number of archers. In the following November, when he was impeached for the failure of his campaign, he was accused of failing to meet even this figure. Probably in the end the force numbered some 4,000–5,000 men.[65] Overall responsibility for leading it lay with the bishop, but from the start it had been envisaged that operational control would be exercised by a secular lord in the office of lieutenant. Finding someone willing to assume the office

that was conferred by these instruments. On one occasion in 1383 Despenser wrote to the chancellor asking for the revocation of a protection granted to one Roger Bedford of London, whom he had discovered to be trying to escape his creditors. Bedford, who was a brewer, had passed himself off as a man-at-arms. The deceit seems to have added to the bishop's indignation: SC8/300/14993; *CPR 1381–5*, 240.

[63] The *Eulogium* writer is emphatic that the king did not want to go: 'Rex laborare noluit' (*Eulogium*, iii, 356). For continuing resistance to the bishop's proposals, see M. Aston, 'The Impeachment of Bishop Despenser', *BIHR*, xxxviii (1965), 138–41. Lancaster probably employed the idea of a royally led expedition simply as a blocking move.

[64] *RP*, iii, 144.

[65] Aston, 'Impeachment', 137. Housley, 'Bishop of Norwich's Crusade', 17, settles for 5,000.

proved difficult. John, Lord Neville of Raby was apparently approached but without success, and no one else could be found of whom the bishop approved. It was almost certainly appreciated that he would be a difficult person to work with. In the end a modified arrangement was agreed whereby the bishop was required to submit the names of four nominees but, if none proved amenable, sole responsibility was to be vested in him. This allowed the bishop a loophole of which he took full advantage. He took with him a number of experienced captains, notably Sir William Elmham, Sir Thomas Trivet and Sir Hugh Calveley, but he constituted none of them lieutenant. This was to form the burden of another of the complaints levelled against him on his return.

The bishop finally crossed from Sandwich to Calais with his force on 16 May. On 19 May they moved up the coast to Gravelines, which was defended by a French garrison. The crusaders stormed the town, slaughtering its inhabitants. Alarmed by this, the people of nearby Bourbourg surrendered, and the English moved on to Dunkirk. They entered the town on 24 May and defeated a large force of French and Flemings mustered by Louis of Mâle. After this a number of Flemish towns, among them Nieuport, Bergues and Dixmude, offered their submission. Thus far the bishop and his men had enjoyed a remarkable run of success, but now some difficult decisions had to be taken. Foremost among these was the future direction of the expedition. The bishop wanted to advance on Artois, a province wholly Clementist in obedience, but his captains' advice was to join the Ghentois in besieging Ypres – a course strategically wise, but diplomatically ill-advised because the inhabitants were Urbanist. The captains had their way, and the English advanced on Ypres, which they invested on 9 June. It was a decision which they were later to regret. Their forces lacked the siege equipment needed to bring the blockade to a speedy close, and before long the unhealthy conditions of the camp led to an outbreak of dysentery. After a final unsuccessful assault on the town on 10 August the bishop and his men decided to withdraw. News had by then probably reached them of the mobilization of a large French army. On 2 August Charles VI had taken the oriflamme at St Denis, and on 15 August a muster was held at Arras.[66] What the English did next is unclear, but almost certainly a request was sent to London for help. A large force was mustered on the Isle of Thanet by Lancaster, and orders were sent out for the arrest of shipping.[67] But so rapid was the collapse of the bishop's army that the force never set sail. On 14 September Elmham surrendered Bourbourg for a payment of 2,000 francs. A few days later Gravelines too was evacuated, after Despenser in fury ordered

---

[66] Ramsay, *Genesis of Lancaster*, ii, 204.
[67] *WC*, 48; E403/496, 15 and 25 Sept.

its sack. In early October the bishop and his men trickled back to England.[68]

The reaction at home was one of astonishment and dismay. People felt betrayed because they could not understand how the expedition could so quickly have foundered after enjoying such spectacular early success. What they did not appreciate was that the early successes had been illusory: they had been gained in the absence of an opposing army. As soon as the French closed in, as they did in September, the bishop's position was bound to become untenable. To say, as Walsingham did, that he should have stood his ground and given battle was unrealistic.[69] The French enjoyed an overwhelming superiority in both manpower and equipment. The result in all likelihood would have been another Roosebeke, not another Crécy.[70] The bishop's decision to withdraw, although obviously difficult and embarrassing for him, was in the circumstances almost certainly right. What made it so unpalatable at home was the clear evidence that it had been accompanied by personal gain on the part of some of his commanders.

Inevitably there were calls for those responsible for the débâcle to be summoned to account, and they were quickly heeded. In the parliament of October 1383 the bishop was impeached by the chancellor, Sir Michael de la Pole, on four main counts: that he had served for less than six months instead of the year to which he was committed; that his army had not reached the agreed total of 5,000 men; that by his extravagant promises he had caused the council to lay aside plans for an expedition led by Richard himself or Lancaster; and that he had brought disaster on himself by refusing to allow a secular lieutenant to assume operational control of the expedition. The bishop put up a spirited defence, answering the charges against him and often causing his accusers some discomfiture. But in the end he was found guilty on all counts and sentenced to forfeiture of his temporalities. Immediately afterwards his captains, among them Elmham and Trivet, were tried, on the lesser charge that they had accepted bribes from the French. Rather than face interrogation, the four threw themselves on the king's mercy, pleading somewhat curiously that they had given the realm good value for money. They were sentenced to imprisonment, but were released shortly afterwards on payment of fines. The bishop's disgrace lasted until 1385, when his service with the king on the Scottish expedition earned him the restoration of his temporalities. The animosity which Gaunt had felt towards him had presumably by that time mellowed sufficiently to allow him to let bygones be bygones.[71]

---

[68] Perroy, *L'Angleterre et le grand Schisme*, 200.
[69] *HA*, ii, 104.
[70] At Roosebeke the Ghentois had been routed by the French (27 Nov. 1382).
[71] For the trial, see *RP*, iii, 152–6; and Aston, 'Impeachment'.

From a study of the background to the crusade it is apparent that the bishop had been made a scapegoat for the errors and omissions of others. He was not the only person responsible for the débâcle, but he was the most convenient on whom to heap the blame. He was arrogant and overbearing. He had relatively few allies and he had made some serious errors of judgement: in particular, he had refused to share command with a secular lieutenant. The officers and council, by shifting the blame on to him, had been able to deflect it from themselves. It was a shabby exercise, but nevertheless a necessary one, for the crusade was in fact a venture of which virtually the whole of the political community had approved. It had been backed by the commons in October 1382, and it had been given full parliamentary endorsement in February of the following year. Consent of a less formal kind had been gained at great councils, several of which had been held in January and February 1383.[72] Certainly dissenters were to be found in the ranks of the higher nobility, chief among them Lancaster, but by the spring of 1383 these few had been overborne by the massive tide of opinion in Bishop Despenser's favour. Religious, political and economic factors combined to swing public opinion behind the bishop. His was the last genuinely popular expedition to be put into the field by an English government for some forty years. Its sudden and unexpected collapse not only bred widespread disillusionment but also contributed to the disarray of the 'war' party. In the years to come the initiative was to pass to those whose preference was for a political accommodation with the French.

[72] *RP*, iii, 122, 144; E403/493, 15 Jan., 5 Feb.

Chapter 6

THE KING AND HIS FRIENDS, 1381–6

In January 1381, when he reached the age of fourteen, Richard passed from 'pueritia' to 'adolescentia', an important step forward in his development. It was at fourteen, according to the medieval theorists, that a boy was held to have left childhood behind. A symbolic entry was made into adulthood. Young nobles, it was believed, could learn to ride and to fight and could even be inducted into such adult institutions as marriage. Young people of all ranks could be held responsible for the payment of taxes. A further seven years were to elapse before full majority was reached, but a definite milestone had been passed in a person's ascent to manhood.[1]

Richard's passage from 'pueritia' to 'adolescentia' was marked in suitably dramatic fashion by his two face-to-face meetings with the rebels in June 1381. The bravery that he showed on those occasions put beyond doubt his claim to a more active role in national affairs. Yet, perhaps strangely, in the twelve months after these meetings there is little evidence that he did become more involved. After the end of the 'bloody assize' at St Albans he spent most of his time itinerating between the hunting lodges of the Thames valley. There are indications that he was instrumental in appointing commissions of oyer and terminer to deal with the rebels, but the warranty evidence on the point is by no means conclusive, and there is a possibility that the commissions were issued not by him but by his ministers.[2] Because of the dearth of evidence from these months it is difficult to form a precise view of the extent of his influence on policy. The likelihood is that it was greater than the surviving evidence suggests; on the other hand, it is doubtful if it was as great as would be expected of a youth growing to adulthood. Steel, noting the king's disappearance from the records, opined that he had been relegated to the background by that very elite whose cowardice and ineptitude he had shown up only months before.[3] Very likely, however, the explanation for the king's disappearance is more humdrum. Richard's attention was increasingly claimed by matters of a

[1] Orme, *From Childhood to Chivalry*, 5–6.
[2] Ormrod, 'The Peasants' Revolt and the Government of England', 21 n.104.
[3] Steel, *Richard II*, 79, 91.

more personal nature. At the end of 1381 he was awaiting the arrival of his bride-to-be and preparing for the marriage and coronation to follow, while in the summers of the two subsequent years he undertook, in his wife's company, two extensive itineraries of his realm: in 1382 he travelled to Woodstock, Devizes and Bristol, and in the following year to Cambridgeshire, East Anglia and York. While he was away, he was kept fully informed of events by the council, and there were times when he fiercely asserted his rights. But the inevitable result was that he was not as closely involved as he might have been in the day-to-day business of government.

Establishing just when he did become more actively involved is a task of some difficulty. Since no provision was made at the beginning of the reign for a minority, there was no formal transfer of power and the stages of the king's growing participation are therefore obscured. One of the few clues to the puzzle is provided by the warrants for the issue of letters under the great seal. As Tout showed long ago, in late 1383 there was a rapid increase in the number of letters issued on the authority of the king's signet. The signet was the smallest of the three seals used to authenticate royal correspondence, and the one which the king kept with him to authorize the dispatch of letters under the other two. Since Richard's accession it had been used extensively only in the first weeks of the reign while a new privy seal was being made. Once that seal was ready, it fell into disuse, and conciliar authorization of correspondence became normal. In late 1383, however, it sprang back into favour, and the king used it to communicate instructions directly to chancery. Whereas in the past he had used it to move the privy seal, which in turn moved the great seal, he now used it to move the great seal directly. In October at least five great seal letters were warranted by the signet, in November at least eight, and in December well over a dozen. By the end of 1383, in Tout's view, the signet had emerged as Richard's favoured instrument 'while he learned to be a ruler': in other words, it had become the instrument of his sovereign will.[4]

Tout's argument can be criticized on a number of grounds. In the first place there is no necessary connection between level of signet use and the king's participation in government. The sudden increase in activity in late 1383 is as likely to have been the result of the appointment in the autumn of 1382 of John Bacon, the king's secretary, as receiver of the chamber. The effect of Bacon's appointment was to make the signet (of which the secretary was keeper) the chief warrant for chamber correspondence, as it had been earlier in the fourteenth century.[5] In other words, it was the link with the chamber

[4] Tout, *Chapters*, iii, 404–5; v, 206–7.
[5] Tuck, *Richard II and the Nobility*, 65–6.

rather than Richard's initiative which explains this greater use of the instrument. Moreover, since there was a further increase in signet activity in 1384, and since much of this later correspondence under the seal was of a routine nature, it could hardly have arisen directly from exercise of the king's will. In that case the question arises of how much of the earlier correspondence actually arose from exercise of the king's will. It may have been very little. The changes of late 1383 noticed by Tout could have resulted in large measure from shifts in bureaucratic routine.

Although for these reasons the level of signet use cannot be said to reflect directly the level of royal participation in government, a looser sort of relationship between the two may still be posited. It is striking that the rise in signet activity should have occurred in the autumn of 1383, just after Richard's return from the north and when he was in a position to involve himself more in government. This coincidence of timing suggests some royal initiative in politics. Richard was after all sixteen years old by now. He was at an age when he would have wanted – indeed, when he would have been expected – to take over more of the responsibilities of kingship. His father was only sixteen when he had won his spurs at Crécy; and his grandfather was just two years older when he had launched the coup against Queen Isabelle which initiated his personal kingship. Richard's own entry into the burdens of office was in a sense long overdue. Even so, it would be wrong to deduce from the absence of earlier signet activity that before 1383 he had entirely neglected those burdens; he had not. A reading of the chronicles shows that he had been intervening intermittently in politics for at least two or three years by then. In 1380, as Walsingham records, he had settled the arguments over his marriage by coming down firmly in favour of an alliance with the emperor.[6] In the following year he had helped to defuse the crisis in London by meeting the rebels at Smithfield. In 1382, in a decisive gesture, he had dismissed his chancellor and replaced him by one more compliant with his wishes.[7] It may only have been from late 1383, as the signet evidence implies, that Richard involved himself in routine matters of government, but for some time he had been intervening in matters of particular interest to him. He was a man who expected to be consulted and deferred to, and he would never allow anyone to cross him or stand in his way. Although little given to immersing himself in administrative details (few kings were), he could act swiftly and incisively when moved to do so. Already in these years there are anticipations of the clashes of will that were to occur later when Richard's interests conflicted with those of others. No epi-

[6] CA, 331; and see above, 92.
[7] CA, 353-4.

sode is more revealing in this respect than the dispute over the Mortimer inheritance that led to Chancellor Scrope's dismissal in July 1382.

Our main source for this episode is Walsingham's chronicle. According to this account, after the death in Ireland in December 1381 of Edmund Mortimer, earl of March, a host of minor but ambitious suitors beat a path to the king's door, begging grants of manors and lordships that pertained to the Mortimer inheritance. Richard in a spirit of generosity acceded to their requests, and sent letters to the chancellor authorizing the preparation in their favour of letters under the great seal. The chancellor, Lord Scrope, however, ardently desiring the king's profit, refused to comply, saying that the king was impoverishing himself by such profligacy. When news of this response reached the king, he was furious. He reproached Scrope, and insisted that he carry out the royal will. Scrope still refused and was dismissed. A long vacancy ensued, and it was not until 20 September that a successor was found in the person of the king's former secretary, Robert Braybrooke, bishop of London.[8]

This account has been criticized on the grounds that it was written long after events and with the benefit of hindsight. It is pointed out that Walsingham subjected his chronicles to stages of revision, and that it is only in the later of these that the extended narrative appears with its clear antipathy to Richard; in the earlier version, written around 1388 before the chronicler's view of the king was fully formed, a shorter, more matter-of-fact account is given in which no hint of bias intrudes.[9] Walsingham certainly invested the episode with greater significance later than he did at the time. But this is not to suggest that his account is without value; clearly it is not. The sequel to Scrope's dismissal shows that a crisis of some proportions had occurred. Not since 1339 had there been an interval of as long as two months between the removal of one chancellor and the appointment of another. Evidently considerable difficulty had been experienced in finding someone of sufficient standing to take Scrope's place. Even when a suitable candidate had been found (in the person of Braybrooke) disquiet remained about the king's attitude to the disposal of wardships. On 14 November an order was issued to the effect that 'all moneys accruing from the Mortimer inheritance and from alien priories in the king's custody by reason of the war' should be applied entirely to the expenses of the

---

[8] Ibid.; *CCR 1381-5*, 214-15. Scrope had left office on 11 July. For a general account of the way in which Richard dealt with requests for bounty, see A. Tuck, 'Richard II's System of Patronage', *The Reign of Richard II*, 1-20.

[9] G.B. Stow, 'Richard II in Thomas Walsingham's Chronicles', *Speculum*, lix (1984), 83-4.

household.[10] This was a measure designed to ensure that good use was made of the windfalls which the crown received. Its origins probably lay in a meeting of the great council held four days earlier on 10 November and attended by members of the nobility.[11] How effectively it would be implemented, however, depended on the willingness of the farmers of the estates to co-operate. Their low standing and many connections with the royal household could hardly inspire the councillors with confidence. On 16 December 1383, therefore, they were replaced. Custody of the inheritance was committed on conciliar authority to a magnate consortium composed of Sir Roger Mortimer, the earls of Arundel, Warwick and Northumberland and John Lord Neville of Raby, 'notwithstanding any grant or gift made by the king to any person after Edmund's death of any manor or lordship from the said inheritance'.[12] These lords retained custody of the inheritance until the heir, Roger, was awarded livery of seisin eleven years later in 1393.[13]

With the lords' appointment the argument over the disposal of the Mortimer inheritance was brought to an end. It had been the first big dispute over counsel and patronage to arise between the king and his ministers, and it was not to be the last. In the five or six years to 1388 criticism of the king's reliance on 'unwholesome' counsel was to be an increasingly discordant theme in political life. In the parliamentary session of October 1383 the lords complained to the king that he did not listen to the advice of the nobility as he should and as his predecessors had. Fourteen months later, at Sheen, Lancaster complained to him of the unsavoury character of those around him, while three years after that the lords and commons together called for the dismissal of his officers and for the wholesale purging of his entourage. It was obvious that the king's choice of counsellors and friends had become a major issue in politics. So who were the king's friends and advisers? And how justified was the criticism that was levelled against them?

Richard's closest confidant at this time was probably his former tutor and magister Sir Simon Burley. Burley had been an influence on him from early childhood: he had supervised his upbringing, guided him on his way to the throne, and masterminded the negotiations leading to his marriage. These and other services Richard recalled in letters patent of 3 November 1382 granting him the lordship of Newcastle Emlyn in South Wales. Simon, he said, had been his constant companion from

[10] CPR 1381-5, 184.
[11] For the date of the great council, see ibid., 201.
[12] CFR 1383-91, 22-3. For discussion, see Tuck, Richard II and the Nobility, 88-9.
[13] CP, viii, 449.

infancy as either chamberlain or vice-chamberlain; he had been on embassies on his behalf to the emperor; he had returned to England with his dear consort Queen Anne; he had made sacrifices on the royal behalf which had plunged him into debt and had forced him to sell lands. He was, in short, Richard's 'well beloved and faithful knight', a man in the highest degree deserving of royal favour. And in recognition of this the king now granted to him in fee simple the castle and lordship of Newcastle Emlyn which earlier he had held only for life.[14]

Burley's career in royal service had certainly been an exceptional one. From relatively obscure origins he had risen to be one of the most powerful men in the realm. As vice-chamberlain from 1377 he had immediate and automatic access to the king; and, more importantly, he had control of others' access to the king. The likelihood is that he was a key figure in the development of court policies in the 1380s. To some he appeared a man of good sense and integrity. The duke of York, at his trial in 1388, was to pay tribute to his loyalty to the king.[15] But to others, the chronicler Henry Knighton for example, he came across as grasping and avaricious, as a man on the make rather than a disinterested royal servant.[16] Certainly he was someone with many sides to his character. There can be little doubt that he held the young king in deep affection: Richard would hardly have returned that affection if he had not. There is no doubt either that he was in constant need of money. Employment in royal service had impoverished him, as it had impoverished many before him, because of the difficulty experienced in gaining reimbursement for expenses from a cash-starved exchequer. His penury was referred to by the king in the letters patent of 1382, and it is significant that at the time of his execution he was still heavily in debt.[17] Unlike other of Richard's friends he was not of well-to-do or magnate descent. His parentage is obscure, but he was probably a scion of a minor Herefordshire gentry family.[18] He had inherited little if any land, and was heavily dependent for income on grants from the crown. From

---

[14] *Foed.*, vii, 370.

[15] *WC*, 328.

[16] *KC*, 500.

[17] Clarke, 'Forfeitures and Treason in 1388', *Fourteenth Century Studies*, 122-3. His cash-flow problems in 1387 were partly attributable to the action of the commission council in cutting off supplies to the household, but it still remains true that he had inadequate cash reserves to live on.

[18] The Burleys took their name from the manor of Birley (Heref.). One John de Burley is recorded as holding an estate there in 1316 (*Feud. Aids*, ii, 387). He was succeeded by another John, and he in turn by Sir John, the chamber knight who was involved with de la Pole in the king's marriage negotiations (see above, 84, 87). Sir Simon was Sir John's younger brother, and the two appear to have made their way in service together. By his marriages Simon won for himself connections but

1374 he was keeper of the manors of Cheltenham and Slaughter in Gloucestershire, forfeited because of the Anglo-French hostilities by the abbot of Fécamp, and from 1377 or earlier he held the castle and lordship of Llanstephan and the castle of Carmarthen. In 1382 he acquired Newcastle Emlyn in fee, and some time before 1384 Robert de Vere granted him the castle and lordship of Lyonshall, Herefordshire.[19] From these estates and from the manor of Castle Frome (also in Herefordshire), which he acquired in 1385, he probably drew sufficient income to maintain himself as a banneret (he also had an annuity of £100 from the estates of the Black Prince); but it is doubtful if he accumulated much of a reserve to invest in land. For someone of his ambition it is striking how little he engaged in buying up manors on the market: almost certainly this was because he lacked the means to do so. From early in the reign he must have realized that his only hope of acquiring an inheritance in fee lay in obtaining one from the king. Richard recognized this by converting his life tenure of Newcastle Emlyn into tenure in fee simple. But he could not be more generous to his friend because of the shortage of suitable forfeitures and escheats, and because of magnate opposition to alienations from the royal demesne. Almost in desperation Burley was driven to entertain a scheme from which a more scrupulous man would have held back – that of laying claim to an inheritance to which he had no title. The legal chicanery and outright intimidation to which he resorted in this cause portrayed him in the worst possible light to friend and foe alike.

The prize in view was admittedly one worth fighting for – the Leybourne inheritance in Kent, a valuable estate, mainly in the west of the county but with outliers elsewhere, worth some £400–£500 annually.[20] The estate had been acquired by Edward III from Juliana de

little land. According to an inscription on his tomb recorded by Weever, his first wife was a Stafford, and his second a daughter of Lord Roos, 'alteram Staffordie, alteram Baronis de Roos': J. Weever, *Ancient Funerall Monuments* (London, 1631), 367. The accuracy of this record, however, is open to question. According to sources in the Archives Nationales, Paris, cited by Luce, he was married to Marguerite de Beausse, widow of the seigneur de Machecoul: *Chroniques de J. Froissart*, ed. S. Luce *et al.* (Société de l'histoire de France, 14 vols, Paris, 1869–   ), vii, liv. Considering his early service in Aquitaine, it is quite likely that he married a lady of French descent. On the other hand, the likelihood that he contracted a match with the second of the two ladies mentioned on the inscription – the Roos daughter – is supported by the fact that his nephew, Sir Richard (d. 1387), also married a lady of the same family – Beatrice, widow of Thomas, Lord Roos (*CP*, xi, 101). The two marriages could have been contracted at the same time.

[19] *CPR 1370–4*, 461; *1377–81*, 223, 262; *1381–5*, 107, 447.

[20] An estimate based on the figures given in C. Given-Wilson, 'Richard II and his Grandfather's Will', *EHR*, xciii (1978), 326 n.2. Given-Wilson gives a full account of the episode.

Leybourne, widow of William Clinton, earl of Huntingdon, for use as the endowment for three of his favoured religious houses – the Dominican house at King's Langley, Hertfordshire, the abbey of St Mary Graces, London, and St Stephen's chapel, Westminster. In his lifetime the king had only partially completed the endowment, and on 5 October 1376, as he lay ill at Havering, he made over the estate to his feoffees, chief among them John of Gaunt, with instructions that they should complete the arrangements in accordance with his will. It seems that until the end of the reign the feoffees enjoyed peaceable possession, but soon after Richard's accession their problems began. A challenge was mounted to their title by the king's council, and their receiver was prevented from making payments according to their wishes without a special mandate from the king. The dispute was referred to the justices and sergeants-at-law, who came down in the feoffees' favour, and in 1382 a compromise was agreed whereby some of the lands were resumed but most remained with the feoffees. There matters rested until the summer of 1383, when the issue was reopened. This time tactics were more aggressive, and the objective was clearly to win control of the estate and make it over to Burley. On 20 August 1383 a licence was issued in his favour allowing him to acquire 'for a term or in fee simple' from the three religious houses the manors of Gravesend, Eastling, Prestbury, Langley and Wateringbury, which were said to be part of the Leybourne inheritance. Then on 28 January 1384 he was granted in tail male the castle and manor of Leybourne and any other lands of the Leybourne inheritance which he wished to acquire, 'on condition that he sue therefor and recover the same at his own cost'. Burley may have had recourse to legal process; but he could not have proceeded very far because on 6 March the king appointed a commission which was to reopen the whole question of the feoffees' title: it was to enquire whether Edward III had or had not died 'seised in his demesne as of fee' of the Leybourne inheritance, Gravesend manor, and the castle and town of Queenborough, because Richard claimed to have information that he had. Burley did not trouble to await its findings – the matter after all had been settled five years before. On the very day that the commission was appointed he ejected the canons of St Stephen's, Westminster from all the Kentish manors which the feoffees had granted to them. By the same method he shortly gained control too of the lands assigned to St Mary Graces. Letters patent of 2 November ratified his tenure of Leybourne castle in fee simple, and he remained in possession until his impeachment in the Merciless Parliament four years later.

The acquisition of the inheritance marked a significant shift in the centre of gravity of Burley's interests. From being a middling proprietor in Wales and the Welsh Marches he was turned into a major one in Kent and the south-east. Kent rather than Herefordshire was henceforth to be the centre of his operations. Early in the New Year a major grant of jurisdictional power lent weight to his position in the county. On 5 January 1384, following the death of Sir Robert Ashton, he was appointed constable of Dover and warden of the Cinque Ports.[21] Tenure of this office gave him not only responsibility for the defence of the Channel coast but also control of the feudal honour of Dover and its courts. Burley attached high enough importance to the appointment to ask Richard himself to attend on his entry into the office, and the king readily agreed.[22] Setting out from Eltham, he reached Dover on 23 January, and at a ceremony on the next day handed over the keys to the new constable. Burley, ever watchful of his interests, took the opportunity to secure reissue of the patents of appointment on clearer terms. In the new letters the proviso was added that if the customs of Sandwich failed to yield the 100 marks per annum originally allowed for, then the shortfall was to be made good from the wool subsidy at that port and, failing that, from the exchequer.[23] It was characteristic of Burley that not even when adequately endowed would he neglect to cover himself against possible financial loss.

The establishment of Burley as a power in Kent both territorially and jurisdictionally was a considerable triumph for the king and his favourite, but it is doubtful if it represented the summit of the ambitions of either. Burley was anxious to acquire an earldom to add lustre to his name, and Richard was apparently hardly less anxious to oblige him. Burley's ability to support a title was no longer in question: with the acquisition of the Leybourne inheritance he had a perfectly adequate endowment and on promotion he could expect a supplement to be made to it. If the account in Knighton's chronicle is to be believed, Richard decided to elevate his friend a year and a half after his entry into Dover. According to the Leicester writer's account, at Hoselaw in Teviotdale, at the beginning of the Scottish campaign, he conferred on him the title earl of Huntingdon.[24] No other chronicler mentions the creation, but there are grounds for taking Knighton at his word. It is highly significant that Richard simultaneously bestowed titles on other lords – dukedoms were given to his uncles Edmund of Langley and Thomas of Woodstock, and Michael de la Pole became an earl; and the tactic may well have been to sneak the controversial honours in with the uncontroversial. What is curious about the episode is that Burley's elevation was never confirmed. Two months later, when parliament

[21] CPR 1381–5, 366–7. For the background, see J.L. Gillespie, 'Dover Castle: Key to Richard II's Kingdom?', Arch. Cant., cv (1988), 179–85.

[22] WC, 56.

[23] CPR 1381–5, 370–1.

[24] KC, 338. For discussion, see J.J.N. Palmer, 'The Parliament of 1385 and the Constitutional Crisis of 1386', Speculum, xlvi (1971), 490.

met, the new dukes and earl were invested, but Burley was not. The sources are silent as to the reasons for the rebuff, but one factor was probably the cost: the supplementary endowments required for four or five creations simultaneously would have placed considerable strain on the exchequer.[25] However, in Burley's case personal objections very likely played a role too. The vice-chamberlain was widely disliked by the parliamentary commons; he was considered ambitious and avaricious, and probably, too, a malign influence on Richard. In addition, his promotion offended against the commons' deeply held and firmly traditional conception of honour. A title in their view was above all a reflection of a man's inherited standing. Burley, being of relatively low birth and having gained his wealth by questionable means, seemed to lack that standing. To advance him in honour would therefore be to disrupt the social hierarchy. In an age already unsettled by change, such a move was one that the commons could not readily endorse. Burley therefore remained, as he had been for two decades, a knight banneret. Though the equal of the higher nobility in power, he was never to be their equal in rank.

Besides Burley there was one other figure of the older generation who was a major influence on Richard. This was Michael de la Pole, Richard's chancellor from 1383, and later earl of Suffolk. The son of William de la Pole, the wool merchant of Hull, and a veteran of the wars, he had been placed in the household by parliament in 1381 to advise and counsel the young king and he had quickly won his charge's trust. On his appointment as chancellor he became one of Richard's most reliable lieutenants. He acquiesced in the king's use of the signet to move the great seal and abetted him in his efforts to evade parliamentary curbs on his expenditure.[26] His service to the crown was rewarded with lavish grants of lands and title. In 1382, on the death of William Ufford, the last earl of Suffolk of his line, he received a grant of the manors of Benhall and Dedham (Suffolk) in fee simple from the escheated portion of the estate. Three years later, in Scotland, he was created earl of Suffolk and awarded the rest of the Ufford inheritance and the reversion of the portion which Ufford's widow held.[27] The lavishness of his endowment provoked the hostility of the nobility, and in particular of Thomas of Woodstock, who was still reliant for income on assignments from the customs. In the next year the new earl's

---

[25] The Westminster writer says, apparently on good authority, that John Neville was given an earldom at the same time as Burley, but his title was not confirmed either (*WC*, 126 and n.).
[26] See above, 109, and below, 198–9.
[27] *CPR 1381–5*, 123, 125–6, 156; *CPR 1385–9*, 18, 24.

brother-in-law, Richard, Lord Scrope, was obliged to come to the defence of his kinsman in a stormy session of parliament. Replying to charges that de la Pole had been 'raised from low estate to the rank of earl', he pointed out that he was a worthy candidate, and that he had possessed more than sufficient means to maintain the estate of banneret, the rank immediately below that of earl.[28] With the backing of his brother-in-law and of the king, de la Pole was able to weather the storm over his elevation. A year later, however, he was at the centre of a fresh controversy – this time relating to his conduct in office as chancellor. In 1385 an ordinance had been passed providing for more adequate supervision of the crown's revenues. Responsibility for its implementation lay with de la Pole, but by the time parliament reassembled in 1386 he had done nothing. The commons were loud in demanding his resignation, 'to allow them', so they said, 'to proceed to other business' – a thinly veiled reference to impeachment.[29] Richard initially held out in support of his officer, but as pressure increased he was obliged to give way. De la Pole resigned on 23 October and shortly afterwards was impeached on seven counts of malfeasance and dereliction of duty. Judgment was given against him on the grounds that he had violated his oath of office and he was sentenced to imprisonment pending payment of a fine. As soon as parliament ended, however, he was released and in the following year he accompanied Richard on his itineration of the realm. His continued influence on the king made him *persona non grata* with the opposition lords, and in 1388, in the wake of the latters' triumph in battle, he was again accused, this time of treason. With the connivance of his brother Edmund, the captain of Calais, he fled from the realm and spent the rest of his life in exile. He died in September 1389 in Paris.[30]

At a number of points over the years de la Pole's career had overlapped with Burley's. In the 1350s and 1360s the two men had served together in the retinues of the Black Prince and the duke of Lancaster. In 1370 they had both gone with Lancaster to lend support to the prince's regime in Aquitaine. After 1377 they had come together in Richard's service and at different times had been involved in the negotiations for his marriage.[31] As a result of their lengthy association the two men had developed an understanding of, and respect for, one another which was to prove invaluable during their years in office from 1383.

---

[28] *RP*, iii, 216–17.

[29] *KC*, ii, 215.

[30] *DNB*, xlvi, 29–33 (by Tout) gives a good account of de la Pole's career. See also below, 157–9.

[31] De la Pole's career, as summarized in *DNB*, xlvi, 29–33, can be compared with Burley's, summarized ibid., iii, 373–4. For de la Pole's role in the marriage negotiations, see above, 84, 87.

They co-operated easily, and succeeded in bringing a coherence to government which had earlier been lacking. Burley himself had long been a major figure in Richard's household and court and had been able to bring his influence to bear on policy with little difficulty. Nevertheless for him to have as sympathetic a figure as de la Pole at his side was clearly of value. It was almost certainly on his nomination that de la Pole was appointed to the post of chancellor on Braybrooke's resignation.

A major factor making for good relations between the two men was their common appreciation of the importance of princely authority in bringing order to a society. Like a number of Richard's leading advisers, they had received their early training in the household of his father the prince. For nearly a decade in the brilliant surroundings of the prince's court at Bordeaux they had witnessed lordship at its most vigorous and assertive. They had seen the order that was brought by the rigorous exaction of the duty of obedience; and they had observed the deference that was shown by subjects and vassals who knew their place in the divinely ordained hierarchy of society.[32] These impressions stayed with them for life and had a powerful influence on their actions in office. Burley from 1381 and de la Pole from 1383 were both to make the subject's duty to obey a cardinal feature of their policies. As de la Pole reminded the commons in October 1383 in his first address to them as chancellor, obedience was 'the foundation of all peace and quiet in the realm', and in its absence there could only be rebellion and disaffection.[33] To ensure the better performance of obedience, he and his colleagues embarked on a policy of strengthening royal government. By reducing hostilities on the continent and seeking an accord with the French they aimed to eliminate the burden of indebtedness which was threatening to make the king the prisoner of his subjects' goodwill; at the same time by placing a new emphasis on the prerogative and strengthening the household organs of government they sought to enhance the dignity of the crown and to raise it in popular esteem.[34] These policies were pursued with a clarity and consistency rare among the governments of Richard's minority. For this de la Pole himself was in large measure responsible. As chancellor he was the minister with overall charge of the government. He received visiting envoys from abroad, presided at meetings of the council and authorized use of the great seal. When parliament met, it fell to him to give the opening address on the king's behalf. The general assurance and authority that he showed in his handling of policy made him probably

---

[32] Ideas which corresponded closely to the precepts of Giles of Rome: see above, 16, and below, 249–50.

[33] *RP*, iii, 150.

[34] See below, 126–8.

the most important single official to serve Richard in the early years of the reign. With Burley he exercised a degree of influence over the king that no other officer in the 1380s could match.

If Burley and de la Pole were the most senior of Richard's advisers in the early 1380s, there was none the less a small group of younger figures who stood high in his affections and by whose opinions he was swayed. These were all up-and-coming knights – men of his own age or generation, with whom he whiled away his leisure hours. Richard appears to have revelled in the company of them all, and it would be unwise to suggest that at this stage he had a favourite. But if there was someone who enjoyed a primacy in his affections, it was a young man whose friendship he was to enjoy but briefly. This was Sir Ralph Stafford.

Ralph, the eldest surviving son of Hugh, 2nd earl of Stafford, had been born in or around 1367. He was of roughly the same age as Richard and would have known him from his upbringing at court. By all accounts he was a bright and promising young man; or at least no one spoke ill of him. But in 1385 he was tragically struck down in an engagement with the king's half-brother Sir John Holand. The incident, which was widely reported by the chroniclers, took place in July near York, as the royal army was making its way north to Scotland.[35] A quarrel of no great consequence had broken out between some rival and intemperate members of Holand's retinue and the earl of Stafford's. Stafford's men had set upon Holand's, killing two of them. Holand went to the king to seek redress, which was promised. But subsequently on the road he chanced upon Sir Ralph, exchanged insults with him and in a fit of temper slew him. Richard was grief-stricken and swore vengeance on Holand. Ralph Stafford had not only been a close friend of his but was also the heir to a loyal comital dynasty.[36] His father was a frequent attender at court and in 1382 had been a witness to grants to Burley.[37] Ralph himself was on the way to becoming a major courtier magnate. With his slaying Richard lost a potential ally and counsellor of importance. By way of compensation he decided to build up the power of his father. A number of grants on the patent rolls bear witness to this. On 20 August 1385 the earl was given custody for life of Macclesfield park and five days later, in addition, was made steward of Macclesfield hundred.[38] On 20 October he was also

---

[35] *HA*, ii, 129–30; Froissart, ii, 50–2; *WC*, 122.

[36] The Westminster writer makes clear the king's affection for Ralph: 'he had loved the lad all the more tenderly for having been a contemporary and comrade in the heyday of his own youth' (*WC*, 122).

[37] C53/159, 160, 161; *CPR 1381–5*, 107.

[38] *CPR 1381–5*, 7, 14.

awarded custody of the county of Chester for three years.[39] The clear purpose behind these grants was to promote the earl as a power in the north-west, but in the following year, still burdened with grief, he left England for a pilgrimage and died before he returned. A vacuum was created in the north-western power structure which it was later given to another of Richard's friends, Robert de Vere, earl of Oxford, to fill. De Vere's rise was in a sense a by-product of Ralph Stafford's premature demise.

After Ralph Stafford, de Vere and his slightly younger contemporary Thomas Mowbray, earl of Nottingham, were probably the two friends whose company Richard enjoyed most. Both were to play a prominent role in the politics of the 1380s, and both were men driven by ambition and lust for power. In de Vere's case the mainspring of that ambition was necessity – financial necessity. His family was one of the poorest in the titled nobility, and by the late fourteenth century they had difficulty in adequately maintaining their rank. Access to royal patronage was essential to their well-being. From the 1360s they had benefited from the brokerage of Sir Aubrey de Vere, a younger brother of Earl Thomas, who had risen in the service of the Black Prince and was a member of the 'continual councils' in the early years of the reign.[40] Through his influence in 1371, when Earl Thomas died and his estates were taken into wardship, Robert, the earl's heir, was received into the royal household and brought up there. Doubtless as intended, he soon met the future king, and the two became inseparable companions. In 1381 they rode out together for the meeting with the rebels at Mile End.[41] Three years later they arranged to meet at Castle Hedingham when Richard was briefly in Essex.[42] So close did the association between the two become that in circles hostile to them it gave rise to allegations of homosexuality. Almost certainly these allegations were baseless.[43] De Vere was in reality something of a womanizer, and in 1387 abandoned his wife, a woman of royal birth, in favour of Agnes Lancecrona, a lady-in-waiting of the queen. His relationship with the king is most likely to have been one of close friendship and no more. All the same, it gave rise to widespread resentment among the nobility. What caused particular annoyance was its exclusivity. While de Vere was in the ascendant few others were able to gain access to the king's favour. He lapped up offices, wardships and grants of land and generally, as

---

[39] *CFR 1383–91*, 113.

[40] Lewis, 'The "Continual Council"', 250–1.

[41] *Peasants' Revolt*, ed. Dobson, 161.

[42] C81/1339/55: an undated signet letter to Michael de la Pole, chancellor, written at 'Hyngham' (i.e. Hedingham), the de Veres' castle. As de la Pole is not referred to as earl of Suffolk, the letter must predate 6 August 1385.

[43] Stow, 'Richard II in Walsingham's Chronicles', 86–7.

Froissart put it, 'bore all the rule around the king'.[44] He was further disliked by the king's uncles for having brought shame upon the royal family through his repudiation of his wife Philippa, a granddaughter of Edward III. Robert de Vere was therefore a man with no shortage of enemies at court, and was reliant for continued ascendancy wholly on the king's favour. When a challenge to the court came, as it did in 1387, he was one of the first to be driven from power, never to return.

Like Robert de Vere, Thomas Mowbray owed his initial association with the court to a wardship. His father, John Lord Mowbray, had died abroad in 1368, when he was only two (and his elder brother just a year older). The inheritance passed to the crown, and custody was granted to Ralph Lord Bassett of Drayton.[45] Provision was probably made for the upbringing of the two wards in the royal household. John, the elder of the two, was knighted with Richard in 1377 and at Richard's coronation later in the same year was made earl of Nottingham.[46] Of Thomas, the younger brother, little is heard before 1383 when, on his brother's death, he succeeded to the title; but the signs are that he too found a livelihood at court. In 1382 in the company of Ralph Stafford, Thomas Clifford and James Berners he was licensed to hunt in the royal parks and chases; and in or before the same year he was formally retained as a king's knight.[47] Thomas's family connections virtually guaranteed him a place at court. On his mother's side he was a direct descendant of Edward I through Thomas of Brotherton, earl of Norfolk, a son by the king's second marriage, while through his father he could claim kinship with the Holands, Richard II's half-brothers. He was a man with high expectations in life. He aspired to a position of honour at court and a share in the distribution of patronage commensurate with his dignity as an earl. For most of the 1380s his expectations appear to have been fulfilled. He was created earl of Nottingham within a few days of his brother's death and, although still a minor, was granted custody of his inheritance almost immediately. In October 1383 he was elected a knight of the Garter, and two years later in 1385 was granted the title of earl marshal for life. Even before he was twenty-one he was guaranteed a secure and assured place at the king's side.[48] By 1387, however, there

---

[44] Froissart, ii, 70.

[45] CFR 1369–77, 8–9.

[46] For John's career, see Goodman, *Loyal Conspiracy*, 156–7; and for Thomas's, ibid., 157–64.

[47] CPR 1381–5, 176; C. Given-Wilson, *The Royal Household and the King's Affinity. Service, Politics and Finance in England 1360–1413* (New Haven and London, 1986), 285.

[48] It is significant that he had an apartment of his own in the royal palace at Eltham along with such other magnates as the duke of Lancaster and the earl of Oxford (*HKW*, ii, 935).

are signs that he was beginning to waver in his allegiance to Richard.[49] After Robert de Vere's defeat at Radcot Bridge on 20 December, he threw in his lot with the Appellants, and appeared with them in parliament the following year when they laid charges against the king's friends. The reason for his defection was almost certainly jealousy of de Vere. He saw that the earl was supplanting him in the king's favour, and felt the loss of place keenly. Unlike de Vere, he did not need access to royal patronage to augment his resources: with an income of at least £2,000 a year he had adequate enough resources already.[50] But he did expect to be given the honour and recognition due to one of his birth. When this was withheld he reacted with a sense of injury. In the more settled conditions of the 1390s he was quickly won back by Richard, for by upbringing and instinct he was a courtier. But his behaviour in 1387 and 1388 had shown how opportunistic he could be. In general, he was a man who inspired little trust and affection, and his presence at court brought an element of unpredictability to an already volatile political situation.

Less exalted in dignity than the earls of Oxford, Nottingham and Stafford were the knightly members of Richard's inner circle. These were for the most part men who had been brought up in the royal household or were employed in the chamber. One of the most distinguished was Sir Thomas Clifford, a scion of a northern baronial family. Clifford was linked closely in Richard's mind with Stafford and Nottingham: in 1382 the king granted all three of them – 'his kinsmen and young knights', as he termed them – permission to hunt in the royal forests and chases.[51] Clifford had become a knight of the chamber by 1382 at the latest and served as governor of Carlisle castle from 1384.[52] A close associate of Clifford's was Sir James Berners, a member of a gentry family of West Horsley (Surrey) and a chamber knight from 1382.[53] Berners, it appears, was a man to whom Richard was closely attached. The Westminster writer tells how during the court's visit to Ely in 1383 he was struck by lightning and left blind, and Richard ordered the monks to pray to St Etheldreda for a cure; by morning his sight had been restored and the king showed his gratitude by confirming the cathedral priory's liberties.[54] There were various other

---

[49] *HA*, ii, 156, dates Mowbray's disaffection to this time.

[50] R.E. Archer, 'The Mowbrays, Earls of Nottingham and Dukes of Norfolk, to 1432' (University of Oxford D.Phil. thesis, 1984), 67–8, revising Goodman, *Loyal Conspiracy*, 158, in significant respects.

[51] *CPR 1381–5*, 176.

[52] *CP*, iii, 292.

[53] He is shown in a stained-glass window in West Horsley church: plate 4. For his career see *House of Commons*, ii, 205–8.

[54] *WC*, 42; *Cal. Charter Rolls 1341–1417*, 288–9.

knights whom the king honoured with his favour, chief among them Sir
John Salisbury, Sir John Clanvow and Sir Richard Stury. These were
generally men of middling gentry stock whose connections earlier in
life had been with the Black Prince. For the most part, their pickings
from the trough of patronage were meagre. Only John Beauchamp, a
chamber esquire from the beginning of the reign, and someone whom
Richard engagingly referred to as 'Jankyn' Beauchamp, made it into the
ranks of the peerage.[55] John had given Richard distinguished service in
a number of offices – first as keeper of the jewels, then as receiver of the
chamber and justice of North Wales, and finally in 1386 as steward of
the household.[56] His landed endowment, however, remained small, and
when Richard raised him to the peerage as Baron Kidderminster in
1387, he did so by the unprecedented method of issuing letters patent.[57] This had the effect of making the barony conferred on him a
personal one, unrelated to the tenure of land. Many of the nobility
reacted with hostility to his elevation, which they saw as conflicting
with traditional conceptions of status. Indeed, there is a likelihood that
it was never accepted by the Appellants, for when at their behest
Beauchamp was impeached in 1388 he was referred to simply as 'John
Beauchamp of Holt'. The new lord's conviction and execution meant
that the promotion was as short-lived as it was unprecedented (it lasted
a mere four months), and it is significant that in the later part of
the reign no similar baronies were conferred.[58] As a candidate
for ennoblement, however, John Beauchamp was by no means as unde-
serving as his detractors made him out to be. He was a hard-working,
perhaps even an efficient, royal servant, and the Westminster chronicler thought that he acquitted himself with distinction in his duties.[59]
His misfortune was to become involved with the court at a time when it
was steering into rough waters. In another reign, and at another time,
he might well have been received as a not unworthy recruit to the
peerage.

   Richard found his associates not only among the gentry and scions of
the nobility at court but also among the clerks and chaplains attached
to the royal household. These were men with many characteristics in
common with the chamber knights and esquires. Most came from
gentry or lesser gentry families, and they performed a variety of admin-

[55] For the diminutive see C81/1343/14 and 42. In the letters patent subsequently
issued it was formalized as 'John' (CPR 1381–5, 474, 516).

[56] His career is summarized in Tout, Chapters, iv, 204–5.

[57] Reports from the Lords' Committees Touching the Dignity of the Peerage (5 vols, London,
1820–9), v, 81.

[58] Though the barony of Kidderminster was revived for John Beauchamp's son,
another John, in 1398 (CP, ii, 46).

[59] WC, 178.

istrative tasks; moreover, they rarely became deeply involved in politics. What distinguished them from the knights was less the matter of their cloth than the nature of the duties that they performed. Unlike the chamber knights, the clerks were nearly always employed to do specific jobs within specific departments, from writing memoranda in chancery to compiling accounts in the wardrobe. In all they amounted to a not inconsiderable labour force. Over 240 men were described as 'king's clerks' in Richard's reign. Only about 90–100 were employed in the household departments; and of these only a relatively small proportion, perhaps no more than a quarter, was resident at court at any one time. The clerks with whom Richard came into regular day-to-day contact were thus a very select group, numbering probably fewer than a dozen.[60] But it was felt that their influence was out of all proportion to their numbers. Particular distrust was shown of Thomas Rushook, the Dominican who was Richard's confessor in the early years of his reign. Described by Gower as 'unctuous, adept at flattery and sedulous in sowing discord', he was banned from court at parliament's behest, but later returned and in 1388 was indicted of treason. Expelled a second time, he eked out his last years in a poverty-stricken Irish see, supported by a £40 annuity granted to him by the king.[61]

Rushook's case is striking, but it is also exceptional. No other clerk who served Richard in the office of confessor aroused even remotely comparable hostility. Generally when contemporaries complained of clerical influence at court it was the seculars whom they had in mind – men like the senior administrative officials and the clerks of the chapel royal. Thomas Favent, the pro-Appellant propagandist, who in the late 1380s wrote a tract on those lords' behalf, identified four such clerks to whom exception was taken. These were Richard Medford, the king's secretary, John Lincoln of Grimsby, chamberlain of the exchequer, Nicholas Slake and Richard Clifford.[62] All four, as Favent noted, were clerks of the chapel royal. Medford was the most senior of them: his connection went back as far as 1375. The others appeared on the lists somewhat later: Slake in 1380, Clifford in 1386 and Lincoln probably in that year too.[63] Their membership of the chapel gave them a corporate identity and an affinity with one another that transcended

---

[60] This quantitative overview is based on Given-Wilson, *Royal Household and the King's Affinity*, 175.

[61] Tuck, *Richard II and the Nobility*, 56, 125. A possible reason for Rushook's unpopularity may have been his assumption of the role of a patronage broker; for examples of grants made by the king at his request see *CPR 1381–5*, 346, 363, 372, 382, 391, 399, 481, 483, 576.

[62] *Historia sive Narracio Mirabilis Parliamenti* attributed to Thomas Favent, ed. M. McKisack (Camden 3rd series, xxxvii, 1926), 13.

[63] A. Wathey, *Music in the Royal and Noble Households in Late Medieval England* (New York and London, 1989), 81 and n.

differences of background and age. Yet it should not be supposed that they were all of equal standing at court. Clifford was at the beginning of his career; his heyday was to come later and in the next reign. Grimsby was rising fast, though only from 1386 was he a significant figure in politics. Slake was closer to the king than either of these two – Walsingham comments on how Richard turned to him for advice at the Salisbury parliament in 1384. Medford was probably the most influential of the four in government. In the administrative field he was one of the key figures of the 1380s. For this reason his career deserves lengthier consideration than the others'.

   Medford's association with the crown had its origins in Edward III's reign. As early as 1352 he had become a fellow of King's Hall, Cambridge, an institution established to groom future clerks of the chapel royal. In 1375 he had been taken on as a king's clerk, and eight years later in 1383 he became chirographer of the Common Pleas.[64] His appointment two years after that as king's secretary brought him to an office with considerable potential for development. Already in Bacon's time the scope of the secretary's work had widened. During his own time it widened still further, and the office became one of the most vital in government. The association that had earlier existed between the secretaryship and the chamber was ended, and the former now emerged as an office in its own right with full control over the signet. There was a massive increase in the volume of correspondence that it dealt with. Between January 1385 and January 1386 nearly 300 letters were sent by signet direct to the chancellor; by the autumn of 1385 as many were warranted by signet as by all other instruments combined, and by the summer of the following year the signet had become the most common of all methods of moving the great seal.[65] This expansion in signet use caused resentment in chancery, and in October 1386, when there was a change of ministers, it was brought to a halt. Bishop Arundel, the new chancellor, insisted that in future only the privy seal be used to move the great seal, and for the duration of his term of office the signet was used simply to authenticate the king's private correspondence and to send instructions to such officials as the chamberlain of Chester.[66] Later chancellors took a less dogmatic line, but the signet never recovered its earlier importance. Between 1388 and 1392, as a consequence of this decline, the secretary's office fell into virtual abeyance, and Medford ceased his employment with the crown. It was not until 1393 when the former treasurer of Calais, Roger Walden, was

[64] Tuck, *Richard II and the Nobility*, 67; Wathey, *Music in Royal and Noble Households*, 80–1. The chirographer was the chief clerk of the court.
[65] Tuck, *Richard II and the Nobility*, 67.
[66] Ibid., 70.

appointed that there was again to be an appreciable upturn in the level
of signet activity.

The emergence of a closely knit group of courtiers, the build-up of the
chamber staff, and the increasing use made of the signet are phe-
nomena that have been invested by some historians with considerable
constitutional significance. To T.F. Tout and the writers on administrative history earlier this century they betokened the establishment of a
royal autocracy. Richard, it was argued, was looking for new types of
servant and new instruments of power. Chancery and the privy seal, the
older departments of state, were no longer responsive to his personal
wishes as king: they had drifted 'out of court' and had become more
subject to baronial scrutiny and control. As a response to their inadequacies Richard built up the power of the household. Finance and
administration he concentrated in the chamber, an office with its own
corps of staff, while written correspondence he directed through the
office of his secretary and sealed with his private seal, the signet. The
older departments were thus left with a purely residual importance.
Chancery still had possession of the great seal and remained a clearing
house of correspondence; but the great seal was moved by the signet
not the privy seal, the latter in effect being bypassed. Bureaucratic
procedures were therefore abbreviated and simplified, and a more
streamlined appearance was given to government. The foundations
were laid for the construction of what in a later age might be termed
'absolutism'.[67]
    In modified form this thesis has been adopted by more recent histo-
rians of the reign. Anthony Tuck, for example, accepting its basic
assumptions, has laid particular stress on the role of the chapel in
furthering Richard's designs. The chapel, he has argued, provided
Richard with a body of trained clerks, many of them graduates, who
could be used to penetrate and colonize other parts of the administration. Through skilful deployment of these men, particularly in the
signet office, he was able to realize the potential of the household and
thus to build up the power of the crown. In this way, he concludes, the
pace of government could be quickened, and the structures of administration made more responsive to the king's will.[68]
    A number of criticisms can be made of these arguments. In the first
place, it now seems that the degree of overlap between the chapel and
the signet office has been exaggerated. Only one clerk can be shown to

---

[67] Tout's views are found in summary form in *Chapters*, v, 207, 229-30.
[68] Tuck, *Richard II and the Nobility*, 66-7.

have been employed in both, and that was Medford. Though a link of some sort probably did exist between the two offices, its strength was less than has been supposed.[69] Secondly, and more fundamentally, the assumption underlying the interpretation can be questioned. There is no evidence that Richard needed to build up a clerically based autocracy. He had perfectly compliant ministers in his service as it was: in the years to 1386 Michael de la Pole at chancery and Walter Skirlaw at the privy seal carried out his instructions to the letter, and there was no need for him to bypass them. The conditions under which Richard might have wanted to create a more 'personal' administration were to arise later, in the two years after 1386 when he was under threat from his opponents. But in that time he did nothing; the signet was allowed to languish. When Bishop Arundel objected to the use of signet warrants he is likely to have done so on grounds that were less constitutional than technical: complaints had been voiced about signet interference with actions at common law, and it is probable that he was trying to respond to these.[70] Richard's preference for the signet seems largely to have been a matter of convenience.

It is difficult not to conclude that the distinction made by administrative historians between household and non-household organs of government is largely illusory. In the middle ages all government was the king's government; every part of it existed to carry out the king's will. Most contemporaries would have conceived of it essentially as a unity. Of course, over time departments 'moved out of court' and developed their own often rigid structures and routines. But this does not mean that the king lost control of them or found it necessary to think of bypassing them. On the contrary, it made him all the more determined to maintain them under his control – which he could do easily through the appointment of dependable officers. Edward III was especially skilful at doing this. By a series of shrewd appointments to the major offices in the 1340s he brought the entire system of government under his control; household and non-household offices were locked together in a common enterprise and jointly entrusted with executing policies agreed in council. Richard may have had his grandfather's success in mind when he made Burley and de la Pole the agents of a not dissimilar co-operative design in the 1380s.

Bringing together the disparate branches of government and ensuring that they co-operated with one another was a relatively easy task: the king had only to appoint the right men to the key offices and then to ensure that there was adequate liaison between them. More difficult, but more important, was the task of tying into the structures of

[69] Wathey, *Music in Royal and Noble Households*, 82–3.
[70] Given-Wilson, *Royal Household and the King's Affinity*, 183.

royal government the informal networks of power centred on the nobility. This was an exercise that made heavy demands on the king's skills of management. The nobility were the principal power-brokers in medieval society. They ranked among the king's leading advisers at court; and locally, through their affinities, they mediated the exercise of royal authority in the shires. Their support was essential to any ruler aspiring to the successful exercise of kingship. Edward III had realized this when he embarked on the renewal of royal authority after the disasters of his father's reign. From the beginning, magnate participation figured as a key element in his programme. Men like Arundel, Warwick and Lancaster were given major responsibilities in the campaigns in France, Aquitaine, and Brittany after 1341, while at home they were employed on a variety of tasks centrally and in the localities. They were honoured and treated with the respect due to members of their class, and in return they lent unstinting support to the crown over a period of time unequalled in the fourteenth century.[71] Edward's success owed much to his easy ways with the nobility: he could identify with their ambitions and mix with them socially. Richard II did not have this advantage. Temperamentally he found himself ill at ease with many of the senior magnates: he found it difficult to establish an *esprit de corps* with them, and he was hampered by being unable to project a vision in which they could share. Politically too he was maladroit in his dealings with them. He failed to maintain that evenhandedness in the distribution of patronage that had been so crucial to the success of his grandfather's governance: he heaped favours and rewards on a small group of courtier nobles – chiefly on Burley and de la Pole in the older generation and Stafford and de Vere in the younger – while offering virtually nothing to everyone else. The result was as disastrous as it was predictable. Between 1382 and 1387 the power base of his regime gradually narrowed, and a rift arose between the courtiers who were richly rewarded and the rest of the nobility who were not. In October 1383 for the first time criticism was voiced of the king's behaviour in parliament. According to the Westminster writer some members of the nobility, whom he does not name, complained that the membership of Richard's inner circle was too narrow and that he listened only to those of his own mind, ignoring the views of those who had brought prosperity to the realm in the past.[72] The king, he says, replied diplomatically to the effect that he would happily accept the guidance of his council – while adding at the same time that he would also take advice from whomsoever he wished. The lords accepted his reply, and for the moment a crisis was averted. But there was no disguising the seriousness

[71] Ormrod, *Reign of Edward III*, ch. 6.
[72] *WC*, 54.

of the issue that had been raised. The behaviour of the king and his
friends had become a matter of major concern in political society, and
criticism was gradually becoming more open. Over the next three years
there was to be a succession of crises provoked by the unsettled relations between the king's friends and the nobility, the first of them
occurring in the parliament held at Salisbury in 1384.

The Salisbury parliament had been convoked with the principal
object of discussing the proposals for peace between England and
France brought back by Lancaster four months before. In the event,
however, its proceedings were dominated by two matters of more
domestic concern – the earl of Arundel's denunciation of the king, and
a Carmelite friar's accusations of treason against the duke. Arundel's
outburst apparently came soon after parliament had opened. According to the Westminster writer, the most reliable source for the episode,
the earl launched into a violent attack on the king and his court. The
country, he declared, stood in peril of destruction because of the lack
of prudent government. Long ago it had begun to atrophy because of
poor governance, but since then the decay had gathered pace, and
unless remedies were applied it would suffer crippling losses and ultimately total collapse.[73] Richard, the chronicler says, went white with
rage. 'If it is supposed to be my fault that there is misgovernment in the
realm,' he cried, 'then you lie in your teeth. You can go to the devil.'
Silence followed, and it was only through the good offices of Lancaster
that the king's anger was assuaged and amity restored.

Arundel's criticism was unspecific, and it is hard to know what concerns in particular moved him to such fury. He was later to favour an
aggressive stance against France, and he may have suspected Richard
and his intimates of nurturing aspirations of peace. Equally he could
have been concerned about the growing cost to the taxpayer of maintaining Richard's court. He was committed to economy in the household, and in November 1381 he had been appointed to a commission
'to survey the king's household and ordain remedies ... so that the
king could live of his own'.[74] The failure of this commission to achieve
any reform is very likely to have lain at the root of his charges of decay
in the realm. For both of these explanations there is a great deal to
be said. Yet neither adequately accounts for the sheer vehemence of
the earl's remarks, which can only be understood in the context of the
burning resentment that he felt at his loss of influence at court. In
the early years of the reign, while Richard was a child, he and his fellow
magnates had been the dominant group in government. They had been
represented on the council, and had been active in leading expeditions

[73] Ibid., 68.
[74] *RP*, iii, 101.

to France. Once Richard had grown to manhood, however, they had found their influence diminished. Burley, de la Pole and de Vere were the men whose views counted for most now, and Arundel and the others were left virtually without a role. Exclusion bred frustration, and frustration boiled over in anger. Lancaster's good offices effected a reconciliation between Richard and the earl at least for a while, and the marriage of Nottingham to the earl's daughter provided a link with the courtier group which had previously been lacking.[75] But the atmosphere of suspicion remained, and the young bloods around Richard did nothing to help dispel it. By 1384 they were engaged in blackening the character of Lancaster himself, who appears to have replaced Arundel as the chief object of their hatred. The duke's wealth and influence, and perhaps too his good sense, aroused their jealousy, and with the passage of time they became steadily bolder in the measures they took to bring about his downfall. An idea of the lengths to which they were prepared to go was afforded by the second of the two *causes célèbres* for which the Salisbury parliament was remembered – the scandal concerning the allegations of a Carmelite friar.[76]

The man at the heart of this curious affair was a Carmelite friar by the name of John Latimer. According to the most reliable account, that of the Monk of Westminster, he went up to the king after celebrating mass and told him that the duke of Lancaster was plotting his death. Richard reacted angrily, and ordered the duke to be executed forthwith. Those in attendance protested at this rashness, saying that it was wrong for anyone to be executed without trial. Richard conceded the point and gave way. He then enquired of the friar if anyone else was involved. The friar replied that Lord Zouche of Harringworth, if asked, would disclose full knowledge of the affair. At this point Richard ordered a proper investigation to be made, and the friar was led away to imprisonment. Once outside, however, he was met by a group of knights, some of them retainers of Lancaster, led by the king's ruffianly half-brother, John Holand. Deeply resentful of the slur cast on the duke's reputation, they assumed custody of the friar themselves and took him away to an obscure cell in the castle. There they subjected him to the most excruciating torture, breaking his limbs and tormenting him with fire. What they suspected was that he had been suborned by someone secretly hostile to Gaunt, but try as they might they could compel him to tell no more than they already knew, and in the end they gave up. The king in the meantime had sent for Lord Zouche, who denied all knowledge of the affair, but the friar, by now at death's door, begged as a last favour that he be allowed a private interview with the lord. Permission was

[75] *WC*, 88.
[76] The best account is ibid., 68–80.

granted, subject to witnesses being present, but nothing of substance emerged from the interview, and within a few days the hapless friar was dead.

The full story of this extraordinary affair will never be known, and there is much about it that remains obscure. Why the friar made the accusation in the first place is never revealed in the sources. It is possible that he was moved solely by personal dislike of the duke. Alternatively he may have borne a grudge against him because of the support that he had given to John Wyclif in the previous decade. A third possibility, and one to which support is given by the narratives, is that he was simply mad. A further issue is whether he was acting in isolation or was being used by others. Under interrogation the friar seemed anxious to implicate Lord Zouche of Harringworth. Lord Zouche was a man with court connections who stood high enough in Richard's favour to incur the ire of the Appellants in 1388, but it is difficult to believe that he was greatly involved in this affair: there is certainly no evidence that he was, beyond the friar's own word. If anyone at court was implicated it is more likely to have been Robert de Vere. Several pieces of evidence point in this direction. According to the Westminster writer, the friar made his allegation after celebrating mass in the king's presence in the apartment of the earl of Oxford. And in the Monk of Evesham's account the friar is made to assert that there was 'a worthy esquire of the earl of Oxford', who would witness the truth of his accusation.[77] These shreds of evidence are hardly conclusive, but they do point to a courtly dimension to an affair for which it is otherwise difficult to find a context. The idea may have been to smear Lancaster and to discredit him in the eyes of the king. The friar's role may have been that of a pawn in a grander game played by the rivals for power at court.

With the ending of the Salisbury parliament on 31 May the tensions that existed between Lancaster and the king and his friends eased a little – or at least were no longer so evident in public. But they were still there, lurking beneath the surface of politics. They came to the fore again in August at a council meeting at Reading at which John of Northampton, the former mayor of London, was tried for inciting disorder after his defeat in the election of October 1383. When the articles of appeal had been read out, the king proposed that the council immediately move to judgment on the accused. John of Northampton, however, stood up and declared, 'I hope, my lord king, that you do not mean to proceed to judgement or to exercise jurisdiction in the absence of your uncle the duke of Lancaster.' Richard flared up and asserted that he was competent to sit in judgment not only on North-

---

[77] Ibid., 68; *HVR*, 81.

ampton but on the duke of Lancaster as well. Only through the intercession of the queen was Richard's temper cooled and the life of the
tactless defendant spared.[78] Three months later in the November parliament differences surfaced again, if in a less dramatic fashion. According
to the Monk of Westminster the proceedings were marked by further
squabbles among the lords and as a result nothing of substance was
decided. By the beginning of 1385 passions could no longer be contained, and a second plot was hatched to dispose of the duke. According to the Evesham writer, the idea was to place him under arrest at a
great council convened at Waltham in early February. Word reached
the duke, however, and he begged leave to be excused attendance, but
Richard insisted that he come – which he did, but only with the security
of an armed escort.[79] The Monk of Westminster's account is slightly
different, but perhaps more plausible. According to the Monk's version, the attempt on Gaunt's life was hatched after and not before the
Waltham council. In the discussions there the differences between the
duke and the king and his friends had emerged more strongly than
ever, and the suggestion was made to arrest him at a tournament to be
held at Westminster on 13 and 14 February and then to have him
arraigned for treason before the chief justice. Gaunt was forewarned of
the plan and fled northwards to Pontefract, but a fortnight later he
returned in order to meet the king at Sheen. Detaching some men to
guard the boat that had brought him, he entered the royal presence
wearing a breastplate under his gown. He reproached the king for
keeping evil counsellors and said it was shameful that he, the lord of all,
should connive in a plot to murder one of his own subjects: rather he
should seek good and loyal advisers by whose counsel he should for-
swear lawless action and do what was best for his people. These were
strong words, but Richard refrained from answering back. Considering
discretion the better part of valour, he spoke 'mild and soothing language' and assured Gaunt that he would act more justly in future. At
this the duke withdrew and made his way via Tottenham to Hertford
where he stayed under the watchful eye of his retainers. In the meantime the princess of Wales, again acting in her accustomed role of
mediator, set to work to effect a reconciliation between her son and his
uncle, and on 6 March, largely as a result of her endeavours, at a
ceremony at Westminster a formal peace was made between the duke
and his enemies.[80]

Of the identity of those behind the plot against Gaunt in February
the chroniclers leave us in no doubt. Walsingham speaks of the young

[78] WC, 92.
[79] HVR, 85-6.
[80] WC, 112-14.

men 'who were the king's accomplices', while Evesham accuses the young men 'who were brought up with the king'.[81] Westminster more specifically singles out the earls of Oxford, Nottingham and Salisbury.[82] It is hard to believe that Salisbury was involved, as he was neither particularly young nor close to the king, and the chronicler may have meant either his brother Sir John Montagu, who was steward of the household, or more likely, as he too was quite elderly, another Sir John, who was to succeed him as earl. Oxford and Nottingham were probably the main culprits. Both had reason to be jealous of the duke. He was a man of greater wealth and experience than themselves, and his views carried greater weight in the councils of the realm. As the Monk of Westminster said, the other temporal lords 'went in constant fear of the duke because of his great power, his admirable judgement and his brilliant mind'.[83] It was difficult for others, like Oxford and Nottingham, to grow up under his shadow. To that extent the tension between Gaunt and these others was largely a factor of his personal standing. But differences of outlook probably made themselves felt as well. Gaunt was a man of broader vision and greater experience than anyone else at court in the 1380s. In a sense he was the political heir of Edward III and the Black Prince. His exalted sense of royal authority, his dynastic ambition and his political adventurism all identified him with the assertive style of kingship associated with his father. Furthermore his interests in the kingdoms of Portugal and Castile were a reminder of the European role that his father had sought for the English crown. Gaunt was in many respects a prince in the mould of Charles VI's uncles, an actor on an international rather than a national stage. This made him unpopular in England, and the suspicion arose that he wanted to corner national resources for the pursuit of largely personal interests abroad. There is no evidence that this was so, and in reality Gaunt was more sinned against than sinning. But the effect was to isolate him in political society. With the exception of his two brothers he had few supporters at the highest level, and when he finally left England for Spain in 1386 it was to obvious relief at court. Gaunt's problem was that he was too important to be ignored, and yet too unpopular to be able to carry many others with him. His presence at court had the unfortunate effect of encouraging a rift in politics which both unsettled English society in the mid-1380s and frustrated the task of formulating a satisfactory response to the recovery in these years in the military power of France.

---

[81] *HA*, ii, 126; *HVR*, 85.
[82] *WC*, 114.
[83] Ibid., 112.

Chapter 7

RETREAT FROM WAR, 1383–5

The collapse of Bishop Despenser's crusade in September 1383 had paved the way for a French military takeover of Flanders. The last English troops, under Elmham, had withdrawn at the beginning of October, and shortly afterwards French forces moved in to occupy the border towns of Bourbourg and Gravelines. Ghent continued its spirited defiance and drew strength from the brilliant night seizure of neighbouring Oudenaarde. But French ascendancy was sealed in the following January when Philip of Burgundy, Charles VI's uncle, succeeded his father-in-law as count.[1] With a prince of the house of Valois ruling in Ypres, the French goal of reducing Flanders to satellite status seemed on the point of fulfilment.

Even before the scale of the débâcle in Flanders became known the English had taken an initiative to bring the hostilities to an end. On 8 September 1383 the chancellor, Michael de la Pole, commissioned Lancaster to treat with the French for peace. The commission was couched in extravagant terms, denouncing war and its attendant evils, and empowering the duke to seek their termination by negotiation if possible and resort to duel if necessary. On 12 September this commission was supplemented by a more conventional one which authorized the duke to conclude a general settlement with both France and her allies on all outstanding issues.[2] In November the duke and his fellow envoys crossed to Calais, and negotiations went on over Christmas into the New Year. The French showed a willingness to compromise because they had their own reasons for ending the war. In the previous year Paris had been rocked by the revolt of the Maillotins, and the government doubted whether popular opinion would any longer endure the taxation needed to pay for war. Progress appears to have been made in the discussions; and to allow time for a deeper examination of the issues a general truce was agreed in January, to last for ten months.[3] By February a rough consensus had emerged, and at the beginning of that month Lancaster was able to cross to England to

[1] Louis of Mâle died on 30 January 1384.
[2] *Foed.*, vii, 407–8, 410.
[3] Ibid., 418–21; *WC*, 58.

show Richard what the Westminster chronicler, who was interested in foreign affairs, called 'the articles of a final agreement'.[4] The king and his councillors were evidently impressed and decided to submit the articles for consideration at the Salisbury parliament, which opened on 29 April.

Unfortunately no text of these articles has survived, and it is difficult to establish their character from the heavily abbreviated record of the parliament roll. Dr J.J.N. Palmer has suggested that they embodied the idea of separating the duchy of Aquitaine from the English crown and of settling it on the duke of Lancaster and his heirs as an apanage.[5] This was an idea that was to surface a number of times in the later fourteenth century. It had initially been proposed by the papal mediators in the negotiations leading to the making of the truce at Bruges in 1375, and it was to be revived in the 1390s as the basis of the proposals which the French were to put to Lancaster at Amiens.[6] Given the likely sympathy with the idea of some of the English council – notably of Lancaster himself – it is possible that it had been given serious consideration at Calais. Certainly the evidence of a couple of contemporary observers appears to support this view. Eustace Deschamps in a poem of c.1384 refers to a demand by the English that homage for Aquitaine should be performed by its duke and not the king, and the seigneur d'Albret in a letter to the count of Armagnac said that he thought that the outcome of the negotiations would be that the two of them 'and all [our] country ... would be given to the duke of Lancaster, who is to be our duke'.[7] It is unfortunate that the absence of any drafts of the treaty or of related documents makes it impossible to say for certain whether a proposal on these lines was incorporated in the terms brought back to London. But there are grounds for thinking that this was not the case. The proposals agreed at Calais provoked remarkably little reaction in England, and certainly no outright hostility, whereas eight years later, when Lancaster acquiesced in the separation of Aquitaine from the crown at Amiens, opposition was vociferous: the commons denounced the proposals at a council at Stamford, and the duke, angry and humiliated, was obliged to withdraw his assent to them.[8] The contrast between the popular responses on these two occasions is surely significant. It suggests that in 1384 some rather less provocative scheme was proposed. It is difficult to say much about the character of the scheme given the poverty of the sources. One possibility is that the English king was conceded a greatly reduced duchy in full sovereignty; another is

---

[4] WC, 58.
[5] Palmer, *England, France and Christendom*, 32–3, 50.
[6] Ibid., 33–4; WC, 490. See below, 213.
[7] Palmer, *England, France and Christendom*, 33.
[8] See below, 213–14.

that he was allowed to retain the duchy more or less as it stood but on condition of performing an oath of liege homage. The majority of the peace proposals made during the war took one or other of these two forms.[9] Whatever the precise terms agreed, however, securing parliamentary assent to them was no easier than it was to be a decade later. The commons at Salisbury, when pressed to declare for or against, sat on the fence. Though owning to a sincere desire for peace, they expressed reservations concerning the proposed oath of homage. For Guienne (i.e. Aquitaine), perhaps, such an oath could be performed, they said, but not for Calais and the other territories won by the sword.[10] When the chancellor pressed them a second time for their opinion, urging them to say simply yes or no, they took shelter behind the earlier, somewhat equivocal, reply of the lords: that without presuming to give counsel either way, their inclination was towards peace.[11] And with that Chancellor de la Pole had to be content.

On 27 May Lancaster and Buckingham were commissioned to treat with the French a second time with a view to securing from them the best terms they could.[12] But when they and their advisers arrived at the meeting place at Leulingham they found that their adversaries' position had hardened. What had been acceptable to them in January was no longer so. The reason for the volte-face was almost certainly the changed situation in Flanders. Count Louis had died, and Duke Philip had succeeded to his inheritance. The French now wanted a free hand to crush the one remaining centre of opposition in the county – the city of Ghent, which looked to the English for protection. The most that Lancaster was able to salvage from the negotiations, and then only in September, was a renewal of the truce to the following May.[13] Ghent was excluded and made the subject of a separate agreement. In England there was a widespread sense of disappointment. The French were thought to have got the better of their opponents, and it was accepted with resignation that in the following year hostilities would be renewed.

The government's response to the collapse of the negotiations was to seek a grant of taxation from parliament in the autumn. An assembly was summoned to meet on 12 November, and in his opening address to the commons three days later the chancellor, Michael de la Pole, pleaded the government's case. He spoke at length of the dangers posed in their different ways by the French, the Spanish and the

[9] For peace proposals in general see J.J.N. Palmer, 'The War Aims of the Protagonists and the Negotiations for Peace', *The Hundred Years War*, ed. K. Fowler (London, 1971), 51–74.

[10] *RP*, iii, 170.

[11] Ibid.

[12] *Foed.*, vii, 428–30.

[13] Ibid., 438–45.

Flemings, and affirmed the king's willingness to embark on the labour and discomfort of a personal campaign.[14] The commons responded by making a grant of taxation, but conflicting accounts of its terms suggest that differences arose over the ends to which it should be put. According to the official account on the parliament roll the commons made a two-part grant, the first confirming the conditional half-subsidy granted at Salisbury and the second making available another half-subsidy to be raised at midsummer (1385).[15] The Westminster writer, in an unofficial but nevertheless well-informed account, confirms the two-part nature of the grant, but adds that the additional half-subsidy was made available only on condition that the expedition led by the king went overseas.[16] The discrepancy between the two accounts points to a growing rift between commons and chancellor over the future direction of policy towards France. The commons had taken an increasingly assertive line ever since the breakdown of negotiations in September. They wanted a major expedition to be sent to the continent – whether to Flanders or elsewhere was not especially important – and they wanted that expedition to be led by the king. The chancellor, on the other hand, wanted to avoid conflict and to acquiesce in France's ambitions. A royally led expedition overseas, in his view, would be counterproductive: it would risk defeat and would occasion the levying of taxation that the realm could ill afford; hard though the conclusion was to accept, the only realistic course lay in retreat from war and disengagement from continental commitments. Little of this thinking was voiced in public; in the speeches that he gave as chancellor, de la Pole said virtually nothing to arouse his audience's suspicion. The evidence for his views was to be found in his actions. During his three years in office he pursued a consistent policy of retreat and withdrawal. He gave way where he should have stood firm, and he remained neutral where he should have taken sides. He did little or nothing which could have offended or given annoyance to the French. The working out of his policy was to be seen in his handling of relations with a number of European rulers. In no area was it more evident than in his dealings with the rulers of the Low Countries.

Despite the failure of Bishop Despenser's expedition there were still compelling arguments for further English intervention in Flanders. English interests in the county were gravely threatened by the succession of a prince of the house of Valois. In particular, the wool trade was put in jeopardy by French control of the cloth-making towns of the county, and a danger was posed to English shipping by French access to

[14] *RP*, iii, 184.
[15] Ibid., 185.
[16] *WC*, 102.

the ports of the Zwin estuary. There was much to be gained from making common cause with Ghent and those of its neighbours opposed to French hegemony in the area – particularly when, as is clear, the latter were keen to form an alliance with England. Between 1383 and 1385 a succession of embassies went to and fro between Ghent and Westminster, and different proposals for joint military action were discussed. The Ghentois suggested that an English prince of the blood be appointed *ruywaert*, or governor, of their city – a move which they hoped would strengthen their ties with England. The English approved the idea; but when it came to making an appointment they named a second-ranking peer, John Lord Bourchier. The impression was given – and it was no doubt intentional – that they did not wish to identify themselves too closely with the city's fate.[17]

A similar reserve was maintained by the government in its dealings with other powers in the area. The king of the Romans, for example, a potential ally because of his interest in the succession to the duchy of Brabant to which Duke Philip also had a claim, was shunned, although he made an extended visit to the Low Countries in 1384, and although he was hastily forging alliances with other princes in the area. The duke of Guelders, a keen protagonist of the English, received somewhat more attention: he was contacted in December 1384 and several times in 1385, but again the negotiations came to nothing and no alliance was formed. A third ruler, Albert of Holland, with whom Duke Philip was anxious to contract a marriage alliance, was almost completely ignored, and allowed to make his own arrangements with the Burgundians.[18] In its dealings with these princes the government could hardly have made its lack of concern any clearer. Whatever the case in the past, no significant military support would be extended in future to any ruler in the Low Countries; and in no event would the king himself be going there at the head of an army. This was not at all to the liking of those on the council who favoured a more assertive policy. Disquiet rapidly spread, and matters came to a head at a meeting of the great council held at Waltham in February 1385.[19]

The agenda for this council comprised all the issues conventionally described as the 'great business of the realm', but the item dominating

---

[17] Palmer, *England, France and Christendom*, 59.

[18] Ibid., 57–8.

[19] It is difficult to determine the exact date of this council, but some time in early February seems likely: payments were made on 11 February for the delivery of summonses to the bishop of London and the earl of Buckingham, and on 16 February for delivery of similar summonses to the earls of Arundel and Stafford and other prelates (E403/505, under those dates). *HVR*, 85, says simply that the council was held after Christmas. *WC*, 110–12, places it before the plot on Gaunt's life at Westminster on 13 or 14 February. See also above, 133.

the discussion was policy towards France. According to the Monk of
Westminster, John of Gaunt took the initiative by arguing the activist
line. The king, he proclaimed, should cross the Channel and crush his
enemies by force. Attack was the better form of defence; if nothing were
done, the French would be free to venture forth and inflict terrible
damage on the English. Others, unnamed by the chronicler, disagreed.
Their argument was that the king should stay in his own country: if he
left it he would simply risk harming his reputation, whereas if he stayed
he would be able to ensure its security and save it 'from the nibbling
attacks of his enemies'.[20] Support for Gaunt came chiefly from his
brothers, Thomas of Woodstock and Edmund of Langley. Woodstock's
relations with his elder brother had previously been strained. The two
had quarrelled over the dispersal of the de Bohun inheritance, a matter
in which their interests had been opposed.[21] But in the spring of 1384
they had jointly headed an expedition against the Scots, and the experience had probably led them to regard each other as brothers-in-arms.
Certainly Thomas reacted violently thereafter to any slur on Duke
John's reputation. His two brothers apart, however, Gaunt found few
supporters. Most of those in attendance preferred a defensive policy.
Seeing which way the wind was blowing, Gaunt left in high dudgeon,
declaring that the king could not expect any assistance from him unless
he made a crossing to France. In his absence (and the absence of his
brothers) a consensus was forged in favour of a defensive policy, and
the trend towards disengagement from continental war became clearer.
No opposition was raised to the tightening of the French noose around
Ghent, and pleas from the city for assistance went unheeded. The
Ghentois concluded that it was time to settle with the French, and on 18
December 1385 by the treaty of Tournai terms were agreed. Given the
Ghentois' weakness, these were remarkably generous. The city was
pardoned and her privileges were confirmed; free commerce was
granted and those banished were allowed to return; the populace's
Urbanist allegiance was to remain unchallenged. In return the
Ghentois were required to make just one concession: to renounce the
alliance with England.[22] It was a concession on paper only, for in

---

[20] WC, 112, is the best source for the council.

[21] For this quarrel, see Froissart, i, 623–4. Thomas had hoped to gain the whole
of the de Bohun inheritance by marrying Eleanor, daughter and co-heiress of
Humphrey, earl of Hereford – Mary, the other daughter, being expected to take the
veil. During Thomas's absence in France in 1380–1, however, Gaunt, through the
agency of a lady of the Arundel family, had Mary spirited away and married to
his son Henry of Derby. Thomas was thereby deprived of half of the de Bohun
inheritance.

[22] Vaughan, *Philip the Bold*, 37–8.

practice the alliance, once the linchpin of English foreign policy, was dead.

So little resistance did the English offer in these years to French expansion that they have been accused of pursuing a policy of appeasement. According to J.J.N. Palmer, the architect of that policy was the chancellor from March 1383, Michael de la Pole. On his appointment, Palmer argues, de la Pole took stock of the situation and decided that he had no feasible alternative to seeking a settlement with France. Over the previous few years the commons had displayed a steady determination to reduce taxation or to refuse it altogether, and the government, already encumbered by years of accumulated war debts, was unable to wage war with any prospect of success. If the situation were allowed to continue, the power and independence of the crown would be gravely endangered. From the chancellor's point of view there were two possible solutions to the dilemma: either to persuade the commons to be more generous, or to end the war. De la Pole opted for the latter.[23]

This is in many ways an attractive and persuasive argument, but it is not entirely convincing. Its principal weakness is that it accords to de la Pole as chancellor a freedom of action which almost certainly he did not possess. He was not a great magnate or prince of the blood, free to follow any path he chose. He was a knight banneret, a man of middling means, throughout his career dependent on the favour and protection of others. Before 1385, when he gained the Ufford earldom of Suffolk, his landed endowment was small, consisting for the most part of manors in Suffolk that he held in right of his wife.[24] He had made his way up the political ladder by service. His main patron was the Black Prince, with whom he had fought several times in France;[25] but he also enjoyed the favour of the duke of Lancaster, and by the 1370s had become one of the duke's fee'd retainers.[26] The duke's interests as well as the king's had a bearing on his policy as chancellor, and on occasion he was willing to adjust policy to suit the duke's convenience. In 1383, for example, when there was pressure from the commons to open negotiations with Castile on terms which would have confirmed the house of Trastamara in possession of the throne, he acquiesced in the

---

[23] Palmer, *England, France and Christendom*, 48.
[24] Pole married Katherine, daughter and heiress of Sir John Wingfield, by whom he held the castle and manor of Wingfield in Suffolk (*CP*, xii, i, 440).
[25] See above, 118.
[26] De la Pole's connection with Gaunt is first documented in 1372: *John of Gaunt's Register 1372–1376*, ed. S. Armitage-Smith, 2 vols (Camden 3rd series, xx–xxi, 1911), ii, no. 969. He also appears in the list of the duke's retainers compiled in around 1382 (*John of Gaunt's Register 1379–1383*, i, no. 22).

nomination of commissioners so favourable to the duke as to ensure that the negotiations were doomed to failure.[27] In the light of this evidence it would be unwise to see de la Pole as entirely his own master in policy-making. He was the agent of those to whom he was answerable: first and foremost the king, but also his fellow councillors and, in time of parliament, the members of the two houses. The conflicts that some-times arose between these personalities and groups help to account for the inconsistencies that can be detected in English foreign policy in this period.

Palmer is on firmer ground when he speaks of the problems posed for English policy by the difficulty of gaining consent to taxation. The Great Revolt had suddenly alerted the lords and commons to the dangers of heavy and recurrent taxation, and after 1381 grants of the levy on moveables were fewer and smaller than they had been before. Three of the four parliaments which had met between November 1381 and February 1383 had refused to make any grant at all, and those which were made in the two parliaments of 1384 were meagre by comparison with what had been granted before.[28] The consequences for the government were serious. While the garrisons of Calais, Cherbourg and Brest, and the garrison of Aquitaine, could be paid for out of customs revenues, the dispatch of an expedition could only be financed by the levy on moveables. A small expedition like Bishop Despenser's had proved costly enough; one led by the king would cost far more. The army would have to be on the grandest possible scale: no corners could be cut in equipping it; its array and accoutrements would have to outshine those of the French. These were heavy demands. The last royally led expedition, Edward III's of 1359–60, had cost the exchequer in wages no less than £134,000; and the one ten years later, which the king was to have led but did not, cost nearly £74,000, or more than twice the yield of a fifteenth and tenth.[29] Sums on this scale were virtually impossible for the government to raise in the 1380s when parliament was conscious of the danger of straining the fiscal tolerance of the people. Military retrenchment was not so much a matter of choice for Chancellor de la Pole; it was forced upon him by circumstances.

Yet there was a dilemma facing de la Pole and his colleagues as they

---

[27] Russell, *English Intervention*, 347.

[28] A. Tuck, 'Richard II and the Hundred Years War', *Politics and Crisis in Fourteenth Century England*, ed. J. Taylor and W. Childs (Gloucester, 1990), 123; idem, 'Nobles, Commons and the Great Revolt', 208–9.

[29] G.L. Harriss, *King, Parliament and Public Finance in Medieval England to 1369* (Oxford, 1975), 346n.; Sherborne, 'The Cost of English Warfare', 136. In 1382 the commons had estimated the cost of an overseas voyage led by the king consisting of 3,000 men-at-arms and as many archers to be at least £60,000 (*RP*, iii, 123).

contemplated the threat of the reviving power of France. National pride and the defence of vital economic interests required that a challenge be mounted to French expansion; yet with manpower and money so limited it was difficult to see how this could be done. De la Pole in a misguided pursuit of retrenchment had neglected the alliances in the Low Countries which would have enabled an anti-French coalition to be mobilized, and no new alliances had been forged in their place. England as a result was left isolated and virtually friendless in Europe. Yet victory in the long Anglo-French struggle could not be allowed to go to the French by default: opinion at home would never stand for it. The commons expected a major expedition to be put into the field; and both within parliament and without people were clamouring for the king to be given the chance to win his spurs. Chancellor de la Pole, in a move to conciliate his critics, promised a royally led expedition in his speech in 1384 – but he carefully refrained from saying where he or the council thought the king should go. Probably at the time he had little idea; with a continental expedition virtually ruled out, it was hard to see where exactly the king could go. Ironically, it was the French who solved his dilemma for him. In the summer of 1384, after months of preparation, the French sent a force of some 1,600 men to Scotland under the command of the redoubtable Jean de Vienne.[30] The expedition was part of an ambitious strategy which was simultaneously to include a landing on the south coast by a force assembled at Sluys. Of the two threats the southern one was much the more serious, but it was the northern one to which the council decided to respond. Preparations were almost immediately put in hand for a major invasion of Scotland to be led by the king in person. The context for the decision was provided by the gradual toughening of English policy towards the Scots which had taken place over the previous two years. In May 1383 English envoys had been given instructions that no English-held land in Scotland was to be surrendered in any settlement with the Scots, and in January 1384 Northumberland and Neville had been ordered to demand reparations for breaches of the truce plus the balance of King David's ransom; if their demands were refused, they were to raise an army and 'hostilely invade Scotland'.[31] Richard and his ministers, in other words, had effectively abandoned their commitment to maintaining peace on the border. War with the French was, at least for the moment, to be replaced by war with the Scots. Unexpectedly the government's strategic dilemma had been resolved.

Before any army could be put in the field, major problems of finance

---

[30] Vienne landed in Scotland at about the beginning of June: WC, 120.

[31] Rot. Scot., ii, 51, 59; A. Grant, 'The Otterburn War from the Scottish Point of View', War and Border Societies in the Middle Ages, ed. A. Tuck and A. Goodman (London, 1992), 41.

had to be overcome. The half-subsidy which the commons had conceded in the previous November for collection at midsummer was
clearly intended for use on an expedition to the continent. Whether or
not that condition was written into the schedule – and it probably was
not – that was the understanding on which it had been granted, as the
Westminster chronicler makes clear.[32] If the money were used on a
Scottish expedition, then, it would be in defiance of the commons'
wishes and to the detriment of good relations with that body in future;
prudence alone suggested that an alternative source of finance be
found. The government's solution was to arrange the collection of
scutage – money in lieu of personal military service – by ordering the
issue of a summons of the English feudal levy. On 4 and 13 June 1385
the writs of summons were sent out, and shortly afterwards a clerk was
ordered to prepare lists of fees for the whole country, so that rear vassals
could be assessed for liability.[33] But shortly afterwards there was a
change of plan. The proposed scutage was abandoned, and the list of
fees was never drawn up. What had gone on behind the scenes is
unclear, but it is likely that there was a crisis provoked by opposition to
the proposed levy. The government quickly backtracked, and in the
session of parliament which met the following November Richard
was asked to confirm that he would never impose a scutage for the
expedition.[34] The sole legacy of the ill-fated scheme was thus the feudal
summons itself, the last such to be issued in England in the middle
ages.

Though it was by this time an archaism, the summons probably had
the beneficial effect of producing a higher turnout than usual by the
tenants-in-chief. The army which mustered with Richard at Newcastle
upon Tyne at the end of July was probably the largest raised on British
soil in the fourteenth century: it numbered some 14,000 men and
included virtually all the magnates and bannerets. As was common in
the middle ages, it advanced in three 'battles': vanguard, middle ward
and rearguard, the main body being covered by wings on both sides.
Lancaster with his brother Gloucester as constable led the van, while
the king and most of the earls were in the main body, and the earls of
Northumberland and Devon in the rear.[35] The plan of campaign was

---

[32] WC, 102.

[33] J.J.N. Palmer, 'The Last Summons of the Feudal Army in England, 1385', EHR,
lxxxiii (1968), 771–5. Palmer's arguments have been challenged by N.B. Lewis,
'The Feudal Summons of 1385', ibid., c (1985), 729–43. Palmer offers a convincing reply: ibid., 743–6.

[34] RP, iii, 213.

[35] For the composition and organization of the army, see N.B. Lewis, 'The Last
Medieval Summons of the English Feudal Levy, 13 June 1385', EHR, lxxiii (1958),
1–26, and Ramsay, Genesis of Lancaster, 223–4.

the traditional one employed by the English in Scotland: to draw their adversaries into battle at the earliest opportunity and to crush them by sheer weight of numbers. But as so often in the past, it misfired. The Scots, seeing the trap laid for them, refused to be drawn. Retreating before the enemy advance they melted into the hills, stripping the countryside of all food as they did so. The English as a result had no enemy to fight and no food to eat. Increasingly hungry and frustrated, they took what revenge they could. In Tweeddale they pillaged and fired the abbeys of Dryburgh and Melrose on the ground that their monks were of the Clementist obedience, and in the lowlands they did the same to Newbattle Abbey.[36] But by the time that they reached Edinburgh, which they did on 11 August, they were developing doubts about the wisdom of the entire enterprise. They found the Scottish capital empty and deserted, and their food supplies were short. There were arguments among the commanders about strategy. News had been received that Vienne and the Scots were heading south through Cumberland and the western march. According to Froissart, Gaunt and his brothers suggested heading south to intercept the force.[37] According to the dubious report of the Monk of Westminster, Gaunt suggested advancing deeper into Scotland.[38] The decision was eventually made to withdraw. On or around 17 August the English left Edinburgh, and by 20 August Richard and his retinue had reached Newcastle.[39] A fortnight later the king was at Westminster giving thanks to St Edward for his safe return.[40]

The diversion to the north of so large a part of the nation's strength had left southern England dangerously vulnerable to a descent by the French. The truces had expired; an armada was gathered in the harbour at Sluys; and since the dispersal of the Channel fleet on 31 July the southern coastline was virtually defenceless. Had the French chosen to mount a landing then they would have encountered little or no active resistance. Yet in the event, and to the government's surprise, no landing was attempted. For this the English had their former allies in Ghent to thank. In an endeavour to break through the French blockade of their city the Ghentois had launched an attack on the port of Damme

---

[36] WC, 126–30, offers the fullest account of the campaign.

[37] Froissart, ii, 53–5.

[38] WC, 128–30. The monk's account of these events is clearly based on the written account of an eyewitness or participant (ibid., xliv). It is evident from the report that the eyewitness was hostile to Gaunt and sought to misrepresent him or to present his advice in the worst possible light. Froissart's account of these discussions is to be preferred.

[39] WC, 130, says that they left Edinburgh on 20 August, but by that date they were at Newcastle (C81/1346/20, where Nottingham is clearly a scribal error for Newcastle).

[40] WC, 132.

and had succeeded in taking it. This was a coup which threatened the French hold on the Flemish coastline, and it had to be reversed before any invasion of England could be attempted.[41] So the mighty host which had been gathering at Sluys was diverted to re-take the town. A swift outcome to the siege had been expected but the Ghentois put up unexpectedly stiff resistance, and by the time that they had evacuated the place – which they did at the end of August – it was too late to attempt a crossing to England. The invasion was called off. Though the fleet remained in readiness for an attempt again the following year, for the moment the English had been given a respite.

The summer's disappointments in the field, the crisis over the attempted levy of scutage, and the growing concern over the cost of the royal household and the king's choice of counsellors all came together to make the parliament which met a couple of months later in October the stormiest that Richard and his ministers had yet faced. The chancellor was keen to obtain an early grant of taxation to ease the government's debts, but the commons were in no mood to oblige him. Resentment was running high in the commons against the king's profligacy – particularly against his mass creation of knights and earls on entering Scotland[42] – and there was concern to ensure that the proposed scutage was killed once and for all. Before considering supply, the commons petitioned the king for enactment of a major body of reforms. The purpose of these was to restrict the king's right of patronage and to ensure the application of crown resources to the common good. Among other measures Richard was urged to put a stop to grants from the royal revenues for the next twelve months and to cease granting hundreds and wapentakes to private individuals, so reducing the sheriff's ability to meet his county farm (or dues) in full. In addition, he was asked to agree to an annual review of the household by the three officers of state and to publish the names of his officers for the year ahead.[43] By a separate proposal a commission was established to enquire into the 'estate' of the king and the kingdom – in other words, into the management of the royal revenues. The ordinance which the commission drew up proposed some sweeping changes: that sheriffs

---

[41] WC, 124–6, 132. For the background, see Vaughan, *Philip the Bold*, 35–6.

[42] For these creations, see above, 116. The titles awarded to Burley and Neville were never confirmed.

[43] RP, iii, 213, 210–11, 213. WC, 146, characterizes the commons' petitions as asking the king to 'revoke grants made imprudently to others out of the possessions of the crown'. This language is highly reminiscent of the language used in the campaign for resumption under Edward II, for which, see Harriss, *King, Parliament and Public Finance*, ch. vii.

and escheators should be appointed not in response to private solicitation but on the advice of the great council; that wardships and marriages should be granted only after their value had been ascertained; that farms from alien priories should be fixed by councillors and the officers of state; and that collectors of the great and lesser customs should be drawn from 'good and loyal people'.[44] These were proposals on which lords and commons were agreed. Overall they represented the most comprehensive reform programme of the reign to date.

Richard's reaction to the commons' petitions was testy. He disliked criticism and resented challenges to his exercise of the prerogative. A public display of hostility tended to lessen rather than increase his willingness to compromise – as the defiant elevation of de Vere to a marquessate shortly before the end of the session so clearly showed.[45] Yet compromise of a sort was essential if a crisis were to be averted. Richard thus assented to some of the petitions while reserving his position on others. He agreed to the ordinance on financial reform and the proposed moratorium on grants, but said that he would take the advice of his council concerning the granting of hundreds.[46] These replies were sufficiently conciliatory to allow the commons to make him a grant of taxation, and a generous subsidy was approved of one and a half fifteenth and tenths – though the condition was attached that the money was to be spent on 'wars to come' and not wars past: the commons wanted no part in shouldering the cost of the Scottish expedition.[47]

How far, if at all, they were justified in giving the king their trust only time would tell. Earlier reforming schemes had foundered on the rock of royal inaction, and so might this one. If Richard did not like what was proposed, he could simply ignore it: he was not obliged to comply, because he did not consider himself bound by promises made to his subjects. It must have been apparent to the commons that the year ahead would constitute a vital test of his kingship. By the time that parliament was likely to meet again, in the following autumn, the outcome of that test would be known.

[44] The ordinance is printed by J.J.N. Palmer, 'The Impeachment of Michael de la Pole in 1386', *BIHR*, xlii (1969), 100–1.
[45] De Vere was created marquess of Dublin on 1 December: *CP*, iv, 473.
[46] *RP*, iii, 213, 210–11.
[47] Ibid., 204.

Chapter 8

HUMILIATION AND CONSTRAINT, 1386–7

On 14 August 1385 at Aljubarrota in Portugal a battle was fought which had far-reaching effects on England's relations with the peninsula. On one side was a Portuguese force of some 7,000 men and, on the other, a Castilian host of perhaps twice that number. The Castilians, under the command of the Trastamaran king, Juan, were heading south from the Montego valley, the traditional invasion route from the east, to encircle and invest the city of Lisbon. Near Leiria they were met by the Portuguese under their newly elected king, Joao of Aviz. Both kings wanted to delay an engagement until the following day. However, as evening approached, a section of the Castilian force prematurely attacked the Portuguese baggage train, and before long the greater part of the two armies had become involved. Details of the fighting, which lasted for about two hours, are obscure, and the chroniclers' accounts are conflicting. But the outcome of the engagement was as clear as it was unexpected. The Portuguese won a resounding victory.[1]

Aljubarrota was a battle doubly significant in the history of the Iberian kingdoms. In the first place, it delivered Portugal from the threat of annexation by Castile which had hung over it for the previous two years. And secondly, it dealt a shattering blow to the power and prestige of the Castilian military elite. According to the Westminster chronicler, Castilian losses in the battle totalled 7,500 men.[2] If the casualty rate was of even remotely this order, there can be little doubt that the Castilian kingdom suffered a blow from which it would take years if not decades to recover.

The outcome of Aljubarrota had major implications for England's relations with Castile. For some years John of Gaunt, who had a claim to the Castilian throne through his wife, had harboured the ambition of leading an expedition against the Castilians to substantiate his title. He had urged the sending of an expedition in the parliaments of May and October 1382, but each time the commons had rejected the idea as

---

[1] Russell, *English Intervention*, 378–99, gives the best account of the battle.

[2] *WC*, 132, clearly drawing on a Portuguese source. Joao himself claimed that some 2,500 Castilian men-at-arms were killed (Russell, *English Intervention*, 396). This would suggest that the Westminster writer's overall figure is broadly correct.

unrealistic.[3] In the wake of the Portuguese triumph over Castile, the objections appeared less weighty. Castilian military strength lay broken, and there seemed a reasonable chance that the duke could, at best, topple King Juan or, at worst, weaken his alliance with France. As a result, the so-called 'chemin d'Espaigne' came to be viewed far more sympathetically. Earlier reservations about the feasibility of the scheme were laid aside and Lancaster found himself the beneficiary of a major shift of opinion in his favour.

News of the Portuguese victory reached England shortly before the end of August. The timing could hardly have been better from Lancaster's point of view because parliament was due to meet in a few weeks, and he could seek its approval for a new expedition. In late November, following settlement of the commons' complaints, he put forward a proposal for an expedition and spoke eloquently on its behalf. On this occasion he encountered no opposition. Virtually unanimous assent was given to his plans and shortly afterwards a generous subsidy was made available which, though not entirely for his use, the duke was able to draw on to a substantial degree. By about 12 January the duke's retainer and confidant Sir William Parr had been sent to Portugal to inform the victorious Joao of what had been decided.[4]

Early in the new year preparation of the great expedition began in earnest. The duke went on a month-long tour of his estates to organize recruitment, and from 12 January a steady flow of protections was issued in favour of those going with him.[5] The leaders of the force were all men with Lancastrian connections. The constable was Sir John Holand, Richard's half-brother and the duke's son-in-law, and the marshals were Sir Thomas Morieux, another son-in-law, and Sir Richard Burley, one of his retainers.[6] The Lancastrian character of the host was reinforced by the large household contingent that went with it. Chaplains, minstrels, painters and embroiderers were included, to allow the duke to establish the semblance of a court when he arrived; and even Juan Gutierrez, the duke's Castilian secretary, was present with a few staff to serve as the nucleus of a Castilian chancery on arrival. Nothing was spared in the effort to make Gaunt appear a convincing Pretender. Yet at the same time, significantly, allowance was made for the

---

[3] See above, 99.

[4] *RP*, iii, 204; *WC*, 142. For Parr, see Russell, *English Intervention*, 403.

[5] Russell, *English Intervention*, 406.

[6] Ibid. Holand found service with Lancaster a convenient escape from the ignominy he had incurred by his murder of Ralph Stafford (for which see above, 120). He married the duke's daughter Elizabeth on 24 June at or near Plymouth, shortly before embarking (see below, 243).

possibility that he might ultimately fail. Gaunt took with him his daughters Philippa and Catalina in the event that he might find it necessary to bargain away his claims in return for a suitable indemnity and the offer of a marriage alliance. While publicly he expressed hopes of victory, privately Gaunt did not rule out the possibility of defeat.

While these military and logistical preparations were being made, so too were those in the diplomatic field. At a ceremony in St Paul's on 18 February Pope Urban's authority to Gaunt to conduct a crusade against the Castilian schismatics was made public, and certain clerks, including Gutierrez and Walter Diss, his confessor, were charged with promoting the expedition as a crusade in England, Gascony and the peninsular kingdoms.[7] In April the bulls themselves, now three years old, were published, and offerings were invited for the benefit of the Lancastrian treasury. At the same time negotiations were opened with Portugal for a naval agreement and treaty of alliance. Parr had first raised such a possibility in January, when he had asked the Portuguese king for a squadron of galleys to escort the expeditionary force to the peninsula. Later, in the spring, formal negotiations between the two kingdoms were opened, and by April a draft treaty had been agreed. Its terms, recited in Richard's presence at Windsor on 9 May and ratified at Westminster a week later, were fairly general. The two kings bound themselves in a perpetual alliance, and each promised to help the other to deal with any political or military movement designed to overthrow the existing dynasty. Attention was paid to the many commercial ties which linked the two realms: the subjects of both crowns were granted the right to trade in either country on the terms enjoyed by the nationals of that country, and freedom of travel for citizens of every rank or status was guaranteed by each country to the nationals of the other.[8] The treaty bore powerful witness to the strength of Anglo-Portuguese friendship and goodwill; but because it initiated what was to be England's oldest formal alliance, it has been invested subsequently with a significance which it almost certainly never possessed. At the time it is likely that it was regarded as less important than the other document which was recited on the same day – the naval agreement between the two kingdoms. The terms of this agreement were simple. In return for the military aid which Gaunt's expedition was construed as giving them, the Portuguese promised to provide ten large galleys to serve with the English for six months at Portuguese expense.[9] To the English this assistance was a godsend. The French were rebuilding their armada at Sluys, and it was feared that a major landing would be attempted later

---

[7] The Castilians supported the antipope.
[8] *Foed.*, vii, 515–21.
[9] Ibid., 521–3.

in the year. In their eyes the treaty of alliance was a small price to pay for the naval assistance they so badly needed. Gaunt himself appears to have valued the alliance chiefly for the safety net that it provided. When he invaded Spain he did so alone and not in company with the Portuguese, because he did not want to offend Castilian susceptibilities by being seen to be in league with their enemies. Only later, after he had suffered disappointments in the field, did he decide to take advantage of the alliance and join forces with King Joao.

By the time that the diplomatic formalities were being concluded at Westminster Gaunt had left court for the west country to supervise the assembly of his great host at Plymouth. The greater part of his force had by now mustered, and it only remained to assemble sufficient shipping to transport them. Orders for the arrest of vessels had gone out as early as 25 February, and it was anticipated that the fleet of transports would be ready by April. As the weeks passed, however, it became clear that there was no possibility of an April deadline being met. On 20 April, in response to a plea from the duke, orders were issued in the king's name for every available craft in the realm to be impressed and sent westwards to Plymouth. From late April vessels began to congregate from the Bristol Channel and the east coast ports. On 13 June ten vessels were hired in Kampen in Holland and another one in the Hanseatic port of Danzig. By 17 or 18 June the fleet was at last virtually complete. Lancaster now awaited only the arrival of the squadron of Portuguese galleys which Parr had requested in January and which was to accompany the fleet on its passage to the peninsula. The squadron appears to have arrived by the end of the month. So in the first week of July the assembled retinues began to embark. Duke John with Dona Constanza his wife, his three daughters and their attendants went aboard the flagship. On the day before departure Henry of Derby, the duke's son – who was left behind to look after the family estates – dined on board with his father and bade him farewell.[10] On 9 July the fleet weighed anchor and set sail. Gaunt was not to see England again until November 1389.[11]

The departure of Gaunt had repercussions for both English domestic affairs and foreign relations. In home affairs the principal effect was to leave a void at the centre of politics. For over a decade Gaunt had been the dominant figure in politics after the king. He had steered the court

[10] KC, 340.
[11] Russell, *English Intervention*, 406–17; J. Sherborne, 'The Defence of the Realm and the Impeachment of Michael de la Pole in 1386', *Politics and Crisis in Fourteenth Century England*, ed. J. Taylor and W. Childs (Gloucester, 1990), repr. in his *War, Politics and Culture in Fourteenth-Century England*, 101–2.

through the crises of Edward's last years, and had been a steadying influence in the early years of his successor. When differences had arisen between the king and his critics, as they had, for example, with Arundel in 1383, he had been quick to smooth over them. Contrary to the opinion of the younger and more irresponsible courtiers, he was a consistent upholder of the prerogative, and throughout the reign he deployed the weight of the Lancastrian inheritance in support of the crown. The duke's departure was undoubtedly a major blow to the king. The latter's position *vis-à-vis* his critics was undermined, and he was deprived of the services of the one magnate who could impose restraint on his enemies. The long crisis from 1386 to 1388, beginning with the impeachment of de la Pole and the attack on the court and culminating in the Appellant takeover, was in a sense the by-product of the duke's prolonged absence.

Abroad the effects of Gaunt's departure were no less significant. The immediate result was a revival of French plans for a major attack on the English south coast. At the beginning of the year such a prospect had seemed unlikely. Contact between the two courts had been resumed, thanks to the mediation of King Leo of Armenia, and the French showed an interest in coming to terms: with Ghent subdued, they were in a strong position and had more to gain from an end to the war than from its continuance. Negotiations were quickly opened, and there was talk of a personal meeting between Richard and Charles VI. But then the news of Gaunt's expedition was received. The French insisted that the duke abandon his plan because Castile was an ally of theirs, and the English, unsurprisingly, refused. In March negotiations broke down, and Charles VI and his advisers returned to Paris. Almost immediately the French resumed their military build-up.[12]

The aim of the French commanders appears to have been largely the same as in the previous year – to deal the English a blow so devastating that they would be forced to capitulate to the French on the latter's terms. To this end a mighty armada was built up in the Zwin estuary in readiness for a crossing of the Channel in the middle or later part of the summer. In the previous year the strategy had come to nothing because the French hold on Flanders had been too insecure. This time, however, its chances of success seemed much greater. The French host was bigger than before: the duke of Brittany who had previously stood aloof, had thrown in his lot with the French and had provided a force of some 500 men. And the French grip on Flanders was much stronger: Ghent had been subdued, and there was no danger that the invasion could be foiled by an attack in the rear. Preparations for muster and embarkation therefore proceeded relatively unhindered. Throughout

[12] Palmer, *England, France and Christendom*, 67–8.

March, April and early May a series of measures was taken to raise money and to concentrate shipping in the area of the Zwin estuary. There was a temporary pause in activity in late May and June caused by rumours that the duke of Burgundy was ill, but in July the build-up was resumed. Jean de Vienne was ordered to arrest all shipping appropriate 'for the crossing', and vessels were dispatched from Brittany and La Rochelle. By late September the mobilization was approaching its climax. Estimates of the size of the force vary, but a figure of 30,000 seems reasonable. By common consent, it was the largest and finest army that had ever been seen in Europe. Ominously for the English, one writer compared it to the great host which had destroyed ancient Troy. In the summer of 1386 England stood in graver danger of being overwhelmed than at any time since the beginning of the long struggle with France in the 1330s.[13]

The English government was not behindhand in taking measures to counter the threat. Acutely conscious of the weakness in the country's naval strength brought about by Gaunt's demands for shipping, it acted swiftly to ensure the safe-keeping of the sea passages. On 22 February two admirals were appointed, Lord Darcy for the north and Sir Thomas Trivet for the west. Four days later contracts were entered into for a two-phase coastal defence operation. The two admirals were to serve from 26 April with 'une petite armée' of 248 men-at-arms and 250 archers serving in ten vessels 'du guerre' for forty days. Subsequently, from 1 July they were to keep the sea for ninety-one days (that is, July, August and September) with 998 men-at-arms and 1,500 archers in 'une grande armée' of 30 large ships, 12 barges, 12 balingers and 8 victuallers. Orders for the arrest of shipping needed for these expeditions went out on 15 March. The vessels for Trivet's use were to assemble by 28 March and those for Darcy's by three weeks later. These deadlines were much too tight given the demands that Gaunt was also making on shipping, and it was not until May that the required number of vessels was assembled in the Thames. Darcy then set sail for Hull and Trivet for Sandwich. The forces at their command were small, each man having a complement of nine ships, one barge and two balingers. In the first phase of their operations, however, they enjoyed a modicum of success. They captured four Castilian vessels, three of which were sold for £1,255 and the fourth more modestly for £100. They also took an Aragonese tarit and a Castilian ship laden with Aragonese goods in the Zwin estuary. With greater resources they could probably have accomplished a lot more. But by midsummer the government was running into a serious financial crisis, and the idea of 'une grande armée' had to be abandoned. Fresh indentures were sealed with Trivet and Darcy

[13] Ibid., 71–5.

providing for them to serve for another forty days with their force almost unchanged except for the addition of some fifty sailors. The admirals' second voyage was uneventful, and when it drew to a close on or before 31 August English naval activity was effectively ended for the year.[14]

The tailing off of naval activity did nothing to reassure opinion of the government's ability to defend the realm. All through the spring and early summer there were rumours of an imminent descent by the French. In March it was Rye that was thought to be at risk, in April it was Sandwich, Portchester and, surprisingly, Trematon in Cornwall, in May it was Thanet and the Isle of Oxney.[15] Around Rye and Oxney concern was particularly great. On 31 April (sic) the people of that area were ordered to retreat within the walls of Dover, Rye or Sandwich and to remain there for safety.[16] Across the Channel concern was also running high in Calais. It was feared that the French were going to launch an attack on the town and then use it as a base for a descent on England. Reinforcements were thrown into Calais in April and May, and a coastal patrol was organized. The town's garrison scored a minor triumph at sea when they captured vessels carrying a prefabricated wooden castle which was to have been erected to cover the French army's disembarkation on English soil.[17]

The government's response to these alarms was to strengthen the system of coastal defence in England. In May new commissions of array were issued for Kent and Essex, and orders for the repair of the king's castles in South Wales and at Leeds and Portchester, and of the urban defences at Sandwich, Rye, Yarmouth and Lynn. New commissions of array were issued for Suffolk and Nottinghamshire in June, and orders for the repair of castles continued to be issued at a steady rate throughout the summer.[18] At the same time special measures were taken to ensure the adequate defence of the capital. On 2 June the London aldermen were ordered to put their wards in array, and on 13 September all London householders were ordered to lay in food supplies for three months.[19] On 6 September a more drastic measure still was taken. The nobility and leading knights were ordered to rendezvous with the king at Westminster by 30 September. By October nearly 4,500 men were in the king's pay and stationed in positions within a 60-mile

---

[14] Sherborne, 'Defence of the Realm', 104–7.

[15] CPR 1385–9, 123, 134, 140, 160, 174.

[16] Ibid., 175.

[17] E403/510, 10 April; E403/512, 4 May, 30 July. For the prefabricated structure: HA, ii, 147.

[18] CPR 1385–9, 160, 175–7, 181, 190, 196.

[19] Calendar of Letter Books of the City of London. Letter Book H, ed. R.R. Sharpe (London, 1907), 283, 285–6.

radius of the capital.[20] The defence of London was understandably considered a priority by the government. The city's fall would have destroyed its credibility in the country and would have undermined, if not broken, the system of national defence. Along the coastline itself, however, policy appears to have been to give ground if necessary. Froissart describes a scheme whereby units were ordered to lure the enemy inland and then turn on them, cutting off their lines of retreat and destroying their landing craft.[21] It was a sensible scheme designed to conserve national resources, yet it was an implicit admission that a French landing, if attempted in sufficient force, could not be prevented at the beachhead itself.

Richard's own role in shaping this defensive strategy is almost impossible to discern, but it is unlikely to have been great. Kings in the middle ages rarely immersed themselves in the day-to-day details of administration, and Richard was no exception. His main interest in the summer of 1386 appears to have been a project for Robert de Vere to lead an expedition to Ireland. On 23 March he had granted de Vere the ransom of Jean de Blois, claimant to the duchy of Brittany, to support 500 men-at-arms and 1,000 archers in Ireland for two years after his arrival there.[22] It is not altogether clear whether de Vere intended going to the lordship in person; but, if he did, he soon abandoned the idea and appointed Sir John Stanley, as lieutenant, to go in his place.[23] All the same, in these early summer months he was deeply involved in organizing the force, and he set up headquarters at Bristol, which was the port of embarkation. Richard travelled to Bristol to be in his company, reaching the town on 16 July.[24] He stayed there for about a week before going northwards to Thornbury, Berkeley and Gloucester.[25] But by August the danger of a French invasion had become so acute that he could no longer ignore it. It was widely known that the armada at Sluys was almost complete, and that only the king's late arrival was preventing its sailing. Panic was taking hold of the south-eastern counties, and the people of London, so Walsingham reports, were behaving like frightened hares: some were fleeing the city, while others were pulling down houses near the walls, the better to resist the enemy.[26] The council

---

[20] E403/512, 6 Sept.

[21] Froissart, ii, 179.

[22] *CPR 1385–9*, 123, 132. For discussion, see M. Jones, 'The Ransom of Jean de Bretagne, Count of Penthièvre: an Aspect of English Foreign Policy, 1386–8', *BIHR*, xlv (1972), 7–26. See also, below, ch. 12.

[23] *CPR 1385–9*, 125.

[24] C81/1352/34.

[25] See Appendix.

[26] *HA*, ii, 145–6. Even monastic landowners – and ones well inland – were involved in the defensive effort. The chapter of Westminster agreed that Abbot Litlington, who was by now at least seventy-five, and two of the monks, John Canterbury and

thought of putting another fleet to sea, but was hampered by lack of money. There was so little cash left that it proved impossible even to provide mariners for the vessels that Gaunt had sent back from Spain – and which as a result had to stand idle. Without the urgent arrival of more money the whole defensive effort would collapse. On 8 August, therefore, at a council at Osney Abbey, Oxford, attended by the king, the decision was taken to summon a meeting of parliament.[27] In the meantime loans were sought on the security of a future grant of parliamentary taxation. During September all the main lenders were approached – the archbishops and bishops, the magnates and the London merchants; but even so only £733 was raised.[28] In desperation the council had to meet the cost of a coastal defence force by making the counties pay for half of the men mustered and by raising forced loans from the towns to pay for the other half.[29] The dubious legality of the measure added to the unpopularity which the government was already incurring as a result of its seemingly never-ending demands for manpower and money.

For another two months the prospect of invasion hung over the country. According to Froissart, the entire population of the southern counties indulged in a frenetic spending spree in an effort to enjoy their worldly goods before they were stripped of them by the French. But as the period of waiting dragged on, and September turned into October, the tense mood began to dissolve: slowly the realization dawned that the French were not going to invade after all. Unknown to their adversaries the French commanders were running into many of the difficulties that the English themselves had. The limits of taxation had been reached, and resort to borrowing had proved only moderately successful. Little or no cash was available to pay wages, and large numbers of troops were pillaging to support themselves. Strong winds and heavy rain had prevented sailing for well over a month, and with winter approaching conditions could only get worse. Doubts began to grow in the French leadership about the wisdom of the whole enterprise and in November the decision was taken to call it off. For the second time in less than a year England had been spared.[30]

John Burgh, should don armour and make haste to the coast because of the urgency of the situation. Canterbury's armour was later put on sale in London, but because he was so tall it would not fit anyone else, and it remained unsold (WAM, Liber Niger, Book I, fo.87^r).

[27] *RP*, iii, 215; C81/1353/4–13.

[28] Sherborne, 'Defence of the Realm', 108.

[29] *CCR 1385–9*, 187, 193–4.

[30] Froissart, ii, 178; Palmer, *England, France and Christendom*, 76–81; Sherborne, 'Defence of the Realm', 112–13.

When parliament met at Westminster on 1 October, however, the threat of a French descent on the realm was still real. As a matter of urgency the government needed a substantial grant of taxation from the commons to enable it to honour its many commitments. The question was whether the commons would be willing to grant one. Only a year previously they had made a grant of a subsidy and a half, part of which had been appropriated to the needs of defence, and they could be expected to argue that this should have been sufficient. A powerful statement of the government's case would be needed if they were to lay aside their reservations. But Chancellor de la Pole signally failed to provide this. Instead of addressing the issues worrying the commons, he dwelt fancifully on the chimera of a royally led expedition: the king, he said, had resolved to cross the Channel in person; he had been hurt by the criticism that he lacked the will to fight and was determined to vindicate his rights in the kingdom of France; to do this, however, he was obliged to ask his subjects for a 'sufficient aid' (i.e. a tax).[31] The chancellor did not say how much he was hoping for, since this was generally left to the commons to settle in association with the ministers, but he let slip the figure of no less than four fifteenths and tenths.[32] Immediately, according to Knighton, there was uproar.[33] Never before had such a sum been demanded of parliament. As a result of either folly or inadvertence de la Pole had misjudged the mood of his audience and had provoked what was to be the worst political crisis of the reign to date.

Given its importance, it is to be regretted that the 'Wonderful Parliament', as it was later known, is not better documented. The official record on the parliament roll is one of the shortest of the reign; and the chroniclers' accounts are generally either brief or inaccurate. The most useful surviving narrative is that of the Leicester chronicler, Henry Knighton, which draws on a contemporary pamphlet or tract. From this a remarkable picture emerges of the confrontation that took place between the king and his parliamentary critics.[34] The opening move was made by the latter. As soon as de la Pole made known his demand for taxation, the lords and commons together called for his dismissal – adding that they had 'business to do with him which they could not transact so long as he remained in office': a veiled reference to impeachment. Richard, of course, refused to give way. Furious at the presumption of his subjects, he retorted that he would not dismiss so

---

[31] *RP*, iii, 215.

[32] A double fifteenth and tenth on moveable property would normally be considered the limit.

[33] *KC*, 354.

[34] Ibid., 354-62. Professor Martin suggests that Knighton's source may have been Gloucester: ibid., lxviii-lxix.

much as a kitchen scullion from office at their request. He ordered
them to return to their business and promptly withdrew from Westminster to Eltham. The members of the two houses stood their ground.
They informed Richard that they would not and could not attend to
normal business until he returned to Westminster and removed
Michael de la Pole from office. The king's response was to ask for a
delegation of forty of the most experienced of their number to come
and discuss their demands with him. The commons, however, feared
that the members of the delegation might be arrested, and the duke of
Gloucester and Bishop Arundel went on their behalf instead. After
presenting themselves, the two lords spoke eloquently, if fictitiously, to
the king of his duties. According to an ancient statute, they said, the
king was bound to summon parliament once a year so that errors in
government might be righted, justice be offered to the poor and the
public burdens be more easily borne; since at the present time the
public burdens were weighing particularly heavily, it seemed to them
only proper that parliament should have the right to enquire how and
by whom the taxpayers' money was spent. For good measure they added
that they had with them another statute, according to which parliament
was able to dissolve itself if the king absented himself without reason for
longer than forty days. These were outrageous remarks. Richard replied
that if they were going to talk of resistance then he could think of no
better response than to call on the assistance of his cousin, the king of
France. To this Gloucester and Arundel reacted with horror. The king
of France, they said, was his greatest enemy; he would advise him to his
ruin. Richard ought to recall the labours of his father and grandfather
in fighting the French and recovering the domains which belonged to
them by right. At the present time, however, such labours were all but
impossible: the realm was impoverished, the magnates saddened and
the whole populace weakened. These ills all sprang from the evil
counsellors who surrounded the king. By way of conclusion they urged
the king to remember yet another statute of old – one which said that
if the king alienated himself from his people and refused to be governed by the advice of his lords, then the people were entitled to
depose him. This unmistakable reference to the fate of Edward II
evidently frightened Richard. He returned to Westminster forthwith
and on 23 October dismissed the offending ministers. On the next
day Bishop Arundel became chancellor and John Gilbert, bishop of
Hereford, treasurer.

  With de la Pole now released from office the commons were free to
go ahead with proceedings for impeachment: that is, prosecution. The
articles appear to have been drawn up fairly quickly. Three (numbers 1,
4, 5) taxed him with peculation in office: namely, that he had purchased lands and other sources of royal income contrary to his oath and
greatly in excess of his deserts; that he had obtained royal confirmation

of the purchase from Tideman of Limburg of an annuity which Tideman had forfeited; and that he had procured a grant of the revenues of St Anthony's Hospital which should have been taken by the crown. Another four articles (2, 3, 6 and 7) charged him with dereliction of duty in office: that he had suppressed the report of the nine lords appointed in the previous parliament to make recommendations for the better government of the realm; that the tax granted in the previous parliament had been spent otherwise than directed with the result that the coast was ill defended; that Ghent had been lost; and that he had allowed a charter conceding franchises to Dover castle to be sealed without adequate authorization.[35] De la Pole's replies to these charges fell under two main headings. To the charges of peculation he said, in effect, that his accusers were expecting a higher standard of morality of him than they expected of other officers of the crown, and that it was wrong of them to single him out; while to the charges of dereliction of duty he said that he alone was not responsible: his fellow counsellors were equally to blame. The lords accepted his arguments up to a point. They agreed that it was wrong to hold him solely responsible for policies on which the council as a whole was agreed. But they found him guilty on the charges of peculation. Richard was obliged to imprison him, pending payment of a fine for his 'defautes et mesprisions'; and it appears that he was held in custody at Corfe castle. By Christmas, however, he was free again, and according to Walsingham he joined Richard for the seasonal festivities at Windsor.[36] He was in Richard's company for the greater part of the year that followed.

The bare record of de la Pole's impeachment – and the bare record is all that the parliament roll affords – leaves a number of vital questions about the case unanswered. Probably the most important of these concerns the role of the commons. Were the commons responsible for launching the attack on de la Pole on their own initiative? Or were they acting largely as proxies for a group of the chancellor's enemies in the lords? It is impossible to give a definite answer to these questions. Certainly the commons had the experience and self-confidence to allow them to act independently: only ten years before in the Good Parliament, using the same weapon of impeachment, they had launched the most devastating assault on a government for nearly forty years. What is in doubt is whether in 1386 they had the leaders to direct them. Their success in 1376 had owed much to the direction of Sir Peter de la Mare, knight of the shire for Herefordshire, whom they had chosen to serve in the office of Speaker. In 1386 no comparable figure came to the fore

---

[35] *RP*, iii, 216–20. For discussion, see J.S. Roskell, *The Impeachment of Michael de la Pole, Earl of Suffolk, in 1386* (Manchester, 1984).

[36] *HA*, ii, 149.

and no Speaker was chosen. It is possible that this left them more
dependent than in the Good Parliament on the leadership of the
magnates. At key points of the crisis they took the precaution of liaising
with the lords. When they issued their call for Michael de la Pole's
dismissal, they did so jointly with the lords; as they did when they
insisted to Richard that he return to Westminster from Eltham. Such
close liaison makes it difficult to distinguish the roles of the two houses
during the crisis. But there is no reason to doubt that responsibility for
impeaching de la Pole was the commons' own: impeachment by its very
nature lay in a prosecution brought by a lower tribunal before a higher.
But with the gradual widening of the crisis in October it is likely that the
leading role came to be assumed by a faction of the nobility. There were
senior figures in the upper house like Gloucester and the two Arundels
who had long voiced their disapproval of the king and who had personal differences with those who surrounded him.[37] They would hardly
have refrained from pressing home their attack when the crisis in
parliament gave them the opportunity to do so.

Coupled with the issue of the commons' role in the crisis is the
equally vexed one of their aims and objectives. It has generally been
assumed that the overthrow of de la Pole was their overriding object
from the outset: Knighton's narrative, which places their call for the
chancellor's dismissal near the start, certainly supports such a view. But
according to a chronicle fragment preserved in Sir Walter Scott's
edition of Somers Tracts, there was initially a move to give priority to an
attack on Robert de Vere.[38] Some of the graver and more experienced
nobility, the narrative says, urged the case for prosecuting de Vere on
account of his overweening influence with the king. At meetings
between the nobility and gentry there was considerable support for this
course of action, but it was eventually rejected on the grounds that de
la Pole, as chancellor, was the easier man to challenge and to bring
down. It is difficult to know what to make of this account. It survives
only in a later transcript, and this may be a forgery. On the other hand,
it carries a ring of verisimilitude. There can be little doubt that at the
beginning of the session there would have been lengthy discussions
about tactics, and almost certainly the impeachment of de Vere was one
of the options considered. Neither the lords nor the commons would
have come along with a strategy already worked out; they would have
liaised with each other on arriving, subsequently adjusting their tactics
in response to changes in the parliamentary situation. What the Somers
fragment probably records is a stage in the negotiations between

---

[37] For Gloucester's personal grievances against the king and Robert de Vere, see
below, 178–9.

[38] Somers Tracts, ed. W. Scott (2nd edn, London, 1809), i, 15–16. For discussion,
see Taylor, English Historical Literature, 272–3.

them on how to mount a successful attack on the government and its policies.

That it was eventually decided to prosecute de la Pole can hardly occasion any surprise, however. By October 1386 the chancellor was totally discredited in the eyes of the commons. His foreign policy had been exposed as a failure by the recent invasion threat, and there was accumulating evidence of his utter disregard for the commons' wish for financial reform. This was a matter of particular concern to the lower house. In the parliament of 1385 a series of reforms had been imposed on the king to ensure the better supervision of the fiscal and other revenues of the crown. It was laid down that advice was to be sought before escheats and wardships were granted out; and a committee was appointed to survey the king's estate and to diminish his expenses.[39] Responsibility for implementing the measures lay with de la Pole as chancellor. Twelve months later, however, it was apparent that virtually nothing had been done.[40] This is why the charge of dereliction of duty figured so prominently in the articles of impeachment (numbers 2, 3, 6 and 7). Doubtless de la Pole was right to argue that he alone could not be held responsible. Almost certainly he was acting on orders from his royal master. But his royal master could not be prosecuted in parliament, whereas he could. In this sense the attack on him was surely exemplary rather than personal: it was the medium through which Richard himself was to be reminded of his responsibilities and brought to terms with the limitations of his own position.

The condemnation of de la Pole brought to an end the first and most dramatic phase of the Wonderful Parliament. The second phase, which opened in mid-November, saw further important concessions made to the commons. On 19 November at their behest a 'great and continual council' with comprehensive powers of government was appointed to hold office for a year. The principal, indeed the overriding, task of the council was to implement the financial reforms that de la Pole and his master had earlier circumvented. To this end it was authorized to survey the estate and condition of the household, to examine all revenue, from whatever source it originated, to look into the cost and expense of defending the realm and to investigate all alienations of land that had been made in the ten years since the coronation. To secure the evidence that it needed, it was empowered to enter the king's household and to compel records and muniments to be produced. Once enquiry had been carried out, it was then authorized to make what reforms it saw fit and to ensure officials' compliance with them.[41]

---

[39] See above, 146-7.

[40] Palmer, 'The Impeachment of Michael de la Pole', 96-101; idem, 'The Parliament of 1385', 477-89.

[41] The letters patent of 19 November appointing the commission are copied in

The powers granted to the commission were far-reaching and virtually without precedent in the fourteenth century. The only consolation for the king was that they were of limited duration. Yet despite their triumph the commons were still not entirely satisfied. Towards the close of the session they launched a renewed assault on the powers of the crown. In an enrolled petition they asked that the three principal officers of state and the steward of the household should be appointed publicly in parliament; that the new council should continue in being, once the twelve months had expired, until the next parliament met; and that both officers and councillors, in order to have access to the records and accounts they needed, should remain in London during their term of office. The key demand here was for the renewal of the commission's life. The commons were concerned not only to lengthen the period of virtual delegation of royal authority but also to overcome any reluctance on the king's part to reassemble parliament. Understandably they encountered strong opposition from the king. Richard rejected outright the demand for an extension of the council's term. The other requests he sidestepped: on appointments to the stewardship he said that he would take the advice of his council, while on the council's place of operation he said nothing at all.[42] Clearly he was shaken by the prolonged attack on his authority, and at the end of the session 'with his own mouth' he made a personal protestation. He disavowed all that had occurred that might be to his prejudice and that of the crown, and added that his prerogative and 'the liberties of the crown' should be preserved and maintained.[43] But this protestation was no more than a hollow gesture of defiance. It availed Richard nothing. By November the conciliar commission was in control of virtually all the organs of government.

The lords who made up the new council were drawn from all parts of the political spectrum. A few of them – but only a few – were friends of the king: notably Alexander Neville, archbishop of York, and Nicholas Morice, abbot of Waltham.[44] Most of the rest were in varying degrees sympathetic with the opposition. William Courtenay, the archbishop of Canterbury, though now reconciled with the king, had clashed with him on several occasions about his reliance on unsound counsel. Two

---

WC, 166–74. They were subsequently enacted as a statute in the form in which they were issued to the sheriffs on 1 December (SR, ii, 39–43). For the significance of their publication as a statute, see D. Clementi, 'Richard II's Ninth Question to the Judges, 1387', EHR, lxxxvi (1971), 96–113.

[42] RP, iii, 221–2.

[43] Ibid., 224.

[44] For Neville, see R.G. Davies, 'Alexander Neville, Archbishop of York, 1374–1388', YAJ, xlvii (1975), 87–101, and below, 184–5. For grants and favours to Abbot Morice, see CPR 1377–81, 84, 353, 438–9. Waltham was an abbey of royal foundation.

other senior prelates, Wykeham of Winchester and Brantingham of Exeter, had been associated with the opposition to Gaunt in the 1370s and had an 'anti-curial aura' about them as a result of their appointment to the (abortive) 1385 commission.[45] Richard, Lord Scrope, the former chancellor, had earned Richard's enmity for his criticism of his profligacy in 1382 and had been rewarded with dismissal for his pains.[46] Thomas of Woodstock, duke of Gloucester, and the two Arundels, Bishop Thomas and Earl Richard, had, of course, been instrumental in foisting the council on Richard in the first place. That left only Edmund of Langley, duke of York, the king's uncle, and two other lords, John Lord Cobham, and Sir John Devereux. Langley was a political lightweight who went along with whoever happened to be in control at court. Devereux and Cobham, however, were men who in other circumstances might be expected to have taken Richard's side. Devereux was an erstwhile retainer of the Black Prince whom he had followed on numerous campaigns in the 1360s and early-1370s, and Cobham a magnate with court connections who had a long record of service in the French wars and had more recently been involved in the peace negotiations with France.[47] The probable cause of these two men's disaffection lay in Richard's attempts to establish Simon Burley and Robert de Vere in influential positions in their own county of Kent. De Vere had been given the constableship of Queenborough in March 1385; Burley had been appointed constable of Dover in 1384 and had also been endowed with the estates of the former Leybourne inheritance.[48] The intrusion of these courtiers, neither of whom had a previous stake in the county, gave offence to established proprietors like Cobham and Devereux and constituted a threat to their own local pre-eminence.[49] Burley's rise seemed particularly threatening. From 1384, when he took over at Dover, Burley was regularly appointed a justice of the peace and commissioner of array for Kent. In June 1386, only months before the

[45] WC, 116. Tuck, *Richard II and the Nobility*, 106–7, offers a good discussion. The quotation is ibid., 106.

[46] See above, 111.

[47] For Devereux's career, see CP, iv, 296–9; and for Cobham's, ibid., iii, 344–5; WC, 24.

[48] CPR 1381–5, 542. For Burley, see above, 113–16.

[49] Cobham had a stronger claim to respect as a county landowner than Devereux; he came of an old and distinguished family with wide estates in north Kent (*Feud. Aids*, iii, 41, 42, 49, 51; T. May, 'The Cobham Family in the Administration of England, 1200–1400', *Arch. Cant.*, lxxxii (1967), 1–31), whereas Devereux only had a stake in the county by right of his wife, Margaret, daughter of John de Vere, earl of Oxford, and widow of Sir Nicholas de Lovein of Penshurst (CP, iv, 298). Devereux was granted a licence to crenellate Penshurst in 1392 (CPR 1391–6, 164). For the background to Kent politics at this time, see B. Webster, 'The Community of Kent in the Reign of Richard II', *Arch. Cant.*, xcix (1984), 217–29.

Wonderful Parliament opened, he had been named as the sole member of the county quorum (the number having previously been nine).[50] Over the summer he had taken a number of high-handed measures to protect the coastline in the event of French attack. He had had the districts of Oxney and Thanet cleared and their inhabitants moved to nearby towns; and he had ordered Becket's relics to be transferred from Canterbury to safe-keeping in Dover castle (a move which the monks, sorely offended, in the end successfully thwarted).[51] Such cavalier disregard for local susceptibilities was unlikely to endear Burley to the people of Kent. Their reaction was to close ranks against him and make him a virtual outcast in his adopted county.[52] Richard's ill-advised attempt to increase his support in the south-east had badly misfired. Instead of strengthening his power base, it had weakened it, fragmenting local society and losing him the support of men who should have been his friends. The defection of Cobham and Devereux was the price that he paid for his folly.

For exactly a year from 19 November 1386 the council of government held office, exercising the powers granted to it by letters patent (and confirmed by statute). The councillors' approach to their work appears to have been brisk and businesslike. Within weeks they were framing a programme to boost the king's revenues and to curb his expenditure. In regard to the former their priority was to maximize the yield from the king's irregular sources of income – feudal incidents and so on. In February groups of commissioners were appointed in each county to assess the true value of lands in royal custody – principally, that is, of wardships and alien priories – and to enquire into the extent of waste and concealment by the escheators who managed them.[53] Associated with this order was a move to impose conditions on those to whom such revenues might be granted. From the spring of 1387 these persons were obliged to enter into recognizances for double the amount of the annual farm, this sum to be levied in the event that the farm was more than a month in arrears.[54] By way of complementing these measures, a

---

[50] *CPR 1381–5*, 348, 590; *1385–9*, 81, 253. See also Roskell, *Impeachment of Michael de la Pole*, 97.

[51] *CPR 1385–9*, 175; *Eulogium*, 358; *William Thorne's Chronicle of St Augustine's Abbey, Canterbury*, 650–4.

[52] Burley is conspicuous by his absence from the groups of Kentish landowners found attesting Cobham family charters in *CCR 1381–5*, *passim*, and BL, Harleian Charters, 48 C41; 48 E35; 48 F15; 54 I32.

[53] *CPR 1385–9*, 317–18, 320.

[54] *CFR 1383–91*, 182–3; *CPR 1388–92*, 24. For discussion, see Given-Wilson, *Royal Household and the King's Affinity*, 118–19.

major effort was put into clearing the backlog of debt in the household. The cash flow to the wardrobe, the household's main financial office, was increased, and some £13,350 was set aside to pay off debts incurred before the 1386-7 accounting period.[55] To prevent a possible build-up of future indebtedness cuts were made in the level of the king's current spending. Wardrobe expenditure was reduced from nearly £17,000 in 1385-6 to only £12,000 in the year of the commission's term of office – a not inconsiderable achievement given the rapid rise in expenditure in previous years.[56] In the area of financial administration the commission went a long way to fulfilling the hopes held out for it by its supporters in parliament.

Measures were also taken by the council to remedy injustices stemming from the misdeeds of those who had benefited from Richard's favour over the years. On 20 March, in response to a petition from the dean and chapter of St Stephen's, Westminster, Sir Simon Burley was ordered to appear before the council to explain his possession of the manors set aside for the performance of Edward III's will.[57] Less powerful now than he had been, Burley came under considerable pressure to surrender the manors, but whether he actually did so is doubtful: the dean and chapter were still petitioning for their recovery in 1388. More successful were the council's efforts to bring his fellow courtier, Robert de Vere, to heel. De Vere had been accused by Philip Courtenay, whom he had replaced in office in Ireland, of harassing him, depriving him of income and plundering his property. The matter was brought before the council, and de Vere was ordered to pay 1,000 marks to Courtenay in compensation. The issue rolls show that the greater part of this sum was paid.[58] There is a possibility that it was in response to grievances like these that ministers decided around this time to make the *sub pena* writ more widely available. The writ had originated in the 1350s as a summons to appear before the council or chancery. Generally it had been issued under the great seal; but from 1386 it was made more widely available under the privy seal. The background to this initiative lay in the growing association between the privy seal and the council, which made the privy seal the regular authority for the council's correspondence. As conciliar jurisdiction gradually widened, it naturally followed that the privy seal *sub pena* writ became the most convenient instrument for bringing cases to that tribunal's attention. By the end of the 1380s

---

[55] But, even so, creditors with tallies who went to the council were to receive only a third of what was owed to them: *CCR 1385-9*, 308.

[56] Given-Wilson, *Royal Household and the King's Affinity*, 118.

[57] *CCR 1385-9*, 222.

[58] Ibid., 232. Payments made to Courtenay in instalments were recorded in E403/519 and E403/521.

the use of such writs, returnable before the council, had become frequent and indeed normal.[59] Though there were later to be complaints about the unfairness of the privy seal procedure, and about the inconvenience that it could cause individuals, its purpose was to assist those who had found it difficult to seek justice under the common law processes.

In the domestic field, then, the councillors had achieved a great deal in which they could take pride. They had reduced the backlog of royal debt and had brought a measure of order to the finances of the household; and they had gone some way to providing remedies for those to whom justice had previously been denied. Their main failure lay in the field of household reform. Here they were hampered by the requirement imposed on them of residency at Westminster. They had no authority to follow the king on his travels around the realm and, as a result, could not gain the access to the household that they needed. They had to be content with influencing the household indirectly through the amount of money that they made available for his use. This was a blunt and unwieldy instrument and one which had distinctly limited effect. There are signs that the king suffered from financial hardship during the year of the council's term of office; but there is no evidence that he responded to that hardship by reducing the size of his establishment.[60]

By the letters which granted them their commission the councillors were only empowered to act in domestic affairs. From the beginning, however, they acted as if they had a more general competence. They took control of the great and the privy seals and directed all correspondence that passed under them; in so doing they arrogated to themselves responsibility for the foreign as well as domestic affairs of the realm. Doubtless this wider competence had been anticipated from the start. Resentment at Richard's policy of 'appeasement' had been a major element in the October parliamentary crisis. Two of the four articles charging Michael de la Pole with dereliction of duty in office had related to his conduct of foreign policy, and the confrontation at Eltham had turned on the king's failure to reconquer his inheritance in France. There was a widespread belief in the commons that the pressure for reform should extend to the foreign as well as the domestic

[59] W.M. Ormrod, 'The Origins of the *Sub Pena* Writ', *HR*, lxi (1988), 11–20.

[60] Tuck, *Richard II and the Nobility*, 110. It is difficult to be certain about the size of the household because no wardrobe book survives for the year. However, it is a fair assumption that if substantial reductions had been made in its size the Appellants would not have found it necessary to purge the household, as they did, on coming to power in 1388 (*WC*, 232).

policies of the crown. Gloucester and the other councillors were in agreement with this and from the outset acted accordingly. One of their first acts was to veto a peace initiative to which Richard had only weeks before given his blessing. In late summer King Leo of Armenia had been encouraged to arrange a meeting between the English and French kings and had written to Richard to request a safe-conduct for a visit to England. In a letter dictated shortly after the council's accession to power Gloucester firmly rejected any such proposition: it was absurd, he argued, that any mediation should be attempted at the present time. The French had assembled a mighty host with which to invade the realm. How could they possibly want to talk peace? If they disarmed, it would be a different matter; but clearly they were not so doing. For the moment negotiations were out of the question.[61]

With this rebuff the council served notice that it intended to renew the war in the coming year. Over the winter it threw itself into making the necessary diplomatic and military preparations. Approval was obtained from parliament for the launching of an expedition to serve in the Channel under the earl of Arundel. On 10 December 1386 the earl was appointed admiral in the north and the west; and a week later on, 16 December, he was retained to serve the king with 2,500 men for three months from 1 March.[62] The intention was that he should conduct a harrying operation along the Flemish coastline, to provoke a rising against Burgundian rule. To provide him with the political and military back-up that he needed the council launched a diplomatic offensive in the Low Countries. Approaches were made to the rulers of Guelders and Ghent to seek their support for the expedition. Duke William of Guelders responded positively and by April had committed himself to forming an offensive alliance with the English. Francis Ackermann of Ghent proved more equivocal. Ackermann was limited in his freedom of action by his obligations under the treaty of Tournai and by his precarious relationship with the Burgundians more generally. Though sympathetic to the English, he probably found it impossible to enter into any definite commitment. He therefore spun out the negotiations over the weeks while never precipitating their collapse entirely.[63]

For the English, Ackermann's tactics were annoying because for military reasons they could not afford long delay. Arundel and his force had to set sail in the spring if they were to have any chance of engaging

---

[61] *DC*, no. 66. The letter was probably written in mid-November, for acknowledgement was made of a letter of Leo's of 2 November. The unfriendly tone adopted is highly suggestive of Gloucester's authorship. For the diplomatic manoeuvrings of these months, see Palmer, *England, France and Christendom*, 85.

[62] C76/71 m.18; E364/21 m.6ᵛ.

[63] Palmer, *England, France and Christendom*, 91–2.

the French fleet in battle. After the dispersal of the land forces in November the greater part of that fleet had made for La Rochelle, where it had refitted and loaded with the French wine harvest. Once laden, it was due to return in March to Sluys, where it would be reassembled for another invasion attempt later in the year.[64] Arundel had to intercept and destroy the fleet if he were to be able freely to ravage the Flemish coastline. For this reason he had to sail in March or not sail at all. There could be no question of delaying in order to suit the needs of diplomatic or military convenience.

In the council's own planning diplomatic priorities certainly yielded precedence to strategic. All through the winter and early spring shipping was assembled at Sandwich for Arundel's use. By February the earl had thirty-six ships at his disposal, and a month later sixty.[65] This was not by any means a large number, but it was as many as he was likely to muster. By the second week of March the earl was ready. On 16 March he arrived at Sandwich to take up command. A week later word was received that the enemy fleet was approaching. Arundel immediately put to sea, and next day battle was joined off Cadzand. The enemy fleet was about 250 strong, some four times the size of Arundel's. The French, however, had put to sea with an inadequate complement of soldiers; and during the course of the fight a number of German and Dutch ships deserted them to join Arundel. In the circumstances Arundel's superior armaments and manpower proved decisive, and after a long fight his victory was complete.[66] The Flemish admiral and some fifty of his ships were captured and another dozen or so sunk or burnt. This was the worst disaster to befall French or Flemish shipping at sea in the second half of the fourteenth century.

In England the most widely noted side-effect of the victory was the subsequent cheapness of wine. Between 8,000 and 9,000 tuns were unloaded at Orwell and sold off at a fraction of the normal price, much to the popularity of the council.[67] Strategically the main result was to pave the way for the second stage of the expedition – the harrying of the Flemish coastline. Immediately after his triumph Arundel pursued what was left of the fleet to Sluys and established himself in the Zwin estuary opposite the harbour. By this time his enemies were in disarray and Sluys itself was at his mercy. Had he seized Sluys castle and town, which were all but undefended, he might have brought the Ghentois into the open and provoked the anti-Burgundian uprising that he desired. But he held back; he decided to launch raids into the surrounding country-

---

[64] Ibid., 92.
[65] For the size of the fleet and of Arundel's force, see E364/21 m.6ᵛ; E101/40/35; E101/40/34.
[66] WC, 182, probably based on a source originating in Arundel's fleet.
[67] Ibid., 184.

side instead. Over a period of two to three weeks the countryside around Sluys was systematically pillaged, and booty worth 200,000 francs was taken. But eventually fevers, ascribed to bad water, broke out among the men, and Arundel was forced to weigh anchor and leave. On 14 April, less than a month after setting out, he arrived back in the Orwell.[68]

Any assessment of Arundel's overall achievement must take due account of his victory at sea. This was not the mere 'massacre of merchants' that those around the king characterized it as. It was a triumph over a large, well-armed fleet. It dealt a mortal blow to French naval strength and delivered the realm from the threat of invasion for the remainder of the king's reign. But the brilliance of the victory should not distract attention from the relative failure of the later stages of the campaign. Arundel had been set the objective of undermining Burgundian authority in Flanders so as to provoke an uprising against it. This he had shown himself unable to do. The Ghentois, despite all the efforts made to draw them into the open, remained stubbornly sphinx-like; and Burgundian authority, though shaken, in the end proved remarkably resilient. No major shift had been brought about in the balance of power between England and France. To this extent the campaign as a whole was a failure. It is true, as has often been observed, that in the remainder of his contracted term Arundel performed useful work in revictualling Brest, which was then under siege by the Bretons.[69] But from a strategic standpoint the moment of greatest opportunity for the earl had passed, and nothing the council might subsequently attempt could alter that fact. Once Arundel had completed his period of service, as he had by mid-June, the military initiative passed back to the French.

Throughout the preparation and course of Arundel's campaign the councillors had made a point of keeping in regular touch with the king. On one occasion, indeed, they were instrumental in passing on to him news from Arundel himself, who was at that time at sea.[70] From the outset they had realized the crucial importance to their work of engaging the king's active assistance and co-operation: after all, the government of the realm was still the king's government even if it was his in name only. Entries on the issue rolls attest their concern to maintain contact with him. Messengers were sent to him at regular intervals with news, and from time to time he was approached for advice on aspects of

---

[68] Palmer, *England, France and Christendom*, 93-5.
[69] *WC*, 184.
[70] *CPR 1385-9*, 323.

government business, in particular on diplomacy.[71] Richard for his part likewise kept open the lines of communication. He regularly trans-mitted instructions to the chancellor, the keeper of the privy seal and the courts of law; and on at least two occasions he had meetings with the officers of state – at Easthampstead on 14 May and at Worcester on about 10 August.[72] But the outward normality of relations between the two parties concealed deep inner tensions. On both sides there was suspicion; and on Richard's side there were also feelings, deeply nur-tured, of resentment and anger. These showed in the periodic gestures of defiance which he made at this time. On 20 November, for example, while parliament was still sitting, he appointed one of his signet clerks, John Lincoln of Grimsby, as a chamberlain of the exchequer in succes-sion to Thomas Orgrave – hardly a tactful choice given the criticism being made of the signet office at the time.[73] Then a little over a month later he named John Beauchamp of Holt, a chamber knight, as steward of the household in succession to Sir John Montagu.[74] The stewardship was an office which the commons had attempted to have filled publicly in parliament, and Richard, if he had wanted to be conciliatory, could have made the appointment while parliament was sitting. But he did not: he waited. This was hardly the behaviour of a man who would willingly share the exercise of power with the council.

Richard showed his frustration with his position in a number of ways. In early 1387 he had a series of trumped-up charges drawn up against Sir Robert Plessington, the chief baron of the exchequer, whom he had dismissed and replaced by a royalist knight, Sir John Cary.[75] The former baron was accused among other things of concealing a marriage, thereby depriving the king of profit from it; of allowing two debtors to go free; of taking a bribe from the archdeacon of Richmond; and of not listening to apprentices and others who pleaded in his court, with the result that the king lost revenue in fines and amercements. These were hardly charges of any great substance. They may or may not have been true; and, even if they were, they scarcely suggested that Plessington had gone much beyond the normal laxity in accepting bribes and douceurs and in showing favour to friends. The reason why the charges were brought was purely political. Richard wanted to demonstrate that Michael de la Pole was not the only official to have been guilty of financial misdemeanours. There is even a possibility that Plessington's prosecution was undertaken in conscious imitation of de la Pole's – Richard was later to show a distinct liking for imitating the legal and

---

[71] E403/515, 11 March; E403/517, 15 June, 17 June, 27 July; CPR 1385–9, 339.
[72] C81/495/4278; C81/1354/1; WC, 186.
[73] Tuck, Richard II and the Nobility, 107.
[74] WC, 178.
[75] E163/6/18. For discussion, see Tuck, Richard II and the Nobility, 107–8.

political tactics of his enemies.[76] Certainly the thinking behind it was largely malicious; its attraction to the king was that it provided him with yet another way of making capital at the expense of the council and its supporters in parliament.

The tension that existed between king and council at the beginning of 1387 was aggravated by the fact that the two operated in such close proximity. The council had its headquarters at Westminster, in accordance with the terms of its appointment; Richard passed his time between Windsor, Westminster and the hunting lodges of the Thames valley. Neither could altogether escape the attentions of the other. For Richard this was particularly annoying because it laid his household open to inspection by the council and its officers. In February, as a final gesture of defiance, he left the capital for a lengthy 'gyration', as Knighton called it, which put him well out of the reach of the council and its officials.[77] He was not to return to Westminster until nine days before the council's authority was due to expire in November.

Richard's itinerary in these spring and summer months can easily give the impression of being no more than a series of fairly aimless wanderings; and certainly that is how it appeared to the chroniclers.[78] In reality, however, it was marked by a degree of coherence. Its first leg took the king and his retinue, the queen included, due northwards from London. They reached Beaumanoir in Leicestershire, Lord Beaumont's estate, on 15 February, and Nottingham a week later.[79] From there they went on to Lincoln and Royston near Barnsley (where the king probably met the canons of Beverley to settle a dispute between them and the archbishop of York) before returning south for the St George's Day ceremonies at Windsor.[80] After a month or so in the Thames valley they set out again on the second leg of their journey, which took them to the central and north-west midlands. Passing through Coventry and Drayton Basset (Ralph, Lord Basset's seat) they reached Lichfield on 29 June, when Richard attended Richard Scrope's installation as bishop in the cathedral; and from there they went on via

[76] In 1397 his courtier allies prosecuted Gloucester, Arundel and Warwick by appeal in imitation of the former Appellants' own use of that procedure.

[77] *KC*, 402-4.

[78] Especially to Knighton: ibid.

[79] Ibid., 388.

[80] It is often said, for example by J.H. Harvey, 'Richard II and York', *The Reign of Richard II*, 205, that Richard visited York during his progress. The only evidence for this is Knighton's statement that he went 'versus Eboracum' (*KC*, 388). There are no letters from the king place-dated from the city. Knighton's 'versus Eboracum' is probably to be understood as meaning 'towards York' rather than 'to York'. It is known that he reached Royston, a Neville manor, where he stayed at least one night, probably as the guest of Archbishop Neville; but there is no evidence that he proceeded any further north or north-east.

Stafford and Stone to Chester, where Richard stayed for a full week in mid-July. During August they undertook lengthy perambulations southwards to Shrewsbury and Worcester and then eastwards to Nottingham. For most of the time, however, they stayed within the area, roughly defined, of the north or the north-west midlands. This was a part of the country where Richard felt secure.[81] He was well away from the prying attentions of the council and its agents. He was also conveniently close to his lordship of Chester where he exercised direct authority as earl. In the company of friends, like de Vere and de la Pole, whom he could trust and in an area where support for him was strong, Richard could begin to think seriously about how to reassert his authority on the expiry of the council's term.[82]

There is strong evidence that from midsummer he was making preparations for the inevitable trial of strength to come. In August he made a vain bid for support in East Anglia. According to the Westminster chronicler he sent an agent into Essex and the eastern counties to retain men in the crown's exclusive service and to give badges to them as a mark of their allegiance. The agent, however, was arrested and thrown into Cambridge prison, and his recruiting efforts appear to have had little effect.[83] More successful were the king's attempts to consolidate his power base in the north-west. By a series of appointments he granted to Robert de Vere wide-ranging, almost proconsular, powers in the area. On 8 September he granted him the office of justice of Chester and a month later that of justice of North Wales as well.[84] De Vere was hardly renowned for the energy which he showed in the execution of his duties, but in these two capacities he acquitted himself well. When the opposition lords took up arms against the king in December, he quickly raised a force in Cheshire and led it south to meet the rebels, albeit unsuccessfully, in a battle at Radcot Bridge.

While rallying his supporters in the country Richard embarked on a policy of consultation with local officials. At a council at Nottingham in August he asked the county sheriffs and a delegation of Londoners what support they could offer in the event of a showdown with the council. The Londoners, recognizing the genuine division of opinion that existed in the capital, gave a noncommittal answer, saying that people could not be trusted one way or the other. The sheriffs were more open and at the same time more discouraging. When asked what

[81] For his residence here in 1398, see below, 392.

[82] For evidence of who was with the king on the 'gyration', see *KC*, 392, 400; *HA*, ii, 161; *CPR 1385–9*, 364 (a council held at Woodstock on 11 Oct., as the king was returning south); Lichfield Joint Record Office, D30/2/1/1, Dean and Chapter Acts Book 1, fo.15^r.

[83] *WC*, 186.

[84] *CP*, x, 229; *CPR 1385–9*, 357.

military support they could give and whether it would be possible to prevent the election of MPs unsympathetic to the king, they said first that raising a force would be impossible since most of the commons were on the side of the barons, and secondly that they would be unwilling to break the long-established custom of freely electing the knights of the shire.[85] Richard dismissed the sheriffs unceremoniously, but did not altogether abandon the idea of influencing future parliamentary elections. When writs for what was to be known as the Merciless Parliament were issued on 17 December, the sheriffs were instructed to return knights who, in addition to the usual qualities, could be reputed 'neutral in the present disputes' – by which the king meant sympathetic to him rather than to the council. Not surprisingly, the offending clause was removed after the Appellants' triumph over de Vere's forces in the field only a day or two later.[86]

The climax of the process of consultation was reached with the two celebrated meetings with the judges at Shrewsbury and Nottingham in August. The purpose of these meetings was to establish whether and to what extent the liberties and prerogatives of the crown had been impaired by the proceedings of the parliament of the previous October. To this end a series of ten carefully drafted questions was put to the judges.[87] They were first asked whether the statute appointing the council was 'derogatory to the regality and prerogative of the lord king'. When they said in reply that it had indeed been derogatory because contrary to the king's will, two further questions were put to them enquiring how those who had procured the statute and compelled the king to assent to it should be punished: to which the judges said that they should be punished 'as traitors'. Next followed questions examining the king's powers in relation to parliament more generally: in reply to these the judges ruled that the king could in law dissolve parliament whenever he wished, and further that the lords and commons had no right to put forward articles of their own and insist on their discussion before dealing with the king's business. These answers cleared the way for the next questions which asked whether parliament could impeach a minister or judge without the king's assent and whether the judgment on Michael de la Pole was erroneous: to which the judges said that

---

[85] *HA*, ii, 161–2.

[86] Tuck, *Richard II and the Nobility*, 112.

[87] The questions are copied in *KC*, 394–8, and *WC*, 196–202. The best discussion of them is S.B. Chrimes, 'Richard II's Questions to the Judges, 1387', *Law Quarterly Review*, lxxii (1956), 365–90, but see also Clementi, 'Richard II's Ninth Question to the Judges'. Much discussion has centred on why Richard chose to put the questions twice. The most plausible answer was given by Tait: Richard wanted all the judges present, and Fulthorpe had been absent at Shrewsbury: J. Tait reviewing Steel, *Richard II*, in *EHR*, lvii (1942), 379–83.

parliament could not impeach a minister without royal assent and that as a result the judgment on de la Pole was erroneous and revocable. Finally it was asked of the judges how those should be punished who had reminded Richard of the statute of Edward II's reign appointing the Ordainers: to which they replied, as they had to so many earlier questions, that they should be punished as traitors.

These answers, which together comprise the most remarkable statement of the royal prerogative ever made in England in the middle ages, provided Richard with a comprehensive riposte to the political arguments of his opponents. They established that it was the king's prerogative to choose his ministers; that those ministers were responsible to him and not to parliament; that parliament was dependent on his will, and his will alone, for summons and dismissal; and that it had no right to initiate business or to impeach officials without his assent. Legally the most questionable aspect of the answers concerned the relationship of the offences to treason. The Statute of Treasons of 1352 had limited the definition of treason to such acts as aiding the king's enemies and levying war against the king in his realm. For this reason it was not possible to accuse those procuring the appointment of the council of treason as such, and the judges, realizing this, were careful to say only that they should be punished 'as traitors'. The distinction was a narrow one, but it showed a concern to stay within the letter of the law. At no point can the judges be accused of misrepresenting the position or of perjuring themselves under oath. Though they were later to claim that they gave their opinions under duress, they appear to have spoken freely and even at times to have enlarged on answers without prompting.[88] There was little in what they said that could not have been held in good faith by any group of men trained in the common law.

In a sense it can be argued that less interest attaches to the answers than to the questions which prompted them – for these were in every sense startling. Judges had been accustomed to answering questions from the king, the council and the lords in parliament for a century or more. But never before had they been presented with issues like these.[89] Instead of technicalities of feudal or fiscal procedure, they were asked to pronounce on the most burning issue of the day: the legality of the parliamentary commission. Who conceived the idea of approaching them in this way is not clear. It may have been Richard; more likely it

[88] Belknap claimed to have been coerced by de Vere and de la Pole (*KC*, 394). His colleagues, while later in confinement in the Tower, put the blame on Rushook (*WC*, 316). In the circumstances, however, they had an interest in claiming that they had not acted as free agents.

[89] T.F.T. Plucknett, 'State Trials under Richard II' *TRHS*, 5th series, ii (1952), 166.

was someone in his circle, perhaps Chief Justice Tresilian.[90] Whoever the person was, he was a thinker of some originality, for he clearly perceived that what had hitherto been a purely political crisis could be redefined as a legal one: that the position of the monarch was an issue to which the lawyers could give an answer. In the long run this was to be a major breakthrough, for it opened the way to the growth of what might be termed constitutional law. In the shorter run it had a less lofty significance, in that it afforded Richard a way of regaining the political initiative: with the information now at his disposal he could bring charges of treason against Gloucester, his fellow councillors and their abettors. For tactical reasons he refrained from showing his hand just yet, and he made the judges and all who had been privy to their statements swear an oath to maintain the secrecy of what had occurred. For a month or two the silence was maintained, but in October or early November news of the opinions leaked out. According to the judges themselves, it was the earl of Kent who broke ranks; but according to the Monk of Westminster it was the archbishop of Dublin, Robert Wickford.[91] Gloucester and his allies were fully alert to the importance of what they had learned. A peaceful accommodation with the king was now impossible: they would have to fight to save themselves from a royalist revanche.

---

[90] Walsingham (*HA*, ii, 162) says that Tresilian brought in one John Blake to draft the questions. Blake is also credited with responsibility in the record of the Merciless Parliament of the following year (*RP*, iii, 240). The precise nature of his role, however, is unclear. Since he was only an apprentice-at-law (*HA*, ii, 162), he could hardly have been the architect of the consultative operation: that is likely to have been someone of higher rank. He was probably employed by Tresilian to advise on technical aspects of drafting.

[91] *RP*, iii, 239; *WC*, 206.

Chapter 9

DEFEAT AND RECOVERY, 1387–9

On the roll of the Merciless Parliament of February 1388 the five so-called Appellant lords – the duke of Gloucester, and the earls of Arundel, Warwick, Derby and Nottingham – left an account of how they prosecuted or 'appealed' the 'traitors' who surrounded the king. On 14 November, they said, at Waltham Cross (Hertfordshire) they met the king's councillors and before them formally appealed Alexander Neville, archbishop of York, Robert de Vere, duke of Ireland, Michael de la Pole, earl of Suffolk, Robert Tresilian, the chief justice, and Nicholas Brembre, past mayor of London. They offered sureties to maintain the prosecution and prayed the councillors to inform the king of their intention – which the councillors did on the same day. Afterwards, on 17 November, the five Appellants repeated their appeal before the king in person at Westminster, and the king assigned them a day for a hearing in the parliament due to assemble in the coming February. Shortly after Christmas the Appellants had a second meeting with the king, in the Tower of London, and repeated their appeal against the traitors. Richard again assigned them a day in parliament to prosecute their appeal, and on the advice of his council had it proclaimed that all the appealed should be present at the said parliament to answer the charges against them. When parliament finally convened, the Appellants submitted their appeal a third time and declared themselves ready to proceed.[1]

As a guide to the events of the autumn and winter of 1387 the Appellants' account leaves a good deal to be desired. In the first place, it is highly misleading. The impression is given that the Appellants' coalition was fully formed from the start; in fact it was not. Only the three senior lords – Gloucester, Arundel and Warwick – were involved from the beginning; their junior partners – Derby and Nottingham – joined later, in December. Furthermore, the account is highly selective. No mention is made of the resistance and dissimulation of the king, of de Vere's resort to arms, of the engagement at Radcot Bridge, or of the threats of deposition in the Tower. These omissions are hardly surprising. The Appellants had to conceal the true nature of their purpose.

---

[1] *RP*, iii, 229.

Like earlier opposition movements, they swore loyalty to the king and committed themselves to upholding the prerogative; yet in reality, to achieve their ends, they had to challenge the king by force and compel him to act against his will. This was an inconsistency of which the Appellants were fully aware, but which they could never resolve. It gnawed away at the integrity of their entire enterprise.

The earliest occasion on which the three senior Appellants – Glouces-ter, Arundel and Warwick – appear to have acted together was in October 1386, in the Wonderful Parliament. According to the *Eulogium* writer, after the chancellor had delivered his address seeking the com-mons' help in resisting the king's external enemies, the three earls retorted that priority should be given instead to dealing with 'the enemies within' – namely, the earl of Suffolk 'and many others'.[2] The value of the passage may be questioned on the grounds that it was written some years after the events it describes, but its witness cannot be dismissed out of hand. The *Eulogium* writer often recorded information not available to, or largely ignored by, others, and it is possible that he was preserving a story that other writers, concentrating on the greater events, were ready to overlook.[3]

Certainly there are powerful reasons for believing that the three senior Appellants harboured resentment against the court by October 1386. Over the previous three years they had seen their influence on policy steadily diminished. The strategy which they had long advocated of taking an aggressive line against France had been disregarded in favour of a policy of conciliation which had weakened the realm and left it virtually defenceless in face of repeated invasion threats. On a number of occasions they had voiced their disquiet about the course of events, only to see their advice flatly ignored. Arundel himself had been consigned to the margins since his outspoken attack on the king in 1384, while Gloucester had become steadily less influential since the departure of his brother for Spain in July. Only Warwick, who had hitherto kept his counsel, had any credit left with the king and his friends.[4]

---

[2] *Eulogium*, iii, 359.

[3] The *Eulogium* continuation was almost certainly written at Canterbury, and the author probably obtained information from the prior of Christ Church, Thomas Chillenden, who attended parliaments. For discussion of the source, see A. Gransden, *Historical Writing in England, II, c.1307 to the Early Sixteenth Century* (London, 1982), 158, 181.

[4] Warwick's views on foreign policy are likely to have been similar to Gloucester's and Arundel's. He came of a family with a tradition of military service, and he had accompanied Gaunt on his great *chevauchée* in 1373. For his career, see Goodman, *Loyal Conspiracy*, 1–2, 135–9.

Superficially at least the struggle between the Appellants and their opponents was about the great issues of politics and diplomacy; but inevitably in a world as small and intimate as that of the medieval court matters of a more personal concern had a bearing on events too. This was particularly so in Gloucester's case. Although Gloucester was sharply divided from the court on issues of policy, the depth and intensity of his feelings owed much to the numerous personal grievances which he had against the king and members of his entourage. Chief among these was the matter of his inadequate territorial endowment.

At the time of his father's death in June 1377 the only lands which the future Appellant held were those brought to him by his wife Eleanor, daughter and co-heiress of Humphrey de Bohun, earl of Hereford. These were worth some £666 per annum.[5] The young Thomas had been given no territorial endowment in his own right by his father. When he was raised to an earldom, at Richard's coronation in July 1377, he was granted an annuity of £1,000 to maintain him in due estate. The annuity was to be collected from the farms of six alien priories, those of Ware, Swavesey, Takeley, Panfield, West Mersea and Stoke-by-Clare.[6] The priories were already in financial difficulties at the time of the grant, and are unlikely to have become more profitable later, so it is doubtful if Thomas ever received his payments in full.[7] In 1385, when he was elevated to a dukedom, he was granted an additional annuity of £1,000 to be taken from the fee farm of Gloucester and from the customs of London, Boston, Hull, Lynn, Ipswich and Yarmouth.[8] Once again he experienced difficulty in collection, and he had to petition the council for remedy. Richard ordered assignment to be made on the wool subsidy in those ports – a more secure source than the customs – but at no time, despite the duke's evident desire, did he show any willingness to exchange the annuities for lands of equivalent value.[9] To a degree exceptional for a royal duke, Gloucester was dependent for his income on exchequer goodwill; and when the exchequer was hard pressed for cash, as it was increasingly in the 1380s, so too was the duke. Small wonder that he quickly became jealous of courtiers like de Vere whose claims on royal favour were more readily satisfied than his own.

[5] *CPR 1374–7*, 337. For the division of the de Bohun inheritance, see above 140, n.

[6] *CPR 1377–81*, 60, 66–7.

[7] A. McHardy, 'The Effects of War on the Church: the Case of the Alien Priories in the Fourteenth Century', *England and her Neighbours 1066–1453*, ed. M. Jones and M. Vale (London, 1989), 284–6. Gloucester's assignments on the alien priories, of course, gave him a vested interest in the continuance of the war.

[8] *CPR 1385–9*, 55.

[9] Ibid., 209.

Coupled with this general sense of resentment against the court was a more specific grudge against de Vere arising from competition with the earl for leadership of county society in Essex. Gloucester and de Vere both had their main seats in Essex, the former at Pleshy, a manor which he held by right of his wife, and the latter at Castle Hedingham, some fifteen miles to the north-east. The presence of the de Vere interest so close to his own constituted a threat to Gloucester's position in the county. The de Veres had never been a richly endowed family and are unlikely to have taken more than a small proportion of the county gentry into their pay, but the pre-eminence which Earl Robert had attained at Richard's court gave them an unaccustomed edge over their rivals. Gloucester resented this. He needed a powerful following of his own both to bolster his own prestige and to keep watch over his interests in the county, but lacking both landed wealth and influence at court he found it difficult to recruit one. His greatest attraction to the gentry was probably his ability to offer them opportunities to seek honour and renown in war.[10] A significant number of those whom he took into his affinity had made their initial association with him as men-at-arms contracted for military service.[11] Very likely an expansion of his role as leader of a military community appeared to him the surest way of giving a secure basis to his lordship in Essex. But with the king and his friends seeking a negotiated end to the war with France, that prospect was looking increasingly remote. Personal grievances thus coalesced with differences of policy to drive him into open opposition to the court.

Thomas, earl of Warwick, in terms of age the most senior of the Appellants, was also a man partly motivated by personal grievances against the king and his entourage. For over a century his family, the Beauchamps, had been the dominant force in political society in the west midlands. They held the bulk of their lands in the midland counties and exercised a controlling influence in the distribution of patronage there. In the 1380s, however, their local pre-eminence came under challenge. In the first place, the rise at court of a collateral member of the family, John Beauchamp of Holt, introduced a new source of patronage in the area, and one that was independent of

---

[10] For Gloucester's military record, see above, 52–3, and Goodman, *Loyal Conspiracy*, 122–7. His abilities as a commander were esteemed as far afield as Gascony. An undated petition from the community of Bordeaux called for him to be appointed lieutenant and governor of the duchy to save it from the attacks of the French: SC8/113/5635.

[11] Among Gloucester's retainers Sir John Gildesburgh, Sir John Harleston, Sir John Lakenheath, Sir John Clifton, John Torell and John Boys can all be shown to have made their initial association with him through military service. For membership of the retinue, see Goodman, *Loyal Conspiracy*, 94–104.

comital power. Secondly, Richard himself ostentatiously began retaining in the midlands during his 'gyration' around the realm in 1387. On 16 August, while at Worcester, Richard took on Sir John Russell, a retainer of the earl's, as a king's knight. The earl was furious and reacted by cutting off Russell's fee – as a result of which Richard had to compensate him with an annuity of £50.[12] Warwick was clearly resentful of any intrusions into what he regarded as his legitimate sphere of influence. He was a vigorous, assertive man, active in the defence of his interests. Adam of Usk's picture of him as a rather pathetic figure, grovelling for mercy when Richard arrested him in 1397, has unduly influenced historians' impressions of his personality. By 1397 Warwick was elderly and probably in ill health. Ten years before he was very much in his prime. He had shown in quarrels with the abbeys of Evesham and Westminster over the exercise of his franchisal rights that he was not a man to be trifled with: he had attacked the property of Evesham and had harassed the abbot of Westminster's tenants at Pershore.[13] His accession to the Appellant cause brought to it the support of a man of somewhat tetchy disposition; but it also secured for it the resources of a major earldom and the repute of a magnate with many years' loyal service to the crown.

In Richard, earl of Arundel, the third of the senior Appellants, it is not so easy to identify personal grievances that could have fuelled the growth of hostility to the court. Arundel was a richly endowed magnate, relatively secure in his power base, and little affected by either the ambitions of Richard's intimates or the burden of exchequer debt. Such grievances as he felt were probably of a fairly general nature. As a major wool exporter he would have been concerned with the loss of the Flemish market resulting from the civil strife there, and as a major landowner in Sussex he would have been troubled by the French raids on the south coast and the poor state of England's defences.[14] The only dispute that he appears to have had with any kinsman or supporter of the king was with the king's half-brother Sir John Holand. In 1380 Richard had granted Holand the lordship of Hopedale, near Chester, which abutted on to Arundel's lordship of Bromfield and Yale, and in the following year he had made him justice of Chester.[15] Before 1384 Holand had laid claim in the county court of Flint to certain townships in Arundel's lordship, which, he maintained, were appurtenances of his

---

[12] For John Beauchamp, see above, 124. For Russell, see CPR 1385–9, 372, and House of Commons, iv, 249.

[13] Usk, 16–17; HA, i, 322; N.E. Saul, 'Richard II and Westminster Abbey', The Cloister and the World. Essays in Medieval History in Honour of Barbara Harvey, ed. W.J. Blair and B. Golding (Oxford, 1996), 196–218.

[14] Goodman, Loyal Conspiracy, 109, 121.

[15] CPR 1377–81, 539, 624.

own, and in 1384 these were adjudged to him.[16] How far, if at all, Arundel's differences with Holand contributed to his larger quarrel with the court is hard to say. Holand was anyway to fall from grace in August 1385 as a result of his murder of Sir Ralph Stafford. On the evidence of Arundel's later career, it was probably unease with the king's foreign policy that was the main spur to his opposition. In 1387 and 1388, in the years of conciliar and Appellant power, he took a leading role in the renewed war against the French. Very likely he felt a longing to distinguish himself militarily which he had been unable to satisfy in the years of truce. Far more than in Gloucester's case, it is difficult to separate the personal and public springs of Arundel's behaviour. The earl gives the impression of having been implacably opposed to the court, and the signs are that his dislike of de Vere and the others ran deep. But he also appears to have acted in considerable measure from principle; his outburst at Salisbury was undoubtedly heartfelt.[17] Quite possibly, to a greater degree than Gloucester and Warwick he took his stand out of genuine concern at the direction of policy.

It is doubtful if any great issues of principle moved the two junior Appellants, Nottingham and Derby. Neither of them joined the coalition out of any particular conviction; each was motivated almost entirely by self-interest. Nottingham, the elder of the two, probably harboured resentment at the growing pre-eminence at court of his rival Robert de Vere. For nearly five years to 1387 he and de Vere had been engaged in a bitter struggle for access to the king's ear. The intensity of the competition between them can be sensed from the eagerness with which they offered their services as patronage brokers at court. First one and then the other, for example, acted as intermediary for John Halsham, a Yorkshire esquire who had seduced and then abducted the wealthy heiress Philippa de Stabolgi, wife of Sir Ralph Percy: de Vere obtained a pardon for the offender in June 1384, and Nottingham did likewise a month later while the king was staying with his father-in-law, the earl of Arundel at Worth.[18] By mid-1387, however, Nottingham appears to have lost, or at least to have given up, the struggle for the king's favour, and Walsingham reports that he deserted the court for his estates.[19] His ally Henry of Derby was less obviously engaged in a struggle of this sort at court, but he too may have resented de Vere's rise. In the Lancastrian domains in the north-west, over which he exercised supervisory control

---

[16] *CPR 1381-5*, 433-4; *1385-9*, 25-6.

[17] See above, 130.

[18] *CCR 1381-5*, 452, 459, 571; *CPR 1381-5*, 399, 423, 439. The Halshams eventually settled at West Grinstead (Sussex), where Philippa is commemorated by a brass.

[19] *HA*, ii, 156.

in his father's absence, he faced a challenge to his authority from de
Vere in his capacity as justice of Chester. De Vere and his deputy Sir
Thomas Molyneux recruited actively in the north-west in 1387, taking
into their lordship men who bore a grudge against the seeming oppres-
siveness of the local Lancastrian administration.[20] It may have been this
activity which led Derby to join forces with the other Appellants in the
brief struggle which ended at Radcot Bridge in December.

The five alleged traitors whom the Appellants named in the appeal
were in some ways a rather surprising group for their opponents to
single out. One or two of them were courtiers of long standing, but
others were relative newcomers to the king's inner circle. The inclusion
of the latter is a mark of the extent to which the court had changed in
composition during the year of the king's 'gyration' around the realm
in 1387.

The most obvious target of Appellant anger was, of course, Robert de
Vere. Over the eighteen months to 1387 he had been raised to unprecedented heights in the peerage. In December 1385 he had been created marquess of Dublin, with the lordship and dominion of Ireland for
the term of his life, and in October of the following year duke of
Ireland, again with the lordship of Ireland attached for his life.[21] His
status and abilities hardly qualified him for such exalted honours. He
was not of the blood royal, and he came from a relatively minor comital
family which over the previous century had played little part in the
political life of the realm. His eminence derived solely from his position
in the king's favour. Grants and privileges were showered on him
seemingly without limit. In June 1384 he was given the wardship of
Thomas Roos of Hamlake – at first on condition of paying rent and
later quit of rent. In July 1384 he was granted the castle and town
of Colchester and in March the following year the castle of
Queenborough in Kent. Later in 1385 came some bigger prizes. In July,
while serving with Richard in the north, he was granted the castle and
lordship of Oakham with the sheriffdom of the county of Rutland; and
in October came the reversion of the wide west-country estates of Sir
James Audley of Heleigh.[22] This flow of grants to de Vere contrasted
sharply with the parsimony shown by the king to other more deserving
lords, notably Gloucester, who was of the blood royal. Many members of
the nobility understandably took offence. Sir Philip Courtenay reacted
to being superseded in Ireland, where he had been lieutenant, by

---

[20] Walker, *Lancastrian Affinity, 1361–1399*, 167–8.
[21] *CP*, iv, 473; vii, 70.
[22] *CFR 1383–91*, 42; *CPR 1381–5*, 442, 542; *CPR 1385–9*, 14, 69–70, 115.

complaining volubly to the king about his treatment by de Vere's officials.[23] Ralph, Lord Basset, a loyal magnate of middling rank, is reported by Knighton to have said that, while he would always be loyal to the king, he would never risk his neck for the duke of Ireland.[24] By 1386 the duke was becoming an increasingly isolated figure in politics. Hostility to him grew sharply in 1387 when he repudiated his wife, a granddaughter of Edward III, in favour of a lady-in-waiting of the queen, Agnes Lancecrona.[25] This was an act which brought dishonour on the king and the royal family who were the countess's kin, and all of the nobility were shocked. For many it was the last straw. There was a feeling that the time had come for the duke to be removed from his position of favour at the king's side.

Two others named in the appeal were disliked almost as widely as de Vere. One was Michael de la Pole, earl of Suffolk, the former chancellor. De la Pole had already felt the strength of popular anger against him in 1386 when he had been impeached and driven from office, but he appears to have been little chastened by the experience. Throughout 1387, when Richard made his itinerary of the shires, he was in the king's entourage, offering him advice and stiffening his resolve. His influence was not, so it seems, used in the cause of moderation. According to Walsingham, he was instrumental in preventing a reconciliation between Richard and the duke of Gloucester when Archbishop Courtenay was promoting peace between them, and according to the Monk of Westminster, he was constantly urging the king to bring about the death of the earl of Warwick, whom he saw as a major fomentor of discord.[26] By his continued interventions in politics he merely added to the unpopularity he had earned in office. Robert Tresilian, the chief justice of King's Bench, was also a man widely disliked. His main offence was to have led the judges in making their submissive replies to the questions the king put to them at Nottingham. But he was also considered oppressive and corrupt. After his downfall a number of plaintiffs filed petitions to seek redress for his various misdemeanours. Sir Philip Medsted, a Sussex knight who was trying to recover the manor of Clawton in Devon, alleged that Tresilian would not hear the case until Medsted agreed, in the event of a successful action, to enfeoff the manor to his own use: which he had had to do. Thomas Treythian, John Trewoyff and other natives of Tresilian's own county of Cornwall joined in complaining that the chief justice had disseised them of pieces of land in the process of building up his own estates in the county.[27] At a

---

[23] CCR 1385-9, 49, 232.
[24] KC, 406.
[25] HA, ii, 160-1; WC, 188-90.
[26] CA, 383; WC, 208.
[27] CPR 1385-9, 517-18, 545-6.

time when the judges were widely criticized for their misconduct it was an easy task for the Appellants to portray Tresilian as a malign and corrupting influence on the king.

The two final defendants named in the appeal were men whose association with the court probably only became controversial in 1385 or 1386. One was the former mayor of London, Sir Nicholas Brembre. Brembre, a rich merchant capitalist and member of the oligarchy of victuallers who controlled the London food trade, rose quickly during the period of crisis to become Richard's chief ally in London. Since the early 1380s he had been a generous provider of loans to the king. In September 1382 he had lent the crown £1,333 6s 8d. In December 1384 he had paid £993 4s 2d into the chamber 'for the king's secret business'. And before March 1386 he lent £666 13s 4d to meet the costs of renewed war. He also lent smaller sums and helped to organize the raising of corporate loans in the city.[28] As a result of his financial links with the crown Brembre became closely involved in court politics. He was present at the council at Nottingham at which the questions were put to the judges, and he appears to have become a trusty confidant of de la Pole.[29] But his intimacy with the king made him many enemies in the city, and the Appellants seem to have had little trouble in soliciting petitions against him from the guilds.

The last of the five courtiers named in the appeal, Alexander Neville, archbishop of York, rose to political prominence barely two years before the onset of the crisis which was to bring him down. He appears to have become a friend of the king's on the occasion of the latter's visit to York in July 1385 on his way northwards to fight the Scots.[30] What drew the two men together is hard to say. The archbishop's reputation before 1385 was that of an irascible and somewhat reclusive diocesan who had a knack of picking quarrels with his suffragans and with powerful collegiate chapters. In the 1370s he had managed to offend the bishop of Durham by attempting a visitation of his diocese before completing the primary visitation of his own diocese, as was canonically required. A few years later he gave grievous offence to the chapter of Beverley when he attempted to secure membership of their body by means of a prebend and in that way to exercise jurisdiction as head of the chapter; the chapter reacted by withdrawing their labour, and the archbishop had to bring in vicars choral from York to perform the services.[31] The archbishop's general tactlessness led to attacks on his

---

[28] *CPR 1381–5*, 164; E403/505, 20 Dec.; *CPR 1385–9*, 121; Bird, *Turbulent London of Richard II*, 90–1.

[29] *KC*, 392; *CA*, 373.

[30] The two had met before, in 1383, but it appears that it was only in 1385 that a lasting association between them was formed.

[31] The archbishop's object appears to have been to challenge the dominance of

property at Bishopthorpe and Cawood and to the submission of petitions against him to the king. One such petition, possibly presented in the parliament of 1382, alleged that he was an oppressor of his diocese and his country, and that he took fees for services, such as proving wills, which he should have provided free. At the time of his condemnation in parliament in 1388 three more hostile petitions were filed against him, two of them, it was said, nailed to the pillar of the chapter house of Westminster, and the third to the walls of the chapter house of St Paul's.[32] The archbishop's character appears from his documented actions to have been brittle and uncompromising, and little suited to the give and take of politics. At court his influence was generally malign. Sir Robert Belknap, a justice of King's Bench, described how he had harangued him in his chamber at Windsor and held him personally responsible for the appointment of the council; in the view of both Walsingham and the Monk of Westminster he was one of those at court most resistant to compromise with the lords.[33] Along with Robert de Vere and Michael de la Pole he formed part of that small inner circle which stiffened Richard's resolve and plotted with him the showdown with the future Appellants.

The crisis in relations between Richard and his opponents came to a head in the late autumn of 1387. By October at the latest Gloucester and his allies had learned of what had transpired at the councils at Shrewsbury and Nottingham. Outwardly at least they maintained their

---

the influential Thoresby faction in the chapter: R.B. Dobson, 'Beverley in Conflict: Archbishop Alexander Neville and the Minster Clergy, 1381-8', *Medieval Art and Architecture in the East Riding of Yorkshire*, ed. C. Wilson (British Archaeological Association., ix, 1989), 149-64. See also Davies, 'Alexander Neville, Archbishop of York, 1374-1388', 87-101; A.F. Leach, 'A Clerical Strike at Beverley Minster in the Fourteenth Century', *Archaeologia*, lv (1896), 1-20; M. Aston, *Thomas Arundel* (Oxford, 1967), 289-91.

[32] SC8/243/12148; W. Illingworth, 'Copy of a Libel against Archbishop Neville, temp. Richard II', *Archaeologia*, xvi (1812), 82-3; SC8/262/13079. It is possible that one of the 'oppressions' referred to in the petition of *c.* 1382 was the construction of a magnate-style affinity: see *CPR 1381-5*, 635; S.K. Walker, 'Yorkshire Justices of the Peace, 1389-1413', *EHR*, cviii (1993), 288, 295n. The archbishop's affinity-building, and later his search for allies at court, were presumably occasioned by the bitter struggle with Beverley: Dobson, 'Beverley in Conflict'. There is a possibility that the archbishop's activities brought him into conflict with the Percys, who were powerful in the East Riding, and whose enmity (in different circumstances) another of Richard's servants John Fordham, bishop of Durham, also incurred: R.B. Dobson, 'The Church of Durham and the Scottish Borders, 1378-88', *War and Border Societies in the Middle Ages* ed. A. Tuck and A. Goodman (London, 1992), 129.

[33] *RP*, iii, 239; *CA*, 384; *WC*, 210.

loyalty to the king. According to Walsingham, Gloucester swore an oath in the presence of the bishop of London and other notables to the effect that he had never plotted dissension in the kingdom, nor would he ever; his objection was solely to the duke of Ireland, whom he would never accept as a friend.[34] To someone as suspicious as Richard this note of qualification was enough: it marked Gloucester out as an enemy. In early November he ordered the earl of Northumberland to arrest Arundel, the duke's ally, at his castle of Reigate. Reigate, how-ever, proved to be more strongly defended than expected, and North-umberland had to withdraw without accomplishing his objective.[35] Arundel, fearful of a royalist revanche, decided to link forces with the other lords. On or shortly before 13 November he marched with his retinue to join Warwick and Gloucester at Harringay park, north of London, and on the 14th the three of them moved to Waltham Cross. Richard, who had by now returned to London, was astonished at the speed of their movement and uncertain how to react. A council meeting was held, and various possibilities were discussed – among them, asking the Londoners for assistance, seeking the help of the king of France, and reaching an accommodation with the lords. Alexander Neville urged the use of force, but calmer counsels prevailed, and the decision was taken to send a delegation to meet the lords. Later the same day the archbishop of Canterbury, the bishops of Winchester and Ely, the duke of York, John Waltham, Lords Cobham and Scrope and Sir John Devereux, all members of the continual council, met the lords at Waltham to arrange a meeting between them and the king. It was at this meeting that the lords made their first formal submission of the appeal of treason, which was probably already in existence in written form. The councillors urged the lords to lay aside their retinues, but promised to arrange an early meeting with the king. Three days later on Sunday, 17 November, the three lords rode to Westminster and were admitted to the royal presence in Westminster Hall. Richard, Lord Scrope, speaking on their behalf, reaffirmed their opposition to the five appellees and confirmed that they intended proceeding against them by way of appeal. Richard assented to this petition and assigned a hearing in the next parliament, due to convene the following February. In the meantime he said that he would take all of the parties, both accusers and accused, into his protection for their own safety.[36]

The rapid escalation of the crisis had undoubtedly caught Richard and his friends unawares. Their reaction was, to say the least, confused.

---

[34] *CA*, 382–3.

[35] Ibid.

[36] *WC*, 210–14; *CA*, 384. The implication of Arundel's dash to Harringay is that the other Appellants had already mobilized there, and were agreed on it as their rallying point.

At one moment they seemed bent on offering resistance: on 12 November letters were sent to the Londoners prohibiting them from selling victuals to Arundel's men. At another they seemed willing to offer conciliation: Richard himself is said to have sipped wine with the lords in his chamber after receiving them in Westminster Hall on the 17th.[37] The decision to refer the appeal to parliament – probably the only one that he could have taken in the circumstances – at least gave him a breathing space, which allowed him to rally his forces and work out a strategy. De la Pole and Neville had probably by this time taken to their heels.[38] De Vere, more courageously, decided to stand by the king. Acting on royal orders, he hurried north to Cheshire and there mobilized an army for Richard. Letters under the king's seal were addressed to the sheriff and to the bailiffs and gentry in the hundreds, and musters were ordered to be held at Flint, Pulford and elsewhere. By mid-December de Vere had an army of perhaps 3,000–4,000 men which he was ready to bring south to rescue Richard from the Appellant yoke.[39]

Word of de Vere's plans reached the Appellants from Arundel's garrison at Holt-on-Dee, which had been watching over events. There was discussion between the lords over how to respond. The hard-liners, represented by Gloucester and Arundel, were minded to depose Richard there and then. Warwick opposed them, saying that their quarrel was with de Vere, not the king. Warwick's view carried the day, and it was decided to concentrate on assembling a force to cut off de Vere's route to London.[40] The three lords moved out of London and headed north. At Huntingdon on 12 December they were met by Derby and Nottingham who, seeing which way the wind was blowing, threw in their lot with them.[41] A brief council of war was held, and the combined forces moved westwards to Northampton and the midlands.

The chroniclers differ considerably in their accounts of the hostilities that followed. Henry Knighton's narrative, deriving clearly from Lancastrian sources, emphasizes the role of Henry of Derby. The Westminster writer, drawing on a source in Arundel's circle, gives precedence to the role of that earl's men. The implication of these differences is that the five Appellant lords must have divided their forces. Their strategy

---

[37] WC, 208; CA, 384.

[38] De la Pole fled across the Channel, only to be arrested at Calais and sent back again (though he escaped a second time): KC, 418; Neville made good his escape to the Low Countries: WC, 214, 492.

[39] P. Morgan, War and Society in Medieval Cheshire, 1277–1403 (Manchester: Chetham Society, 3rd series, xxxiv, 1987), 188. The evidence for royal complicity in de Vere's plans is provided by the correspondence allegedly shown by the Appellants to Richard in the Tower at the end of December: HA, ii, 169, 172.

[40] WC, 218.

[41] RP, iii, 376.

was to encircle Robert de Vere's force and cut off its line of retreat. Gloucester, Arundel and probably Warwick occupied Banbury, Chipping Campden and the country in the north Cotswolds behind the line of the duke's advance; Derby occupied the bridgeheads across the Thames so as to deny his adversary the chance to escape south.[42] The strategy worked brilliantly. De Vere advanced south-eastwards through Evesham, reaching Chipping Campden, according to the Worcester register, by the night of 19 December. Ahead of him, Moreton-in-Marsh was occupied by the duke of Gloucester.[43] On the morning of 20 December de Vere made an effort to challenge the duke somewhere in the region of Bourton-on-the-Hill, but many of his men deserted. He then decided to make a dash for the river crossings. Heading south-east through Stow-on-the-Wold he came into the Windrush valley. At Burford – the Monk of Westminster says Witney, but Burford is more likely – he was met by Arundel's forces.[44] A brief skirmish occurred, in the course of which his lieutenant, Sir Thomas Molyneux, was killed by Arundel's chief steward, Thomas Mortimer and his servant William Curtis.[45] De Vere, now growing desperate, was able to press on, but at Radcot Bridge, on the Thames, his path was blocked by Derby. Another brief skirmish was fought, this one in thick fog, and de Vere's men were routed. The duke made good his escape; most of his men, however, were made captive, stripped of their possessions and sent home.[46] Next day the Appellants made their triumphant entry into Oxford.[47]

With the defeat and disintegration of de Vere's army Richard's last hope of resisting the Appellant tide was lost. The king retreated from Windsor to the greater security of the Tower of London, there to await his fate.[48] A number of his councillors were with him, and when the Appellants arrived, on or around 27 December, a delegation led by the duke of York and the bishops of Ely, Hereford and Winchester went out to negotiate with them.[49] A meeting with the king was quickly arranged,

[42] WC, 220; KC, 420–2.

[43] Information on events at Chipping Campden and Moreton comes from the Worcester register, in R.G. Davies, 'Some notes from the register of Henry de Wakefield, bishop of Worcester, on the political crisis of 1386–1388', EHR, lxxxvi (1971), 547–58.

[44] WC, 222. CA, 385, mentions Burford, but otherwise confuses the story. Witney is too far from Moreton: de Vere could not have done the journey there in the day. For a discussion of the sources, see J.N.L. Myres, 'The Campaign of Radcot Bridge in December 1387', EHR, xlii (1927), 20–33.

[45] KC, 422; J.L. Gillespie, 'Thomas Mortimer and Thomas Molineux: Radcot Bridge and the Appeal of 1397', Albion, vii (1975), 161–73.

[46] KC, 422–4.

[47] Usk, 145; WC, 224. At Oxford the Appellants concerted their future plans.

[48] WC, 220, 224. Measures were taken to strengthen the Tower at this time: Given-Wilson, Royal Household and King's Affinity, 84.

[49] Davies, 'Notes from the Register', 557.

and on 30 December the five lords entered the Tower with 500 heavily armed followers, ensuring that the gates were firmly closed behind them. Richard received them with apparent courtesy and took them into the privacy of his chapel. What happened next is obscure but of the highest importance. According to Walsingham, the lords reproached the king for his treachery, showing him correspondence with de Vere that had fallen into their hands and accusing him of wanting to call on the king of France to procure their destruction.[50] When the king was suitably chastened, they made a number of demands of him. Knighton reports their insistence on the arrest and imprisonment of the five appellees. Walsingham, offering a different view, says that they required him to attend a council meeting at Westminster the next day: Richard, lachrymose and confused, initially agreed, but then changed his mind and in the end only submitted under threat of deposition.[51] The suggestion of deposition is picked up by the Westminster writer, who gives a picture of a difficult and prolonged crisis. The lords, the writer says, rebuked Richard for his duplicity and misgovernance, and gave a clear warning that he must correct his mistakes and rule better in future: they reminded him that he had an heir of full age and that this heir was fully prepared, if need be, to take on the governance of the realm in accordance with their advice. Taken aback by these words, the king said that he was prepared to defer to the lords' wishes and 'to be guided by their wholesome advice . . . without prejudice to his crown'. On the next day he made his way reluctantly to the palace of Westminster.[52]

The consensus of these various writers is that throughout the long ordeal the king and the lords managed to retain an understanding with one another. Gloucester and his allies severely reproached Richard and may even have threatened him with deposition; but ultimately they were able to achieve their purposes without violating his regality. Directly conflicting with this view, however, is a narrative which presents a very different account of the crisis. This is the chronicle of Whalley Abbey, Lancashire, which suggests that for a brief while Richard actually ceased to reign. On entering the Tower, the chronicler says, the lords deposed Richard and for some three days he was deprived of his crown. Gloucester and his nephew Derby, however, could not agree on which of them was to take his place and in the end he was restored to his title.[53] This is a remarkable story, and one without parallel in the other narratives, but support for it can be found in the later confession of the duke of Gloucester. When interrogated at Calais shortly after his arrest in 1397, the duke admitted that he and his fellow Appellants had

[50] *HA*, ii, 172.
[51] *KC*, 424–6; *HA*, ii, 172.
[52] *WC*, 226–8.
[53] BL, Harley MS 3600, in Clarke, *Fourteenth Century Studies*, 91.

'assented ther to [i.e. to the king's deposition] for two dayes or thre and than we for to have done oure homage and our oothes and putt him as heyly in his estate as he ever was.'[54] This confession was extracted under duress, but it carries the ring of truth. Rumours of Gloucester's designs on the throne were circulating so widely at the time that he was obliged to deny them publicly when parliament opened in February.[55] King and lords both had an interest in suppressing the true nature of what had occurred; but in the circumstances there can be little doubt that for a period of some two or three days Richard ceased to rule.[56] In the light of this it is easy to understand why in later years Richard should have been so preoccupied with his regality. In December 1387 he had suffered a blow to his prestige which was to leave him psychologically scarred for life.

The crisis in the Tower had exposed the divisions, both actual and potential, that threatened the unity of the Appellant coalition. The two junior Appellants, Derby in particular, had shown themselves less hostile to the king than their seniors. They wanted to see the court purged and de Vere removed, but that was all. They had no sympathy with Gloucester's plan to remove the king and put himself in his place. Richard observed these divisions and played on them. According to Walsingham, he persuaded Derby to stay behind in his chamber and dine with him; according to Knighton, he persuaded Nottingham to do the same.[57] Doubtless he had hopes of detaching the two from their partners, but at this early stage his chances of success were slight. The Appellants were united in their commitment to take over the government and to bring their enemies to trial. On 1 January they made the journey to Westminster and assumed control of the royal household. With conciliar approval they purged a number of the more prominent royal servants, arrested others, and required various courtier lords and their wives to abjure the court.[58] They also began the systematic amassing of evidence for use in the trials to come. On 14 January the ports were sealed and the constable of Dover ordered to collect 'all writs, writings, orders and commands addressed from 20 November 1386 to 14 January 1388 . . . on behalf of the king . . . for passage of all who have passed from the realm overseas for whatever cause'.[59] Four days later a meeting was held with the London guilds at which the opportunity was taken to solicit indictments against the former mayor Sir

---

[54] *RP*, iii, 379; *Chrons. Revolution*, 81.

[55] Favent, *Historia*, 14–15; *WC*, 234.

[56] It is perhaps also significant that no letters bearing the dates of the last three days of December were enrolled on the close and patent rolls.

[57] *HA*, ii, 172; *KC*, 426.

[58] *WC*, 228–30.

[59] *CCR 1385–9*, 388.

Nicholas Brembre.[60] The Appellants took every step to ensure that they did not enter the coming hearings inadequately prepared.

The trials of the five accused opened with due ceremony in the White Hall at Westminster on 3 February 1388. Thomas Favent, the Appellant pamphleteer, gives a vivid account of the scene. The room was crowded: every space was filled. First the king made his entry, and then the five Appellants, the latter arm in arm to show their solidarity, and wearing cloth of gold. The chancellor, as was customary, gave an opening address, 'to expound the causes and matters of the present parliament'. When he had finished, Sir Robert Plessington, on the lords' behalf, asked for the duke of Gloucester to be given the opportunity to clear himself of treasons imputed to him by the courtiers – a veiled reference to the events of a month earlier in the Tower. The chancellor replied that the king held him blameless, and then Geoffrey Martin, the clerk of the crown, proceeded to read out the appeal of treason – a task that took him two hours.[61]

The aim of the appeal was to set out in general and particular terms the offences of which the appellees stood accused. This it did in the form of some thirty-nine lengthy and sometimes overlapping articles arranged in no particular order.[62] Clauses 1–4 dealt with the undue influence of the accused over the king. Clauses 5–10, 22, 23 and 36 accused the favourites of abusing their power and 'taking advantage of the king's tender years' for personal gain. Clauses 15–21 and 25–32 arose out of Richard's defiance of the council of 1386–7 and referred in particular to his bid for French help. Most of the remaining clauses dealt with the events of autumn 1387 and purported to show that the accused had encouraged the king to take military action against the Appellants. If there was a theme running through the counts, it was the familiar one of medieval oppositions, that the accused had taken advantage of the favour shown to them 'to accroach the royal power': that is, to gain such a hold over the king as to allow them to make illegitimate use of his authority. Earlier royal favourites had been accused of the same, notably Edward II's friends, the Despensers, in the 1320s. It is almost certain that the Appellants were aware of these precedents as they drew up the charges against Richard's own favourites.

The crimes alleged in the appeal were so grave that king and lords had been agreed from the outset that they could only be heard in parliament. Parliament by the later fourteenth century had established

[60] WC, 232–4.
[61] Favent, Historia, 14–15.
[62] RP, iii, 230–6; WC, 236–68; KC, 452–96.

for itself a recognized position as the only appropriate setting for major state trials. The precedent had been set by Mortimer's trial in 1330. It had been followed in the trials of 1376 in which the weapon of impeachment had been forged, and it had won general acceptance by the time of the arraignment of de la Pole in 1386.[63] There is little merit in the suggestion that the lords wanted the trials to be conducted in the court of chivalry.[64] The court of chivalry operated according to civil law, and the lords had made it perfectly clear in their original submission that they wanted their enemies to be punished according to the common law of the realm.[65]

Transplanting the processes of common law to a parliamentary setting, however, involved the Appellants in a major difficulty of procedure. The lords' political agenda called for the early, if not immediate, condemnation of the accused; yet of the five, only one, Nicholas Brembre, was present, and under common law defendants could not be condemned in their absence. This difficulty threatened to upset the Appellants' entire strategy, and it had to be speedily overcome. The Appellants turned for advice to the judges and sergeants, but the latters' replies were hardly encouraging. The appeal, they said, belonged to neither the one law nor the other: it was a procedure unknown to the common law, yet the civil law, which recognized the procedure, had no cognizance of the crimes alleged in the appeal.[66] To solve the conundrum the Appellants in the end resorted to a legal sleight-of-hand. In a celebrated declaration they said that in the case of crimes as high as those alleged in the appeal, which touched the king's person and were committed by peers of the realm, the trial should be held in parliament and be conducted there according to the law of parliament; it was never their intention either that England should be subjected to civil law or that the appeal should be governed by the process of any lower court of the realm.[67] The implication of this lofty if somewhat ambivalent statement was that parliament could make up the rules as it went along: which is precisely what it did. The principle of conviction by default was borrowed from Roman civil law to deal with the problem of the appellees' non-attendance. On three successive

---

[63] A. Rogers, 'Parliamentary Appeals of Treason in the Reign of Richard II', *American Journal of Legal History*, viii (1964), 102.

[64] Clarke, *Fourteenth Century Studies*, 134–5.

[65] WC, 214.

[66] RP, iii, 236. The statement that the appeal did not belong to the common law is puzzling because appeals were a recognized method of initiating personal actions under common law. It is possible that the judges meant that the appeal had never before been used to initiate a prosecution in parliament. Alternatively, they could have been alluding to the fact that the crimes alleged in the appeal fell outside the Statute of Treasons, 1352.

[67] RP, iii, 236.

occasions in early February the five were summoned; and when all but one of them failed to appear they were found guilty and condemned in their absence. De Vere, de la Pole and Tresilian were sentenced to death and to the forfeiture of their lands, and Neville to the loss of his temporalities.[68] A week later on 17 February proceedings were initiated against the final defendant, Sir Nicholas Brembre. In his case a mixture of common and civil law procedures was followed. In accordance with common law he was asked how he pled. He declared himself innocent and offered to prove this by battle; but 'although more than a hundred gloves were cast against him' he was denied his request by the lords on the grounds that, in accordance with civil law procedure, trial by battle was allowed only when there were no witnesses. This decision put the Appellants in a difficult position, because they were doubtful of obtaining sufficient depositions to secure a conviction. They made an approach to the city guilds, but this was evidently of little value. In the end they turned to the mayor and aldermen of London, who gave it as their belief that Brembre was 'rather aware than ignorant of the crimes of which he stood accused'. On this flimsy basis he was found guilty and sentenced to death.[69]

Having secured the conviction of the five principal accused, the Appellants now turned their attention to the secondary objects of their anger, the officials and chamber knights who had served the king. For the trials of these men the Appellants reverted to the method of impeachment. Appellate process had shown itself to be an awkward and ineffective instrument in practice: it was not easily adapted to parliamentary use, and the advantage that it offered of dispensing with royal participation seemed less important once the king was virtually powerless. There appears to have been no opposition to the idea of using impeachment for those trials which remained. The first cases to be heard were those of John Blake, the lawyer who had drafted the questions to the judges, and Thomas Usk, the under-sheriff of Middlesex, who had tried to secure London for the king in 1387; both men were found guilty and executed. The second case to be heard was that of Thomas Rushook, bishop of Chichester, the king's confessor, who faced charges unspecified in the parliament roll: he was found guilty, but was spared the death penalty because of his cloth and was sentenced to perpetual exile in Ireland. A day or two later, on 6 March, the cases of the six judges were taken. The judges were a group viewed with

[68] WC, 308. Tresilian was subsequently found in hiding in Westminster and executed at Tyburn (WC, 310–12).

[69] WC, 308–14. The petitions printed in RP, iii, 225–7, and wrongly assigned there to 1386, probably have their origins in the Appellants' search for evidence against Brembre. The evidence solicited was clearly less conclusive than the Appellants had at first supposed.

particular dislike by the Appellants because of their apparent duplicity in denouncing the 1387 council to the king only months after advising the lords on the terms of its appointment. Like Blake and Usk they were condemned to death, but after the clergy and lords had interceded on their behalf with the king their sentences were commuted to exile in Ireland.[70]

Six days later, on 12 March, the series of judicial hearings entered its final phase. Four of Richard's chamber knights, Sir Simon Burley, Sir John Beauchamp, Sir John Salisbury and Sir James Berners, were impeached on sixteen counts of treason. They were said to have taken advantage of the king's youth to turn him against his proper counsellors, to have obstructed the work of the continual council, and to have assisted the favourites in conspiring and treating with the king of France. Burley was additionally accused of assisting in Suffolk's escape from the realm, encouraging the king to keep company with de Vere, filling the household with Bohemians, and making illicit use of the great seal.[71] All four denied the charges against them, and none was found guilty on more than two counts. The case of Burley, who offered to defend himself with his body, aroused much controversy, and his fate was not decided until after the adjournment from 20 March to 5 May. The three senior Appellants were determined to see him condemned, but their junior colleagues and a sizeable body of neutral opinion argued for mercy to be shown. Gloucester and York disagreed publicly over his fate. York said that Burley had always been loyal to the king, to which Gloucester replied that on the contrary he had been false to his allegiance. York retorted that his brother was a liar and Gloucester returned the insult: only the king's intervention succeeded in calming them down. Richard and his queen, the latter on bended knees, interceded on behalf of the former chamberlain, but Gloucester, strengthened by the support of the commons, refused to give way. On 5 May the knight was condemned to death 'by parliamentary process', and on the same day he was executed on Tower Hill.[72] A week later the other three knights suffered the same fate.[73]

[70] *RP*, iii, 240–1; *WC*, 314–18.

[71] *RP*, iii, 241–3; *WC*, 268–78. For the charge of making illicit use of the great seal, see Roskell, *Impeachment of Michael de la Pole*, 87–96.

[72] *RP*, iii, 243; *WC*, 328–32. Gloucester was to say after his arrest in 1397 that he had told Richard that he would have to choose between Burley and his crown (*RP*, iii, 431). It is unclear how much weight can be attached to this statement considering that it was made under duress. To threaten the king so directly would have been impolitic in the light of what had occurred in the Tower. However, it is evident that Gloucester and his allies were under considerable pressure to speed up the trials and to press on with reform. There were risings in the south in April, and shortly afterwards the commons submitted a petition highly critical of the Appellants: *KC*, 442–50.

[73] *WC*, 332. It had been apparent to some of the knights since the beginning of the

With the destruction of the court's inner circle the main work of the aptly named 'Merciless Parliament' was done. On 1 June the king entertained the lords at the banquet customarily given at the end of a parliament. Two days later, in a symbolic act of reconciliation, he and they attended a solemn mass in Westminster Abbey. During the service Richard renewed his coronation oath while the lords renewed their oaths of homage.[74] The suggestion was put about by the Appellants that the renewal of oaths was necessary because Richard had acceded to the throne as a minor;[75] but a further consideration must have been an awareness on all sides of the treasonable events that had occurred the previous December in the Tower. Both the king and his opponents among the lords must have felt the necessity for a symbolic reaffirmation of the proper relationship between the king and the law to remove any lingering taint of disloyalty and deposition.

The period of the Appellant coup and its aftermath was the most anguished and harrowing that Richard had yet lived through. He had seen his policies reversed, his household taken over and purged, and his friends either exiled or sent to their deaths. He himself had been subjected to humiliation and constraint. Sadly, evidence for his reaction to these events is hard to come by. Few insights are provided by the chroniclers. Walsingham records his tearfulness when confronted by the Appellants in the Tower, while the Monk of Westminster comments on the alarm that he felt at the Appellants' threats.[76] Neither of these writers nor any other, however, has anything to say on the subject of his mood during parliament. One reason for this may lie in the relative ignorance of the chroniclers, few of whom appear to have been well informed about events at Westminster. Another and more significant reason, however, was Richard's own inscrutable behaviour at the time. On only one occasion during the three months of the parliament did he allow himself to give outward expression to his feelings. This was in May when he intervened to try to save the life of Simon Burley. The rest of the time he kept the secrets of his mind firmly to himself. The result is that it is impossible to judge the exact nature of his reaction to events. It may be surmised that initially his emotions were confused and that he found it difficult to come to terms with what had happened. It may be surmised too that he was embittered by the judicial destruction of his party, but that his bitterness was tempered by a consciousness of the need to trim to the Appellant wind. Beyond such vague and

---

year that their lives were in danger. In January John Beauchamp wrote from the Tower to the prior of Worcester asking him to safeguard the valuables which he had entrusted to his keeping (Worcester Cathedral Library, Liber Albus, fo.331ᵛ). It was in Worcester Cathedral six months later that he was buried (plate 5).

[74] WC, 340, 342.

[75] Favent, Historia, 24.

[76] See above, 189.

inadequate generalizations, however, the evidence does not allow us to go.

In the three or four months following the end of the Merciless Parliament Richard appears to have taken little or no active role in politics. He presided over a meeting of the great council at Oxford in July, but otherwise, according to the Monk of Westminster, largely abandoned himself to the pleasures of the chase.[77]

The business of government at this time was carried on under the Appellants' direction by the three senior officers of state acting in liaison with the members of a number of overlapping councils. Responsibility for watching over the king was vested in a council composed of the bishops of London and Winchester, the earl of Warwick and Lords Cobham and Scrope, which was appointed at the end of the Merciless Parliament.[78] The direction of policy more generally appears to have been assumed by a body variously referred to in the sources as a 'continual council' or a 'council appointed in parliament'.[79] The membership of this body is nowhere stated, but a leading role on it is likely to have been played by Gloucester and Arundel, the two most vigorous and committed of the five Appellants. Gloucester was in a sense the unofficial leader of the Appellants by virtue of his royal birth and long record of criticism of the court.[80] Arundel, a man with an even longer record of criticism, was his close ally. The two were very similar in outlook and political beliefs. They had both been bitterly opposed to the dominance of the court in the mid-1380s by de Vere and the other favourites; and they both favoured an early renewal of the war with France. By the late spring of 1388, with Burley and the king's other friends gone, they could consider the purging of the court largely accomplished. It was to the matter of renewing the war that by the summer they were directing their energies and attention.

By the end of 1387 the military endeavours of the council had petered out in anticlimax. Arundel's expedition, though it had scored a major victory over the French at Cadzand, had failed in its central objective of provoking a rebellion against the French in Flanders. Hotspur's relief of the beleaguered garrison at Brest offered some

---

[77] WC, 344, 342. Richard was at the royal hunting lodge of Beckley intermittently in July and early August: CPR 1385–9, 495, 499.

[78] WC, 332.

[79] RP, iii, 246.

[80] Significantly, he was the only one of the five Appellants to whom the dean and chapter of York considered it worth paying a fee: they paid him the substantial sum of £40 in 1387–8 (York Minster Library, Dean and Chapter chamberlains' accounts, E1/9).

consolation. But this was a local success; it had no effect on the overall outcome of the war.[81] Effectively the two sides had reached stalemate again. Richard's response was to initiate behind-the-scenes moves for peace in the expectation that he would shortly be back in control.[82] The Appellants' coup in December put paid to his plans, and Gloucester's and Arundel's response was very different: it was to order the planning of a fresh expedition. It was to the task of achieving this that they applied themselves in the late winter and early spring.

The strategy conceived by the two lords was an ambitious one. It involved a three- or even a four-pronged assault on the French. The main thrust was to be provided by another naval expedition under Arundel, but secondary thrusts, it was hoped, would be provided by forces under the leadership of the duke of Brittany, the Ghentois and John of Gaunt, who had by now left Castile for Aquitaine.[83] A major diplomatic offensive was launched in January in an effort to persuade these rulers and princes to participate, but the results were considerably more meagre than the lords had expected. Only with the duke of Brittany was a formal treaty concluded. The text of the document does not survive, but it seems that the English committed themselves to sending a considerable force to the duchy in return for the duke's participation first in an attack on Jean de Blois, his rival, and then in an invasion of the French heartland.[84] With the other parties who were approached no agreements were made. The Ghentois were sympathetic, but after seven years of struggle lacked the stomach for war. John of Gaunt, having bartered away his claim to the Castilian throne, was now more interested in consolidating his position in Aquitaine.[85] The last thing that either party wanted was the renewal of a war from which they would both emerge the losers.

The failure to win widespread diplomatic support was disastrous for Gloucester's and Arundel's plans. What had been conceived as an ambitious and wide-ranging campaign was in danger of degenerating into a sideshow. The most Arundel could hope for was the support of the duke of Brittany in an attack on the north-west of France. But even that modest assistance was denied him. When the duke heard of Gaunt's refusal to become involved he began to have doubts about his own participation. Using the late departure of Arundel's fleet as an excuse he left the duchy for a meeting with the French dukes at Blois;

---

[81] Palmer, *England, France and Christendom*, 100–2.

[82] Ibid., 105–21.

[83] Ibid., 122–30.

[84] Ibid., 127. Jean de Blois had been released in accordance with the terms of an agreement between him and Robert de Vere, to whom Richard had granted his ransom. On this, see above, 155.

[85] See below, 209.

and from there he made his way to Paris to enter into an accommodation with Charles VI. Arundel, who was unaware of what had happened when he set sail, heard the news only when he arrived off the Breton coast. He hung around for several weeks in the vain hope that the duke might change his mind. When it became clear that he would not, he weighed anchor and headed south. Probably at this stage he still entertained hopes of effecting a junction with Lancaster; but these hopes too were to be disappointed. The duke did not show up, and the earl had to content himself with launching raids on the countryside around La Rochelle. These were favourably reported by the English chroniclers, but strategically of little value. On 3 September the earl returned to England having failed to achieve any of the objectives set for him.[86]

Only a matter of days after Arundel had taken so optimistically to the sea at Southampton, the Appellants found themselves engaged in the north. On 29 June, after the expiry of the latest in a series of truces, the Scots – evidently catching the English unawares – launched an ambitious two-pronged invasion of the northern counties, ostensibly in retaliation for the English invasion of 1385. The offensive was said by the Monk of Westminster to have been the largest for many years. One force under the earl of Fife cut its way through Cumberland and Westmorland, while the other under the earl of Douglas broke into Northumberland through Redesdale. Douglas ravaged the river valleys of the borders, and inflicted a heavy defeat on an English force under Hotspur at Otterburn on 5 August. This was a severe blow to English prestige, and Hotspur himself was captured, but the battle was of limited strategic significance. More serious in many ways was the western assault on Cumberland and Westmorland. Much of the country north of Shap was systematically devastated; Carlisle itself held out, but Appleby was sacked and the villages of the Eden valley suffered serious damage. Richard's response to the incursions was to order an immediate retaliatory attack on the Scots, but at a great council at Northampton on 20 August it was decided to defer any such action until the following year. Reprisals for the moment were left to the local nobility, who successfully repulsed raids on Berwick and Carlisle and burned Peebles in the summer of the following year.[87]

---

[86] The best account of the expedition is *WC*, 350–2; see also *HA*, ii, 175.

[87] For the fighting in the north, see *WC*, 346–50, which may be supplemented by information in SC8/304/15167 and Edinburgh University Library MS 183, fos 94^r–94^v. For the background to the fighting, see A. Goodman, 'Introduction' and A. Grant, 'The Otterburn War from the Scottish Point of View', *War and Border Societies in the Middle Ages*, ed. Tuck and Goodman. Otterburn is the battle commemorated by the Chevy Chase ballads. The name 'Chevy Chase' refers to the chase or hunt in the Cheviots.

The Appellants' failures in France and on the borders did much to discredit their regime in the eyes of their supporters in the commons. The commons had entertained high expectations that the Appellant council would be able to step up the war and bring them the victories that had proved so elusive in the past. By the end of the season it was clear that their expectations were to be disappointed. The upturn in military activity had lasted no more than a few weeks, and the results achieved in the field had been meagre. There was no sign of the breakthrough in the war for which the Appellants and their supporters had hoped. Not surprisingly, the result was growing disenchantment with a regime that had promised so much but had delivered so little.

Military failure was one reason for the commons' disenchantment with the Appellants. A second and related factor was the problem of public finance. The Appellants had expected to meet most of the cost of renewed war from the crown's own resources, for a large amount of property had come into royal custody as a result of the sentences imposed in the Merciless Parliament. The earldoms and inheritances of Oxford and Suffolk, the temporalities of the sees of York and Chichester, and the lands and goods of convicted judges, officials and chamber knights had all been seized and taken into royal keeping. A statute passed at the end of the parliament provided that these properties were either to remain in the king's hands or, if necessary, to be sold on the authority of the council and the proceeds used to pay off the king's debts.[88] The Appellants availed themselves of the latter option as a way of simultaneously solving their financial problems and creating a vested interest in the permanence of their regime. Accordingly, from July 1388 the greater part of the lands were auctioned off, and by midsummer 1389 almost £10,000 had been paid or promised to the exchequer. This was a somewhat lower sum than had been anticipated, because entailed land and land held in jointure was excepted.[89] Moreover it afforded little immediate help to the Appellants because the receipts from sales trickled in slowly. The Appellants thus found themselves driven, however reluctantly, to seek parliamentary taxation. In March a half-subsidy was sought from the Merciless Parliament to pay for Arundel's expedition; and six months later at Cambridge a full fifteenth and tenth were sought to pay for the defence of the north. These taxes were granted with considerable reluctance. At Cambridge it is likely that only half of the sum that the chancellor had initially asked for on behalf of the government was made available.[90] The commons' had expected the Appellants to pay for the renewal of the

[88] *SR*, ii, 52.

[89] C.D. Ross, 'Forfeiture for Treason in the Reign of Richard II', *EHR*, lxxi (1956), 560–75.

[90] A. Tuck, 'The Cambridge Parliament, 1388', *EHR*, lxxxiv (1969), 232.

war out of the crown's own resources without burdening the people
with further imposts. That expectation, like the expectation of military
success, was disappointed, and by autumn there was evidence that
disillusionment with the regime was setting in.

With the gradual weakening of the alliance between the Appellants
and their commons supporters Richard found his political prospects
significantly improved. By autumn he could entertain the thought of
playing the commons off against the lords and of presenting himself as
the political champion of the former. He could not achieve much so
long as the political agenda was dominated, as it had been, by issues of
war and foreign policy, which favoured the Appellants. But in the
autumn an issue came to prominence which he could turn to his
advantage. This was the matter of liveries and their relation to public
order.

The commons had grown increasingly restive about the state of
public order since the early years of the reign. The violence of the Great
Revolt had unnerved them, and they felt uneasy about the continuing
high level of lawlessness in the shires. The evidence of their parliamentary petitions suggests that they viewed the problem of disorder, or
'misrule' as they called it, in social rather than strictly legal terms. They
saw lawlessness as a consequence of the breakdown of the social hierarchy and the failure of the estates to perform their appointed roles.
The lower orders, they believed, were aping the manners and lifestyle of
the magnates, while the magnates themselves were aggravating the
problem by practising unlawful maintenance and failing to preserve the
peace. Symptomatic of the general decay was the magnates' distribution
of badges, or 'signs' as they were known, to those on the fringes of their
affinities. Bestowal of these marks of favour emboldened the wearers
and encouraged them in their misdeeds. If public order were to be
restored and the established hierarchy reaffirmed, badge distribution
would have to be curbed and the badge-wearers themselves subjected to
discipline.[91] It was to the attainment of these objects that the commons
applied themselves at the parliament which met at Barnwell Priory,
Cambridge, in September.

The commons stated their main demand clearly in the first clause of
their roll of petitions – that 'all liveries called badges, whether given by
the king or the lords, of which use has begun since the first year of King
Edward III (1327), and all other lesser liveries, such as hoods, shall
henceforth not be given or worn but shall be abolished upon the pain
specified in this parliament'. To this they added the further demand,
intended to reduce corruption in the courts, that justices of assize and

[91] On this theme see N.E. Saul, 'The Commons and the Abolition of Badges', *PH.*,
ix (1990), 302–15.

the peace should have power to investigate and try cases of maintenance, bribery and other means of corrupting juries.[92] The Appellants
were taken aback by the comprehensiveness of these demands. Their
immediate response was to ask the commons to hand over any
offenders known to them for exemplary punishment. This proposal
failed to impress the commons, who reiterated that law and order could
only be restored if badges were abolished. The two sides seemed to be
heading for deadlock. At this point Richard himself decisively intervened. Stressing his desire for peace, he offered to lay aside his own
badges as an example to others. This was a clever move, designed to
wrongfoot the lords, and the latter not surprisingly were reluctant to
accept it. Richard then donned the mantle of conciliator and offered to
bring the two sides together. He said how anxious he was to avoid
dissension, and that he wanted to see them living together in harmony.
He therefore suggested that the whole matter be deferred for consideration in the next parliament, while in the meantime he would ordain
a provisional remedy in co-operation with the lords. His proposal was
accepted, and an ordinance was agreed the terms of which were re-
hearsed on the roll of the following parliament (January 1390): no man
of whatever condition could wear a lord's livery badge unless retained
for life by indenture, and no person of lesser estate than esquire could
wear a lord's badge unless he was a household servant of that lord.[93] It
was these provisions which formed the basis of the final settlement of
the issue ordained at the great council of April 1390.[94]

Richard's skilful handling of the badges issue bore witness to a new
assurance and sophistication in his kingly style. All of a sudden it
seemed that he had shed the brittle and inflexible behaviour of his
adolescent years and was assuming the character of a mature and
reasonable young ruler, willing to listen and eager to learn. The causes
of this transformation have been much debated. Anthony Steel suggested that Richard was made 'more or less numb', as he put it, by what
had happened in 1388: he could not respond coherently to the crisis
that beset royal authority and instead found refuge in appeasement – in
other words, in humouring the Appellants and in going along with
whatever they required of him.[95] The difficulty with this theory is that it
underestimates the measure of Richard's achievement in late 1388 and
1389. A man who could recover power as smoothly and as comprehensively as Richard did in these months could hardly have been 'more or
less numb' from shock a few weeks previously. An alternative, and in
many ways a more plausible, theory is that of the late K.B. McFarlane

[92] *WC*, 356–8.
[93] *Ibid.*, 356; *RP*, iii, 265; Given-Wilson, *Royal Household and the King's Affinity*, 239.
[94] Storey, 'Liveries and Commissions of the Peace', *The Reign of Richard II*, 145–6.
[95] Steel, *Richard II*, 173–4.

that Richard was dissimulating – concealing his true feelings, which were always hostile to the Appellants, under a façade of reasonableness and moderation.[96] There is much to be said for this view, not least that it helps to account for the further change that occurred in Richard's behaviour in 1397. But one major objection can be raised against it: if Richard had been dissimulating, he would surely have let the mask slip occasionally, revealing himself in his true colours. In fact, however, nothing of the sort ever happened. Richard's behaviour over the subsequent eight years was as calm and generally consistent as anyone's ever could be.

The most likely explanation of Richard's behaviour suggested by the evidence is that it was what psychologists call 'situation dependent': it varied according to the circumstances in which the king found himself. In one psychological environment he might display one set of reactions consistently over time, while in another he might display a quite different set. The responses that he made would in large measure be dependent on his appraisal of the situation and his reactions to it.

An analysis of Richard's behaviour in these terms can help to make sense of a good deal that would otherwise be inexplicable. The sudden changes in Richard's behaviour can be seen as shifts from one psychological environment to another, and the periods of stability in between as responses to a basic stability of environment. The psychological environments themselves can be seen in chronological terms as phases in Richard's development from adolescence to manhood. The first such environment was probably that in which Richard grew up between 1377 and 1387. Spatially this was defined by the structures of the court and the royal household, and socially by the dominant influence in it of Burley, the king's tutor, and de Vere, his closest companion. The stability of this environment was shattered by the destruction of the court in 1388, and its successor was markedly different in character. The dominant influences now were those of his uncle, John of Gaunt, newly returned to England, and a tightly knit group of officers of state and chamber knights. These were men of a more mature and balanced outlook than their predecessors in royal favour, and their influence on the king's conduct quickly became noticeable. In council Richard showed a new willingness to heed criticism, listen to advice and refrain from unwise or controversial measures. To the extent that he was rewarded for his more amenable manner, he was encouraged to reproduce it in a variety of other settings and it became his uniform style of behaviour. Had there been no further changes in psychological environment it is possible that he would have continued to act in this way and would never have suffered the unhappy fate of deposition. But

[96] K.B. McFarlane, *Lancastrian Kings and Lollard Knights* (Oxford, 1972), 36.

towards the end of the 1390s it seems that a further change did occur, and as a result there was a second major shift in his behaviour. It is this shift that forms the background to the years of 'tyranny' after 1397 and Richard's eventual overthrow in 1399.[97]

In late 1388 and 1389, however, it was Richard's stability and moderation that impressed people. The tide of opinion was moving in his favour, and by autumn there was little to prevent him from flexing his political muscles again. There were no longer any unpopular favourites at court to give unity and point to the forces of opposition. All that stood in the way of the king's formal recovery of his power was the solidarity of the Appellants themselves. During the winter and spring of 1389 Richard worked to break up that solidarity by winning over Nottingham and Derby, the least committed of the five lords. At a great council on 20 January he appointed Nottingham warden of the eastern march towards Scotland, with effect from 1 June.[98] The appointment was of considerable importance, given the turbulent state of the border, and it was Nottingham's first independent command. Doubtless the earl took the intended hint that Richard now had more to offer him than did the Appellants. His former ally Henry of Derby made his way back to royal favour without the aid of inducements and douceurs. He was a courtier by instinct, and once his enemy Robert de Vere had gone he was happy to return to the fold. A gift to him from the king of a valuable breastplate marked the growth of a warmer and more intimate relationship between them.[99]

By May Richard was ready formally to reassert his authority and bring the period of Appellant rule to an end. At a council meeting in the Marcolf chamber at Westminster on 3 May he announced his assumption of personal responsibility for the governance of the realm. For twelve years, he said, he and his kingdom had been ruled by others, and his people had been oppressed by taxation. But now he was of mature age, and he intended assuming the burden of government in person and working tirelessly for the well-being and prosperity of his people.[100] On the next day he dismissed the ministers imposed on him by the Appellants. Arundel was replaced as chancellor by the aged bishop of Winchester, William of Wykeham, and Gilbert as treasurer by the equally aged Brantingham of Exeter; Gloucester and Arundel were removed from the council. Four days later Richard made a further announcement in the form of a proclamation to the sheriffs. He declared his intention of ruling in such wise as to bring better peace and justice to the realm. The sentences of 1388, he said, would be

---

[97] See below, 366–75.
[98] WC, 376–8; Rot. Scot., ii, 96.
[99] Goodman, Loyal Conspiracy, 52.
[100] WC, 390–2.

upheld; riots, oppressions and unlawful assemblies would be suppressed; and complaints about unlawful behaviour would be given immediate attention by the officers and council.[101] This second proclamation complemented the first, and together they amounted to a comprehensive programme of reform. What Richard was offering his subjects was the promise of better governance, lower taxation and speedier access to justice. This was a programme broadly similar in character to the Appellants' of a year earlier. In one significant respect, however, it differed. Whereas the Appellants had premised their policies on a commitment to renewing the war with the French, Richard did not. He had long been opposed to the war, and saw the obstacle it posed to lowering the level of taxation. His own commitment was to reaching an accord with the French as speedily as possible. So much was implicit in the decision he made on 16 May to remit the second half of the subsidy granted at the Cambridge parliament on condition that a satisfactory truce was made with the French.[102] Lower taxation and the absence of war, he was saying, went hand in hand. This was a connection that he hoped his subjects would remember when he began the quest for a final settlement of the long conflict with France.

[101] *CCR 1385–9*, 671; *Foed.*, vii, 618–19.
[102] *Foed.*, vii, 620–1.

Chapter 10

THE QUEST FOR PEACE, 1389–98

Little more than a month after Richard's recovery of power a truce was agreed between the English and the French at Leulingham near Calais. The negotiations leading to this outcome had been long and tortuous. Philip of Burgundy had made the first move in December 1387 when he had written to Gloucester to enquire if he would be interested in a proposal for a long truce. Gloucester, who was committed to war at the time, had no interest and did not reply. Six months later, however, after the failure of Arundel's expedition, his attitude changed, and he saw in Duke Philip's enquiry a way of reopening contact with the French without loss of face. Apologizing for his delay in replying on the grounds that he had been occupied with other business, he accepted the proposal for a truce and suggested that the captain of Calais be used as an intermediary. Negotiations were apparently begun in the autumn, when the English appointed their envoys, but their course was halting and slow. The French were responsible for delays in the early stages while Duke Philip, who had invaded Guelders in October, tried to consolidate his position there. Later the English raised objections when the French wanted the Scots and Castilians to be included, and for a couple of months the talks were adjourned while the two groups of envoys referred to their respective monarchs. In the spring, after this issue had been settled, largely to the advantage of the French, events moved more rapidly. Safe-conducts for the French envoys were renewed by Richard on 5 May. A commission to conclude a truce was issued nine days later; and the truce itself was sealed a little over a month after that, on 18 June.[1]

The truce inaugurated the longest break in hostilities since the resumption of the war in 1369. Initially the agreement was that it should last for three years until August 1392; but in 1392 it was renewed until 1393, in 1393 until 1394, and so on. Neither of the two protagonists had any interest in resuming hostilities. The pressures of war over the previous twenty years had severely strained both kingdoms. In France wide areas of the countryside lay devastated, and the burden

---

[1] *CPR 1385–9*, 502–3; *WC*, 376; *HA*, ii, 179–80. For discussion see Palmer, *England, France and Christendom*, 138–9, 142.

of taxation was provoking resistance from the people. In England physical damage was slighter, being confined mainly to the south coast, but
resistance to taxation had grown equally strong. Three of the four
parliaments from 1381 had refused to make any grant of direct
taxation, and the grants made thereafter were usually small. Even the
Appellants, who had come to power on a tide of popular goodwill,
were unable to extract more than a half-fifteenth and tenth from the
Merciless Parliament and a single one from the parliament held at
Cambridge. The Appellants' inability to maintain the momentum of
war resulted in large measure from their failure to command adequate
financial resources.

Behind parliament's resistance to further taxes lay a growing disenchantment with the war. People were worried and perturbed by the
failure of English arms to make any headway against the French. For
twenty years there had been no victories to celebrate, nor even many
feats of arms to cheer the soul. The lands conquered by Edward III had
slowly but seemingly inexorably been whittled away. Reactions to the
tale of unending woe varied. One response, strongly articulated in
parliament, was to blame the court for corruption and failure of leadership and to call for reforms which would lessen the need for taxation.
Another, widespread among the educated and articulate elite, was to
question the justness of the war and the righteousness of those who
waged it. Sir John Clanvow, one of Richard's chamber knights and a
poet of distinction, pointed to the self-indulgence of the knights, who
wasted and destroyed lands and spent their gains on food, drink, clothing and living in ease. John Gower, echoing these sentiments, went
further and attacked the very waging of war which, he said, was condemned by God in both the Old Law and the New.[2] Occasional echoes
of these views are found in the work of Chaucer, while across the
Channel similar sentiments were expressed by Philippe de Mézières and
Christine de Pisan.[3] The war was condemned not – or not only – because
it was expensive but because it was savage, immoral and unjust.

Richard's own dislike of the conflict is attested by a number of

---

[2] 'The Two Ways', ll.4–10, *The Works of Sir John Clanvow*, ed. V.J. Scattergood
(Cambridge, 1975); John Gower, 'Vox Clamantis', Bk. 5, ch. 8, in translation in *The
Major Latin Works of John Gower*, ed. E.W. Stockton (Seattle, 1962); Gower, *Confessio
Amantis*, Book 3, l.2277, in *The Complete Works of John Gower*, ed. G.C. Macaulay
(Oxford, 4 vols, 1899–1902), ii, 287.
[3] For Chaucer's outlook see his short poem 'The Former Age' in *The Works of
Geoffrey Chaucer*, ed. F.N. Robinson (London, 2nd edn, 1957), 534. For discussion
see V.J. Scattergood, 'Chaucer and the French War: *Sir Thopaz* and *Melibee*', *Court
and Poet*, ed. G.S. Burgess (Liverpool, 1981), 287–96; and J.A. Burrow, *Ricardian
Poetry: Chaucer, Gower, Langland and the Gawain Poet* (London, 1971), 57, 93–4. For
Christine de Pisan see *Le 'Livre de la Paix' of Christine de Pisan*, ed. C.C. Willard (The
Hague, 1958); and for de Mézières see below, 207–8.

contemporary writers. Froissart recalled a conversation with Sir Jean de Grailly in which the latter told him of the king's ardent desire to end the war. Richard, Grailly told the chronicler, believed that the war had gone on for too long, that too many brave men had been killed in it, too many evil deeds perpetrated, and too many Christian people ruined or destroyed, to the detriment of the Christian faith. It was his hope that a lasting peace could be established between himself and the king of France and between their two peoples.[4] Froissart's testimony, which, it is true, is not always reliable, is here supported by Philippe de Mézières, the former chancellor of Cyprus who was seeking Richard's support for an Anglo-French crusade to the Holy Land. In his famous letter to Richard II, the *Épistre au Roi Richart*, he praised the king for his affection for his fellow monarch, Charles of France, and spoke of the desire that he had always shown to make peace with his brothers, the French, and with all Christian peoples.[5] If the evidence of these writers is to be believed, Richard's opposition to the war was not just a matter of policy. To say this is not to suggest that he was entirely oblivious to the case for peace on tactical grounds: the Westminster chronicler says that in 1387 he had been worried that, if war continued, 'he would be compelled for ever to be burdening his people with new imposts, with damaging results for himself'.[6] Almost certainly, he saw a settlement with France as a means of relieving the fiscal burden on his subjects and removing the opportunities which the crown's financial weakness offered to its opponents. But considerations of this kind seem to have weighed with him a good deal less than those of a loftier nature. The king was moved by a genuine abhorrence of the shedding of blood between Christians. It may well have been on his initiative that in the 1380s a change was made in the diplomatic formulae of chancery correspondence which gave expression to this sentiment. Hitherto in the instructions drawn up for their envoys he and his predecessors had expressed their desire for peace in very general terms. From 1384, however, a formula was employed by which Richard referred expressly to his 'wish to bring peace and tranquillity to his people and to end the shedding of Christian blood'.[7] This is language highly reminiscent of that employed

---

[4] Froissart, ii, 573-4. Froissart stresses Richard's support for peace at other points in his narrative, e.g. 548, 558, 560.

[5] P. de Mézières, *Letter to King Richard II*, ed. G.W. Coopland (Liverpool, 1975), 19, 32.

[6] WC, 204.

[7] *Foed.*, vii, 429, 431, 433. Horror of bloodshed had been invoked in preambles on a few occasions before – in 1340, 1356 and 1374 (*English Historical Documents. IV: 1327–1485*, ed. A.R. Myers (London, 1969), 67; *Foed.*, v, 851; vi, 760–1), but it was only from 1384 that it was used regularly. It is tempting to wonder whether Richard's abhorrence of 'the shedding of Christian blood' could help to account for his reluctance to press far into Scotland in 1385.

by Philippe de Mézières. What lay behind it was a growing appreciation
of the folly of Christians waging war with Christians at a time when
Christian kingdoms in the east were being overrun by the Turks. By the
1380s the greater part of south-eastern Europe lay exposed to the
Turkish advance. In 1385 Sofia had fallen, in 1386 Nis and in 1387
Thessalonika. In 1389 at Kossovo the kingdom of Serbia was destroyed.
The danger posed to Christian Europe by the infidel advance could no
longer be avoided. Richard, keenly aware of his responsibilities as a
Christian ruler, fully realized this – as Charles VI of France did too. Both
kings were accordingly anxious to bring an end to the long-running
dispute between them. A settlement of that dispute was a precondition
of a wider settlement of the divisions of Christendom; and once the
divisions of Europe were healed the way would be open for the organization of a crusade to the East.

The broad outlines of Richard's attitude to the Anglo-French war are
thus fairly clear. What is less easily established is the king's role in the
diplomacy designed to bring it to an end. The difficulty here lies in the
nature of the sources. The instructions to envoys and letters to foreign
rulers which are the raw materials of the study of diplomacy, though
issued in the king's name, were never drafted by him. They were the
work of his clerks, many of them experienced administrators and men
with a legal training, like Richard Ronhale and Edmund Stafford.[8] How
far these sources reflect the king's thinking, as opposed to that of those
who advised him, is hard to say. The king would have been regularly
consulted on all the major questions of policy. Payments on the issue
rolls to messengers taking letters to him bear witness to ministers'
anxiety to keep him informed. But the more technical aspects of policy
were dealt with by the council. The council at this time was a working
body which met in regular session at Westminster, usually without the
king.[9] The most frequent attenders in the 1390s were the officers
of state, a few magnates such as Lancaster and Northumberland, and
a group of chamber knights led by Sir Edward Dallingridge, Sir John
Clanvow and Sir Richard Stury. Dallingridge and the knights attended
for anything up to 200 days a year.[10] Administratively their presence
on the council was indispensable, but politically they did not carry
great weight. The most influential members of the body were the

[8] Ronhale was a BCL and a former warden of King's Hall, Cambridge, and
Stafford a DCL (A. Cobban, *The King's Hall within the University of Cambridge in the
Later Middle Ages* (Cambridge, 1969), 281–2; *BRUC*, 487–8; *BRUO*, iii, 1749–50). In
his will Ronhale left a collection of books of canon and civil law to Newnham Priory
(Beds.) (Lambeth Palace, Reg. Arundel, i, fo.178ᵛ).
[9] See below, 251–3.
[10] J.F. Baldwin, *The King's Council in England during the Middle Ages* (Oxford, 1913),
133. For a detailed discussion of the council, see below pp. 251–3.

officers, in particular the chancellor Thomas Arundel, and the king's uncle John of Gaunt and the earl of Northumberland. Of these men Gaunt was probably the most important. It is likely – indeed, it is almost certain – that where foreign affairs were concerned his was the decisive voice.

Gaunt's interest in matters outside the realm was, of course, of long standing. He had been an influential force in debates on foreign policy since the later years of Edward III's reign. His views, however, had changed a great deal since the time, only a few years before, when he had clashed with de la Pole and other royal councillors about whether or not there should be a royally led expedition to France.[11] In the 1380s Gaunt had been a keen advocate of aggressive action against France and her allies. He himself had a claim to the crown of France's ally Castile, and he saw his pursuit of that claim as a way of breaking the deadlock between the two sides in the larger conflict. The expedition to the peninsula, which he led in 1386, however, had enjoyed mixed fortunes. Disease had badly ravaged the ranks of his forces and those of the king of Portugal, and he had had little success in breaking through the Castilian defences in Leon.[12] Little more than a year after landing in the peninsula the duke judged it expedient to submit to a settlement with the Castilian king. At Trancoso terms were agreed whereby Gaunt surrendered his claim to the throne in return for an initial payment of 600,000 francs and an annual pension thereafter of 40,000 francs; at the same time a marriage alliance was arranged between his daughter Catalina and Juan's son and heir Henrique.[13] Once these terms were ratified at Bayonne on 8 July 1388, Gaunt's attitude to the Anglo-French conflict changed. Instead of favouring the extension of the war he now favoured its limitation. Any renewal of the conflict would threaten both the receipt of his pension and the position of his daughter, shortly to become queen of Castile. The gradual development of his interests in Aquitaine, whither he had withdrawn after his settlement with Juan, also disposed him towards peace. In 1388, while the Appellants were in power, he had been granted the office of lieutenant of Aquitaine. Two years later in March 1390 Richard bestowed the duchy on him for life as a personal apanage. The grant of this dignity did much to satisfy Gaunt's yearning to make himself a semi-independent ruler in the manner of Philip of Burgundy. Almost as soon as he had arrived in the duchy (he reached Bayonne in September 1387) he set about buttressing his lordship there. On 18 August at Blaye he agreed

---

[11] On this see above, 140.

[12] *WC*, 190 gives a list of magnate and gentry casualties in Spain. For discussion of Gaunt's military fortunes see Russell, *English Intervention*, chs xvii, xviii.

[13] The successive drafts of the treaty are printed in *The Treaty of Bayonne (1388)*, ed. J. Palmer and B. Powell (Exeter, 1988).

a six-month truce with the representatives of the duke of Berry, ending all acts of war south of the River Loire. A little later he negotiated an extension of the truce until July.[14] A cessation of French military activity in the south-west was therefore essential to Gaunt if he was to establish himself in his duchy. Equally, a final settlement of the war was essential to him if he was to augment the territorial extent of the duchy.[15] Like Richard, but for different reasons, he had a powerful interest in peace.

One problem in particular, however, stood in his way, as it had stood in the way of others before him: the seemingly insoluble dispute over the duchy's status. Aquitaine had come to the English crown by the marriage of Eleanor to Henry of Anjou, the future Henry II, in 1152. In the twelfth century the duchy had been ruled as an *allod*, an independent territory held of no feudal lord and effectively outside the kingdom of France. This situation had been transformed by the treaty of Paris of 1259. Henry III, as a condition of being allowed to retain his duchy, was required to enter into feudal dependence on the French king: henceforth he and his successors had to perform an oath of liege homage each time there was a change of either king or vassal. The effect of this was seriously to limit the king-duke's exercise of authority in his duchy. Vassals who were dissatisfied with his justice could take their cases on appeal to Paris, thus removing themselves from his jurisdiction and offering the French king every excuse to intervene. It was the execution of a sentence given in the *parlement* at Paris that provided the French king with a pretext for confiscating the duchy in 1294, 1324 and 1337. In the eyes of the English king – who was after all a sovereign lord in his own kingdom – the anomalies of the English position in Aquitaine were intolerable. The central demand of English negotiators at successive conferences in the Hundred Years War was therefore that they be eliminated: that the duchy be detached from the kingdom of France and be held 'from God alone'. The French steadfastly refused to accede to this request, but in 1360 at Brétigny, at a time of unusual national weakness (King John was a prisoner in England), they were obliged to give way. The duchy was granted to the English king in full sovereignty in return for his renunciation of his claim to the French crown. The settlement was effective for a while, but it was too one-sided to be enduring, and nine years later the French tore it up. In all subsequent negotiations they stood rigidly by their earlier position: that Aquitaine must remain within the kingdom of France, and that the king of England, as a vassal of his French overlord, must perform liege homage

---

[14] C.J. Philpotts, 'John of Gaunt and English Policy towards France, 1389–1395', *JMH*, xvi (1990), 367–8.
[15] Ibid., 376.

for it. To Edward III and his ministers, as to his successors, these terms were unacceptable. In their view, performance of liege homage would place the English crown in subjection to the French, and some at least of Aquitaine must be held in full sovereignty. Upon the rocks of these two irreconcilable positions all discussions between the two sides foundered.

During the hundred years or so that the war lasted a number of proposals were put forward to break the deadlock. In the 1340s it was suggested that the English surrender Aquitaine in return for compensation elsewhere. A century later what was called a 'half-peace' was mooted, the aim of which was to combine territorial concessions by one side with a long truce.[16] Neither of these proposals ever gained widespread acceptance. In the later fourteenth century, however, according to Dr J.J.N. Palmer, a scheme was put forward which stood a much better chance of settling the problem and bringing the long struggle to an end. This was to separate England and the duchy by conferring the latter on an English prince (John of Gaunt being the favoured candidate) either for a number of years or in perpetuity under the sovereignty of the French kings.[17] The scheme suffered from a number of drawbacks, chief among them the probable opposition of the English parliament and the certain opposition of the duchy's inhabitants. But against these were to be set certain advantages. The first was that only in this way would the English government be reconciled to the idea of French sovereignty – for under the arrangement homage to the French king would be done by the duke (be it Gaunt or anyone else) and not by the king of England, thus removing the humiliation implied by the feudal subjection of the English crown. Secondly, and no less importantly, the proposal would appeal to the French. The principle of liege homage, which they regarded as fundamental, would effectively be conceded, and there was a reasonable possibility that over time the ducal dynasty would become assimilated to Valois France. Not surprisingly it was from the French side that the proposal for separation first emanated. It was put forward, according to Dr Palmer, in the Anglo-French negotiations of 1375, and it formed the basis of the abortive settlement of 1384. In the following decade, in Palmer's view, it was the essential foundation of the various proposals that culminated in the draft peace of 1393.

A central position in Palmer's interpretation is occupied by Richard's creation of his uncle as duke of Aquitaine for life in 1390, shortly after his return to England. This move, Palmer believes, was 'a declaration

---

[16] For these proposals see Palmer, 'The War Aims of the Protagonists', 53–6.

[17] Palmer, *England, France and Christendom*, ch. 2. For an earlier discussion of Palmer's views in the context of the proposed settlement of 1384, see above, 136–7.

of intent', 'the earliest hint' of a policy that was to come to fulfilment in the draft treaty agreed in 1393.[18] Certainly the timing of the announcement suggests a connection with the negotiations with the French, which were shortly to resume at Leulingham: Gaunt was created duke on 2 March; a month later the English envoys to the conference were issued with instructions which (it is argued) implicitly envisaged a final settlement based upon Gaunt's life tenure of the duchy.[19] A connection with the search for peace is suggested too by the terms of the grant. Richard invested his uncle with the duchy using the title of king of France: Gaunt was to hold the duchy from the king and his heirs 'as kings of France' and to pay homage to them in that capacity. This choice of formula seems to imply the existence of some hidden agenda in the grant of the duchy to Gaunt, for if Richard were to relinquish the title of king of France Gaunt would be left holding his duchy from Charles VI. No neater way of effecting the transfer could be conceived.

In the light of this evidence it is easy to see why Dr Palmer believes that the grant to Gaunt was very likely the starting point for the implementation of the proposed peace settlement with France. However, the argument is by no means as clear-cut as it seems. There is a plausible case for supposing that there was no connection at all between the grant and the resumption of the peace process. The grant could have been made solely in order to please Gaunt. Gaunt was an ambitious man, and his aspirations had to be satisfied. Since returning from Spain he had been without any clearly defined role in politics; the grant in his favour of Aquitaine provided him with such a role, and in a part of the world in which he had long been interested. It is true, as Palmer says, that the Gascons were to be loud in their objections to the grant. But the ultimate origin of these objections lay less in the fear of an Anglo-French accord than in the nature of the grant itself. Aquitaine had since 1254 been annexed to the English crown, from which it had been separated only as an apanage for the king's eldest son. The grant to Gaunt – the uncle and not the son of the reigning king – was in Gascon eyes quite simply an illegal step: in contravention of the terms of earlier grants and in violation of their privileges and liberties. It was for this reason and not because of any peace proposals, as yet unformulated, that the Gascons complained so volubly. Significantly, in their petitions to the crown they never mentioned the possibility of peace once. They were equally silent on the issue of the king's seemingly portentous use of his French rather than his English title. This probably had a quite

[18] Palmer, *England, France and Christendom*, 144; idem, 'The Anglo-French Peace Negotiations, 1390–1396', *TRHS*, 5th series, xvi (1966), 85.
[19] *Foed.*, vii, 659–60; *PPC*, i, 19–21.

different meaning for them from the one that it has for us. Richard could have been seen to be restating his claim to the French throne rather than laying plans to renounce it. Both before and after the donation he appointed judges to hear appeals in Aquitaine to him as king of France according to the procedures of his court of France.[20] He probably thought it appropriate to use his French title as well when investing his kinsman with a French apanage.

When all the evidence is considered, it seems unlikely that the grant to Gaunt had quite the significance that Palmer assumed that it did. However, his case does not rest entirely on this one piece of evidence. He finds further support in a quite different quarter – the Monk of Westminster's account of the proposals which John of Gaunt brought back from Amiens in 1392. The Monk was a well-informed writer, and one with a particular interest in foreign policy. What he has to say is deserving of respect. According to the Monk's account, it had been proposed by the French that Richard should renounce his claim to the crown of France and the old Angevin empire, in return for which the French would concede that, after the death of the duke of Berry, Aquitaine and Gascony and their appurtenances should revert to the duke of Lancaster *and his heirs* for ever, provided that the duke and his heirs performed the customary homage to the French king (i.e. liege homage).[21] These proposals, subsequently modified in detail, in Palmer's view formed the basis of the eventual settlement put to parliament in 1394. Again the Monk of Westminster provides the main support for the argument. In his account of the parliament the Monk reports the proposal that the dukes of Berry and Burgundy should have a life interest in the parts of Aquitaine which they held, and that on their deaths the reversion should devolve on the duke of Lancaster *and his heirs*.[22] The implication of these proposals was that an hereditary apanage would be created for the duke. In other words, the dispute between England and France would be settled by means of the permanent separation of Aquitaine and the English crown – the outcome which, Dr Palmer argues, Richard had in mind from the beginning.

There are a number of difficulties with this argument, just as there were with its earlier stages. In the first place, the Amiens proposals of 1392 could not have formed the basis of the final peace, because they were rejected by the English shortly after being negotiated. In May, only weeks after Gaunt's return, a great council was convened at Stamford to discuss them, and widespread opposition was

---

[20] Philpotts, 'John of Gaunt and English Policy towards France', 367.
[21] WC, 490.
[22] Ibid., 518.

voiced. The Monk of Westminster reports members of the commons as saying that it was absurd that for the benefit of a single person (i.e. Gaunt) the king should suffer the loss of such a fair and extensive domain, which had long been his by hereditary right. The king had probably lent his support to Gaunt, but faced with opposition of such strength he had no alternative but to back down. Fresh envoys were then sent to France to seek an extension of the truce and to negotiate an improvement of the proposed terms.[23] The Amiens proposals were effectively dead.

The second reason for doubting Dr Palmer's argument is that the Monk's account of the proposals tabled in parliament in January 1394 bears little or no relation to the text of the draft peace as it survives in a contemporary copy in the British Library. There are times, indeed, when the two sources seem to be referring to quite different agreements. The Monk talks of provision for the life interest of the duke of Berry, of tenure of the duchy by Lancaster and his heirs, and by implication of the permanent separation of Aquitaine and the crown. None of these proposals appears in the draft treaty, which is almost wholly preoccupied with the details of the territorial settlement between the two countries and the future of Calais and its march.[24] Almost the only feature common to both sources is the recognition of French sovereignty and acceptance of the principle of liege homage. Dr Palmer, recognizing the difference between the sources, has argued that the separation of Aquitaine from the crown is implied in the treaty by the fact that the French concessions were made to 'the king of England, his heirs and successors and those having cause of him' ('*aiains cause de lui*').[25] But to argue on these lines is to make a virtue of special pleading. The phrase 'having cause of him' was inserted for one reason only: to allow Richard a way of avoiding having to perform liege homage in person. It was never intended to allow Lancaster to perform the oath of homage as duke. The clear implication of the terms of the draft peace is that that document was founded on very different principles from those espoused by Lancaster in the previous year. The idea of permanently separating England and Aquitaine was taken off the agenda. Certainly proposals were considered to allow Lancaster to do homage for the usufruct of the duchy, but the union of Aquitaine with the crown after Lancaster's death was never called into question. All this is very different from the impression given by the otherwise reliable Monk of Westminster. It is hard to avoid the conclusion that on this occasion the Monk must be judged in error. He may have misunderstood the

---

[23] Ibid., 490.

[24] J.J.N. Palmer, 'Articles for a Final Peace between England and France, 16 June 1393', *BIHR*, xxxix (1966), 180–5.

[25] Palmer, 'The Anglo-French Peace Negotiations', 88.

proposals; alternatively he could simply have confused them with those of 1392.

The existence of these various difficulties makes it impossible to accept, or to accept in its entirety, Dr Palmer's thesis that the separation of Aquitaine from the crown was 'the fundamental basis' of all the peace proposals formulated between 1390 and 1394. It is true that separation was one of the options considered by the two governments – the idea was espoused by Lancaster at Amiens in 1392 – but it was subsequently rejected by the council at Stamford and thereafter appears to have been discarded.

In reality it seems unlikely that there was ever any single idea, or 'settled policy' in Dr Palmer's phrase, to which the two governments and their envoys adhered in all the meetings of this period.[26] Governments and envoys in the middle ages rarely approached their work in such terms. Diplomacy, like war, still retained many of the attributes of a lawsuit. It was concerned not so much with principles or policies as with the assertion and defence of rights. Negotiations were conducted in a highly legalistic manner, commonly employing the forms and techniques of the courtroom. The two sides would parley with one another, progressively reducing the differences between them until either an agreement was reached or the differences could be reduced no further. In the latter event the two sides would refer back to their respective monarchs for fresh instructions, and when these had been received they would meet again and the whole process would be resumed.

When medieval diplomacy is viewed in these terms it becomes possible to see that, in so far as there were any fixed points or 'settled policies' in the negotiations of the 1390s, they were to be found less in policy objectives spanning the national divide than in the negotiating positions of the two governments. The English position can be defined as embracing two principles: that the boundaries of the reconstituted Aquitaine should be defined as closely as possible to those agreed at Bretigny in 1360; and that the king or his assign should be required to perform only simple and not liege homage. These were the initial positions adopted by the English at the conferences held at Amiens in 1392 and Leulingham in 1393. A review of the outcome of those conferences will indicate the success which they achieved in adhering to them.

Settling the boundaries of the new Aquitaine, although a difficult matter technically, was in fact the easier of the two issues to resolve. The French showed themselves willing to make generous concessions. In

[26] For 'settled policies' see Palmer, *England, France and Christendom*, 143.

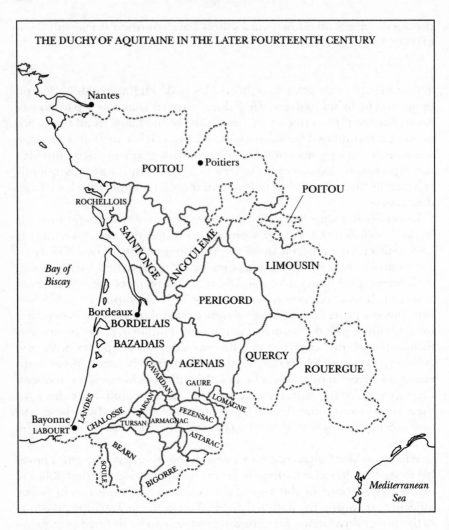

THE DUCHY OF AQUITAINE IN THE LATER FOURTEENTH CENTURY

1392, in reply to an English demand for the whole of Aquitaine, including Poitou (which was held by the duke of Berry) they offered the greater part of the old duchy – that is, the Gascon heartland, the Agenais, Périgord, Saintonge south of the Charente, Angoulême, Rouergue, Quercy and Bigorre; only Poitou, Saintonge north of the Charente, Aunis and Limoges were held back. In the following year at Leulingham the offer was improved. La Rochelle and the Limousin were added; so too was the homage of the counts of Armagnac, Foix and Périgord.[27] The English could count themselves well satisfied with

[27] H. Moranvillé, 'Conférences entre la France et l'Angleterre (1388–1393)',

what they had won. Negotiating from a relatively weak position militarily, they had gained all of the territories granted to Edward III except for Aunis, Poitou and northern Saintonge.

Greater difficulty was encountered in reaching agreement on the other issue, that of homage. For both sides this issue was fundamental, because it determined the relative standing of the two rulers, the king and the king-duke. The English government by this time had given up hope of retaining the duchy in sovereignty. The chief matter to be decided was whether the king should perform simple or liege homage. The difference between the two was greater than it seemed. Simple homage was merely an acknowledgement of lordship: it scarcely, if at all, limited the freedom of the vassal. Liege homage was a very different concept. It implied acceptance of the allied notions of sovereignty and *ressort*; sovereignty was an expression of the French king's claim to be 'emperor in his own kingdom', and *ressort* the right of the French king to be the ultimate arbiter of justice – the final 'resort' of appeals against judgments in lower courts.[28] To the English crown the performance of liege homage, though accepted by Henry III in 1259, was anathema. In the first place, it implied the subordination of the English king to the French, a humiliating condition that no English king could happily endure. And, in the second, it restricted the king's exercise of his authority in his capacity as duke: not only was there a risk that if he disciplined his vassals they would appeal against him to Paris; there was also the danger that he would be summoned by the French king to perform obligations – for example, of military service – that conflicted with his interests as king of England. For these reasons English envoys had long refused to submit to the French insistence on liege homage. In 1390, for example, they had objected that liege homage had not previously been discussed, and that the French should offer some territorial concessions before raising the terms on which the territory should be held.[29] In 1392 they sought to circumvent the problem by proposing that Lancaster should perform the oath of homage as duke. But a year later, by which time the French had made substantially greater territorial concessions, they shifted their position. In the articles of agreement drawn up at Leulingham they indicated their acceptance of 'la foy et hommage lige, le ressort et le soveraineté'.[30] This was the vital concession for which the French had been pressing.

The result was that by the summer of 1393 agreement had been

Bibliothèque de l'École des Chartes, i (1889), 371–3; Palmer, *England, France and Christendom*, 145–7.

[28] M. Vale, *The Angevin Legacy and the Hundred Years War, 1250–1340* (Oxford, 1990), 48–50.

[29] Moranvillé, 'Conférences entre la France et l'Angleterre', 368.

[30] Palmer, 'Articles for a Final Peace', 182.

reached on the two main issues in the way of a settlement. The English, on Lancaster's advice it seems, had signalled their acceptance of liege homage, but the French had gone a long way to satisfying their adversaries' demands in regard to territory. A document variously referred to by historians as a 'draft treaty' or 'articles of agreement' was drawn up to which the dukes of Berry and Burgundy, Lancaster and Gloucester put their seals; and a conference of legal experts was arranged to resolve the various technical matters that remained for consideration.[31] It seemed likely that the next stage would be the arranging of a meeting of the two kings to turn the draft into a final treaty of peace. In the event, however, no such meeting was held. In late 1393 there was a postponement because of a recurrence of Charles VI's bouts of insanity. In the following year the proposal for a meeting was dropped altogether. The two kings and their uncles went their separate ways – Richard and the duke of Gloucester to Ireland; Lancaster to Aquitaine; Orleans, Berry and Burgundy to Avignon.[32] After three years of intermittent negotiation the peace process was indefinitely suspended.

The causes of the impasse are difficult to pin down. Few insights of value are provided by the chroniclers. Walsingham asserts, with disarming simplicity, that Richard was unwilling to accede to the demands of the French – in effect restating the problem rather than resolving it. The Monk of Westminster, more helpfully, stresses the opposition to the proposed terms of the commons in parliament – although he confuses the terms on offer with those of two years before. Froissart – unusually – confesses himself completely puzzled. He says that at Abbeville, where he was staying, it was rumoured that peace had been made, but in the event, as he found, agreement was secured only to a renewal of the truce.[33] The inadequacy of these accounts is patent. To some extent the writers were suffering from ignorance, for they knew little of what was going on behind the scenes. But there was a certain opacity about the events themselves. No one cause, or set of causes, stood out as having precipitated the breakdown; contemporaries were at a loss to explain how it could have occurred. The Monk of Westminster's account of the problems that the government had in securing parliamentary ratification of the proposed peace highlights one area of difficulty faced by Richard and his ministers, but it does not offer a complete explanation of the crisis. Opposition to the proposed peace had been articulated in various quarters well before parliament met in January 1394. Froissart notes the hostility that the commons – by

---

[31] Ibid., 182–5; idem, *England, France and Christendom*, 149.

[32] Palmer, *England, France and Christendom*, 149.

[33] *Annales*, 157; *WC*, 518; Froissart, ii, 561–2. The St Denis chronicler was similarly ignorant: *CRSD*, ii, 82.

which he meant chiefly the gentry – showed in 1392 and 1393: he reports them as saying that 'they preferred peace to war, because war with France was more beneficial to them than otherwise'.[34] Froissart adds that the reservations of the English had by no means been overcome by the negotiations at Leulingham. Differences remained between them and the French over the status of Calais. At the same the English suspected the French of duplicity, and Gloucester was still of the view that the terms proposed were too favourable to the French.[35] Froissart's knowledge of the particular points at issue at Leulingham may well have been inaccurate and incomplete, as commentators have pointed out.[36] None the less it has to be recognized that the Hainaulter was a writer peculiarly sensitive to the popular mood. What he was reflecting was a genuine and growing unease in England at the prospect of peace – a fear widespread among the gentry and professional men-at-arms that livelihoods were going to be threatened. This unease was articulated, at least until about 1392, by Gloucester. Once the duke had become compromised by his involvement in the negotiations, however, as he had by 1393, it lacked a highly placed spokesman.[37] A sense of frustration developed which finally broke into the open in 1393 in an important but ill-documented episode: the rebellion of the commons of Cheshire. It was this episode which first made the government aware of the scale of the popular opposition to peace.

The best – indeed, the only detailed – account of the rising is found in Walsingham's longer chronicle.[38] This was written a decade or more after the events it describes, but it nevertheless draws on a number of well-attested contemporary traditions. The main point to emerge is that the origins of the rising lay in opposition to Richard's proposals for peace with the French. The rebels, according to the chronicler, accused Lancaster, Gloucester and Derby of being intent on depriving the king of his French title and of seeking to abolish the ancient liberties of their county. Under the leadership of Sir Thomas Talbot and Sir Nicholas Clifton, two veterans of the war, they nailed manifestoes to church doors and quickly attracted a large following. The government, despite being aware of the scale of the rising, was slow to respond. Some time in the spring the earl of Huntingdon and Sir John Stanley were sent to Cheshire to convey the king's displeasure and to suppress illegal assem-

---

[34] Froissart, ii, 548.

[35] Ibid., 559–60.

[36] J. Sherborne offers a devastating critique in 'Charles VI and Richard II'.

[37] WC, 518, comments on Gloucester's loss of influence with the commons as a result of his involvement in the negotiations.

[38] Annales, 159–62. For discussion see J.G. Bellamy, 'The Northern Rebellions of the Later Years of Richard II', BJRL, xlvii (1964–5), 254–74.

blies and gatherings.[39] The choice of Stanley, a local lord, showed sensitivity to rebel feelings; but the government's fairly mild reaction proved insufficient. In May Lancaster and Gloucester were summoned back from Leulingham, and on the 6th writs were issued to the former, as palatine lord, and to the latter, as justice of Chester, commanding action against the insurgents. The lords went about their task briskly but with moderation. Using force only occasionally, they succeeded in pacifying the county and offering reassurance to the rebels. Lancaster made a point of recruiting as many rebels as possible into a force that he was taking to Aquitaine. In this way he was able to allay the distrust that had fuelled the rising and had kept it alive. The restraint that he showed earned its reward. In the summer, when he started recruiting, the countryside was still in turmoil, but by November, when he left, conditions had largely returned to normal.

Fear of possible loss of livelihood, though the main, was not the only grievance that the rebels had against Lancaster and the king's ministers. Local factors had added to their discontent. Four years before the rising Richard had demanded a subsidy of 3,000 marks from the Cheshire community in return for granting a charter confirming the county's liberties. From the judicial records of Cheshire it is clear that collection of the subsidy was unpopular and that considerable opposition was provoked.[40] To the north, in neighbouring Lancashire, the position of the Lancastrian retinue as sole mediator of patronage bred resentment among those not privileged to be within its embrace. Two Lancashire knights who were excluded were the rebel leaders Talbot and Clifton. Talbot had found an alternative outlet for his energies as a professional soldier and garrison captain in France, and Clifton had followed his example; but with the successful conclusion of the duke's negotiations with the French, it looked as if even this avenue of employment was going to be closed. In the minds of soldiers like Talbot and Clifton dislike of the duke mingled with more principled opposition to peace.[41] But among the rebels as a whole, as Walsingham rightly pointed out, it was the threat of peace alone which was the main spur to rebellion. Cheshire had long been a recruiting ground for soldiery in the king's wars. Edward I had recruited 1,000 archers there for his Welsh campaign in 1277, nearly twice as many as in any other county, and in 1361 Cheshire sent three times the average number of soldiers raised from

---

[39] C47/14/6/44: a copy of an undated privy seal letter. The letter is remarkably complacent in tone, enjoining the two lords to offer redress of grievance to the rebels. Huntingdon and Stanley had set out for the county by 16 May (E403/543, 16 May).

[40] CPR 1391-6, 77–8. For discussion see Morgan, *War and Society in Medieval Cheshire*, 193–4.

[41] Walker, *Lancastrian Affinity*, 171–3.

each county to Ireland. The tradition of military service almost certainly had its origins in the county's proximity to Wales, but it was greatly strengthened in the 1360s by the Black Prince's tenure of the earldom of Chester, which gave the county a personal connection with the foremost soldier of the day.[42] There can be little doubt that the peace proposals of the 1390s constituted a major threat to the well-being of the Cheshire military community, and it is hardly surprising that the latter's reaction to them was so hostile.

Elsewhere in England the level of gentry participation in war was far lower than in Cheshire. In the midlands and south it is doubtful if more than about a quarter of the knights and richer esquires saw active service in the French wars in the 1370s and 1380s.[43] Men with such limited military experience lacked the direct interest in the continuance of war of their more battle-hardened colleagues, but they were probably no less committed to supporting the king's endeavours to recover his legitimate inheritance. The commons had said in parliament in the 1340s that the king's quarrel was 'a just one', and that 'they would support him in it with all their heart and to the best of their power'.[44] To the commons – and probably to the gentry in general – the king's quarrel was essentially a dispute over rights. The king was to be seen in the role of a dispossessed landowner whose honour and good name required him to vindicate his claim and who was obliged by his foe's recalcitrance to use arms to do so. The quarrel, like many such in gentry society, was long-drawn-out and complex. At times there had seemed a likelihood that it would end in victory: indeed, the Brétigny treaty of 1360 had been a victory of sorts. But by the 1380s England had suffered a series of reverses, and the outlook appeared less promising. Despite this, the commons were little inclined to advise compromise. In their view, the king should uphold the rights and liberties of his crown, for these were the essential guarantee of their own liberties. The articles negotiated at Leulingham in 1384 had put those rights and liberties in jeopardy, and for that reason they had been rejected. It remained to be seen whether the terms negotiated a decade later would be any better. In January 1394 those terms were submitted to parliament for ratification.

Two accounts survive of the proceedings of the 1394 parliament, neither of them satisfactory. The first is the official record on the parliament roll, and the other a brief narrative in the Westminster

---

[42] Tuck, *Richard II and the Nobility*, 166; Morgan, *War and Society in Medieval Cheshire*, chs 2–4.

[43] Calculating the level of participation in the wars is not easy, but a rough estimate can be made on the evidence of the retinue rolls in E101 in the Public Record Office.

[44] *RP*, ii, 159.

chronicle.[45] The parliament roll suffers from all the usual weaknesses of
that source: it is highly edited; it is composed mainly of memoranda and
petitions to which the king gave his reply; and it contains few reports of
speeches or discussions. Despite these problems, it is possible to learn
a little of what had been going on behind the scenes. When the parliamentary session ended in March, two memoranda were enrolled
recording the outcome of the discussions on the proposed treaty. The
first noted that the two houses gave their assent to the treaty, but only
on certain conditions – that the homage performed by the king should
be simple and not liege; that the king should reserve the right to
resume his French title 'if the peace were infringed by his adversary';
and that modifications should be made to the treaty to prevent
the future confiscation of Aquitaine. Immediately after this memoran-
dum a second one was entered recording a protestation by the
commons' Speaker, Sir John Bushy. Bushy stressed the commons' reluctance to take on the burden of offering advice, for the 'three points' as
he called them – of liege homage, sovereignty and *ressort* – were too
weighty for the commons to discuss. Nevertheless, if it was the view of
the king and the lords that under due definition homage could be
rendered for Aquitaine, then for the sake of 'good peace' he and his
colleagues were prepared to lend their assent. What mattered most
to them was that the king and his heirs should be as free as their
ancestors in their enjoyment and exercise of their traditional rights and
liberties.[46]

It is evident from these memoranda that both houses of parliament,
and in particular the lower, had substantial reservations about the
treaty. This is borne out by the brief narrative in the Westminster
chronicle, which makes clear, as the parliament roll does, that the
commons' worries centred on the issue of homage. According to the
Westminster writer, the knights, when they heard the treaty, declared it
absurd 'for the king of England to do homage and fealty to the French
king for Aquitaine and other overseas territories and in fine become his
liegeman, with the corollary that every Englishman would pass under
the heel of the French king and be kept in future under the yoke of
slavery'. If men of modest station and not princes of the blood had
proposed such an idea, 'they would have been immediately, and deserv-
edly, branded traitors on the spot. But the duke of Lancaster does as
he likes, and even dupes his own brother [Gloucester], and nobody
upbraids him.' In the light of these and other considerations the
commons found it impossible to give their assent to the agreement 'on

---

[45] Ibid., iii, 309–23; *WC*, 516–18. For earlier discussion of the Westminster narrative, see above, 214–15.
[46] *RP*, iii, 315–16.

such terms'.[47] To simple homage they would assent – but liege homage was tantamount to slavery.

The Westminster chronicler's account, like that of the official record, leaves little doubt that the sticking point for the two houses was the issue of liege homage. Liege homage carried with it implications that were unacceptable to the commons. Not only was there a serious danger that English foreign policy would be subordinated to French; there was also a worrying possibility that English liberties would be undermined by French demands for military service. The commons could not accept the proposals as they stood. In a protestation that Speaker Bushy read on their behalf they insisted that 'the king, his crown, his realm and his subjects of England, their goods and chattels, should not be burdened or in any way abandoned as a result of the said homage and *ressort*'. This was a stipulation that echoed *mutatis mutandis* a petition of the parliament of 1340, to which Edward III had given his assent, that no 'subjection or obedience' should be exacted from the realm of England to the king in his capacity as king of France.[48] Among the commons there was a widespread suspicion that the performance of liege homage, no less than the assumption of the French title half a century before, would bring with it precisely such 'obedience and subjection'. The commons were looking for an assurance that the rights of the crown would be upheld: if that were the case, then the liberties of the subject would be safe too; the latter were but an extension of the former.

The commons' refusal to entertain the idea of liege homage dealt a devastating blow to the government's plans for making the draft treaty the basis for a final settlement. As the government well knew, the French would never agree to the commons' request for the performance of simple homage. They were therefore in a difficult position. They could not override or disregard the commons' views for fear of forfeiting any chance of securing ratification in future; but equally they could not reopen discussions with the French on the matter of principle. There was only one course available to them, and that was to see if the French would accept modifications to the way that liege homage was applied in practice. Lancaster and Gloucester were sent back to Leulingham in the spring, when parliament had ended, to look into this possibility. Initially their talks with the French appeared to go well, and plans were made for a committee of legal experts to meet in the summer to hammer out details. But by late spring there were signs that

[47] The writer was probably in error in supposing that the draft treaty envisaged the permanent separation of Aquitaine from the crown (above, 214). However, there is no reason to doubt the truth of his observations concerning the commons' opposition to liege homage.

[48] *RP*, iii, 315–16; *SR*, i, 292.

the talks were faltering, and in June they broke up altogether. Why this sudden impasse occurred is not completely clear. Dr Palmer has suggested that the difficulty lay in the outbreak of a rebellion against Lancaster's rule in Aquitaine.[49] In April 1394, just after the negotiations at Leulingham had reopened, the archbishop of Bordeaux and a group of nobles, townsmen and ecclesiastics of the duchy solemnly renounced their allegiance to the duke and swore henceforth to be governed only by the king and his crown. The reason they gave for their action was their unhappiness with the terms of the grant of the duchy to Lancaster in 1390.[50] What was probably of greater concern to them, Dr Palmer argues, was the fear that a settlement would be made on the basis of the permanent separation of the duchy from the English crown. That such a settlement was at least being considered is suggested by a report of Froissart's. According to Froissart, quoting his friend Sir Richard Stury, Richard granted the duchy at this time to his uncle in perpetuity, presumably as the first step to effecting a settlement based on separation.[51] The Gascons, argues Dr Palmer, would almost certainly have known of Richard's move; and the aim of their disavowal of Lancaster's rule was to obstruct any further moves in the same direction. They quickly achieved their objective: Lancaster's authority collapsed over the summer and the government had to abandon its treaty.

Dr Palmer's argument is an attractive and ingenious one, and it has the advantage of explaining the coincidence of timing between the revolt and the end of the Leulingham talks. But there are difficulties with it. In the first place, there is no evidence in the record sources that a grant in perpetuity to Lancaster was ever made, and the likelihood must be that Froissart was reporting hearsay. And secondly, as we have seen, the surviving draft of the Leulingham terms affords no hint of a settlement based on the permanent separation of Aquitaine from the crown. So it is doubtful if there was any connection between the outbreak of the disturbances in Aquitaine and the breakdown of the talks at Leulingham. If an explanation is to be offered for their breakdown, it is probably to be found in the essential incompatibility of the two governments' positions. The English were asking for concessions which the French would never allow, while the French were taking up positions which the English – since the parliamentary débâcle – would never accept. Given the gap between the two sides, the talks were probably doomed to failure from the beginning.

The collapse of the Leulingham talks and the outbreak of the

---

[49] Palmer, *England, France and Christendom*, 149, 152–65.
[50] E30/1232. For discussion, see Palmer, *England, France and Christendom*, ch. 9.
[51] Froissart, ii, 574.

rebellion in Aquitaine had a damaging effect on the once close relationship between Richard and his uncle of Lancaster. In November 1389, when the duke had returned to England from Spain, he had been received by Richard with warmth and affection: he had been accorded a position of honour at court, and his views on foreign policy had been listened to with respect. On his return to England at the end of 1395 his reception was much cooler. Walsingham reports that the king received him properly 'but, so men say, without love'.[52] In the final years of the reign Richard was to rely far less on Duke John's support than he had. He was to pursue his own diplomatic initiatives and to seek friendship in and counsel from the younger, more venturesome, generation of magnates.

By the latter half of 1394 diplomatic exchanges between the governments of England and France had virtually ground to a halt. The leading figures on each side found themselves engaged in a variety of other business – Richard in subduing the Irish, Gaunt in re-establishing himself in Aquitaine and, on the French side, Burgundy in planning a crusade. Direct contact between the two courts was resumed only in the spring of 1395. What brought the two together again was an entirely new factor in the diplomatic equation – Richard's need to find a new bride. Anne of Bohemia had died on 7 June 1394, shortly before Richard was due to set out for Ireland. Richard's grief was intense: he and his late wife had been close.[53] But the king knew that he had to remarry. His marriage to Anne had been childless, and he needed to produce an heir of his body. In the winter of 1394 the council, acting on his behalf, initiated the search for a suitable bride. A number of possible matches were considered, among them a daughter of the king of Scotland, but by February 1395 their choice had fallen upon Yolande, daughter of King John of Aragon.[54]

The choice of Yolande was dictated largely by the diplomatic situation in Europe, in particular by the need to strengthen the English position *vis-à-vis* the French. The ending of the war in 1389 had led to a resurgence of French power on the continent, and there were signs that the dukes of Bourbon and Anjou were looking for fresh outlets for their energy. The English council were determined to contain their ambitions, and the way in which they sought to do this was by making alliances with rulers on France's borders. They concentrated their

[52] *Annales*, 188.

[53] For the relationship between Richard and Anne, see below, 455–6.

[54] For this and the following three paragraphs see J.J.N. Palmer, 'The Background to Richard II's Marriage to Isabel of France (1396)', *BIHR*, xliv (1971), 1–17; idem, *England, France and Christendom*, ch. 10.

diplomatic efforts on two main areas: the north-west of Germany and
the Low Countries, and Iberia. In the former area the English had
already negotiated an alliance with the duke of Guelders and were in
the process of doing the same with Rupert of Bavaria, count palatine of
the Rhine.[55] In the south their position was less strong. They had an
alliance with the king of Portugal, contracted in 1386, but they needed
another. The approach to the king of Aragon represented an attempt
to achieve this aim.

What Richard's ministers and councillors had not reckoned with
when launching their initiative was the likely reaction of the French.
Charles and his ministers disapproved, for two reasons. First, Yolande
was already engaged to a French prince, Louis II of Anjou, titular king
of Naples. Louis was counting on this match to bring him Aragonese
support in his bid for the Neapolitan throne, and Richard's intervention threatened to frustrate this ambition. Secondly, Richard's initiative
opened up the possibility of a personal union between the English and
Aragonese crowns. Yolande had no brothers, and her only sister had
renounced her claim to the throne on her marriage to the count of
Foix. She therefore had a plausible claim to succeed her father. It is
highly unlikely that Richard had any designs on the Aragonese throne,
and in any case King John intended his brother to succeed him; but in
the light of Gaunt's recent attempt on the Castilian throne Charles's
alarm was understandable.

When Charles heard of Richard's bid, in February, English envoys
were passing through his realm on their way to Spain. They were
persuaded to delay their journey to allow time for the king to contact
Richard in Ireland. A French embassy was then dispatched to Dublin to
offer three of Charles's cousins as alternatives to Yolande. In the meantime diplomatic pressure was put on Aragon to reject an English alliance, and Charles himself made a highly personal appeal to Richard to
abandon his marriage plans in the interests of peace between their two
countries. As a final gesture to win the king over, he made an offer in
May of the hand of his six-year-old daughter Isabella.

Richard and his ministers wasted little time in deciding how to
respond to the French overtures; by the beginning of July, if not earlier,
they made known their acceptance of Isabella. On 8 July powers were
granted to the archbishop of Dublin, the bishop of St Davids, the earls
of Rutland and Nottingham, Lord Beaumont and Sir William Scrope
to negotiate the terms of the match.[56] The envoys were instructed to
contract either an engagement or a marriage with the princess, to

---

[55] J.J.N. Palmer, 'English Foreign Policy, 1388–1399', *The Reign of Richard
II*, 84–5.
[56] *Foed.*, vii, 802–5.

negotiate the size of her dowry and the terms of payment, and to settle such matters as her expenses and the date of her delivery to her husband. For her dowry they were to demand initially 2 million gold francs (£333,333 6s 8d), a sum which could be progressively reduced to one million, at which point they were to hold firm. Provided this figure were agreed, they were to insist on a down payment of 400,000 francs (£66,666 13s 4d), with the balance to be paid in three annual instalments. They were to ask additionally that Isabel be brought to Calais at her father's expense, and that an indemnity of 3 million francs be paid if she subsequently broke the contract or engagement. Richard for his part offered to endow Isabella with lands worth £6,666 13s 4d a year, and to take another of her father's close relatives in marriage if she died before she was thirteen.

As well as receiving these powers and instructions the English envoys were also authorized to conclude a final treaty of peace with the French. The instructions given to the envoys show how far English ambitions had grown since the ending of the Leulingham talks two years before. After making the customary protestations the envoys were to ask for the duchy of Aquitaine as granted to Edward III by the treaty of Brétigny and without homage; Calais and Ponthieu also without homage; the arrears of King John's ransom, plus reparations for the damage done to England since the war began; and the cession of Normandy, Anjou and Maine as an apanage for the king's eldest son by Isabel.[57] The extravagant nature of these demands reflected the greatly improved negotiating position in which the English now found themselves. The Anglo-Aragonese match had unsettled the French and made them vulnerable to English pressure. The English, realizing this, pitched their demands high in the expectation that the French would respond with a proposal of their own, out of which a compromise would emerge. The French, however, simply rejected the English demands and refused to negotiate: their envoys made it plain that they were only prepared to discuss the terms for a long truce. The English did not entirely abandon hopes of a peace, and empowered their envoys to extend the existing truce for only a further five years. But the French would not shift their position, and by the end of the year the English had decided to give in. When their envoys made their third and final visit to Paris in January 1396 they were empowered to conclude a 28-year truce. A document to this effect was duly sealed in Paris on 9 March 1396.[58]

The outcome of the negotiations was in some ways a disappointment to the English. The council had obviously hoped to secure a treaty of

---

[57] BL, Cotton MS, Vitellius C XI, nos 2–3, in Palmer, *England, France and Christendom*, Appendix 5.
[58] Palmer, *England, France and Christendom*, 171–2.

peace and not just an extension of the truce. An extension, however, carried with it certain advantages that a treaty did not. To secure a treaty the English would have had to offer concessions to the French, notably on the issue of liege homage, which would have reopened old wounds and provoked fresh outcry in the country. By giving its consent to a truce the government managed to avoid these pitfalls. In fact it was in the fortunate position of gaining most of the benefits, while incurring few of the risks, of peace. English possession of Aquitaine was assured (even if it was possession of a much-reduced duchy), and the prospect was held out of continuing relief from taxation. The 'barbicans' of Cherbourg and Brest were surrendered, ending an outlay on their garrisons which had amounted to over £40,000 between 1378 and 1381;[59] and no more costly military expeditions would need to be put into the field. With the gradual easing of the pressures of war, and the consequent lessening of tensions in the realm, Richard could look forward to enjoying the greater affection and goodwill of his subjects.

On the same day as the negotiations for the truce were concluded, so too were those for the king's marriage. The size and nature of Isabella's dowry and the renunciations required of her – the two principal features of the marriage contract – had already been agreed, and it only remained to settle the terms of payment and the problems which would arise in the event of the premature death of either bride or groom. The dowry was fixed at 800,000 francs, 300,000 to be paid when the pair were married and the balance in annual instalments. If the king were to die childless before her twelfth birthday, Isabel was to have 500,000 francs of her dowry for her own disposal; if she died childless, the king could retain 400,000. If she refused consent to her marriage on reaching her twelfth birthday, the king was entitled to take the whole of her dowry; if, on the other hand, he rejected her when she reached the age of consent, he was not only to return the dowry but to add another 800,000 francs of his own as compensation. In the event of the king's death Isabel was free to return to France with her jewellery.[60]

For the most part the terms reflected the preoccupation with property and financial arrangments common to all marriage agreements between princes and nobles at the time. One of the instructions that Richard gave to his envoys in January 1395, however, was of a quite different order and has understandably provoked comment.[61] This was

[59] Tuck, 'Richard II and the Hundred Years War', 128.
[60] *Foed.*, vii, 813–20.
[61] See, for example, Steel, *Richard II*, 212–13; M.H. Keen, *England in the Later Middle Ages* (London, 1973), 289. The present discussion follows Palmer, *England, France and Christendom*, 173–4.

the king's request for French military assistance. The request was made in the context of negotiations over the payment of Isabella's dowry. In reply to the French offer of a down payment of 200,000 francs and the balance to be paid in annual instalments, Richard gave his envoys a series of counter-proposals, the third of which was a down payment of 200,000 francs and the option of French assistance against his subjects should he need it. The bid for French military assistance has been cited as evidence of Richard's despotic intentions, and in a sense it is; but the point needs to be made that Richard did not attach a high importance to it. It figures as the third and last of the series of counter-proposals that he gave to his envoys, and when the French settled for the first (a down payment of 300,000 francs) it promptly disappeared from the agenda. Nothing in a similar vein is to be found in the final accord. If Richard had seriously wanted French military aid he would surely have bid for it more purposefully. The likelihood is that his main object in the negotiations was simply to milk the French for as much silver as he could.

Once the diplomatic preliminaries were settled, Richard's thoughts turned to taking delivery of his wife. He was anxious for the young queen to be handed over to him as quickly as possible. After sending William Scrope to Paris on his behalf to sound out the French, he travelled to Calais in August to meet the duke of Burgundy, who had custody of Isabel, and it was agreed that she should be given away by her father at a ceremony in or near Calais later in the year.[62] The task of preparing for the ceremony occupied the two sides for most of the next two months: food had to be ordered, transport arranged, accommodation requisitioned, pavilions and tents assembled. The work went ahead more speedily on the English than on the French side, and Richard was ready to cross the Channel by late September. Charles and his entourage do not appear to have set out from Paris until October: moving through Amiens and Thérouanne they finally arrived at St Omer on the 17th. Both kings brought enormous retinues. Richard was attended by the dukes of Lancaster and Gloucester and their families and by the earls of Nottingham and Northumberland, and his father-in-law by the dukes of Berry, Bourbon, Burgundy and Orleans, as well as the counts of Harcourt and Sancerre and their retinues. On Thursday, 26 October, in the morning, the kings made their way to the great encampment that had been prepared for them near Ardres. Richard was accompanied by the dukes of Berry and Orleans, and Charles by Lancaster and Gloucester. On the following day at 3 p.m. the two kings met each other for the first

---

[62] L. Mirot, 'Isabelle de France, reine d'Angleterre', *Revue d'histoire diplomatique*, xviii (1904), 71–2.

time.[63] Richard was dressed in a long scarlet gown bearing the white hart; the French king wore a similar but shorter gown emblazoned with a bend sable engrailed argent in memory of Richard's late queen. Advancing over an equal distance the kings met at a central post, and all in their respective retinues knelt as the pair doffed their hoods, shook hands and kissed.[64] Wine and sweetmeats were offered by the attendant dukes and presents were exchanged.[65] Charles then took Richard to his marquee, and afterwards accompanied him on a return visit to his. At the end of the day's proceedings the two kings kissed once more and took leave at the halfway point. On the following day there were further formalities at the halfway point, but on this occasion they were interrupted by a downpour which soaked many of the lords and swept away some of the French pavilions. (The English pavilions were shielded by a slope.) The greater part of the day was occupied by a four-hour conference between the two kings in the French king's pavilion which resulted in agreements between the two rulers on resuming talks for peace and ending the schism in the papacy. There were no meetings on the following day, which was a Sunday, but on the 30th, a Monday, proceedings reached their climax when the little queen was brought to the central spot and there formally delivered to her lord. Richard thanked Charles for his precious gift, and then entrusted her to the duchesses of Lancaster and Gloucester and the countesses of Huntingdon and Stafford. She was taken to Calais with a train of ladies, and there on 4 November, in the church of St Nicholas, Richard married her.

The junketings at Ardres bear comparison with a later and more celebrated Anglo-French extravaganza – the Field of Cloth of Gold, which was held on the same site in 1520.[66] The later, like the earlier, meeting was intended to set the seal on an Anglo-French reconciliation. Henry VIII and Francis I, like Richard and Charles, decked themselves out in fine clothes, embraced each other lovingly and swore eternal friendship. Henry and Francis, like their predecessors, showered gifts and goodwill offerings on each other. And Henry and Francis, again like their predecessors, entertained one another to a magnificent round of banquets, dances and other spectacles. There were differ-

---

[63] There are accounts of the conference in *Annales*, 188–94, and *CRSD*, ii, 450–71. An eyewitness account by a member of the English delegation survives in Oriel College, Oxford MS 46, in P. Meyer, 'L'Entrevue d'Ardres', *Annuaire Bulletin de la Société de l'Histoire de France*, xviii (1881), 209–24.

[64] The anonymous English eyewitness adds that at one point the French king showed signs of fainting and that Richard took him by the arm and comforted him (Meyer, 'L'Entrevue d'Ardres', 213).

[65] For discussion of the presents, see below, 353–4.

[66] For the Field see J.G. Russell, *The Field of Cloth of Gold* (London, 1969).

ences between the two occasions, of course. Chivalric entertainments played a much larger role at the Field than at the earlier conference: special lists were built in which jousting could take place, and Henry and Francis themselves jousted regularly for a fortnight. Almost certainly there was also a greater emphasis on sports: Henry and Francis, both keen sportsmen, wrestled with each other, which Richard and Charles would never have done. These differences apart, however, the two meetings were broadly similar in character and purpose. Indeed, it is possible that Henry and Francis took the earlier meeting as their model. Significantly the two kings, like Richard and Charles before them, vowed to build a chapel on the spot where they had met. They dedicated it, as their predecessors had, to Our Lady of Peace.[67]

Historians have been quick to dismiss the Field of Cloth of Gold as an exercise in 'vain posturing . . . and a huge, expensive game'; and it is easy to speak as disparagingly about the meeting between Richard and Charles.[68] The meeting between Richard and Charles, like the later one, was enormously expensive. While it cannot be costed precisely, the total outlay could hardly have fallen short of £10,000–£15,000.[69] Simply assembling the retinues and transporting them across the Channel was equivalent to mounting a moderately sized military expedition. Expenditure on this scale placed a severe strain on the king's finances. Even after the ending of hostilities Richard was suffering acute shortages of money, and by the mid-1390s the annual deficit at the exchequer had reached nearly £2,000.[70] But despite this Richard had to spend lavishly on the ceremonies because of the considerations of power play involved. To be effective on the international stage a king had to appear kingly. If he arrived at a conference poorly arrayed, as an English observer says that Charles VI did at Ardres, he would have been written off as a ruler of no consequence.[71] Spending lavishly was a

---

[67] For Richard's and Charles's promise to found a chapel, see *Annales*, 191.

[68] J.J. Scarisbrick, *Henry VIII* (London, 1968), 79, provides a summary of opinion.

[69] Unfortunately, there is a dearth of financial information for this year of the reign. No wardrobe book survives, and the relevant issue roll of the exchequer is missing. Thus the only figures that we have are those in Walsingham's chronicle. Walsingham, with pardonable exaggeration, estimated the total cost of the conference at 300,000 marks (£200,000). He also said that Richard gave gifts to the French worth 10,000 marks (*Annales*, 194). It is possible that there is some truth in the latter figure since the anonymous English observer says that Richard gave Charles a collar of pearls and other precious stones of the late queen's livery which alone was worth 5,000 marks (Meyer, 'L'Entrevue d'Ardres', 217). There is evidence that the crown resorted to borrowing to meet the cost of the conference: see *CPR 1396–9*, 29.

[70] Given-Wilson, *Royal Household and the King's Affinity*, 270–1. In the year after Ardres the deficit jumped to over £11,000 (ibid.).

[71] Meyer, 'L'Entrevue d'Ardres', 217. For the sartorial contest between the two kings, see below, 354.

means to the end of creating an image of power. Ardres was the first great high-level meeting with another king that Richard had attended, and he was determined to make a vivid and lasting impression on those present. Massive spending on gifts and fine clothing ensured that he did so.

Any assessment of the significance of the Ardres conference must also take into account its serious side. In the course of the four days of meetings agreement was reached on two important acts. The first of these, dated 28 October, committed Richard to aiding his father-in-law against all men and to settling any differences that might arise with him by consultation within and between the two royal families. The second, agreed on 5 November, pledged the two kings to common action on two issues: the making of a final peace and the ending of the papal schism.[72] It was intended that the kings would proceed simultaneously on both issues. An Anglo-French peace conference would be convened for 1 April 1397, and at the same time a delegation from the two kingdoms would be sent to Rome and Avignon to force the resignation of the two popes. The support of the king of the Romans was to be solicited by both parties; and it appears from a later document that the two kings agreed to withdraw their obedience if the popes did not satisfy their demands.

Only a part of this wide-ranging programme was put into effect. Measures were taken to heal the wounds of the schism: Richard and Charles both wrote to Wenzel, and in April a joint Anglo-French embassy was sent to Rome and Avignon to lay the kings' demands before the two popes. A few weeks later, in May, a second Anglo-French mission was sent to Frankfurt, where the imperial diet was assembling, to win the backing of the German princes for the two kings' initiatives. Together these measures amounted to a not inconsiderable effort to heal the schism. Rather conspicuously, however, there were no equivalent measures to promote a final peace between the two kingdoms. Charles VI kept on raising one problem or difficulty after another. First he asked for a postponement of the opening date of the conference arranged for the spring; then he would not agree to the proposed new date, and finally he returned an evasive answer to Richard's request for the conference's immediate summoning. Part of the problem was that plans for the conference were becoming entangled with the concurrent moves to heal the schism. By the end of the summer the joint embassy had returned empty-handed from its consultations with the popes, and the question arose of how to bring further pressure to bear. The French were anxious to go ahead with a simultaneous withdrawal of obedience by the two kings, and on 27 July 1398 Charles VI and his uncles

---

[72] Palmer, *England, France and Christendom*, 176–7.

unilaterally withdrew their obedience from Benedict. Richard, however, contrary to their expectations, proved reluctant to follow suit. In a letter to Charles explaining his position he said that he wanted to refer the matter to the masters of the universities before acting; but since he had already been given the universities' views his statement was clearly a fiction. The real reason for his hesitation was probably that his own commitment to the 'voie de cession' was waning.[73] In the previous twelve months a number of his nominations to the episcopal bench had been blocked by Boniface, and he wanted to obtain a clarification of his rights over the Church. In the summer of 1398 he accordingly opened negotiations with the pope, and in November a concordat was agreed between them defining their respective rights in the making of appointments. News of the agreement came as a bitter blow to the French, who had expected the English to follow the line agreed at Ardres, and their anger is evident in the tone of their correspondence with Richard. In 1398 Charles wrote an angry letter to the king about his failure to implement the terms of the 1396 truce in Gascony: English garrisons there, he said, were continuing to levy tribute, and there was a real danger that war in the duchy might be renewed. As relations between the two kings and their respective advisers grew steadily worse there was little possibility that new initiatives would be taken to heal the schism or to promote a full peace. The spirit of Ardres was dead. The programme of joint action to which the two sides had committed themselves at the conference, so far from bringing them closer together, had simply driven them further apart again.[74]

Though the material fruit of the Ardres initiatives was meagre, the conference marked the high point of Richard's diplomacy in the 1390s. It set the seal on his reassertion of control over policy and brought to an end the long period of tension between the kings of England and France. Richard was in a sense only bringing to completion the work that had been started by his uncle of Lancaster. Lancaster's diplomacy between 1390 and 1393 had paved the way for an accord between the two kings, and his summit with the French at Amiens provided the model for the extravaganza staged at Ardres. It was Richard's own personality and tastes, however, that stamped themselves on the

---

[73] I.e., the simultaneous withdrawal of obedience.

[74] Perroy, *L'Angleterre et le grand Schisme*, 376–87, offers the fullest narrative. J.J.N. Palmer, 'England and the great western Schism', *EHR*, lxxxiii (1968), 516–22, puts the blame for the breakdown in relations on the French. Given-Wilson, whose views are in part followed here, emphasizes the problems caused by the differing aims of the English and the French (*Chrons. Revolution*, 24–8). For the background to the concordat and the difficulties that Richard experienced over episcopal appointments see R.G. Davies, 'Richard II and the Church in the Years of Tyranny', *JMH*, i (1975), 344–61.

proceedings that culminated at Ardres. The conference was the fruit of an initiative of his, arising out of his meeting with the duke of Burgundy at Calais. It bore witness to the faith that he had in the community of interest binding together fellow monarchs; and with its accompanying pageantry and entertainments it allowed him ample opportunity to indulge his fondness for drama and stage-play. Ardres was the epitome of Ricardian kingship in action.

Chapter 11

PATRONAGE AND POWER, 1389–96

The early to mid-1390s was a period of relative calm in English domestic politics. There were no major crises or upheavals, apart from the quarrel in 1392 between Richard and the Londoners; and relations between the king and the nobility were more harmonious than they had been for a decade. The memory of the Appellant period, while still recent, was quickly fading. After 1389 the Appellants themselves virtually ceased to exist as a faction. Derby and Nottingham, the two junior Appellants, had drifted back to the court; Warwick was no longer a significant force in politics, and Gloucester and Arundel kept such resentments as they had to themselves. Open opposition to Richard's rule had largely melted away.

Richard himself contributed to the restoration of harmony by showing greater sensitivity to his subjects' feelings than he had in his youth. He was more sparing, and also more evenhanded, in the distribution of patronage, and he accepted that no grant which had financial implications should pass without the advice of the council and the assent of his uncles and the chancellor.[1] There are significant indications that he went some way towards implementing the promises he had made in May 1389 when declaring himself of age. He showed a new and unaccustomed vigour in enforcing the law and eliminating corruption, and in November he took a personal interest in the appointment of new sheriffs.[2] In addition, he made a gesture in the direction of relaxing the financial demands which had earlier burdened his subjects. On 16 May 'of his own mere motion, without advice from anyone' he remitted collection of the second instalment of the subsidy granted at the Cambridge parliament.[3] In the wake of the agreement with the French at Leulingham he was able to reduce the burden still further. He postponed the levying of another subsidy on moveables until 1391 and after that he did not ask for one until 1393. There was considerable evidence that sound government and the establishment of domestic and external peace were flowing from the king's assumption of the duties of his

---

[1] *PPC*, i, 18a–b.
[2] *WC*, 404; and see below, 262–3.
[3] *CCR 1385–9*, 679; and see above, 199.

office. To many it must have appeared that Richard had learned the error of his ways and would offer better and more abundant governance in future.

The more conciliatory style of Richard's rule at this time led T.F. Tout to interpret the period as an 'age of compromise'.[4] Undoubtedly there is much to be said for this view. For the first time a degree of pliability and moderation was evident in Richard's public behaviour. No longer was he apt to react with hostility whenever criticism was offered. He showed a willingness to accept the advice of his councillors, and he even recognized that there might be limits to his independence of action as king. It is instructive to note the calmness with which he reacted in 1392 when the council rejected his request that Robert de Vere and Alexander Neville be allowed to return to England. 'The king graciously bowed to their insistence,' reports the Westminster chronicler, 'and he accepted that the banishment of the two should be permanent.'[5] There was no angry display of temper, and the matter of the favourites' return was never raised again.[6] Richard saw the validity of his councillors' viewpoint and accepted that it might be better for him gracefully to give way.

To acknowledge the restraint and moderation of Richard's behaviour after 1389 is not, however, to suggest that the king had either forgotten or abandoned the aims of his earlier years: for almost certainly this was not the case. He was as convinced as he had ever been of the unique God-given nature of his office. He regarded it as a duty laid on him by the Almighty to maintain the rights, liberties and privileges pertaining to his office – in other words, the body of rights known as the prerogative.[7] Whenever he felt that the prerogative was in danger of encroachment by his subjects he reacted promptly and with firmness. He was particularly on his guard against the ambitions of the parliamentary commons. In the January 1390 session, when the resignation and reappointment of the ministers gave the impression that these officials were answerable to parliament, he insisted that the action was not to be interpreted as a precedent, and that he was to be free to appoint and remove officers as he pleased.[8] Seven years later, when the commons presumed to criticize the size and composition of his household, he

[4] Tout, *Chapters*, iii, 454. Steel, more provocatively, characterized the period as one of 'appeasement' (Steel, *Richard II*, ch. vii). J. Taylor commented that it was 'baffling': 'Richard II's Views on Kingship', *Proceedings of the Leeds Philosophical and Literary Society*, xiv (1971), 199.

[5] *WC*, 484–6.

[6] Not at least in council: see the further discussion of this issue below, 255.

[7] As he said in a letter in 1398, 'the king's will is to preserve the rights of the crown, as he [the king] is sworn to do': *CCR 1396–99*, 354.

[8] *RP*, iii, 258.

reacted with far greater severity; he said that it was not for lieges to speak on a subject which pertained to his regality, and he demanded that the knights and burgesses identify and hand over the sponsor of the petition – which they did.[9] Richard demonstrated by the vigour of his reactions on these occasions that his political stance had little to distinguish it from that which he had adopted in the 1380s; it was only the tactics that had changed. It is interesting to note that, even as he was wooing the commons with his promises and fine words, he was reflecting on how he might strengthen his kingly authority. Some time around 1389 – and apparently no later than 1390 – he commissioned a volume of statutes which contained implicit hints of a possible desire on his part to throw off earlier restraints (plate 12).[10] The volume, which brought together an exceptionally wide-ranging collection of statutes, included the *Articuli super Cartas* of 1300, the Ordinances of 1311 and the *statutum come Hugh le Despenser*: measures by which, in the first case, Edward I and, in the latter two, Edward II had been shackled, and to which Richard himself took exception. A couple of years earlier, in the questions to the judges, Richard had indicated how fascinated he was by the politics of Edward II's reign, for in the ninth question he had enquired into the punishment appropriate for those who had imposed the Ordinances on the king: to which the answer was given that they should be punished as traitors.[11] Almost certainly, by commissioning the volume, Richard was inwardly reliving the struggles of his great-grandfather's reign. His identification with the king is hinted at in the appearance of the royal arms in the margin against his name; and his appreciation of his place in the royal line of descent is suggested by the painting of portraits of his predecessors in the historiated capitals. But, for all the evidence in its contents of historical awareness, the book was conceived to serve an essentially present purpose. It represented a stage in the fashioning of a more assertive, more legalistic, style of governance. Commonly in the middle ages, when an institution such as a monastery set about recovering its rights, it began by gathering evidences in a cartulary or landbook. Richard was undertaking a not dissimilar exercise: the book of statutes was to serve as a personal book of precedents. At one level in his mind the book bore witness to the fullness that royal authority achieved in law. At another it indicated what had been lost and still needed to be recovered. It was a kind of manifesto for the reassertion of royal power.

---

[9] Ibid., 339; and see below, 368–9.
[10] St John's College, Cambridge, MS A 7. On fo.133ʳ is a painting of Richard receiving a presentation copy of the volume (plate 12). For discussion of the book, see *A Descriptive Catalogue of the Manuscripts in the Library of St John's College, Cambridge*, ed. M.R. James (Cambridge, 1913), 8–9.
[11] Clementi, 'Richard II's Ninth Question to the Judges', 96–113.

Richard's aim of rebuilding and reasserting royal power was one that was utterly unexceptional. Every late medieval king who, for whatever reason, had suffered a temporary setback or reverse strove to win back what had been lost. Edward I had vigorously reasserted the prerogative after being forced to give ground in the 1290s; and Edward III had done the same after having to cede to Archbishop Stratford and his allies in 1340.[12] In many ways there was a good deal in common between Richard's outlook and policies and those of his predecessors. But there was also a major difference. Richard's kingship was marked by a self-consciousness entirely lacking in his predecessors'. Richard showed an almost obsessive interest in projecting and manipulating his own image. In every artistic medium – in sculpture, writing and in painting – he flaunted an idealized royal image before his subjects. He regularly had himself portrayed as a ruler-in-majesty, a remote, godlike monarch to whom obedience was due. None of the three Edwards – nor even the allegedly 'absolutist' Henry III – had done this. The explanation for the king's obsession is fairly straightforward. The speed and thoroughness of the Appellants' triumph in 1387 had exposed the essential hollowness of royal power. When confronted by a ruthless and determined baronial faction, as he had been in that year, Richard had had no alternative but to give way. He had no readily available army to call on, and the militia levies in the shires were inadequate. Effectively, he was without coercive strength. If he was to re-establish his authority and power, Richard needed not only to build up support and win friends, but also to do something more: to convince his subjects that he was mightier than he was. Around 1395 Richard commissioned a massive portrait of himself for Westminster Abbey, in which he was shown crowned and holding an orb and sceptre, staring out frontally like an iconic close-up of the face of Christ (plate 21). Around the same time, in the Wilton Diptych he was shown in an angelic and heavenly company, sponsored by the Baptist and two kings and facing the Virgin and Child (plate 13). These powerful artistic images were complemented by the verbal elevation of the king. From around 1391 a richer and more formal language of address to the king was introduced. For example, the commons' petitions were now addressed to 'your highness and royal majesty' or to 'your most excellent and powerful prince', instead of, as they previously had been, to 'your rightful and gracious lord'.[13] Simultaneously, servants and friends of the king began to (or were encouraged to) address him in more exalted terms. Bishop Waltham,

---

[12] Edward III had also commissioned a book of statutes: Harvard Law School, MS 12.

[13] *RP*, iii, 290, 305, 318, 344. For further discussion see N.E. Saul, 'Richard II and the Vocabulary of Kingship', *EHR*, cx (1995), 854–77; and see also below, 249, 340–1.

the treasurer, writing to him in 1394, while using the language of lordship in his opening address, switched to 'highness', 'majesty' and 'your high royal presence' later; and, according to Walsingham, the commons' Speaker, Sir John Bushy, addressed Richard in similarly grandiloquent terms in parliament in September 1397.[14] The effect of the use of this language, no less than that of the visual images, was to distance the king from his subjects. Richard was seen in ritualistic terms as a sacred icon, supreme and all-powerful. He was invested with a mystical, almost a godlike, quality. It is clear that the implied identification of Richard with the Godhead was deliberate.[15] The men who crafted these images saw it as their object to encourage the king's subjects to direct towards him the responses that had once been reserved for God. By that means it could be impressed on them that, although the king might be gracious towards them, and although he might willingly remedy their grievances, their only proper relationship with him was one of obedience; resistance to his authority was tantamount to resistance to the will of God. Given the uncompromising nature of this message, and considering also Richard's lofty attitude to parliament, there could be little doubt as to the true character of Richard's kingship in these years: it was to be vigorous, masterful and assertive. Overriding all other objectives was to be the defence and maintenance of the powers of the prerogative.

The creation of this new, more authoritarian style of kingship was a task on which Richard embarked shortly after the end of the Merciless Parliament. The first steps that he took to achieve it were necessarily modest, for the Appellants were still dominant, and the ministers whom they had appointed occupied all the major offices. Richard's chief aim was to recover the power that he had lost two and a half years before. In the winter of 1388–9 he assiduously gnawed away at the unity of the Appellant coalition. He played on the differences between the junior and the senior members of the coalition and he detached the commons from their adventitious alliance with the lords. By the spring of the next year, when he had won over the two junior Appellants, he was able to throw off the Appellant yoke. On 3 May at the council meeting in the Marcolf chamber he declared himself of age and appointed his own ministers.[16] By this one dramatic act he recaptured the political initiative. Nevertheless, he was still a long way from establishing a firm power base for his kingship. His following in the country remained small, and

[14] *Anglo-Norman Letters and Petitions*, ed. M.D. Legge (Anglo-Norman Text Society, iii, 1941), no. 24; *Annales*, 210.

[15] F. Hepburn, *Portraits of the Later Plantagenets* (Woodbridge, 1986), 15.

[16] *WC*, 390–2; and see above, 203.

he had few allies among the higher nobility. It was only when John of
Gaunt returned to England in November that the balance of power
shifted materially in his favour. Gaunt was an unswerving supporter of
the prerogative, and he gave Richard his full backing throughout the
remainder of his active career. Probably to a greater extent than
Richard's declaration of age it was Gaunt's re-entry into politics which
marked the beginning of a revival in royal power.

The alliance between Richard and Gaunt was one of the most
remarkable features of English political life in the 1390s. For much of
the previous decade relations between the two had been cool. Richard
appears to have seen his uncle's enormous wealth and influence as
constituting a challenge to his royal authority, and must have been
relieved when the duke set sail for Spain in July 1386. However, with the
passage of time and in the light of his subsequent misfortunes, the
king's attitude gradually softened, and by October 1389 he was writing
to his uncle to request his urgent return.[17] The change of attitude to the
duke that Richard underwent was shared by many in English political
society. It can be sensed in the writings of some of the major chroniclers
of the time. Thomas Walsingham, for example, having poured obloquy
on Gaunt in the 1380s, suddenly took a more favourable view of his
subject in 1390, transforming him almost into a pillar of the state.
Walsingham's justification for his change of heart was an alleged refor-
mation in the duke's morals. Gaunt, he said, had turned over a new leaf:
he had reflected on his disloyalty to his wife, and had resolved to acquit
himself more honourably in future.[18] Walsingham, brought up to see
history as a branch of theology, could be expected to have offered an
explanation couched in moralistic terms. The more worldly of his
contemporaries, however, would have recognized that there were
other, more material, factors which had a bearing on popular attitudes
to the duke. First his renunciation of his claim to the crown of Castile
meant that he could no longer be accused of manipulating policy, or of
cornering national resources, in the pursuit of aims that were essentially
personal. Secondly, and no less importantly, there was the fact that his
departure from the realm had been followed by – indeed, might have
contributed to – the outbreak of political turmoil. Even the duke's
bitterest enemies now had to admit that his political skills, and the sheer
weight and power of his inheritance, were stabilizing factors in the
political life of the realm. The effect of these two considerations was to
bring about a major shift in the popular perception of Gaunt. No
longer was he viewed as a political outcast. He was fêted and honoured
by those who had previously spurned him and found himself moving

[17] *Foed.*, vii, 648.
[18] *HA*, ii, 194.

almost effortlessly into the role of a respected elder statesman. Significantly, his first public act on his return involved him in promoting an act of reconciliation. Richard had summoned a meeting of the great council at Reading for 9 December to effect a symbolic healing of the nation's wounds, and he invited Gaunt to join him there. According to the Westminster writer, the duke was received by the king two miles from the town, and the two men exchanged a kiss of peace. On the following day the duke attended his first session of the council. Right at the outset he reconciled the king and the former Appellant lords. Then, on the king's initiative, he was himself reconciled to his former adversary, the earl of Northumberland.[19] By these symbolic acts of goodwill former enemies were brought together and a measure of harmony was restored to national life.

Gaunt's backing provided the essential underpinning of Richard's regime for the next eight or nine years. Gaunt knew only too well how important his influence was to the king and he made sure to extract concessions in return. Initially his aims were confined to securing and, if possible, expanding the Lancastrian inheritance. Thus in February 1390 he successfully obtained a grant of the duchy of Lancaster as a palatinate entailed on his heirs male, and in the following month he received a grant for life of the duchy of Aquitaine. Almost certainly in later months, however, he aspired to a more general influence over government. This seems to be implied by the lengths to which he went to cultivate and win the friendship of the young king. In July 1390 he played host to both Richard and Anne at a magnificent hunting party at Leicester. As the Westminster chronicler attests, the duke spared no expense in making a success of the occasion. Lavish banquets were laid on, 'and such was the succession of festivities that several days on end were devoted to amusement and gaiety'.[20] At the end of the party a council was held at which the duke, ever mindful of the interests of his clients, requested that John of Northampton and his associates might be permitted to return to London and have their rights as citizens restored. Richard declined the request, saying that it was not at present in his power to grant this, but Gaunt, skilfully pandering to the king's self-regard, said that on the contrary he could do not only that but even more: God forbid, he declared, that your power should be so cramped that you could not extend grace to your subjects when circumstances demanded it.[21] Richard reminded him that friends of his own were living in exile too; but he agreed to a conditional pardon for Northampton provided he did not enter, or hold office in, London.[22] In

[19] WC, 406-8.
[20] Ibid., 440.
[21] Ibid.
[22] CPR 1388-92, 297.

general Richard was sympathetic to his uncle's cause and tried his best
to accommodate him. Increasingly he took to displaying his friendship
and affection for him. He publicly wore the Lancastrian collar of SSs,
while at the same time he allowed the duke to have his own badge of the
white hart embroidered on choir copes worn by his clerks.[23] By the
middle of the decade the alliance between the king and the duke was
being flaunted so openly that it provoked angry criticism from their old
adversary, the earl of Arundel. In the parliament of January 1394 the
earl complained of the duke's arrogance at the council table, of his
presumption in walking arm in arm with the king, and of the wearing of
his livery by the king and members of the royal household. These were
charges that sprang largely from personal pique. Richard answered
them one by one, and the earl was obliged to apologize and retract.[24] By
speaking so tactlessly the earl had simply underlined how isolated he
was among the nobility.

As time was to show, Richard's defence of his uncle against the earl
marked the high-water mark of relations between the two men. After
1394 they were still on outwardly good terms, but the close bond that
had tied them began to weaken. One reason for this was the exposure
of the fragility of Gaunt's rule in Aquitaine. Richard had initially
been a keen supporter of the duke's bid to establish a principality
for himself in the duchy, but after the ructions at Bordeaux he developed doubts. His confidence in his uncle's judgement was undermined,
and he began to distance himself from him. Walsingham reports
that when Gaunt returned to England Richard received him politely
'but not, so men say, with love'.[25] At the same time, Richard's domestic
political position was growing steadily stronger, and his need for his
uncle's support was correspondingly reduced. Over time the alliance
was drained of all but symbolic importance. The duke exerted less
and less influence over the course of policy, and in the end could not
even save his own son from sentence of exile.[26] Assiduously though he
cultivated the alliance with Richard, it was not he who benefited from it;
it was the king.

Richard's need for his uncle's backing in the years after 1389 had
sprung from his lack of a clear power base among the nobility.
The circle which had gathered around him in the 1380s had been
destroyed by the Appellants in the Merciless Parliament. Burley,
Beauchamp and Berners were all dead, and de Vere, de la Pole and

---

[23] *RP*, iii, 313; Goodman, *John of Gaunt*, 144.
[24] *RP*, iii, 313.
[25] *Annales*, 188; and see above, 225.
[26] See below, 401.

1. Tomb of the Black Prince, Canterbury Cathedral. The prince had requested burial in the chapel of Our Lady Undercroft, but instead he was interred in the Trinity Chapel, near the shrine of Becket. His effigy looks up to a painting of the Trinity on the tester above.

2. Miniature of Joan of Kent (*top*), Richard's mother, from the St Albans Book of Benefactors. The drawing, although contemporary, is probably not an authentic likeness.

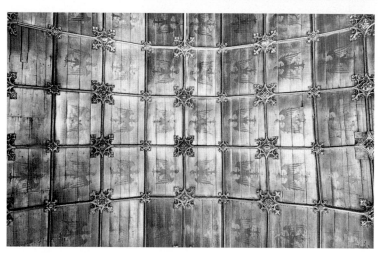

3. The roof of the chancel of the Great Hospital (formerly St Giles' Hospital), Norwich. The Hospital was built between 1381 and 1383, partly at the expense of Henry Despenser, bishop of Norwich. The lavish display of eagles is probably a reference to the visit to Norwich in 1383 of Richard and his queen, Anne, the daughter of the Emperor Charles IV.

24. Canterbury Cathedral, the nave. Probably designed by Henry Yevele, the nave is one of the most elegant and inspired designs of the age. Richard II contributed generously to the cost.

25. Tomb of Edward II in Gloucester Cathedral. Richard's interest in promoting the cult of his murdered great-grandfather is attested by the white harts painted on the capitals of the adjacent columns.

22. Westminster hall, looking south-east. Richard rebuilt the hall from 1394. A possible source of inspiration was Gaunt's rebuilding of the hall and state apartments at Kenilworth in the 1380s. There was originally a throne at the far end. The statues of kings on the end wall reinforced the authority of the royal presence.

23. Westminster Abbey, the nave. Work on the nave, broken off in 1272, was resumed in the 1370s and carried forward in the 1390s when Richard made financial provision for it. The design is a simplified version of that of the choir.

20. Tomb of Richard II and Anne of Bohemia, Westminster Abbey. Contracts for the tomb and effigies were placed in 1395, and work was probably completed by 1398. The figures were shown holding hands: a conventional posture in contemporary effigial sculpture.

21. Portrait of Richard II, Westminster Abbey. The portrait was probably commissioned in the mid-1390s. Richard is shown seated in state, regally and frontally, crowned and holding the symbols of royal authority.

18. (*left*) Brass of John Waltham, bishop of Salisbury, 1395, Westminster Abbey. Waltham's burial, on Richard's orders, in the Confessor's chapel of the Abbey, where hitherto only members of the royal family had been buried, aroused the hostility of the monks.

19. Brass of Sir Simon Felbrigg K.G. and his wife, 1416, Felbrigg, Norfolk. Felbrigg's wife, the duke of Teschen's daughter, was a lady-in-waiting to Queen Anne; Felbrigg himself was Richard's standard bearer. The brass, laid down fifteen years after the king's death, is rich in symbolic reference to Richard's kingship.

16. Crown made for a princess, *c.* 1370–80. The crown, a masterpiece of the goldsmith's art, came to Bavaria as part of the dowry of Blanche, daughter of Henry IV, on her marriage to Ludwig III in 1401. It is likely, though not certain, that it belonged to Anne of Bohemia.

17. Brass of Sir William Bagot and his wife, 1407, Baginton, Warwickshire. The appearance of the Lancastrian collar of 'SS' on the figures attests Bagot's success in surviving Richard's fall and making his peace with the new regime.

15. Illuminated initial 'R' in the Shrewsbury charter showing Anne of Bohemia interceding with her husband on behalf of the citizens of Shrewsbury. The likeness of Richard is consistent with that in the *Book of Statutes*. Unusually, Anne is shown with long plaited hair.

13. The Wilton Diptych, interior of wings. On the left, Richard is shown with Saints Edmund, Edward the Confessor and John the Baptist, while, on the right, an angel hands a banner to the Christ Child, who is held in the arms of his Mother and attended by other angels.

14. The Wilton Diptych, exterior. On the left wing, a white hart lies among branches of rosemary on a flowery bank; on the right wing are the royal arms of England and France ancient impaled with the arms of Edward the Confessor.

11. The crown of thorns linking the crown of France (*left*) and England (*right*), from Philippe de Mézière's *Épître au Roi Richart* (*Letter to King Richard*). The letter proposed a joint crusade to the Holy Land to be undertaken with Charles VI of France.

12. Illuminated initial 'R' showing Richard receiving a presentation copy of the *Book of Statutes*. The book was probably compiled around 1390.

10. A presentation copy of Dymock's *Liber contra XII Errores et Hereses Lollardorum* (*Treatise against the Twelve Errors and Heresies of the Lollards*). Richard is shown enthroned and wearing the crown in a miniature on the richly decorated opening folio. In the border are the royal arms, and at the foot two white harts chained and lodged.

8. Roof boss showing the white hart, Dartington Hall, Devon. When John Holand, earl of Huntingdon, rebuilt the old manor house at Dartington in the 1390s, he included this boss as a mark of his Ricardian allegiance.

9. Copper alloy badge of the white hart. The badge is now in the Musées de Troyes. It probably found its way to France in the baggage of Richard's second wife Isabella, who returned to France after his death.

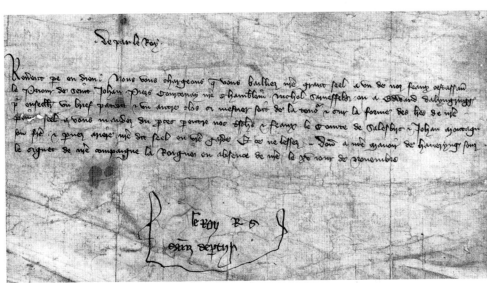

6. Autograph signature of Sir Simon Burley. The signature appears on a petition to the king which was subsequently transmitted to chancery for the issue of letters patent.

7. Signed letter of Richard II ordering the chancellor to deliver the great seal to one of the persons named in the letter. The words 'le Roy R[ichard] S[econd] sau[nz] dep[ar]tyr' are in the king's own hand ('saunz departyr' being a kind of motto).

4. Stained glass figure of Sir James Berners, West Horsley, Surrey. Berners, one of Richard's chamber knights, is shown kneeling, in armour, with the family arms on his jupon. The inscription says that he was patron of the church.

5. Tomb of Richard's friend Sir John Beauchamp (later John, Lord Beauchamp of Kidderminster), Worcester Cathedral. The tomb is generally thought to be Beauchamp's, although in the absence of an inscription the identification cannot be conclusive. Shortly before his arrest in 1387, Beauchamp entrusted his worldly goods to the prior and convent of Worcester.

26. Episodes in Richard's deposition from an early fifteenth-century manuscript of Creton's *Metrical History* (BL, Harley MS 1319):
(*from top and continuing overleaf*) a) the arrival of the earl of Salisbury at Conway; b) the earl of Northumberland received by Richard at Conway; c) the earl of Northumberland swearing an oath; d) the capture of Richard near Conway.

Neville were in exile, never to return. Richard was isolated; he was lacking in close friends – in particular, friends of his own generation and age. One of his first tasks after dismissing the Appellants, therefore, was to assemble around him a new courtier nobility. In the space of no more than two or three years from 1389 he had drawn into his service the men who were to remain his closest allies until the closing days of the reign.

Probably the earliest (and ultimately one of the most richly rewarded) recipients of his favour was his half-brother John Holand, earl of Huntingdon. Holand was in many ways an extremely unlikely man to win the king's friendship. Froissart portrays him as a violent ruffian, delighting in nothing more than a good fight.[27] His unruly ways had landed him in trouble more than once in the past. In 1385, while accompanying the royal army to Scotland, he had quarrelled with the king's close friend Sir Ralph Stafford and killed him.[28] Probably to escape the resulting obloquy he enlisted to serve with Gaunt in Spain in the following year, but while waiting to embark at Plymouth he had sullied his reputation a second time. He eloped with the duke's twenty-two-year-old daughter Elizabeth, and seduced her; and Gaunt, to save his daughter's honour, had to arrange a hasty marriage between the two.[29] There appears to have been little abatement in Holand's raffish behaviour when he finally arrived in Spain. Though appointed to the constableship by his father-in-law, he showed little military competence and failed to maintain discipline in the English forces. It was only when he returned to England in April 1388 that he began the climb-back to respectability and favour.[30] The uncertain political situation prevailing at the time played into his hands, and he was aggressively courted by the Appellants because of his kinship with Gaunt. It was probably at the Appellants' behest that on 2 June, with Warwick and Salisbury as his sponsors, he was created earl of Huntingdon and endowed with an ample estate to the value of £1,333 6s 8d per annum.[31] The Appellants' vigorous courtship of him made it essential for Richard to follow suit and in 1389, after recovering power, he began his own campaign of wooing. In May 1389 he gave him Arundel's offices of admiral of the fleet in the west and captain of Brest, and by February 1390 at the latest

[27] Froissart, ii, 50.
[28] See above, 120.
[29] WC, 192.
[30] But it is worth noting that at the end of the reign he was still heartily disliked by some. The anonymous author of the Chronique de la traison et mort de Richart II, ed. B. Williams (London, 1846), who probably served for a time in his household and knew him personally, never missed an opportunity to blacken his character (J.J.N. Palmer, 'The Authorship, Date and Historical Value of the French Chronicles on the Lancastrian Revolution, I and II', BJRL, lxi (1978–9), 165–8.
[31] RP, iii, 250–1; CPR 1385–9, 494–5.

he appointed him chamberlain of the royal household.[32] The bestowal of these offices drew Holand closer to the king, and for the remainder of his career he was to be a thoroughgoing royalist. Richard rewarded him for his loyalty with a whole series of grants. Over the four years from 1389 he granted him life interests in the castles of Berkhamstead (Hertfordshire), Tintagel (Cornwall), Horston (Derbyshire) and Trematon (Cornwall), and in the honours of Rockingham (Northamptonshire) and Haverford (Pembrokeshire).[33] In 1393 he granted him the wardship of the substantial west country estates of the de Briens and two years later that of the Sharnsfield estates in Cornwall.[34] The effect of these grants was to make the earl a substantial landed proprietor, especially in the west country, where the bulk of his comital inheritance lay. He established himself at Dartington, near Totnes, and from about 1390 undertook a lavish rebuilding of the manor house there. In a striking gesture he had Richard's badge of the white hart carved on the central boss of the vault over the main porch (plate 8). This was the kind of architectural labelling for which the Tudor courtiers were to show a liking, and its purpose was to 'turn the house into a hymn of gratitude' to the ruler or dynasty that had made the fortunes of the owner.[35] In a sense Dartington manor was made not only Huntingdon's house but Richard's too – an outpost of Ricardian lordship in a county where royal power had hitherto been weak. The implications of the emblematic labelling were not lost on the Courtenay earls of Devon, who had long been the greatest landowning family in the county, and in the 1390s the Courtenays' relations with Huntingdon became testy. It is true that there were no outbreaks of violence or blood-letting, and Huntingdon was careful to avoid challenging local interests, but in 1399 the Courtenays were to side with Bolingbroke. There can be little doubt that Huntingdon's arrival in Devon had given them offence.[36]

[32] C76/73 mm.4, 26; WC, 414; CPR 1388–92, 252. For Richard's use of patronage in this period see R.A.K. Mott, 'A Study in the Distribution of Patronage, 1389–99', Proceedings of the Leeds Philosophical and Literary Society, xv (1974), 113–33.

[33] CPR 1385–9, 518, 537; CPR 1388–92, 372, 394, 488; CPR 1391–6, 15, 70, 357.

[34] CPR 1391–6, 218, 600. Holand's estates and income are considered in detail in A. Emery, Dartington Hall (Oxford, 1970), Appendix 2.

[35] The phrase 'hymn of gratitude' is D. Starkey's, in 'The Age of the Household: Politics, Society and the Arts, c.1350–c.1550', The Later Middle Ages, ed. S. Medcalf (London, 1981), 273. Starkey was speaking of Sir Richard Clements's Ightham Mote (Kent), but the phrase is equally applicable to Dartington.

[36] For Holand's role in the politics of the period see M. Stansfield, 'The Holand Family, Dukes of Exeter, Earls of Kent and Huntingdon, 1352–1475' (University of Oxford D.Phil. thesis, 1987), 71–102; and for his relations with the Courtenays: M. Cherry, 'The Crown and the Political Community in Devonshire, 1377–1461' (University of Wales Ph.D. thesis, 1981), 155–64; and idem., 'The Courtenay Earls of Devon: the Formation and Disintegration of a Late Medieval Aristocratic

Second only to Huntingdon in the extent to which he benefited from Richard's generosity in these years was Richard's cousin Edward of Rutland, son and heir of the duke of York. Edward was a more assertive man than his father. Able, ambitious and unscrupulous, he was typical of those curialists who sought fulfilment in a career of service to the crown. Richard early on recognized his claims to a place in the peerage. On 25 February 1390 he created him earl of Rutland for the term of his father's life, with a grant of the castle and lordship of Oakham, the forest of Rutland and the sheriffdom of that county for the support of his title.[37] In the four or five years that followed the king found outlets for his talents in a variety of employments. On 22 March 1391 he appointed him admiral of the northern fleet, and in the following November sole admiral, an office which he retained until 1398. In the spring of 1392 he named him as an envoy to accompany John of Gaunt to the negotiations with the French at Amiens; and around the same time he appointed him to succeed the earl of Kent as constable of the Tower of London.[38] The king's dependence on Rutland appears to have increased as his relations with the former Appellants grew more strained. Rutland was a regular companion of his at court, and according to Creton 'there was no man in the world whom Richard loved better'.[39] When Richard went to Ireland in 1394 the earl accompanied him as one of his leading commanders, and he was rewarded with a grant of the earldom of Cork.[40] With his slightly older contemporary John Holand, he was one of the rising stars of the court in the early 1390s.

The promotion of John Holand and Edward of Rutland to high honours in the peerage formed part of Richard's larger policy of raising the royal stock in dignity and elevating it in public consciousness. There was a clear justification for such a policy. Richard had remarkably few close kin: his only brother Edward of Angoulême had died as a boy, and his marriage to Anne was without issue. He could not draw the strength that his father or grandfather had from the presence of a large and supportive family. To compensate for this weakness he chose to raise the collaterals and the half-blood as a distinct estate in the

Affinity', *Southern History*, i (1979), 90–3. It is significant that the constable of Bristol who surrendered Bristol castle to Bolingbroke (or, in theory, to the keeper, the duke of York) in 1399 was a Courtenay – Sir Peter Courtenay, the earl's uncle (Cherry, 'The Crown and the Political Community', 166, 346).

[37] *RP*, iii, 264.

[38] *CP*, xii, ii, 899–900.

[39] Creton, 309. According to Sir William Bagot in 1399, Richard even considered abdicating in favour of Aumerle once he had restored the authority of the crown. The statement affords a useful insight into Richard's regard for Aumerle even if it is of doubtful worth regarding the king's actual intentions (*Chrons. Revolution*, 211).

[40] *CP*, xii, ii, 900.

peerage.[41] His half-brothers, the Holands, were treated as if they were royal kin: John and his brother Thomas, the earl of Kent, were allowed to use the distinctive royal arms impaled with those of the Confessor; and Thomas, when he died in 1397, was granted the honour usually reserved to members of the royal family of a funeral in Westminster Abbey (even though he was buried at Bourne). The Beauforts, the illegitimate offspring of John of Gaunt, were also drawn more closely into the royal circle. In 1397 they were legitimized, and in the letters of legitimation Richard referred to them as 'our most dear kinsmen . . . sprung from royal stock'.[42] As a witness to their blood they too were allowed to impale their arms with those of the Confessor. What Richard saw himself as doing was enhancing his own dignity by drawing attention to the dignity in the peerage enjoyed by his kinsmen of royal blood.

Because of this shortage of close kin Richard had to devolve more responsibility at court on to magnates and lords who were not of royal birth. One of the most prominent of these men was the younger brother of the earl of Northumberland, Sir Thomas Percy. Percy was essentially a soldier by background.[43] He had served under the Black Prince in Gascony in the 1360s and had been present at the sack of Limoges in 1370. In the winter of 1380–1 he had accompanied Buckingham on his great chevauchée across France, and in 1386 he had gone to Spain with Lancaster. On returning from the peninsula he embarked on a new career at court, probably under Lancaster's patronage. In February 1390 he secured the position of vice-chamberlain of the household, and three years later became steward of the household in succession to Sir John Devereux. By 1392 he had also become a regular attender of meetings of the king's council, and was one of relatively few members of that body to benefit to any extent from royal patronage. He received the custody of two castles in South Wales, the office of justice of South Wales and, for a time, the office of forester of Inglewood in Cumberland.[44] In September 1397, after Richard's coup against the former Appellants, he was raised to the earldom of Worcester, and in the final two years of the reign was one of the most loyal and hard-working of the king's advisers. Though he was to desert Richard after the latter's return from Ireland, it is possible that he still had sympathies with the king, for in 1403 he lent his support to his family's rebellion against Richard's supplanter.

---

[41] R.A. Griffiths, 'The Crown and the Royal Family in Later Medieval England', King and Nobles in the Later Middle Ages, ed. R.A. Griffiths and J. Sherborne (Gloucester, 1986), 15–26.

[42] Ibid., 19; for Kent's funerary obsequies see E403/555, 6 June.

[43] The best account of his career is CP, xii, ii, 838–42.

[44] CPR 1391–6, 208, 413–14, 507; 1388–92, 249.

A younger contemporary of Percy's, and a man whose career followed broadly the same course, was Sir William Scrope, son and heir of Richard, Lord Scrope, the king's former chancellor. Scrope, like Percy, had spent his formative years on more or less continuous active service abroad.[45] For nearly a decade from 1383 he had served in Bordeaux as seneschal of Aquitaine. Between 1386 and 1389 he had combined with this office the captaincy of Cherbourg, and from the latter date the captaincy of Brest. He returned to England to settle down in 1392, and in the following year Richard appointed him vice-chamberlain of the household. Scrope quickly won the friendship and favour of the king. In the space of a few months in 1394 he was made a knight of the Garter and appointed constable of the castles of Dublin and Beaumaris in Anglesey. In October 1394, when Richard crossed to Ireland, he went with him and was promoted to chamberlain of the royal household and six months later chamberlain of Ireland; some time before June 1395 he was also appointed justiciar of Ireland. To judge from the comments made about him by contemporaries, Scrope was an ambitious man whose personality was marked by a streak of coldness. Walsingham in the *Annales* calls him 'providus et praedives' (prudent and very rich).[46] He was a highly successful courtier and a rising star at the court of the 1390s, but the true measure of his character and the secret of his relationship with Richard remain obscure.

Scrope, Percy and the Holands were the leading members of the new courtier nobility that Richard built up in the early to mid-1390s, but there were others who played a lesser, if still important, role. Of these the nearest in blood to the king was his uncle, Edmund, duke of York. York was not the most assertive or determined of the nobility, and he suffered from being overshadowed by his more spectacular brothers, but he was probably as strongly royalist in outlook as Lancaster. He was a regular attender of the council and he witnessed nearly all of the charters granted by the king in these years.[47] Also related in blood to the king was Thomas Mowbray, earl of Nottingham, the former Appellant who had been weaned from his allegiance in 1389. Nottingham was a fickle man, but a courtier by inclination, and he served Richard on a number of embassies in France and Germany between 1394 and 1397. Like York, he regularly attested charters in the mid-1390s.[48] Less exalted in rank was John, Lord Lovell, a proprietor in Wiltshire and the east midlands who had been associated with the court in the 1380s. Lovell had been expelled from the household in 1388 by the Appellants, but

---

[45] For the details of his career see *CP*, xii, ii, 730-4.

[46] *Annales*, 157.

[47] Tuck, *Richard II and the Nobility*, 142; Given-Wilson, 'Royal Charter Witness Lists', 77.

[48] *CP*, ix, 602; Given-Wilson, 'Royal Charter Witness Lists', 77.

in the 1390s he staged a comeback and in 1395 was retained to stay with the king for life. He was a regular trier of petitions in parliament, and there are signs that he was actively involved in government, both locally and at the centre. The elaborate new castle that he built at Wardour in Wiltshire survives as a monument to his political ambitions and to the refinement of his architectural taste.[49]

In Lovell, Rutland, Huntingdon and the other lords Richard created a body of men bound to the crown by common interests and by the loyalty created by extensive endowments. The men's identification with the crown is indicated by their pattern of service. Several of them, like Huntingdon and Scrope, held high office at court, and four of them – Lovell, Rutland, Percy and Scrope – accompanied the king on one or both of his expeditions to Ireland. In character and employments the men were obviously in the tradition of the courtier nobility of the 1380s. Socially, however, they were of far higher standing. Three of them had royal blood in their veins, and another two were scions of comital or senior baronial lines. They could not be denounced as unworthy of their titles in the way that de la Pole and de Vere had been in the previous decade. More than a few of them would have succeeded to titles in the peerage in the natural course of events anyway. The fact that they received them from the king's hands arose from Richard's desire to create a new courtier nobility in his image. Richard had little respect for the link hallowed by time between nobility and the tenure of land. Nobility in his view was not a reflection of territorial wealth but of a lord's standing in royal favour. As he had said in the patent ennobling de la Pole in 1385, 'we believe that the more we bestow honours on wise and honourable men, the more our crown is adorned with gems and precious stones'.[50] The nobility, that is to say, were the gems in the royal diadem – luminaries who cast their light on the king. The process of creating and endowing a peer did not impoverish the crown; it enriched it. At one level the crown benefited from the new lord's service; at another it benefited from the lustre shed by his new status.

Richard's exalted view of the crown as a source of honour and nobility had its origins in his overall conception of the kingly office. Richard saw

---

[49] Through his wife Lovell was related to the Holands (*CP*, viii, 219–21). For Wardour castle see R.B. Pugh and A.D. Saunders, *Old Wardour Castle* (London, 2nd edn, 1991) and M. Girouard, 'Wardour Old Castle', *Country Life*, 14 Feb., 1991. It is possible that the architect of this remarkable building was William Wynford, Wykeham's master mason at Winchester Cathedral and College and New College, Oxford (J.H. Harvey, *English Medieval Architects. A Biographical Dictionary down to 1550* (Gloucester, 2nd edn, 1984), 354–5).

[50] *Reports from the Lords Committees Touching the Dignity of the Peerage*, v, 64–5.

the office of king as the sole legally constituted source of authority in society. The other necessarily subordinate sources of authority, he believed, owed their existence to it, and whatever honour these conferred yielded precedence to that conferred by the crown. In a realm united in obedience to a king, title and land were received from the king's hands and held by his continued favour.

This conception of the kingly office formed the basis of Richard's ideas on governance more generally. Richard aimed to create what was recognized in the late middle ages as a 'regal regime' ('regimen regale'), in which the will of the king predominated. The sources of Richard's political ideas appear to have been principally twofold – the teachings of the civil lawyers, and Giles of Rome's *De Regimine Principum*. The influence of the civilians is evident in Richard's development of a more elaborate vocabulary of address. Richard liked to be referred to in formal addresses as a 'prince'. A 'prince' to the civil lawyers was a sovereign ruler, someone who acknowledged no earthly superior. Richard also liked to be addressed as 'your majesty'. 'Majesty' was a civilian concept largely interchangeable with sovereignty. While originally referring to the total power possessed by a ruler, it gradually acquired a religious gloss, and in the late middle ages the crime of 'lèse-majesté' was considered an offence against the semi-religious aspect of the royal persona.[51] There are signs that Richard's familiarity with the civil law was widely recognised and viewed with concern. In the deposition articles of 1399 he was accused of quoting the civilian adage that 'the laws were in his mouth . . . or alternatively in his breast'; and very likely the charge was true.[52] Civil law was a vital element in the king's apparatus of power, for it strengthened and legitimized his role as a supreme law-giver. Its influence overlapped with that of the other main source of his ideas, Giles's *De Regimine Principum*, a work written in the 1270s which enjoyed a wide circulation in later medieval Europe.[53] Correspondences are to be observed at a number of points

[51] Saul, 'Richard II and the Vocabulary of Kingship', 864. For suggestive remarks on the importance of civil law to late medieval kings, see Cobban, *The King's Hall*, 256–8.

[52] *Chrons. Revolution*, 177–8.

[53] For Giles's ideas see J. Dunbabin, 'Government', *The Cambridge History of Medieval Political Thought, c.350–c.1450*, ed. J.H. Burns (Cambridge, 1988), 483–5. The circulation of Giles's treatise in England is touched on by Jones, *The Royal Policy of Richard II*, 161 n.45. Richard's tutor, Sir Simon Burley, is known to have owned a copy of the *De Regimine Principum*: see above, 16. Jones suggests that it was from Simon that Richard picked up his knowledge of the work. This may have been the case, but it cannot be proved. There were others in Richard's entourage who showed a knowledge of civilian ideas, notably Michael de la Pole in the 1380s and Edmund Stafford in the 1390s. For the origins and sources of Richard's political ideas, see also Saul, 'Richard II and the Vocabulary of Kingship', 863–70.

between Giles's maxims and Richard's statements and policies. Thus Giles had emphasized that all honour and privilege in society flowed from the king; and Richard said very much the same in the patents of ennoblement that he issued.[54] Giles had said that the king should be powerful enough to govern; and Richard claimed to exercise all the powers of the prerogative that he had sworn to uphold.[55] Giles had said that all the king's subjects should be obedient to him; and Richard's ministers had stressed the need for obedience in a number of speeches in parliament. Richard's exercise of his kingship in the 1390s was almost a case study in the deployment of Giles's ideas in action. Richard saw the principal object of his government as the establishment of what he referred to as 'peace' – unity, in other words – in his realm.[56] And, following Giles, he believed that he could only achieve this if he, the king, was strong and his subjects were obedient to his will.

The body of ideas which Richard gleaned from Giles and the civilians, and which was sharpened and refined by the humiliations of the 1380s, lay at the heart of the policies which he pursued from 1389. Throughout this period his aim was to strengthen royal government and to make it a more effective instrument of his will. His methods were conservative and traditional: there was no return in the 1390s to the administrative novelties of the 1380s.[57] Richard worked through the existing agencies of government: he simply subordinated these to the control of ministers and officials whom he could rely on. As soon as he declared himself of age in 1389 he purged the Appellant ministers and councillors and replaced them with men more to his liking. Later, as his position strengthened, he replaced these in turn with men who either identified with his outlook or had a tie of loyalty to him personally. These officers, who had all come to the fore by the middle of the decade, were a small and fairly tightly knit group. One of the most important was Edmund Stafford, the keeper of the privy seal from 1389 to 1395 and subsequently chancellor. Stafford was a son of one of the Black Prince's most faithful retainers, and his career at Oxford had given him a training in civil law. In both the offices that he held he was a consistent defender of his master's acts, and in the second of them it fell to him to deliver the authoritarian opening address to the parlia-

[54] See above, 248. Cf. also Richard's grant of arms to one John de Kingston in which the king said that he 'received him into the estate of gentleman and made him an esquire' (CPR 1388–92, 72).

[55] RP, iii, 347.

[56] Giles too had stressed the prince's duty to maintain the peace: Dunbabin, 'Government', 484. For Richard's understanding of 'peace' as unity, see below, 387.

[57] Tout, Chapters, v, 209–10, 219–20.

ment of September 1397.[58] Another who was to prove himself a loyal servant of the king in these years was the former treasurer of Calais, Roger Walden. Walden was Richard's secretary from 1392 to 1395 and subsequently treasurer of England. He was one of the king's closest advisers from the mid-1390s and during his period as secretary reorganized his office so as to make it more responsive to his master's wishes.[59] Probably more important than either of these men, however, was Walden's predecessor as treasurer, John Waltham, bishop of Salisbury. Waltham was a man who earlier in his career had been identified with the Appellants. He was an associate of Archbishop Arundel's, and between 1386 and 1389, while Arundel was chancellor, had held the office of keeper of the privy seal. Dismissed with Arundel when Richard recovered power, he nevertheless worked his way high into royal favour and was appointed treasurer when Brantingham retired in 1391. He proved himself a brisk and efficient holder of that office, and when he died in 1395 Richard honoured him with the privilege of burial in the Confessor's chapel of Westminster Abbey, much to the annoyance of the monks.[60] A certain likeness is to be observed between Waltham's career and those of such administrators of knightly rank as Dallingridge, Bushy and Bagot. Waltham, like these three, was initially of baronial sympathy, in so far as he was of any sympathy at all, but he was quickly won over by the king and later identified with him more strongly than did many whose service to him had been longer. His was without doubt the strongest clerical voice at court in the early and middle years of the decade.

Stafford, Waltham and Walden were valued by Richard not only for the work that they did in their own departments but also for the more general administrative services they rendered. Probably the most significant of these was regular attendance at sessions of the council. By the beginning of the 1390s the council – the future privy council – had established itself as the principal executive agency of royal government. Sitting on a regular basis at either the London Blackfriars' or the Star Chamber at Westminster, it handled a wide variety of business and made decisions that had a bearing on nearly every aspect of political life.[61] As a branch of the old curia regis it was in theory a body entirely

---

[58] *BRUO*, iii, 1749–50; Tout, *Chapters*, iii, 462–3. Stafford was probably one of the men from whom Richard picked up his knowledge of the civil law.

[59] Tout, *Chapters*, iv, 7; v, 221. Walden was rewarded with the see of Canterbury on Arundel's exile in 1398.

[60] Tout, *Chapters*, iii, 216, 461–2; Ormrod, 'Origins of the *Sub Pena* Writ', 11–19; S.K. Walker, 'Richard II's Views on Kingship', *Rulers and Ruled in Late Medieval England. Essays Presented to Gerald Harriss*, ed. R.E. Archer and S. Walker (London, 1995), 55–6. For the circumstances of Waltham's burial see *HA*, ii, 218.

[61] For the 'professionalism' of the council, see Baldwin, *The King's Council*, 499,

dependent on the royal will: its authority came from the king, and its members were appointed by him. In practice, however, by Richard's reign it increasingly acted as if it were a largely autonomous body. It met in regular session away from the king; it not infrequently ventured to disagree with, and even to criticize, the king; and it demonstrated an awareness of a responsibility not just to the king but to the community of the realm as a whole. As K.B. McFarlane once observed, it was 'developing its own distinct constitutional position *vis-à-vis* the king'.[62]

The pressures leading the council in the later fourteenth century to take this more independent view of its role came largely, it seems, from within the council itself. By the 1390s the council was casting off its earlier informal character and turning itself into a more professional, tightly organized body. Moreover, it was settling into fairly definite rhythms of work. Customarily it met on a daily, or near-daily, basis during term; and it had a small, but clearly defined, body of members. As Tout observed, it was even acquiring some of the characteristics of an embryonic cabinet.[63] There is evidence that by Richard's reign the councillors were giving thought to how best they might transact their business. In March 1390 an 'ordinance for the government of the king's council' was drawn up which laid down guideliness for procedure and functions.[64] Business was, as far as possible, to be departmentalized. All that touched the common law was to go to the justices of the two benches, and all that concerned the office of chancellor to the chancery; financial business was to go to the treasurer, to be determined by him in the exchequer. All other matters which required the 'special grace and permission of the king' were to be explained to him, so that his pleasure might be learned. However, the king could not do what he liked. 'No gift or grant which might tend to reduce the king's resources' was to pass without the advice of the council and the assent of the royal uncles and the chancellor, or of any two of them. Business of any importance, it was laid down, was to be determined by council and ministers; bills of individuals and matters of lesser importance might be examined and determined by the keeper of the privy seal and other councillors then present. Regular hours were ensured by the provision that the council was to assemble 'between eight and nine o'clock at the latest'. There is no evidence that many of these rules were innovations:

504; J. Gillingham, 'Crisis or Continuity? The Structure of Royal Authority in England 1369–1422', *Das Spätmittelalterliche Königtum im Europäischen Vergleich*, ed. R. Schneider (Sigmaringen, 1987), 68–70. For where the council sat, see *PPC*, i, 12c, 14c.

[62] McFarlane, *Lancastrian Kings and Lollard Knights*, 86.

[63] Tout, *Chapters*, iii, 467.

[64] *PPC*, i, 18a–18b. For discussion see Tout, *Chapters*, iii, 465–7.

it is more likely that they drew on and codified what was already existing practice. What they did was bring a more businesslike air to the council's business. The object of greater efficiency was also achieved by the taking of minutes of the council's decisons. The minute book kept by John Prophet, the first known clerk of the council, is the earliest surviving record of that body's deliberations.[65] By the 1390s the council had become a clearly and efficiently organized body entrusted with the day-to-day conduct of government.

The second factor that contributed to the growing self-awareness of the council was stability and cohesiveness of membership. Although numbers were swelled from time to time, especially when negotiations with the French were under consideration, routine business was handled by a small group of men who had in effect the status of professional administrators. There are two periods for which a systematic body of evidence about membership survives – the seven months from August 1389 to March 1390, and the period of just over a year from January 1392 to February 1393 covered by Prophet's journal. In the first period the chancellor and treasurer, the great officers of state, were regularly in attendance; of the lay lords, York, Northumberland, Nottingham and Lancaster (after his return) attended most frequently; while at a lower level the chamberlain and steward of the household and a group of knights led by Sir Edward Dallingridge, Sir William Neville and Sir Richard Stury were also present for a large number of sessions.[66] In the second period the officers of state and the knights Dallingridge and Stury were again regularly present. It can be established from the arrangements made for payment of wages that Dallingridge attended the council for 207 days between 8 January 1392 and 21 February 1393, and Stury for 159 days. Among others who attended regularly in this period were two bishops, Wykeham of Winchester and Scrope of Lichfield, and the steward and the vice-chamberlain of the household, John Devereux and Thomas Percy respectively.[67] Through the presence of these latter (as of the chamber knights Dallingridge and Stury) regular informal communications were maintained between the council and the king. The council in the 1390s was in no sense deliberately hostile to the king, and the majority of its members wished for no more than to work harmoniously with him.

Richard appears to have accepted the need for a measure of conciliar supervision of his activities after he regained power. As we have seen, the ordinances of 1390 envisaged that no grant with financial implica-

[65] Baldwin, *The King's Council*, Appendix II.
[66] *PPC*, i, 6–18; Tuck, *Richard II and the Nobility*, 141–3.
[67] Baldwin, *The King's Council*, 132–4 and Appendix II.

tions was to pass without the assent of the royal uncles and the chancellor, or any two of them.[68] There is abundant evidence from the 1390s that the consent of the council was regularly sought for royal grants which affected the revenue, and there are signs that Lancaster himself personally intervened to ensure that royal wishes were put into effect.[69] Naturally, there was tactical advantage to the king in bowing to conciliar supervision of patronage, for parliamentary criticism of patronage could thereby be deflected from him on to the council. But it is doubtful if Richard willingly submitted to supervision when he suspected that his wishes were being thwarted or his interests threatened. In November 1389 he reacted angrily when the chancellor, Bishop Wykeham, refused to issue letters patent or close in accordance with his command: he ordered the chancellor to hand over the seal to the prior of the Order of St John and three of his knights, so that they could authorize it instead.[70] This was an episode which had echoes of the quarrel that had led to Lord Scrope's dismissal from the chancellorship in 1382.[71] A month earlier there had been a more dramatic demonstration of the tensions that could arise between the king and his officers and council. The earl of Nottingham had requested reappointment as warden of the East March, and at new, and higher, rates of pay. The council refused to negotiate a fresh agreement until the old one had expired, because they did not want to be charged with wantonly adding to the realm's financial burden. The king took Nottingham's side and tried to induce the council to agree to his request, but Chancellor Wykeham, speaking for them all, declined to do so. The king, who was present at the meeting, stormed off to Kennington, but the council held firm and next day the king suggested that Nottingham's term of office should be extended, but that he should be paid at the old rates. This was a compromise that the council immediately accepted.[72]

What emerges from these exchanges is that, if Richard was happier than before to compromise and accept conciliar advice, he did not invariably give way. Nor would he readily surrender on issues which he considered of particular importance to himself and his friends. In the

---

[68] See above, 252.

[69] Tuck, *Richard II and the Nobility*, 140.

[70] C81/1354/15, in H.C. Maxwell-Lyte, *Historical Notes on the Great Seal of England* (London, 1926), 321.

[71] See above, 111.

[72] *PPC*, i, 12b–12d. For discussion see Tuck, *Richard II and the Nobility*, 139–40; R.L. Storey, 'The Wardens of the Marches of England towards Scotland, 1377–1489', *EHR*, lxxii (1957), 600–2. One final instance of conciliar initiative may be noted. On 22 September 1393 the council overrode a signet letter to the mayor and bailiffs of Northampton, urging the election of a certain person as mayor, on the grounds that the king, advised by his council, now regarded the nominee as incompetent for office (*CCR 1392–6*, 167).

following two years his relations with the council appear to have become more harmonious: at least Prophet's journal affords no evidence
of an open rift between them. Not until the spring of 1392 did another
major difference of view occur. This time the cause of the trouble was
the fate of Richard's exiled friends. According to the account in the
Westminster chronicle, which is supported by the journal minute,
Richard put a request to the councillors that the judgments on Alexander Neville and Robert de Vere be reversed and that the two be allowed
to return to England. The lords, however, says the chronicler, maintained that on no account could this be allowed. The king then 'graciously' gave way, and accepted that the banishment should be
permanent. The lords, reassuring him of their loyalty, promised to join
him in arms against any who broke these engagements, and Richard
himself gave a pledge that it was not his intention to restore anyone who
had been sentenced in parliament to forfeiture.[73]

The terms of these delicately phrased exchanges are so guarded that
it is difficult to establish what lay behind them. One point that emerges
is the lingering suspicion with which the two sides viewed each other.
The king suspected the councillors of wanting to encroach on the
prerogative, while the councillors were suspicious of the king calling
into question the settlement of 1388. The fact that the exchanges
ended in a compromise may well be evidence of the king's willingness
to accept a measure of conciliar supervision. But against this has to
be set the evidence from other sources of the king's determination
to pursue the matter of his friends' return. Twice over the previous
fifteen months, and each time clearly on royal initiative, the commons
had submitted parliamentary petitions requesting that the king should
be as free in his 'liberty, regality and royal dignity' as any of his predecessors.[74] It is hard to account for these petitions, and especially the
second submission in November 1391, other than on the supposition
that Richard felt that his 'liberty' had been encroached upon in some
way and that he was seeking the commons' support in reclaiming
it. Richard's tactic was evidently to play off the commons against the
councillors and the lords. It was a tactic that was bound to fail given
the strength of the councillors' feelings on the issue, but the fact that
he attempted it at all bears witness to the shrewdness and calculation
with which he could play the political game. Richard never readily

---

[73] WC, 484–6; Baldwin, *The King's Council*, 495.

[74] RP, iii, 279, 286. Evidence that the petitions were 'planted' is afforded by the
1399 deposition articles, which allege that 'whereas various statutes were made
in parliament, which ought to remain in effect until revoked by a later
parliament . . . the king craftily arranged for a petition to be put forward by the
commons in parliament that he should be granted the right to enjoy the same
liberties as any of his predecessors' (*RP*, iii, 419; *Chrons. Revolution*, 178).

acquiesced in the loss of his rights. Time and again, he was testing the
ground to see how far he could go. He was as assertive, and yet as
flexible, in his tactics as his grandfather Edward III had been in his
heyday.

The kind of day-to-day problems which Richard faced in his dealings
with the council were replicated in his dealings with the highest consultative and judicial forum in the land – parliament. After his recovery
of power Richard was keen to assert his rights over parliament, most
obviously because it was that body which granted him extraordinary
taxation, but also because it was in a parliamentary setting that his
authority found fullest expression. His assertion of his rights, however,
led in the middle and later years of the decade to a straining of relations
with the commons. In January 1397 there was criticism of his refusal to
accept requests for curbs in the size of his household; and well before
then there was controversy over his continuing demands for taxation.
Strikingly, when he was deposed in 1399, one of the charges laid against
him related to attempts, made in the course of the 1390s, to coerce
parliament into making grants of subsidies in time of truce.
    At the beginning of the decade Richard had shown himself deeply
concerned to conciliate the commons. On recovering power in 1389 he
had promised to ease the burden of taxation on his people, and on the
making of the truce with the French he was able to go some way to
honouring that commitment. On 16 May he remitted collection of the
second instalment of the subsidy granted at the Cambridge parliament,
and in the two years to 1391 he made no further demands for the levies
on moveables.[75] Nevertheless, as the chancellor frequently reminded
the commons, the ending of formal hostilities did not mean an end to
the king's need for his subjects' aid. There was a variety of defensive
charges to be borne. The English Channel had to be patrolled, the
Scottish Marches defended, and the garrisons at Calais and Brest maintained. The annual cost of defending Calais alone came to between
£10,000 and £20,000; the wages of the wardens on the Scottish Marches
and their garrisons came to another £4,500, and those of the garrison at
Brest to perhaps £3,000.[76] Sums on this scale could only be afforded if
the king received adequate financial support from his subjects.

[75] See above, 235.
[76] In 1378 Calais had cost the English government £24,000 per annum (*RP*, iii,
34). By the 1390s, as a result of the truce, the cost had come down. In 1397–8 John
Bernard, the treasurer of Calais, received £18,000; and his predecessor a year
earlier rather less (E403/556). The wages of the wardens of the Marches towards
Scotland had been fixed in 1389: the warden of the Eastern March was to receive
£3,000 per annum in time of truce, and his colleague in the west half that sum
(Storey, 'Wardens of the Marches', 600). For his captaincy of Brest John Holand
took a fee of 3,000 marks (Jones, *Ducal Brittany*, 148, 221).

In the 1390s considerable pressure was exerted on the commons to continue granting subsidies despite the fact that formal hostilities had ended. Chancellor Wykeham's plea to the commons in the parliament of January 1390 was typical of many heard in the course of the decade. The realm, he said, was surrounded by enemies: there were threats to the king in France, Spain and Aquitaine in the one direction, and Scotland and Ireland in the other; there was no certainty that the truce would hold. At the same time provision had to be made for the safe-keeping of the Scottish Marches and of the outposts at Calais, Brest and Cherbourg; and the peace had to be kept in Ireland and Aquitaine. The king, he concluded, could not support these burdens without financial aid from his faithful lords and commons.[77] In January 1390, however, as so often later, the commons took little notice of the plea. They took their stand on the Romano-canonical principle, according to which public taxation could only be demanded in the event of 'necessity' or special need. Generally in the fourteenth century a 'necessity' was identified with a state of war, since war threatened the very existence of the realm.[78] In the 1390s there was little certainty as to whether – or how far – subjects had a responsibility for defence in time of peace or truce. Before these years the most pertinent precedents came from the decade after the signing of the treaty of Brétigny in 1360. Although Brétigny had established a full peace, the crown was still obliged to maintain garrisons in Calais, Ireland and elsewhere, and successive ministers tried persuading the commons to support these financially on the grounds that to do so accorded with their own interests as well as the king's. The commons responded by renewing the subsidy on wool exports, but repeatedly designated these grants as made 'for the estate and honour of the king' to show that they did not acknowledge a general obligation to support the standing charges of peacetime defence.[79] In the decade from 1389 the government again put pressure on the commons to shoulder a proportion of the costs of 'peacetime' defence, while the commons resisted this pressure and limited the number and size of grants. As in the 1360s, the commons distinguished sharply between the wool and leather subsidies, on the one hand, and the levies on moveables, on the other. They were prepared to concede the former on a regular basis, but they would only grant the latter if exceptional need were demonstrated – in other words, if the realm was at war or on the brink of war; and it was their practice when making a grant to 'appropriate' it for a specific purpose. Thus in November 1391 the commons granted a half-subsidy to pay for a projected conference

[77] *RP*, iii, 257.

[78] G.L. Harriss, *King, Parliament and Public Finance*, 509–17; idem, 'War and the Emergence of the English Parliament', *JMH*, ii (1976), 35–56.

[79] Harriss, *King, Parliament and Public Finance*, 470.

between Richard and the king of France and a whole subsidy to be levied if hostilities resumed and if Richard led an expedition in person to either Scotland or France.[80] In January 1393 the commons were equally specific in their terms. They made available three half-subsidies – the first unconditional, the second for a 'voyage' to either Ireland or Scotland (and to be kept in hand if that 'voyage' were cancelled), and the third for an expedition to be led in person by the king. At the commons' request the king's officers were instructed to record all three of these stipulations on the parliament roll.[81]

The commons' insistence on restricting the use of public taxation to certain limited and approved purposes made it increasingly difficult for Richard's government to pay its way, and as early as 1389 there are signs that it was resorting to irregular exactions. In the spring and early summer of that year wide-ranging 'trailbaston' enquiries were conducted by Arundel in South Wales; and in August and September enquiries into waste at the king's expense, which the Westminster writer called 'trailbastons', were ordered in the south-eastern counties.[82] In the winter of 1389–90 a subsidy of 1,000 marks was levied on the people of North Wales, and in the following year the men of Cheshire were constrained to make a grant to the king of 2,000 marks.[83] On a lesser scale, in February 1392 a general distraint of knighthood was ordered, to generate an income in fines from those seeking exemption from the rank.[84] At the same time, to ease its cash-flow problems, the council resorted to widespread borrowing. In the summers of 1391 and 1394 the king solicited loans from a wide variety of individuals and borough communities, though only in the latter year does he appear to

[80] *RP*, iii, 285–6.

[81] Ibid., 301–2.

[82] The commission to Arundel was issued on 18 February 1389 (*CPR 1388–92*, 55–6; *WC*, 382); proceedings appear to have got under way by May (E403/524, 18 May). For the commissions in the south-eastern counties see *CPR 1388–92*, 140–2; *WC*, 406.

[83] E403/532, 9 Feb. 1391; E403/536, 12 Dec. 1391. It may be the latter fine which the king was still trying to collect in 1393, when three esquires were sent to Wales 'pro £1,600 assignatis ad expensas hospitii querendas et usque hospitium predictum salvo ducendas': E101/403/22, fo.17ʳ. The king's need for money appears to have become acute by 1393, and it may have been for that reason that in July and August he undertook an extensive itinerary of southern England, moving between monastic or episcopal manor houses at Farnham, Alton, Winchester, Downton, Wimborne, Salisbury, Beaulieu and Sutton (E101/402/10, fos27ʳ–31ʳ: see Appendix). Despite living partly at his subjects' expense he still had to send out messengers to seek money to meet the expenses of his household (E101/403/22, fo.17ʳ). A year or two later further efforts were made to raise money in South Wales: see R.A. Griffiths, 'Gentlemen and Rebels in Later Medieval Cardiganshire', *Ceredigion*, v (1964–7), 154–5.

[84] Baldwin, *The King's Council*, 494.

have encountered anything like a satisfactory response.[85] In 1392, to supplement these efforts, the council approached the mayor and aldermen of London for a substantial loan. Somewhat unwisely, and contrary to their usual practice, the Londoners refused, and Richard retaliated by confiscating the liberties of the city. From June until the middle of September London was ruled by a royally appointed warden, and the mayor and aldermen were restored to office only when they agreed to pay a corporate fine to the king of £10,000.[86] Richard in the end obtained the money that he wanted, but the price he paid for his high-handed behaviour was a substantial loss of popular goodwill in the city.

The increasing predatoriness of Richard's government bore witness to the underlying deterioration in his financial position in the early to mid-1390s. At the start of the decade Richard had enjoyed a small surplus of income over expenditure; by 1392 that surplus had turned into a deficit. For a while in 1393 and 1394 there was a surplus again, thanks to the settlement with London and the imposition of extraordinary taxation. But after 1395 the deficits returned, and by 1398 the king was spending over £11,000 a year more than he received.[87] It is not hard to find the reason for this worsening situation. In October 1390 the king, following the example of the nobility, had begun to establish his own 'bastard feudal' affinity, and by the late 1390s he was paying fees to over 80 knights and some 210 esquires. The effects of this outlay soon registered in the accounts. The expenditure of the great wardrobe, which was responsible for the distribution of livery to royal dependants, rose from £8,000 over the period from November 1390 to September 1392 to almost £16,000 by September 1394. The expenses of the household as a whole also grew in the same period. Between 1389 and 1394 there was a slow but gradual increase from roughly £16,000 a year to a little over £19,000, but after 1394 the increase was much sharper and total expenditure in 1395 was £26,000 and in 1396 nearly £38,000.[88] Some of the increase in the latter year

[85] Tuck, *Richard II and the Nobility*, 144; A. Steel, *The Receipt of the Exchequer, 1377-1485* (Cambridge, 1954), 71.

[86] C.M. Barron, 'The Quarrel of Richard II with London, 1392-7', *The Reign of Richard II*, 173-201. There was a sting in the tail of the settlement with the king: Richard restored the city's charter only on conditions – 'until it shall be otherwise ordained for them', as the letters patent said. The Londoners had to make a loan of 10,000 marks to the king in August 1397 to have their liberties restored to them in full: C.M. Barron, 'The Tyranny of Richard II', *BIHR*, xli (1968), 6. It is clear from the accounts of both Walsingham and the Westminster writer that the origin of the quarrel was the Londoners' denial of a loan (*HA*, ii, 207-8; *WC*, 496).

[87] Given-Wilson, *Royal Household and the King's Affinity*, Appendix I, provides a convenient summary of the king's financial position.

[88] Ibid.; Tout, *Chapters*, vi, 108.

can be accounted for by the cost of the Ardres conference, but the underlying trend was upward. Richard could no longer manage to live 'of his own'.

Richard's response to this predicament was to appeal to his subjects for financial support. To do so, of course, he had to break, or at least seriously to weaken, the identification of a 'necessity' with war or the threat of war. The first occasion on which his ministers, acting on his behalf, attempted to do this was at Winchester in 1393. Chancellor Arundel in his opening address simply made a general plea to his listeners to assist the king with his 'costs and charges', regardless of 'whether it was a time of war, truce or peace'.[89] The commons responded by making a series of grants, two of which they assigned to particular purposes but one of which (a half-subsidy) significantly was unconditional. Their recognition of the very different nature of his plea is evident in the preamble to the schedule in which they stressed that they were acting not out of recognition of a necessity but more out of affection for the king:

> To the reverence of God and for the weal and tranquillity of the realm and for the great trust that the commons of the realm have in our lord king and in his royal majesty, and for the great dearness and tenderness that the king has to his crown and to his said commons by surrounding himself with good government to discharge them as far as possible from any impositions or tallages in time to come, and to maintain and sustain them in his right laws, both rich and poor, the said commons by their good grace and free will and by assent of the lords spiritual and temporal have granted . . . [There follows the grant of indirect taxes.]
>
> And also the commons have granted to our lord king by the assent aforesaid for the defence of the realm, and for the costs and charges of the king, and to honour the person of the king, be there truce, peace or suffrance of war . . . [There follows the grant of a half-subsidy.][90]

The chancellor's plea in the next parliament, that of January 1394, was couched in traditional fashion because the king needed money for a military expedition to Ireland, but there was further resort to novelty in 1397. In his opening address to the parliament of September that year the chancellor entirely disregarded the doctrine of 'necessity'; his talk was all of the subject's duty of obedience. The peace, he said, ought

---

[89] *RP*, iii, 300.
[90] Ibid., 301–2. For discussion see G.L. Harriss, 'Thomas Cromwell's "New Principle" of Taxation', *EHR*, xciii (1978), 724–5.

to be better kept, and the laws better executed; the king should be powerful enough to govern, and his subjects should be obedient to his will. The effect of this strongly authoritarian address was to evoke a generous response from the commons. At the end of the session they made two grants to the king – the first, an unprecedented one of the wool and leather subsidies for life, and the second a subsidy and a half conceded in similar terms to those of 1393 in return for the granting of a general pardon.[91] The size and terms of the grants represented a major victory for the king. He had successfully overridden the view of taxation as justified only by the exceptional needs of the realm and had opened the way to the imposition of taxation in time of truce or peace. It was the notoriety of these happenings which Henry IV exploited in 1399 when he accused Richard of taxing his people 'while the kingdom was not burdened with the expense of war'.[92] An extension of the grounds of public taxation to meet the peacetime costs of government was seen as a threat to the property and liberty of the subject.

In his efforts to secure the commons' acquiesence to public taxation in time of truce the king was able to draw on the services of those members in the lower house who had links with the crown. Such men were more numerous in the parliaments of the 1390s than ever before. In the Merciless Parliament of 1388 there had been nine. In the two parliaments of 1390 the number rose to thirteen and twelve respectively. In 1391 there were as many as twenty-two, and in the four parliaments that followed sixteen, twenty, nine and fourteen.[93] Many of the knights with royal connections were among the most experienced and frequently returned of all the members. Both Sir John Russell and Sir Henry Green had represented their counties twice before entering the king's service; Sir John Bushy had represented his four times, and Sir James Pickering and Sir William Bagot theirs no fewer than ten times.[94] It was the experience which these men had built up over the years which made their service so valuable to the king: they could act as a cadre of 'king's men' in the house. There can be little doubt that Richard expected them to be active in managing the commons in the way that he wanted; but how, and with what degree of success, they went about their task it is almost impossible to say. In only one area can the working of their influence be detected, and that is in elections to the office of Speaker. Significantly the only man to have served more than once in

---

[91] *RP*, iii, 347, 368-9.
[92] Ibid., 419; *Chrons. Revolution*, 177.
[93] Given-Wilson, *Royal Household and the King's Affinity*, 247.
[94] *House of Commons*, iv, 248-51; iii, 225-8; ii, 449-54; iv, 77-80; ii, 99-103.

the 1390s as Speaker was one of Richard's most active and experienced
retainers, his councillor Sir John Bushy. Bushy served in the office in
1394, and again in the two parliaments of 1397. Walsingham said that
Richard actually 'appointed' ('constituit') Bushy as Speaker in September 1397.[95] It is unlikely that this was the case, because the right of
choosing their own Speaker was one which the commons jealously
guarded. A more plausible explanation is that the king's knights were
active in lobbying on his behalf. Cohesive, well connected and well
organized, they were in a strong position to influence opinion in his
favour.

Richard's appreciation of the importance of the commons and of the
gentry class whom they represented is one of the most striking characteristics of his rule in the 1390s. In part it was a product of his growing
political maturity: for now in his late twenties he was developing some
skill in the arts of management. Much more, however, it was a response
to the setbacks that he had suffered at the hands of the Appellants. His
inability to resist the Appellant coalition or to do anything effective to
save his councillors and friends from their fates had brought home to
him the consequences of his lack of a substantial following in the
country, and he realized that he needed to take action to broaden the
base of his regime. There were various ways in which he could go about
doing this. The first was by establishing a personal following – an affinity
– just as the magnates had long done. The other – less direct – was
by championing the interests of the gentry in parliament. It was the
second approach which he put into effect first. Shortly after resuming
power in the spring of 1389 he made a deliberate bid for an alliance
with the commons, and the bait that he offered was a commitment to
implement the commons' programme on public order.[96]

Richard had given an earnest of his commitment to enforce better
order in the realm in his manifesto of 7 May 1389. Riots, oppressions
and illegal assemblies, he said, would be suppressed, while complaints
about unruly behaviour would be given immediate attention by the
officers and council.[97] In the weeks that followed he acted swiftly to give
effect to these promises. Between 10 May and 1 June he sent no fewer
than three judicial commissions to enquire into various offences in
Gloucestershire, Norfolk, Kendal and Westmorland – in other words, as
many as the total number of general commissions of enquiry issued
since the appointment of the council in November 1386; and between
July 1389 and June 1390 other general commissions were issued for

---

[95] *Annales*, 209.

[96] For disagreements between the commons and the lords at Cambridge on the
issue of public order see above, 200–1.

[97] *CCR 1385–9*, 671.

Somerset, Dorset, Shropshire, Surrey and Kent.[98] A month and a half later, on 15 July, the king issued new commissions of the peace in every shire.[99] Their appointment was the first general review of the commissions of the peace for nearly seven years, and a striking innovation was the omission of members of the nobility. In the past magnates with a territorial stake in a county, even if they rarely resided, had headed that county's commission; on this occasion, however, they were omitted, presumably in a conscious bid by the king to win gentry support. Four months later, in November, the king further demonstrated his concern with public order by comprehensively reviewing the membership of the July commissions. Some of the smaller commissions were enlarged by the addition of one or two new members, while the larger ones suffered losses as the king weeded out unsatisfactory justices.[100] At the same time a new procedure was introduced for the appointment of the sheriffs. According to the Westminster chronicler, it was ordained that the sheriffs, instead of being appointed by the officers of state and exchequer judges as in the past, were to be chosen by the king in his privy council and made to swear that they would faithfully perform their duties.[101] The purpose of the new arrangement was to impress on the new appointees that the king was personally concerned about their performance in office, and the absence in the next parliament of any complaints about shrieval malpractice suggests that the message had got through. At least for the moment, the king's measures appeared to be having an effect.

The one issue on which Richard had so far refrained from taking action was that of the distribution of badges. As a result of his inactivity the commons were beginning to grow restive again. In the parliament of January 1390 they reminded him that the Cambridge accord had been provisional; and, according to Walsingham, they issued a fresh call to him to abolish badges altogether.[102] Richard's response to their urgings was to promise to refer the matter to the council. In April the councillors gave it their attention, and in the following month the well-known ordinance 'of livery and maintenance' was published. By the terms of this measure the right of giving 'livery of company' was restricted to those of the rank of banneret and above, and that of

[98] R.L. Storey, 'Liveries and Commissions of the Peace, 1388–90', *The Reign of Richard II*, 136.

[99] *CPR 1388–92*, 135–7.

[100] Ibid., 137–9.

[101] *WC*, 404. On 13 November payments were made to messengers to summon all the newly appointed sheriffs to attend a meeting of the council – presumably so that they could take the oath (E403/527, 13 Nov.).

[102] *HA*, ii, 195–6.

receiving it to domestic staff and knights and esquires retained for life
by indenture.[103] In broad outline the measure followed the terms of the
provisional agreement made at Cambridge, but in a couple of respects
it parted company from its exemplar: in the first place, it spoke of 'livery
of company' and not, as the provisional agreement had, of badges
(*signes*); and secondly it confined the distribution of livery to those of
the rank of banneret and above. Both of these changes favoured the
lords, and their inclusion must have bitterly disappointed the commons. The message was clearly signalled that Richard was backing
away from the commitment that he had earlier made to reform.[104] The
most likely explanation for the king's change of heart is that he was
coming under pressure from the magnates. Since parliament had
ended in March the magnates had steadily reasserted their influence in
government, and the council in April at which the terms of the ordinance were agreed was a magnate-dominated assembly attended by
Lancaster and his two brothers.[105] Richard, to judge from the speedy
retreat on which he now embarked, found it difficult to hold out against
their pressure. In the weeks after the ending of the council he made
further concessions to their interests. On 16 May, as part of a general
statute regulating the work of the peace commissions, he waived the
prohibition on magnate stewards on the commissions which had
been ordered at Cambridge in 1388.[106] A month later on 28 June new
commissions were issued on which over half a dozen stewards were
present, at least five of them Gaunt's.[107] In the light of these moves
Richard's wooing of the commons looked less and less convincing.
Five months later in November the policy was abandoned. At the end
of the parliamentary session of that month a statute was published
readmitting the magnates to the commissions. On 24 December
new commissions were issued, and all but four of them were headed by

---

[103] *English Historical Documents*, 1116. Storey, 'Liveries and Commissions', 147, says
that 'evidence of prosecutions for violation [of the ordinance] still awaits discovery',
but for one instance of a conviction see *CPR 1391–6*, 249.

[104] The omission of any reference to badges in the ordinance is crucial. As the
careful reportage of the Westminster writer makes clear, it was the distribution of
badges (*signa*) which the commons had been complaining about in 1384 and 1388
(*WC*, 82, 356); and it is evident from the commons' petition of January 1390 that
it was the distribution of badges (*signes*) that had been regulated by the Cambridge
agreement: 'livery of cloth' is nowhere mentioned in the document (*RP*, iii, 265;
and see above, 201). The failure of the ordinance to make any reference to badges
is therefore a clear measure of the council's retreat. This is a point glossed over in
the otherwise useful discussion in Given-Wilson, *Royal Household and the King's
Affinity*, 239.

[105] Storey, 'Liveries and Commissions', 146.

[106] *SR*, ii, 62–3.

[107] *CPR 1388–92*, 341–4. For discussion see Storey, 'Liveries and Commissions',
148–9.

magnates.[108] With this concession Richard's dalliance with the commons may be said to have ended.

If Richard felt it necessary to shy away from supporting gentry authority in the shires, so too, it appears, did the commons. The initiative in restoring the magnates to the peace commissions had actually come from the commons in the meeting of parliament in November.[109] What had probably become clear to the commons was that gentry JPs alone could not adequately enforce the law. The involvement of the magnates – who were after all the most influential men in the shires – was essential if the justices' authority was to be put into effect. Lancaster probably argued this very point at the April council at which the change in policy on public order was agreed. Richard raised no objection because he had developed doubts of his own about the course on which he had embarked. After two years it seemed to have brought him few political dividends. He had not created a new power base for himself; nor had he deprived his opponents in the nobility of theirs. The aim that he had set himself of harnessing the power of the gentry was an understandable one; moreover, it was one that would appeal to later rulers, in particular Henry VII. But the problem that faced him was that gentry power was diffuse: it was spread thinly and widely across the political landscape. If its potential was to be realized, it was essential that royal favour and patronage be directed not indiscrimately but at the leaders of gentry communities – at those who would bring others in their wake. Richard's appreciation of this point led him fundamentally to change his policy to the gentry in the latter half of 1390. Instead of wooing the class as a whole through the commons he now wooed selected members. In other words, he embarked on the formation of a royal affinity – an affinity made famous by its use of the king's badge, the white hart.[110]

Richard's initiative in forming this affinity was an entirely new one for a medieval king. Until the last quarter of the fourteenth century direct relationships between the king and the knightly class had been in the main confined to the military sphere. Kings had retained a fairly large, but fluctuating, corps of 'knights of the royal household' to serve as the nucleus of the armies which the king led in war, and from the 1340s there was additionally a small number of knights or esquires 'of the chamber', whose employments were largely domestic; neither the chamber staff nor the knights of the household were recruited by the king to serve as agents of the royal will in the shires. In the 1360s

---

[108] *CPR 1388–92*, 344–6.
[109] *RP*, iii, 279.
[110] The white hart was first used by Richard at the Smithfield tournament of October 1390: *HVR*, 132; *An English Chronicle of the Reigns of Richard II, Henry IV, Henry V and Henry VI*, ed. J.S. Davies (Camden Society, 1856), 6.

this long-established system began to break down. With the realm at peace, it was no longer necessary for the crown to retain a large number of knights for service in war. The corps of household knights therefore faded away, and after 1360 no such knights are recorded in the wardrobe books of the household.[111] What remained was the small body of knights and esquires of the chamber. These men were employed chiefly at court, as councillors, special commissioners and envoys to foreign rulers; there was emphatically no role for them in the shires. It was the crises of 1387 and 1388 that alerted Richard to the need to build up a wider following in the country. In the summer of the former year, when it was clear that a struggle for power could no longer be delayed, Richard sent a sergeant-at-arms around East Anglia handing out livery badges to the local gentry. The sergeant was arrested, and subsequently disappeared from view, but his efforts represented the first attempt by his master to mobilize the power of the gentry.[112] Later in the year the king took on an important west midlands knight, Sir John Russell, a retainer of the earl of Warwick and a man who was to be one of his closest councillors in the final years of the reign, and in the years after he recovered power he recruited more extensively.[113] Between 1389 and 1393 he took on no fewer than thirty-six knights, and in the six years that followed a further forty-six. He also took on a large number of esquires. Between his accession and his defeat in 1387 he had retained hardly any esquires at all for life. By the time he was deposed, however, he had taken on 125 for life, and it is likely that he took on nearly as many again for shorter terms.[114] In the space of less than a decade the character of the royal affinity had been transformed. Its military aspect had been shed, and it had become an active 'civilianized' force with representatives in every shire in the land.

The men whom Richard attracted to his service were for the most part substantial figures in their communities. Most were the lords of two, three or four manors or more. One or two, like Sir Gerard Braybrooke senior or Sir William Sturmy, were wealthy men with strings of manors scattered across several counties.[115] Almost all had had, or were to have, some experience of local administration. A number, as we have seen, were regularly returned to parliament, where they were

[111] C. Given-Wilson, 'The King and the Gentry in Fourteenth-Century England', *TRHS*, 5th series, xxxvii (1987), 88–93.

[112] *WC*, 186.

[113] *CPR 1385–9*, 372.

[114] These figures are taken from Given-Wilson, *Royal Household and the King's Affinity*, 214–15. To the list of Richard II's knights ibid., Appendix V, add Sir Ivo Fitzwaryn (*CPR 1391–6*, 577).

[115] For these men see respectively *House of Commons*, ii, 343–6; iv, 520–4. For Sturmy see also J.S. Roskell, 'Sir William Sturmy', Roskell, *Parliament and Politics in Late Medieval England* (3 vols, London 1981–3), iii, 91–105.

probably active on the royal behalf. The precise mechanics of recruitment to the affinity are unclear, and it is not really possible to say how
the initial contact with the knight was made. A few of the group had had
earlier connections with the king's household. Sir Robert Bardolph, Sir
Thomas Barre and Sir Richard Redman are referred to as 'king's
knights' between 1386 and 1388: Richard probably retained them on
a more formal basis later to comply with the terms of the 1390 ordinance.[116] A somewhat higher proportion had already distinguished
themselves in the service of other lords. Sir John Bushy and Sir Henry
Green, for example, were long-standing retainers of John of Gaunt, and
it is likely that their entry into royal service was a by-product of the close
relations between the king and his uncle after 1390.[117] Less predictably,
a number of knights came to the king from the service of the former
Appellant lords. Sir Simon Felbrigg and Sir William Arundel, for example, had connections with Gloucester, Sir William Bagot with Nottingham and Warwick, and Sir Edward Dallingridge with Arundel.
Dallingridge and Bagot may very well have been active militarily on the
Appellants' behalf in 1387.[118] Whether it was Richard's policy deliberately to seek out men of former Appellant allegiance is hard to say. It
would obviously have suited him to do so on opportunistic grounds, but
there was a danger that he could have given offence to the former
Appellants. Warwick reacted furiously when Richard poached Russell
from him in 1387: he cut off the knight's fee and conducted a campaign of harassment against him through the agency of his retainers.[119]
Richard had no desire to provoke this sort of outcome because he did
not wish to fuel the fires of factionalism locally, so he is likely to have
refrained from deliberate poaching. What evidence there is suggests
that he had little difficulty in attracting enough of the sort of men that
he wanted in the natural course of events anyway. The fees that he
offered were generous – almost certainly more generous than those
offered by most private lords: Dallingridge, William Arundel and
Nicholas Hawberk, for example, all received 100 marks per annum.[120]
Moreover, wider horizons were opened by entry into royal than into
private service: the new retainer could look forward to more extensive
involvement in government and perhaps, if he wished, to promotion at

[116] Given-Wilson, *Royal Household and the King's Affinity*, 215.

[117] Walker, *Lancastrian Affinity*, 266, 270 and the references there cited.

[118] Goodman, *Loyal Conspiracy*, 38, 102, 148–9, 159–62, 115–16; *House of Commons*,
ii, 99–103, 738–42.

[119] Goodman, *Loyal Conspiracy*, 150–1.

[120] *CPR 1388–92*, 102; *CPR 1391–6*, 178, 352. The range of fees paid by the king
varied widely, but the average was still high: the knights generally received 40 marks
or £40 per annum (*House of Commons*, i, 199). Most knights in the service of private
lords would have received £20.

court. The rewards of royal service were thus adequate enough to draw to the king men who had already proved themselves in the service of other lords. To the extent that a number of these men were former retainers of the Appellants, the latter obviously suffered some loss of repute. In Sussex, for example, Arundel's influence was reduced by the emergence of Edward Dallingridge as a patronage broker in the east of the county. Developments of this kind were to benefit the king in the long term, but it is doubtful if Richard intended them from the outset; political targeting played no part in his calculations.

The expansion of the royal affinity was the most striking and innovative of the measures that Richard took in the 1390s to reassert his power. It gave the king what he had previously lacked – a wider following among those who were socially and politically influential in the shires. Richard probably did not see the functions of his men as primarily military. Relatively few of them accompanied him on his two expeditions to Ireland, and hardly any new knights were taken on when these expeditions were planned.[121] The likelihood is that it was for peacetime, not wartime, service that the majority of the knights were recruited. Richard looked to the men to act as an informal network linking the household and court to the outlying regions of the realm. Significantly, a higher than average proportion of his recruits came from the northern and western counties and the Welsh Marches, where royal authority was weaker.[122] There was a particular need in these areas a long way from Westminster for a body of men who could watch over royal interests and defend royal rights. Such a function had been performed in the past by the justices in eyre; but since the demise of the eyre in the second quarter of the century responsibility had devolved on to the sheriff and the escheator, and the duties of these officials were too many and too burdensome to allow them to exercise such oversight effectively.

Richard's formation of a magnate-style affinity represented an intelligent and practical response to the problems raised by the exercise of royal authority in the later middle ages. It set the seal on the long process of re-establishing and reasserting royal authority that the king had begun in 1388. In the immediate aftermath of the Appellant coup Richard's prospects had looked unpromising. His power base at court had been destroyed, and he had forfeited the goodwill of his subjects; it was the Appellants who held the fortunes of the nation in their hands. Yet within less than a year Richard had recaptured the initiative. He had undermined the Appellant coalition and weaned the two junior lords from their allegiance; and he had embarked on his policy of wooing the

---

[121] Given-Wilson, 'King and the Gentry in Fourteenth-Century England', 97–8.
[122] Given-Wilson, *Royal Household and the King's Affinity*, 219–21.

commons. In the years that followed his grip on the realm grew progressively stronger. He sealed an alliance with Gaunt and embarked on the construction of a courtier nobility. He kept up the pressure on the commons for taxation and had some success in obtaining grants of the moveables levy in time of peace. In the space of some four or five years he had successfully restored the fortunes of his kingship and condemned the memory of his failures to the past. With the realm at peace and his authority re-established, he could think of devoting attention to the problems of the further parts of his realm. In 1394 he set out for Ireland.

Chapter 12

RICHARD IN IRELAND

Richard II was the first English king to visit Ireland since John in 1210; and he was the last to do so until William III in the 1690s. Irish affairs did not rank high in the priorities of England's medieval rulers. Most of the Angevin kings were more interested in the pursuit of continental ambitions. Henry II and his sons sank all in the defence, and later the attempted recovery, of the Angevins' lands in France; and Edward III and the 'Plantagenets' doggedly pursued their claim to the crown of France. Edward I, almost alone among Richard's predecessors, showed an interest in extending his dominion within the British Isles. Richard, of course, was not wholly averse to upholding the wider European interests of his dynasty. In 1390 he offered to take the county of Flanders into his personal protection, and in 1397 he made a bid for the imperial crown. But from the middle of the 1380s he seems to have been increasingly attracted by the idea of deepening his lordship within the British Isles. The idea of the 'wider realm' appealed to him. He conceived of his crown as a congeries of lordships, with the core and the peripheries on a sort of continuum, and it is possible that he had in mind the 'imperial' notion of a crown possessed of many dependencies.[1] In the 1390s, as soon as the lull in Anglo-French hostilities gave him the opportunity, he began building up his power in the non-English parts of the British Isles. He spent more time in the Marcher lordships and the Welsh borderlands. He elevated Chester and the adjoining county of Flint to a principality.[2] And, most strikingly of all, he undertook the two great expeditions to Ireland. His fascination with Ireland formed part of a broader commitment to a kingship extending beyond the south-east and midlands of England.

The attention that Richard paid to Irish affairs was in a sense long overdue. For nearly half a century the English position in Ireland had been steadily weakening; and by the 1380s there were many in the Dublin administration who feared that, unless urgent relief were given, the colony would cease to exist. The period of accelerated decay had

---

[1] M.J. Bennett, 'Richard II and the Wider Realm', *Richard II. Power and Prerogative*, ed. A. Goodman (Oxford, 1997).

[2] See below, 392–3.

begun in the wake of Edward Bruce's invasion of 1315. On the eve of
this assault English power in Ireland had been at its height. The area
under English lordship was well defended, and the Dublin exchequer
handed over a reasonable surplus to its counterpart at Westminster. At
the same time, in the areas beyond the lordship the chiefs had submitted to, or had been brought within the influence of, English earls or
the English king directly. Edward Bruce's invasion had fatally undermined this supremacy. Bruce's aim in crossing to Ireland had been to
provoke a rebellion against English rule and to use the province as a
springboard from which to invade Wales. He failed in his ultimate
objective, and was defeated and killed in a skirmish near Dundalk in
1318. But the consequence of his activities was to provoke a revival in
the self-confidence and sense of identity of the Gaelic Irish. Irish lords
and chieftains from now on campaigned actively to recover lands which
had been lost to the colonists. In 1342, according to the annalist John
Clyn, Laoighseach O Mordha 'violently ejected almost all the English
from their lands and inheritance' and in one night burned eight
of their castles, among them Roger Mortimer's 'noble castle' of
Dunamase. In other parts of the province Irishmen forcibly took possession of castles built by Anglo-Norman magnates – as at Sligo, Ballymote,
Cloughoughter and Donaghmoyne. At the same time, the more assertive of the Irish chieftains were entertaining kingly ambitions. It is
recorded that in 1327 'the Irish of Leinster came together and made a
king of Donal, son of Art MacMurrough who, when he had been made
king, ordered that his banner should be placed within two miles of
Dublin and should afterwards travel throughout all the lands of
Ireland'. It may have been the memory of this episode which inspired
O'Brien of Thomond in 1374, so the council alleged, 'to claim falsely
and without title to have the lordship of Ireland'.[3] The later fourteenth
century was a period of high ambition among the Irish chieftains and
'kings', and the victories and ancestry of these men were celebrated by
bards and *seanchaidhe* (traditional historians) in ornate verse. It is
hardly surprising that one poet should have claimed, as he did in 1364
in an inauguration ode for Niall Mor O'Niall, king of Tir Eoghain, that

> Ireland is a woman risen again
> from the horrors of reproach . . .
> she was owned for a while by foreigners,
> she belongs to Irishmen after that.[4]

---

[3] For these episodes see J.F. Lydon, 'The Impact of the Bruce Invasion, 1315–27',
A New History of Ireland, II. Medieval Ireland, 1169–1534, ed. A. Cosgrove (Oxford,
1987), 302; K. Simms, 'The Norman Invasion and the Gaelic Recovery', *The Oxford
Illustrated History of Ireland*, ed. R.F. Foster (Oxford, 1989), 89.

[4] Simms, 'The Norman Invasion and the Gaelic Recovery', 88–9.

A phenomenon which both added to and aggravated the effects of the Gaelic revival was the gradual retreat from Ireland of the once largely resident Anglo-Norman nobility. In the thirteenth century Irish society had been led by families like the Genevilles, the Verdons and the de Lacys and the de Burghs, who also held lands in England but spent much of their time in Ireland. By the fourteenth century virtually all these families had gone. Richard de Burgh, earl of Ulster, had been killed in 1333, leaving a baby daughter who took her estates in marriage to Lionel of Antwerp, an absentee. The families of Verdon, Geneville, de Clare and de Valence also became extinct in the male line in the early decades of the fourteenth century. The places of these lords were for the most part taken by absentees. Estates were inherited by heiresses or co-heiresses, and the husbands to whom they were given in marriage usually held the bulk of their interests in England. Not uncommonly they parted with their Irish estates by sale. The effects of this disengagement were twofold. In the first place, a more distinctively Anglo-Irish aristocracy emerged: various branches of the Geraldine (Fitzgerald) and Butler families, for example, acquired earldoms and played a more prominent role in the mediation of patronage and favour.[5] Secondly, and more seriously for the Dublin administration, the colony's ability to defend itself was weakened. There were no longer enough lords with either the means or the commitment to muster a force in time of need. Increasingly, military assistance had to be sought from without.

It is easy to exaggerate the scale of the lordship's decline at this time. The English community had passed through difficult times before. In the 1250s there had been a revival in Gaelic self-confidence, and a native ruler, Brian O'Neill, had styled himself high king of Ireland; yet in time the threat receded, and the colony had flourished again. Hardly ever had the struggle for power in Ireland resulted in outright victory for one side and outright defeat for the other; generally it had issued in compromise and in the formation of a new balance of power. The Dublin government had for some time been reconciled to the existence of severe limits on its power. Large parts of the north and west were effectively beyond its control; in many other areas the main hope of exerting influence lay in co-operation with the more reputable of the magnates, who could construct regional supremacies and deal with the native chieftains rather in the manner of the pre-Conquest over-kings. In a semi-colonial society like Ireland's the state of politics fostered, and eventually demanded, the consolidation of lordships, the exercise of

---

[5] For the self-image of these people see R. Frame, ' "Les Engleys Nees en Irlaunde": The English Political Identity in Medieval Ireland', *TRHS*, 6th series, iii (1993), 83–103.

power locally and resort to self-help. The more successful of the Dublin justiciars realized this. Sir Thomas de Rokeby, who was justiciar in 1349–55 and 1356–7, co-operated with the nobility, built up an elaborate system of alliances and proved a masterly exponent of the art of frontier management.[6] But in the later decades of the century there were few justiciars who could match Rokeby in calibre or experience. Indeed, the problem faced by the government was that of getting anyone to hold the office of justiciar at all. In 1382, following the death of the earl of March, both Ormond and Desmond declined the office, and it was eventually taken by the chancellor John Colton, dean of Dublin, only on sufferance and on condition that he should be allowed to relinquish it in the next parliament or great council.[7] The reason for the unpopularity of the justiciar's office was the financial burden that it imposed on the holder. As the treasurer made clear in 1382, there was no money in the Dublin exchequer to meet even the ordinary costs of government, let alone those of military activity. Rokeby had had to rule in the 1350s with inadequate funds at his disposal: often he had had to negotiate with, rather than confront, his enemies. Thirty years after his time the financial crisis had become considerably worse. The evidence of the Irish pipe rolls bears witness to this. Over the half-century to the Bruce invasion the Dublin exchequer had yielded a surplus annually to Westminster of some £5,000–£20,000; by the 1350s it rarely yielded a surplus of more than £1,000–£2,000; and by the early years of Richard's reign it constituted a net drain on English resources.[8] Informed opinion in England was well aware of the deterioration. Walsingham noted that, whereas Edward III had received annually £30,000 from his Irish lordship, his successor not only received nothing but had to spend roughly the same amount on the lordship's defence.[9] This situation could not be allowed to continue indefinitely. By the 1380s there was strong pressure on the Westminster government to take action to restore the colony to fiscal and military self-sufficiency.

The idea that the king himself should cross with a force to Ireland had initially been floated by a council held at Dublin in 1385. The proposal had its immediate origins in the widespread dissatisfaction felt with the policies of the lieutenant, Sir Philip Courtenay, the uncle of the earl of

---

[6] R. Frame, 'English Officials and Irish Chiefs in the Fourteenth Century', *EHR*, xc (1975), 748–77.
[7] A.J. Otway-Ruthven, *A History of Medieval Ireland* (London, 1968), 316.
[8] H.G. Richardson and G.O. Sayles, 'Irish Revenue, 1278–1384', *Proceedings of the Royal Irish Academy*, lxii (1962), 87–100.
[9] *Annales*, 172.

Devon.[10] Courtenay had run into difficulties in his relations with the Anglo-Irish and appears to have aroused opposition with his taxes and demands for military service. In December 1384 complaints about his behaviour were made to the king, and in the following year there were demands for his removal from office. Courtenay's position was a diffi-cult one, because he was an outsider. The informal leadership of Irish political and aristocratic society lay with the Mortimer earls of March, the leading landowners in the province, but Edmund, the third earl, had died suddenly in 1381 leaving a seven-year-old boy as his heir. In the 1380s there was thus a vacuum at the highest level of Irish society. Courtenay, a mere scion of a comital family, was ill qualified to fill this. At a council held at Dublin in 1385 the request was put that the king should come in person to the province: or that, if he could not, he should send the greatest and most trustworthy lord in his place. Richard, as it happens, was already thinking along similar lines himself; but his response was not what the Dublin council had in mind. On 12 October he announced that he intended shortly to bestow the title of marquess of Dublin on his favourite Robert de Vere, earl of Oxford, and on 1 December the formal patent of creation was issued granting de Vere for life the land and lordship of Ireland, with all that pertained to it, saving only liege homage and superior lordship. All writs from now on were to run in the marquess's name, and the marquess's arms – newly created for the occasion – were to replace the king's in Ireland. It is unlikely that Richard was responding directly to the initiative of the Dublin council because he did not receive the envoys from Ireland until early in the New Year, but he was well aware of the general movement of opinion in the province. The Dublin administration could only have been shocked and disappointed by his decision. De Vere had no terri-torial interests in Ireland; he was totally lacking in military and admin-istrative experience, and his rise to power was entirely the product of royal favour. To many his appointment afforded proof of Richard's intention of building Ireland up as a bastion of royal power, closely linked with Cheshire and North Wales, where the marquess and other favourites already held office.[11] In reality, the king was probably influ-enced more by a desire to enhance his friend's dignity in the English aristocratic hierarchy. De Vere came from a modest background, and his family was the least distinguished of the comital lineages. By creat-ing him a marquess, and then in the following year a duke, Richard was giving him equality of status with Lancaster and placing him, at least nominally, above the other two royal dukes, York and Gloucester,

[10] For what follows see A. Tuck, 'Anglo-Irish Relations, 1382–1393', *Proceedings of the Royal Irish Academy*, lxix (1970), 15–31.

[11] This was how the Appellants saw the appointment: see clauses 7, 22, 38, 39 (*WC*, 244–6, 256, 266–8).

neither of whom enjoyed palatine powers over their inheritances. Of course, in terms of the influence that he wielded in his domains, de Vere was substantially less powerful than Gaunt, because his titles were empty ones. To give substance to the titles he would have had to carry out a war of conquest in Ireland, and there is little evidence that he intended to do this. In spring 1386 preparations were made to supply him with shipping to Ireland, and on 23 March that year he was granted the ransom of Jean de Blois, claimant to the duchy of Brittany, for the maintenance of 500 men-at-arms and 1,000 archers in Ireland for two years after his arrival there.[12] But at the same time letters patent were issued appointing Sir John Stanley as his lieutenant in the lordship, and it seems likely that the duke's intention was to stay in England while Stanley went with the force to Ireland.[13] Within a matter of months domestic political problems were to frustrate the king's plans for his friend. In the October parliament the 'continual council' was appointed to hold office for a year, and the king and his household left Westminster for the midlands. In the autumn of the following year de Vere raised a force in Cheshire with which to challenge and destroy the Appellants. While leading it south, however, he was trapped by the earl of Derby and defeated, and in the Merciless Parliament the grant to him of the duchy was annulled.

These events in England had an unsettling effect on political life in Ireland. The rhythms of administration were disrupted, and substantial changes were made in the personnel of government. De Vere's officers and dependants in Dublin were removed by the Appellants in early 1388, and shortly before that Stanley had returned to England.[14] The idea appears to have been considered of reviving the duchy in favour of the duke of Gloucester, but nothing came of this and in July 1389 Stanley was reappointed lieutenant for three years. In the early months of 1390 Stanley led a vigorous campaign against the O'Neills in Ulster. His conduct of the campaign, however – and, indeed, his handling of government more generally – gave rise to criticism in both Dublin and London. It was alleged that he had mismanaged the revenues of the Irish exchequer, maltreated prisoners taken on campaign, and failed to observe the terms of his indenture. An enquiry into the charges was ordered and, following this, on 11 September 1391 he was removed from office. As a stopgap measure the bishop of Meath was reappointed justiciar, but the government, seeking a longer-term solution to the problem, now revived the idea of sending Gloucester to the province. Around the beginning of October Gloucester was appointed lieutenant

[12] See above, 155.
[13] CPR 1385–9, 125.
[14] Ibid., 441; Tuck, 'Anglo-Irish Relations', 27.

and shortly afterwards the terms of an indenture were agreed with him. He was to hold office for five years, for the first three of which he was to receive 32,000 marks from the English exchequer; he was also to have all the issues and profits of the lordship, but after three years the government of the country was to pay for itself.[15] Preparations for the duke's passage to Ireland were set in hand in May; but in July the appointment was suddenly cancelled. The reasons for the change of plan are obscure. It is possible that Gloucester considered that the lieutenancy would be too expensive and politically unrewarding. On the other hand, it is possible that Richard had other plans for his uncle. Negotiations with the French had been resumed in earnest in 1392, and he may have had in mind including his uncle in future embassies: Gloucester was indeed to be a member of the team that concluded the draft treaty at Leulingham in the summer of 1393.[16]

In 1392, then, arrangements for the government of Ireland were brought under review yet again. On the day that Gloucester was discharged Richard announced the appointment as lieutenant of the new earl of March, Roger Mortimer, who was only nineteen. As a temporary measure, until March could come over, the earl of Ormond was given the office of justiciar. Ormond found himself holding office for much longer than he had anticipated, and more than two years elapsed before March actually arrived. The reason for the delay is almost certainly to be found in a controversy between the earl of Kent, on the one hand, and the earls of Arundel, Warwick and Northumberland, on the other, over the terms on which March was to leave the country while still under age. Kent was the guardian of the young earl himself, but Arundel, Warwick and Northumberland had received custody of his inheritance after the dispute over its control in 1382.[17] In a document probably drawn up soon after the announcement of March's appoint-

---

[15] It used to be believed that the indenture with Gloucester was made in about May 1392, when there is evidence that an expedition to Ireland was being organized. The undated document which survives, however, specified that part of the duke's stipend was to be paid on the approaching 23 April, provided that the king was informed before Easter (1392) of the duke's return to England and willingness to go – and assuming that he actually made his proposed voyage to Prussia in the first place. From this wording it is apparent that the indenture must have been drawn up before Gloucester's departure for his abortive Baltic crusade; and the Westminster chronicler says that he set sail for the Baltic in mid-October 1391 (*WC*, 480). A further difficulty is presented by the fact that the existing document is clearly a draft: it is covered with erasures and additions. No final version survives, and it is doubtful if one was ever agreed: D.B. Johnston, 'Richard II and Ireland, 1395–9' (Trinity College, Dublin, Ph.D. thesis, 1976), 34; idem, 'The Draft Indenture of Thomas, Duke of Gloucester, as Lieutenant of Ireland, 1391', *Journal of the Society of Archivists*, vii (1983), 173–82.

[16] Tuck, 'Anglo-Irish Relations', 28; Otway-Ruthven, *Medieval Ireland*, 321–3.

[17] For this, see above, 111–12.

ment Kent put forward certain articles concerning the earl's proposed expedition to Ireland. The first and most important of these was that the earl should receive livery of his inheritance even though he was under age. In another document Arundel, Warwick and Northumberland opposed the proposal on the grounds that they were the lawful guardians of the inheritance and could see no reason why they should be ousted against their will. They were also doubtful about the propriety of March using the resources of his inheritance to finance the expedition. The matter remained in dispute for some time. In June 1393 the king granted March livery of his Irish lands, but the three earls had never had custody of these and they were not referred to in the documents submitted to the council. Not until the following February did the king allow the earl livery of his English and Welsh estates. It is possible that Richard deliberately delayed coming to a decision on Kent's proposals in order to avoid giving offence to Arundel, Warwick and Northumberland. By February 1394, when their custody had little more than a year to run, the earls may have moderated their objections, but even so the decision had in the end gone against them. They complained that they had been 'ousted from their estate', but apparently to little effect: it seems that no special arrangements were made to protect the Mortimer inheritance while the earl was in Ireland. The earls' opposition had perhaps prevented Kent's proposals being implemented in 1392 or 1393, but they had failed to get their way on the substantive issue; and their unease may have been a contributory factor to the renewal of political tension in 1397.[18]

The dispute over the March inheritance had dragged on for so long that by the time it was resolved Richard's plans for the government of Ireland had changed yet again. In letters published on 16 June 1394 the king announced his decision to cross to Ireland in person. The timing of the announcement was probably influenced by the loss of his queen, Anne, who had died at Sheen only nine days before, but it is likely that the ambition of going to Ireland in person had been forming in his mind for some time.[19] Over the previous four years there had been a rapid improvement in relations between England and France, and it was possible to consider the diversion of resources to Ireland without endangering national security. The aim of the king's expedition was simple. As he put it in a letter to the duke of Burgundy, it was to secure 'the punishment of our rebels there and to establish good government and just rule over our faithful lieges'.[20] To attain these

[18] For this dispute see Tuck, 'Anglo-Irish Relations', 29–31.

[19] Significantly, Stanley's indenture of 1389 included the condition that he relinquish office in the event of an expedition led by the king himself (E101/247/1/3). I am grateful to Dr D. Johnston for drawing this point to my attention.

[20] *Anglo-Norman Letters*, no. 3

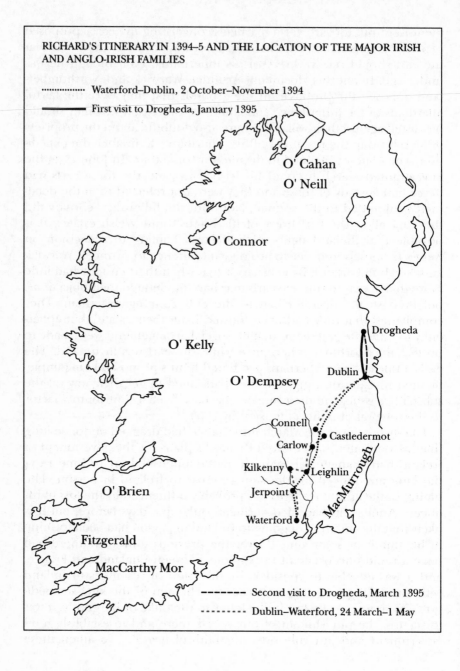

RICHARD'S ITINERARY IN 1394–5 AND THE LOCATION OF THE MAJOR IRISH
AND ANGLO-IRISH FAMILIES

················· Waterford–Dublin, 2 October–November 1394

————— First visit to Drogheda, January 1395

O' Cahan

O' Neill

O' Connor

O' Kelly

O' Dempsey

Drogheda

Dublin

Connell

Carlow

Castledermot

Kilkenny

Leighlin

Jerpoint

MacMurrough

Waterford

O' Brien

Fitzgerald

MacCarthy Mor

- - - - - - Second visit to Drogheda, March 1395

········· Dublin–Waterford, 24 March–1 May

objectives Richard took with him an exceptionally large and well-equipped army. It is difficult to be sure about its size, but it could hardly have numbered less than 7,000–8,000 men. The core of the force was a substantial household contingent, numbering some 4,000–5,000, of the kind that had been familiar in the Welsh and Scottish wars of Edward I.[21] The leaders of the main contingents were all Richard's friends. Among them were the earl of Rutland, shortly to be made earl of Cork, the earl of Nottingham, the earl of Huntingdon, the heir to the earl of Kent, Sir Thomas Despenser, Sir Thomas Percy, Sir William Scrope and Sir John Beaumont; Huntingdon was chamberlain of the household, Scrope the vice-chamberlain, and Percy the steward. Among the older or non-courtier nobility the only participants were March and Gloucester, the latter probably an unwilling participant. Lancaster was in Aquitaine; York remained in England as keeper of the realm; Northumberland, Arundel and Warwick either had responsibilities elsewhere or preferred not to take part.

The progress of the expedition can be charted from contemporary narratives and from Richard's correspondence with the council in London.[22] Richard made the crossing from Milford Haven to Waterford, in southern Ireland, on 1 October. He spent about three weeks at Waterford while he worked out his strategy. His main aim at this stage was to round up Art MacMurrough, the self-styled king of Leinster and the Irish chief whose removal from Leinster he was especially anxious to achieve. MacMurrough's power base lay in the difficult hilly country to the west and south-west of Dublin. Richard's strategy for bringing the Irishman to heel was effectively to starve him into submission. A naval blockade was mounted along the Irish coastline; and a series of strongpoints, or 'wards', was established on the perimeter of his lordships cutting him off from the rest of Ireland.[23] At the same time his tenants were subjected to a campaign of constant raiding and harassment. On one of the raids MacMurrough was himself nearly captured. The earl of Nottingham chanced upon his house by night, and the Irishman had to leap from his bed while the English seized his possessions and put his property to the flames.[24] But MacMurrough could not hold out indefinitely against the forceful deployment of the English, and before

---

[21] The figure is derived from the accounts in the wardrobe book, E101/402/20. The wardrobe book is incomplete, however, and there are no entries for men taken on by the king after he had arrived in Ireland.

[22] The fullest account of the expedition is now Johnston, 'Richard II and Ireland', 66–182.

[23] J.F. Lydon, 'Richard II's Expeditions to Ireland', *Journal of the Royal Society of Antiquaries of Ireland*, xciii (1963), 135–48.

[24] E. Curtis, 'Unpublished Letters from Richard II in Ireland', *Proceedings of the Royal Irish Academy*, xxxvii (1927), 292–3; *Anglo-Norman Letters*, 207–8.

Christmas he was suing for terms. On the English side the negotiations were conducted by Nottingham, who as lord of the liberty of Carlow had a special interest in the outcome, and on 7 January agreement was reached. 'In a field between Tullow and Newcastle' MacMurrough was received into the English king's peace; he swore to restore to the English king everything which he or his men had lately occupied in Leinster, and undertook that all his subjects and tenants in these places would swear fealty to the king. He swore further that before the first Sunday of Lent he would leave all Leinster to the true obedience, use and disposition of the king, and that he would deliver his brother to the king as a hostage. In return he was guaranteed an annual payment of 80 marks to him and his heirs for ever, and his wife's inheritance in the barony of Norragh (the withholding of which had been a major source of grievance to him). He was followed in making these undertakings by his *irrachts*, or leading vassals, and by all the petty chieftains of Hy Kinsella.[25]

The submission of MacMurrough was a major triumph for Richard, and it was shortly followed by agreements of a similar nature with other chiefs. By early to mid-February all the *irrachts* of Leinster, with their hereditary king at their head, had made their submission to Richard or to one of his captains and Richard was also receiving submissions from chieftains of other parts of the country. On 8 January he could write to the council: 'From day to day we have, thank God, pleasant news, and that is, that O'Neill and our other Irish rebels will come to surrender to us, submit, recognize their offences, and receive for them whatsoever we will devise.'[26]

Richard was particularly anxious to secure the submission of O'Neill, because it would then be possible for him to effect a settlement of Ulster, where the earl of March, nominally earl of Ulster, also had claims. The younger O'Neill, a powerful figure, in the event held back; but on 19 or 20 January his father, both for himself and as proctor for his son, submitted. At the house of the Dominican friars at Drogheda he performed homage and fealty in person to Richard, undertaking to surrender to March the *bonnacht* or fealty of the Irish of Ulster and all other services which he or his ancestors had owed to the earl's ancestors. This was a promising development; and, though it yet remained for the younger O'Neill to appear, a step had been taken towards working out a settlement of the problems of Ulster.[27]

[25] E. Curtis, *Richard II in Ireland, 1394–5, and Submissions of the Irish Chiefs* (Oxford, 1927), 80–5.

[26] *Rotulorum Patentium et Clausorum Cancellarie Hibernie Calendarium*, ed. E. Tresham (Irish Records Commission, 1828), 154.

[27] Otway-Ruthven, *Medieval Ireland*, 328–9; Curtis, *Richard II in Ireland*, 105–7, 144–6, 190–2, 223–4.

Considerable progress was also made in these weeks in securing the submission of leaders in other parts of Ireland. By the end of January the king had heard that 'our rebels who call themselves kings and captains of Munster and Connacht' were ready to do homage to him. The report was a little premature, because heavy fighting was still going on around Cork in March; but by 4 February Richard had received from Brien O'Brien of Thomond a letter in which O'Brien undertook to find pledges for his fealty to the king. On 1 March O'Brien, the self-styled 'prince' of Thomond, submitted to the king at Dublin; and three days later 'in a field called Maghadir by the town of Quin' he publicly repeated his oath of allegiance and was followed in so doing by the rest of the Irish of Thomond.[28]

By the early spring of 1395 Richard had gained recognition of his authority from the native leaders in all parts of his Irish lordship. Well before this time he was giving consideration to the nature of his relationship with these men. In a celebrated letter to the English council he distinguished three categories in the Irish population: he said that 'there are the wild Irish our enemies, the rebel Irish, and the obedient English'.[29] He went on to outline his policy towards the second group, the rebel Irish. He explained that their rebellion arose from past failures of government; and warning that, unless mercy were shown to them, they would ally with the enemy, the 'wild Irish', he proposed taking them into royal protection until their past rebellion had been either purged or excused. Readings of this letter have sometimes taken the 'rebel Irish' to mean the 'Anglo-Irish', with the implication that Richard saw the degeneracy of the Anglo-Irish as the main problem facing the lordship. But there are strong grounds for believing that it was actually the native Irish who were uppermost in his mind. In the first place, there is the evidence of the king's priorities over the previous four months: ever since he had arrived in Ireland it had been the 'rebel Irish' whom he had been striving to bring back into his obedience. And, secondly, there is the evidence of terminology in the lordship at the time. In official correspondence and memoranda ethnic origin was always distinguished very precisely, and if a writer meant someone of English origin he invariably described him as such: which in this case Richard did not.[30] For each of these reasons it seems highly unlikely that, when speaking as he did in his letter to the council of the 'Irish', Richard really meant the 'English'. What he was outlining was a policy of conciliation towards those members of the native Irish who had

---

[28] Curtis, *Richard II in Ireland*, 93–4, 137; Otway-Ruthven, *Medieval Ireland*, 329, 331.
[29] *PPC*, 56.
[30] Otway-Ruthven, *Medieval Ireland*, 333; D.B. Johnston, 'Richard II and the Submissions of Gaelic Ireland', *Irish Historical Studies*, xii (1980), 6–7.

broken away from their allegiance and whom he wanted to win over
again. Unlike the Dublin administration he did not regard a subject's
race as relevant to the matter of his obedience. The 'land of Ireland'
was in his eyes a single lordship: all who lived in it were potentially his
subjects, whatever their racial origin. In other words, implicit in the
king's policy was a legal redefinition of the crown's relations with its
Gaelic subjects. The lordship of the crown was being asserted as an
indivisible whole: it could be enjoyed by all in the king's protection
regardless of race. From now on there were to be 'liege Irish' just as
there had always been 'liege English'.

From the perspective of the native Irish there was a great deal to be
gained from this process of redefinition. Probably of greatest value to
them was the fact that as subjects they were given access to the fountain-
head of royal justice. Many of the Irish had grievances against leading
Anglo-Irish lords who had encroached on their lands or rights of lordship, and they now had the opportunity to take these grievances to the
king himself for redress. In an undated letter, probably of early 1395,
Niall Mor O'Neill of Ulster wrote to Richard of the 'joy' that he felt at
the news of the king's coming; for now, he said, he knew that he would
be able to obtain justice for the injuries done to him and his people by
those whom he called 'the English of the Marches' – in other words, the
nominal earls of Ulster, the earls of March. O'Neill and his family had
long been engaged in fierce competition for power with the earls of
March, and they saw the coming of the English king as potentially
making the contest more even. Others who petitioned Richard looked
to him to provide remedy for more specific grievances. Maghnus
O'Cahan, lord of Cianacht in Derry, demanded the return of cattle
seized by men in the pay of the Englishman Edmund Savage. Felim
O'Toole of Kildare was worried that his licence 'peacefully to enjoy
buying and selling in your markets and towns' had not been honoured.[31] To these men and others of similar background Richard's
promise to listen sympathetically to his Irish subjects offered an unprecedented chance to challenge the power of the English.

However, the benefits offered by Richard's coming and the extension
of English lordship were by no means limited to the possible remedying
of grievances. Entry into the English king's allegiance offered the
additional prospect of raising the chiefs' standing as rulers. This
was a powerful attraction to the chiefs because they wanted to become
the equals of the earls and to challenge their ascendancy. Art
MacMurrough's aspirations to greatness, for example, are aptly illustrated by his adoption of a seal on which he styled himself 'by the grace

---

[31] Curtis, *Richard II in Ireland*, 131–2, 211–12, 142–3, 220–1, 125–7, 206–8. For
discussion see Johnston, 'Submissions', 9–10.

of God, king of Leinster'.[32] In the eyes of a native ruler like Art entry into the allegiance of the king of England could be considered the equivalent of entering into the state known in Gaelic as *comairce*, or 'protection'. In a *comairce* agreement the status of the submitting man could be raised if his partner in the agreement was a man of superior standing to himself. This was clearly the case when an Irishman entered into the lordship of the king of England, a ruler of vastly superior standing to any native chieftain or 'king'. The Irish lord's status was enhanced, and some of the aura of his new overlord rubbed off on to his own person. The effect was to strengthen the chief's hold over his vassals: he could become a 'king' in the more generally accepted sense of the time.[33]

The precise terms on which the Irish established their new relationship with the king were laid down in the oaths which the king exacted when they submitted to his obedience. The texts of the oaths and the instruments that accompanied them were formal documents, drawn up by notaries and subsequently transcribed on the memoranda roll of the English exchequer. Their diplomatic form was closely modelled on that of the feudal oath of liege homage. The new vassal bound himself to become the liegeman of the king, to be faithful to him and to render him assistance against his worldly enemies; to be obedient to his laws, commands and ordinances, and to come to him and his heirs and to their parliaments when summoned; and finally 'to do in all and singular that which a good and faithful liegeman ought to do and is bound to do to his natural liege lord'.[34] These terms, or terms very similar to them, were sworn by virtually every Irishman who submitted to the king: they were the essential preliminary to the formal settlement of grievances that followed. It is hardly surprising that they should have been cast in a feudal form, because feudal concepts provided the conventional framework for the expression of relationships of lord and man at the time. Nevertheless the relationship created by the agreements bore little resemblance to the early medieval notion of liege homage. By the middle to later fourteenth century that earlier notion of 'ligeantia' was hardening into the idea of 'allegiance', or obedience to the ruler.[35] A stage in the evolution of the concept can be seen in the letters patent

[32] Curtis, 'Unpublished Letters', 293.

[33] K. Simms, 'Gaelic Lordships in Ulster in the Later Middle Ages' (Trinity College, Dublin, Ph.D. thesis, 1976), 115–17.

[34] Curtis, *Richard II in Ireland*, 58–9, 150–1. Richard also required the principal chiefs to agree to pay sums of money to the papal Camera should they break their oaths. This was a significant reinforcement of the normal sanctions for oath-breaking and indicated the seriousness with which he took the agreements. For discussion of the forms of wording see Johnston, 'Richard II and Ireland', 51–4, 64–5.

[35] Johnston, 'Submissions', 12.

issued to a Scotsman resident in England in 1385.[36] The Scotsman, it was said, had 'become the king's liege and had done homage'; and for that reason he was 'admitted to the king's allegiance to live during good behaviour within the realm'. The overlap between homage, allegiance and obedience had become much clearer a decade later, when the Irish submission oaths were drawn up. The terms accepted by Donough O'Byrne made perfectly clear that liege homage carried with it obligations of obedience. O'Byrne swore, as his fellows did, to become the king's faithful liegeman; but he went on to promise to 'serve and obey the king against all men as every faithful man is bound to his liege lord, with every kind of submission, service, obedience and fealty, and to keep his laws, commands and precepts, and continually to obey them without complaint'.[37] The similarity of meaning between 'liege' and 'subject', highlighted in the oaths, was also exhibited by the variety of ways in which vassals described themselves – 'vester ligeus homo', 'vester subditus ligeus', 'vester humilis obediens', and even 'vester humilis subditus et homo ligeus'.[38] Significantly, in a number of instruments ancillary to the oaths vassals submitted to the king in terms of extreme humility and subjection. A not untypical example is a letter written by Brien O'Brien of Thomond. O'Brien wrote 'to the most excellent lord the king, with all humility, reverence and honour', saying that he would have submitted 'heartily and humbly and with all subjection' if he had been apprised earlier of the king's arrival, 'wherefore in this regard deign to hold me excused'; moreover, if he had 'sinned in any regard against the king's most noble lordship or his allegiance, [he] would amend to the king's wish and honour and bind himself and all who were subject to him in pledges and other obligations befitting the king's majesty'.[39] Submissiveness of a different order was expressed by a handful of chieftains who had given offence to Richard in some respect. One such chieftain, Art O'Dempsey of Clanmalier in Leinster, was led before Richard 'with a cord round his neck and the palms of his hands joined'. 'Fearing that his guilt could not be purged by imprisonment of the body . . . he prostrated himself at the feet of the Lord King . . . and humbly begged forgiveness, and the Lord King, suffused with the glow of mercy . . . and overflowing with pity, and so that no pride in his

---

[36] *CPR 1385–9*, 53.

[37] Ibid., 61, 152–3. The essentially non-feudal character of the oaths was noted by Johnston, 'Submissions', 12. Johnston saw them as involving elements of 'citizenship', but there are dangers in employing a term so strongly associated with the ideas of a later age. The context for the oaths is clearly provided by Richard's evolving idea of 'obedience': for which see above, 119, and below, 385–6.

[38] Curtis, *Richard II in Ireland*, 88, 114, 121, 122, 129, 131. For discussion see Johnston, 'Richard II and Ireland', 60–1.

[39] Curtis, *Richard II in Ireland*, 74–5, 163–4.

former deeds should reassert itself, granted life and mercy to the said Art.'[40] The elaborate – not to say extravagant – language in which these instruments of submission were couched bears a strong similarity to the language of address to the king the use of which Richard was encouraging in England at this time. O'Brien, O'Dempsey and the others addressed Richard as 'your highness', 'your majesty' and 'most serene prince and lord'; plaintiffs and correspondents were doing the same in England.[41] The justification for such language was that it distanced the king from his subjects; Richard was seen by his subjects not so much as a 'good lord' but rather as a sovereign law-giver – a ruler clothed, quite literally, in majesty. On the evidence of the use that he made of language in the submissions it is clear that Richard's approach to the problems of Ireland, while conciliatory, was also authoritarian. Richard saw his primary task as being to restore and to exalt the liberties of the crown in Ireland. It followed from this that he had to remind the Irish of their obligations as subjects: obedience had to be given and homage and services performed. Only when these obligations had been fulfilled could redress of grievance be offered. This was a body of ideas that was to be central to the policies that he pursued in England after 1397.[42] It was in his Irish settlement that they found earliest mature expression.

The task of implementing the Ricardian settlement was left after the king's departure to March, in his capacity as lieutenant. March was young and inexperienced, and the difficulties he faced were daunting. Richard had left a host of disputes to be resolved, many of them between English and Irish over lands occupied by the latter but claimed, often with good title, by the former. The most explosive dispute was one in which the earl was himself involved. This centred on the struggle for pre-eminence in Ulster. Since the 1330s the Ulster earldom had been held by the Mortimer earls of March, a family which had experienced several lengthy minorities and whose heads were generally absentee. In the absence of an effective Mortimer presence the leading role in Ulster society had been assumed by the O'Neills, who were headed in the 1390s by Niall Mor and his son Niall Og. For the O'Neill clan and their allies Richard's coming had spelled disaster, for there could be little doubt that its consequence would be a Mortimer restoration. Not long after the king arrived Niall Mor had written to him requesting protection against the earl 'in case he be provoked by stern advice to exact more from me than by right he should'.[43] In January, when he had made his submission to the king, the

---

[40] Ibid., 62–3, 154.
[41] See above, 238–9.
[42] See above, 249–50, and below, 385–7.
[43] Curtis, *Richard II in Ireland*, 131–2, 211–12.

matter of his dispute with the earl was raised, and Niall promised to
surrender to the latter the *bonnacht* of all the Irish of Ulster and other
unspecified services. This concession involved him in considerable loss
of face, and he later repented of it. Niall found himself in a genuine
difficulty here. If he declined to offer resistance to March he risked
losing the respect of his own people; yet if he took up arms against him
he would 'become a rebel and traitor to your majesty which, God be
witness, I never intended to be'.[44] In a letter to Niall in 1395 Richard
deferred judgement on the issues separating him from March until he
could come to England. None the less, he stressed the obligation that
the Irishman was under to stand by the terms of his submission at
Drogheda.[45] Niall Mor, while scrupulous in his observance of the peace,
still clung on to his rights of *bonnacht* and refused to give ground. March
then at some stage launched a raid on the O'Neills' tenants. Sporadic
raiding followed, and in 1396 March in partnership with Ormond and
Kildare launched a much larger attack on the O'Neill lands. By the
beginning of 1397 the peace in Ulster was strained almost to breaking
point.[46]

The situation was scarcely more promising in Leinster, the province
in the east. The issue here centred on implementation of the agreement made between Art MacMurrough and Nottingham. Art had
agreed to a very precise series of terms. He was guaranteed payment of
an annuity of 80 marks at the Dublin exchequer; and he was granted
possession of his wife's barony of Norragh which, technically, he was
disqualified from holding by the Statute of Kilkenny. In return for these
concessions he was required to surrender lands that he had conquered
and to be willing to leave Leinster at the king's wages.[47] It seems that
MacMurrough went at least some way towards honouring his side of the
bargain: he withdrew from the barony of Idrone, to which Thomas
Carew successfully asserted his title, and he probably also withdrew
from other lands.[48] Unfortunately, however, the Dublin administration
made little effort to honour its side of the bargain. MacMurrough was
never paid his annuity at the exchequer, and difficulties were placed in
the way of his entering his wife's inheritance. The narrative known as
the *Four Masters* says that he quickly became resentful and reneged on

---

[44] Ibid., 134–5, 214–15.

[45] For the texts of the two surviving drafts of the letter see Johnston, 'Richard II
and Ireland', Appendix VIII.

[46] Otway-Ruthven, *Medieval Ireland*, 335–6; D.B. Johnston, 'The Interim Years:
Richard II and Ireland, 1395–1399', *England and Ireland in the Late Middle Ages:
Essays in Honour of Jocelyn Otway-Ruthven*, ed. J.F. Lydon (Dublin, 1981), 179–82.

[47] Curtis, *Richard II in Ireland*, 81–4, 169–71; and see above, 280.

[48] Johnston, 'Submissions', 16 and n.

his oath to the king.[49] By 1397 Leinster, like Ulster, was once again spiralling into war.

Richard was kept in touch with events in Ireland by letters from the justiciar or his deputy and by personal visits by the lieutenant, the earl of March.[50] March was in England in the first half of 1397 and does not seem to have returned to Ireland before the end of July. He made a second visit to England in January 1398, when his council took on captains to serve in the Irish war: the retinue of 100 men-at-arms and 600 archers which he had taken with him in 1394 was almost certainly by now much depleted. In April 1398 March's appointment as lieutenant was renewed for another two years, the unexpired portion of the appointment of the previous year.[51] But by this time the earl's relations with Richard were becoming strained. The king appears to have seen the earl as a possible rival and focus for discontent. The Mortimers stood next in line to the throne and exercised wide territorial power in the Welsh Marches. To assure himself of the earl's loyalty Richard made him attend the adjourned session of parliament at Shrewsbury and swear an oath to uphold the work of that parliament. But he could hardly have been encouraged by the reception that the earl received. According to Adam of Usk, who was admittedly sympathetic to his cause, he was 'greeted joyfully by the people', who 'hoped through him for deliverance from the grievous evil of such a king'.[52]

In the summer of 1398 Richard began to think of alternative arrangements for the government of Ireland. On 26 July, only three months after renewing the earl's appointment, he named his nephew the duke of Surrey as lieutenant with effect from 1 September; the earl was thus in effect dismissed. Surrey crossed to Ireland in the autumn and was sworn in on 7 October. His position in Ireland bore an obvious similarity to de Vere's a decade earlier. He came as an outsider; he lacked any inherited estates in the lordship; and he owed his appointment entirely to royal favour. But whereas the earlier courtier had been supported in office by the grant of palatine powers, Surrey was maintained by a subsidy from the English exchequer. According to the terms of his appointment the duke was entitled to draw a fee of 11,500 marks

---

[49] *New History of Ireland*, 392; Johnston, 'Submissions', 16–17.

[50] Shortly before leaving Ireland in April 1395 Richard had divided the responsibility for government between the lieutenant, March, who acted in Ulster, Connacht and Meath, and the justiciar, Sir William Scrope, who acted in Leinster, Munster and Louth. Scrope, who was at court most of the time, appointed a deputy to exercise his responsibilities – his brother, Stephen. The territorial division lasted until April 1397, when March assumed responsibility for the whole lordship (Otway-Ruthven, *Medieval Ireland*, 335; Johnston, 'Richard II and Ireland', 184–93).

[51] Otway-Ruthven, *Medieval Ireland*, 336.

[52] Usk, 19, 164.

annually.[53] This was a huge sum, and it would have been impossible for the exchequer to meet it indefinitely.[54] Perhaps Richard intended eventually to endow Surrey with major estates in Ireland, but in the light of his subsequent plans for the lordship it is more likely that he conceived of his lieutenancy as an interim one. In the summer of 1397 Richard had announced his intention of crossing to Ireland once again in person. In the short term domestic affairs[55] prevented him from giving effect to his aspiration, but in the spring of 1399 preparations for the expedition began in earnest. Surrey's task was almost certainly to pave the way for the king's arrival. The grant to him in late January of significant new powers strongly suggests this. On 22 January the duke was authorized to investigate the financial resources of the lordship, to secure what improvement in them was possible, and to expend the revenue at his discretion to deal with the lordship's military crisis; and by separate letters of the same day he was instructed to receive the homage of tenants-in-chief succeeding to their estates.[56] The implication of both of these orders is that a second royal expedition was imminent. The order for the duke to take homages is particularly instructive, for in the past tenants-in-chief had been required to cross to England to do homage to the king. Obviously, if the king was now coming to Ireland himself, this would no longer be necessary. In other words, behind Surrey's appointment lay the king's initiation of moves to lead a second expedition to the lordship. The duke's role was, in effect, to be a stalking horse for Richard himself.

The first orders for the preparation of a new expedition were given in the early months of 1399. On 1 February letters were sent to the heads of monastic houses requesting horses for the king's use in Ireland, and six days later writs were issued for the arrest of shipping.[57] Unfortunately, it is impossible to say as much about the preparation of this

---

[53] E403/559, 24 July, 23 Aug. March, by contrast, had been given a stipend of 5,000 marks per annum in April 1397 (E403/555, 25 May; E403/556, 8 Oct.). For discussion of the terms of Surrey's appointment see Stansfield, 'The Holand Family', 108–12.

[54] Financial considerations had stood in the way of Surrey's appointment a year earlier. The terms of an indenture had been agreed whereby the duke would serve at a stipend of 6,000 marks per annum for nine years. The indenture was subsequently cancelled because March would serve for 4,000 (later raised to 5,000) marks (Johnston, 'Richard II and Ireland', 193, 379). There can be little doubt about the exchequer's concern at the cost of operations in Ireland.

[55] Principally the suppression of the former Appellants.

[56] CFR 1391–9, 293; CPR 1396–9, 476. For discussion see Johnston, 'Richard II and Ireland', 211–16.

[57] Worcester Cathedral, Liber Albus, fo.396ʳ; BL, Cotton MS Faustina C.V, fo.87ᵛ (letter book of the prior of Rochester); CPR 1396–9, 511. The letters to the priors of Worcester and Rochester show that the king's decision to go to Ireland predated the death of Gaunt and the prospect of the seizure of the Lancastrian estates.

expedition as of the earlier, because no wardrobe book for the year survives. All the same it is clear that it was again conceived on the largest scale.[58] Roughly a dozen magnates accompanied the king, among them the dukes of Aumerle, Exeter and Surrey and the earls of Salisbury and Worcester. There was a large household element: many of the king's knights and Cheshire archers were present. There were also no fewer than six bishops, a host of court chaplains and the staff of the chapel royal.[59] Foreign visitors joined the throng, anticipating brave deeds and perhaps, like Creton, a little 'merriment and song'.[60] Richard appears to have had in mind a fairly lengthy stay. Not only did he formally make his will at Westminster before leaving; he also took with him his jewellery, at least some of his relics and his regalia.[61] In so doing he could hardly have anticipated the eventual outcome of his visit.

Richard crossed, again to Waterford, on 1 June. His main aim was probably to compel Art MacMurrough to submit. In its early stages his expedition enjoyed a measure of success. Not long after arriving Richard wrote to the regent, the duke of York, informing him that Surrey had led a foray into MacMurrough's territory, killing 162 armed men and kerns.[62] But, as the weeks passed, the campaigning became more desultory. In a parley arranged by the earl of Gloucester MacMurrough made clear his refusal to submit; indeed, he allegedly claimed to be the rightful king of Ireland.[63] Richard pressed on northwards to Dublin, which he reached by 1 July. It must have been a few days after that that he received the news of Bolingbroke's landing in England. Orders were given for the assembly of shipping, and some time before 20 July he made the return journey from Waterford.[64]

Richard's departure, and his subsequent deposition, left Ireland in a state of confusion. It seems that Surrey's brother Edmund Holand, later

[58] The force is likely to have numbered 4,500 men at the minimum (D. Johnston, 'Richard II and Ireland', 446–55).

[59] Tout, Chapters, iv, 53–5. The size of the entourage gave rise to logistical problems. As late as 1 May the king was writing to heads of monastic houses requesting assistance with transport (BL, Cotton MS Faustina C.V, fo.88ᵛ). For the armour that Richard took to Ireland see E101/403/20.

[60] Creton, 60.

[61] He made his will on 16 April (Foed., viii, 75). The allegation that the king took his jewellery, relics and regalia to Ireland is Walsingham's (HA, ii, 232). It may well be true. In 1388 Richard had granted to the abbot and monks of Westminster a ring worth 1,000 marks with a ruby in it on condition that he could resume it whenever he left the realm: apparently he did so resume it in 1399, and the abbey did not recover possession until Henry V's reign: H.F. Westlake, Westminster Abbey (2 vols, London, 1923), i, 139.

[62] Curtis, 'Unpublished Letters', 289, 297–8.

[63] Creton, 37–42.

[64] For the circumstances and timing of the king's return see D.B. Johnston, 'Richard II's Departure from Ireland, July 1399', EHR, xcviii (1983), 785–805.

earl of Kent, acted for a while as deputy; later the bishop of Meath was
appointed justiciar. MacMurrough continued his advance in Leinster.
According to the Dublin government, MacMurrough was in alliance
with the earl of Desmond in a campaign against the earl of Ormond
and was afterwards intending to turn with all his power against the
English lordship; at the same time, it was alleged, O'Neill was massing
his forces to make war in Ulster.[65] Henry IV's government lacked both
the money and the commitment to counter the threats from the native
chieftains in Ireland. Accordingly, the local nobility were left to
shoulder most of the burden themselves. In December 1399 Henry
ordered implementation of the Absentee Act of 1380. This required all
who held lands or offices in Ireland to reside there and defend them
and all who held castles to repair and maintain them.[66] It is doubtful if
the order could have had a great deal of impact in practice, because so
many licences of exemption were granted. But the general drift of royal
policy is evident: from now on the local nobility would have to accept
greater responsibility for their own defence.

In the light of subsequent events it is difficult not to conclude that
Richard's expeditions made little difference to the political condition
of the lordship. Even if he had remained king, it is unlikely that his
policies would have greatly affected the balance of power between the
English and the native Irish. By the end of the fourteenth century
the position of the English in Ireland had become dangerously weak:
the administration in Dublin was bankrupt, and most of the main
landowners were absentee. The sending of a major expedition could
have had only a transient effect. For any settlement to be effective there
needed to be a longer-term investment of resources, and this the Westminster exchequer was either unwilling or unable to provide. Richard's
experiences in Ireland would hardly encourage his successors to emulate him; yet the ultimate failure of his policy does not mean that it was
entirely without merit. Richard established an imaginative new framework for relations between the crown and the native Irish. He articulated a vision of Ireland as a single lordship, with its inhabitants all his
liege subjects, regardless of race. Through the widening of his lordship
he was able to accord the chieftains a status equivalent to that of the
English elite: the chieftains were offered redress of grievance, and they
were involved in the government of the province through participation
in councils and parliaments. Implementation of the plan was frustrated
by the bitter rivalries and incompatible claims of English and Irish; but
its memory lived on, and in many of its features it anticipated the

[65] Otway-Ruthven, *Medieval Ireland*, 339.
[66] A. Cosgrove, 'England and Ireland, 1399–1447', *A New History of Ireland*, 526.

policies of later kings, in particular the scheme of surrender and regrant put forward by Henry VIII a century and a half later.[67]

However limited a place it may occupy in the history of the lordship, Richard's involvement in Ireland bore powerful witness to his perception of a 'British' dimension to his kingship.[68] Richard in his maturity never allowed his activities as ruler to be confined to the largely south-eastern power base cultivated by his predecessors; his ambition was also to tap the resources of allegiance in the further-off parts of his realm. He achieved this by a variety of means. In the first place, he undertook several lengthy itineraries. In 1385 he led a major expedition to Scotland. In 1394 he travelled extensively in South Wales while on his way to Ireland; and in the final two years of the reign he spent long periods at Nottingham and Lichfield and in the Welsh Marches.[69] At the same time he was active in constructing power bases for himself and his friends on the fringes of his realm: in the 1380s and early 1390s he built up his half-brother John Holand as a major figure in the south-west, and in 1397 he raised his demesne earldom of Chester and the adjacent county of Flint to the status of a principality.[70] A number of contemporaries suspected him of wanting to abandon England altogether for a base in the Celtic lands. In 1399, when he crossed to Ireland, it was rumoured that he was going to tyrannize his English subjects from the province.[71] The curious suggestion was even ventured that he intended to crown the duke of Surrey as king of Ireland.[72] These and other fears which were voiced of the king's intentions were almost certainly groundless; but contemporaries were right to appreciate a growing drive on the king's part to dignify the non-English parts of his realm. There are signs that he toyed with the idea of creating client principalities. It seems that a semi-viceregal role was envisaged in Ireland for de Vere in 1386; and possibly something of the same sort was planned for Gloucester in 1389.[73] In 1392 Richard's friend William Scrope was

[67] Ibid., 525.

[68] Bennett, 'Richard II and the Wider Realm'.

[69] See below, 392, and Appendix.

[70] For Holand, see above, 244; and for Cheshire, below, 393. Holand's connection with the west country had begun with the grant to him of the estates of the Audley family in 1384. It is possible that he was endowed with these lands simply because they were the only ones that happened to be available, but his position in the south-west was confirmed by further grants in the 1390s. The grandeur of the rebuilding he undertook at Dartington certainly confirms his own sense of playing a major role in the political geography of that part of the world: see Emery, *Dartington Hall* (plate 8).

[71] *Annales*, 239–40.

[72] Usk, 36, 190.

[73] Cf. Walsingham's remark *sub anno* 1386 that Richard would have made de Vere

allowed to acquire for himself the lordship of the Isle of Man with its
concomitant claims to a kingly title.[74] Further afield a life interest was
granted to Gaunt in the duchy of Aquitaine, which had previously been
appurtenant to the crown. It is possible that Richard saw his dominions
much as the Angevins had seen theirs, as a loose 'empire' of principalities, duchies and lordships. In the middle ages the splendour of a
monarchy was held to lie less in its integrity and cohesion than in the
number of its dependent peoples. Richard's fascination with Ireland
could have owed something to an acceptance of this view. When
Philippe de Mézières addressed him, as he did in his *Epistre* of 1395, as
'King of Great Britain, Prince of Wales and North Wales, Lord of Great
Britain and King of Cornwall', he was not indulging in mere flattery; he
was acknowledging the importance which Richard himself attached to
the further, and in some places non-English, parts of his realm.[75]

king of Ireland if he could (*HA*, ii, 148). This anticipates Usk's remark about
Surrey.
[74] *HA*, ii, 213.
[75] Mézières, *Letter to King Richard II*, 101.

Chapter 13

PIETY AND ORTHODOXY

According to an early fifteenth-century preacher a king mediated the flow of God's favour to his people; his love of God and defence of the Church were the channels through which peace and prosperity were granted to his realm.[1]

The preacher's view of the kingly office, fairly commonplace by the fifteenth century, corresponded closely to Richard's own. Richard saw himself as the dispenser of divine favour to his subjects. Whether he was successful in his task depended on the acceptability of his government to God. If he ruled justly and defended God's Church, then the benefits of divine favour would flow. If he allowed heresies and errors to multiply, his kingdom would wither and collapse.

For the greater part of Richard's reign the English Church was in desperate need of a strong guardian. In the 1370s, for the first time since the Pelagian controversies of the fifth century, a fundamental challenge had been mounted to the Church's teaching and authority. The initiator of the challenge was the Oxford master John Wyclif. Wyclif was one of the most distinguished and controversial scholars of his age. A vigorous and prolific writer, his intellect was admired even by his enemies. To John Kenningham, a Carmelite opponent, he was the 'wise clerk', and to Archbishop Arundel, 'a great clerk'; while to the chronicler Henry Knighton he was 'the pre-eminent doctor of theology in those days, considered second to none in philosophy and unmatched in skill in the schools'.[2]

Wyclif was probably born in the early 1330s in Yorkshire. He was briefly a Fellow of Merton in the 1350s and in 1360 was Master of Balliol. By 1372, when he supplicated for his doctorate, he had established himself as the leading theological master in the university. The background to his views lay in the arguments between the rival nominalist and realist schools of philosophy. The nominalists, who drew their inspiration from William of Ockham and his disciples, held that abstract concepts or 'universals' were merely linguistic devices and had

---

[1] R.M. Haines, ' "Our master mariner, our sovereign lord": a Contemporary Preacher's View of Henry V', *Medieval Studies*, xxxviii (1976), 85–96.

[2] P. Heath, *Church and Realm, 1272–1461* (London, 1988), 167; *KC*, 242.

no independent reality. The realists, with whom Wyclif identified, asserted in opposition that universals were as real as specific objects
observed by the human senses. Wyclif's commitment to realism was
evident in his theory of cognition. Wyclif believed that a person's knowledge of things derived not from the senses – from sight or touch – but
from something in them, or about them, that rendered their being
intelligible. In Wyclif's view by peering under the surface of things to
the underlying reality one could savour an understanding of God,
whose universal knowledge made a knowledge of some of these things
accessible to those fashioned in his image. Wyclif's metaphysical teaching, unlike Ockham's, created a significant opening for human speculation in theology. But it carried with it, as a by-product, a commitment
to predestination. An element of predestinarianism had been present
in Catholic belief from the time of Augustine, and in the 1340s it had
been given new emphasis in the work of Bradwardine; but Wyclif now
pushed this strand of thought to extremes. Omniscient God, he argued,
knew from the beginning of time who was going to be saved and who
would be damned. It followed that there could be no justification for
the visible Church and its hierarchy. Only those with a standing in grace
could be accounted in a true sense members of the Church; the
Church, in other words, was the body of the elect, among whom the
pope and the clergy might or might not be numbered. The Church, in
the sense of the Church on earth, had no claim to divine authority.
Authority lay solely in the scriptures, which accordingly ought to be
made available in the vernacular. Wyclif's metaphysical system also
coloured his view of lordship, or possession. Following and adapting the
view of Giles of Rome and Archbishop Fitzralph, he argued that lordship depended on grace, and that righteousness was the only genuinely
valid title to lordship; if the clergy were unrighteous, they had no right
to their temporalities. Wyclif's apparatus of realist metaphysics, and in
particular his predestinarianism, had a crucial influence on the development of his thought. But it is open to question whether it alone was
responsible for leading him down the road to heresy. At the time that
he was writing his metaphysical works he was still a teacher in the arts
faculty. His challenges to the Church's eucharistic teaching only came
later when he took up theology. The date of composition of his eucharistic works points to his close reading of the Bible and of the early
Church fathers as being primarily responsible for the doubts that he
developed about the central miracle of the mass. When the fathers
spoke of the mass, he pointed out, they invariably mentioned bread.
When Christ said, 'This is my body' ('hoc est corpus meum'), he did not
mean 'hoc corpus est corpus meum', which would be tautological, but
'hic panis est corpus meum'. When he turned from the Gospels to
Augustine, Wyclif found support for his reading. 'What we see,' argued
Augustine, 'is the bread and the chalice that the eyes announce; and

faith receives that the bread is the body and that in the chalice is the blood of Our Lord.' There were no grounds, maintained Augustine, for supposing a change in substance. Wyclif never denied the importance of the mass, or even the real presence of Christ at the eucharist: he readily admitted that the sacrament was founded on Christ's scriptural injunction – 'Do this'. But Christ's presence, he believed, was sacramental and spiritual – in the sense, 'I am with you always'. The significance of the mass for Wyclif was that it represented the spiritual union of all the faithful in Christ's sacramental presence. There was no reason in his view for seeing in it the miracle of transubstantiation.[3]

Wyclif's arguments, although superficially persuasive and vigorously deployed, were by no means as logical or internally consistent as they seemed. It might be supposed that, in the light of his predestinarianism and his emphasis on the primacy of the scriptures, Wyclif would have rejected the whole ecclesiastical establishment; but he did not. While he always maintained that the body which called itself 'the Church' had no right to that title, he stopped short of advocating its outright abolition. He believed that it had a role provided that it could be reformed. In common with his one-time allies, the friars, he saw the cause of the Church's problems as lying principally in its possession of wealth. If the Church could be stripped of its enormous endowments, and its clergy relieved of their temporal duties and responsibilities, it could be restored to the purity of life described in the Book of Acts. But his espousal of this argument merely gave rise to fresh problems. Who was to carry out the disendowment, and on what basis? It went without saying that the clergy could not be entrusted with the role, for they were among the damned. Wyclif held that the task should fall to the king. However, if the logic of Wyclif's own earlier arguments were followed, there was no way of telling whether the king himself was one of the elect or one of the damned. If, unknown to his subjects, he was one of the latter, what right did he have to exercise lordship over property? These were difficult issues which Wyclif never adequately addressed. It was not so much the inner logic of his many works that accounted for their enormous success as their relation to issues of contemporary concern. In the later fourteenth century there was growing criticism of the Church and its role in society. Anti-clerical sentiment, for example, was gaining ground in parliament. In 1371 the bishops of Winchester and

---

[3] For Wyclif's thought see J.A. Robson, *Wyclif and the Oxford Schools* (Cambridge, 1961), chs v–ix; P. McNiven, *Heresy and Politics in the Reign of Henry IV. The Burning of John Badby* (Woodbridge, 1987), 12–18; M. Keen, 'Wyclif, the Bible and Transubstantiation', and A. Kenny, 'The Realism of the *De Universalibus*', both in *Wyclif in his Times*, ed. A. Kenny (Oxford, 1986); J.I. Catto, 'Wyclif and Wycliffism at Oxford, 1356–1430', *The History of the University of Oxford, II. Late Medieval Oxford*, ed. J.I. Catto and T.A.R. Evans (Oxford, 1992), 175–262.

Exeter, respectively the chancellor and treasurer, were removed from office at the behest of the commons, who wanted their ministers to be answerable in the courts for their conduct. Five years later the same bishop of Winchester was sentenced to the forfeiture of his temporalities largely at the behest of his enemy, Wyclif's patron, John of Gaunt. At the same time there were ever louder demands from the commons for the Church to pay a greater share of public taxation. In 1371 the commons made a grant of £50,000 conditional on the same amount being made available by the clergy. In 1380 the commons insisted that, since the clergy possessed a third of the land, they should pay a third of the £100,000 being demanded in taxation.[4] It is against the background of these recurrent arguments over the clerical contribution to taxation that the Wycliffite demands for disendowment have to be understood. There was a well-established doctrine that in time of necessity ecclesiastical possessions could be used for the common good. Two Austin friars were commissioned to argue this case before parliament in 1371. Their arguments were based not simply on the need to find money to pay for the war but also on the ground that the lay power, which had originally given property to the Church, might take it back and use the revenue for secular ends. This was reasoning which appealed to a laity convinced that it was already paying more than its fair share in taxation; and Wycliffite doctrine tapped much the same vein of frustration. People felt that the clergy were evading their responsibilities; if clerical wealth could be plundered, the burden which they themselves shouldered might be reduced.

While there was a powerful undercurrent of self-interest making for the popular success of Wycliffism, there were also considerations of a more purely spiritual nature that gave it a wide appeal. By the later fourteenth century it was becoming clear that the Church was failing to satisfy the spiritual aspirations of the laity. Piety was taking a more personal, introspective and evangelical form. The rapid spread of literacy among the laity partly contributed to this; so too, at least among the nobility, did the increasingly regular practice of confession, which encouraged penitents to examine their consciences systematically. The response of the Church to these changes was slow and often inadequate. The Church was an institution that had become ever more bureaucratic over the years; change was physically difficult to accomplish. At the same time, as the use of canon law had spread in the twelfth century, it had become more legalistic in its attitudes and more anxious to impose theological definitions on the faithful. One of the

[4] For these events see M. McKisack, *The Fourteenth Century 1307–1399* (Oxford, 1959), 291.

attractions of Wyclif's teaching was that it promised a move away from the rigidity of this hierarchical, institutionally based religion. In place of sacerdotalism it offered personal, immediate contact between the believer and his Creator. The theological drift of Wyclif's teaching might have been unacceptable to many: a list of twenty-four of his conclusions was condemned at the Blackfriars council of 1382. But the moral and ethical content of his thought had deep roots in contemporary lay piety. Lollardy was in the strict sense of the word a movement for 'reform':[5] it sought not the destruction of the Church but its regeneration on lines that corresponded to new attitudes of mind and accorded a new recognition to the laity. It was merely one manifestation, albeit an extreme one, of the ascetic, evangelical and anti-sacerdotal mood of contemporary lay piety.[6]

Prominent among the early supporters and sympathizers of Wyclif were a group of knights who were active at court in the early years of Richard's reign. The names of these half-dozen or so veterans were well known to contemporaries: Walsingham gave one list of them and Knighton another.[7] They were a fairly discrete and closely knit group of men. Three or four of them had passed into Richard's service from that of Edward III or the Black Prince. Sir Richard Stury had been an esquire of Edward III in the 1350s and early 1360s and from 1366 was one of his knights; additionally he had connections with the prince, and in 1376 had passed from the latter's service to his son's. Sir Lewis Clifford had been in the prince's service for nearly twenty years before serving in turn his widow and his son. Sir John Clanvow, a knight of Edward III, was attached to Richard's chamber from 1381. Sir John Cheyne, an esquire of Edward III's by 1374, was knighted by 1378, and in 1380 had become a 'king's knight' retained for life. A smaller number of knights had established themselves at court as a result of family ties rather than service in the previous reign. Sir John Montagu, for example, later earl of Salisbury, was a scion of a comital line, and the son of a former steward of the household. Sir William Neville, a close associate of Clanvow's, was a brother of both Ralph Neville, the future earl of Westmorland, and Alexander, archbishop of York, the king's close ally. Sir Thomas Latimer, Sir John Trussell and Sir John Pecche – the last two mentioned only in Knighton's list – had much looser ties with the court. Latimer was a servant of the princess of Wales, while

[5] The etymology of 'Lollard' is uncertain. The term had been used to describe heretics before; it appears to have meant 'mumblers'.
[6] McFarlane, *Lancastrian Kings and Lollard Knights*, 224–5.
[7] *HA*, ii, 159, 216; *KC*, 294.

Pecche as a boy had been brought up as a ward of Sir Richard Stury.[8] Besides these half-dozen knights, there were two others whom the chroniclers appear not to have noticed. One was Sir Robert Whitney, a king's knight and harbinger of the household, who lent support to the Lollard preacher William Swinderby; and the other, Sir William Beauchamp, brother of the earl of Warwick and captain of Calais, whose manors in Worcestershire were visited in the early 1400s by Czech scholars looking for Latin copies of Wyclif's works. It is possible that Beauchamp owned a small library of Lollard tracts and devotional pieces; certainly his cultural affinities appear to have been with that group of well-lettered religious radicals which centred on Clanvow and Montagu.[9]

The presence of this body of knights at court, and before that in the household of the prince and princess of Wales, suggests that Richard may have grown to manhood in a distinctly radical religious atmosphere. The Black Prince's sympathies seem to have been strongly anticlerical, like those of his younger brother Gaunt. The prince was critical of those churchmen, including Archbishop Whittlesey, whom he suspected of a reluctance to help pay for the war; and he presided over an assembly in which Wyclif's anti-papalist arguments were either anticipated or echoed.[10] The evidence of his wife's sympathies is still more explicit. In 1378, according to Walsingham, the princess sent a directive to the bishops, delivered by Clifford, ordering them to halt their proceedings against Wyclif.[11] And seven years later, when she drew up her will, she conspicuously named as her executors the three knights in her entourage who were most closely connected with Lollardy: Sir Lewis Clifford again, Sir John Clanvow and Sir Richard Stury.[12] Virtually nothing is known of the inner piety of the prince and princess beyond the fact that the prince was devoted to the Trinity; but the general character of their personal religion seems clear: it was informed by the same moralistic, anti-clerical, and possibly anti-papal sentiments as that of the other leading *dévots* of the day.[13]

---

[8] For the careers of these knights see McFarlane, *Lancastrian Kings and Lollard Knights*, 161–76.

[9] *House of Commons*, iv, 838–40; J.I. Catto, 'Sir William Beauchamp between Chivalry and Lollardy', *The Ideals and Practice of Medieval Knighthood*, iii, ed. C. Harper-Bill and R. Harvey (Woodbridge, 1990), 39–48.

[10] K.B. McFarlane, *John Wyclif and the Beginnings of English Nonconformity* (London, 1952), 58–9.

[11] *CA*, 183.

[12] *Testamenta Vetusta*, ed. N.H. Nicolas (2 vols, London, 1826), i, 13–15.

[13] Barber, *Edward, Prince of Wales*, 240–1. There is a possibility that the prince may have been an admirer of the Carthusians. The evidence for this is indirect but suggestive. In 1387 the prince's one-time retainer Sir Peter le Veel granted the advowson of his manor of Norton Fitzwarren (Somerset) to the London

How much of this sensibility rubbed off on the young Richard is hard to say. Richard's religious sympathies before the late 1380s are difficult to fathom: the wardrobe books are uninformative, and no devotional books of his survive. There is circumstantial evidence, however, that while his outward observances were by all accounts impeccably orthodox, inwardly he may have been sympathetic to some of the opinions of his parents. In the first place, and most obviously, there is the evidence that he retained the service of the Lollard knights. Clifford, Stury, Clanvow, Beauchamp, Whitney and Neville all served in the innermost sanctum of the king's chamber; Montagu and Cheyne were king's knights, retained for life; and Stury was in addition an active councillor. All eight of them were well rewarded for their service. Clanvow was granted Haverford castle together with the stewardship of its lordship in 1381; Clifford exchanged an annuity for a grant of Princes Risborough in Buckinghamshire and Mere (Wiltshire) in 1377 and 1381; and Beauchamp obtained the valuable farm of the estates of the Hastings earls of Pembroke.[14] There is no sign that before the 1390s any disciplinary action was taken against any of these men; Montagu, indeed, despite the nonconformity of his observances, was to be one of the closest of the king's allies to the very end of the reign. Secondly, and scarcely less strikingly, there is the evidence of the king's failure, in the first decade of his rule, to lend any active assistance to the ecclesiastical arm in its fight against heresy. Before 1388 only one legislative initiative was taken. In May 1382, as a response to the panic caused by the Great Revolt, power was given to the chancellor, on certification by the bishops, to issue commissions to the sheriffs or other royal officers to arrest unorthodox preachers and to detain them until their appearance before a Church court.[15] This measure offered a speedy and effective mechanism to the authorities for dealing with preachers who had escaped attention by moving between dioceses. But in the legislation of the early years of the reign it stands strangely alone. It was not until 1388 that any further initiatives were taken. In the course of the

---

Charterhouse: *Feet of Fines for the County of Somerset, 21 Edward III to 20 Richard II*, ed. E. Green, Somerset Record Society, xvii, 1902), 132. This is a striking gesture, and it may have had its origins in a group mentality. Support for the Carthusians was strong among the courtier elite. Richard himself was associated with the foundation of the Coventry Charterhouse: see below, 322. For court patronage of the Carthusians, see A. Tuck, 'Carthusian Monks and Lollard Knights: Religious Attitude at the Court of Richard II', *Studies in the Age of Chaucer Proceedings, I, 1984: Reconstructing Chaucer*, ed. P. Strohm and T.J. Heffernan (New Chaucer Society: Knoxville, Tennessee, 1986), 149–61. The Black Prince's moral puritanism is also suggested by the contempt for the flesh shown in the epitaph on his tomb at Canterbury, which he personally chose.

[14] *CPR 1377–81*, 627, 157–8, 159, 511.
[15] *RP*, iii, 124–5.

Merciless Parliament of that year commissions were issued for the seizure of Wycliffite writings for examination by the council and for the arrest of those handling such material and the imprisonment of the same at the king's pleasure.[16] This initiative represented a significant tightening of policy against heresy, and the fact that it was taken by the Appellants suggests that the latter may have been concerned at the failure of Richard's governments to be more vigorous in their backing of the ecclesiastical arm. Richard himself could hardly have been ignorant of the advances made by the heretics over the previous ten years. Yet, if he was moved by any concern at the dangers these advances posed, he scarcely displayed it by the vigour of his actions.

Richard's relative indifference to matters of religious conformity appears to have been overcome in the course of the mid- to late 1380s. By 1389 he was the vigorous and articulate defender of orthodoxy that he was to remain until his death. The reasons for his change of attitude are hard to establish, given the lack of evidence for his private opinions; but it is likely that, in common with many of his contemporaries, he was fearful of a possible connection between Lollardy and social unrest. In the aftermath of the Great Revolt there was considerable alarm in government about the unsettling effects of Lollard preaching. In the preamble to the Statute of 1382 it was asserted that the preachers 'made discord and dissension between the various estates of the realm, both spiritual and temporal, to the commotion of the people and the great peril of the whole realm'; and Adam of Usk, a generation later, said that Wyclif's disciples, 'by preaching things pleasing to the rich and powerful, namely the withholding of tithes and offerings', had sown the seed of 'many disasters, plots, disputes, strife and sedition which last to this day'.[17] Lollardy was in a sense the victim of the timing and circumstances of its birth. Appearing as it did in the early 1380s, it quickly became associated with the phenomenon of popular unrest; and, once that association was established, upper-class support for it ebbed away. Gaunt appears to have abandoned his interest from about 1382, and Richard probably did so a year or two later.[18] Richard's progress to orthodoxy may have owed a little to the influence of Archbishop Arundel, the Appellants' chancellor. Arundel, though an active pastoral bishop, was also socially and politically a conservative.[19] In the 1390s, when he served Richard for a second time as chancellor, he

[16] *CPR 1385–9*, 430. For discussion of measures against heresy see H.G. Richardson, 'Heresy and the Lay Power under Richard II', *EHR*, li (1936), 1–26.

[17] *RP*, iii, 124–5; Usk, 3–4. For discussion see Aston, 'Lollardy and Sedition', 276, 278.

[18] For Gaunt, see Goodman, *John of Gaunt*, ch. 11.

[19] The pastoral aspect of Arundel's work as archbishop of York is considered by J. Hughes, *Pastors and Visionaries. Religion and Secular Life in Late Medieval Yorkshire*

yielded nothing to his master in his insistence on obedience.[20] In
Arundel's view heretics were guilty of conspiracy, and were thus
enemies of the social order. As letters on the close rolls show, by the
early 1390s this was Richard's view too.[21] It is possible, indeed it is likely,
that the king's eyes were opened by a man with whom on more general
issues of governance he was often at variance.

Evidence of the king's new preoccupation with heresy can be found
in his correspondence from these years. Before the late 1380s the
matter of heresy had rarely if ever figured in his letters. After this time
it became a recurrent theme. In 1393, for example, when he thanked
the archbishop of Canterbury for news of a miracle at the shrine of
Becket, he dwelled on its value in combating heresy. When the Church
was threatened with so many enemies, he said, miracles were essential
for converting men 'from their errors back to the way of salvation'.[22]
Four years later, in responding to the archbishop's letters of submission
carte blanche, he stressed his role as protector of the Church. 'As to the
maintenance of the Catholic faith and destruction of damnable opinions,' he wrote, 'if there be such working contrary to our creed, we
desire for the future, just as we have always done so far as we could, by
the grace of God, without feigning, to do our duty; and the more
Almighty God strengthens us with his power, the more we intend to
strive and labour to show honour to the Holy Mother Church and to
cherish and strengthen the faith.'[23] This same theme of the responsibility of the king for the spiritual welfare of his people crops up in a
letter which he sent to the bishop of Chichester a few months before.
Urging the bishop to arrest all Lollards and other heretics in his diocese, Richard spoke with contempt of the 'damnable errors repugnant
to the faith . . . which would bring ruin to the diocese if not resisted by
the arm of the king's majesty'; and he stressed how he longed for the
diocese to be purged 'of such heresies, lest the wickedness of the
lurking enemy thereby infect the people of the whole realm, the ruling
whereof is committed to the king from on high'.[24] Towards the end of
his reign, probably in spring 1398, Richard expressed fears for the

(Woodbridge, 1988), 177–87. An indication of the conservative nature of
Arundel's – indeed, the Appellants' – political thought is afforded by the chantries
inquest of 1388, which was prompted to some degree by a fear of illicit associations
of the kind believed to have lain behind the Great Revolt: C.M. Barron, 'The Parish
Fraternities of Medieval London', *The Church in Pre-Reformation Society,* ed. C.M.
Barron and C. Harper-Bill (Woodbridge, 1985), 20.

[20] See below, 386.

[21] See below, 301–3.

[22] *Literae Cantuarienses,* ed. J.B. Sheppard (3 vols, Rolls series, 1887–9), iii, 26–8.

[23] Ibid., 50. For the letters of submission *carte blanche,* popularly known as 'blank
charters', see below, 388.

[24] *CCR 1396–9,* 158.

safety of the Church under any other defender than himself. Speaking
to Sir William Bagot, he said that he was afraid that if Derby became
king he would be 'as great a tyrant to the Holy Church as there ever
was'. He and his ancestors, by contrast, had been 'good confessors, who
never persecuted the Church'.[25] They had utterly 'cut off and abolished
errors and heresies by the secular arm'.[26]

The king's 'zeal for the catholic faith, whereof he is the defender'
manifested itself in the more vigorous deployment of the secular arm
against heresy in the final decade of the reign.[27] While it is true that no
new legislative initiatives were taken, the existing legislation was
enforced more thoroughly. The council, using the powers given to it by
the legislation of 1388, had little hesitation in arresting and interrogating traffickers in heretical writings. It appears to have been particularly watchful of activities in Oxford. In 1392 a writ was sent to the
chancellor and proctors of the university stating that the council had
learned that the Cistercian doctor, Henry Crumpe, had been teaching
heretical doctrines; the university was required to suspend him from
scholastic acts and order him to appear before the council. Three years
later, in July 1395, a further writ was sent to the chancellor and proctors: they were instructed to expel all who, after enquiry, were found to
be of Lollard sympathy; and anyone opposing the proceedings, it was
said, was to be brought before the council for punishment.[28] It is clear
from this evidence that the council was prepared, when necessary, to act
on its own initiative. But there were times when Richard himself was
expected to offer the realm leadership. Such a time came in January
1395. During a session of parliament held while Richard was in Ireland
Lollard sympathizers nailed manifestoes to the doors of Westminster
Hall and St Paul's. The officers and council wrote to Richard urging his
return, and by the beginning of May he was back. Immediately he took
steps to restore confidence. Walsingham tells how he made one of
the 'Lollard knights' in his service, Sir Richard Stury, swear an oath
to abjure the heresy, warning him that if he went back on his word
he would have him executed.[29] The king also took measures against
lesser officials in his service. A household esquire by the name of John
Croft was arrested and examined before the council as a preliminary to

---

[25] *Chrons. Revolution*, 211.

[26] *CCR 1392–6*, 437–8.

[27] For the quotation, see ibid., 438.

[28] *CCR 1389–92*, 453; *CCR 1392–6*, 434. The 1395 writ was chiefly directed against
Robert Lechlade. For discussion of these cases, see Richardson, 'Heresy and the Lay
Power', 18, 20; Catto, 'Wyclif and Wycliffism', 230–1.

[29] *Annales*, 183. In July Stury was ordered to appear before Richard at Eltham on
15 August to answer 'certain matters objected to him' (E403/551, 19 July). Presumably these 'certain matters' related to his Lollardy.

appearing before the king at Windsor on 29 August, when he formally submitted and renounced his heretical opinions.[30] From references in the chancery rolls it is apparent that Richard continued to be vigilant against Lollardy even after the 1395 scare was over. On 10 March 1397, for example, he ordered Sir William Scrope to bring before him for his own examination all the Lollards in his custody.[31] But by the later 1390s the authorities were looking for new measures to stem the spread of the heretic weed. In one of the two parliaments of 1397, almost certainly in the January assembly, a petition was submitted by the clergy asking for heresy to be made a capital offence. No statute to this effect appears to have been passed, and the suggestion has been made that Richard was too busy with other matters to take action.[32] However, there is also a possibility that he was personally uneasy with the idea of the death penalty. A decade earlier, in instructions given to envoys negotiating with the French, he had expressed horror at 'the shedding of Christian blood in war'; and he may have had misgivings of a similar nature in the quite different context of the debate over penalties for heresy.[33] Whether or not he urged caution on the issue, however, there can be little doubt that he was a zealous defender of orthodoxy. Over the previous ten years he had given ample evidence of his support for the Church, and the popular perception of him was as an orthodox ruler: it was for this reason that Roger Dymock presented to him a copy of his anti-Lollard *Treatise against the Twelve Errors* (plate 10).[34] While Richard may not have 'laid low the heretics, and scattered their friends', as he boasted on his tomb epitaph in Westminster Abbey, he had done all that could reasonably be expected of him to give the ecclesiastical arm secular backing.[35]

Richard's growing preoccupation with orthodoxy bears witness to the individual stamp of his religion in the second half of the reign. Before the late 1380s his religion was probably for the most part formed in the image of his parents'; his whole outlook had been shaped by his parents and those, like the knights, who attended them, and he is known to have been especially fond of his mother. It is true that he was beginning to develop some of the tastes that were to characterize his piety later. By

[30] Richardson, 'Heresy and the Lay Power', 18.
[31] *CCR 1396–9*, 37
[32] Heath, *Church and Realm*, 186.
[33] See above, 207.
[34] Cambridge, Trinity Hall MS 17. For an edition of the volume, see *Rogeri Dymmok liber contra XII errores et hereses Lollardorum*, ed. H.S. Cronin (London, 1922).
[35] *Royal Commission on Historical Monuments. Westminster Abbey* (London, 1924), 31.

1381, for example, he was already devoted to the cult of the Virgin, for Froissart says that he prayed before the Virgin's image in the chapel of Our Lady of the Pew, Westminster Abbey, before riding out to meet the peasants at Smithfield.[36] And two years later, when he visited the shrine of St Etheldreda at Ely, he was evincing an interest in the saints of pre-Conquest England which was to become more pronounced later.[37] But probably only after the upheaval of the Great Revolt, with all the self-questioning that it prompted, did he develop a clear religious person-ality of his own. From the middle of the 1380s the secular and spiritual aspects of his life were fused in a single vision. His piety came to have an 'ardour' and intensity that it had earlier lacked.[38]

The evidence for Richard's personal religion in his maturity is to be found chiefly in the exchequer issue rolls and the 'alms' sections of the wardrobe books. From the payments recorded in these sources it is possible to get an idea of how he arranged his expenditure for the benefit of his soul. The picture offered by the sources is a sadly imper-fect one. Not only is the record of the king's pious oblations incom-plete, for the separate almoners' accounts have not survived;[39] the sources themselves highlight only the external manifestations of the king's devotions. Personal religion in the later fourteenth century was by its very nature introspective, and its deeper instincts are hidden from view. In the case of the nobility, service books and devotional tracts go some way to making good the absence of other sources, but for Richard no such appear to have survived. The most valuable non-documentary sources are the physical objects that he owned or commissioned – vestments, altarpieces and objets d'art. Some of these are lost and are known only from inventories or antiquaries' descriptions. A few, how-ever, survive. Of the works of art which he commissioned the most beautiful and celebrated is the Wilton Diptych in the National Gallery (plates 13 and 14).

The Diptych, one of the outstanding works of European art of the middle ages, is a portable and folding altarpiece which the king would have used as a focus for his private devotions. Commissioned probably in the late 1390s, it consists of two panels painted on both their inner and outer sides. The decoration on the outside is entirely secular. Painted on the side uppermost when the Diptych is closed is Richard's emblem of the white hart lying on a bank of foliage among branches of

---

[36] Froissart, i, 661.

[37] WC, 42; and see below, 309–11.

[38] In a notarial instrument of 1395 Richard pardoned William and Mayv Baret, 'rebels of English birth in Ireland', 'through the immense ardour of his piety' ('immenso pietatis ardore'): Curtis, Richard II in Ireland, 73.

[39] Which makes it difficult to discuss Richard's personal religion in as much detail as, say, Henry III's.

rosemary; while on the other side is a set of heraldic emblems personal to Richard: at the top a lion passant guardant and, below, a red cap of maintenance and silver helmet and the royal arms of England and France impaled with the mythical arms of Edward the Confessor. On the inside the subject matter is entirely religious. In the left-hand panel Richard is shown kneeling crowned, with his hands open and extended upwards. Behind him three saints – Edmund, Edward the Confessor and John the Baptist – present him to the Virgin and Child, opposite, who are surrounded by angels, one of whom carries a white banner with a red cross of the type normally borne by Christ in scenes of the Resurrection. Incised within the Child's halo are a crown of thorns and three nails, symbols of Christ's Passion. The Child's movements are a complex fusion of gestures, but it seems clear that one of them involves giving a blessing to the king.

The significance of the Diptych has been much disputed. Borenius and Tristram suggested that the panel was commissioned to commemorate the king's coronation.[40] The youthful appearance of the king and the allusions to his kingship and the coronation certainly make this an attractive theory. But counting against it is the variety of the symbolism, which suggests a celebration of kingship more generally. John Harvey, who was also impressed by the symbolism of kingship, saw it as a focal point for the devotions of a secret order which Richard had in mind to found 'for the maintenance of divine government in England'; the eleven angels, he argued, stood for the eleven companions whom Richard intended to appoint to the order.[41] This is an altogether less probable suggestion, because there is no evidence that Richard ever founded, or intended to found, such an order. More promisingly, Dr J.J.N. Palmer has argued that the Diptych was a crusading icon.[42] At first sight, this is the most plausible theory advanced to date. The years from 1396 to 1398, to which the Diptych can be assigned, witnessed vigorous lobbying for a crusade: Robert the Hermit was seeking recruits to a new crusading order, the Order of the Passion, and Philippe de Mézières had written his *Épistre* to Richard urging him to join the king of France in a joint expedition to the east.[43] If the Diptych is seen as an expression of the king's commitment to a crusade, much that is otherwise unaccountable about its symbolism makes sense. It becomes clear, for example, why the angels are shown wearing the badges of the two kings:

[40] T. Borenius and E.W. Tristram, *English Medieval Painting* (repr. New York, 1976), 27–8.

[41] J.H. Harvey, 'The Wilton Diptych – a Re-examination', *Archaeologia*, xcviii (1961), 19.

[42] Palmer, *England, France and Christendom*, 242–4.

[43] For the date of the Diptych see M.V. Clarke, 'The Wilton Diptych', *Fourteenth Century Studies*, 272–92.

for the latter were engaged in an enterprise, the recovery of the Holy Land, which justified what would otherwise have seemed a sacrilegious gesture. There is also an explanation for the appearance of the banner of Redemption: Richard and Charles were committing themselves to redeem Christ's patrimony. However, as always in discussions of the Diptych, there are arguments on the other side to be considered. First, if the Diptych was conceived in association with the Order of the Passion, it is surprising that Richard is not shown wearing the robes of the order as, for example, a prince in the *Épître* is. And secondly, the banner in the Diptych, though possibly included as a symbol of redemption, is not specifically the banner of de Mézières' order, which had a quatrefoil containing the Lamb at the intersection of the red cross. These two objections substantially weaken the theory of a crusading context for the Diptych. It might also be added that the theory takes no account of the complex symbolism of kingship which seems so important to an understanding of the Diptych's inner meaning.

Significant new insights have been afforded into the Diptych by a discovery made in the course of cleaning and conservation in 1992, when it was observed that within the upper of the two orbs above the banner is a minute painting, only a centimetre across, of an island.[44] At the centre of the island stands a white castle with two turrets and black vertical windows. Behind it are trees set against a blue sky, and in the foreground is a brown boat in full sail with black masts sailing in a sea made of silver leaf, now tarnished to brown. A clue to the meaning of the drawing is provided by a lost altarpiece showing Richard II which, in the seventeenth century, was in the English College at Rome. From two seventeenth-century descriptions the antiquary Charles Coupe reconstructed the altarpiece as consisting of five panels showing the Virgin and Child at the centre with Saints George, John the Baptist and two other saints presenting Richard and his queen, Anne. According to the earlier of the two descriptions, recorded in a manuscript of *c.*1606, Richard was 'lifting his eyes and hands' to the Virgin and offering her a 'globe or patterne of England'; and at the foot of the panels, according to Silvestro Petrasancta in 1638, was this inscription:

Dos tua, Virgo pia
Haec est, quare rege, Maria.
(This is your dowry, O holy Virgin, wherefore O Mary, may you rule over it.)[45]

---

[44] D. Gordon, 'A New Discovery in the Wilton Diptych', *Burlington Magazine*, cxxxiv (1992), 662–7. And see also now *The Court of Richard II and the Artistic World of the Wilton Diptych*, ed. L. Monnas and C. Barron (London, 1996).
[45] Gordon, 'A New Discovery', 665–7.

On the basis of this analogy it can be suggested that the drawing in the Wilton Diptych was intended to represent the island of Britain. Richard was shown offering his kingdom to the Virgin as her dowry; the banner which the king has surrendered has been received by the Child, who has handed it to an angel and is now about to bless the king; and the king waits to receive it back in order to rule under the protection, and with the blessing, of the Virgin. The idea of England as the Virgin's dowry enjoyed a wide currency at the end of the fourteenth century. In a letter which he sent in 1400 to the bishop of London Archbishop Arundel said, 'We are the humble servants of her [the Virgin's] inheritance and the liegemen of her especial dower, as we are approved by common parlance.'[46] Fifteen years later at the battle of Agincourt the priests invoked the mediation of the Virgin on behalf of her English dowry, and in 1416, when the English won a naval victory on the vigil of the Assumption of the Blessed Virgin, the notion was invoked again by the author of the *Gesta Henrici Quinti*.[47] In the work of Thomas Elmham, another biographer of Henry V, England is referred to as the 'Dos Mariae' in terms remarkably close to those on the Rome altarpiece:

Anglia Dos tua fit, Mater pia, Virgo Maria,
Henrico rege, tu tua jura rege.[48]

The idea of a Marian context for the Diptych makes sense in the light of the other evidence of Richard's interest in the Virgin's cult. In 1383, while he was in East Anglia, the king visited the shrine of Our Lady at Walsingham.[49] Four years later, in the course of his 'gyration', he and his queen were admitted to the confraternity of Lincoln Cathedral, a church of which the Virgin was patroness.[50] In 1396, while going from monastery to monastery in the west midlands, he made an offering of 6s 8d at an image of the Virgin in Tewkesbury Abbey, another house of which the Virgin was patroness.[51] Richard's devotion, though fairly characteristic of fourteenth-century piety, was formed in sharp contrast to the tastes of his father. The prince showed little interest in the Virgin; his own interests had drawn him to the cult of the Trinity.[52] Among Richard's immediate forebears the man with the strongest commitment to the Virgin was his grandfather, Edward III. Almost every year Edward visited or sent oblations to the shrine at Walsingham, the statue of Our

---

[46] Ibid., 667 n.22.
[47] *Gesta Henrici Quinti*, ed. F. Taylor and J.S. Roskell (Oxford, 1975), 88 n.1, 144.
[48] Gordon, 'A New Discovery', 667.
[49] *WC*, 42. In 1392 he gave £6 13s 4d to the friars minor at Walsingham: E403/538, 6 July.
[50] J.W.F. Hill, *Medieval Lincoln* (Cambridge, 1948), 258.
[51] E101/403/10, fo.35ᵛ.
[52] See above, 298.

Lady in St Paul's Cathedral, and the Lady Chapel in Christ Church, Canterbury. He also patronized a remarkable number of regional, and sometimes rather obscure, Marian cults and during the Scottish wars gave alms before statues of the Virgin at Scarborough, Darlington and York.[53] It is possible, though it cannot be proved, that both kings were steered to the cult by their wives. Noble-born women in the middle ages were well known for their devotion to the Virgin, and Richard's queen, Anne, is thought to have fostered in England the cult of St Anne, the Virgin's mother.[54]

Richard's devotion to the Virgin Mary formed part of a much wider interest in the saints and their relics. Richard, like most of his contemporaries, saw the saints as mediators between man and God. Conventionally, he believed that the saints, by their lives or the manner of their death, had made themselves pleasing to God and were therefore in a position to intercede with him on behalf of the living faithful. Often he turned to the saints for aid in time of danger: in 1381, for example, he prayed to the Virgin in Westminster Abbey before going out to meet the rebels.[55] He was also given to invoking the anger of the saints as a sanction against his enemies: in 1385, when granting Queenborough castle to Robert de Vere, he proclaimed, 'the curse of God and St Edward and the king on any who attempt aught against this grant!'[56] As was common in the middle ages, whenever possible, he sought the favour of the saints by visiting their shrines. It is striking how often his longer itineraries accommodated visits to churches well known for their shrines. In 1383, when in East Anglia, he visited Bury St Edmunds, Ely, Norwich and Walsingham.[57] In 1387, on the 'gyration', he fitted in Lincoln, Lichfield, Chester and Worcester. In 1393 he went to Rochester, Canterbury and Winchester, and four years later to Gloucester, Hereford, Worcester, Evesham and again Lichfield; before leaving for Ireland in 1399 he made a point of visiting Becket's shrine at Canterbury.[58] Predictably, he was keen to hear news of miracles. When Archbishop Arundel sent him news of a miracle that Becket had wrought, he wrote back effusively saying that 'we are strictly bound to thank the High Sovereign Worker of Miracles and to offer gratitude and thanks, which we desire to do unfeignedly and with all our power'; and he added that he believed that the faith of those who criticized the

---

[53] W.M. Ormrod, 'The Personal Religion of Edward III', *Speculum*, lxiv (1989), 857–8. It might be added that a devotion to the Virgin is one of the few pietistic traits which Richard did share with his grandfather.

[54] Froissart, i, 661.

[55] See above, 324.

[56] *CPR 1381–5*, 542.

[57] *WC*, 42–4.

[58] For Richard's itinerary see Appendix.

Church would be strengthened by news of what had happened.[59] There can be little doubt that his own faith was strengthened by the working of miracles. In 1383, when he and his household were at Ely, one of his chamber knights, Sir James Berners, had his sight restored to him by the intercession of St John the Evangelist and Ely's patroness, St Etheldreda, and Richard showed his gratitude by granting to the monks of Ely confirmation of their right to all forfeitures within the liberty of St Etheldreda. In the letters patent making the grant, clear reference was made to the occurrence of the miracle.[60]

The saints to whom Richard paid the greatest respect were for the most part ones already popular with his contemporaries. It is noticeable that he shared in the widespread late medieval devotion to St John the Baptist. This is hardly surprising since he had been born on 6 January, the feast of the Baptism of Christ, and became king on 22 June, the eve of the vigil of the saint's nativity. Evidence of his devotion to the saint is abundant. He is shown kneeling before the Baptist in a stained-glass window in Winchester College chapel commissioned in about 1390, and the Baptist figured as one of his sponsors in both the Wilton Diptych and the lost Rome altarpiece.[61] Richard was a keen collector of relics of the Baptist. In 1386 the vicar of All Saints, Pavement, York gave him the dish on which the Baptist's head had lain, and in 1398 he acquired a tooth of the Baptist, for which the bearer received a pension of 4d a day for life.[62] Significantly it was the Baptist whose intercession Richard besought on the inscription on his tomb. The words chosen for this epitaph seem almost consciously to echo the scene on the Diptych: 'O clemens Christe – cui devotus fuit iste; Votis Baptiste – salves quem pretulit iste' ('O merciful Christ, to whom he [Richard] was devoted, save him through the prayers of the Baptist, who presented him').[63]

Richard's devotion to the Baptist was fairly characteristic of mainstream lay piety in the late middle ages. So too was the interest that he took in the English saints of the pre-Conquest period. The English pre-Conquest saints enjoyed especial vogue at this time because of the revival in national self-consciousness. Probably the most notable cult to benefit in this way was that of St Edmund, the East Anglian king who

[59] *Literae Cantuarienses*, iii, 26–8.
[60] WC, 42; Maxwell-Lyte, *Historical Notes on the Great Seal*, 225; *Calendar of Charter Rolls 1341–1417* (London, 1916), 288–9. See also above, 123.
[61] D. Gordon, *Making and Meaning. The Wilton Diptych* (London, 1993), 55–6.
[62] *CPR 1385–9*, 194; *CPR 1396–9*, 329.
[63] Gordon, *Making and Meaning*, 61. It is worth noting, too, that 'By St John the Baptist' was the king's habitual oath (*Annales*, 202, 204, 212, 220; *Traison et Mort*, 148). Richard Maidstone notes Richard as saying in 1392 that the Baptist was his 'special patron saint': *Political Poems and Songs Relating to English History*, ed. T. Wright (2 vols, Rolls series, 1859–61), i, 296.

had been martyred by the Danes in *c.* 870. Edmund was widely regarded in the fourteenth century as an English patron saint, and his shrine at Bury became the focus of considerable pilgrimage traffic in the period.[64] Richard himself visited the shrine in 1383, and in 1396 he provided the abbot with a writ of aid for the construction of a new cloister.[65] Richard is likely to have felt a particular affinity with the saint because the latter's slippers formed part of the regalia which he had worn at his coronation. According to the *Anonimalle* chronicle, through inadvertence one slipper fell off immediately after the ceremony, and in 1390 Richard presented Westminster Abbey with a replacement pair, embroidered with fleurs-de-lis, which had been blessed by Pope Urban VI.[66] In the same year, according to the Westminster chronicler, Richard celebrated St Edmund's feast at the abbey: he attended vespers and midnight matins in the conventual church on the vigil of the feast, and on the day itself he was present at the procession and at high mass. Afterwards he presented the convent with 10 marks for its pains.[67]

St Edmund of East Anglia was only the most distinguished of a whole company of pre-Conquest saints to whose cults Richard evidenced a devotion. Among the others, Saints Winifred, Etheldreda, Ethelburga and Edward the Martyr seem to have stood high in his favour. Richard's devotion to St Etheldreda has already been noted.[68] The cult of this foundress and patroness of Ely appears to have been an active one in the later fourteenth century, and the miracle which she performed on the occasion of Richard's visit to her church was one of several which caught the attention of contemporaries.[69] The cult of St Winifred was probably one in which Richard developed an interest as a result of his travels to the north-west in the final years of his reign. Winifred had lived the greater part of her life at Holywell, in Flint, and her burial place was Shrewsbury Abbey. It is recorded that Richard visited the Holywell shrine in 1398, and Archbishop Walden's order for the celebration of her feast (along with those of David and Chad) almost certainly reflects royal patronage.[70] Richard's devotion to St Edward the Martyr was obviously part of his wider interest in the lives of his saintly

---

[64] For St Edmund's cult in the late middle ages see D. Farmer, *The Oxford Dictionary of Saints* (Oxford, 2nd edn, 1987), 131. The saint was included in a series of forty royal figures in windows in the choir clerestory at Gloucester, glazed *c.*1350–60: R. Marks, *Stained Glass in England during the Middle Ages* (London, 1993), 88.

[65] *WC*, 42; *HA*, ii, 96–7; *CPR 1396–9*, 24.

[66] *Anon.*, 111; *WC*, 414–16.

[67] *WC*, 454.

[68] See above, 309. For further evidence of Richard's devotion to St Etheldreda, see *CPR 1381–5*, 300.

[69] For other reports of miracles see *HA*, ii, 183–4, 185.

[70] E403/559, 24 July; BL, Cotton Charters XV/12.

royal forebears. Edward, like Richard, was a boy king, and was canonized following his death at the hands of assassins in 979 at Corfe, Dorset. Richard spent a lengthy sojourn at Corfe in the summer of 1393, and during that time he probably visited the saint's burial place at Wareham.[71] Two years later, at his request, the prior and convent of Canterbury agreed to celebrate the saint's Martyrdom and Translation as principal feasts in the cathedral.[72] By comparison with the cults of these saints, that of St Ethelburga, a contemporary of Etheldreda, was probably of lesser importance to Richard. Ethelburga, who was buried at Barking, afforded no demonstrations of her power in this period. Nevertheless Richard saw fit to make an offering of 6s 8d to her on 4 September 1396.[73]

The cult of a pre-Conquest saint which elicited the most personal response from the king was, of course, that of his royal forebear, St Edward the Confessor. Henry III and possibly Henry V apart, Richard demonstrated a greater commitment to the Confessor's cult than any other late medieval ruler. It is true, of course, that most late medieval rulers from Henry II showed at least a formal devotion to the cult: Edward I gave the crown of Llewellyn and the spoils of his Scottish victories to the saint's shrine, and Edward III, who had been baptized on the Confessor's feast day, made regular oblations at the shrine.[74] But after Henry III no ruler could match Richard in either the depth or the intensity of his devotion. Richard saw his relationship with the saint as one akin to marriage. From around 1397 he impaled his own arms (of England and France ancient) with the mythical arms of the Confessor, in the manner of husband and wife.[75] He saw the Confessor as his partner: his mentor in spirituality and guide in matters of government.

The origins of Richard's devotion lay in part in his strong – not to say, all-consuming – sense of lineage. From his earliest ascent to adulthood

---

[71] See Appendix.

[72] *CCR 1392–6*, 473.

[73] Farmer, *Oxford Dictionary of Saints*, 147; E101/403/10, fo.36ᵛ. It is also worth noting the interest that Richard showed in the cult of St Erkenwald, the distinguished bishop of London, who died at Barking in 693. St Erkenwald's day became a major festival in 1386, and Richard visited the saint's shrine in St Paul's in 1392 (*Political Poems and Songs*, i, 293).

[74] P. Tudor-Craig, 'The Medieval Monuments and Chantry Chapels', C. Wilson, R. Gem, P. Tudor-Craig, J. Physick, *Westminster Abbey* (London, 1986), 117; Ormrod, 'Personal Religion of Edward III', 858–9. For a full discussion of the cult of St Edward, see P. Binski, *Westminster Abbey and the Plantagenets. Kingship and the Representation of Power 1200–1400* (New Haven and London, 1995), ch. 2.

[75] Clarke, 'The Wilton Diptych', 274–6.

Richard had seen his ancestors and predecessors in the royal line as a presence in his midst, and he was keen to associate himself with their spirituality. His devotion to the Confessor was inseparable from his campaign for the canonization of Edward II. In each case he was motivated by a desire to draw down the blessings of holiness on the royal line.

But there was another reason for his interest in the Confessor: his identification with what the saint was perceived to stand for. In the late middle ages the Confessor was intimately associated with the notion of 'peace'. Ailred of Rievaulx and Matthew Paris in their influential 'lives' of the king had both stressed the 'glorious peace' of his reign. Ailred had said that, 'since the pacific king had reigned for so long, all things met together within one bond of peace'; and Matthew emphasized the peace, in the sense of harmony, that the king brought to his realm by loving and cherishing his nobility.[76] It was the Confessor's reputation for peace that had recommended him to Henry III, his first great late medieval patron. Henry, like Edward, was a 'vir pacificus', and in the biographies of the saint he found the legitimizing imagery that he needed for his rule. Edward I and his immediate successors, inclined as they were to a more aggressive style of kingship, found less in the saint's career to attract them, and accordingly turned to other cults for legitimation – Edward I to that of Arthur, and Edward III to that of St George. Among late medieval monarchs it was undoubtedly Richard who found most in the Confessor's perceived career to identify with. Richard, like the Confessor, was a peace-loving king. Externally his main objective was to end the war with France, which Froissart reports him as saying had gone on for too long; and internally his rule was characterized by a quest for 'peace' in the sense of unity. Like the Confessor of literary myth, Richard wanted to see factional strife ended and his subjects united in willing submission to his rule. It was for this reason that he ordered the arrest of the former Appellants in 1397. As he wrote to Manuel Paleologus, the Byzantine emperor, early the following year, he had trodden down his enemies and thus brought to his people a 'peace' which, he hoped, would last for ever.[77] 'Peace' was the Confessor's ideal; and so too was it Richard's.

Richard's devotion to the Confessor found expression in a number of ways, most notably in the lavishing of gifts on his shrine in Westminster Abbey, which the king did with little regard for cost. According to a document now lost, the king on one occasion gave a magnificent port-

[76] *Lives of Edward the Confessor*, ed. H.R. Luard (Rolls series, 1858), 179, 198, 204; D. Carpenter, 'King, Magnates and Society: the Personal Rule of King Henry III, 1234–1258', *Speculum*, lx (1985), 61–2.

[77] For the various notions of 'peace' see above, 207, and below, 387. The letter to Manuel is printed in *English Historical Documents*, 174–5.

able altar ('tabula') of silver enamelled with the well-known story of the Confessor and the pilgrims.[78] At various times he also made gifts of jewellery. On 14 November 1388, while visiting the shrine, he presented a ring of gold with what the abbey chronicler called 'a costly and valuable' ruby set in it. This was a gift made on unusual terms. In the charter confirming it Richard said that for as long as he lived he would retain the use of the ring, but whenever he left the realm he would restore it to the shrine and then recover it on his return.[79] By rights according to this arrangement the ring should have been restored when he crossed to Ireland in 1399, but apparently it was not: it fell to Henry V to return it after 1413.[80]

Hardly less costly than the gifts which Richard made to St Edward's shrine were those which he made to the abbot and convent who guarded it. These were spurred partly by a concern to earn remission from the trials of purgatory, but much more by a desire to enrich the setting of the abbey's liturgical life. On a number of occasions Richard presented to the monks magnificent sets of vestments. On 28 May 1389, 'at the shrine of St Edward the Confessor', he donated a set consisting of a chasuble, three copes, three albs, three maniples and two stoles. The chasuble, an exceptionally fine garment, was woven of gold cloth: in the orphreys on one side were figures of the Virgin Mary, the Confessor and St Edmund, and the arms of the king and queen; on the other were figures of the Virgin, St John the Baptist and an abbess, with the royal arms repeated.[81] In 1395, in somewhat bizarre circumstances, Richard gave the house another rich and costly garment. As Abbot Colchester was later to recall, when the king's friend and former treasurer Bishop Waltham was being buried, in the Confessor's chapel, Richard was so moved when looking at the body that he promised to give in the bishop's memory a magnificent vestment embroidered with the tree of Jesse.[82] Unfortunately, it is not clear from the abbot's account whether the vestment was a cope or a chasuble; but it was certainly a valuable item: the abbot estimated its worth at no less than 1,000 marks. Over the years Richard gave many other vestments,

---

[78] J. Perkins, *Westminster Abbey. Its Worship and Ornaments* (Alcuin Club, xxxiv, 1930), ii, 58. Perkins does not state his source, and no reference to the 'tabula' survives in the abbey muniments. The story of the Confessor and the pilgrims centres on the gift of a ring that the king made to a beggar near Westminster. Two years after the gift was made some English pilgrims in the Holy Land were met by an old man who said that he was John the Apostle. He gave them the ring and told them to return it to Edward, whom they were charged to warn of impending death in six months' time (Farmer, *Oxford Dictionary of Saints*, 134).

[79] WAM 9473; *WC*, 372.

[80] Westlake, *Westminster Abbey*, i, 139.

[81] *Calendar of Charter Rolls 1341–1417*, 311.

[82] WAM 5262A.

altarpieces and liturgical banners to the abbey which, all told, must have been worth several thousand marks.[83]

Richard's interest in the abbey and the shrine of its second founder was chronicled over more than a decade by the writer known to historians as the Monk of Westminster. Almost certainly a senior member of the convent – he has been identified as Richard Exeter, a former prior[84] – he wrote from a unique and exceptionally well-informed vantage point. He must have seen the king on many occasions; he may even have met him. Certainly he was sensitive to his changes of mood. In the earlier part of the chronicle he sees the king as a rather petulant, hot-tempered young man, quick to lose self-control: his abuse of Lancaster is recorded, and so too is his threat to draw his sword on the archbishop of Canterbury.[85] Later, however, he portrays the king more favourably. He shows him consenting to reconciliation with the Appellants, responding to criticism of his harshness towards the Londoners and even showing alarm at the danger of jousting with unrebated lances; twice at least he praises him for his love of the Church.[86] The shift in the Monk's perception was partially a reflection of changes in the community's relationship with the king over the years. In the early to mid-1380s the relationship had been soured by a number of unhappy incidents. In 1383 the abbey suffered the loss of its temporalities because it had appealed to the pope, in defiance of a royal prohibition, at one point in the long dispute with the dean and canons of St Stephen's. Three years later the king took offence when the community elected William Colchester as their new abbot in preference to John Lakenheath, a one-time conventual treasurer and a man with strong royal connections.[87] As a result of these incidents there was a cooling of the traditional goodwill that the community felt for the king, and it was only in the early 1390s that relations materially improved. It is very likely that the initiative for the improvement came from the king. In the wake of the successive assaults on his authority Richard had developed a new appreciation of the value of conventual support and of the legitimacy which it conferred on his rule. Strikingly, from the late 1380s he made the abbey the focus of many of his most significant actions as king. He processed there, accompanied by de Vere and de la Pole, when he returned to the capital in November 1387 after his 'gyration' around the realm; and he performed his devotions there at the end of the day of celebrations marking his reconciliation with the Londoners in August 1392.[88] In October 1392 he even associated himself with the

[83] For more details see Saul, 'Richard II and Westminster Abbey', 196–218.
[84] WC, xl–xliii.
[85] Ibid., 130, 116.
[86] Ibid., 406–8, 502, 436, 326, 338–40.
[87] Saul, 'Richard II and Westminster Abbey'.
[88] WC, 206–8, 506.

monks in a major act of public ceremonial: on the eve of the Confessor's feast day (13 October) he walked barefoot in procession with them from the abbey precinct westwards to St James's and then northeast to Charing Cross and back southwards along the line of present-day Whitehall – a distance of 2–3 miles. In the abbey church he then spent time on devotions before returning to the palace.[89] Richard could hardly have demonstrated more dramatically the importance of public religion to his perception of his role and obligations as king.[90]

So important was Westminster Abbey to Richard – both as the burial place of his patron, the Confessor, and as the focal point of his own cult of kingship – that in the second half of his reign he made the embellishment of its fabric the supreme expression of his religious and architectural patronage. By the 1380s the state of the fabric had become something of an embarrassment to the monarchy. The rebuilding which Henry III had initiated in 1245 had halted after his death, for the three Edwards had lacked either the money or the commitment to bring it to completion. Thus for a century a huge Gothic choir towered over the more modest Romanesque nave of the Confessor. The first step to resuming work on the fabric had been taken by Cardinal Langham, a former monk of the house in 1375. To stimulate activity Langham had promised the sum of £200 a year to a building fund should work on the 'novum opus' be set in hand.[91] Within months a site was cleared, and in March 1376 Abbot Litlington laid the first stone of the new building. However, work proceeded slowly, and after ten years relatively little had been accomplished. In 1386 Richard decided to step in. On 7 July he granted to the abbot and convent the sum of £100 a year 'in aid of the "novum opus" [i.e. the nave] of the monastery out of devotion to the shrine of St Edward the Confessor'.[92] From the abbey's point of view the timing was somewhat unfortunate because Richard's political problems were gathering pace, and only three months later the continual council was appointed with a brief to curb royal expenditure. It is doubtful if the convent was ever able to collect more than a fraction of the sums due to it. When Richard recovered power in 1389 he decided to put financial provision for the project on a firmer basis. He made over to the abbey two alien priories which were

---

[89] Ibid., 508–10.

[90] Richard's commitment to the abbey also found expression in his support for its liberties. He defended the abbot's possession of franchisal rights in Worcestershire against a claim by the earl of Warwick; and he lent support to a bid by the abbot to win precedence in parliament from the premier English abbot, the abbot of St Albans: Saul, 'Richard II and Westminster Abbey'; *Annales Monasterii Sancti Albani a Johanne Amundesham*, ed. H.T. Riley (2 vols, Rolls series, 1870–1), i, 414–17.

[91] R.B. Rackham, 'The Nave of Westminster', *Proceedings of the British Academy*, iv (1909–10), 38–9. For the nave in general see C. Wilson, 'The Gothic Abbey Church', Wilson et al., *Westminster Abbey* (London, 1986), 31–4.

[92] *CPR 1385–9*, 188.

in his custody because of war – Folkestone, worth £20 a year, and Stoke-by-Clare, worth £100 – and the income from these establishments was to be the mainstay of the 'novum opus' for the next ten years.[93] Periodically it was supplemented by further payments from the king. In 1394, following Queen Anne's death, he paid a total of £106 13s 4d to the fund from his own pocket, and in the following year the sum of £100 exactly.[94] Furthermore, he helped with the provision of raw materials for the work. In March 1393, in response to a petition from the abbot and convent, he granted authority to two masons of the abbey, John Mayhew and John Russe, to impress labourers in Dorset to hew the Purbeck marble for the columns and carry it down to the sea.[95] Two years later in 1395 Peter de Combe, the abbey sacrist, and William Colchester, the mason, were given full authority to find the workers that they needed to speed up their work.[96] Evidently after the Black Death it was hard to find labour and to retain it – which is probably the main reason why progress was so slow. By the time of the king's deposition only the skeleton of the building stood complete. The aisle walls had been laid out and carried to triforium level and the double row of marble pillars had been erected to the greater part of their height, but the clerestory, vaults and higher parts of the west front had not even been started.[97] In his will, made just before he sailed for Ireland, Richard made generous provision for continuation of the work: so strongly did he identify with it that he referred to it as having been 'by us begun', which was not strictly correct.[98] But after his death, despite this provision, the momentum was not maintained. In Henry IV's reign little was done, and only in the brief reign of Henry V was there another major upturn in the level of activity (plate 23).[99]

Richard's promotion of the rebuilding of the abbey bore witness to his desire to provide the shrine of his favourite saint with surroundings of appropriate magnificence. Richard, no less than Henry III before him, saw the building or rebuilding of a church as a way of honouring a saint: it bore outward and visible witness to the saint's inner grace. To say this is not to imply that saintly piety was the only spur to the king's architectural patronage. Richard, like many another patron, was well aware of

[93] *CPR 1388–92*, 230; *CPR 1385–9*, 188; WAM 6226.
[94] WAM 23464, 23466. Richard also gave £60 in 1393–4 (WAM 23463).
[95] The abbey's petition to the king is E28/2 m.21. For Richard's response see *CPR 1391–6*, 244.
[96] *CPR 1391–6*, 643, 647.
[97] Rackham, 'The Nave of Westminster', 43–4.
[98] *Foed.*, viii, 76.
[99] Rackham, 'The Nave of Westminster', 43–9.

the benefit that building, a meritorious act, might bring in drawing down the mercy of the Almighty: his endowment of soul masses is witness to his fear of the pains of purgatory.[100] All the same, such indications as there are point to a simple, if deeply intense, devotion as being the main spur to his patronage. A particular aspect of his piety that suggests this is the fascination that he showed for saints' relics. Much of Richard's devotion was focused on churches which either possessed relics or were the centres of major cults. Westminster Abbey was one such church – and obviously the most important. Two others were the metropolitan churches of York and Canterbury.

Richard's interest in the church of York was probably awakened by his visit to the city in June 1392, when the organs of government were removed thither from London. Seven or eight years before his visit work had begun on a new choir to link the early fourteenth-century nave with Archbishop Thoresby's Lady Chapel, built in the 1360s, to the east. In 1385 the chapter secured a stone supply by taking a lease on a quarry at Huddleston, but by 1390 there were complaints that little had been achieved.[101] Richard first came to the chapter's assistance in 1395. According to an entry on the exchequer issue roll, on 12 July that year he gave 100 marks 'to sustain and pay for operations at the church of the blessed Peter of York'.[102] His gift, which was marked by the carving of a white hart on a capital above the entry to the south choir aisle, was soon followed by another of still greater value. In 1396 he presented to the Minster the relics of one of the Holy Innocents, which the chapter then had enclosed in a silver and gilt shrine and borne into the church in full procession by four choristers on Holy Innocents Day.[103] The offerings at the shrine of such a major relic (and the Minster already had the relics of St William) must have substantially assisted in enabling building work to move forward more swiftly, and by 1400 the choir was virtually completed.

Richard's generosity to York Minster was eclipsed by the support he gave over a number of years to operations at the rival church of Canterbury. Canterbury had a twofold claim on his attention. It was the burial place of his father, Edward the Black Prince, whose anniversary he punctiliously observed; and it housed the shrine of St Thomas Becket, to whose cult he was deeply devoted. Richard went in pilgrimage to Becket's shrine on a number of occasions in his reign. On his second visit, in 1384, he made offerings of 6s 8d at the shrine itself and at the

---

[100] CPR 1396–9, 452, 464, 477, 565, 580.
[101] Harvey, 'Richard II and York', 208.
[102] E403/551, 12 July.
[103] Historians of the Church of York, ed. J. Raine (3 vols, Rolls series, 1879–94), ii, 426. For Richard's ceremonious visit to the city, see York City Chamberlains' Account Rolls 1396–1500, ed. R.B. Dobson (Surtees Society, cxcii, 1978–9), 1–8.

tomb of Becket's head, and of 3s 4d at the martyrdom in the north transept; he also offered 6s 8d at an image of Our Lady in the Undercroft.[104] When he went back in 1393, he not only made oblations at the shrines; he also attended Trinity Sunday mass in the cathedral and a day or two later a requiem mass for his father.[105] It was probably on the occasion of this latter visit that he was persuaded to lend his support to the rebuilding of the nave which the newly elected prior, Thomas Chillenden, had resumed with vigour a couple of years before.[106] According to the cathedral's calendar of obits Richard gave 'to the fabric of the high altar and of the nave, beyond various jewels which he presented, and to the Blessed Virgin Mary in the crypt more than £1,000 sterling'.[107] This was a huge sum, but it did not exhaust Richard's fund of generosity. When the work reached the west front, he offered further support. In 1397, 'out of special devotion to the martyr Thomas', he exempted the chief masons and surveyors of the works from being put on assizes and commissions against their will; and at about the same time he discharged the prior and chapter of £160 in taxes owed by them for the year 1396 'in aid of building of the west front'.[108] The glazing of the west window may also have benefited from his generosity: the upper lights contained shields of his arms and those of Queen Anne and his second wife, Isabel.[109] Richard was a keen supporter of the rebuilding programme at the cathedral: in all probability he was the largest individual contributor to its cost.[110] Christ Church, Canterbury may have lacked the exclusive association with the crown that Westminster Abbey had, but it benefited as much as the latter from royal generosity (plate 24).

Richard also lent his support to other, generally smaller, building programmes in various parts of the country. He was particularly generous to religious houses in the north which had suffered either direct damage or loss of revenues as a result of war. In 1393 he contributed

[104] E101/401/2, fo.37ʳ. The chapel of Our Lady Undercroft, in the crypt, contained one of the principal cult altars of the cathedral. The Black Prince had chosen it as his intended burial place although, in the event, his wishes were ignored and he was interred in the Trinity Chapel.

[105] E101/402/10, fo.34ʳ.

[106] Payments for the rebuilding of the nave are recorded from 1379, but the pace of work on the project greatly quickened after Chillenden's election in 1391 (F. Woodman, *The Architectural History of Canterbury Cathedral* (London, 1981), 151–4).

[107] *Inventories of Christ Church, Canterbury*, ed. J. Wickham Legg and W. St John Hope (London, 1902), 109.

[108] *CPR 1396–9*, 79; E159/172, *Brevia directa*, Easter rotulus 9.

[109] Woodman, *Architectural History of Canterbury Cathedral*, 249.

[110] There are signs that interest in the cathedral may have been widely disseminated in the court circle: Richard's friend Joan, Lady Mohun chose to be buried there, by the chapel of Our Lady Undercroft in the crypt (ibid., 254).

£10 to the repair of Grey Friars, Carlisle; and in the previous year, at the request of the dukes of Gloucester and Lancaster, he gave no less than £100 for the rebuilding of Tynemouth priory, a dependent house of St Albans.[111] His support for the abbey of Bury St Edmunds, which had been strong in the 1380s, continued to show itself in this decade: in 1396 he granted a writ of aid to the abbey for the construction of a new cloister and other works.[112] Almost certainly too he contributed to the fabric fund at Lichfield Cathedral. He was very interested in the cult of St Chad; he paid many visits to the city from 1387, and in the final years of his reign the see was occupied by his friend and former confessor John Burghill.[113] Unfortunately there are no accounts to illuminate the building history of the cathedral, but the three spires which dominate its skyline appear to have been under construction from 1385.[114] Quite possibly other churches in the north-west benefited from the king's generosity during his sojourns in the area in 1398 and 1399. Richard rarely showed hesitation in assisting religious communities that turned to him for aid.

The king's belief in the intercessory power of the saints, his fascination with miracles, and his generous support for ecclesiastical building programmes: these are all marks of the strongly conventional nature of Richard's piety. Yet the later fourteenth century was a time when, among the upper classes at least, piety was rapidly losing its conventional character. New patterns of devotion were forming, and new modes of religious expression being opened up. Religious observances were assuming a more personal and introspective turn. Men of sensibility among the laity were seeking approaches to salvation that allowed them greater opportunity for individual expression. Encouraged by

---

[111] E403/543, 13 May; E403/541, 12 Nov.

[112] *CPR 1396–9*, 24. Richard had visited Bury in June 1383: *CPR 1381–5*, 280; *HA*, ii, 97; *WC*, 42. Because of the sufferings of the abbey in the Great Revolt, the townsfolk of Bury had been excluded from the general amnesty issued to the rebels in November 1381 (*RP*, iii, 118). The Bury rebels had to sue for a separate pardon, which was granted in 1383 and involved the payment of compensation to the abbey (Oman, *The Great Revolt*, 136–7).

[113] For his interest in the cult of St Chad see below, 323; and for his visits to Lichfield, below, 392.

[114] It is difficult to establish an adequate chronology for the building of the cathedral. The core of the fabric is thirteenth and early fourteenth century, and the presbytery and Lady Chapel were finished by 1350. Yet it is clear that work of some sort was in progress (or being contemplated) in March 1385 when Gilbert the Mason, master of the masons at the cathedral, was assigned two other masons to work under his direction (Harvey, *English Medieval Architects*, 117). Harvey is inclined to associate this appointment with the construction of the spires: J. Harvey, *English Cathedrals* (London, 2nd edn, 1956), 139.

their confessors, such men were systematically searching their consciences and performing penitential exercises. Richard's great-uncle, Henry of Grosmont, duke of Lancaster, wrote a remarkable treatise, the *Livre de Seyntz Medicines,* which almost certainly had its origins in such an exercise.[115] The more refined and reflective of the nobility, like Henry, Lord Scrope of Masham, and perhaps even Thomas of Woodstock, were turning to the works of the mystics. Richard, as he grew older, was moving in the company of magnates and gentry who exhibited these more advanced tastes. What evidence is there that his own piety was influenced by them?[116]

There can be little doubt that Richard's piety took the more individual and introspective form characteristic of the age. Not only was he a man by nature introspective and even secretive; his devotional practices were shaped by the private confessors who played a vital role in shaping the devotional lives of the nobility. Most of his confessors, like those of the nobility, were drawn from the ranks of the Dominicans. At the beginning of the reign he was advised by William Siward, an Oxford graduate, prior of the King's Langley convent and later the Order's English provincial. Siward attended the Blackfriars council in 1382, and in 1399 was summoned with other scholars to attend a council at Oxford to advise the king on policy regarding the schism.[117] Later in the reign Richard was served, among others, by Thomas Rushook, Alexander Bache, John Burghill and possibly John Gilbert, bishop of Hereford, all of them Dominicans.[118] It is hardly surprising that the king's chaplains and other clerks of his household were required to read 'the canonical hours according to the Dominican use, that being the one which the king reads daily'.[119] John Harvey has ventured the suggestion that the Dominican confessors played a key role in shaping Richard's political and religious outlook.[120] Confessors were men who

[115] *Le Livre de Seyntz Medicines,* ed. E. J. F. Arnould (Anglo-Norman Text Society, ii, 1940).

[116] For late fourteenth-century lay piety see J.I. Catto, 'Religion and the English Nobility in the Later Fourteenth Century', *History and Imagination. Essays in Honour of H.R. Trevor-Roper,* ed. H. Lloyd-Jones, V. Pearl, B. Worden (London, 1981), 43–55; J. Hughes, *Pastors and Visionaries.*

[117] *BRUO,* iii, 1704; C.F.R. Palmer, 'The King's Confessors', *The Antiquary,* xxii (1890), 264–5.

[118] Palmer, 'The King's Confessors', 265–6; *CPR 1388–92,* 15; *CPR 1391–6,* 694; Goodman, *John of Gaunt,* 254. Gilbert had been a confessor to the Black Prince and served Richard in many diplomatic capacities from 1377. There is a possibility that Thomas Brinton, bishop of Rochester, was a confessor to the king in the early years of the reign. Benedictine tradition maintained that this was the case, but there is in fact no evidence: see *The Sermons of Thomas Brinton, Bishop of Rochester (1373–1389),* i, ed. M.A. Devlin (Camden 3rd series, lxxxv, 1954), xvii.

[119] *Calendar of Papal Registers, v, 1396–1404* (London, 1904), 67.

[120] Harvey, 'Richard II and York', 203.

were constantly in the king's company, and their influence on Richard was widely recognized by contemporaries.[121] Two at least of them appear to have incurred widespread opprobrium. Alexander Bache was criticized by the Westminster chronicler in the 1390s for the haughtiness of his bearing in royal service, and a decade earlier Thomas Rushook had been twice banished from court because of his baneful influence over the king.[122] These men may have been exceptional, and it is difficult to establish in more general terms how far the confessors contributed to the shaping of the king's political mentality. Commonly in the later middle ages royal confessors had little or no impact on the making of policy, and this may have been the case in Richard's reign. Certainly it is possible to find other, and more plausible, sources for the king's political ideas.[123] In the absence of conclusive evidence, the case for significant Dominican influence on his kingship must remain unproven.[124]

There remains, however, the matter of the confessors' influence on the more private and other-worldly aspects of the king's thinking. Dr Catto has argued that confession, by drawing attention to the individual conscience, altered the whole scope of a person's moral life.[125] This may have been the case with some of the nobility, but it is doubtful – even allowing for the inadequacies of the evidence – if the same could be said of Richard. Richard's piety was almost certainly not of the unsettling or questioning sort. In contrast to a number of his contemporaries, the king never gave any sign of the anguish or self-doubt that characterized the spirituality of those to whom inward reflection was central. All the same, the indications of a sharpened conscience can be detected in aspects of his piety. Richard, like several of the nobility, developed a respect for anchorites and holy men. In 1381 he sought the advice of Westminster's anchorite, John of London (perhaps John Murimuth), before meeting the rebels at Smithfield, and later in the reign he made payments to support anchorites in various towns.[126] Interestingly, he also shared the contemporary enthusiasm for ascetic monasticism. He took a personal interest in the establishment of the

[121] Richard had his confessor with him at Winchester in July 1393, which suggests that the latter accompanied him on his travels (Winchester College Muniments, 1).

[122] *WC*, 434; and see above, 125.

[123] See above, 16, 249–50, and below, 385–8.

[124] There may be some significance in the fact that a Dominican, John Deeping, regularly preached to Richard on St Edward's Day, 13 October (E101/402/5 fo.26ʳ; E101/402/10, fo.33ʳ; E101/403/10, fo.35ʳ⁻ᵛ); Deeping, however, is not known to have served as a confessor. What little is known about him is gathered in *BRUO*, iii, 2169.

[125] J.I. Catto, 'Religion and the English Nobility', 50.

[126] D. Knowles, *The Religious Orders in England* (3 vols, Cambridge, 1948–59), ii, 220; E403/549, 3 April.

Charterhouse which his friend William, Lord Zouche had founded at Coventry. In 1385, when returning from Scotland, he stopped at Coventry to lay the foundation stone of the church, and it is reported that he said that he would be the founder of the convent and would bring it to perfection.[127] Subsequently he honoured his promise by granting to the house the priory of Edith Weston in Rutland.[128] Richard's taste for the ascetic may have been aroused by reflections in the confessional on the transience of earthly glories: the vanity of material wealth was a common theme in penitential writing. However it would be wrong to discount the influence of other, and possibly more important, factors. The encouragement of the Carmelite and Austin friars who preached before the king at the principal feasts of the year may have counted for something.[129] The Carmelites were an order renowned for their asceticism, and John Kenningham, their English provincial from 1393, has been credited with arousing John of Gaunt's respect for the eremetical tradition.[130] It seems almost certain, too, that allowance should be made for the influence of the patrons of asceticism among the gentry and nobility. As numerous scholars have pointed out, the impetus behind the late medieval flowering of the Carthusian Order was provided by members of the higher nobility.[131] The London Charterhouse had been founded in 1371 by Sir Walter Mauny, Edward III's captain, the Hull Charterhouse in 1379 by Michael de la Pole, the Axholme Charterhouse in 1395 by Thomas Mowbray, earl of Nottingham, and Mount Grace, Yorkshire in 1398 by Thomas Holand, duke of Surrey.[132] De la Pole, Nottingham and Surrey were men who were close to Richard; the last two, indeed, were his kinsmen. Quite possibly the late fourteenth-century patronage of the Carthusians was a manifestation of courtly taste.[133] Richard's interest may have been encouraged,

[127] W. Dugdale, *Monasticon Anglicanum* (6 vols, London, 1846), vi, i, 15. *Victoria History of the County of Warwick*, ii, ed. W. Page (London, 1904), 84.

[128] *CPR 1388–92*, 317, 361.

[129] The Carmelites noted in the wardrobe books as preaching before Richard are Robert Yvory, John Woodcote, John Kenningham, Robert Marshal and John Colton (for whom, see E101/402/5, fo.26^r; E101/402/10, fo.33^r; E101/403/10, fo.35^v). The Austin friars noted are Thomas Winterton and John Brenchley (E101/402/5, fo.26^r; E101/403/10, fo.35^r; E101/402/10, fo.33^v). Winterton had written a polemic against Wyclif: H.B. Workman, *John Wyclif* (2 vols, Oxford, 1926), ii, 146–7. For Richard's tastes in preaching, see Walker, 'Richard II's Views on Kingship', 58–9.

[130] Goodman, *John of Gaunt*, 245, 247–8. Kenningham was the duke's confessor; for his career see *BRUO*, ii, 1077.

[131] Catto, 'Religion and the English Nobility', 52.

[132] Knowles, *Religious Orders in England*, ii, 130–3. William, Lord Zouche, who had founded the Coventry Charterhouse, also tried to secure the conversion of the Benedictine priory of Totnes (Devon) into a Carthusian house (E326/8661).

[133] Tuck, 'Carthusian Monks and Lollard Knights', 154–8.

even if it was not initially aroused, by de la Pole and Zouche; and that interest could in turn have spurred Nottingham and Surrey when they were thinking of establishing their own houses.

It may be a further indication of Richard's occasionally avant-garde tastes that he actively encouraged the recognition of new saintly cults. Among those in the courtier elite who were sympathetic to the new puritanism attitudes to the saints varied. Some, like Sir William Beauchamp, the former chamberlain of the household and intimate of the Lollard knights, appear to have been enthusiasts for new cults.[134] Others, however, like Sir John Clanvow, rejected the veneration of the saints in favour of biblical prescription and a more personal relationship with the Almighty.[135] Richard's religion, as we have seen, was firmly based on the cult of the saints: the interest that he took in sponsoring new cults was of a piece with his personal religion as a whole. The most notable new cult that he sponsored was probably that of John Thweng of Bridlington. Thweng was a canon, and later a prior, of Bridlington Priory, who enjoyed a wide repute as a holy man and a healer.[136] Soon after his death in 1379 miracles were reported at his tomb, and Richard petitioned the pope on his behalf.[137] Partly as a result of the king's interest, canonization was conceded in 1401, two years after his fall.[138] Of a more self-interested character were Richard's efforts to secure the canonization of his great-grandfather Edward II, who was buried at Gloucester Abbey. In the summer of 1390 Richard commissioned a book of supposed miracles performed at the king's tomb, which five years later he sent to Pope Boniface IX. The pope, however, was unimpressed and, despite the efforts of a second embassy in 1397, nothing came of the initiative.[139] Richard may also have been instrumental in pressing for better observance of the cults of a number of old English saints. In spring 1398 orders were issued at Archbishop Walden's behest for the celebration of the feasts of Saints David, Chad and Winifred, and for the better commemoration of the feast of the Translation of St Thomas.[140] David, Chad and Winifred were saints to

[134] Beauchamp was an early devotee of the cult of the Holy Name of Jesus (Catto, 'Sir William Beauchamp', 47).

[135] McFarlane, *Lancastrian Kings and Lollard Knights*, 205.

[136] Hughes, *Pastors and Visionaries*, 98–9, 302–3.

[137] *Calendar of Papal Registers, iv, 1362–1404* (London, 1902), 378–9. In 1397 Richard made a grant to Robert Waldeby 'out of reverence to St John of Beverley' (*CPR 1396–9*, 170).

[138] Hughes, *Pastors and Visionaries*, 99.

[139] *WC*, 436–8; *Issues of the Exchequer*, ed. Devon, 247–8, 259, 264. For discussion, see A.R. Echerd, 'Canonization and Politics in Late Medieval England: the Cult of Thomas of Lancaster' (University of Chapel Hill, NC, Ph.D. thesis, 1983), 232–6.

[140] BL, Cotton Charters XV.12: a letter to the dean of London enjoining observance of a decision of the Canterbury convocation.

whose cults Richard was devoted, and it is difficult not to see the king's hand behind the order.[141] There can certainly be little doubt that it was royal backing that secured wider recognition of the cult of St Anne, the Virgin's mother, in England. The cult, which was commonly observed on the continent, had attracted little interest north of the Channel before the later fourteenth century. According to the Evesham Abbey writer, it was on Queen Anne's initiative that it was finally given official backing. Shortly after her marriage to Richard, Anne sought from the pope that the feast be 'more solemnly' observed in England, and in 1383 Urban acceded to her request, in honour, so he said, of her marriage.[142] Anne was clearly a devotee of the cult, and it may be significant that the chronicler should have reported, albeit in error, that her funeral took place in Westminster Abbey on St Anne's Day, in 1394.[143]

So there is reasonable evidence that Richard, or, perhaps more precisely, Richard and his queen, lent their support to some of the newer, if not of the more radical, currents of the day. Richard manifested a clear taste for the ascetic and eremitic. He gave his patronage to the Carthusians, and he sponsored the adoption of new cults. All this accords well with what is known of the sentiments and practices of his friends in the higher nobility. Probably more idiosyncratic was the king's recourse to supernatural help. Richard appears to have paid a considerable amount of attention to astrological predictions. A beautifully produced book of divinations, the *Libellus Geomancie*, was presented to him 'for his solace' by one of his servants, probably John Thorpe, the treasurer of Ireland, in 1391.[144] Brought together in the volume are a treatise on physiognomy, a 'Philosophy of Dreams', a long geomantic tract, and a 'Rosary of King Richard', the last consisting of diagrams determining whether certain actions could be permitted according to the position of the planets. The whole volume is pervaded by a deep trust in the power of the planets to influence lives. The king's dependence on the 'judicial of astronomy' is further indicated by the highly wrought horary quadrant made for him in 1399 and now in the

[141] Richard visited St David's in September 1394 on his way to Milford Haven to embark for Ireland (*CPR 1391–6*, 474).

[142] *HVR*, 134. For discussion see R.W. Pfaff, *New Liturgical Feasts in Late Medieval England* (Oxford, 1970), 2; W. Scase, 'St Anne and the Education of the Virgin: Literary and Artistic Traditions and their Implications', *England in the Fourteenth Century*, ed. N. Rogers (Stamford, 1993), 81–96.

[143] *HVR*, 134. St Anne's Day was 26 July. The queen was interred on 3 August (*Foed.*, vii, 776).

[144] Oxford, Bodleian Lib., MS 581. Another copy is BL, Royal MS 12 C.V.; this lacks the portrait of the king found in the Bodleian version. For a discussion of the authorship of the volume see *Four English Political Tracts of the Late Middle Ages*, 23–30.

British Museum. On the reverse of the quadrant is a table showing the sun's noon altitude for a selection of 96 days of the year, and above this is a circle of dominical letters for 28 years beginning with the letter 'e'.[145] The relation of Richard's astrological interests to his actions is unclear and is unlikely ever to be resolved.[146] Probably the most that can be said is that those interests were not peculiar to him. Others of his immediate circle appear to have shared them. His mother, for example, commissioned a set of astrological tables from a mendicant, John Somers. Chaucer demonstrated more than a passing interest in astrology in his writings: he alludes to the influence of the stars in 'The Knight's Tale', and his *Treatise on the Astrolabe* would presumably have been used, if completed, for predictive purposes.[147] It is an interesting comment on contemporary taste that a number of carefully executed astrological manuscripts such as Bodleian Library MS Digby 41 should have been produced in this period. Evidently there was a ready market for this sort of literature among the well-to-do clergy and the aristocracy. What motivated these people to read it can only be guessed at. Richard may have turned to it for a modicum of guidance to rulership; others may simply have wanted to fathom the uncertainties and unpredictability of the times in which they lived.

What overall impression can be formed of Richard's piety? To an even greater degree than was common in men born to kingship in the middle ages, the king's personal piety was inseparable from his public religion. Sacred and secular ideas were fused in his mind in a single vision. When he wrote to Albert, count of Holland, in 1397 to explain why he had arrested the former Appellants, the content of the letter was political but the tone religious. Richard rendered 'thanks to the highest observer of human minds', and expressed the hope that 'those who contrived wickedness against King Christ the Lord would be hammered back into confusion'.[148] To Richard rebellion against a king was equivalent to rebellion against God, and was therefore liable to be punished as such. Rebellion and heresy in his mind went together. Both were a threat to the established order and a danger to the people's favour with God.

In its outward manifestations Richard's piety was entirely conven-

[145] *The Age of Chivalry. Art in Plantagenet England, 1200–1400*, ed. J. Alexander and P. Binski (London, 1987), no.724. A quadrant (probably not this one) is listed in an inventory of Richard's jewels and plate: E101/411/9 m.33.

[146] What are we to make of Usk's remark that Richard was told by a 'sortilegio' (soothsayer) that Norfolk would win the duel at Coventry in 1398 (Usk, 24, and see below, 400–1)?

[147] Catto, 'Religion and the English Nobility', 48. For the subject more generally see H.M. Carey, *Courting Disaster. Astrology at the English Court and University in the Later Middle Ages* (London, 1992), ch. 6.

[148] Harvey, 'The Wilton Diptych', 27–8.

tional. Richard shared his contemporaries' devotion to the cult of the saints; he looked to them for intercession, and he was a frequent visitor to their shrines. Relics were central to his thinking. He was heir to one of the largest relic collections in Europe, and he made several additions to it: his delight was evident when a German merchant gave him a relic of the Holy Innocents.[149] Like the nobility, he lavished favour on religious houses; he had an especially close tie with Westminster Abbey and he actively assisted in the abbey church's rebuilding. In all these and other ways there was little to distinguish his outward piety from that of his immediate predecessors. His grandfather Edward III had been devoted to the saints and had often turned to them for assistance; Edward III, too, had been a keen collector of relics.[150] But Edward III's piety – like Edward I's – appears to have lacked any hidden depths. Richard's piety was very different. Richard's piety ran deep. It was marked by an inner power and intensity that his grandfather and great-grandfather could never summon. Richard entered into his devotions with passion. He cherished his relations with the saints. He felt the sufferings of Christ on the Cross as his own. He had a bitter hatred for the heretics. A pained, almost an embattled, tone can be felt in his correspondence as he denounces the evils of heresy. Not for Richard the consolatory side of religion: Richard's was a restless and agonized spirit. His religion was cathartic. He appears to have seen himself as engaged in a struggle – a struggle of the righteous against the unrighteous, the orthodox against the heterodox. Although he professed himself a lover and a bringer of peace, it is doubtful if temperamentally he was ever at ease with the idea. Inwardly he was longing for a fight. It is possible that the struggle against the heretics answered some deep inner need in his being. Could he have found in it a substitute for the struggle against his internal and external foes that for so much of his reign he was unable to engage in?

[149] *Anglo-Norman Letters*, no. 23. This is probably to be identified with the relic that he gave to York Minster: see above, 317.

[150] Ormrod, 'Personal Religion of Edward III', 853–62.

Chapter 14

THE KING AND HIS COURT

In the late middle ages the social and ceremonial setting of monarchy was provided by the court. It was at sessions of the court that the king received envoys from abroad, dispensed favours to his magnates, arranged marriages for his kinsfolk, and performed the myriad other duties of an active ruler. At the same time, it was from the rituals and ceremonies of the court that his subjects, and those who visited or watched him, gained an impression of his wealth and splendour, and thus of his power. The court was the most vital institution of medieval monarchy. It was simultaneously the means and the expression of royal power.[1]

The material foundations of the court were provided by the departments and offices of the household. Broadly speaking, these can be divided into two areas of responsibility – the 'below stairs' offices referred to in the 'Black Book' of Edward IV's reign as the 'domus providencie' and the 'above stairs' offices referred to as the 'domus magnificencie'. The 'below stairs' offices were the responsibility of the steward and were divided into three main groups. First, there were the buttery, bakehouse and pantry; secondly, the kitchen, including the poultry, larder, scullery and saucery; and thirdly, the marshalsea, which looked after the several hundred horses attached to the household. Within each of these sub-offices there was at least one sergeant, supported by a staff of purveyors , valets, carters and grooms. The clerks of these sub-offices were accountable to the cofferer, who in his turn was accountable to the controller of the household and, above him, the keeper. Linked to the 'below stairs' structure for accounting purposes but otherwise separate from it was the 'above stairs' world controlled by the chamberlain. In part this comprised a variety of specialist agencies such as the jewel house and the chapel royal. Its central component, however, was the personnel of marshals of the hall, esquires, sergeants-at-arms and ushers and valets of the chamber – a body of staff to whom

---

[1] For the role and functions of the court, see R.A. Griffiths, 'The King's Court during the Wars of the Roses', *Patronage, Princes and the Nobility. The Court at the Beginning of the Modern Age*, ed. R.G. Asch and A.M. Birke (Oxford, 1991), 41–67; and R. Horrox, 'Caterpillars of the Commonwealth? Courtiers in Late Medieval England', *Rulers and Ruled in Late Medieval England*, 1–16.

the demarcations of 'office' did not readily apply. The chamberlain himself was a major figure, usually a senior knight and always a close friend of the king: Sir Simon Burley held the office in the 1380s and John Holand for a long period in the 1390s. Superior to the chamberlain was the steward, the officer who had overall responsibility for management of the household. By tradition the steward was one of the five great officers of state. In Richard's reign royal familiars were prominent among the holders. In the 1380s Sir John Montagu and Sir John Beauchamp of Holt held the office, and in the next decade Sir Thomas Percy, later earl of Worcester.[2]

The organization and structure of the household have received far greater attention than the structures of the court itself. Tout and others subsequently who have studied medieval administration have analysed the household in detail;[3] but rarely have they cast more than a passing glance at the court. Perhaps historians' long neglect is understandable, given the nature of the subject, for the court, unlike the household, lacked an institutional character. Contemporaries could recognize the court, and very often they could describe it. But in the last resort it was a mental or perceptual construct – the rationalization of those who beheld it; and, because of its artificiality, it left no records. For the household a variety of sources are extant. There are the wardrobe books, which form a long but intermittent series in the later middle ages; and there are the ordinances issued periodically which offer descriptions of household organization. For the court there are only incidental sources: one or two chroniclers' vignettes, a few visitors' narratives and the occasional comments of critics. Taken together they hardly amount to a great corpus.

So shadowy is the documentary existence of the later medieval court that a number of historians have doubted whether it existed at all. Sir Geoffrey Elton has summarized the case from the perspective of an early modernist. A 'true court', he argues, 'could not exist until the crown had destroyed all alternative centres of loyalty or all alternative centres of worldly advancement. So long as there were magnates [holding sway in the shires], their patronage and standing took away from the king's patronage and sovereignty, and their residences from the uniqueness of his court.' In Sir Geoffrey's view, the origins of the court are to be found in Henry VII's reign, when the rival centres of power were all but eliminated. In his son's reign the court's ascendancy was sealed when it became the focus of the realm's social and political life. In Sir Geoffrey's words, 'the work of raising the king . . . above all

[2] For household structure, see Given-Wilson, *Royal Household and the King's Affinity*, 1–22. For the officers see Tout, *Chapters*, vi, 24–50.

[3] Tout, *Chapters, passim*; S.B. Chrimes, *An Introduction to the Administrative History of Medieval England* (Oxford, 1952).

his subjects was not completed until the second Tudor added the visible enjoyment of his position to the reality created by the first'.[4] This is a viewpoint to which Mr D.A.L. Morgan has recently given qualified support. Mr Morgan shares Sir Geoffrey's belief that there was no 'court' as such in the middle ages. But he differs from him in seeing the crucial period of its emergence as the Yorkist, rather than the early Tudor, period. In the years after 1471, he argues, Edward IV achieved a monopoly of power never given to his predecessors; and he used this to assimilate the older, 'local pattern of land-based lordship to the more emphatic ascendancy of the Yorkist dynasty'.[5] This was a change so major as to call for the adoption of a new vocabulary of personnel. The royal household was from now on referred to as the 'court'; and the continental literature of the 'court' was borrowed or adapted to describe it. 'Curialis' was translated as 'courtier' in a dictionary of 1483; and in *The Curial, a prose epistle,* it was 'court', rather than 'household', which was employed to describe 'a convent of people that under fantasy of common weal come together to deceive each other'.[6]

These arguments provide a valuable corrective to the hitherto rather indiscriminate use made of the word 'court' by historians. Medievalists have too often been tempted to use 'household' and 'court' as if they were synonymous: which clearly they were not. None the less there is a serious difficulty with the argument. To acknowledge the distinction between household and court is one thing; to go on to deny the existence of the medieval court is quite another. Courts of a sort undoubtedly existed in the middle ages, and contemporaries knew how to describe them. From roughly the latter part of the ninth century the word 'curia' was used to describe a 'court', and 'curialis' a 'courtier'. The usage of these terms was not continuous. In the post-Carolingian period what contemporaries recognized as a court was often referred to as a 'palatium' or 'aula', which reflects some weakening of the notion of courtliness. But in the later eleventh century the word 'curia' came back into use and it was never subsequently dropped. 'Curialis' appears in a letter of Lanfranc of *c.*1063, and 'curialitas' (courtliness) in a text of 1080 by a chronicler of the church of Hildesheim.[7] The meaning of these terms could often be wide. For example, there was no assumption that only the king could hold a court: a 'curia' in the high middle ages

---

[4] G. Elton, 'Tudor Government: the Points of Contact. III. The Court', *TRHS*, 5th series, xxvi (1976), 211–28, in particular 212.

[5] D.A.L. Morgan, 'The House of Policy; the Political Role of the Late Plantagenet Household', *The English Court from the Wars of the Roses to the Civil War*, ed. D. Starkey (London, 1987), 64.

[6] Ibid., 68–9.

[7] For these examples, see A. Scaglione, *Knights at Court* (Berkeley, 1991), 47, 64–6.

was simply a major administrative headquarters, generally with juridical functions attached, over which a king, magnate or ecclesiastic could preside. But gradually, as 'curialitas' became fused with courtesy, so the 'curiae' came to be identified with locations or environments where courteous behaviour was most likely to be found – in other words, kingly or princely courts. By the middle of the twelfth century, in most parts of Europe, a courtly literature was coming into existence: poets patronized by princes began celebrating the polite and courtly values of love, sacrifice and chivalry. At the same time, and doubtless reflecting the courtiers' self-consciousness, a literature about courts came into existence as well. A celebrated example from the Angevin world is Walter Map's *De Nugis Curialium*. Walter began by saying that he found the court an elusive concept: 'I am now in the court,' he wrote, 'and I speak of the court, but – God knows – I have no idea what the court is.'[8] Since he subsequently built an elaborate comparison between Henry II's court and hell, his confusion was clearly a literary conceit: he knew perfectly well what the court was. Walter's friend and associate Gerald of Wales too pondered contemporary courtly life, comparing the Angevin and Capetian courts and awarding the palm to the latter because it was more tranquil and less pompous.[9] References to the court also become common in the chronicle narratives. This is an important development because the chroniclers were to a large extent drawing on the language of everyday political life. One or two particularly interesting usages of 'court' are found in the chronicles of Richard II's reign. The Westminster writer, for example, describing the Appellants' purges in 1387, noted that the bishops of Durham and Chichester and various knights and ladies were ordered to 'abjure the court' ('curiam abjurare').[10] This wording suggests that the writer had a strong sense of the real existence of the court. Alongside the passage can be set an entry in the Evesham Abbey chronicle noting that after Richard's deposition Bishop Tideman of Worcester was never again seen at the king's court ('in curia regis').[11] Here again the court is seen, if not precisely in physical terms, then as having an actual existence. The clerks of the wardrobe and exchequer displayed a similar understanding of the word. In 1397 a note was made on the exchequer issue roll of a payment to a sergeant, John Swift, for bringing messages to Roger Walden, the treasurer, and then returning with

---

[8] Walter Map, *De Nugis Curialium*, ed. M.R. James (revised edn, Oxford, 1983), 248.
[9] J.W. Baldwin, 'The Capetian Court at Work under Philip Augustus', *The Medieval Court in Europe*, ed. E. Haymes (Munich, 1986), 71.
[10] *WC*, 230. See also ibid., 370.
[11] *HVR*, 165.

replies 'to the king's court' ('versus curiam regis').[12] Four years earlier, and still more illuminatingly, a payment was made in a wardrobe account to a messenger, Nicholas Inglefield, for going 'from the court' ('de curia') to London and Bristol to seek cash to meet the expenses of the household ('ad expensas hospicii').[13] In this entry the choice of words leaves little doubt that the clerk had a sense not only of the existence of the 'court', but also of the difference between the 'court' and the 'household'. In the light of this, and bearing in mind the chroniclers' perception of the 'court', it seems casuistical of historians to deny the court an actual existence. Mr Morgan makes the point that only in the following century did a clear language of 'court' and 'courtier' emerge. This is certainly true in the limited sense that it was only then that these terms were widely used in the vernacular. But 'court' and 'courtier' were simply vernacular renderings of 'curia' and 'curialis'; and these were terms that had a long history of use. The change that is occurring here may only be one of language and not in the underlying realities being described.

The argument about the medieval origins of the court is not, of course, entirely about technicalities of language or meaning. The doubts that Sir Geoffrey Elton has expressed go deeper. Sir Geoffrey has questioned whether a 'court', properly understood, could exist in the medieval polity. A court, he argues, was by definition the centre of the social and political life of the realm. Thus it could exist only where the king had a monopoly of power; and in the middle ages no such monopoly existed, for the king had to share the exercise of power with his nobility. In Sir Geoffrey's view, a court in the later sense could emerge only when the partnership between king and nobility was dissolved. Obviously, there is a measure of truth in this argument. It is clear that the crown did not permanently assimilate local centres of power to itself until the later fifteenth or early sixteenth centuries; the process was probably begun under Edward IV and brought to completion under the early Tudors. But attempts to construct a royal monopoly had been made in at least two earlier periods. The first such period was in the 1320s, when Edward II and the Despensers had established a powerful court-centred regime after Lancaster's defeat at Boroughbridge; the estates of the dissident, or 'contrariant', nobility were seized and confiscated, and the local informal networks of power subordinated to those of the court; in effect the independent power of the nobility was eliminated. The second period when such a regime was created came three-quarters of a century later in the 1390s, when Richard

---

[12] E403/556, 4 Dec.
[13] E101/403/22, fo.17ʳ.

re-established his authority. Through the formation of a baronial-style affinity the king provided himself with a major new power base in the shires while later, by crushing the former Appellants and redistributing their lands, he was able to assimilate the local power structures to those of the centre.[14] For at least the final ten months of his reign Richard was effectively without internal challenge to his power. The aspirations of the ambitious were focused exclusively on his court, and the households of the magnates were left high and dry.

There can be no doubt that in its main characteristics Richard's court-centred regime differed little from the more lasting one created by the Tudors; probably only the personality of the king distinguished it from Henry VIII's. Indeed, the similarity between the two courts appears the more striking when attention is directed to their social and cultural life. A characteristic of the Tudor, especially the later Tudor, court was its essentially civilian aspect. The military atmosphere which had characterized the medieval court had been shaken off, and court life became more refined: there was a cult of good manners; a premium was put on patronage of the arts, and women exercised a civilizing influence on their male colleagues. The shift to this more sophisticated environment was a long drawn-out and, at times, halting process. It probably began in the thirteenth century under Henry III, a patron of art and culture; it slowed under the impact of the continuous warfare around 1300. But it picked up again in the second half of the fourteenth century. The changes that occurred at that time were made possible by the court's gradually diminishing involvement in war. Edward III in his later years and Richard subsequently rarely campaigned in person and, as a result, had little need of a large corps of household knights. The knights' numbers were quickly run down, and ultimately their place was taken by the chamber staff, whose duties were mainly administrative.

Against this background of civilianization a further stimulus was provided by Richard's own personality and tastes. Richard was a highly fastidious man, with an interest well in advance of his times in cleanliness and hygiene. It is known that he had bath-houses constructed at Eltham and Sheen, and it has been suggested that he invented the handkerchief.[15] The more elegant and sophisticated air that he brought to court life is reflected in the improvement in manners. At dinner it became normal for people to eat with spoons rather than with their

[14] See above, 265–8, and below, 381–4.

[15] At Eltham the bath-house was made 'on the king's order': *HKW*, ii, 934; at Sheen 2,000 painted tiles were provided 'for paving a chamber assigned for the king's bath': ibid., 998. For the handkerchief, see Clarke, *Fourteenth Century Studies*, 117–18; G.B. Stow, 'Richard II and the Invention of the Pocket Handkerchief', *Albion*, xxvii (1995), 221–35.

fingers.[16] The presence of women at court became more common,[17] and from the beginning of the reign women were regularly elected to the sorority of the Garter.[18] By the middle of the 1380s a new and more lively interest was being taken by the courtiers in letters, and writers like Chaucer and Gower were producing works in a courtly ambience.[19] These were changes that did not go unnoticed by contemporaries. Walsingham caustically observed that Richard's knights were 'knights of Venus rather than of Bellona: more effective in the bedchamber than the field'.[20] The comment was made by one who was a hostile witness but it highlighted an important truth. By Richard's reign the court was shedding the character of a military household; it was evolving into the sophisticated, civilianized, court of the Renaissance. It is doubtful whether a direct line of descent can be traced from Richard's court to that of the early Tudors, but developments in Richard's reign certainly pointed to the shape of things to come.

The elegant new court of Richard II was born within the shell of the older administrative structures. Over the course of the two or three centuries from Henry III's reign to Bosworth the organization of the household appears to have changed relatively little. Certainly it became more complex: offices were subdivided and chains of command lengthened. But the basic outlines of the structure remained much the same. Probably the only change of significance that occurred was in size. The household became bigger – much bigger. Between the twelfth century and the fourteenth it seems that its numbers at least doubled. Henry I's household had numbered 150 or so.[21] Two centuries later Richard II's was nearly three times that number. Admittedly, it is difficult to be sure exactly how many people were at court at any one time. Nominally permanent officials such as the chamber knights, esquires and purveyors would often be away on the king's business while members of the

---

[16] The evidence for the use of spoons rather than hands is to be found in the court recipe book, The Forme of Cury, ed. J. Nichols (London, 1780). Meat was rarely served whole: there were directions as to how it should be 'teysed' or 'morterysed' before being cooked. The meal, as served, must have resembled 'a gigantic pâté': G. Mathew, The Court of Richard II (London, 1968), 24.

[17] Haxey's petition of 1397 complained about the number of women at court: RP, iii, 339, and below, 369. For an invitation from the king to Lady Poynings to spend Christmas 1398 with the court, see Anglo-Norman Letters, no. 25.

[18] CP, ii, 591–4. For discussion, see J.L. Gillespie, 'Ladies of the Fraternity of St George and of the Society of the Garter', Albion, xvii (1985), 259–78.

[19] See below, 359–60.

[20] CA, 375. For contemporary criticism of new fashions of clothing at court, see 'On the Times', in Political Poems and Songs, i, 270–8.

[21] Given-Wilson, Royal Household and the King's Affinity, 259.

nobility, foreign dignitaries and envoys would be arriving on visits to the
king, bringing their retainers and servants with them. The evidence of
the wardrobe books suggests that there was a normal staff complement
of between 400 and 700. But it is not hard to imagine that at times this
could have risen to 800 or 1,000.[22]

The great majority of the people thronging the court were officials or
menial staff, like purveyors, harbingers, ushers and kitchen boys. The
number of people who would have been recognized as 'courtiers' was
relatively small – probably no more than a few dozen. Chief among the
elite would have been the higher nobility, the king's leading councillors
and the senior chamber staff. It was especially important for a king to
have a respectable showing of nobility at his court. Not only were this
group the leading players in political life; their regular attendance on
the king helped him to convey an impression of splendour and power,
thus enhancing his standing as a ruler. When he went on major itineraries of his realm, Richard always took care to have a reasonable
number of nobility with him. On his visit to Downham and Ely in 1383,
he was accompanied by Thomas Mowbray, earl of Nottingham, his half-
brother Sir John Holand, the duchess of Brittany, the countess of
Pembroke, and various 'other lords'.[23] Four years later, when staying at
Lichfield in the course of his 'gyration', he had with him a still more
impressive company: the archbishops of York and Dublin, the bishop of
Chichester, the dukes of Ireland and York, the earl of Suffolk, Lords
Basset, Beaumont and Zouche, and Sir Simon Burley.[24] His visits to Ely
and Lichfield were both of a highly ceremonious nature, and he was not
always so well attended. Most of the higher nobility did not normally
reside at court: they had estates of their own, and they needed to return
home periodically to attend to them. To form an impression of the
number and identity of the courtiers more generally attendant on the
king it is necessary to turn to the witness lists appended to the royal
charters. In the witness lists of the 1380s the names that occur regularly
are those of the dukes of Lancaster, Gloucester and York, the earls of
Arundel and Suffolk, and, among the officials, Sir John Montagu and
Sir Hugh Segrave. In the lists of the following decade the names of the
dukes of Lancaster and York are still prominent, but others have come

[22] Ibid., 74. A massive rise in the size of the household is certainly suggested by the
escalation of expenditure. In the early 1390s the household spent roughly £18,000
per annum; at the end of the decade twice that amount: ibid., 270–1.

[23] Cambridge University Library, Ely diocesan records, D5/7a.

[24] Lichfield Joint Record Office, D30/2/1/1, Dean and Chapter Acts Book 1,
fo.15[r]. On the household account roll of Bishop William of Wykeham there is a
brief note of those accompanying the king on a visit to Winchester in July 1393: the
queen, the earl of March, Lord Beaumont, the king's confessor 'and others' are
mentioned (Winchester College Muniments, 1).

to the fore – most notably, the earls of Nottingham, Huntingdon and Rutland and among the officials the steward Sir Thomas Percy.[25] These men were all 'courtiers' in the sense that they were frequently at court. Some of them, of course, were members of the royal kin, while others played an active role politically. Not all of them, however, were necessarily 'familiars' or intimates of the king. Some, indeed – notably Gloucester and Arundel in the 1380s – were often bitterly at odds with him, and a few, like Warwick, in the end virtually withdrew. Very likely the men closest to the king at court were not so much these very grand figures as the more middle-ranking men who attended him – the household officials, chamber staff and knightly councillors. Some of these, it seems, could be on terms of the highest intimacy with him. Sir William Bagot, a leading councillor in the 1390s, was to recall a conversation in which Richard spoke to him frankly about his hopes and fears for the future: Richard, he said, maintained that he wanted to live long enough to see the crown held in high esteem and obeyed 'with lowly humility by all lieges' and, once this had been achieved, he would be prepared to renounce his crown on the following day; but he did not want Hereford to become king, for 'Hereford would be as great a tyrant to the church as there ever was'.[26] If Richard could unburden himself so frankly to a man of this rank, it is hardly surprising that he could mourn the loss of a chamber official as much as, or more than, that of a lord. When his trusty knight Sir John Golafre died in 1396 Richard, in disregard of the knight's wishes, had him buried in Westminster Abbey immediately beside his own tomb.[27] It seems very likely that feelings of similar intensity existed between the king and Sir Simon Felbrigg, the royal standard bearer. Richard had arranged for Sir Simon to be married to the most distinguished of the queen's ladies-in-waiting, the daughter of the duke of Teschen; and in 1416, when the knight laid down a brass to her memory, he had it strewn with Ricardian symbolism (plate 19).[28] It is probable that Richard was also on close, perhaps even intimate, terms with his confessors and with the clerks of his chapel. One of the earliest confessors to serve him, Thomas Rushook, was a key influence on Richard until his expulsion by the Appellants in 1388. In the following

---

[25] Given-Wilson, 'Royal Charter Witness Lists, 1327–1399', tables 6 and 7.

[26] *Chrons. Revolution*, 211.

[27] The burial is discussed by N.E. Saul, 'The Fragments of the Golafre Brass in Westminster Abbey', *Transactions of the Monumental Brass Society*, xv, i (1992), 19–32. In his will Golafre had requested burial at Grey Friars, Oxford. Golafre's attachment to the king is indicated by the many bequests that he made to him. These included his best horse, a device engraved with a white hart, a golden cup again engraved with the white hart, and a ring with a diamond engraved with the words 'saunz departier' (Lambeth Palace Library, Reg. Arundel, i, fos155^r–155^v).

[28] J.D. Milner, 'Sir Simon Felbrigg, KG: the Lancastrian Revolution and Personal Fortune', *Norfolk Archaeology*, xxxvii, i (1978), 84–91.

decade the chapel clerks Tideman of Winchcombe, Richard Maudelyn, Thomas Merks, William Ferriby and John Ikelington all stood high in royal favour: Tideman was the king's physician and, according to the Evesham writer, he and Merks spent the greater part of their nights in a state of stupor with the king.[29] In the final years of the reign the number of clerks among the king's closest companions and advisers was considerably greater than the number of knights: clerks predominated among those whom he named as his executors.[30] Several of the group, notably Ferriby and Maudelyn, joined in the earls' rebellion in 1400. They were in no wise fair-weather friends. Their devotion to their royal master well outlasted his ability to reward and promote them.

It is easier to reconstruct the membership of the court than to say anything of value about its daily routines or the details of its ceremonies. The administrative sources, of which the most important are the wardrobe books, shed little light on these matters. For the most part they are accountants' records – subjecting the household's annual income and expenditure to review, and that is all. A general impression of the splendour of the king's person and surroundings is given by the inventories of his jewellery and plate compiled in or after 1399: these are some of the fullest such records to survive from the middle ages.[31] But there is an unfortunate dearth of well-informed descriptions of the court by insiders. For Richard's reign there are no eyewitness accounts to compare with Christine de Pisan's biographical memoir of Charles V. Compensation of a sort is afforded by vignettes of the chroniclers. The Monk of Westminster, probably the best-informed writer of the reign, provides a remarkable description of the king's reception of the exiled king, Leo of Armenia in 1385: Leo 'was welcomed by the king', he says, 'and was enriched by a quantity of truly splendid gifts and presents, given not only by the king but by the queen and the nobles who were there. . . . Later [Richard], donning his more impressive finery, escorted the Armenian to Westminster where, although dusk was coming on, he nonetheless took him to the monastery by candlelight . . . and showed him the royal insignia with which he had been invested at his coronation.'[32] An attractive account is also given by the same writer of the duke of Guelders's reception in London in 1390. The duke, he says, was personally greeted by the king, 'who feasted him sumptuously and plied him with lavish entertainments, including dancing and a

---

[29] *HVR*, 165.

[30] Nine of the fifteen executors were clerks. These were the bishops of Salisbury, Exeter, Worcester, Carlisle and St David's, Richard Clifford, the keeper of the privy seal, Richard Maudelyn, William Ferriby and John Ikelington (*Foed.*, viii, 77).

[31] *The Ancient Kalendars and Inventories of the Treasury of His Majesty's Exchequer*, ed. F. Palgrave (3 vols, London, 1836), iii, 309–61; and see below, 354–5.

[32] *WC*, 154–6.

pleasing variety of instrumental music and paid him every flattering attention'.[33] To set alongside these vignettes are the occasional eyewitness accounts of visitors to the court from abroad. Possibly the most valuable is the account of Raymond, *vicomte* of Perelhos and Roda, who came to England in 1397. Raymond's purpose was to make a pilgrimage to St Patrick's shrine in Ireland, but near Oxford he caught up with the court, and was received by Richard himself. The king bestowed gifts on him, and he was lavishly entertained for ten days. When he finally left for Ireland, he was provided with guides and letters of introduction to the earl of March, the king's lieutenant there. From this account and from the Westminster writer's notices an impression is gained of the splendour and variety of spectacle at the court. There was always something to attract the eye or to engage the attention. People were coming and going, formal ceremonies unfolding, and feasts and entertainments being prepared. Courtly life can be seen as a series of unfolding set-pieces or occasions: occasions at which visitors were received, business transacted, gifts bestowed and the splendour of the king's majesty revealed to his subjects.

The great spectacle of courtly theatre was staged wherever the king happened to be, whether at Westminster, Windsor, Woodstock, Oxford, or any of the other staging-posts on the royal itinerary: for the king was constantly on the move. The Christmas festivities of the court were generally held at Westminster, Windsor or Eltham, where the grandest surroundings were to be had.[34] Usually in the spring the king moved out into the provinces. In 1382 he undertook a lengthy journey to Bristol and the surrounding towns, and in the following year he went to East Anglia. In April it was invariably his habit to return to Windsor for the annual Garter ceremonies. Then in May or June he would set out on his travels again. By tradition he held his midsummer court at a major town – in 1392, for example, at Nottingham, in other years at Canterbury, Windsor or Lichfield.[35] Generally he devoted part of each summer to the pleasures of the chase. In 1384 and 1393 he went to the New Forest. In other years he spent two or three weeks at Woodstock or one of the hunting lodges in the adjoining forest. At the beginning of autumn he would return to the south-east, often calling *en route* at his manor of King's Langley. In October and November he would fit in visits to Kennington or Sheen; and in December he would move on to Westminster for Christmas. For the most part, this was a pattern of movements characteristic of most late medieval rulers: its hub was the

---

[33] Ibid., 434.

[34] For details of the king's itinerary, see Appendix.

[35] The Westminster writer records that at Nottingham on the Nativity of St John the Baptist (24 June), 1392, Richard 'seated himself on the royal throne' (*WC*, 498).

lower Thames valley. But towards the end of 1397 there was a sudden
change. After the end of the September parliament Richard went off to
the midlands and hardly ever returned. He spent the Christmas of 1397
at Lichfield and in the following spring moved on to Shrewsbury. After
briefly returning to Westminster in April he spent the late summer and
autumn moving restlessly around the Welsh Marches. It seems that he
was irresistibly drawn to this remote area, where he felt happier or more
secure than he did in the south-east.[36] He briefly returned to the south-
east in early spring 1399, when he visited Becket's shrine, but at the end
of April he was off again – this time on his ill-fated expedition to
Ireland.

Richard's constant journeyings, particularly in his final years as king,
inevitably limited the opportunities given to him for display. Jewellery,
hangings and altar vessels all had to be packed or unpacked every few
days, and ceremonies had to be staged in cramped or inadequate
surroundings. Accommodation was often difficult to find. Sometimes it
was possible for the king to stay in a sizeable abbey or castle: in 1383, for
example, he stayed at Ely and Bury St Edmunds, and in 1396 and 1398
in the abbeys of the Severn valley. But even at abbeys accommodation
could be confined, and there might be an unseemly scramble for
lodgings.[37] On many itineraries the king had to be satisfied with the
shelter of a small manor house or priory. On the route that he took
from Woodstock to Oakham in 1390 there was virtually nowhere suitable for him to stay. The towns were all very small; and there were few
monasteries or manor houses large enough to serve his needs. At
Daventry, on the second night, he probably stayed at the priory. But at
Brackley, on the first night, and at Lutterworth and Market
Harborough later on he would have had to seek such lodgings as
he could among the townsfolk while his menial staff camped out.[38]
Whatever its many drawbacks, however, the itinerant lifestyle was not
always incompatible with the projection of an image of splendour.
Richard had several fine palaces in which to stay: Westminster was a
large, sprawling complex with a magnificent hall which the king rebuilt
(plate 22); Windsor had a grandiose set of apartments in the upper
bailey; the manors of Sheen, Eltham and Leeds (in Kent) all offered

---

[36] For the final years of the reign, see below, ch. 16.

[37] When a parliament was held at Gloucester Abbey in 1378, the monks found
themselves temporarily displaced: *Historia et Cartularium Monasterii Sancti Petri
Gloucestriae*, ed. W.H. Hart (3 vols, Rolls series, 1863–7), i, 53. Walsingham
complained of the impositions occasioned by Richard's stay at Bury in 1383 (*HA*, ii,
96–7).

[38] E101/402/5, fos23ʳ–23ᵛ; for discussion, see Given-Wilson, *Royal Household and
the King's Affinity*, 36–7.

ample accommodation.[39] Occasionally the friends with whom he stayed were prepared to extend or renovate their accommodation in readiness for his coming. In the later 1390s successive bishops of Lichfield rebuilt the episcopal palace in the cathedral close to accommodate the court on its increasingly frequent itineraries to the midlands.[40] It was at a session of the court at Lichfield that Richard received a kinsman of the emperor of Constantinople and a papal envoy, the bishop of Dax.[41]

Within such surroundings as he could find Richard cultivated a courtly style that suited his tastes and reflected his lofty conception of his office. To judge from the chroniclers' comments, his court was characterized by richness of ceremony and heavy emphasis on deference. Courts had always been formal and deferential societies: successive ordinances for the household had been preoccupied with the relative standing of officials and their position in the courtly hierarchy. But Richard's insistence on deference appears to have been exceptional even by the standards of his age. As early as 1385 the Westminster writer had commented on Richard's 'lust for glory and eagerness to have from everyone the deference properly due to his kingship'.[42] In later years his ceremoniousness was the subject of comment by a number of writers. The *Eulogium* writer, in a famous passage, recorded his stately demeanour at formal crown wearings when he would sit enthroned from dinner till vespers, conversing with none but watching all.[43] The Evesham chronicler, in his account of the year 1390, noted

---

[39] Richard rebuilt the great hall of Westminster palace from 1394: *HKW*, i, 527–33 (plate 22). At Windsor the royal apartments in the upper bailey had been magnificently rebuilt by Edward III between 1357 and 1365: ibid., ii, 876–80. Eltham had also been the subject of extensive building works in the 1350s and 1360s: ibid., 931–4. At Sheen Richard carried out a series of works intermittently in the 1380s and had a timber-framed lodging called 'la Nayght' constructed on an island in the river: ibid., 998. Outside Westminster, probably the most ambitious programme that Richard undertook was the rebuilding of the domestic apartments in the inner bailey at Portchester between 1396 and 1399: ibid., 790–1. Since he apparently never once visited Portchester, and at the time of these works had largely abandoned southern England for the midlands, it is not clear what the purpose of the rebuilding was. One possibility is that the works were initiated for the benefit of Roger Walden, the treasurer and later archbishop of Canterbury, who, with his brother, was keeper of the castle from 1395: *CPR 1391–6*, 568, 572; *CPR 1396–9*, 64. A grant made by Richard to Walden and his brother of lands in the Portchester area refers to 'their purpose to urge the king to repair the castle' (ibid., 274). I am grateful to Justine Cooper for discussing Portchester with me.

[40] *Victoria History of the County of Stafford*, xiv, ed. M.W. Greenslade (London, 1990), 14, 59. Richard's friend Richard Scrope was bishop from 1386 to 1398, and his former confessor John Burghill bishop from 1398.

[41] *HVR*, 151.

[42] *WC*, 138.

[43] *Eulogium*, 378; *Chrons. Revolution*, 68.

that at the end of the Smithfield tournament Richard gave a magnificent banquet at which, in order to demonstrate his royal dignity to foreign visitors, he sat enthroned, in full regalia and wearing his crown.[44] The Westminster writer, reviewing the events of the same year, noted that when the king visited the abbey on St Edward's Day he was attended by the whole of his chapel and sat in the choir during mass wearing his crown, with the queen, also wearing her crown, beside him.[45] The growing frequency of comment on Richard's highly formal and self-conscious behaviour suggests that he was deliberately fostering a more elaborate and ceremonial style of monarchy, and evidence from non-narrative sources confirms this. How then did the protocol of Richard's court change over the years? And what sort of aims was Richard trying to achieve? It is not easy to answer these questions, given the limitations of the evidence, but a general impression can be formed both of the pattern of change at court and of the thinking behind it.

Indications of an elaboration of protocol are to be found in a number of areas of court life. Some of the most striking evidence is afforded by the development in the second half of the reign of the lofty new vocabulary of address to the king.[46] Traditionally in England subjects had addressed their remarks to the king in the everyday language of lordship. In other words, they addressed, or petitioned, the king in much the same way as they would a great lord. In the years around 1390, however, a major change occurred. Subjects began to address the king in loftier and more exalted terms. The king was referred to as a 'prince' and addressed as 'your majesty' and 'your highness'. An early example of the new style is found in the roll of the parliament of 1391. The heading of the commons' petitions reads, 'To the most excellent and most renowned and most excellent prince, and most gracious lord, our lord the king, pray your humble lieges the commons of your realm of England, that it should please your highness and royal majesty . . . to grant the petitions which follow.'[47] For the roll of the Winchester parliament of 1393 an abridged form of the same was employed: 'To the most excellent and most powerful prince, our lord the king, pray your humble commons . . . that it should please your highness . . . to

---

[44] HVR, 132. For a similar account of Richard and Anne dining in state at Salisbury in 1392, see *Eulogium*, iii, 369.

[45] WC, 450. Two years later the king's 'great crown' was brought from Queenborough to Westminster for his use in the St Edward's Day mass: E403/541, 30 Oct.

[46] Saul, 'Richard II and the Vocabulary of Kingship'; and see above, 238–9.

[47] RP, iii, 290. The original is in French: 'A tres excellent et tres redoute et tres puissant Prince, et tres gracious seigneur, nostre seigneur le Roi, supplient voz povres liges, communes de vostre roialme d'Engleterre, qe plese a vostre hautesse et roiale mageste . . . graciousment granter les petitions souz escriptz.'

grant the petitions which follow.'[48] A similar degree of elaboration is found in correspondence sent to the king in the 1390s. A good example is a letter which John Waltham, bishop of Salisbury, wrote in 1394. Beginning 'Tresexcellent, tresredoubte et mon soverein seignur, je me recommanc a vostre haut roiale majeste', the bishop went on to say that he had received the letters of credence 'from the king's royal highness' ('de par mesme vostre hautesse'), and that he had made his way to the Welsh coast by the nativity of Our Lady, but had been detained from coming 'to the king's high royal presence' ('devers vostre haut roiale presence') by contrary winds; all the same, further news of his movements would be given by the carrier of the letters, 's'il soit plaisir a vostre hautesse'.[49] In the middle and later years of the decade a number of other correspondents were writing to the king in similar vein.[50] The effect of the adoption of this lofty new language – which, according to the *Brut* chronicler, was encouraged by the king[51] – was to widen the distance separating the king from his subjects. The king was raised to a higher level and wrapped in mystique, while his subjects were reminded of their inferiority to him. The lofty language complemented such other expressions of deference as bowing or averting the gaze.[52]

Coupled with the use of the new vocabulary of address was a second development which added to the formality of the court. This was the lengthening of the hierarchy of degree. The process of lengthening had been started in the 1330s by Edward III when he introduced the title of duke for the benefit of his eldest son. The pace of change, however, greatly accelerated under Richard. In the mid-1380s several new ranks appeared. The title of marquess was introduced in 1385 to dignify the king's close friend Robert de Vere, earl of Oxford, while two years later the first barony by patent was created for the chamber knight, John Beauchamp of Holt. By a parallel, and perhaps slightly later, process the untitled lords – the 'barons' – were differentiated more sharply from the gentry. Thus in the later 1390s the word 'sire' was increasingly used as a title in its own right, meaning 'lord'.[53] At the same time the position of the royal family within the peerage was being

[48] Ibid., 305. The French original reads: 'Al tres excellent et tres puissant Prince nostre seigneur le Roi supplient humblement voz povres Communes . . . qe please a vostre Hautesse . . . granter les petitions souz escriptz.'

[49] *Anglo-Norman Letters*, no. 24.

[50] See, for example, ibid., nos 27, 198, 207.

[51] Some of the most obsequious forms of address were found in the so-called 'blank charters' of 1398, which the author of the *Brut* continuation says that 'King Richard made and ordained' (*Brut*, ii, 356). For the 'blank charters', see below, 388.

[52] For examples of bowing, see *WC*, 112, 226.

[53] J.E. Powell and K. Wallis, *The House of Lords in the Middle Ages* (London, 1968), 420–1.

given clearer and more precise definition. The Holands and Gaunt's illegitimate offspring, the Beauforts, were allowed to adopt the king's distinctive arms impaled with the arms attributed to Edward the Confessor, and in 1397 the royal earls' superiority was recognized by their creation *en masse* as dukes.[54] It is possible that concomitant moves were made to elaborate the ceremony of investiture of lords. When John Beaufort was created earl of Somerset in January 1397, it was noted on the official roll that he was not only girded with a sword by the king, but was attired in a cloak of velvet as a garment of honour.[55] Even if such a garment had been worn in earlier ceremonies of investiture, it is significant that at this time it was considered worthy of mention in the record.

The elaboration of courtly protocol received a stimulus from a third development – the growing emphasis on ceremonial. While still a teenager, Richard had taken great delight in ceremonial. According to the Westminster writer, who was in a position to know, in the mid-1380s he expected a show of deference from all who approached him.[56] In the later years of the reign his preoccupation with ceremonial became appreciably greater. The *Eulogium* writer gives a celebrated description of his demeanour at the thrice-yearly crown-wearing ceremonies, when 'he ordered a throne to be prepared for him in his chamber on which he sat ostentatiously from after dinner till vespers, talking to no one but watching everyone; and when his eye fell on anyone . . . that person had to bend his knee to the king'.[57] The tradition of thrice-yearly crown-wearing sessions stretched back to early Norman times. However, no previous chronicler had commented on the extreme formality of such occasions, so there is a possibility that Richard's lofty demeanour was new. Outside the highly formalized rituals of the court the same novel emphasis on ceremonial was to be observed. Tournaments became more elaborate. The great series of tournaments held at Smithfield in October 1390 were preceded by a procession through the streets in which each of the knights was led by 'cheynes of gold' by a lady of the sorority of the Garter.[58] The practice of staging 'joyeuses entrées' – formal royal entries into cities – also made its appearance. The earliest such entry to be recorded was that of July 1377, when Richard rode with a large company through London to Westminster on the day before his coronation.[59] A second grand entry was staged in January 1382 to mark Anne of Bohemia's arrival in England: according to the *Brut* writer, the Londoners formally met the queen at Blackheath, and a series of pag-

[54] Griffiths, 'The Crown and the Royal Family', 18–19; and see above, 245–6.
[55] *RP*, iii, 343.
[56] *WC*, 154.
[57] *Chrons. Revolution*, 68.
[58] *Brut*, ii, 343. I am grateful to Hugh Collins for this reference.
[59] *CA*, 154–5; *Anon.*, 108.

eants was constructed to mark her passage through the city.[60] The third and most extravagant of the ceremonial entries was that of 1392, to celebrate the settlement of Richard's quarrel with the Londoners. There are descriptions of the entry in the chronicles and in a poem by Richard Maidstone.[61] According to Maidstone, Richard took a route westwards along Cheapside which was marked by a series of pageants. The pageants were carefully co-ordinated to present a celestial theme. On the first of them, which was atop a conduit, a choir of singers was costumed to resemble one of the heavenly orders of angels. At the second, technically the most ambitious, a castle-like turret was erected from which a youth handed down chalices of wine to the king while a maiden disbursed golden crowns. At the third, a pageant throne was fixed to the Little Conduit and surrounded by three circles of angels, symbolizing the three angelic orders in attendance before the throne of the Almighty. The fourth and last depicted a scene of John the Baptist preaching in a wilderness teeming with wild beasts.

These pageants formed a tightly organized and iconographically powerful series of spectacles. The general aim appears to have been to present London in the role of the new Jerusalem. Richard, like Christ at the Second Coming, was entering his kingdom for the second time. At his first coming – on the eve of the coronation – he had been received by the citizens dressed as angels and disbursing wine. But since then his people had broken their faith by refusing him a loan, and the question arose of how he should receive them. In the pageantry he was cast in the role of the forgiving bridegroom of an errant but penitent spouse, taking the city back to himself. This was a portrayal of which he would have approved: as his surviving iconography shows, he was given to seeing himself in Christ-like terms.[62] Typologically, the pageants fall

---

[60] Little is known about this entry. For the meeting at Blackheath, see *Brut*, ii, 338–9; and for the making of a pageant castle by the goldsmiths: W. Herbert, *The History of the Twelve Great Livery Companies* (2 vols, London, 1836–7), ii, 217–18.

[61] Maidstone's poem offers the fullest account: *Political Poems and Songs*, i, 282–300; for a modern edition of the poem see C.R. Smith, 'Richard Maidstone, *Concordia facta inter Regem Riccardum II et Civitatem Londonie*' (Princeton University Ph.D. thesis, 1972). The other sources are *WC*, 504–8; *KC*, 546–8; and a contemporary newsletter: H. Suggett, 'A letter describing Richard II's reconciliation with the city of London, 1392', *EHR*, lxii (1947), 209–13. The best discussion of the pageants is Kipling, 'Richard II's "Sumptuous Pageants"', 83–103. For the little that is known of Maidstone's career see *BRUO*, ii, 1204; and C.R. Smith, 'Richard Maidstone', 1–10. Maidstone was close to the court: in the early 1390s he was confessor to John of Gaunt. But he was also an academic controversialist: in about 1390 he was involved in a dispute over poverty and dominion with John Ashwardby, vicar of St Mary's, Oxford. Could he have composed the striking epitaph of Richard's tomb (for which see below, 357)? For help with Maidstone I am indebted to Wendy Scase.

[62] On this theme, see the discussions of the Wilton Diptych and Westminster Abbey portrait, above, 304–5, and below, 384–5.

roughly halfway between civic pageant and courtly ritual. A plausible hypothesis would be to see the tasks of staging and organization as being assumed by the citizens, while the thematic inspiration was provided by the king. Certainly the context in which the pageants were conceived was provided by the striking growth of pageantry and spectacle more generally at court.

The phenomenon of civic pageantry reinforces the impression given by the sources as a whole that there was a growing emphasis at Richard's court on formality and the observance of hierarchy. Undoubtedly, a number of the changes of his reign had been anticipated by his predecessors. The process of elevating the royal kin had been begun by Edward III in the 1340s; and the introduction of new titles can be dated to the same reign. But much else in the life of Richard's court was new. The processes of elaborating the language of address, of distancing the king from his subjects, of organizing ceremonial pageants were ones for which there was no precedent in England. What, then, were the sources for Richard's ideas? And what sort of aims was the king trying to achieve?

The first and most immediate source of the new formalism was almost certainly the Black Prince's court in Aquitaine. Richard could hardly have recalled much about the court himself, for he was only four when the prince returned to England, but he would have heard much about it from his elders. In its heyday the prince's court had been one of the most magnificent in Europe. Froissart said that the prince's and the princess's 'estate' was so splendid and rich that no other ruler or lord could begin to match it.[63] The prince had taken a particular delight in the staging of lavish entertainments. In 1365, to mark the birth of his eldest son and the churching of the princess, he held a series of tournaments. According to one eyewitness account, the tournaments were attended by 154 lords, 706 knights and 18,000 horses, the latter stabled at the prince's expense. Twenty-four knights and twenty-four lords formed the princess's retinue, and the tourneying, jousting and other amusements lasted for ten days.[64] The impression is given by other sources that the prince was equally ceremonious when he undertook itineraries of the duchy. In the light of subsequent developments in England, it is instructive to note that his entries into major towns were marked by impressive pomp. According to an entry in the cartulary of St Severin's collegiate church, on his entry into Bordeaux in 1355 he was 'attended by a great retinue of the earls and barons of England'.[65] Moreover, at formal sessions of his court he insisted on an

[63] Froissart, i, 383.

[64] Barber, *Edward, Prince of Wales*, 184.

[65] *Cartulaire de l'Eglise collegiale Saint-Seurin de Bordeaux*, ed. J.A. Brutails (Bordeaux, 1897), 4–5.

extravagant display of deference. According to the *Anonimalle* writer, probably drawing on an eyewitness report, it was his habit to keep the Aquitanian nobility waiting for days on end for an audience, and then only to admit them to his presence on bended knee.[66] This was behaviour of a kind that directly anticipates his son's at the festival crownings described by the *Eulogium* writer. Quite possibly, in assuming a more formal style, Richard was drawing on what he knew of the protocol of his father's court.

While the prince's court was a major influence on his son's, particularly in the early years of the reign, it should not be supposed that it was the only one. In the later fourteenth century developments broadly similar in character to those in England and Aquitaine were occurring at a number of European courts. At Paris and Prague, for example, there was a growing preoccupation with protocol and etiquette.[67] In the courts of provincial France princes were cultivating a more formal and consciously 'distant' style. It is interesting in the latter connection to compare Froissart's description of the behaviour of Gaston III of Foix, *vicomte* of Béarn, with the *Anonimalle* writer's of the Black Prince's: Gaston, he says, sat apart from his courtiers on formal occasions and was addressed by them only when he himself opened the conversation.[68] Increasingly, rulers would address petitioners only through intermediaries. It seems likely that these moves evolved in response to the growing social unrest of the time. All over western Europe in the final quarter of the century the lower orders were becoming more assertive. There were popular or artisan uprisings in Florence in 1378, France in 1382 and, of course, England in 1381. Representative assemblies and estates were making unprecedented bids for power; everywhere the social order seemed under strain. Rulers reacted to these challenges in broadly the same manner: by formalizing the old hierarchies and emphasizing people's obligation of obedience. This was the case in Richard's England no less than in France – or for that matter Béarn.

The trend to uniformity was reinforced by the rapidly increasing range of contacts between courts which was characteristic of the period. Contacts were fostered most obviously by diplomacy. Heralds, publicists and envoys went backwards and forwards between courts on missions. Kings undertook visits to one another;[69] and periodically they and their nobles attended high-level conferences. At the same time, informal contact was stimulated by the holding of tournaments. The largest tournaments of the time, like the one staged at St Ingelvert in 1390,

---

[66] *Anon.*, 55–6.
[67] See below, 347, 350.
[68] Froissart, ii, 95.
[69] A notable example being the visit of the Emperor Charles IV to Paris in the winter of 1377–8.

were attended by princes and lords from all over the continent. Those who participated could converse with one another and take note of each other's appearance and manners. In any or all of these ways the styles and fashions of one court could be observed and followed in another. As a result, there was a near synchronism in the developments in the courtly life of the period. Courts in every part of the continent became more formal, and more formally organized. Ambitious rulers presented themselves as patrons of letters and exemplars of chivalry and courtesy. The presence of women at court became more wide-spread. A new interest was shown in fashion – and fashion not only in clothes but in food and drink. Most dramatically of all, there was a cult of the king as a figure in majesty. All these are characteristics of what has been termed the 'international' courtly culture of the late four-teenth century; and they are found to a greater or lesser degree in all the main European courts of the day.

In an influential study Gervase Mathew traced the origins of the new courtly style to the Neapolitan court of the early fourteenth century.[70] In Mathew's view many of the style's characteristic elements first came together in Naples in the reign of King Robert of Anjou (1309–43). Mathew singled out the use of sinecures and high office as rewards, the seeking after luxury and the cult of fashionable dress, the presence of women at court with all that this implied for sensibility, and, above all, the leadership of a scholarly king who lent a civilian character to his court and bestowed patronage on men of letters. From the Neapolitan court, in Mathew's view, a taste for the new courtly style spread quickly to other parts of Italy. It was noticeable by the middle of the century at the Visconti court of Milan and at the Carrara court at Padua. Perhaps through the agency of the Avignon papacy, it was transmitted thence to northern and central Europe. By the third quarter of the century it was observable at the Emperor Charles IV's court at Prague and at Charles V's at Paris. Mathew tentatively suggested that it was from the emperor's court that it was transmitted to Richard II's in England: Richard, he argued, 'modelled himself on what he had heard of his father-in-law Charles IV, not on what he had heard of his own grandfather, Edward III'.[71]

There is much in Mathew's reconstruction to command acceptance. There can be little doubt that, as Mathew argued, civilized and culti-vated rulers were responsible for bringing about a major change in courtly manners and sensibility in this period; there can also be little doubt that a greater emphasis was placed in court life on the patronage of letters and of the arts generally. On the other hand, as has often been

[70] G. Mathew, *Court of Richard II.*
[71] Ibid., 17.

pointed out, Mathew tended to exaggerate the importance of the developments in Angevin Naples. Many of the characteristics of King Robert's court were anticipated three-quarters of a century earlier by the Emperor Frederick II's court in Sicily. Frederick's court, like Robert's, was a 'school of manners'. The emperor himself was a learned and lettered man: he read in six languages, wrote poems and made translations of Aristotle. He lent patronage to scholars, jurists and academics: he built up the celebrated medical school at Salerno and founded a university at Naples. His court at Palermo was a magnet for nobles and intellectuals from all over Europe: the doctor Master Theodore came to work there, and so too did the astrologer Michael Scott.[72] If a search is to be made for the ultimate origins of the sophisticated style of the late middle ages, it is probably to Frederick's court rather than Robert's that it should be directed. Robert's court was but a revival of the former; probably in southern Italy the memory of it had never faded.

If Mathew seriously postdated the appearance of the new style, he may also have misrepresented the means of its transmission across Europe. Mathew assigned a pivotal role to the court of the Emperor Charles IV at Prague: he tentatively suggested that it was from Charles's court that the new styles were carried to England, after Richard's marriage to Charles's daughter Anne. It is easy to see why he should have taken this view. Charles's court, like Richard's later, was highly stratified. There was a rigid insistence on the observance of etiquette, and a major role was accorded to pomp and ceremony. The emperor himself took a close interest in elaborating the liturgical ritual. According to the chroniclers, he swelled the ranks of the Bohemian clergy by introducing a graded system of canons, altarists and choristers in the larger churches, expecially those in Prague. His belief in order and rank found expression in the buildings that he commissioned. The majestic castle at Karlstein, begun in 1348, was conceived according to a master plan in which each of the component parts had an allotted place: the palace, the residence of a mere mortal, was placed at the lowest level, the chapel of the Virgin and St Catherine's chapel in the middle, and the chapel of the Holy Cross, with its relics of the Cross and the crown of thorns, at the top in the great tower.[73] This carefully graded scheme

---

[72] For an illuminating discussion of Frederick's court, see A.G. Dickens, 'Monarchy and Cultural Revival', *The Courts of Europe. Politics, Patronage and Royalty, 1400–1800*, ed. A.G. Dickens (London, 1977), 22–8. Only one characteristic of the late medieval and Renaissance court was missing in Frederick's: the presence of women: each of the emperor's three wives lived separately from her husband (ibid., 26).

[73] The best account in English of Charles's court is V. Dvořáková and others, *Gothic Mural Painting*, 41–65. See also S.H. Thomson, 'Learning at the Court of Charles IV', *Speculum*, xxv (1950), 1–20.

reflected his hierarchical conception of the world – a conception that bears more than a passing resemblance to Richard's own.

Superficially, the case for Bohemian influence on England seems a compelling one. Richard and Charles IV shared broadly the same outlook on the world; and after Richard's marriage to Charles's daughter in 1382 the way was open for the entry of Bohemian culture and ideas into England. Yet, strangely, evidence for direct Bohemian influence on English courtly life is hard to come by. In Mathew's view the English insistence on protocol had Bohemian roots; but when so many other courts were elaborating their protocol, it is difficult to be sure that Bohemia was the sole or exclusive source of influence. There is evidence that Bohemian painting exerted an influence on English court art of the period: the formal 'coronation portrait' of Richard in Westminster Abbey has antecedents in the portraits of the Bohemian kings in the great hall at Karlstein, and affinities have been observed between a number of English manuscripts, notably the *Liber Regalis*, and Bohemian mural and manuscript painting.[74] But these are relatively minor connections, considering the closeness of ties between England and Bohemia in the years after Richard's marriage.[75] Against them has to be set the fact that contemporary English chroniclers were unaware of any widespread imperial influence. The most that the well-informed Evesham writer could find to comment on was the introduction to his country of some new and exaggerated styles of attire.[76] It is possible that the elaboration of the vocabulary of address to the king owed something to imperial influence: for the royal chancery would have been used to addressing the emperor as a 'prince' and as 'your majesty'. On the other hand, the timing of such elaboration hardly lends support to such an idea. Richard's marriage took place in 1382, while the changes in vocabulary were initiated some seven or eight years later. Moreover, there were other sources than the imperial diplomatic for the new and richer vocabulary. The senior clergy in England had long been accus-

---

[74] Like the figure of Richard in the 'coronation' portrait, the kings in the Karlstein series were shown almost frontally and holding the orb and the sceptre (Dvořáková, *Gothic Mural Painting*, plates 69, 70). For the *Liber Regalis*, see Binski, *Westminster Abbey*, 194–5. Bohemian influence has also been detected in the Cambridge Old Proctor's Book: N.J. Rogers, 'The Old Proctor's Book: A Cambridge Manuscript of *c.*1390', *England in the Fourteenth Century*, ed. W.M. Ormrod (Woodbridge, 1986), 213–23.

[75] Simpson, *The Connections between English and Bohemian Painting*, found little or no Bohemian influence on English visual and plastic arts in the fourteenth century.

[76] *HVR*, 134. There are references to gowns 'in the Bohemian style' ('modo Boem') in the livery rolls of the great wardrobe (e.g. E101/401/6 m.1; E101/401/16 m.4). The fact that these were singled out for mention suggests that they were seen as out of the ordinary.

tomed to using the terms 'prince' and 'majesty'.[77] And across the Channel, nearer to England than the empire, was another monarchy which was using the language of 'prince' and 'majesty', and that was the French.

Mathew paid relatively little attention to the role the French monarchy may have played in European courtly development. He cited the French court in passing as an example of one that was influenced by the styles spreading from Italy.[78] But he did not examine its characteristics in any detail; nor did he consider it as a source for the formalism of Richard's court. There are signs that the role of the French court in shaping European courtly culture was of considerable importance. The taste of the imperial court in the early fourteenth century was heavily influenced by French models. The Emperor Charles IV as a young man had been a devoted admirer of French art and culture. In the 1330s and early 1340s he had paid many visits to France with his father, who was a francophile. In the course of his visits he acquired numerous French manuscripts, which found their way into his collection at Prague. Charles's architectural tastes were revealed by his choice of a French master mason, Matthew of Arras, to design his new cathedral of St Vitus at Prague.[79] Only in later years, as his interests and ambitions turned eastwards, did the burden of French influence on the emperor lessen.

The leadership of the French court had been a characteristic of the artistic and cultural life of Europe for well over a century. St Louis's fame and success had made the French monarchy the most widely admired in Europe: Henry III and Edward I of England had both in their different ways looked to the French court as a model for their own. The personal style of the French kings until the middle of the thirteenth century had been relatively simple. Access to the king appears to have been fairly unhindered, and the etiquette of the court generally informal. From Philip III's reign, however, there was a move to a more ceremonious style. It was no longer considered appropriate for the king to dispense justice sitting under a tree in his garden, as Joinville says that St Louis had done; and a new image of remoteness was cultivated. From roughly the mid-fourteenth century, in particular from the 1360s, there was a shift to much greater elaboration. The spur to these further moves came from the shock administered to the French monarchy by the defeats of the 1340s. At the beginning of the decade

[77] Saul, 'Richard II and the Vocabulary of Kingship'.
[78] Mathew, *Court of Richard II*, 8.
[79] Matthew had earlier worked at the cathedral of Narbonne. For relations between Charles and the French court more generally, see Dvořáková and others, *Gothic Mural Painting*, 41–3.

the French navy had been destroyed in the Zwin estuary at Sluys; six years later came the humiliating defeat of Crécy and in the following year the loss of Calais. Cumulatively, these setbacks had dealt a shattering blow to the Valois monarchy's prestige. Among the courtiers there was a widespread feeling that steps were needed to build up the monarchy in popular esteem. The first important steps were taken by the second Valois ruler, John II, 'the Good' (1350–64).[80] Like Edward III of England in similar circumstances earlier, John began by harnessing the power of chivalry to his cause. In 1352 he founded an order of chivalry – the Company of the Star – to serve the dual ends of glorifying the crown and tying the knightly class more closely to the dynasty.[81] In later years, as he sought to project a new image of culture and sophistication, he took writers and artists into his service. The poet Guillaume de Machaut was invited to reside at his court, and Petrarch accepted an invitation to visit. By 1352 he was employing a painter, Girard d'Orléans, and the likeness of him in the Louvre attests his interest in portraiture.[82] John's son, the more obviously successful Charles V (1364–80), continued his father's policies, but carried them very much further. Charles consciously cultivated an image of himself as a 'sage', a wise ruler. He made a point of attracting scholars and men of letters to his court. In his palace of the Louvre he assembled a great library of nearly 1,000 volumes, and he was active in commissioning vernacular translations, in particular of Latin texts on government. As a way of bearing visible witness to his power, he also spent lavishly on painting and building. He refurbished the Louvre to make it a suitable setting for courtly pomp and ceremony. He commissioned a magnificent tomb (in due course to be a double tomb) of himself and his queen at the abbey of St Denis. Perhaps more remarkably still, he seems to have encouraged the making and circulation of representations of himself: Charles the royal 'sage' appears in dedication miniatures, donor and devotional portraits, and historiated charters.[83] Charles believed that a policy of exalting the monarchy would contribute to the rebirth of French power, and he was almost certainly justified in this view. The many successes that he enjoyed against the English owed less to his prowess in arms than to the recovery of his subjects' confidence and the restoration of his monarchy's prestige. Contemporaries were quick to observe, and to adjust to, the change in French fortunes. The Emperor

---

[80] For John's policies, see R. Cazelles, *Société politique, noblesse et couronne sous Jean le Bon et Charles V* (Geneva, 1982).

[81] D'A.J.D. Boulton, *The Knights of the Crown. The Monarchical Orders of Knighthood in Later Medieval Europe 1325–1520* (Woodbridge, 1987), 208–10.

[82] M. Meiss, *French Painting in the Time of Jean de Berry. The Late XIV Century and the Patronage of the Duke* (2 vols, London, 1967), i, 31, 100.

[83] C.R. Sherman, *The Portraits of Charles V of France (1338–1380)* (New York, 1969).

Charles IV, in the final years of his reign, began to turn his attention westwards again. The visit that he made to Paris in the winter of 1377–8 was an implicit recognition of the fact that French cultural leadership of the west had been restored.

Richard and his counsellors were fully aware of these developments at the French court. They had had ample opportunity to observe them. Many of the older generation of courtiers, like Burley and de la Pole, had spent long periods on active service in France. Many more of Richard's nobility and civil servants had had contact with the French court through the workings of diplomacy. High-level English missions had been sent to France on many occasions in the 1380s; and in April and May 1392 John of Gaunt and Thomas of Woodstock attended a two-week conference at Amiens, at which they had been lavishly feasted and entertained. In the years of truce from 1389 there was a burgeoning of informal contact between the two sides. Waleran, count of St Pol, a leading French courtier and Richard's brother-in-law, for example, came to England twice, in 1389 and 1390.[84] At the St Ingelvert tournament in 1390 knights from England, France, the Low Countries and elsewhere gathered to joust, converse and socialize for nearly a month. And in the early to middle years of the decade the knights Louis de Giac and Otto de Granson were active in England recruiting for Philippe de Mézières's crusading order.[85] Relations between England and France had hardly ever been closer.

There is ample evidence that the information which Richard picked up about the French court was a major influence on the evolution of his own courtly style. Sometimes it is possible to pinpoint the connection directly. According to Froissart, for instance, the spur to the holding of the Smithfield tournament in 1390 was the news of Queen Isabella's ceremonious reception a few months earlier at Paris. Isabella, Froissart records, had made a formal entry into Paris – a 'joyeuse entrée'. A magnificent procession had been organized, led by the queen and consisting of the duchesses, countesses and ladies, in due order of precedence. At stages along the route a series of biblical and historical pageants was enacted. At the first there was a scene of the Nativity, at the second a joust between Saladin and the Christians, and at the third a representation of the heavenly kingdom. All the streets of the city were richly decorated, with bunting and trimmings hanging from the windows.[86] The Parisian festivities made an enormous impression on contemporaries. Froissart says that 'Richard and his uncles received the fullest information about them: for some of his knights had been

---

[84] *WC*, 400–2, 450. The Smithfield tournament of 1390 attracted a large attendance from abroad: ibid., 450.

[85] Palmer, *England, France and Christendom*, 188.

[86] Froissart, ii, 398–405. Thomas Johnes misdated this episode to 1399.

present, and they reported all that had passed with the utmost fidelity.'
Then 'in imitation of them, the king ordered great tournaments and
feasts to be held in London. . . . Sixty knights and sixty ladies were to be
present; and the knights were to tilt for two days: that is to say, on the
Sunday after Michaelmas and on the Monday following, in the year
1390.'[87] These tournaments that Richard ordered were the ones shortly
held at Smithfield and commented on by the chroniclers.[88] Very likely
it was the French inspiration behind them that accounts for the
decision to hold a major procession through the city beforehand.[89]
There seems a reasonable possibility that the influence of the Paris
spectacle was a factor in the staging of other public ceremonies of this
time. In 1392 Richard made his own 'joyeuse entrée' into London to
mark the settlement of his quarrel with the Londoners. Pageants were
staged, the conduits decorated, and the streets hung with bunting.[90]
Solemn entries of this sort had been held in England at least twice
before, in 1377 and 1382, but the spur to elaboration, so evident in
1392, may well have been an awareness of the Parisian spectacular of
three years earlier.[91]

   In other areas it is possible to discern English indebtedness to French
courtly practice. There is a powerful case for supposing that the growing emphasis on protocol at the English court owed a great deal to
French inspiration. John II and Charles V had both been highly ceremonious princes, and Charles in particular insisted on a show of
deference from all who approached him. Charles's style appears to have
been a major influence on the Black Prince's court in Aquitaine, which
was similarly ceremonious; and Richard's court in turn owed much to
the prince's.[92] In the later years of the reign the influence of France can
be seen in the elaboration of the language of address to the king. For a
century and more the kings of France had been referred to as princes
and had been addressed as 'your majesty'.[93] Richard and his clerks
would have been well aware of French practice, for they they were in
frequent and regular communication with the French court. There are
also signs of the working of French influence in the very different area
of personal attire. For example, the high collars and long houpelandes

---

[87] Ibid., 477.

[88] *Brut*, ii, 343; *WC*, 450; *HVR*, 132; Froissart, ii, 477–81. There was a diplomatic
purpose to the junketings. Richard was hoping to entice the count of Ostrevant,
one of the participants, into an alliance with England.

[89] J. Stow, *A Survey of London*, ed. C.L. Kingsford (Oxford, 1908), i, 245. S.
Lindenbaum, 'The Smithfield Tournament of 1390', *Journal of Medieval and Renaissance Studies*, xx (1990), 4, posits a Low Countries origin for the procession.

[90] See above, 343.

[91] See above, 342.

[92] See above, 344–5.

[93] Saul, 'Richard II and the Vocabulary of Kingship'.

(gowns), sported by Richard and the nobility in the manuscript of Creton's *Metrical History* (plates 26b,c), were styles which were initially made popular by the Parisian *couturiers*; and it seems on the evidence of illuminations generally that there was probably little to distinguish the fashions worn by the upper classes of England and France at this time.[94] Similarly, in regard to the plastic and decorative arts, the evidence suggests that the main influence on taste was that of France. The statues of kings which Richard commissioned around 1385 for Westminster Hall were inspired by a series made half a century earlier for the great hall of the Louvre.[95] There are also strong indications that the jewellery and hanaps (goblets), of which Richard amassed a considerable collection, were influenced by the styles of the Parisian workshops.[96]

The admiration that Richard felt for things French was thus amply demonstrated by his patronage and taste. It was admiration which turned first into emulation and later into competition. Probably by the mid-1380s, and certainly by the 1390s, Richard and the French were vying with each other in the splendour of their courts. Their rivalry reached its climax at the conference held at Ardres in 1396. The purpose of the conference was to ratify the terms of the marriage alliance negotiated at Paris in March, but the series of encounters between the two courts quickly turned into a game of one-upmanship. The account of an English observer provides a vivid insight into the proceedings.[97] Richard, the observer narrates, opened the bidding by giving presents to the royal uncles – a buckle worth 500 marks to Berry, and a hanap and a ewer worth £200 to Orléans. On the following day, when Richard and Charles met for the first time, more, and more valuable, presents were exchanged. Richard gave his royal brother a gilt cup, worth 700 marks, and a gilt ewer; and Charles replied, more generously, with (again) a gilt cup, a ewer adorned with pearls and other precious stones and a gilt 'nief' (ship), at each end of which was a carving of a tigress looking into a mirror; a little later, when the kings retired to the English king's pavilion, Richard, not to be outdone, added a buckle worth 500 marks to his earlier offerings. On the next day, when there were further meetings between the kings, Richard

---

[94] Harvey, 'The Wilton Diptych', 15 n.7.

[95] *Age of Chivalry. Art in Plantagenet England 1200–1400*, nos 708–9.

[96] J. Cherry, 'Late Fourteenth-century Jewellery: the Inventory of November 1399', *Burlington Magazine*, cxxx (1988), 137–40. The list of areas in which European, and more particularly French, influence on the court is evident can probably be extended. Hilary Carey singles out the case of astrology. Astrology had held no interest for Edward III. Richard II, however, was fascinated by it. His fascination seems to have formed part of a much wider European courtly phenomenon (Carey, *Courting Disaster*, 22; and see above, 324–5).

[97] Meyer, 'L'Entrevue d'Ardres', 209–20. There is a shorter account from the French side in *CRSD*, ii, 457–71.

entered into a new area of competition, that of sartorial attire. Charles,
as the English observer critically observed, wore the same outfit of red
velvet as he had worn on the previous day; Richard, however, had
changed into a magnificent gown of white velvet and red sleeves.[98]
Towards the end of the day the two kings met to exchange yet more
presents. Charles gave Richard two magnificent gilt 'niefs' and a host of
religious tableaux, worth, so it was said, no less than 16,000 francs;
Richard, aware of the need to cap this, replied with a collar of pearls
and other precious stones, worth the huge sum of 5,000 marks. On
Monday, 30 October, the final day of the conference, Richard again
outshone his fellow monarch in the splendour of his attire. According
to the English observer, Charles VI turned out for yet a third time in his
familiar red gown, while Richard donned a magnificent new outfit from
his wardrobe, this one of blue velvet and gold 'molle'. At the end of the
first of the day's meetings Richard took Charles and a select group of
the French lords into his tent, where his new queen was sitting, and
bestowed more gifts on them. He gave the king a hanap, a gilt ewer and,
best of all, a crystal bottle with precious stones set in it, worth 500
marks. Later in the day Charles received Richard in his own pavilion
and replied in kind with gifts of a clasp, a gilt plate loaded with spices
and a horse surmounted by a silver saddle. The two sides then parted.
The contest between them had been closely fought. So far as the
exchange of gifts was concerned, the honours were probably fairly
evenly divided; but in the sartorial stakes Richard emerged the clear
winner.

As the series of encounters at Ardres had shown, Richard, as he grew
older, developed an enormous fondness for personal display. In
common with his father and grandfather, he was an extravagant, luxury-
loving prince. His tastes were expensive and he took a delight in beautiful objects. He owned a large and valuable collection of goldsmiths'
work and plate.[99] He was lavish in his spending on clothing, jewellery,

[98] The observer had commented on the splendour of Richard's attire on the first
day of the conference. Richard had then worn a long gown of red velvet and a hat
loaded with pearls, while around his neck he sported the French king's collar
(presumably the broom-pod collar): ibid., 212. Understandably, in the account of
the St Denis writer there is less emphasis on the splendour of the English king's
attire.

[99] Much of his collection is listed in inventories. Palgrave published some of these
in *Ancient Kalendars and Inventories*, iii, 309–61. But Palgrave overlooked the largest
inventory: E101/411/9. For a discussion of this, see U. Ilg, 'Ein wiederentdecktes
Inventar der Goldschmiedearbeiten Richards II von England und seine Bedeutung
für die Ikonographie des Wiltondiptychons', *Pantheon*, lii (1994), 10–16. Ilg dates
the inventory, on the evidence of the badges and devices mentioned in it, to 1398,
but her argument is not entirely convincing. Several of the lords who are recorded
as donors are referred to by both their pre- and post-1397 titles; and Walden, who

tapestry and *objets d'art* generally:[100] according to the Evesham chronicler, on one occasion he spent no less than £20,000 on a robe lined with precious stones.[101] There was a touch of the spendthrift, even of the profligate, in his character. However, it would be erroneous to suppose that his spending was motivated entirely by personal whim or wanton extravagance. There was an element of political calculation in his conduct. Richard's aim, like that of any prince in these circumstances, was to present a particular set of messages about himself.

The first, and most obvious, message that he sought to convey was that of the reality and effectiveness of his power. In the middle ages it was common for the power of kings to be measured by reference to the size and splendour of their courts. Kings with poor or inadequate courts were considered impotent, while those with rich and impressive ones elicited respect. Appearances mattered in politics. In diplomacy decisions about tactics – even, on occasion, decisions about war and peace – hinged on perceptions of the other side's wealth and potential power. Similarly, in regard to the internal governance of a realm appearances were vital. A king who was poorly attired or accoutred would sooner or later forfeit the allegiance of his subjects – as Henry VI was to find in the next century. In the middle ages, projection of a rich and splendid image implied the possession of power. There can be little doubt that the cultivation of such an image constituted a vital element in Richard's programme for the restoration and reassertion of royal authority.

Allied to this was a second reason for Richard's fondness for display. This was the belief, widespread among contemporaries, that display

---

was archbishop of Canterbury in 1398, is nowhere referred to as such. The inventory appears to be a collation of several earlier ones. Possibly it was put together after 1399 on the orders of Henry IV. One of the most splendid objects that Richard acquired was not listed in any of the inventories. This was a golden altar cross, set with nearly 400 pearls, a few gems and images of the Virgin, St John the Baptist and white harts, all enamelled, and weighing 74 ounces: M. Campbell, 'Gold, Silver and Precious Stones', *English Medieval Industries*, ed. J. Blair and N. Ramsay (London, 1991), 154.

[100] *Ancient Kalendars and Inventories.* For a list of Richard's cloths of Arras (i.e. tapestries) see E101/403/19 no. 67; interestingly, the subjects were mainly historical ones. Towards the end of the reign Richard was buying jewellery from the Mannini of Florence: E403/562, 20 June 1399. In December 1399 Henry IV had to pay an outstanding bill of 500 marks to the Mannini for a gilt collar set with 58 pearls which Richard had ordered: E403/564, 10 Dec.

[101] *HVR*, 156. It is easy to dismiss this figure as a chronicler's exaggeration, but it is worth recalling that in the final years of the reign, of which the chronicler was writing, Richard was wealthy and had the cash to spend on luxuries. In Ireland in 1399 Richard delivered no less than £14,148 6s 0d 'of the king's gold' to the custody of Surrey, the lieutenant. The origin of this sum of money was almost certainly Queen Isabella's dowry (Johnston, 'Richard II and Ireland', 412–13).

bore visible witness to wisdom. The clearest articulation of this view is found in a treatise dedicated to the king and presented to him in about 1395 – Roger Dymock's *Liber contra XII errores et hereses Lollardorum.*[102] Dymock's main aim in writing and presenting the tract was to rebut the main tenets of Lollardy. Most of the arguments, inevitably, were concerned with theology and ecclesiastical organization; but in dealing with the twelfth Lollard error Dymock found himself straying into the area of politics. The twelfth error had maintained that all trades providing luxuries should be abolished because they give rise to sin through 'wast, curiosite and disgysing'. Dymock, in his discussion, took 'disgysing' to mean 'disfiguring by wearing overly elaborate clothes'; and on that basis he launched into a defence of the luxurious dress style at court. Founding his argument on Aristotle's discussion of 'magnificence' or 'the art of spending money lavishly' in the *Nicomachean Ethics*, Dymock argued that spending on display was a virtuous activity. Not only did it buttress the social order by teaching the common people to respect their superiors; it also had a beneficial effect in disarming a king's rivals for power. In support of the latter argument Dymock recounted part of the biblical story of King Solomon and the Queen of Sheba. The Queen of Sheba, having heard of the wisdom for which Solomon was renowned, had resolved to travel to Jerusalem to test it for herself. She travelled with 'a great train, and riches, and camels that carried spices, and an immense quantity of gold and precious stones'. Clearly it was her intention to impress the king with the evidence of her power. 'But when she saw the house that Solomon had built,' wrote Dymock, quoting 2 Chronicles 9: 4–5, 'and the food set on his table, and the apartments of his servants, and the order of his ministers and their apparel . . . she no longer had any spirit in her; and she said to the king, "The report is true, which I heard in my own country, concerning thy words and concerning thy wisdom."' 'Thus it is clear,' Dymock concluded, 'that a king should be in possession of sumptuous and beautiful buildings, excellent meals, and ornate clothing, since it was because of these things that the wisdom of Solomon received great praise.'[103] The story of Solomon and the Queen of Sheba enjoyed considerable favour in the late middle ages with defenders of courtly splendour. In the 1470s it was to be used by the compiler of the *Black Book* of Edward IV as evidence that magnificence implied possession of wisdom.[104] Richard himself would have taken a particular delight in the story because it reinforced his own self-image. His perception of himself

---

[102] *Rogeri Dymmok liber contra XII errores et hereses Lollardorum* (plate 10).

[103] P.J. Eberle, 'The Politics of Courtly Style at the Court of Richard II', *The Spirit of the Court. Selected Proceedings of the Fourth Congress of the International Courtly Literature Society*, ed. G.S. Burgess and R.A. Taylor (Woodbridge, 1985), 173–7.

[104] *The Household of Edward IV*, ed. A.R. Myers (Manchester, 1959), 81.

was as a latter-day Solomon. On the epitaph on his tomb in Westminster Abbey he had himself described as 'prudens et mundus' (prudent and refined), and later as 'animo prudens ut Omerus' (prudent in mind like Homer).[105] In contemporary terms, prudence was the quality of a 'sage'. What Richard was seeking was recognition from contemporaries of his 'sagesse', his wisdom as a ruler; and through the fashioning of a magnificent court on the model of Solomon's, he hoped, in some degree, to achieve this.

Richard's carefully contrived self-image as a 'sage' was almost certainly modelled on that of Charles V of France. Charles, through his patronage of the visual arts and literature, had striven to portray himself as a wise and majestic ruler. He had encouraged the presence of scholars, lawyers and theologians at his court. He had built up a magnificent library. He had used classical and early Christian texts to buttress the intellectual foundations of his rule. And what evidence there is, though it is not much, suggests that his efforts had a significant effect on popular perceptions of his rule. Writers and translators competed with one another in paying tribute to the king's wisdom. Philippe de Mézières had referred to him as 'le sage Salemon'; and Nicholas Oresme and Denis de Foulechat had adapted the words of Ecclesiastes in thanking God for a prince endowed with such wisdom.[106] There can be little doubt that Richard would have known of Charles's initiatives in image-making, for he was perfectly familiar with developments at the French court. There can equally be little doubt, on the evidence of his actions in the 1390s, that he wanted to be seen in similar terms to Charles. The strong emphasis in his epitaph on his 'prudence', his use of 'reason', and 'truthfulness of speech' contrasts sharply with the heroic qualities stressed in Edward III's tomb epitaph of a few years earlier.[107] These same qualities of prudence and reason were ones for which he was praised in a literary compilation that he commissioned

[105] *Royal Commission on Historical Monuments. Westminster Abbey*, 31. A difficulty is raised by the comparison with Homer. According to the *Brut* tradition, the English monarchy was descended from Trojan Aeneas, whom the Greeks, celebrated by Homer, drove from his city. To introduce this comparison is odd, for Homer was on the wrong side. Perhaps the panegyrist simply needed a phrase like 'ut Omerus' to complete the rhyme. But even if the force of the analogy is weakened, there is no need to doubt the emphasis in the epitaph on prudence: Richard remains 'prudent', even if not exactly 'as prudent as Homer'.

[106] Sherman, *Portraits of Charles V*, 82.

[107] Edward, according to his epitaph, was 'a ruler triumphant in war' ('armipotens rexit'); he was the 'unconquered leopard, as powerful in arms as the Maccabees' ('Invictus pardus – bellis pollens Machabeum'): *Royal Commission on Historical Monuments. Westminster Abbey*, 30. Edward's tomb was being prepared in 1386: *CPR 1385–9*, 127. Richard's epitaph – composed as it was in his lifetime – can reliably be taken as a guide to his self-image.

around this time – the collection of tracts in Bodley MS 581. In a prefatory dedication the compiler wrote: 'I have put together this present book of geomancy . . . at the special request of our most excellent lord Richard, the most noble king of the realms of England and France, who governs in sublime fashion not so much by force of arms as by philosophy and the two laws; and indeed he has not declined to taste the sweetness of the fruit of the subtle sciences for the prudent government of himself and his people.'[108] In this dedicatory passage, as in the tomb epitaph, there is a strong emphasis on the king's wisdom and far-sightedness. Richard was pictured not as a warrior prince but as a 'sage'. He was cast in the role of a philosopher king – one who was in tune with the traditions of his people, and could shape them to his visionary ends.

This was a powerful and, in English terms, a highly singular self-image. How far it conformed to reality is another matter. It is doubtful if in its intellectual distinction Richard's court could be considered a match for Charles's. Charles's court was thronged by jurists, scholars and translators of repute; Richard's, somewhat conspicuously, was not. Certainly there were graduate masters and doctors of laws in Richard's service, but these men were chiefly occupied in the work of administration; they were never conceived as an adornment of the court. Richard seems to have had little or no ambition to be a patron of learning.[109] On the other hand, it is clear that Richard's governance was more 'bookish', more legalistic, than his predecessors'. Richard, like Charles, was interested in the law. The book of statutes (St John's College, Cambridge MS A7) is obviously a presentation copy which he commissioned.[110] Richard was familiar with some of the basic concepts of civil law: he made skilful use of the ideas of sovereignty and majesty in elaborating the language of address. The author of the dedication in Bodley MS 581 was probably recognizing his legal expertise when he said that he governed 'by philosophy and the two laws'. It is difficult to be sure how Richard could have picked up his knowledge of the language and concepts of law. Probably he relied on the advice and instruction of legists like Edmund Stafford, his chancellor from 1396. But it is equally likely that he dipped into glossators himself. At the very least, it can be said that his legal interests led him in the direction of reading and study.

Richard's interest in law – and particularly in civil law – was excep-

---

[108] *Four English Political Tracts of the Later Middle Ages*, 22–3. For discussion, see M.J. Bennett, 'The Court of Richard II and the Promotion of Literature', *Chaucer's England. Literature in Historical Context*, ed. B. Hanawalt (Minneapolis, 1992), 16.

[109] The absence of a university in London may help to account for this: at the rival capitals of Paris and Prague major schools lay close to the court.

[110] See above, 237 and plate 12.

tional for an English late medieval ruler, and it marked him out as a man of some originality. All the same, if he elicited respect from contemporaries for wisdom or prudence, it was probably less as a result of his own endeavours than by virtue of his association with the work of others. It was during the middle and later years of his reign that there came together at court a group of littérateurs more gifted and talented than any before seen in England. The names of the leading members of this group are well known. The most distinguished was, of course, Geoffrey Chaucer. Chaucer, a king's esquire since 1367, was a minor office-holder who had served in a number of posts, chiefly in London and Kent, but had never risen high and by the 1380s had chosen to concentrate on writing. His first major work had been the *Boke of the Duchesse* (c.1368–9). A decade later came the *Hous of Fame* (c.1380) and the *Parlement of Foules* (c.1382); from approximately 1387 he was occupied on his greatest work, *The Canterbury Tales*, but this was unfinished at his death.[111] Chaucer's circle of acquaintances at court included a number of other writers of distinction. One of the most talented was the chamber knight, Sir John Clanvow (d. 1391), a Lollard sympathizer who was the author of an elegant lyric called the *Booe of Cupide*, at one time thought to have been written by Chaucer.[112] Another acquaintance – indeed, perhaps, a friend – was someone on the fringes of the court, John Gower. Gower, an independent-minded man with legal connections, wrote extensively in English, Latin and French, his finest work probably being the love poem, the *Confessio Amantis*.[113] Nearer the heart of the court was another chamber knight, Sir John Montagu, later earl of Salisbury, none of whose work has survived, but who received the compliments of no less a critic than Christine de Pisan.[114] Chaucer, Gower, Clanvow and Montagu were the principal 'polite' poets, or 'makers', at court but there were others of courtier rank with a literary penchant. Edward of Aumerle, the duke of

[111] Among the many studies of Chaucer, the most useful are D.S. Brewer, *Chaucer* (London, 3rd edn, 1973); D. Pearsall, *The Life of Geoffrey Chaucer* (Oxford, 1992); and P. Strohm, *Social Chaucer* (Cambridge, Mass., 1989). For Chaucer's discretion in the political struggles of the reign, see S. Sanderlin, 'Chaucer and Ricardian Politics', *Chaucer Review*, xxii (1987), 171–84.

[112] For Clanvow see *The Works of Sir John Clanvow*, ed. Scattergood; McFarlane, *Lancastrian Kings and Lollard Knights*, 162–3, 165–6, 177, 199–206; L. Patterson, 'Court Politics and the Invention of Literature: the Case of Sir John Clanvowe', *Culture and History, 1350–1600. Essays in English Communities, Identities and Writing*, ed. D. Aers (Detroit, 1992), 7–41.

[113] J.H. Fisher, *John Gower. Moral Philosopher and Friend of Chaucer* (London, 1965).

[114] N. Wilkins, 'Music and Poetry at Court: England and France in the Late Middle Ages', *English Court Culture in the Later Middle Ages*, ed. V.J. Scattergood and J.W. Sherborne (London, 1983), 188–9. In 1398 Salisbury and Christine had met: J.C. Laidlaw, 'Christine de Pizan, the Earl of Salisbury and Henry IV', *French Studies*, xxxvi (1982), 129–43.

York's son and a friend of Richard, translated Gaston Febus's *Book of Hunting* into English and added to it some chapters of his own.[115] Other members of the court were distinguished as readers rather than writers. Simon Burley possessed a collection of books that included nine French romances, a *Brut* chronicle, the *Prophecies of Merlin*, and a copy of Giles of Rome's *De Regimine Principum*.[116] Sir Richard Stury, an associate of Burley's, was familiar with the works of Froissart and Eustace Deschamps and was probably the possessor of a copy of the *Roman de la Rose*. Another chamber knight, Sir Lewis Clifford, inherited a book on 'vices and virtues' from the duchess of York.[117] Virtually all the king's inner circle of chamber knights were known to Chaucer and would have been familiar with his works. There was a range of ability and interest in this circle which had no precedent in the fourteenth-century court.

It is perfectly possible – indeed, it is likely – that Richard saw the fame and distinction of his courtly littérateurs as contributing to others' perception of him as a 'sage'. However, it is curiously difficult to identify the contribution, if any, which he himself made to their achievement. Part of the problem lies in the fact that the sources for the king's patronage are disappointingly few. In the small and intimate world of the late medieval court a commission from the king to write or to present a work would almost certainly have been given orally; nothing would have been written down. Possibly, after the work had been completed, the king would have offered a money reward to the author; but, if so, payment would have come from the chamber accounts, which are no longer extant. Thus it is very difficult to form a clear picture of the king's role as a patron. Discussion tends to centre on possibilities and probabilities and rarely, if ever, on certainties.

It is true that a reasonable case can be made out for the king's interest in letters on circumstantial grounds. M.J. Bennett has posited a connection between the breakthrough in the vernacular at court in the mid-1380s and Richard's emergence as a patron.[118] In the mid-1380s, he points out, a number of major vernacular works were produced, among them such Chaucerian masterpieces as *Troilus and Criseyde*, *The Legend of Good Women* and some of *The Canterbury Tales*, Thomas Usk's *Testament of Love* – the work of a poet who had connections with the court – and Clanvow's *Boke of Cupide*. Since Richard was growing to maturity at this time and giving expression to his will in patronage, it is tempting to think that his interest and encouragement had something

---

[115] *The Master of the Game*, ed. W.A. and F. Baillie-Grohman (London, 1904).

[116] Clarke, *Fourteenth Century Studies*, 120–1.

[117] For Stury and Clifford see V.J. Scattergood, 'Literary Culture at the Court of Richard II', *English Court Culture in the Later Middle Ages*, 29–41.

[118] Bennett, 'The Court of Richard II and the Promotion of Literature', 11.

to do with their composition. Dr Bennett has also suggested that a courtly context should be sought for another major poem of the time, *Sir Gawain and the Green Knight*.[119] The subtlety and elegance of *Sir Gawain* mark it out as a product of a cosmopolitan courtly milieu, although the dialect suggests that the author came from Cheshire or the north-west. In the late 1390s Richard spent a great deal of time in the midlands and the north-west, and it is possible that the author was introduced to the court by a local patron, perhaps the controller of the household Sir John Stanley. As Derek Pearsall has suggested, the poem would have made an excellent entertainment for a Christmas or New Year 'house party' for the court.[120]

There is much to be said for circumstantial arguments of this kind. The natural presumption must always be that the character and atmosphere of the court were shaped by the tastes of the king who presided over it. What is known of Richard's character and interests certainly suggests that he could have taken a positive role as patron. Richard was a man of taste and refinement. He was fluent in two languages – English and French – and he probably had at least a superficial knowledge of a third, Latin. He showed a polite interest in letters: he responded favourably when Froissart presented him with a volume of love poems. He commissioned at least two books – the St John's College book of statutes and the collection of tracts of pseudo-science and advice in Bodley MS 581. Moreover, he enjoyed the company of men of a literary disposition: Clanvow was a friend, and Montagu possibly a close friend, of his. If a man can be judged by the company that he keeps, Richard deserves to be seen as a patron of letters.

None the less the difficulty remains: there is little or no evidence directly to connect the poetry of the court with Richard's patronage. The problem cannot be wished out of existence by reference to the loss of sources. Chaucer's career is well documented. The details of his life have been uncovered more effectively than those of any other late fourteenth-century gentleman or littérateur. On the issue rolls of the exchequer there is a host of references to his relations with the king,[121]

---

[119] Ibid., 13–15. M.J. Bennett, '*Sir Gawain and the Green Knight* and the Literary Achievement of the North-west Midlands: the Historical Background', *JMH*, v (1979), 63–85. Idem, *Community, Class and Careerism. Cheshire and Lancashire Society in the Age of Sir Gawain and the Green Knight* (Cambridge, 1983), 231–5. Bennett's arguments find general support in J.M. Bowers, '*Pearl* in its Royal Setting: Ricardian Poetry Revisited', *Studies in the Age of Chaucer*, ed. L.J. Kiser (New Chaucer Society, xvii, Columbus, Ohio, 1995), 111–55.

[120] D. Pearsall, 'The Alliterative Revival: Origins and Social Backgrounds', *Middle English Alliterative Poetry and its Literary Background*, ed. D. Lawton (Cambridge, 1982), 51.

[121] The materials have been gathered in *Chaucer Life-Records*, ed. M.M. Crow and C.C. Olson (Oxford, 1966).

yet not once is there a record of a reward to him as a poet.[122] The problem is exactly the same when approached from the complementary perspective of the internal evidence of the poems. It was normal in the middle ages for a 'courtly maker' to pay tribute to his patron in a dedication. So it might be supposed that if Chaucer had benefited from Richard's patronage, or if he had received a commission for a poem from him, he would have expressly acknowledged as much. Yet he never does; nowhere in Chaucer's works is there a single reference to patronage from the king. It seems likely that only one major poem of the period had its origins in a royal commission. This was Gower's *Confessio Amantis*. In a prologue, which he later replaced, Gower says that he was travelling with the king in the royal barge when Richard asked him to write a poem about love; and, in obedience to the royal will, he did so.[123] It is possible that one slighter poem originated in a royal commission – Chaucer's early 'Tale of Melibee', later used in *The Canterbury Tales*. The poem was based on a French original, and in his rendering of it Chaucer omitted an uncomplimentary reference to boy kings: implying that his own patron was just such a king.[124] But these are just two instances in a large corpus; elsewhere there is nothing. Perhaps it is this absence of reference to the king which explains why no foreign visitors or littérateurs ever paid tribute to Richard's patronage of letters. Writers like Eustace Deschamps, Philippe de Mézières and Christine de Pisan were well aware of the literary distinction of the English court; and Christine once paid tribute to the work of John Montagu. But none of them ever praised Richard for his favour to writers. It is difficult not to mark the contrast with the praise heaped by contemporaries on Charles V.

If Richard's patronage was so insignificant, how is the literary flowering of his court to be explained? A possible solution lies in distinguishing between the king and his court. Courts everywhere and at all times in the middle ages derived their existence from the king. But by the early to mid-fourteenth century, certainly in England, they were also developing an existence apart from the king. The main reason for this is that they were becoming larger and more stable in composition. In

---

[122] It is worth remarking that every time that Chaucer received a reward or mark of favour from the king he had to petition for it. On one occasion, in 1398, he even took the precaution of having the grant enrolled on 13 October, St Edward's Day, to ensure that it had a special place in Richard's memory: S. Ferris, 'Chaucer, Richard II, Henry IV and 13 October', *Chaucer and Middle English Studies in Honour of Rossell Hope Robbins*, ed. B. Rowland (London, 1974), 210–17.

[123] J. Gower, *Confessio Amantis*, ed. R.A. Peck (Toronto, 1980), 494.

[124] *The Works of Geoffrey Chaucer*, 741. Against the possibility of royal sponsorship has to be set the evidence of criticism of the king in the poem: L.S. Johnson, 'Inverse Counsel: Contexts for the *Melibee*', *Studies in Philology*, lxxxvii (1990), 137–55.

the two or three centuries to 1400 most west European courts doubled or nearly trebled in size. The English court went up in number from 150 or so in the reign of Henry I to 400–700 in that of Richard II.[125] At the same time, and partly as a result of this, the institutional aspect of the royal entourage became more complex and highly developed. In the course of the later twelfth and thirteenth centuries a hierarchy of offices and departments had come into existence to minister to the king's needs, each of them employing a settled body of staff. In consequence of this, recognized career patterns began to emerge, and it became common for senior officials to pass from the service of one king to the next. Over time, the effect of these processes was to encourage in the officials and administrators who worked and lived together at court the growth of a group identity. In the early fourteenth century this identity seems to have taken the form of simple group interaction. The mens' families intermarried; they assisted one another; and they promoted each others' careers. Later on, however, as they grew in confidence and self-consciousness, they developed a range of interests in common. The novelty of the 1370s was that among an elite group of chamber and household staff these interests took a strongly literary form. In many ways, this was a less remarkable phenomenon than it appears. The men were all literate, and they probably had a measure of formal education. Moreover, they enjoyed contact with foreign writers of distinction like Eustace Deschamps in France.[126] All the same, aspects of their achievement were distinctly novel. In the first place, it is significant that they chose to write in English. In the course of the fourteenth century English had been making rapid headway as a general vernacular, but among the gentry and aristocracy it was still normal to write, and to use records, in French. The decision of Chaucer and his contemporaries to use English was thus a highly self-conscious one: it distinguished their work very sharply from the courtly literature of the past. A measure of self-consciousness is also to be found in the concerns and preoccupations of the men's poetry. Chaucer and his friends turned their backs on the heroic themes of earlier writers. They chose rather to dwell on issues of a more personal or intimate nature – chiefly the ethical basis of behaviour, the joy and the pain of love and the relationship between the transient and the eternal.[127] These were issues touched on hardly at all in the epics and courtly romances which appear to have formed the staple reading of the royal family and aristocracy at this time. It has been suggested, in the light of this evidence, that Chaucer's and his contemporaries' work found only a

[125] See above, 333.

[126] Scattergood, 'Literary Culture', 39.

[127] Burrow, *Ricardian Poetry*. For Chaucer in particular, see N.E. Saul, 'Chaucer and Gentility', *Chaucer's England. Literature in Historical Context*, 41–55.

limited readership in the aristocracy: that it circulated chiefly among the middle-ranking courtiers of Chaucer's own type.[128] This is very likely to be true. The aristocracy, to judge from their library lists and from the books which they bequeathed in wills, were rarely attracted by the new lyrics: Thomas of Woodstock had a book of 'tretes amoireux et moralitez et de caroll' in French, which may have been a book of lyrics or shorter poems;[129] but Richard, according to a list of 1384, had nothing at all in the new idiom.[130]

Thus it appears that there was a division of taste between the middle-ranking officials at court and the higher aristocracy – the former preferring the newer lyric poetry and the latter the more traditional romances and chivalric works. It is possible that Richard's own tastes extended across the divide, for a man who was known to Chaucer and Clanvow, and was on friendly terms with them, could hardly have been ignorant of their works. But, whether or not this was the case – and it is only a possibility – it is clear that his role as a patron was limited. He commissioned little or no poetry from these men; and his interest in letters was largely polite.[131] Chaucer, Clanvow and Gower found their primary audience in each other and in fellow officials of their type. The court was important to them as a source of employment and livelihood; but it was of little significance as a source of patronage.

The role that literature and learning played in the life of the court and, in particular, in shaping the royal image was of lesser importance than in contemporary France. In France in the later fourteenth century the patronage of letters figured prominently in Valois royal policy. Charles V consciously set out to use literature to buttress his rule. He employed writers who would honour and justify his achievements, and scholars, philosophers and translators thronged his court. Richard's attitude to the cult of letters was very different. There was never any 'official' royal literary programme. Letters were enjoyed by the

---

[128] D. Pearsall, 'The *Troilus* Frontispiece and Chaucer's Audience', *Yearbook of English Studies*, vii (1977), 68–74.

[129] Scattergood, 'Literary Culture', 34–5.

[130] For Richard's books, see E. Rickert, 'Richard II's Books', *The Library*, 4th series, xiii (1933), 144–7; R.S. Loomis, 'The Library of Richard II', *Studies in Language, Literature and Culture of the Middle Ages and Later*, ed. E.B. Atwood and A.A. Hill (Austin, Texas, 1969), 173–8; R.F. Green, 'King Richard II's Books Revisited', *The Library*, xxxi (1976), 235–9. It needs to be stressed that the list was compiled near the beginning of Richard's reign and reflects his predecessor's tastes more than his own. But the acquisitions that Richard made later do not significantly modify the picture: Scattergood, 'Literary Culture', 32–3.

[131] R.F. Green, *Poets and Princepleasers. Literature and the English Court in the Late Middle Ages* (Toronto, 1980), 109, considers the possibility that the comparison of Richard to Homer on the tomb inscription means that he wrote poetry. This is highly unlikely. The context of the passage suggests that reference to the king's prudence and far-sightedness was intended.

courtiers for their own sake – for the joy that they brought or the light that they shed on the human condition – and not for the lustre that they shed on the king. Significantly, there was no court chronicle in England; nor, with the possible exception of Richard Maidstone, were there any official royal panegyrists. Richard, of course, was fully alive to the importance of image-making, but his efforts were directed more to the visual than the literary dimension. It was painting and architecture that attracted him, not letters. In this respect, as in others, he invites comparison with a later ill-fated ruler of eclectic taste and autocratic temperament, Charles I.

Chapter 15

MAJESTY, DOMINION AND MIGHT, 1397–9

In a celebrated passage of his chronicle Thomas Walsingham reports that in 1397 Richard 'began to tyrannize' his people.[1] What occasioned his remark was Richard's demand that summer for 'forced loans'. Richard, Walsingham says, sent agents out with letters under the privy seal specifying the sums which were to be lent but leaving the names of the lenders to be filled in after it had been established who was in a position to lend. This was a course of action that constituted 'tyranny' in the sense of misuse of the subject's property. In a broader sense, however, Richard began to rule tyrannically in 1397. On 10 July he suddenly and without warning ordered the arrest of the three senior Appellants. Warwick was seized at the end of a banquet in London to which he had been lured by a ruse. Gloucester was detained in the small hours of the following morning at his castle of Pleshy. Arundel was persuaded to surrender himself at Reigate by his brother, the archbishop. Two months later in September the three lords were put on trial by appeal in parliament. Arundel was executed, and Warwick sentenced to life imprisonment; Gloucester was already dead by the time he was ordered to appear. Truly, as Walsingham wrote, 'was the kingdom suddenly and unexpectedly thrown into confusion'.[2]

The explanations of contemporaries for Richard's dramatic actions varied widely. Walsingham suggested that Richard decided to act when envoys from Germany who had come to offer him the imperial crown implied that he was not fit to wear it if he could not control his subjects at home.[3] Other writers, less hostile to the king, said that he was motivated by revenge: the Evesham and Kirkstall writers both prefaced their accounts of the arrests with comments to the effect that Richard 'recalled to mind' his earlier humiliations and 'determined to right those injuries and bring the country back under his control'.[4] A third explanation was that Richard was acting to head off a plot. According to the *Traison et Mort* Richard had been apprised that the three senior Appellants and other lords were conspiring against him and decided to

[1] *Chrons. Revolution*, 71.
[2] Ibid.
[3] Ibid., 70–1.
[4] Ibid., 55, 94.

nip their plans in the bud.[5] Walsingham went some way to endorsing this line when he said that Richard had proclaimed that the lords were arrested for 'recent offences which they had committed against the king'.[6] But he never made clear how he reconciled this possibility with his earlier emphasis on the influence of the German electors.

Richard's own explanation of his actions was curiously enigmatic. In a proclamation on 15 July he said that the lords had been arrested 'for the great number of extortions, oppressions, grievances etc. committed against the king and people, and for other offences against the king's majesty, which shall be declared in the next parliament, and not for the assemblies and ridings' occasioned by the uprising of 1387 and 1388.[7] Though the implication of this statement is that the king had acted in response to warnings of a plot, when parliament assembled no evidence of a plot was produced; all the charges related to the events of a decade before. Perhaps the proclamation was intended to be no more than a cover for an exercise in exacting revenge. There are signs that resentment against the Appellants was a powerful element in the king's thinking at the time. At Pleshy he is said to have taunted Gloucester with the remark, 'I'll show you such mercy as you showed to Simon Burley'. And in the following year he afforded a striking indication of how vivid the memory of Radcot Bridge still was to him: he arranged for a sum of no less than 4,000 marks to be stored at Chester and distributed among the Cheshiremen who had fought for de Vere at the battle.[8] On the other hand, there are reasons for doubting whether revenge could have been the only, or even the main, reason for his action, for it leaves unexplained the matter of timing. Richard could have destroyed the Appellants as easily, indeed perhaps more easily, in 1395, when he had just returned from Ireland and had a substantial army behind him. In 1397 he had to recruit a force of Cheshiremen especially to achieve his end. It is possible that the exaction of revenge was more a by-product than a cause of his action.

In personal terms, the most plausible explanation for Richard's coup is that he had experienced a change in his 'psychological environment'. As we have seen, since 1389 Richard had inhabited a fairly stable and secure environment.[9] The friends of his youth had been dispersed, most of them never to return, and he was guided by the advice of a more mature and experienced group of counsellors. He was guaranteed the support of Lancaster; and by skilful management he had been able to achieve his aim of strengthening the crown without provoking dissent

[5] *Traison et Mort*, 117–27.
[6] *Chrons. Revolution*, 73.
[7] *CCR 1396–9*, 208.
[8] *Chrons. Revolution*, 65; E163/6/12; E403/561, 28 Oct., 18 Nov.
[9] See above, 202.

or confrontation. By 1397, however, his world was being disturbed and upset. It has been suggested that the main reason for this was the death of his wife Anne.[10] Anne, however, had died three years before, and the effects of her loss on his behaviour might be expected to have shown themselves well before 1397. An altogether more plausible explanation is that in the early part of the year the political consensus that had prevailed since 1389 began to break down. For the first time for a decade the king was being subjected to outspoken criticism. He felt vulnerable and exposed, and in consequence he reacted unpredictably.

The first signs of renewed tension were felt in the January parliament. The session had been summoned for much the same reason as usual – the king's need for taxation. At the conference at Ardres Richard had committed himself to collaborating with Charles VI in an expedition against the Milanese the following spring. Ostensibly the purpose of the expedition was to promote a compromise solution to the schism, but it seems that the French also had in mind to punish the Milanese for allying with their enemies, the Florentines. The chancellor, doubtless anticipating opposition, concealed Richard's true purpose in his opening address, and his remarks largely centred on the well-being of the Church, the better government of the realm and the need for more justice. Only a couple of days later did it emerge that the king's real object was to mount an expedition. The commons immediately expressed unease. Pointing out that many of the peers were still absent, they asked for a delay before giving a response. Richard grudgingly acquiesced, but sent the chancellor to enquire who had stirred the commons to resist his 'honourable purpose'. The commons protested that no one had moved them to resist his 'purpose', but as he had acceded to the 'voyage' of his own volition they must be excused any responsibility for its financing. Richard then took up the defence of his policy 'with his own mouth'. He argued that it was necessary by common action to demonstrate the reality of the Anglo-French accord, and that he intended to be 'at liberty to order his people to go to the support of his friends, and for that purpose to dispose of his goods as and when he pleased'.[11] It was arranged that the ministers would convene with the commons a week later to receive their reply to these points. In the meantime, however, it emerged that the commons had certain matters which they wanted to lay before him. At his command the chancellor then gave an account of four articles of petition that had

---

[10] Steel, *Richard II*, 203.
[11] *RP*, iii, 337–8.

been tabled. The first complained that the sheriffs and escheators were not men of substance as required by the law, and that they were kept in office beyond their yearly term. The second complained of the unprotected state of the Scottish Marches, the third of the continued distribution of badges ('liveree de signes') to esquires who were non-resident in households, and the fourth and final one of the 'great and excessive' cost of the royal household and of the 'multitude' of bishops and ladies maintained therein.[12]

Richard, perhaps to the commons' surprise, condescended to reply to the articles point by point. The issue of badges he sidestepped by agreeing to re-enact the existing legislation on the subject. Regarding the first charge – about local government – he argued, with justice, that a sheriff could not learn the duties of his office properly in a year and that once he had gained the experience he should use it to the king's advantage. As to the defence of the Marches he said that he would be glad to do anything the lords might suggest, if only the means were provided. To the fourth article, however, he reacted with 'deep grievance'. He said that it was contrary to his 'regality' that subjects should presume to govern the royal household or to criticize persons of quality whom he was pleased to retain in his company; and in trespassing on this area the commons had offended against 'his majesty and the liberty which he had inherited against his ancestors'. He demanded to know who had handed in the offending remonstrance. Shocked by his response, and doubtless skilfully managed by their Speaker Sir John Bushy, the commons quickly complied with his wishes. The next day they appeared before the lords and delivered up the petition with the name of 'Thomas Haxey, clerk'. The lords then declared that whoever engaged in such criticism was guilty of treason, and the commons, abjectly apologizing, handed over the unfortunate clerk, who was sentenced for treason but later pardoned because of his cloth. As an act of grace, and to conciliate the commons, Richard then remitted his request for taxation.[13]

It is evident that Richard had been intensely annoyed by the criticisms in Haxey's petition. Yet, if the complaint in the last clause is set aside, there was little in the petition that was new. The first demand – for the sheriffs' term to be limited – was one that had been made by the commons and the county elites for more than a century. The second complaint – about the unregulated granting of liveries – had a shorter pedigree but had nevertheless been heard in parliament on several occasions in the 1380s and again in 1393. The fourth and final complaint, about the size of the king's household, also touched on an issue

[12] Ibid., 339.
[13] Ibid.

on which the commons had been petitioning since at least the beginning of the reign.[14] The only significant new element in the petition lay in the emphasis on the number of 'bishops and ladies' at the court. Why Haxey or his commons backers chose to highlight this issue is unclear. It is true that the number of bishops with curial connections was increasing sharply in the 1390s, as several of Richard's former chaplains and ministers were promoted to the bench, but it would be difficult to prove that more than a few of them spent the greater part of their time at court.[15] Equally it would be difficult to show that the female aristocratic element at court was increasing significantly. Haxey may have singled out the 'bishops and ladies' for criticism merely because these groups had been targeted by the Appellants in their purge of the household nearly a decade before.[16] If, as is likely, the real cause of his complaint was the rising cost of the household and its burden on the taxpayer, he should have directed his criticism not at the resident but the non-resident element of the household – the king's affinity in the shires. This was the biggest cause of the increase in expenditure. Yet it was not even mentioned in the petition. When there was so little in the document to give offence, it is reasonable to conclude that it was its symbolic rather than actual importance which led Richard to react so strongly. Almost certainly he sensed that the petition presaged a revival of the wounding criticism of the 1380s; and for that reason he decided that it warranted a doctrinaire reassertion of the prerogative.

Richard's reaction to Haxey's petition had distracted attention from the original issue of contention – the king's foreign policy, and in particular his *rapprochement* with Charles VI. By early 1397 the consensus on foreign policy which had prevailed for the greater part of the decade was close to breakdown. Richard's idea of mounting a joint military expedition against Giangaleazzo Visconti with Charles encoun-

---

[14] *RP*, iii, 101; Palmer, 'The Impeachment of Michael de la Pole', 96–101; *SR*, ii, 39–43.

[15] The only significant contemporary comment concerns the bishops of Carlisle and Worcester, respectively Thomas Merks and Tideman of Winchcombe who, according to the Evesham writer, spent nights of orgy with Richard at court (*HVR*, 165). The evidence of Bishop Tideman's register confirms that he was largely absent from the diocese before 1399 (*ex inf.* Professor C. Dyer). Of the other bishops, the only one who can be shown to have been almost wholly absent is Robert Waldeby, who was briefly archbishop of York in 1397 (R.G. Davies, 'Richard II and the Church', 336–7). It is possible that what underlay Haxey's concern was less the actual number of bishops at court than the growing dominance of the episcopal bench by the curialists. Senior figures in the administration like himself could no longer expect the usual preferment. I am grateful to Dr A. McHardy for advice on Haxey.

[16] *WC*, 230. Significantly Joan, Lady Mohun, one of those expelled in 1387, was back in favour in the 1390s. For gifts which Richard gave to her and other ladies see E403/555, 16 May 1397.

tered fierce opposition from the commons, who told him that if he wanted to take an army to Milan he could pay for it himself. Milan had enjoyed good relations with the English and with the English-supported pope, and an expedition against her would have conflicted with English interests. According to Froissart, particular opposition to the scheme was voiced by Gloucester, who had ties with the Milanese through the marriage of his elder brother Lionel to Giangaleazzo's daughter Violanta.[17] Gloucester's opposition to Richard's policy had sharply increased since the making of peace, and Richard was anxious to learn, through visitors to Pleshy, what the duke was thinking. Robert the Hermit, conversing with him in 1395, found him vehemently opposed to friendship with France, and Froissart implies that he reported as much to the king. Other visitors to Pleshy came away with the same impression and, again according to Froissart, Richard's courtiers and friends were pressing the king to take measures against him.[18] Doubtless the courtiers remembered how the duke had treated his own enemies in 1388. In the opinion of the French chroniclers, Gloucester was particularly incensed at the surrender of Brest in June 1397,[19] and the seemingly poor condition in which the town's garrison had returned home. The author of the Traison et Mort says that the duke complained to the king that they had been badly paid.[20] A few weeks later, according to the same writer, the duke in collaboration with Arundel began to hatch a plot against the king. Dining at St Albans with the abbot of St Albans, his godfather, the duke promised to remedy the surrender of Brest, and invited all present to meet him at Arundel in a fortnight's time. At Arundel, the chronicler relates, the duke and his fellow accomplices – Warwick, Derby, Nottingham and the prior of Westminster – prepared a plan to seize the king and his uncles and imprison them for life. The plan, however, was revealed to the king by Nottingham, and shortly afterwards Richard arrested the duke at Pleshy.[21] The chronicler's story is fleshed out with considerable circumstantial detail and has enormous dramatic power; but, as it stands, it cannot be accepted. There is no evidence in other sources that a plot against the king was being hatched in the summer of 1397. It is true that, according to Adam of Usk, Warwick during his trial said that he had been encouraged to join the other lords 'by the duke of Gloucester and by the then abbot of St Albans and by a monk recluse of Westminster', but it is

[17] Froissart, ii, 637. Froissart is in error in saying that Gloucester had a Milanese nephew: Clarence's marriage to Violanta was without issue.
[18] Ibid., 586-7, 610. For evidence of French envoys visiting Gloucester at Pleshy see E101/402/15 m.5.
[19] Brest had been leased to the English in 1378.
[20] Traison et Mort, 117-21.
[21] Ibid., 121-30.

almost certain that this statement refers to the events of 1387 and not to those of ten years later.[22] Significantly the abbot of St Albans who stood godfather to Gloucester was not John Moot, the abbot in 1397, but his predecessor Thomas de la Mare, who had died a year earlier. The chronicler's account therefore conflates the genesis of the Appellant uprising with the events of a decade later. There are grounds for thinking that the chronicler's confusion was deliberate and not accidental. Without supposing a plot to imprison the king he was at a loss to explain Richard's action in arresting Gloucester and the two other lords. His fictional reconstruction both accounted for the arrest and provided a dramatic opening to his account of Richard's tyranny and fall.[23]

But if the reality was that no plot existed in 1397 there was reason to suppose that there might be one. Gloucester and the other senior Appellants had no shortage of grievances against the king. Not only were their views on foreign policy being disregarded and ignored; the three of them had been marginalized politically. Gloucester was of little or no account in the king's counsels, and whatever influence he still exerted he owed to the sponsorship of his uncle, Lancaster. Arundel's power base in the localities was disintegrating as one after another of his retainers deserted him for lords of greater influence.[24] Warwick, so far as can be discerned from the fragmentary evidence, was denied any active role in politics at all.[25] In Warwick's case the frustration bred of exclusion was exacerbated by personal grievances. In June 1397 Richard and his judges had awarded the earl's lordship of Gower in South Wales to his rival Nottingham. The Beauchamp and Mowbray families had been disputing ownership of the lordship for nearly three-quarters of a century. The Beauchamps claimed descent from William, third earl of Warwick, who had held the lordship in the late twelfth century; the Mowbrays staked their claim on the gift which the last de Braose lord of Gower had made to his elder daughter Alina and her first husband John Mowbray (d. 1322). The Mowbrays held the lordship

---

[22] Usk, 161.

[23] J.J.N. Palmer, 'The Authorship, Date and Historical Value of the French Chronicles', 145–81, 398–421, in particular 402–5.

[24] Arundel lost the services of Sir Edward Dallingridge in 1389, Sir William Heron in 1394 and possibly John Cocking by about 1395. He also lost the services of an important retainer, Sir John Fallesle, by death (*House of Commons*, ii, 741; Goodman, *Loyal Conspiracy*, 116, 117–19).

[25] The last references to his involvement come in 1394–5. On 5 December 1394 he lent the king £200, presumably for the Irish expedition. Four months later, while the king was still in Ireland, he was summoned, along with some of the other magnates, to a great council in London (E403/549, 15 Feb., 1 March). Unlike Lancaster, Gloucester and Nottingham he was not involved in any of the foreign policy initiatives of the period.

from 1331, but in 1354 the then earl of Warwick had been awarded possession on the largely arbitrary grounds that his opponent could not prove that his grandfather's alleged gift to his parents had in fact been carried out. Nottingham's hope was that his friendship with Richard II would ensure that that decision was overturned. In 1396 he brought an action for recovery in King's Bench, and in June the following year the judges, influenced as much by political as by purely legal considerations, found in his favour. For Warwick the outcome was doubly disastrous. Not only did he lose his single most valuable lordship (in 1367 it had yielded a profit of over £600 a year); he was ordered to pay to his rival all the issues and profits that he had received from the lordship in the thirteen years since it had come into his inheritance. Moreover, the judgment on Gower was not the only sign of royal displeasure given to the earl. Only six months earlier he had been worsted in another case. In the January parliament the new bishop of Llandaff, John Burghill, had complained that during the recent vacancy of the see Warwick, as a Marcher lord, had appropriated custody of the episcopal manor of Bishopston in Gower and still retained possession of it. Burghill was a former confessor of the king, and the success of his petition was guaranteed. Warwick was fined for his intrusion and contempt of the crown's rights and ordered to restore the manor to the bishop.[26]

By the spring and early summer of 1397, then, Richard's relations with the three former Appellants had become tense. There was an atmosphere of suspicion in the air, and Richard began to feel threatened. Very likely he suspected that Warwick was bound, sooner or later, to take action to restore his lost fortunes; and very likely too he felt the same way about Gloucester. It is easy to see how, in these disturbed and unsettled conditions, he decided to launch a pre-emptive strike. The indications are that he made his decision quickly. Consultation was minimal and probably only his closest associates – men like Rutland and Scrope – were told in advance of what he planned.[27] The three lords themselves were taken by surprise: Gloucester was lying ill at Pleshy; and

[26] For these cases see J.B. Smith and T.B. Pugh, 'The Lordship of Gower and Kilvey', *Glamorgan County History, III: The Middle Ages*, ed. T.B. Pugh (Cardiff, 1971), 249–54; *RP*, iii, 341.

[27] In letters of 13 July Richard said that he had arrested the lords with the assent of Rutland, Kent, Nottingham, Huntingdon, Somerset, Salisbury, Despenser and Scrope: the future counter-Appellants (*CCR 1396–9*, 197). However, it is unclear from this whether those lords were consulted beforehand. R. Mott has argued that Richard procured Lancaster's and York's prior support. He points out that on 6 July, four days before Gloucester's arrest, the king confirmed Lancaster in his position as duke of Aquitaine, and that on the 17th he made grants to York: R.A.K. Mott, 'Richard II and the Crisis of July 1397', *Church and Chronicle in the Middle Ages: Essays presented to John Taylor*, ed. I. Wood and G.A. Loud (London, 1991), 171–2.

Warwick and his countess had only recently received a visit from the queen.[28] The details of Richard's detention of his enemies vary from one chronicle to another. The fullest and most highly coloured account is Walsingham's. According to this version, Richard invited the three lords to a banquet in London on 10 July.[29] Only Warwick attended; Gloucester pleaded ill-health, while Arundel, who earlier in the year had declined to attend a council meeting, stayed in his castle at Reigate. Richard pretended friendship to the earl over dinner, but at the end had him arrested. Almost immediately he gave orders for the arrest of the other two. Archbishop Arundel was induced to persuade his brother the earl to give himself up. Richard himself undertook to bring Gloucester to heel. Walsingham gives a graphic account of the king's journey out to Pleshy. An enormous retinue of peers, household men and London artisans was assembled. The force set out by dead of night – many of them ignorant of where they were going – and arrived at the castle before dawn. Gloucester was roused from his sleep and came down attended by only a few clerks (the rest of his household was on leave).[30] Richard bowed to him, exchanged a few courtesies and then personally arrested him. A small section of the royal retinue entered the castle with the king, inspected the chapel and took breakfast. Richard then ordered the duke to make his farewells; and the latter, after packing his bags, was taken away. He was shortly entrusted to Nottingham's custody at Calais.

Walsingham's narrative of the arrests, though partisan and richly embroidered, is probably accurate in broad outline. Richard had in mind to detain the lords by a ruse; and when that plan misfired he resorted to other means. Confirmation of the archbishop's role in the arrest of his brother is found in other narratives, notably that of the Canterbury-based *Eulogium* writer, while it is evident from the record sources that the three lords were soon in custody.[31] Public reaction to

---

Against this suggestion must be set the evidence of the letters of 15 July in which Richard said that Gloucester had been arrested with the assent of the lords previously named, *and* Lancaster, York and Derby 'after they repaired to the king's person' (*CPR 1396–9*, 241). Thus it is possible that the two uncles were only told after the event.

[28] *Chrons. Revolution*, 71; A.F.J. Sinclair, 'The Beauchamp Earls of Warwick in the Later Middle Ages' (University of London Ph.D thesis, 1987), 230. Gloucester was receiving grants from the king almost to the time of his arrest: R.A.K. Mott, 'Richard II's Relations with the Magnates, 1396–9' (University of Leeds Ph.D. thesis, 1971), 20.

[29] *Annales*, 201–6, extracts of which are in *Chrons. Revolution*, 71–3. The *Traison et Mort* says that the banquet was held at Cold Harbour, Huntingdon's house in Lombard Street (*Traison et Mort*, 127).

[30] A further indication that no hostile action by the king was anticipated.

[31] *Eulogium*, 371–2; *Annales*, 203; *CCR 1396–9*, 172.

the king's action is difficult to gauge, but there are indications that there was a mood of alarm.[32] Richard offered reassurance to the lords' retainers and dependants. On 15 July he ordered the sheriffs to proclaim that the lords had been arrested for new offences and not for their role in 1387-8, and that those who had ridden with them in that year had no cause for alarm.[33] At the same time he took a series of measures for his own security. On 13 July an order was sent to the sheriff of Cheshire to recruit 2,000 archers as a matter of priority and with all possible haste.[34] A month later, on 20 August, further orders were sent to the sheriffs to arrange for all those in the king's pay to array themselves and assemble at Kingston upon Thames on 15 September.[35] In the meantime a session of the king's council was convened at Nottingham to decide how the three lords should be prosecuted. On the advice of the king's friends it was decided to act on Gloucester's own precedent and to proceed by means of a parliamentary appeal. Writs were issued for parliament to meet at Westminster on 17 September. In the Ricardian camp there was a mood of expectancy and anticipation.[36] The stage was set for Richard's exaction of revenge on his former opponents.

The parliament that met on St Lambert's Day 1397 was by any standard an exceptional assembly. Even its setting was bizarre. Westminster Hall, under reconstruction at the time, could not be used, so a temporary wooden structure had to be erected in the palace yard.[37] Contrary to what had become usual practice the magnates were allowed to bring their retinues with them; and Richard himself assembled a force of over 300 Cheshire archers to overawe the gathering: he had the men flanking the open-sided building.[38] Predictably the commons were in a compliant mood. In membership and outlook they differed sharply from their predecessors – so sharply that it was suggested that the elections of

---

[32] This is suggested by a letter from Abbot Colchester to the prior of Westminster dated only 31 August (no year). The abbot advised his correspondent to act with restraint at the present troubled time. Pilgrimages and journeys abroad were to be avoided; the monks, he advised, should be enjoined to process every fourth day round the abbey precincts and every sixth day through the town of Westminster to pray for the common good of the king and realm. The day and the month of the letter suggests that it may belong to 1397 (WAM 6221).

[33] *CCR 1396-9*, 208.

[34] CHES 2/70 m.7d.

[35] *CCR 1396-9*, 210.

[36] *Annales*, 207. For the mood of the king's supporters, see the Kirkstall writer in *Chrons. Revolution*, 96.

[37] *Annales*, 209; *Eulogium*, 373.

[38] *Foed.*, viii, 14; Usk, 154.

the previous month had been rigged. Arundel himself, facing his accusers, famously asked, 'Where are the faithful commons?'[39] Certainly few who had been there in the January assembly were there nine months later. No fewer than 86 out of the 203 members had never been in the house before; and as many as twenty-one constituencies (six of them shires) returned *two* individuals with no previous parliamentary experience. In the deposition articles two years later it was alleged that Richard had manipulated parliamentary representation by appointing creatures of his as sheriffs; but it is doubtful if this could have been the case. The sheriffs who made the returns in September were men who had been appointed in the previous year, before Richard embarked on the widespread reshaping of local government. The most likely explanation for the changed complexion of the assembly is that experienced parliamentarians were reluctant to put themselves forward, knowing that the three lords had been arrested and that a political crisis was brewing. In several constituencies the normal pattern of representation was disrupted. In Wiltshire, for example, the newly appointed sheriff, Richard Mawarden, one of the king's retainers, returned a councillor, Sir Henry Green, in company with a chamber knight, Sir Thomas Blount, neither of whom had shown any previous interest in the county's affairs. When so many of the MPs were newcomers, or lacking in parliamentary experience, it was easy for those with curial connections to provide the lead. Numerically those of a curial background formed a sizeable minority. There were 25 fee'd royal retainers or servants, among them Bagot and Green, 22 associates of the new appellants (Nottingham, Huntingdon, Salisbury, Rutland, Despenser, Scrope and Kent) and no fewer than 85 who held crown offices of some sort.[40] The Speaker himself, Sir John Bushy, was of course one of the king's most active and trusted councillors.[41] With so many experienced managers in the house, the king had little reason to fear the emergence of opposition to his will.

The sermon at the opening of the session was preached by the new chancellor, Bishop Stafford of Exeter; in it he set out the doctrines which were henceforth to inform the king's governance. Taking as his theme Ezekiel 37: 22, 'There shall be one king over them all', he said that 'for the realm to be well governed, three things were needed: first, the king should be powerful enough to govern; secondly, his laws should be properly executed; and thirdly, his subjects should be duly obedient'. These themes he then treated at greater length. If the king

---

[39] *Chrons. Revolution*, 59.

[40] For an analysis of the composition of this parliament see *House of Commons*, i, Appendix C3.

[41] J.S. Roskell, 'Sir John Bussy of Hougham', Roskell, *Parliament and Politics*, ii, 45–63.

were to be powerful enough to govern, he must be in full possession of
'his regalities, prerogatives and other rights', and it was the duty of the
estates to report if these were encroached upon or under attack. Likewise, if his laws were to be duly executed and enforced, they needed to
be backed with the appropriate punishment; and the estates should
advise him if this was not the case. The king was naturally anxious that
his subjects should be in full possession of their liberties and franchises,
as they had been under his ancestors; but he was also aware of the many
misdeeds and offences which were daily being committed to their peril.
To strengthen his subjects in their goodwill towards him, he wanted to
afford them a demonstration of his affection. Accordingly he would
grant a general pardon 'to all his lieges . . . except for fifty persons
whom it would please the king to name and those who were to be
impeached in the present parliament'.[42] Stafford's was an uncompromising and authoritarian address, loftier in tone than anything the
commons had heard for a decade and a half. What caused his audience
particular alarm was the exception of fifty individuals from the terms of
the general pardon. The Speaker at the commons' behest urged
Richard to disclose the names of these fifty, but Richard consistently
refused to do so. By keeping the names to himself he acquired a new
power over his subjects: men with guilty consciences might be persuaded to come forward and to identify themselves by seeking individual pardons; and in the next twelve months a good number of them
did so. By September 1398 over 500 individual pardons had been
enrolled on a supplementary patent roll.[43] Richard had succeeded in
discovering who his enemies were; and he had enabled the exchequer
to profit handsomely from their insecurity.[44]

On the next day Bushy was elected Speaker, and the real business of
parliament began – the legalizing of Richard's revolution. Bushy first
drew the king's attention to the derogatory council of 1386, 'appointed
when the present archbishop was chancellor'. The document establishing the council was produced, read and repealed by acclamation as
having been extorted by force; and the repeal was then extended to the
pardons granted to Gloucester, Arundel and Warwick in 1388. With the
revocation of the pardons Archbishop Arundel rose to make an objection, but Richard put him off to the next day, and two days later warned
him not to appear at all. On 20 September, in his absence, the clergy
appointed a general proctor to act on their behalf and immediately
afterwards Bushy, in the name of the commons, impeached him of
treason for his share in the events of 1386-8. It was useless for Arundel

[42] *RP*, iii, 347; Usk, 152.
[43] C67/30.
[44] Barron, 'The Tyranny of Richard II', 7-9. Beneficiaries had to pay for individual
pardons. It is hard to say how much money was raised in all.

to deny his involvement, and on the 25th he was condemned to exile and forfeiture.[45] Roger Walden, the king's treasurer, was appointed to the see of Canterbury in his place.

On Friday, the day after the archbishop's first appearance, the new appellants formally appealed Gloucester, Arundel and Warwick of treason in deliberate imitation of the procedure of the Merciless Parliament. Arundel's trial immediately followed. It provided the occasion for a brilliant display of repartee. Lancaster, presiding as high steward, told the earl, 'Your pardon is revoked, traitor.' 'Truly, you lie,' replied the earl; 'never was I a traitor.' 'Why in that case did you seek a pardon?' asked the duke. 'To silence the tongues of my enemies, of whom you are one,' retorted the earl. 'Answer the appeal,' interjected the king. 'I see it all now,' said the earl. 'You who accuse me, you are all liars. I claim the benefit of my pardon, which you granted when you were of full age.' 'I granted it provided it were not to my prejudice,' replied the king. Whereupon Lancaster declared, 'The pardon is worthless'; and Bushy added, 'The pardon has been revoked by the king, the lords and by us, the faithful commons'; to which Arundel retorted 'Where are the faithful commons?'[46] Arundel undoubtedly got the better of the exchanges, but his eloquence was of no avail. Lancaster declared him guilty of treason, and the same day he was taken to Tower Hill and beheaded.[47]

Warwick's turn came on Friday, the 28th. The earl, who may have been ill by now, cut a pathetic figure. 'Like a wretched old woman', in Usk's words, he broke down, and confessed his guilt, 'sobbing and whining'. Richard, taking pity on him, commuted the initial sentence of death and banished him for life to the Isle of Man.[48] There was then only one defendant to be dealt with, the most important of all – Gloucester. On 21 September a writ was issued to Nottingham as captain of Calais ordering him to produce the duke at Westminster, but three days later the earl returned that his prisoner was already dead. Gloucester was condemned as a notorious traitor none the less, and on

[45] RP, iii, 351; Usk, 155–6. For Richard's denunciation of the archbishop after he left the country see A.L. Brown, 'The Latin Letters in MS. All Souls College 182', EHR, lxxxvii (1972), 565–73.

[46] The best accounts of the trial are those of Adam of Usk and the Monk of Evesham (Usk, 157–8; Chrons. Revolution, 58–9). Both draw on a third account, now lost, which was probably the work of an eyewitness. For the relationship between the sources, see C. Given-Wilson, 'Adam Usk, the Monk of Evesham and the Parliament of 1397–8', HR, lxvi (1993), 329–35.

[47] Gaunt and Arundel, of course, had long been at odds: see above, 242. Walsingham, possibly drawing on a contemporary tract, reports that Arundel was soon venerated as a martyr and that pilgrimages were made to his tomb (Annales, 218–19).

[48] Usk, 161; RP, iii, 379–80.

the next day a highly abbreviated version of a confession by him was produced to justify the sentence. Considerable confusion seems to have existed as to the date and circumstances of the duke's death. As early as the middle of August rumours were circulating in England of his demise. However, on 17 August one of the king's justices, Sir William Rickhill, was sent to Calais to converse with the duke, and on 8 September he received the confession from him. It was only two and a half years later, in Henry IV's first parliament, that the full story of how the duke met his end emerged. A former valet of Nottingham's, by the name of John Hall, was charged with his murder. In a confession, read out in parliament and recorded on the parliament roll, Hall described how on royal orders he and half a dozen accomplices had dragged the duke from his cell and suffocated him under a featherbed in the back room of a Calais hostel. The deed appears to have been committed on the night of 8 September, but there is a possibility that Richard had ordered summary dispatch much earlier. In spring 1398 Nottingham was to tell Bagot that he had kept Gloucester alive for 'three weeks or more' after first receiving the order from the king to be rid of him. It was presumably the king's belief that Gloucester was dead in August that accounts for the rumours to that effect that were circulating at that time. Richard had wanted to avoid the duke's appearance in parliament at all costs: not only might his eloquence make a favourable impression on his listeners; there was the danger that his brother, the steward, might refuse to pass judgment on him. Once it was learned that he was still alive, therefore, a second order was sent to Calais, and Hall and his accomplices did their worst.[49]

When the trials and proscriptions were over, one further task was accomplished in the session: that of ensuring the permanence of the new political order. 'At the request of the commons', as the parliament roll says, two complementary statutes were passed to bring this about. The male issue of the defendants were declared incapable of sitting in parliament or council; and all future peers were required to swear to maintain the Acts of the session before receiving livery of their temporalities or estates. When these measures were passed, on 30 September, the estates made their way to Westminster Abbey where, before the shrine of St Edward the Confessor, they swore to observe in perpetuity the laws and judgments passed in the parliament, saving only to the king his regality. Sir Thomas Percy took the same oath on behalf of the

---

[49] For Gloucester's death see J. Tait, 'Did Richard II Murder the Duke of Gloucester?', *Historical Essays by Members of the Owens College, Manchester*, ed. T.F. Tout and J. Tait (Manchester, 1902), 193–216; A.E. Stamp, 'Richard II and the Death of the Duke of Gloucester', *EHR*, xxxviii (1923), 249–51; R.L. Atkinson, 'Richard II and the Death of the Duke of Gloucester', ibid., 563–4; *Chrons. Revolution*, 14–15, 79–83, 211–12, 219–23.

clergy, and the bishops pronounced excommunication on all who might presume to reverse the parliament's proceedings.[50] Later on the same day the customary banquet was held; and parliament was then adjourned to meet again on 27 January 1398 at Shrewsbury.

It is not immediately apparent why Richard found it necessary to defer some of the business in hand to a second session away from London. One possibility is that he had been distracted by the unravelling of the settlement in Ireland. Relations between the Dublin administration and the native Irish had deteriorated since his visit in 1394, and in July he had announced his intention of making a personal visit to the province again. If he wanted to combine the dispatch of parliamentary business with the preparation of a new expedition, Shrewsbury was as good a place at which to do so as any.[51] A second, and perhaps a more likely, explanation is that policy differences had begun to emerge within the courtier elite. Among the group of eight major lords who had been associated in the coup against the former Appellants there were two whose attitude to the proceedings in parliament must have been highly ambivalent. These were the earls of Derby and Nottingham, the two junior Appellants of 1388. Derby and Nottingham had a clear interest in limiting the scale of the counter-revolution for fear of their own role in events ten years before being called into question. Nottingham for one openly counselled caution on the king. In the sentence passed on him in the following year Richard said that 'both in public and in private' the earl had argued against annulling the Acts of the parliament of 1388, and that he had even 'maintained the validity of the wicked and unlawful appeal'.[52] In the face of this opposition from a leading member of the elite Richard probably deemed it expedient to interrupt proceedings temporarily to seek a breathing space. Even in January, however, when the estates reassembled, his collaborators were far from united. A statute repealing the judgments and Acts of the Merciless Parliament was proposed and approved on the very first day of the session; but only seven of the eight new appellants put their names to it: Nottingham did not. It must have been apparent by now to Richard that he was running into difficulties in his relationship with Nottingham. In the course of the session these were compounded

---

[50] *RP*, iii, 352, 355–6.

[51] On 23 July the keeper of the wardrobe was ordered to disburse wages to the mariners engaged for the king's Irish expedition ('pro viagio domini Regis in propria persona sua versus Hiberniam'): E403/555, 23 July; *CCR 1396–9*, 154, 157; and see also above, 288. Richard did not in the end go to Ireland until 1399. There is no truth in the *Traison's* suggestion that Shrewsbury was chosen to punish the pride of the Londoners (*Traison et Mort*, 140).

[52] *Chrons. Revolution*, 91.

when a quarrel broke out between the earl and his former ally Derby.[53] Probably to save himself from further embarrassment Richard halted the proceedings of the parliament after only four days. But in the space of that period he was able to achieve virtually all of the objectives that he had set himself. Arraignments were brought against two more of his enemies – John, Lord Cobham, a member of the council of 1386, and Sir Thomas Mortimer, who had killed Thomas Molineux, one of the leaders of de Vere's forces, at Radcot Bridge.[54] A new definition of treason was also approved. And, perhaps most useful of all, a subsidy of unprecedented generosity was conceded by the commons: the king was granted the wool and leather duties for life. On the last day a parliamentary committee was appointed to determine certain outstanding petitions. The king then thanked the estates for their co-operation, and on 31 January the session was brought to a close.[55]

Despite the difficulties that he had encountered at Shrewsbury Richard had enjoyed a remarkably easy triumph over his opponents. Gloucester and his former allies were by 1397 no longer in a position to mount a challenge to him. Gloucester himself had forfeited the commons' goodwill by allowing himself to become associated with the policy of *rapprochement* with France; Arundel had given offence by his tactless behaviour in parliament and elsewhere; and Warwick, who was by now probably ill, had ceased to be an important, or at least an active, force in politics. Richard, on the other hand, was in a stronger position than he had been in for some years. Many of the younger nobility identified with his general objectives, and senior figures like York and Lancaster had lent him significant support. There was little or no danger that he would encounter opposition to his plans.

In the wake of his triumph Richard embarked on a major remodelling of the peerage. His first and most immediate aim was probably to honour and reward his chief supporters. But it was almost certainly a subsidiary objective to enhance the glory and renown of the crown. As he said in his patents of ennoblement, he saw the role of the lords as being to 'reinforce and fortify the king's sceptre'.[56] On 29 September,

---

[53] See below, 395–401.

[54] Gillespie, 'Thomas Mortimer and Thomas Molineux', 161–73. There is evidence that a third knight was proceeded against – Sir John Cheyne of Beckford (Gloucs.), a king's knight who had earlier been associated with Thomas of Woodstock: see, on this, J.S. Roskell, 'Sir John Cheyne of Beckford', *Parliament and Politics in Late Medieval England* (3 vols, London, 1981–3), ii, 79–80.

[55] For the enactments of the Shrewsbury session, see *RP*, iii, 355, 356–69; *Chrons. Revolution*, 91; J.G. Edwards, 'The Parliamentary Committee of 1398', *EHR*, xl (1925), 321–33, repr. in *Historical Studies of the English Parliament*, I, ed. E.B. Fryde and E. Miller (Cambridge, 1970), 316–28.

[56] *RP*, iii, 355; for Richard's attitude to nobility see above, 248.

the final day of the parliamentary session at Westminster, there was an unprecedented distribution of titles. Three of the king's closest allies were given earldoms. William Scrope became earl of Wiltshire, Thomas Percy, earl of Worcester, and Thomas, Lord Despenser, earl of Gloucester. Others already ennobled were raised to higher dignities in the peerage. Nottingham became duke of Norfolk, Rutland duke of Aumerle, Huntingdon duke of Exeter, Derby duke of Hereford, and Kent duke of Surrey. At the same time John Beaufort, earl of Somerset, Gaunt's eldest son by Katherine Swynford, became marquess of Dorset. Others outside the closely knit circle of the court were also included in the distribution of honours. Ralph Neville, a northern lord and a long-standing rival of the Percies, was made earl of Westmorland; and Nottingham's mother Margaret, countess of Norfolk, was granted the title of duchess in her own right.[57] Never before had so many honours been dispensed at once, and Walsingham referred disparagingly to those raised to the highest dignity as the 'duketti'.[58] But the titles that Richard bestowed were by no means empty ones. All the new dukes or earls were endowed with forfeited lands of the Appellants to a level appropriate to their dignity. Huntingdon was given Reigate and the bulk of Arundel's Sussex properties, and Percy the bulk of the same earl's Welsh Marcher property; Kent received Warwick castle and extensive Beauchamp properties in Worcestershire, and Despenser Elmley Castle, not far from his own lordship of Tewkesbury, along with other Beauchamp properties. Rutland was granted Gloucester's great lordship of Burstwick-in-Holderness, and York the duke's Norfolk estates.[59]

In the allocation of these lands it was Richard's policy to divide up the inheritances in such a way that they ceased to exist as social and economic units. The Arundel estates, for example, were split no fewer than four ways, between Huntingdon, Nottingham, York and Percy. At the same time, however, it was also the king's policy to ensure that the beneficiaries themselves had relatively compact blocks that allowed them to bear the rule over their respective 'countries'. Despenser, for example, endowed with his extensive Beauchamp lands, emerged as the dominant influence in the Severn valley counties. Kent, taking over the

---

[57] *RP*, iii, 355.

[58] *Annales*, 223. But the creations were consistent with Richard's policy of raising to ducal status those of royal blood.

[59] *CPR 1396–9*, 200–10, 213–16, 220, 280–1. It is striking that in this redistribution of estates Nottingham, or Norfolk as he had now become, gained relatively few manors and lordships in areas where he was already strong. In Warwickshire, for example, where he was a major landholder, he conspicuously failed to get the lordship of Warwick itself, which went to Surrey. A grant of the Warwick lordship would have consolidated his hold on the county; but his only gains in the area were outlying rural manors like Brailes, Tanworth and Berkswell. There may be evidence here that Richard was already distrusting the earl.

Beauchamp *caput honoris* of Warwick, emerged as the controlling influence in Warwickshire. The territorially based lords who had previously been influential in these counties found themselves to a large degree sidelined. The Courtenays were forced to cede precedence in Devon and the west country to Exeter, and the Berkeleys to do likewise in Gloucestershire to the Despensers.[60] In the space of little more than a year the political geography of the realm had been completely reshaped. Old families had been eclipsed by the rise of new, and long-established networks of influence had been upset and replaced. Out of the turmoil and disruption of this brief period emerged the outlines of a new tenurial order.

The political and territorial revolution which Richard unleashed in 1397 formed part of a much wider strategy of subordinating the local structures of power to those of the centre. Another, and scarcely less vital, element in it was the strengthening of the king's control over local government. By comparison with other European rulers, the English king already exercised considerable control over the work of his officials in the localities. The sheriff was subject to a rigorous process of accounting at the exchequer, while other officials such as the justices of the peace were liable to have their activities reviewed by the central courts. Occasionally, in addition, justices of 'trailbaston' were appointed to make visitations of specific regions or shires. This was a system of control ideally suited to supervising the performance by the local officials of their everyday duties. It was altogether less effective, however, in guaranteeing those officials' loyalty or obedience to the king. In the conditions of late 1397 and 1398 it was chiefly the matter of loyalty that was of concern to the king: he needed to know that the oaths he required his subjects to take would be exacted, and that unpopular or controversial orders would be carried out; and the only way of ensuring this was to see that men of proven loyalty and commitment were given office. From autumn 1397, therefore, Richard began to 'politicize' the ranks of local officialdom. As articles 13 and 18 of the deposition articles were to allege, the king appointed sheriffs 'who were either his familiars or who, so he knew, would be entirely amenable to his will . . . and caused them to retain their offices, some for two years, some for three, contrary to the letter and spirit of the statute'.[61] At least eleven of the twenty-seven sheriffs who were appointed in November 1397 had connections with the household or royal affinity. These were John Worship (Beds), John Golafre (Berks), Andrew Newport

---

[60] For Devon see Cherry, 'The Crown and the Political Community', 161–2; and for Gloucestershire, R. Hanna, 'Sir Thomas Berkeley and his Patronage', *Speculum*, lxiv (1989), 889–91; N.E. Saul, *Knights and Esquires. The Gloucestershire Gentry in the Fourteenth Century* (Oxford, 1981), 80, 113. See also above, 244.

[61] *Chrons. Revolution*, 176–7.

(Cambs), John Colshull (Cornwall), Thomas Clanvow (Heref), Henry Retford (Lincs), John Mulsho (Northants), Adam Peshale (Salop), William Walsall (Staffs), Richard Mawarden (Wilts), and John de Eynsford (Warks).[62] In counties for which no suitable royal servant could be found a retainer of a courtier magnate was named. In Gloucestershire John Brouning, a retainer of the new earl of Gloucester, was appointed; in Norfolk and Suffolk William Rees, a retainer of the earl marshal; and in Rutland Thomas Oudeby, an associate of Lord Zouche.[63] Simultaneously Richard filled the lesser offices and commissions such as those of the bench according to similar principles: household men were appointed where they were available, and dependable retainers where they were not. Thus on the Herefordshire peace commission, a body with a total membership of ten, there were two courtier magnates, two justices and three knights with who had connections with the household.[64] By the end of 1397 the government of counties as diverse as Gloucester and Norfolk, Warwick and Devon had been almost wholly assimilated to the structures and political imperatives of the courtier-led regime.

With the destruction of the former Appellants and the dramatic reassertion of the prerogative Richard brought to fulfilment the most deeply held aspirations of his kingship. Nearly a decade after the Merciless Parliament he could feel that he had at last wiped away the stains of his earlier humiliation. Given the importance that he had always attached to the sacred nature of his office, it is likely that he saw the recovery of his rights as an obligation laid on him by God. The religious dimension to his outlook is highlighted by the symbolism of the Wilton Diptych, which was probably commissioned around this time.[65] Richard, in the left-hand panel, is shown delivering to the Virgin a banner of the resurrection, in the orb of which is depicted his kingdom, the Virgin's

---

[62] Tout, *Chapters*, iv, 43–4; *House of Commons*, ii, 633–5; iii, 804–6; iv, 201–2. There is an element of doubt concerning John de Eynsford because more than one man of that name was active in the 1390s. It seems, however, that the John who was sheriff of Warwickshire was the king's knight because the latter is known to have died by early 1399 at the latest, and a new sheriff for the county was appointed on 17 November 1398 (*CPR 1391–6*, 336; *CCR 1396–9*, 468; *CPR 1396–9*, 278). Eynsford's successor, Aymer Lichfield, was a thoroughgoing royalist (*House of Commons*, iii, 601–2).

[63] *CFR 1391–9*, 221, 240; *House of Commons*, ii, 389–92; iii, 884–5; iv, 187–9. Saul, *Knights and Esquires*, 113, 139.

[64] *CPR 1396–9*, 227. The courtier magnates were Lancaster and Norfolk, the two justices Hill and Huls, and the three knights with royal connections Walter Devereux, Robert Whitney and Thomas Clanvow.

[65] See above, 304–5.

dowry. The banner is then passed to the Christ Child, who is in the act of returning it to Richard, to enable him to rule under the Virgin's protection. The meaning of the complex symbolism of the Diptych seems fairly clear. Just as Christ had brought hope of renewal to the world, so Richard was to do likewise to his kingdom. He was a ruler who had been redeemed by God's saving grace. Received into the Virgin's protection, and blessed by the Christ Child, he could rededicate himself to his task and begin his reign anew.

The association between the Almighty and Richard's kingship was a theme frequently emphasized in the literary and artistic imagery of the court in the later years of the reign. In paintings like the Diptych (plate 13) and the 'coronation' portrait in Westminster Abbey (plate 21) Richard's person appears to undergo a virtual apotheosis. In the abbey portrait, a remarkable and audacious work, Richard is shown frontally, as in an iconic close-up of the face of Christ – a position which, it is reasonable to suppose, was intended to suggest a conception of the king in Christ-like terms.[66] Richard himself in letters for a wider audience employed phrases or formulae that suggested an association between his royal authority and the authority delegated by God. In a letter to Albert, count of Holland, written in 1398, Richard described those who resisted his royal authority as 'contriving wickedness against King Christ the Lord'.[67] The Christological strain so evident in this and in other letters bears witness to the role that piety played in shaping the character of the king's political vision.[68] Nevertheless it should not be supposed that piety, however intensely felt, was the only, or even the chief, influence on the ultimate working out of that vision. Like other contemporary rulers, notably the princes of France, Richard readily resorted to the ideas of the legists and political theorists to buttress his authority.[69] Two ideas in particular seem to have had a major influence on his thought in 1397. The first was the belief that the subjects of a ruler had an obligation of obedience to him, and the second that he was establishing 'peace' in a united realm.

The notion that the subjects of a king had a binding obligation to obey him was one that had been circulating at Richard's court for some time by the 1390s. The origins of the idea in its late medieval form were

[66] The date of the abbey portrait is uncertain, but there are strong grounds for associating it with a commission of December 1395: *Age of Chivalry*, no. 713. Other mid- to late fourteenth-century portraits of secular subjects had shown the sitter in profile: see Meiss, *French Painting in the Time of Jean de Berry*, ii, plates 505-8.

[67] Harvey, 'The Wilton Diptych', Appendix II.

[68] See above, 238. It is worth noting that Christological imagery figured prominently in the triumph that marked Richard's reconciliation with the Londoners in 1392: see Kipling, 'Richard II's "Sumptuous Pageants"', 83-103.

[69] See above, 248-51.

to be found in Giles of Rome's *De Regimine Principum* (*c*.1277–9). Giles had stressed the clear obligation on a ruler's subjects to obey him. Obedience, he said, was the source from which the values of the commonwealth were derived, and honour, safety and abundance of prosperity were the rewards of an obedient citizenry.[70] These were arguments which powerfully attracted the Black Prince and his servants, chief among them Simon Burley, who owned a copy of Giles's treatise, and Michael de la Pole. Significantly it was the latter – Richard's chancellor between 1383 and 1386 – who provided the first, and the clearest, statement in England of the meaning of obedience when, addressing parliament in 1383, he said that proper obedience to the king was 'the sole foundation of all peace and quiet in the realm'.[71] De la Pole's speech was made in the aftermath of the Great Revolt and with the events of that upheaval in mind; a decade later, in the aftermath of another crisis – the Appellants' coup – other officers spoke in a similar vein. Archbishop Arundel, as chancellor, addressing parliament in 1395, declared that subjects had a general obligation 'to honour, cherish and obey the king, and to employ all their power in his service'.[72] Two years later, in the parliament of September 1397 at which Richard's *coup d'état* was ratified, Arundel's successor Bishop Stafford declared that in a well-governed realm 'every subject should be duly obedient to the king and his laws'.[73] An interesting parallel to these ideas is found in a contemporary text, the 'De Quadripartita Regis Specie', which was presented to Richard in 1391 or 1392. Though the greater part of the tract is unoriginal, there is a striking passage in which the writer says that nothing is more likely to force a king to impose penalties on his subjects than an act of disobedience.[74] This view corresponded very closely to Richard's own. Richard, a man with a highly developed sense of regality, saw disobedience as an act of rebellion. In a letter to Manuel Paleologus, the Byzantine emperor, written in 1398, he vented his hatred of what he called the 'wantonness and rebellion' of his enemies among the magnates: this had led him, he said, to stretch forth his arm, tread on the offenders' necks and grind them down, even to the root.[75] Richard was here employing Old Testament language to describe Old Testament

---

[70] Jones, *The Royal Policy of Richard II*, 156–7; Dunbabin, 'Government', 483–5. For lengthier discussion, see above, 250.

[71] *RP*, iii, 150; and see above, 119–20.

[72] *RP*, iii, 329. The language of obedience was also used in the letters of submission offered by the Irish chieftains to Richard: see above, 284.

[73] *RP*, iii, 347.

[74] *Four English Political Tracts of the Later Middle Ages*, ed. J.-P. Genet (Camden 4th series, xviii, 1977), 35–6.

[75] *English Historical Documents*, ed. Myers, 174–5.

vengeance – with the former Appellants cast in the unfortunate role of his victims.[76]

The second factor which weighed with the king in accomplishing his design was the need to establish what he called 'peace' in his realm. This is a point which emerges clearly from the letters that he wrote to foreign rulers in the wake of his coup. To Albert of Holland, he wrote that he had punished the malice of those treacherous nobles whom he had raised to the highest peaks of honour, and by adjudging them to natural or civil death he had brought to his subjects a peace which, by the grace of God, would last for ever.[77] To Manuel Paleologus, in the letter already quoted, he wrote in a similar vein. Being unable, he said, to endure any longer the 'wantonness and rebellion' of his magnate enemies, he had stretched forth his arm and, with the aid of God's grace, had trodden on their necks and ground them down, not only to the bark but also to the root, so restoring to his subjects the peace which they longed for and which by God's blessing should last for ever.[78] By 'peace' in these letters Richard did not mean an end to external hostilities. Hostilities with both Scotland and France had been effectively ended by the truce agreed at Leulingham eight years earlier. What he had in mind was the establishment of internal unity. It was in this sense that 'peace' was understood by contemporary academics and writers. Jean Gerson, chancellor of the University of Paris, enjoined 'peace' on the competing factions at the French court in a sermon in November 1408 in which he stressed the danger to the realm of the evils of internal discord and dissent. Peace, he said, was the guarantee of internal unity; it should exist between those of the same blood, even those of the same royal blood; if it did not, the realm would never be able to resist its enemies.[79] This was a doctrine of unexceptional character; indeed, it ranked as one of the commonplaces of the age. In 1433 it was to be enjoined upon the competing factions at another court – that of King Henry VI, in a speech delivered by Chancellor Stafford.[80] But in Richard's hands it was turned into a doctrine almost absolutist in tone. Its essence was conveyed by Richard's chancellor, Bishop Stafford in his speech to the parliament of September 1397, when he said that, to ensure the good government of the realm, three things were needed: the king must be powerful enough to govern; the laws by which he governs should be well kept; and his subjects should duly obey him and

---

[76] But also cf. the New Testament allusions of the Magnificat: 'He has put down the mighty from their seats' (Luke 1: 52).

[77] Harvey, 'The Wilton Diptych', Appendix II.

[78] *English Historical Documents*, ed. Myers, 174–5.

[79] C.M.D. Crowder, 'Peace and Justice around 1400: a Sketch', *Aspects of Late Medieval Government and Society*, ed. J.G. Rowe (Toronto, 1986), 59.

[80] Ibid., 53–4.

his laws.[81] Unity – that is, peace – was incompatible with dissent; what the king required was unquestioning acceptance of his rule and submission to his will.

Over the following two years a series of measures was taken to assist the king in the realization of his vision. Sheriffs were required to take new and more stringent forms of oath on assuming office. The county communities were prevailed upon to appoint proctors to seal charters on their behalf submitting themselves and their goods to the king's pleasure, giving him *carte blanche* to do what he wished to them. And oaths were demanded from the king's 'spiritual and temporal lieges' to ensure the upholding of the acts of the Westminster-Shrewsbury parliament. At the same time, the council was instructed to keep a watch on letters coming into and going out of the country, while the court of chivalry was given a brief to deal with traitors found anywhere in the kingdom.[82]

The effect of these and the other measures taken in 1397 and 1398 was the exact opposite of what Richard intended. Instead of confirming and strengthening the king's subjects in their affection for him they brought about their alienation. It is difficult to survey in detail the popular response to Richard's rule because of the shortage of evidence, but it is clear that many who had once borne the king goodwill now felt repelled and estranged. One of those to speak out against him was the writer John Gower, whom Richard had earlier commissioned to write the *Confessio Amantis*. In his poem *O Deus Immense* Gower appealed to the king to see the error of his ways. The people were suffering, he said, because of the wrongs that he had committed. Instead of initiating purges and imposing censorship, he should hasten into the highways and byways and listen to what his subjects had to tell him. He should let them speak openly, for to suppress their talk was to store up danger. Above all, he should avoid avarice, for the treasure to be collected in people's hearts was more valuable than any amount of treasure he could collect in coin.[83] The obvious unhappiness that Gower felt was shared by another writer, the author of *Richard the Redeless*, who wrote at the time of the king's downfall. Richard had come to the throne, he said, with the goodwill of his people, but since then he had fallen under the influence of foolish counsellors who had led him to abuse the law, over-tax his subjects, and maltreat the commons; he should repent of his errors and endure his imprisonment with fortitude if he wished to

---

[81] *RP*, iii, 347; and see above, 376–7.

[82] Barron, 'The Tyranny of Richard II', 1–18; *CCR 1396–9*, 288; *Chrons. Revolution*, 181–2. The oath of the men of Worcestershire to uphold the legislation of the Westminster-Shrewsbury parliament is transcribed in the Worcester Liber Albus (Worcester Cathedral Library, Liber Albus, fo.398ʳ).

[83] *Complete Works of John Gower*, ed. Macaulay, iv, 362–4.

be sure of the salvation of his soul.[84] A third contemporary, the anonymous author of the satire *On the King's Ministers*, picked up the theme of the foolishness of the king's counsellors. Directing his criticism particularly at Bushy, Bagot and Green, whom he identified by puns on their names, he denounced the counsellors for their arrogance and highlighted the causes of their downfall.[85] The works of all three writers bear witness to the growing dissatisfaction felt with Richard's rule after 1397. Further evidence of that dissatisfaction is found in the works of the chroniclers, in particular in the successive recensions of Thomas Walsingham's works. The argument has been put that the chroniclers' coolness towards Richard should be treated sceptically because the majority of extant narratives were written after 1399.[86] It is true that the accounts of Richard's reign written after his downfall are generally more critical than those written while he lived. All the same, there are contemporary accounts, Walsingham's early ones being the most notable, which show disenchantment setting in well before the king's downfall.[87] It would be wrong to dismiss the chroniclers' witness merely because they were writing in the very different climate of Henry IV's reign. The chroniclers were not – or, at least, the majority of them were not – political time-servers, and it is likely that their views on Richard were formed well before they felt free to express them.

Further insights into attitudes to Richard's government are afforded by the scattered evidence of popular unrest. From this, one can sense the tensions and unease that lay beneath the surface of ordinary life. Of particular interest is the uprising at Bampton, Oxfordshire in 1398. According to several west Oxfordshire juries, on the night of Palm Sunday 1398 a group of insurgents led by John Milford, a weaver of Cogges, rose in rebellion and plotted the death of the king and the destruction of the magnates. Assembling about 200 fellows, they met at Cokethorpe and chose as their leader one Gilbert Vaughan, to whom as a symbol of authority they gave a pair of gilt spurs. They then marched to Yelford and Aston, collecting others as they went, and finally to Bampton, where they encountered more supporters. At Bampton Henry Roper, another of the insurgent leaders, rallied the men, crying

---

[84] *Mum and the Sothsegger*, ed. M. Day and R. Steele (EETS, cxcix, 1936). The poem was published by Day and Steele alongside *Mum* but, as D. Embree shows, (' "Richard the Redeless" and "Mum and the Sothsegger": A Case of Mistaken Identity', *Notes and Queries*, ccxx (1975), 4–12), it is almost certainly a separate poem. The work was addressed to Richard, and was probably composed in autumn 1399.

[85] *Political Poems and Songs*, i, 363–6.

[86] C. Barron, 'The Deposition of Richard II', *Politics and Crisis*, 132–4.

[87] Stow, 'Richard II in Walsingham's Chronicles', 83, notes that successive revisions of his chronicles reveal 'Walsingham's growing criticism of, and gradual alienation from, Richard and his policies'. For further discussion see below, 437.

'Arise all men and go with us, or else truly and by God ye shall be dead.'
William Barbour and one or two others who resisted were beaten and
threatened with death. Roper was then chosen by the rebels as their
spokesman, and given instructions to seek the king 'and his government' at Bristol or Gloucester. He set out the following day, and his aim,
the indictment concludes, was to destroy the king, the peers and magnates, and the laws of the kingdom.[88] The later progress of the rising,
and the measures taken to suppress it, are matters on which the indictments are silent, and it is virtually impossible to determine how serious
a threat was posed to the government's authority. A letter which the
treasurer, the bishop of St David's, sent to the king, however, shows that
the officers and council were seriously concerned about the situation:
the bishop, writing in May, after the worst was over, reported with relief
that order was restored.[89] It is hard to say whether there were any other
serious disturbances before Bolingbroke's landing, but on balance it
appears unlikely. None the less, there is evidence of an undercurrent of
popular unease. The Dieulacres chronicler, a writer sympathetic to
Richard, admitted that in the wake of the king's exactions 'evil rumours
began to spread because of the harsh bondage to which the whole
community was being subjected'; and he adds that because of the
extortions of the Cheshire archers the king was 'held in fatal odium
by his ordinary subjects'.[90] Some of the rumour-mongering to which
the chronicler alludes was brought to the attention of the council.
In 1398, according to Walsingham, two 'well-known friars and doctors
of theology' who spoke out against the poor governance of the realm
by the king and his councillors were disciplined and sent to prison.[91]
In December of the same year three otherwise obscure men, John
Dyne, Richard French and William Pilkington, were hauled before the
earl of Wiltshire and other members of the council for slandering the
king, and they too were imprisoned.[92] These two cases indicate
the anger and unease spreading in the realm. That there was not a
greater body of complaint should not be taken to indicate uncritical
acceptance of Richard's tyrannical rule; rather it affords proof of
his success in stifling dissent. People wisely kept their opinions to
themselves.

---

[88] *Oxfordshire Sessions of the Peace in the Reign of Richard II*, ed. E.G. Kimball (Oxfordshire Record Society, liii, 1983), 82–5. The insurgents were well informed as to the
king's movements: he was at Gloucester and Bristol at roughly the times that they
supposed he was: see Appendix.
[89] *Anglo-Norman Letters*, no. 198.
[90] M.V. Clarke and V.H. Galbraith, 'The Deposition of Richard II', *BJRL*, xiv
(1930), 170, 172.
[91] *Annales*, 223.
[92] A. Tuck, *Richard II and the Nobility*, 198.

There is no reason to suppose that Richard was greatly concerned by his subjects' attitude, favourable or otherwise, towards him. Such evidence as there is suggests that he was disdainful of the opinions of others. He made little attempt to seek his subjects' goodwill and affection, and he showed himself indifferent to their aspirations. As he became more powerful in the 1390s, so he became more aloof, and possibly also more arrogant. There was a degree of contrivance in his demeanour for, like other contemporary rulers, he consciously 'distanced' himself from his subjects so as to promote an attitude of obedience.[93] However, the signs are that for the most part his behaviour was 'genuine'. The spur to Richard's actions is to be found in his personal psychology. Early in 1397 he had suffered a disturbance to his psychological environment. He had suspected his former enemies of plotting his downfall and had reacted, unpredictably it seems, by crushing them. In the aftermath of his coup he had retreated inwards and become more self-absorbed. He had always been introspective to a degree, but in the final two years of his reign this tendency became more pronounced. The change manifested itself in a number of ways. Most obviously, there was the king's fondness for the self-dramatization afforded by ceremonial. As the *Eulogium* writer narrates, it became his practice to sit enthroned from dinner till vespers, observed by his courtiers, who were expected to bend the knee whenever his gaze fell on them.[94] At the same time the chroniclers tell how he was increasingly given to spending his time in the company of sycophants and cronies. The most regular attenders at his court now were the courtier bishops, household officials like Scrope, and the 'duketti' – men who could be counted on to agree with him.[95] He rarely summoned a 'great council' of magnates or turned to a wider circle of friends for advice. Earlier in the decade the council had provided an independent forum of criticism and advice,[96] but after 1397 the body was little more than a sounding board for his own views. The councillors who attended most often were the three officers of state, the notorious trio of Bushy, Bagot (plate 17) and Green, Laurence Drew, a lawyer, and the cleric Ralph Selby.[97] All were either dependent in some way on the king or

---

[93] For Richard's kingship of 'distance' see above, 238-9, and below, 453.

[94] *Chrons. Revolution*, 68; and see above, 342.

[95] Among the nobility, Walsingham singled out Aumerle, Norfolk and Exeter as the king's principal advisers (*Chrons. Revolution*, 75). Froissart mentioned Exeter, Aumerle and Salisbury as being 'especially in his favour' (Froissart, ii, 664). See also above, 335-6.

[96] See above, 252-4.

[97] Attendance at sessions of the council can be reconstructed from the material in C81/1394; SC8/214, 215 and 221. For discussion of this, see Tuck, *Richard II and the Nobility*, 198-9. Possibly the most intriguing of the group of councillors is Ralph Selby. From 1391 to 1398 Selby was warden of King's Hall, Cambridge, a college of

were on the most intimate terms with him. There was virtually no possibility that they would challenge his will or express an opinion contrary to his own.

The king's tendency to draw on his innermost reserves of strength can also be sensed in his itinerary at this time. Before 1398 he had followed a fairly normal itinerary for a late medieval king, moving chiefly between the palaces and hunting lodges of the south-east, and making only occasional forays further afield. At the beginning of 1398, however, this itinerary changed. The king now spent his time almost wholly in those parts of the country where support for his rule was strongest – in the midlands and west. After the ending of the Shrewsbury parliament he undertook an extensive itinerary along the Welsh Marches, calling at Oswestry, Worcester, Gloucester and Bristol.[98] There was a clear logic in his choice of stopping places. Worcester was the episcopal seat of his friend and former physician, Tideman of Winchcombe; Gloucester was the burial place of his great-grandfather, Edward II; and Bristol had formed part of the estates of his deceased queen, Anne. In the summer he undertook a second extensive itinerary of the midlands and Welsh Marches. This time the focus of his movements was further north, at Lichfield. Lichfield was the episcopal seat of his close friend and former confessor, John Burghill. He stayed in the episcopal palace there a number of times – in May, when envoys from the duke of Brittany visited him to conclude a treaty, in September, when he attended Burghill's enthronement, and in December, when he held his Christmas court in the newly enlarged great hall.[99] In the late spring and summer he made a number of visits from Lichfield to places further north. In July he went to Nottingham for a week, in August to Shrewsbury, Macclesfield and perhaps Chester and Holywell (Flint), and in September to Newcastle under Lyme.[100] Many of these places lay within, or very close to, the boundaries of the royal earldom of Chester.

In the final two years of his reign Richard was to demonstrate great

royal foundation whose members specialized in the study of civil law (*BRUC*, 517; Cobban, *The King's Hall*, 255–6, 282–3). Very possibly Selby was one of the group of legists who supplied Richard with the civil law vocabulary and maxims that are a characteristic of his later years.

[98] See Appendix.

[99] *Victoria History of the County of Stafford*, 14, 59; *Annales*, 224; *HVR*, 151; Lichfield Joint Record Office, D30/2/1/1, fo.52ᵛ.

[100] Richard's movements in the latter half of 1398 are unfortunately ill documented. The main sources are: *CPR 1396–9*, 376, 381, 384–5, 411–15; *CCR 1396–9*, 339; *Anglo-Norman Letters*, 69; C81/1354/28, 29; C81/1355/20; C270/25/38; E403/559, 24 July. It is not clear whether Richard actually went to Chester itself: he tended to hover on the borders of the county. The exchequer thought that he might have gone there: E403/559, 24 July.

affection for the Chester earldom and its 'loyal subjects'. This affection was partly the product of filial piety, for Cheshiremen had been prominent in the service of his father for nearly thirty years. However, to a greater extent it was born of the gratitude that he felt to the Cheshiremen for their loyalty to his cause at Radcot Bridge. How much the recollection of that battle meant to the king is suggested by his establishment in November 1398 of a fund of 4,000 marks for distribution among those who had fought in the engagement. Petitions for payment were requested from the veterans and their relatives, and the whole sum was disbursed in December. This extraordinary act of remembrance was but one of a host of favours that the king showed to Cheshire at this time. Constitutionally the most significant of these was his raising of the county to a principality by statute in September 1397. The effect of this measure was to elevate Cheshire above the county palatines of Lancaster and Durham, and to give it a status shared only with the principality of Wales. Hardly less striking was the annexation to Cheshire of the former Arundel lordships of Oswestry, Chirk, and Bromfield and Yale, which briefly made the county the largest territorial complex in the kingdom. In addition to these corporate privileges, the people of Cheshire were the recipients of a host of lesser favours: pardons, offices, and grants of land and confiscated goods were bestowed upon them; general pardons were granted to the counties of Flint and Chester; and the charter of the city of Chester was confirmed and its privileges extended. Richard saw himself as enjoying a special relationship with the principality and its 'loyal subjects'. Cheshire was the inner citadel of his kingdom; it was the county in which he found a security and inner contentment that stubbornly eluded him elsewhere.[101]

Richard's growing affinity with the north-west at this time is also evidenced by his tendency to concentrate his retaining in that area. Before the end of 1397 he had taken into his service men from virtually every part of the country.[102] After that time the great majority of those whom he took on came from the north-west, in particular from Cheshire. Eleven of the 28 new knights retained in the last two years of his reign came from Cheshire or Lancashire, and no fewer than 140 of the 170 or so esquires did so. By September 1398 the total number of Cheshiremen in the king's pay came to some 760. The core of this group was the famous bodyguard, which comprised 311 archers and was divided into seven 'vigilia' or watches. In addition to this elite group there was also a reserve bodyguard of 101 archers retained for life, and

[101] R.R. Davies, 'Richard II and the Principality of Chester', *The Reign of Richard II*, 256-79.

[102] He had shown a slight bias to retaining in the Welsh Marches and north: see above, 268.

a further 197 who were retained during pleasure.[103] These numbers represented an unprecedented build-up of royal power in one county. Never before had a king surrounded himself by so massive a personal bodyguard, let alone one so exclusively recruited. Edward I and his successors had retained a corps of 'king's archers' or 'archers of the crown', though at no time had these been numerous: in Edward III's reign they numbered a mere handful at most.[104] The force that Richard called into being had all the appearance of a private army. It was the task of its members to protect the king by day and by night.[105] According to the witness of the Kenilworth chronicler, the corps leaders said to Richard, in terms of remarkable intimacy, 'Dycun, slep sicury quile we wake, and dreed nouzt quile we lyve sestow.'[106] The archers' commitment to stand by their promise need hardly be doubted. So long as the Cheshiremen were at his side, King 'Dycun' could sleep safely in his bed.

The impression that Richard gave by his actions and movements after 1397 was that of a man who was living increasingly in fear. Though supreme in the realm, he exhibited a distrust of all but the closest of his courtly intimates. To a greater degree than his predecessors, he distanced himself from his subjects; he elevated himself above them and did everything in his power to impress the duty of obedience upon them. Wherever he travelled in his realm, he surrounded himself with his Cheshire archers, who ate and slept with him and instilled terror into every community through which they passed.[107] He took every measure to buttress himself by a system of pledges, oaths and other

---

[103] Given-Wilson, *Royal Household and the King's Affinity*, 222–3; J.L. Gillespie, 'Richard II's Cheshire Archers', *Transactions of the Historic Society of Lancashire and Cheshire*, cxxv (1974), 1–39.

[104] J. Gillespie, 'Richard II's Archers of the Crown', *JBS*, xviii (1979), 14–29.

[105] According to notes in a St Albans Abbey calendar, 'every night during [the September 1397] parliament was the king watched at Westminster, that is to say, a lord of his retinue on one night, another lord on another night and so forth' (BL, MS Harley 3775, fos87ʳ-87ᵛ).

[106] Clarke and Galbraith, 'Deposition of Richard II', 163–4.

[107] The mayor and council of Canterbury bought the favour of the Cheshire archers when Richard visited their city in April 1399: they spent £3 0s 8d on wine 'for the men of the county watching over him' ('pro vino dato viris de comitatu Cest' vigilantibus circa dominum Regem in adventu suo'): Canterbury Cathedral Library, Canterbury city accounts, FA1, fo.40ʳ. The Canterbury-based *Eulogium* chronicler also commented on the size of the Cheshire retinue that accompanied the king on the visit (*Eulogium*, 380). According to the Dieulacres writer, they habitually stood guard on the king with axes: Clarke and Galbraith, 'Deposition of Richard II', 172. Contemporaries would have agreed with J. Gillingham: 'Richard lived as if in enemy country': 'Crisis or Continuity?', 65.

forms of obligation. His signal triumph over the former Appellants in 1397 had apparently done little to allay his sense of insecurity. Yet paradoxically the measures that he took at this time were all in the end misdirected, for when a challenge to his authority came, it came not from without – not from the mass of his ordinary subjects – but from within, from the elite of the courtier nobility.

The event that brought the royal house of cards tumbling down was the quarrel that broke out during the winter of 1397-8 between Thomas Mowbray, the newly created duke of Norfolk, and Henry Bolingbroke, the newly created duke of Hereford. The background to the quarrel is difficult to disentangle, and historians' assessments of the motives of the two lords have varied considerably. However, Dr Given-Wilson is probably right to argue that the affair was a product of much wider disagreements among the king's supporters about the direction of royal policy, and that it was Richard's inability to keep these rivalries in check that was ultimately to bring him down.[108]

Only one side of the tangled story is known, that of the duke of Hereford. Hereford had unburdened himself to the king at Great Haywood, Staffordshire on about 20 January, and on the latter's instructions he repeated what he had told him to the Shrewsbury parliament.[109] The gist of his tale was as follows.[110] Hereford had been riding between Brentford and London one day in December when Norfolk approached him in haste and warned him that the two of them were about to be 'undone' by the king for their part in the events of 1387-8. Hereford expressed disbelief, saying that they had both been pardoned. Norfolk nevertheless persisted, arguing that the pardons were worthless, and in the end Hereford was provoked to make his famous remark that 'it was a funny old world'. Norfolk went on to allege that 'had it not been for certain people, your father the lord of Lancaster and you would have been either seized or killed when you came to Windsor after the parliament [of September 1397]'. These 'certain people', he continued, were the dukes of Aumerle and Exeter, the earl of Worcester and himself, who had jointly sworn an oath that in future 'they would never assent to the ruin of any lord without just and reasonable cause'. The chief conspirators whose 'malice' lay behind the plot against Lancaster were the duke of Surrey and the earls of Wiltshire, Salisbury and Gloucester: these four had sworn to destroy six other lords, namely Gaunt, Aumerle, Exeter, the marquess of Dorset and themselves. Furthermore, he claimed, it was the conspirators'

---

[108] *Chrons. Revolution*, 17.

[109] *RP*, iii, 382; *Chrons. Revolution*, 86. The 'Haywode' referred to is Great Haywood, a manor of the bishop of Lichfield, and not Heywood-in-Cheswardine, as ibid., and *CPR 1396-9*, 700.

[110] *RP*, iii, 360; *Chrons. Revolution*, 86-7.

intention to reverse the judgment of 1327 which had restored the
Lancastrian inheritance: an act 'which would result in the disinheritance of us and of several others'; to which Hereford replied, 'God
forbid!' Finally, alleged Norfolk, the king – whom he at this point
identified with the plotters – was trying to lure the young earl of March
into joining the conspiracy against the lords. If this was indeed the case,
replied Hereford, then no trust could be placed in any of them. Indeed
not, concluded Mowbray; they would never sleep easily again.

So ran Hereford's story; and the question arises of how much weight
can be attached to it. K.B. McFarlane maintained that the story was
incredible. He believed that Hereford would never have relayed Norfolk's story to the king after what the duke had told him of the latter's
duplicity. In his view it made better sense to suppose that it was Hereford who had voiced his misgivings to Norfolk.[111] This is an ingenious
theory, but its only contemporary foundation is afforded by Froissart;
and Froissart systematically reverses the roles of the two lords throughout.[112] In reality there is probably more to be said for Hereford's version
than McFarlane (and others) have supposed. At the heart of the duke's
account was the allegation of a plot against his father. In the circumstances of late 1397 it is perfectly possible to suppose that such a plot
was being hatched.[113]

The background to the hostility to John of Gaunt lay in the enormous
power and wealth of the Lancastrian house and, in particular, in the
uncertainty hanging over the succession. Richard by 1397 was aged
thirty. His marriage to Anne of Bohemia had been childless, and there
was no immediate prospect of issue by his marriage to the seven-year-
old Isabella. Thus it was hardly surprising that the thoughts of many of
those closely involved turned to the question of the succession; and
there is evidence that they did. According to Walsingham, Bagot, when
tried in 1399, reported a conversation with Richard in which the latter
apparently toyed with the idea of resigning the crown and handing
power to his cousin Aumerle, as being 'the noblest and wisest man in
the whole kingdom'. Mowbray, present with Bagot, retorted that it
would be more appropriate for him to be succeeded by Hereford,
because Hereford was more closely related to Richard. Whether or not
these exchanges actually unfolded as reported (and it is possible that
they did not), it is clear that talk about the succession was in the air, and
that the claims of Lancaster were being voiced. By tradition, if not by
law, the throne of England descended by primogeniture; and if tradition were followed, and Richard were to remain childless, the heir

---

[111] McFarlane, *Lancastrian Kings and Lollard Knights*, 44–6.
[112] Froissart, ii, 661–6.
[113] The following reconstruction largely follows C. Given-Wilson, 'Richard II,
Edward II, and the Lancastrian Inheritance', *EHR*, cix (1994), 553–71.

would have been the young earl of March, Roger Mortimer. March's claim came through the female line. On the other hand, in the four-teenth century an increasing number of great estates were being 'entailed' on the male line, and Gaunt, whose family stood to benefit should inheritance to the crown be similarly restricted, could claim that the same principle should apply to the kingdom as well. There is some evidence that he did make such a claim: both Hardyng and the *Eulogium* writer report that in one of the parliaments of the 1390s he petitioned that his son Henry be recognized as Richard's heir, to which the earl of March replied that he was the rightful heir. Richard ordered them both to be silent: not surprisingly, as he would not have wanted to encourage discussion on the subject.

Gaunt not only aroused hostility because of his interest in the succes-sion; he also aroused jealousy because of his vast wealth and power. The Lancastrian inheritance was by far the most extensive in England, worth at least £12,000 a year, and there must have been many who coveted a share in it. It is on this matter that Hereford's narrative of his encounter with Norfolk is of such singular interest. According to Norfolk, the four lords who were at the heart of the plot were Surrey, Wiltshire, Salisbury and Gloucester. These four had one main characteristic in common: they were all 'new men'; or, as Dr Given-Wilson puts it, men who had been 'born again'. Wiltshire, Salisbury and Gloucester received their earldoms between July and September 1397; Surrey, who was already an earl, received his dukedom in the distribution of honours in Sep-tember. They were the rising stars at court, and they saw access to royal favour as the means to augment their personal and family fortunes. Some of them had inherited claims from their ancestors which it was their every intention to pursue. Salisbury, for example, had a claim on the great Marcher lordship of Denbigh, of which his uncle had been deprived in favour of the earl of March in 1354, while Gloucester, a descendant of the two Despensers who had been Edward II's favourites, had claims on lands once held by his forebears which he was granted royal permission to pursue. Beyond these lands to which they had a legitimate claim the four lords appear to have set their sights on the inheritance of Lancaster. The six lords whose downfall they allegedly encompassed were all connected in some way with the house of Lan-caster: Hereford was Lancaster's son, Dorset his bastard son, Exeter his son-in-law and Aumerle his nephew. If the reversal of the sentence of forfeiture passed on Thomas of Lancaster were overturned, an outcome which Richard might well desire given his devotion to the memory of Edward II, then the Lancastrian inheritance would fall to the crown, and the lords could all stake their claims.

Evidence that a plot of some sort was being hatched in early 1398 is not hard to uncover. Most strikingly there is the evidence of the two recognizances, enrolled on the close roll, into which Bagot was obliged to enter in March of that year. By the first of these Bagot agreed to pay the king £1,000 if it were proved at any time in the future that he had brought about the disinheritance of Gaunt, his wife, or any of his children; by the second, dated two days after the first, Bagot submitted to be executed without further judgment or process against him if at any time in the future he were to kill or put to death Gaunt, his wife, or any of his children.[114] The implication of these two extraordinary documents is that Bagot was suspected of being implicated in a plot, the chief architects of which were probably men mightier than he. Rumours of his involvement were still circulating a year or more later. According to Walsingham, Bagot admitted at his trial that he had once planned the death of Gaunt, but claimed that he had been pardoned by both Gaunt and the king.[115] A London chronicler, also reporting the trial, records the duke of Exeter as saying that it was Bagot, Norfolk and Richard himself who were behind the plot, Bagot allegedly declaring that, 'we shulde never have oure purpos but affter the deeth off John, late Duk off Lancastre'.[116] In the light of this evidence it is easy to understand why Lancaster and his son should have found it necessary, in February 1398, to secure from the king, 'with the full assent of the council after mature deliberation', an undertaking that he (the king) would not attempt to use the judgment against Thomas of Lancaster as a way of claiming any of the Lancastrian lands.[117] Quite understandably they feared that Richard and his friends had in mind using the judgment to enter just such a claim. The attractions to the king of such a course were not inconsiderable. Not only would he be able to dispose of a rival source of authority to his own; he could also augment the royal demesne, replenish his reservoir of patronage and exalt still further the power and authority of his crown.

Analysis of the background to the allegations that Norfolk made in his conversation with Hereford suggests, in other words, that there was probably a substantial measure of truth to them. But why did the two principals behave in the curious way that they did? And why, in particular, did Norfolk divulge his fears to Hereford rather than take them directly to the king?

Norfolk's position by 1398 was in fact ambivalent. On the face of it he stood high in royal favour. His role in the unhappy events of 1387–8 had been forgotten – or, at least, formally forgiven; he had been elevated to a dukedom in the distribution of honours; and he had been given extensive grants from the lands of the former earldoms of Arundel and Warwick. But, on the other hand, there are signs that his

---

[114] *CCR 1396–9*, 291–2.
[115] *Annales*, 308.
[116] *Chronicles of London*, ed. C.L. Kingsford (Oxford, 1905), 54.
[117] *CPR 1396–9*, 285.

position in royal favour was not as well established as it seemed.[118] He had caused difficulties for himself by his ambivalence towards the proceedings in parliament in 1397–8; and he had failed to attend at Westminster 'on the day that the appeal against the three lords was to be decided', despite the fact that he was one of the appellants himself. Three months later at Shrewsbury he added to his sins by failing to join in the call for the repeal of the legislation of the Merciless Parliament. The reason for his equivocal behaviour was of course his own past involvement in the events of the Appellant period; and it was the fact that Hereford was in the same position that led him to divulge his fears to him. What he seems not to have anticipated was that Hereford would break his confidence and report the allegations to his father. Once he discovered what had happened, he panicked. He knew that parliament was due to reassemble at Shrewsbury on 27 January, and that Lancaster would almost certainly tell the king about the allegations – if he had not already done so. The duke, therefore, tried to waylay or assassinate Lancaster. According to Adam of Usk, he 'laid snares of death' for the royal uncle as he travelled to the Shrewsbury parliament, but the latter was forewarned and avoided the trap. Intelligence of a similar sort seems to have reached the author of the *Traison*, who says that Norfolk later admitted having 'laid an ambush to kill my lord of Lancaster'.[119]

Norfolk had fatally damaged himself by his irresponsible conduct in January; Bolingbroke now had a free hand to present his side of the story, and he did so in full parliament at Shrewsbury. Richard reacted in a way that strongly implied his belief in the other's guilt. Norfolk was stripped of his offices of earl marshal and admiral of England, and a writ was sent to the sheriffs ordering them to compel his appearance before the king within fifteen days.[120] Norfolk quickly gave himself up, and was imprisoned in the great wardrobe in London. On 23 February he was brought before the king at a council held at Oswestry. He denied everything that Hereford had alleged against him; the king in consequence ordered the two men to appear before the parliamentary committee, which had been assigned responsibility for resolving the dispute. The meeting took place at Bristol on 19 March. In the absence of conclusive proof of either man's guilt, it was decided that the dispute between them should be resolved 'according to the law of chivalry' – in other words, by wager of battle.[121] A month later, however, a further

---

[118] It may be a mark of the king's misgivings about Norfolk that he did not make grants to him of former Appellant lands in counties where he was already strong. See above, 282n.

[119] Usk, 169; *Traison et Mort*, 148.

[120] *RP*, iii, 368; *CCR 1396–9*, 281–2.

[121] *RP*, iii, 383; *Chrons. Revolution*, 89.

meeting was held, at Windsor, at which Hereford considerably enlarged his earlier charges. He now accused his opponent of misappropriating funds during his period as captain of Calais; of being 'at the bottom of all the treasons committed in the kingdom these last eighteen years'; and of ordering the murder of the duke of Gloucester.[122] Hereford's reasons for bringing these new allegations were probably twofold: to draw Richard into proceeding to judgment against Norfolk as quickly as possible, and to exact retribution for the death of Gloucester, to whom he and his father had been socially, if not politically, close.[123] His tactics, however, largely misfired. Richard had absolutely no interest in reopening discussion of the circumstances of Gloucester's death, lest his own role in the affair be called into question; and at the same time it was clear from Norfolk's replies to the new charges that there was no case for proceeding to an immediate judgment against him. The duke resolutely defended himself against the charges of his opponent. He argued that Calais was as well guarded as it had ever been, and that he had never received any payment for embassies he had undertaken on the king's behalf. He therefore insisted on trial by battle. Every effort to reconcile the two having failed, it was ordered that such a trial should take place in the lists at Coventry on 16 September.

Preparations for the engagement began almost at once. The two rivals sent abroad for their armour – Hereford to Milan and Norfolk, it appears, to Bohemia.[124] Neither spared any expense in accoutring himself as lavishly as possible. As both were aware, the contest between them was attracting enormous popular interest. Visitors poured in from all parts: Sir Walter Stewart, the duke of Albany's son, came from Scotland, the count of St Pol from France, and others from further afield still.[125] As the chroniclers indicate, the entire realm was gripped with excitement. According to Walsingham, the majority sentiment in the country favoured Hereford, on the grounds that he was the more likely to avenge the dead Gloucester.[126] Richard, however, perhaps wrongly, was suspected of favouring Norfolk.[127]

On the night before the engagement Richard stayed with the ubiquitous Bagot at his manor house at Baginton. The following morning he

[122] *Traison et Mort*, 146–7. The new charges do not appear in the record of the parliamentary committee's deliberations on the parliament roll: not surprisingly, given Richard's interest in stifling all reference to Gloucester's murder.

[123] A. Goodman, 'John of Gaunt', *England in the Fourteenth Century*, ed. W.M. Ormrod (Woodbridge, 1986), 86.

[124] For Hereford's armour, see Froissart, ii, 663. Norfolk's use of Bohemian armour may be inferred from the fact that a Bohemian esquire attended him at Coventry (*Traison et Mort*, 149).

[125] *Traison et Mort*, 150, 153.

[126] *Annales*, 226.

[127] Froissart, ii, 665.

made his way to the tournament green at Gosford, on the edge of Coventry, where the magnates and knights, the archbishop of Canterbury and the visiting dignitaries were already assembling. The author of the *Traison et Mort*, who was probably an eyewitness, gives a vivid account of the morning's proceedings.[128] Hereford arrived at nine, accompanied by six mounted attendants. Challenged by the constable and marshal as to his name and business, he said that he was Henry, duke of Hereford, come to do his duty against the false traitor Thomas, duke of Norfolk. He then took an oath to uphold his claim, crossed himself and rode to a pavilion at the far end of the lists. After the entry of the king, his retinue and the Cheshire archers, Norfolk duly appeared. He took the same oath and with the cry, 'God speed the right!' rode over to his pavilion. The lances were then measured; the champions' tents were removed, and Hereford made the first advances towards his opponent. Norfolk remained motionless. But then, suddenly, the king rose up and cried, 'Hold!'; and the proceedings were immediately halted. Hereford and Norfolk returned to their pavilions, and for two hours the crowd waited. In due course Brittany herald climbed the tribune and prayed silence. Sir John Bushy came forward to announce the king's decision: Hereford was to be banished from the realm for ten years, and Norfolk for life. A huge outcry accompanied the announcement of Hereford's sentence, for the duke was the popular favourite. When calm was restored, the king made the two rivals swear to abide by his award; and shortly afterwards he left the green.

There can be little doubt that Richard's intervention had spoiled what promised to be the outstanding chivalric occasion of the year – indeed, of the age; and the disappointment can be sensed in the writings of the chroniclers. The difficulty for Richard, however, was that a resolution of the issue by arms would have exposed him to intolerable difficulties. A victory for Norfolk would have revived criticism that he wanted to stifle enquiry into Gloucester's murder, while a victory for Hereford would have added to the renown of a man whom he

---

[128] As J.J.N. Palmer has argued ('The Authorship, Date and Historical Value of the French Chronicles'), the *Traison* is for the most part a source of little historical worth. However, it is clear that the passage describing the Coventry tournament is the work of an eyewitness. Not only is the narrative at this point informed by a wealth of circumstantial detail (for example, the comment that Norfolk remained motionless when Hereford advanced); it is also surprisingly accurate on topographical observation. The writer says that Richard stayed at Bagot's 'tower-house' (at Baginton) a little way out of the city (149). Excavations carried out at Baginton in the 1930s confirmed that the house was indeed of tower design, a form common in the north, but unusual in the midlands (Emery, *Dartington Hall*, 112, 126–7). Wrottesley's statement that it was Hereford who stayed with Bagot is based on a misreading of the *Traison* (G. Wrottesley, 'A History of the Bagot Family', *Staffordshire Historical Collections*, new series xi (1908) 47).

increasingly disliked and whom by now he probably also feared. Neither outcome would have been in the least acceptable to the king. Some other solution had to be found. The king of France's advice, communicated through the count of St Pol, was to continue to press for a reconciliation.[129] A number of attempts, however, had already been made to bring the two men together, and all of them had failed. The decision to hold the tournament, but then to stay it, was one that, according to Froissart, Richard probably took on the advice of his intimates.[130] It was a course entirely permissible under the procedures of the court of chivalry. Richard was the combatants' liege lord: he was entitled to take their quarrel into his own hands and settle it without letting them fight to a finish.[131] There was no suggestion from contemporaries, even hostile contemporaries, that he had acted in any way contrary to the law of arms. In only one respect can Richard's handling of the affair be faulted, and that was in his decision to punish Hereford. To condemn the duke to a period of exile, albeit a briefer one than Norfolk's, was to cast doubt on his integrity and honour. Richard acknowledged this when he said that the sentence was 'not given on account of any misdemeanour committed by the said duke of Hereford in matters concerning his appeal'; rather it had been imposed because of the need 'to bring peace and tranquillity to the realm' and to avoid 'future disagreements . . . between the two dukes'.[132] This was a highly apologetic line of defence. By its very evasions it merely highlighted the real reason for the sentence, which was the king's desire to see off a man whom he saw as a threat to his security. Procedurally, Richard had acted at Coventry with exemplary correctness; in imposing the sentence that he did on Hereford, however, he surrendered to the almost inevitable temptations of *realpolitik*.

Richard could be forgiven for thinking, as he left Coventry, that his ascendancy over the realm was finally complete. Gloucester and Arundel were dead; Warwick was in prison; and Hereford and Norfolk had been condemned to exile. Financially, he was secure. His wife's dowry and the confiscated wealth of the former Appellants had replen-

---

[129] H. Wallon, *Richard II* (2 vols, Paris, 1864), ii, 211.

[130] Froissart, ii, 665. There is no reason to believe that Richard made the decision 'impulsively', as McKisack suggested (*The Fourteenth Century*, 488).

[131] Forty years earlier, King John of France had taken this action in a quarrel between Henry of Grosmont, duke of Lancaster, and the duke of Brunswick: he had the two combatants led out of the lists and then settled their quarrel himself: K. Fowler, *The King's Lieutenant. Henry of Grosmont, First Duke of Lancaster 1310–1361* (London, 1969), 105–9.

[132] *Chrons. Revolution*, 90.

ished his coffers.[133] Parliament had shown itself agreeably compliant in enacting his will; and the nobility, and political society more generally, had been reshaped in his image. Never before had the power of the crown been raised to such dizzy and exalted heights.

In part, Richard's achievement was a tribute to his singlemindedness and clarity of purpose. However, in part it reflected the support given to him by his uncle, the duke of Lancaster. For nearly a decade the weight of the Lancastrian inheritance had been placed at the king's disposal. It had been instrumental in buttressing the king's authority in the early 1390s, and it had contributed to the maintenance of stability in the aftermath of his coup against the Appellants. As 1398 drew to a close, however, it was by no means clear how much longer its resources would be at Richard's disposal. Lancaster was growing old, and there was the prospect that his position would shortly be taken by a son a good deal less sympathetic to the king than his father. From being the principal buttress of the monarchy, the Lancastrian power could easily become the cause of its downfall: a potential focus for disaffection which could prove fatal to Richard's exercise of authority. This was a worrying prospect for a king obsessed with his own security. But in the later months of 1398 it does not appear that Richard was greatly perturbed by such a possibility. In the wake of the Coventry award he explicitly reaffirmed Hereford's right to succeed; and on 3 October he issued letters in the duke's favour authorizing him to receive livery of his inheritance in the event of his father's early demise.[134] Richard probably expected Gaunt to survive, and to be reasonably active, for some years to come: he had stayed with him at Leicester in September, and at that time apparently he had still been in good health.[135] Early in the New Year, however, it seems that the duke succumbed to a serious illness; and on 3 February he died. A decision had to be made quickly on whether or not Hereford should be allowed to inherit. The

[133] In 1399 Richard was probably wealthier than any king since Edward II on the eve of his downfall. It is impossible accurately to assess Richard's income because of the absence of chamber accounts. However, an indication of his wealth is given by the wardrobe evidence. In 1398-9 the wardrobe's income was sharply up on the previous year's - £56,000 as against £29,349. The increase was largely accounted for by 'foreign receipts' - that is, non-exchequer income. Richard was evidently receiving large cash inflows from somewhere other than the exchequer. Almost certainly the source was his wife's dowry, which had been fixed at £133,333. Richard probably received £83,000 of this sum between 1396 and 1399. In this way he was able to pay for his second Irish expedition. By 1399 he had amassed a huge cash reserve at the former Arundel stronghold of Holt, near Chester. According to his clerk John Ikelington, £43,964 had been deposited there, along with many goods and jewels (Given-Wilson, *Royal Household and the King's Affinity*, 90, 271; Davies, 'Richard II and the Principality of Chester', 271).

[134] *CPR 1396-9*, 417.

[135] Ibid., 388, 412-15; Goodman, *John of Gaunt*, 166.

arguments on the two sides were evenly balanced. To deny Hereford his inheritance would be to commit an act more flagrantly at odds with the law and customs of his realm, and more offensive to the deepest instincts of landowning society, than anything the king had hitherto done; furthermore, it might provoke Hereford into coming back to reclaim his rights. On the other hand, to admit the duke to his inheritance, even *in absentia*, would be to undo all that the king had achieved over the previous fifteen months. In the event the king decided to take the risk of keeping the duke out. On 18 March, six weeks after Lancaster's death, he revoked the letters that he had granted in the previous October; and at the same time he caused the terms of reference of the parliamentary committee to be altered to allow a sentence of perpetual banishment to be imposed on the duke.[136] Richard softened the blow in one significant respect. When apportioning the forfeited lands of the duchy, he granted the beneficiaries possession only 'until Henry of Lancaster, duke of Hereford, or his heir, shall have sued the same out of the king's hands according to the law of the land'.[137] In other words, he held out the possibility that either Hereford or his son might one day be restored. Very likely the object of his hopes was the duke's son, the future Henry V, whom he looked on favourably and whom he was shortly to knight in Ireland.[138] In a sense, then, there was a silver lining to the grey cloud of the king's dramatic action. But in the uneasy conditions of March 1399 it was the darkness of the storm-cloud that loomed larger in the perceptions of English landowning society. Richard had taken a step which struck at the heart of the aristocracy's most vital interests. The chain of events had been set in motion which only seven months later was to culminate in the king's deposition.

---

[136] *RP*, iii, 372. Richard's action was not entirely without precedent. In the 1380s the king had shown a remarkable contempt for legal title when he assisted Burley in his attempt to grab the lands which Edward III had set aside for the performance of his will (see above, 114–15). A precedent from an earlier reign is afforded by Edward II's seizure of the estates of his queen, Isabella, in 1324 (*CFR 1319–27*, 302).

[137] *CFR 1391–9*, 293.

[138] Creton, 29–30.

Chapter 16

DEPOSITION AND DEATH, 1399–1400

Duke Henry was in Paris when he heard the news of his father's death. He had left England to begin exile in the previous October.[1] According to Froissart, he had originally intended going to the count of Ostrevant's court in Hainault, but on his father's advice he had headed instead for Paris.[2] At Paris he was warmly welcomed by Charles VI and his uncles, and he and his retainers were handsomely dined and plied with gifts. Froissart says that the Hôtel de Clisson was assigned to him as a residence.[3] Since he was able to continue drawing money from England, he had little difficulty maintaining himself in style and cutting a grand figure at the French court.[4]

From the moment of his arrival opinion at the French court had been broadly favourable to him. It was widely felt that he had been punished without due cause and that the sentence imposed on him was unjust. In the following year, when his inheritance was confiscated and his period of exile extended from ten years to life, opinion moved still further in his favour. The chronicler of St Denis spoke for many when he said that Richard's action made a mockery of his earlier promises.[5] Duke Henry was shown considerable sympathy by the duke of Berry and other princes of the royal blood.[6] But Richard had a powerful ally in Philip of Burgundy, who was effectively the head of the French government at the time. Burgundy's interest lay in maintaining good relations with England, because the cloth industry in his county of Flanders was dependent on the steady supply of English wool.[7] In order to show Richard his goodwill, Burgundy kept a watchful eye on Henry's activities in Paris. In autumn 1398, when the duke began negotiating for the hand of the duke of Berry's daughter and Richard made his disapproval

---

[1] But it is possible that he came back for the funeral in March: J.B. Post, 'The Obsequies of John of Gaunt', *Guildhall Studies in London History*, v (1981), 4.

[2] Froissart, ii, 667–8.

[3] Ibid., 676, 684.

[4] He was allowed an annuity of £2,000 for the duration of his exile. For payments to him, see E403/561, 14 Nov.; E403/562, 15 April.

[5] *Chrons. Revolution*, 105.

[6] Ibid., 106.

[7] Burgundy had succeeded to the county of Flanders on the death of his father-in-law, Louis of Mâle, in 1384.

known, Burgundy intervened on Richard's behalf.[8] Burgundy had considerable reservations about the proposal himself and Charles VI was less than enthusiastic. Berry appreciated the folly of promoting an alliance to which Richard was opposed, and eventually the scheme was dropped.

So long as Burgundy was in control of the French government, Richard could be confident that his interests would be adequately safeguarded. In 1399, however, Burgundy was increasingly threatened by his nephew and rival, Louis, duke of Orléans.[9] Duke Louis's political objectives were very different from his kinsman's. For over a decade he had harboured the ambition of carving an empire for himself in central Italy at the expense of the states of the Church. Such a policy, if implemented, would inevitably bring him into conflict with the English government, which was opposed to French expansion south of the Alps. Towards the end of the 1390s Orléans also had ideas of establishing a presence in the county of Périgord, west of his own lands in France, but in this area too he ran into opposition from the English. Périgord lay on the borders of English-held Aquitaine, and only in the event of a more general renewal of hostilities would it have been possible for him to bring his plans to fruition.[10] By early 1399 it was apparent to the duke that he needed to end the Anglo-French *rapprochement* if he was to advance his territorial interests. In the late spring of that year he entered into negotiations with Duke Henry; and on 17 June, after Philip of Burgundy had left Paris for Artois, and Berry had gone to Bicêtre for the summer, the two men entered into a treaty of friendship. The terms of the treaty seemed innocent enough: the dukes swore to be each other's friends and well-wishers and to maintain each other's honour, estate and well-being; and the kings of England and France and the duke of York, the keeper of England, were specifically excluded.[11] But it is difficult not to believe that, however obliquely, the Englishman had given his ally an indication of the nature of his plans. It is doubtful if he manifested a design on the crown, for as yet his ambitions probably did not extend that far; more likely, he simply indicated a desire to regain his inheritance. Orléans, whether or not he

---

[8] Salisbury was sent to complain in November 1398; for the date of his visit, see Laidlaw, 'Christine de Pisan, the Earl of Salisbury and Henry IV', 131–2. Salisbury's role in this episode helps to explain why the duke was so cool towards him when the two met at Flint in the following August (below, 416). For the story of the negotiations and Henry's subsequent coolness, see Froissart ii, 678–80; *Chrons. Revolution*, 150; F. Lehoux, *Jean de France, Duc de Berri* (3 vols, Paris, 1966), ii, 406–7; M.W. Warner, 'The Montagu Earls of Salisbury, c.1300–1428: A Study in Warfare, Politics and Political Culture' (University of London Ph.D. thesis, 1991), 82–4.

[9] Lehoux, *Jean de France*, 416.

[10] Ibid.

[11] *Chrons. Revolution*, 112–14.

fully trusted the duke, gave him his blessing; and other leading figures, notably Charles himself, did not stand in his way. Unwittingly, Richard himself played into his adversary's hands by provoking disagreement with the French on a number of sensitive issues. In November 1398 he had concluded a concordat with the papacy while the French were still negotiating a simultaneous withdrawal of obedience by the two kings.[12] And in 1399, shortly before departing for Ireland, he dismissed Margaret, Lady Courcy, his wife's governess, and several of her staff, allegedly for extravagance and lack of discretion.[13] In the light of these actions the French probably saw little point in shielding him any longer from the machinations of his aggrieved cousin.

Henry began preparing for his departure almost at once. At the beginning of May Richard had sent a letter to his father-in-law advising him that he would shortly be setting out for Ireland. Henry would have realised that he had an opportunity to strike. By late spring two other exiles – the Arundels, Thomas, the archbishop, and his nephew and namesake, the earl – had joined him from Germany. The duke already had with him the dozen or so Lancastrian retainers who had accompanied him into exile. Thus in the modest surroundings of the Clisson he had the nucleus of a force to take to England. Hardly anything can be said of the details of the duke's preparations, for these were necessarily secret. According to Froissart, he travelled from Paris to Nantes, where he conferred with the duke of Brittany before embarking for Plymouth.[14] Froissart's account is unsupported by other sources, and Froissart is anyway an unreliable witness to the usurpation. The better-informed St Denis writer offers a more plausible narrative. The duke, he says, made his way to Boulogne, putting it about that he was embarking on a pilgrimage. His sympathizers in England, forewarned of his plans, arranged for a 'sizeable fleet' to cross the Channel to meet him, but the duke of Burgundy, alarmed by the arrival of so much shipping, wrote to the townsmen of Boulogne warning them to be on their guard. Henry, however, had little difficulty in evading the duke's watch and, establishing contact with the masters, embarked with his men-at-arms and sailed for England.[15] The details of the chronicler's narrative may be a little embroidered, but its essence appears sound. Walsingham confirms that Henry went from Paris to Boulogne and was carried by English shipping.[16]

The keeper of England, the duke of York, and his council were kept informed of Henry's movements by reports that they received from

[12] See above, 232–3.
[13] *Chrons. Revolution*, 30; E403/562, 10 June.
[14] Froissart, ii, 685–8.
[15] *Chrons. Revolution*, 110–11.
[16] Ibid., 116–17.

merchants and other travellers to France. There is evidence that they were aware of the possibility of a descent on southern England. On 28 June the duke wrote to the sheriffs telling them that an armed force was gathering in Picardy with a view to invading England, and ordering them to raise forces and join him with all possible haste at Ware, Hertfordshire.[17] Henry appears to have been uncertain where to make a landing. According to Walsingham, he sailed up and down the coast-line trying to discover where the defences were weakest.[18] An advance guard under his retainer John Pelham put ashore at Pevensey and took the castle, a duchy property, by surprise.[19] But the duke himself and the larger part of his force sailed northwards and disembarked at Ravenspur on the Humber estuary, probably in the last few days of June.[20] In Yorkshire the duke could be sure of receiving a sympathetic reception. There were extensive duchy estates in the area, and he was within easy reach of some of the most powerful duchy castles. He headed first for Pickering,[21] to cover his flank, and then turned west-wards to Knaresborough. By 13 or 14 July he was at Pontefract. It is not known how many supporters he had with him when he first arrived, but the figure of sixty given by the Evesham writer is probably about right.[22] As he made his way slowly across Yorkshire, his numbers swelled. The duchy accounts record that some thirty-seven knights and esquires came to him with their companies and attendants.[23] At Doncaster on or around the 16th he won the backing of the earl of Northumberland and his son, Henry 'Hotspur'. The terms on which the two lords com-mitted themselves to his cause are unclear, but according to John

[17] Ibid., 32.

[18] Ibid., 117.

[19] CPR 1396–9, 596; Walker, 'Letters to the Dukes of Lancaster', 75–9.

[20] The date 30 June is suggested by a payment in a duchy of Lancaster account book to one John Davy for travelling from London to Dover 'on hearing of the lord's arrival at the end of the said month [June]' (DL28/4/1, fo.15ʳ). A date of a week earlier is suggested by a note in the Westminster Abbey Liber Niger (WAM, Book 1, fo.86ᵛ), which says that Henry 'came to England' ('venit . . . versus Angliam') on 23 June. A compromise would be to settle for a date somewhere between the two: the phrase 'versus Angliam' in the Liber Niger could imply travelling *to* England rather than actual arrival. The chroniclers mostly put Henry's arrival in early July: see Tuck, *Richard II and the Nobility*, 214.

[21] Which he had reached by 4 July (WAM, Book 1, fo.86ᵛ).

[22] *Chrons. Revolution*, 126. The Louth Park chronicle says that he had 100 men with him: *Chronicle of Louth Park Abbey*, ed. E. Venables (Lincolnshire Record Society, i, 1889), 43.

[23] Tuck, *Richard II and the Nobility*, 214. Tuck says that most of these men came from Lancashire and Yorkshire, but nearly twenty came from Nottinghamshire and Derbyshire: S. Payling, *Political Society in Lancastrian England. The Greater Gentry of Nottinghamshire* (Oxford, 1991), 135. According to a York writer, people referred to Henry as earl of Derby, ignorant that he was now duke of Hereford (*Historians of the Church of York*, ed. Raine, ii, 430).

Hardyng, writing forty years later, they said that they would support the duke in his endeavour to recover his ancestral estates.[24] The defection of the Percys, who were disenchanted with Richard's management of the north, gave Henry a considerable psychological boost.[25] With the most powerful of the northern lineages behind him, he could be seen as constituting a convincing challenge to the authority of the keeper of England and his council.

On 4 July the keeper had sent a messenger to Richard in Ireland to inform him of Duke Henry's landing.[26] It is likely that the king received the news no later than the 10th. However, it was nearly a fortnight before he undertook the return journey to Wales. The chroniclers offer a variety of explanations for the delay. Jean Creton, a Frenchman who was in the king's party, found a villain in the duke of Aumerle. Aumerle, he says, advised the king against any hasty action: after the councillors had decided on a speedy return he went 'secretly' to the king and urged him to hold back, saying there was a shortage of shipping; the best course, he suggested, was for an advance guard to be sent under Salisbury, while the king himself mustered his shipping at Waterford.[27] Creton was, of course, writing with the benefit of hindsight: he was aware that Aumerle was to play an ambivalent role in the revolt of the earls in January 1400, and he probably suspected that his deceitful behaviour went further back. But it is striking that other chroniclers offer confirmation of a change of plan. Walsingham says that 'just when everything was ready, Richard ordered that the horses and provisions, which had already been loaded on to the boats, be unloaded again and taken to a different port. As a result of this it was another seven days before the horses and other apparatus could once more be assembled on board ship.'[28] The problem, as both writers appear to have realized, lay in Richard's difficulty in mustering shipping. When the royal army had disembarked at Waterford in June, most of the vessels had been dispersed. Some of them had gone on to Dublin; others had been sent back to England. A return in force was impossible.[29] In the circumstances, sending an advance guard was probably the only practicable course. Thus, around 17 July Richard dispatched Salisbury to North Wales with a small retinue, probably giving him instructions to head for,

[24] *Chrons. Revolution*, 192–7.

[25] From 1396 Richard had appointed three courtier lords in succession to the wardenship of the Western March, which Hotspur had held – first Lord Beaumont, and then Huntingdon and Aumerle: Tuck, *Richard II and the Nobility*, 201; Tuck, 'Richard II and the Border Magnates', *Northern History*, iii (1968), 22–39.

[26] E403/562, 4 July.

[27] *Chrons. Revolution*, 138.

[28] Ibid., 121.

[29] Johnston, 'Richard II's Departure from Ireland', 793.

and to secure, Chester. Creton, who went with him, records the sequel. The earl summoned the Welsh gentry to a muster, promising that he would destroy the invader in three days. But the Welshmen had little confidence in him. They said, 'the king is not here . . . we believe that he is dead. We will no longer fight for you.' Fearful and demoralized, they broke ranks. Some of them returned home, while others gave their allegiance to the duke.[30]

Duke Henry's spies are likely to have kept him informed of the difficulties attending Richard's return to Wales. The duke was by this time making his way across the midlands. After his meeting with the Percys at Doncaster he moved slowly south, probably reaching Leicester, a duchy manor, on 20 July. At Leicester he paused to consider his future strategy. A number of possibilities lay open to him. He could carry on southwards to London, to take the capital, or head southwestwards to Bristol, to cut off Richard's return, or he could occupy Chester, the king's 'inner citadel'. Initially, he appears to have intended heading for London. But around 20 July York, as keeper, began moving slowly to the west in the hope of linking up with Richard, and Henry decided to follow him. Making his way through Coventry, Warwick and Evesham, he reached Gloucester on 25 or 26 July.[31] On the 27th he caught up with York at Berkeley. In Berkeley parish church, the monk of Evesham says, the two men had a meeting and came to an agreement.[32] The terms of the agreement are unrecorded, but their essence is clear: York offered his capitulation to the duke. Precisely why York gave in so easily is hard to say. Walsingham says that he was reluctant to stand in the way of one who had come to claim his rightful inheritance.[33] Very likely there is a measure of truth in the report, but there are signs that he was also experiencing trouble in holding his forces together. Although over 3,000 men had initially responded to his summons, many of them had deserted before 27 July, and it was left to a handful of diehards, notably Henry Despenser, bishop of Norwich, to offer resistance.[34] Whatever the justification for York's action, the meeting at Berkeley was a turning point in the duke's campaign. From this time on Henry and the keeper were to act in unison. On the

---

[30] *Chrons. Revolution*, 138–9.

[31] At Warwick he had removed Richard's badge of the white hart from the gateway of the castle: *Chrons. Revolution*, 135–6; J.B. Post, 'Courts, Councils and Arbitrators in the Ladbroke Manor Dispute', *Medieval Legal Records Edited in Memory of C.A.F. Meekings*, ed. R.F. Hunnisett and J.B. Post (London, 1978), 323–4.

[32] *Chrons. Revolution*, 127.

[33] Ibid., 118. For an analysis of the duke's conduct and motives, see D. Biggs, '"A Wrong whom Conscience and Kindred bid me to right": A Reassessment of Edmund of Langley, Duke of York, and the Usurpation of Henry IV', *Albion*, xxvi (1994), 253–72.

[34] *Chrons. Revolution*, 35.

following day the two men led their forces southwards to Bristol. The constable, Sir Peter Courtenay, immediately surrendered the castle, and Richard's councillors, Wiltshire, Bushy and Green, who had fled there from Oxford, were captured. On the next day, to the delight of the crowd, the three were executed.[35] York's presence at the executions could only have been seen as publicly committing him to Duke Henry's cause.

Within barely a month of his landing, Henry had won control of most of central and eastern England. Richard's delay in returning had been the cause of a massive haemorrhaging of his support. Many of his backers believed that he had either died or taken to flight, and retainers who would have fought for him laid down their arms. By the time that he finally landed in Wales, on or around 24 July, his position was critically weak. According to Adam of Usk, he immediately dispatched the earl of Gloucester to muster his tenantry in Glamorgan, but Gloucester's efforts were unavailing: the tenantry refused to fight.[36] Adam reports that the king was dismayed on hearing the news. Richard had probably anticipated making an advance east through Glamorgan to southern England, but in the light of the intelligence there now seemed little point. Richard lingered for some days near the coast. On 29 July – the day that Wiltshire, Bushy and Green were executed – he was at Whitland Abbey, near Carmarthen, where he managed to establish contact with some of York's officials.[37] Two days later he was at Carmarthen itself. Around then he must have received the news of York's defection and possibly too of the surrender of Bristol. Walsingham suggests that by this time he was suffering rapid changes of mood. Initially, the St Albans writer says, the king had declared that he would meet Duke Henry in battle, but later, and on reflection, he backed away from the idea.[38] Rumours began to circulate of a plot to capture him.[39] In the tense and febrile atmosphere of the camp Richard abandoned his earlier plans. Instead of advancing through Glamorgan, he decided to link up with Salisbury in the north. According to the Dieulacres writer, he fled in the dead of night attended by only fifteen companions.[40] Creton, who was with Salisbury, largely confirms the account. Richard, he says, fled at midnight disguised as a poor priest.

[35] Ibid., 128, 133–4. They were tried under the legal authority of the constable and marshal, the earls of Northumberland and Westmorland respectively: ibid., 128, 166–7.

[36] Usk, 177. For discussion of the narratives, see J. Sherborne, 'Richard II's return to Wales, July 1399', *WHR*, vii (1975), repr. in his *War, Politics and Culture in Fourteenth-Century England*, ed. Tuck, 119–29.

[37] Johnston, 'Richard II's Departure from Ireland', 795; *Chrons. Revolution*, 37.

[38] *Chrons. Revolution*, 122. Walsingham implies cowardice on the king's part.

[39] Ibid., 156.

[40] Ibid., 154.

Creton identifies his companions as including the dukes of Exeter and Surrey, the earl of Gloucester and the bishops of Carlisle, Lincoln and St David's.[41] When Richard's departure was discovered the next morning, the steward of the household, Thomas Percy, earl of Worcester, formally broke his rod of office and told the king's followers that they were free to disperse. It was an emotional occasion. Worcester, according to Walsingham, wept bitterly: he knew that the end of the reign was near.[42]

Richard's movements across central and northern Wales are only vaguely recorded by the chroniclers. All are agreed that the king ultimately reached Conway; Dieulacres has him passing through Harlech and Caernarfon; Walsingham also fits in a visit to Anglesey.[43] The journey, a distance of nearly 200 miles across difficult country, must have taken nine or ten days. All the while, the king's movements were shadowed by those of his adversary. Bolingbroke left Bristol on 29 or 30 July and headed northwards to Chester. He was at Hereford by 2 August, at Ludlow by the 4th, and at Shrewsbury, where he spent two days, by the 5th. At Shrewsbury he received a delegation from Chester led by Sir Robert Legh, the sheriff of Chester, which offered terms for the submission of the city.[44] Four days later Duke Henry made a ceremonial entry into Chester, to a welcome from the monks of St Werburgh and the other clergy of the city. The so-called 'inner citadel' of Richard's kingdom had fallen without a fight.

Richard's response to these events is described in detail in the *Metrical History* of the Frenchman, Jean Creton. Creton had returned to North Wales with Salisbury, and was at Conway with the earl when Richard arrived there. Creton describes the emotional first encounter between the two men. Both were tearful and distressed. 'Truly,' he wrote, 'it was a piteous sight to behold their looks and countenance.' Salisbury at once told Richard about his attempts to muster a force and the tale of desertions that had followed.[45] The king was miserable and downcast. Later there was a discussion about how best to proceed. Creton reports that the duke of Exeter took the lead and suggested that

---

[41] Ibid., 139–40. The bishops of Carlisle and St David's, respectively Thomas Merks and Guy Mone, were both Ricardian loyalists; the bishop of Lincoln was Henry Beaufort, Henry of Lancaster's half-brother. Sherborne, 'Richard II's Return to Wales', 124–5, errs in arguing that the Dieulacres writer has Richard taking his Cheshire retinue with him northwards. The chronicler only mentions the presence of the retinue at Carmarthen. It is clear from his account that when Richard went north he had with him only the fifteen companions.

[42] *Chrons. Revolution*, 122.

[43] Ibid., 154, 122.

[44] Henry's movements are detailed by Adam of Usk and the Evesham writer: ibid., 158, 128–9.

[45] Creton, 96–8.

envoys be dispatched to the duke at Chester to ascertain his intentions. Richard and his advisers went along with Exeter's suggestion, and the duke himself and his nephew Surrey were given authority to make the journey.[46] The two men probably arrived at Chester on 9 August. When they entered the castle, however, they were arrested and were never allowed to return. The duke took the line that any negotiations with the king must be conducted by men of his own choosing. On or around 10 August he appointed Northumberland to undertake a mission to Richard. Northumberland and his retinue probably arrived on the east bank of the Conway estuary on the 12th. Richard, of course, was unaware of their coming. So as not to alarm the king, Northumberland stationed the bulk of his men some way short of the estuary. He crossed to the other side with a handful of attendants and sent a herald to the king to request a meeting. On Salisbury's advice, according to Creton, Richard decided to admit him.[47]

The series of conferences that unfolded at Conway effectively sealed Richard's fate as king, and by the end of them his will to fight on had gone. However, reports of the exchanges are sketchy. There is no consensus on who was present or what was agreed. According to Creton, Kirkstall and John Hardyng, who wrote later, Northumberland was the only spokesman for the duke.[48] Dieulacres, Walsingham and the official account on the parliament roll, on the other hand, all have Archbishop Arundel present as well.[49] The discrepancy between the authorities is puzzling and not easily resolved. However, there are grounds for believing that Northumberland travelled to Conway alone. If the archbishop had been at his side, Creton, an eyewitness, would surely have said so; and he did not. Very likely, as J.W. Sherborne suggested, a role was created for the prelate in the later narratives to lend a measure of legitimacy to the proceedings.[50]

Accounts of the negotiations at Conway fall essentially into two groups – those of Lancastrian origin which maintain that Richard freely resigned his crown to the duke; and those written independently, which imply his surrender of something less.[51] The archetype of the first group is the official Lancastrian narrative of the deposition, the so-called 'Record and Process'. The essence of this version is that Richard

---

[46] Ibid., 106–9.

[47] Ibid., 121–2, 131–2.

[48] *Chrons. Revolution*, 135, 144–8. For discussion, see J. Sherborne, 'Perjury and the Lancastrian Revolution of 1399', *WHR*, xiv (1988), repr. in his *War, Politics and Culture in Fourteenth-Century England*, ed. Tuck, 131–54.

[49] *Chrons. Revolution*, 123, 155; *RP*, iii, 416.

[50] Sherborne, 'Perjury and the Lancastrian Revolution', 229.

[51] For a general discussion of the sources, see Taylor, *English Historical Literature*, ch. 9.

informed Northumberland and the archbishop that he would 'willingly yield up and renounce his crowns of England and France and his royal majesty, on account of his own inability and insufficiency, which he admitted'; and, furthermore, that he asked for the surrender to be done 'in the best manner and form that could be devised according to the counsel of learned men'.[52] The 'Record' is a purely propagandist account and its multitude of fictions was exposed long ago.[53] A very different picture is given by the writers who did not draw on Lancastrian propaganda. A couple of these were of French origin, but the majority were Englishmen who had access to local information. Predictably Jean Creton's narrative is the fullest and most circumstantial. Creton maintains that Northumberland told Richard that the duke would accept a peaceful settlement on three conditions: that his inheritance be restored to him; that a parliament be summoned over which he would preside as steward; and that five of the king's councillors – the dukes of Exeter and Surrey, the earl of Salisbury, the bishop of Carlisle and Richard Maudeleyn – be put on trial for treason.[54] Richard, according to Creton, spent several days considering these terms and decided in the end to accept them – subject to one condition: that the earl swore on the host that the duke intended 'no deceit'. When this act was done, 'agreement was made', and Richard voluntarily quitted the castle.[55] Creton's version of events is broadly corroborated by the witness of another non-Lancastrian writer, the Dieulacres chronicler. According to Dieulacres, while the king was at Conway, 'the duke sent an embassy with the request that he [the king] should present himself voluntarily to the duke who was then steward of England by hereditary right and to the commons without fear'.[56] The terms as summarized in this account are very similar to those described by Creton. The chronicler goes on to say that 'the archbishop of Canterbury and the earl of Northumberland as chief negotiators both promised, indeed they swore on the host, that the king would be permitted to retain his royal power and dominion'. Here the writer is confirming a point implicit in Creton, namely that Henry disavowed any bid for the crown.[57] Adam of Usk, who had accompanied Henry in his progress across England, made essentially the same

---

[52] *Chrons. Revolution*, 169–70.

[53] Clarke and Galbraith, 'The Deposition of Richard II', 125–55.

[54] *Chrons. Revolution*, 144–5.

[55] Ibid., 146–7.

[56] Sherborne's translation in 'Perjury and the Lancastrian Revolution', 232. The Latin reads: 'Interea dux regem audiens apud Conway prestolari misit legacionem ut se sponte duci tunc Anglie senescallo iure hereditario et communibus secure presentarent.' This hardly makes sense as it stands, and Sherborne plausibly suggests that 'presentarent' is a copyist's error for 'presentaret': which would give the meaning in the translation.

[57] *Chrons. Revolution*, 155.

point: Northumberland and the archbishop gave a promise to Richard that he would be able 'to save his dignity'.[58] The impression is given by all three writers that Henry was still limiting his ambitions. His goals at this stage were probably twofold: to obtain possession of the king's person and to procure the summoning of a parliament; beyond that, his plans were as yet uncertain. Little or no evidence is afforded by the accounts that he was dissimulating. Indeed, if anyone was dissimulating, it is likely to have been Richard. As Creton makes clear, Richard gave in to Northumberland only because he had to. 'Truly I swear to you', Creton reports the king telling his friends, 'that whatever assurances I give him [Northumberland], he will be put to bitter death for this outrage that he has done to us. Doubt not, there will be no parliament held at Westminster on this matter . . . I will muster men from all over Wales.' Richard was not interested in a genuine accommodation with his challengers; he was hankering after revenge.

However, by the end of the exchanges at Conway it must have been clear to the king that the struggle was as good as over. His army had dispersed; he had been deserted by his friends and supporters, and supplies were short. The duke, on the other hand, had the tide of events in his favour. Theoretically it was open to the king to stay in the safety of Conway, obliging the duke to challenge him. But Richard does not seem to have considered this option. Probably he found his circumstances too depressing.[59] The chroniclers suggest that he hesitated for a day or two before letting Northumberland know his decision.[60] On or around 15 August, he agreed to leave.[61] An arrangement was made whereby Northumberland would go ahead, to prepare dinner at Rhuddlan, while Richard followed. Richard duly set out and crossed to the other side of the estuary. But a few miles further on an incident occurred which convinced him that he had been tricked (plate 26d). Northumberland, on the outward journey, had stationed the bulk of his retinue a mile or two short of Conway in a valley. Richard, now breasting a hill, suddenly caught sight of the force. Creton, who witnessed the incident, was frightened. Richard was not only frightened but angered; and immediately he demanded that they go back to Conway. Northumberland resisted the demand and protested his innocence, saying that the king dishonoured him. For a second time he swore an oath on the host.[62] The journey was resumed and in the

---

[58] Ibid., 159.

[59] There was probably little food in the castle.

[60] Dieulacres says three days, but this is too long (*Chrons. Revolution*, 155).

[61] From 16 August letters were issued at Chester in the king's name: *CPR 1396–9*, 586–97.

[62] *Chrons. Revolution*, 147–8. For discussion of the incident, see Sherborne, 'Perjury and the Lancastrian Revolution', 148.

evening the party reached Flint. Throughout the day's proceedings Northumberland had treated the king with courtesy; but, as both men were well aware, the king was now effectively the earl's prisoner.

Before leaving Conway, Northumberland had sent a messenger to Bolingbroke with the news of Richard's surrender. On Saturday, 16 August, the duke moved with his force to Flint, a distance of eight miles, to meet the party. Creton, who had accompanied Richard, gives a vivid account of the day's proceedings.[63] Richard, he says, rose early in the morning, looking doleful and depressed. He lingered over his breakfast, because he had no appetite. After hearing mass he climbed to the battlements and from there he caught his first sight of Bolingbroke's host making its way along the coast. The sight alarmed him. 'Now I can see the end of my days coming,' he told Salisbury. Later, he saw a small group of men leave the host and spur their horses to the castle. Among them were Archbishop Arundel, the duke of Aumerle and the earl of Worcester.[64] Richard ordered the three lords to be admitted to the castle and he conversed with them in the keep. While the men were talking, the Lancastrian forces disposed themselves more closely around the castle. Richard climbed to the battlements again and looked out. When he saw the show of force, he complained to Northumberland, who persuaded the duke not to enter the castle until the king had eaten. The duke was by now standing only a few yards from the entrance. Creton records that he and a companion of his were introduced to him by Lancaster herald. 'Have no fear, young men,' the duke told them. 'Keep close to me, and I will answer for your lives.' A little later, the duke finally entered the castle. Richard was still in the keep, where he had taken dinner. At Northumberland's request he came down. As soon as the duke saw him, he bowed low to the ground and, as the king came closer, he bowed a second time with his cap in his hand. The king took off his hood and welcomed him. The duke, still bowing, said, 'My lord, I have come sooner than you sent for me, and I shall tell you why. It is said that you have governed your people too harshly, and that they are discontented. If it is pleasing to the Lord, I shall help you to govern them better.' Richard answered, 'If it pleases you, fair cousin, then it pleases us well.' The exchange then ended. The duke turned briefly to the bishop of Carlisle and to the knights; then he ordered horses to be prepared. Later the same afternoon the two sides set out for Chester.

On his arrival at Chester Richard was treated a good deal less defer-

---

[63] Creton, 149–73; extracts in *Chrons. Revolution*, 148–51. Cf. Shakespeare, *King Richard II*, Act III, scene iii.

[64] Arundel had thus clearly not been at Conway. Worcester had joined Henry's ranks after the dispersal of Richard's household near Carmarthen.

entially than he had been at Flint. He was taken straight to the highest tower of the castle and entrusted to the care of the sons of Gloucester and Arundel, who, Creton says, 'hated him more than anyone because he had put their fathers to death'.[65] In a tiny room nearly opposite his own he could see the duke of Exeter but was unable to speak to him. On or around 20 August Duke Henry and his retinue, with the king, set out for London. They spent the first two nights at Nantwich, and then made their way south through Stafford, Lichfield and Coventry.[66] According to the author of the *Traison et Mort*, the Cheshiremen made an abortive attempt to rescue the king somewhere near Lichfield.[67] The *Traison* is a source rarely to be trusted on matters of detail, but it is possible that the attack is to be identified with one which, according to a later indictment, was made by Richard's Cheshire affinity at Cholmondeston near Nantwich.[68] After they resumed their journey southwards, the party passed through Northampton, Dunstable and St Albans. At some point along the way a delegation of Londoners came out to offer the submission of their city.[69] By about 1 September the party had reached the capital. The duke went to the bishop of London's palace near St Paul's, while Richard was quickly dispatched to the Tower.[70]

On 19 August, before he left Chester, the duke had issued summonses in the king's name for a parliament to assemble at the end of September.[71] It is fair to assume that the duke intended presiding over the assembly in his capacity as steward. The earls (or the dukes) of Lancaster had been stewards of England for over a century, and Henry's plan was probably to use the powers given to him by the office to inflict appropriate punishment on the courtiers. But some time towards the end of August he changed his mind and revealed loftier ambitions. Walsingham says that on his return to Chester the duke sent messengers to every abbey with orders that histories be combed for matters touching the state and governance of the English realm since the Conquest.[72] A couple of weeks after this, a committee was appointed of 'certain doctors, bishops and others', of whom Adam of Usk was one, to

---

[65] Creton, 173–4; *Chrons. Revolution*, 151.
[66] The party's itinerary can be charted from the evidence of the Evesham writer (*Chrons. Revolution*, 130) and the chancery enrolments (*CPR 1396–9*, 590–3).
[67] *Traison et Mort*, 211.
[68] Walsingham also mentions attacks on the duke's train: *Chrons. Revolution*, 124. For discussion of the incident, see Morgan, *War and Society in Medieval Cheshire*, 204.
[69] Barron, 'The Deposition of Richard II', 142–3.
[70] *Chrons. Revolution*, 131. The Evesham writer says that Richard wore the same simple set of garments for the whole journey (ibid., 130).
[71] *CCR 1396–9*, 520–1.
[72] *Chrons. Revolution*, 124–5. Walsingham makes this contemporaneous with the summons of parliament (19 Aug.).

consider 'the matter of setting aside King Richard, and of choosing the duke of Lancaster in his stead, and how it was to be done'.[73] By these two initiatives the process was set in motion leading to the deposition.

Just when the duke became committed to his new course is hard to say. It was not until 10 September that he openly signalled his ambition by ceasing to employ Richard's regnal year in his duchy of Lancaster letters.[74] But the general drift of his thinking was probably known to his supporters well before then. The reasons for his change of mind can only be surmised. Doubtless he had been encouraged by the warmth of his reception and the rapid triumph of his cause: his ambition may have been fed by the heady brew of popular favour. But it is also likely that to some extent he was acting defensively. He knew Richard to be vengeful and untrustworthy. Barely a couple of years before, he had witnessed the terrible punishment the king had inflicted on the former Appellant lords for challenging the prerogative and executing his friends. There was no guarantee that if he were left on the throne he would not inflict similar punishment again. In all probability it was self-preservation rather than vaulting ambition that was the main spur to his action. But whatever the balance of motives in his mind, the illegality of the duke's intended course was clear. The duke was only too conscious of this himself. That was why he ordered the searches of the chronicles: he wanted his agents to come up with suitable precedents for his actions. His aim was to make a wholly illegitimate act appear as nearly legitimate as possible.

Finding a watertight way of setting aside the king, however, was more easily said than done. Richard was crowned and anointed, and his right to remain on the throne had been recognized by Northumberland under oath at Conway. Contrary to the impression already being put about by the Lancastrian propagandists, and reported by Usk,[75] there was little evidence that Richard was prepared freely to surrender his crown: indeed, right to the end he was to take a principled stand on his anointed status. Even if he had been willing to oblige his supplanter by resigning, this would not have settled the problem of the transfer of power, for resignation was an act that could be withdrawn: there needed to be formal proceedings of deposition as well. But then such questions arose as: deposition on what grounds? and by what means? An obvious precedent was provided by the deposition of Edward II three-quarters of a century earlier. The case against Edward had been that he had been 'insufficient to govern': it was alleged that he was unduly

[73] Ibid., 160.

[74] Sherborne, 'Perjury and the Lancastrian Revolution', 152.

[75] *Chrons. Revolution*, 160.

influenced by others, that he had lost Scotland and Gascony, and that he was guilty of neglect and dilapidation.[76] Approval of these charges was followed by the king's formal removal and the succession of his son. However, there was a difficulty with this precedent, for it was by no means clear that the king had actually been deposed. Parliamentary acceptance of the articles had been followed by the king's statement of abdication; there had been no formal deposition in the legal sense. Possibly a more useful precedent was found in the papal deposition of Frederick II in 1245. Frederick had been deposed by Innocent IV on grounds of a long list of crimes, ranging from tyranny and perjury to sacrilege and suspicion of heresy. The sentence had been published in a bull *Ad apostolice dignitatis*, a copy of which, Adam of Usk says, was used by the committee.[77] It was the precedent of the pope's deposition of Frederick which appears to have provided the model for the lengthy catalogue of crimes – thirty-three in all – with which Richard was charged. Adam makes clear that these crimes constituted legal grounds for deposition. There was an echo, conscious or unconscious, of the articles of 1327 in the emphasis in the opening declaration on the king's insufficiency, but the case against Richard was essentially one that had its basis in canon law.[78]

In addition to finding an acceptable way of deposing Richard, the committee had to invent a suitable title for Duke Henry. This too was a task that bristled with difficulties. Henry was not Richard's nearest male heir. That position was occupied by Edmund, earl of March, who was descended in the female line from Edward III's second son, whereas Duke Henry was descended from the third. To circumvent the problem, the committee, according to Usk, investigated the 'Crouchback legend': the story that Edmund 'Crouchback', earl of Lancaster, had been the elder rather than the younger brother of Edward I, but had been passed over for the throne because of deformity. Various chronicle accounts were consulted, but no evidence for the legend was found.[79] Walsingham says that Henry seriously considered claiming the throne by right of conquest, but was discouraged from doing this by Sir William Thirning, the chief justice of King's Bench, on the grounds that to do so would create insecurity in men's minds about their property.[80] Henry's claim, when it was eventually framed, bore all the hallmarks of a compromise. There was a vestigial reference to

[76] *Select Documents of English Constitutional History, 1307–1485*, ed. S.B. Chrimes and A.L. Brown (London, 1961), 37–8.

[77] *Chrons. Revolution*, 160.

[78] G.E. Caspary, 'The Deposition of Richard II and the Canon Law', *Proceedings of the Second International Congress of Medieval Canon Law* (Boston, 1965), 189–201.

[79] Usk, 182–4.

[80] *Annales*, 282.

conquest and to the need to reform the realm,[81] but the main argument was an hereditary one: that Henry was 'descended by right line of the blood coming from the good Lord Henry third'. Possibly Henry was making a vague allusion in this statement to the Crouchback legend, but more likely he was laying claim as the nearest heir in the male line. By the later fourteenth century it was becoming common for the private estates of the nobility to descend in the male line rather than through the heir general, and Henry may have been implying that it was appropriate for the crown to do the same.[82] Three-quarters of a century earlier the French monarchy had successfully applied this doctrine on the extinction of the direct line of the Capetians. It could be argued that Henry was only following continental practice by doing the same.

By the last week of September the committee appears to have reached agreement on a way of proceeding. The first step, it was proposed, was to obtain a formal renunciation of the crown from Richard. This could be presented to the session of parliament due to meet on 30 September and, once it had been accepted, Henry could be acclaimed king. According to the 'Record and Process', the formal Lancastrian narrative of the deposition, the procedure was put into operation without hitch. On 29 September a delegation headed by Bolingbroke visited Richard in the Tower and the latter, 'with a cheerful countenance', resigned in the duke's favour and as a token of goodwill gave him his signet ring.[83] It is unlikely that this narrative can be accepted. The 'Manner of King Richard's Renunciation', the account of an eyewitness, probably from Christ Church, Canterbury, gives a very different picture of events. According to the 'Manner', Richard resisted his supplanter and only gave in under sustained pressure.[84] The narrative says that there was a series of meetings spread over two days. On Sunday, 28 September, a delegation headed by the earl of Northumberland was sent to Richard to determine whether or not he was willing to resign. Initially, it says, the king was reluctant to give a response: he asked for a copy of the proposed resignation and said that he would reflect on it overnight. On the following day the delegation returned and put the

---

[81] '. . . God of his grace hath sent me, with helpe of my kyn and of my frendes to recover it; the whiche Rewme was in poynt to be undone for defaut of governance and undoyng of the gode lawes' (RP, iii, 422–3).

[82] A. Tuck, Crown and Nobility 1272–1461 (London, 1985), 221.

[83] Chrons. Revolution, 169–70.

[84] Ibid., 162–8. The 'Manner of King Richard's Renunciation' was first published by G.O. Sayles, 'The Deposition of Richard II: Three Lancastrian Narratives', BIHR, liv (1981), 257–70. Sayles supposed that it was an early draft of the official Lancastrian narrative. Almost certainly, however, it was the work of an eyewitness with associations with Canterbury – possibly Thomas Chillenden, the prior of Christ Church: C. Given-Wilson, 'The Manner of King Richard's Renunciation: A "Lancastrian Narrative"?', EHR, cviii (1993), 365–70.

matter to the king a second time. This time Richard was resolutely defiant: he said that he would not resign in any circumstances, and added for good measure that 'he would like it explained to him how it was that he could resign the crown, and to whom'. When further arguments were put to him, Richard softened his stance, and said that he would resign if Bolingbroke himself visited him. Later the same day, accordingly, 'after dinner' Bolingbroke came to the Tower at the head of a third delegation. The question was once more asked whether Richard was willing to resign his right to the crown. Richard replied that he would 'willingly do so in the interests of his dear cousin of Lancaster but only on certain conditions'. The duke, however, would not accept this: Richard, he said, must resign 'simply, and without conditions'. At this point Richard finally gave in. Under pressure he read out the schedule which had been prepared for him and asked only for one favour: that he retain the lands which he had acquired in order to endow an anniversary for his soul in Westminster Abbey; this request was conceded. The names of the witnesses were then added to the schedule. Shortly afterwards the meeting ended.

For Richard the agreement of 29 September marked the effective end of his long struggle against fate. For nearly two months he had watched the life-blood of his kingship drain away. The leadership that he had given since returning from Ireland had been mediocre and erratic, and his behaviour in public had alternated between the angry and the despairing. But throughout those seven weeks he had fought tenaciously to cling on to at least the outward vestiges of his regality. Never once did he contemplate freely resigning the crown. At Conway he had given in to Northumberland only on condition that he remained in his kingly estate; and thereafter he was consistent in arguing that his kingly dignity be respected. The narrative of the Canterbury eyewitness gives an idea of the many difficulties that he placed in the usurper's path. A recurrent theme in his pronouncements was his insistence on the inalienable nature of his kingship. According to the Evesham writer, he said in the Tower that he could not renounce the 'characters' impressed on his soul: the sanctity of his anointing was indelible.[85] At no time in the lengthy exchanges with his interlocutors did he accept the idea of directly transferring his rights to his supplanter. According to the Dieulacres writer, when he surrendered his crown, he 'placed it on the ground and resigned his right to God' – from whom he had received it.[86] Richard's conception of his royal office was an exalted, but in legal terms an entirely correct, one. The difficulty

---

[85] *HVR*, 159. For discussion, see H.G. Wright, 'The Protestation of Richard II in the Tower in September, 1399', *BJRL*, xxiii (1943), 151–66.

[86] *Chrons. Revolution*, 155.

facing him was the embarrassing, even painful, disparity between that
exalted conception and the circumstances in which he found himself.
With Bolingbroke in the ascendant and controlling the levers of power,
little beyond the shadow of his kingship was left to him. In his prison
cell he could only console himself by musing sorrowfully on his fate.
When Usk paid him a visit, he reflected, 'what a strange land this is, and
a fickle, which has exiled, slain, destroyed or ruined so many kings,
rulers and great men, and is ever tainted with strife and envy'; and he
went on to recount the histories and names of sufferers from the
earliest habitation of the kingdom.[87] Richard's fascination with English
royal genealogy never deserted him. But whereas in times gone by it
had been a source of strength – a mainspring of both action and piety
– now it was only a cause of doleful reflection.

In the wake of the meetings in the Tower, the record of the king's
resignation was presented to parliament in Westminster Hall on
Tuesday, 30 September. John Burbach, a doctor of laws, read out the
schedule of resignation, using the copy that Richard himself had used,
and the assembly shouted their approval, 'Yes, yes, yes.' After this, John
Ferriby, a notary, read out a summary of what the 'Manner of King
Richard's Renunciation' calls 'the points given as reasons for the king's
deposition': namely 'the things that he had done which were contrary
to the crown . . . the vengeful sentences given against the lords and
other points, including the will which he had made before he went to
Ireland'.[88] The archbishop of Canterbury asked the assembly for their
approval of the proposed deposition, and again there were cries of 'Yes,
yes, yes.' According to the Traison et Mort, Thomas Merks, the bishop of
Carlisle, stood up at this point and declared that Richard should not be
condemned unheard. No other source, however, mentions the bishop's
intervention, and it seems that the story should be regarded as a fiction.[89] None the less there is evidence of an undercurrent of unease in
the assembly. According to the 'Manner of King Richard's Renunciation', Bolingbroke asked the lords whether they assented to his kingship 'with their hearts as well as their mouths': for, if they did not, he
went on, 'it would not be any great surprise to me'. The duke was then
given the reassurance that he was seeking. According to the writer,
another cry of 'Yes, yes, yes' went up.

On the following day (1 October) the proctors of the estates brought
news of the deposition proceedings to Richard in the Tower. Sir

[87] Ibid., 160–1; cf. Shakespeare, Richard II, Act III, scene ii, 155–60.
[88] This was presumably an early draft of the deposition articles.
[89] Palmer, 'Authorship of the French Chronicles of the Revolution', 411–12;
Chrons. Revolution, 190–1. Shakespeare used the Traison's witness (mediated
through Holinshed) to dramatic effect in Richard II, Act IV, scene i, 114–49. For
Merks's career, see BRUO, ii, 1263–4.

William Thirning, the chief justice, speaking 'in the name of the estates and the people', renounced their homage and allegiance.[90] Richard, according to the parliamentary record, said simply that he 'looked not hereafter, but hoped that his cousin would be a good lord to him'.[91] In Walsingham's version of the episode there were some lengthier exchanges. The St Albans writer says that Richard maintained that he could never renounce the characters of a spiritual nature which had been bestowed on him at his coronation. Thirning replied that he had himself admitted that he was unfit to govern. Richard's retort was that this was not true: what had happened was that his government had been rejected by his people. Thirning then reminded him of his signed renunciation. Richard managed a thin smile; he had no answer to this. He merely asked the chief justice to ensure that he had the means to support himself honourably.[92] By now his honour was all that was left to him. He was a simple knight: Sir Richard of Bordeaux, as he had been as a boy.

The end of Richard II's twenty-two-year reign was deemed to have occurred on 29 September. Accordingly, on the 30th the parliament which had been summoned in his name was dissolved and a new assembly summoned in the name of his successor. The elected membership of the new assembly was the same as that of the old. On the opening day of the session (6 October) Archbishop Arundel gave an address on the text 'vir dominabitur populo', justifying the rejection of Richard the childlike and the selection of the manful Henry. After the archbishop's address the proceedings were adjourned for a week until after the new king's coronation. The coronation was staged on a day of particular significance to Richard – St Edward's Day (13 October). A number of changes were made to the traditional ceremonial. First, and most significantly, according to Froissart, a closed crown, 'a crown with arches in the shape of a cross', was used.[93] If Froissart is right, the crown was of imperial type, and Henry's purpose in using it must have been to stress the sovereign nature of his kingly authority. The second innovation was made in the ceremony of anointing. For the first time, use was made of the miraculous phial of oil said to have been presented to Becket by the Virgin Mary, and afterwards hidden at Poitiers, until discovered there by Henry's grandfather, Henry of Grosmont. According to Walsingham, Richard had come across the phial while searching in the Tower a year or two previously and had asked Archbishop Arundel to anoint him with it. The archbishop had

---

[90] *Chrons. Revolution*, 187.
[91] Ibid., 188.
[92] Ibid., 188–9.
[93] Froissart, ii, 700. For a discussion, see W.H. St John Hope, 'The King's Coronation Ornaments', *The Ancestor*, i (1902), 153–4.

refused.[94] There is an irony in the fact that the first king to use the oil should have been Richard's supplanter; but, given the dubious nature of his title, it is hard to think of anyone in greater need of the attributes of legitimation.

In the wake of his accession Henry had to decide what to do with the person of his predecessor. The issue was a difficult one. Richard was young, and there was every expectation that he would live for some time. He could easily become the focus for disaffected elements, as Edward II had been in 1327. Henry's intentions regarding his predecessor are difficult to establish. It is possible that he considered putting him on trial for his crimes. In October the commons in parliament petitioned him to hold a trial, but he gave an equivocal reply, saying that 'he did not wish to respond until all the prelates were present'; possibly he was worried that a trial could lead to a reopening of old wounds. A couple of days after this Archbishop Arundel and the earl of Northumberland asked the lords what they thought should be done, 'for the king does not wish to deprive [his predecessor] of his life'. The lords' reply was that he should be imprisoned in a secret and secure location, where he could be guarded by trustworthy persons and waited on by strangers.[95] Some time towards the end of October he was finally removed from the Tower. According to the *Traison*, he was dispatched first to Gravesend and later, in the disguise of a forester, to Leeds in Kent.[96] From Leeds, probably at the beginning of December, he was sent northwards to the mighty Lancastrian fortress of Pontefract.[97]

It was presumably Henry's expectation that at Pontefract his predecessor would be quietly forgotten: that with the passage of time the memory of his rule would fade and affection for his person weaken. However, the king's somewhat naive optimism was not to be borne out. There was no early closing of the political ranks. Richard's former courtiers, despite their generous treatment by the new king, continued to grieve over his loss and hankered after his restoration. By early to mid-December a group of these began hatching a plot. The ringleaders were the earls of Salisbury, Huntingdon, Rutland and Kent, and Lord Despenser.[98] The details of their plans are obscure, but it seems that

---

[94] *Chrons. Revolution*, 201; T.A. Sandquist, 'The Holy Oil of St Thomas of Canterbury', *Essays in Medieval History Presented to Bertie Wilkinson*, ed. T.A. Sandquist and M.R. Powicke (Toronto, 1969), 330–44.

[95] *Annales*, 311, 313; *RP*, iii, 426.

[96] *Traison et Mort*, 228. The *Brut* and an anonymous York writer also say Leeds: *Brut*, 359; *Historians of the Church of York*, ed. Raine, ii, 430.

[97] The Kirkstall chronicler says that he was taken first to Knaresborough: *The Kirkstall Abbey Chronicles*, ed. J. Taylor (Thoresby Society, xlii, 1952), 82.

[98] Huntingdon, Rutland, Kent and Despenser were the former dukes of Exeter, Aumerle, Surrey, and earl of Gloucester respectively. Demotion to their former ranks was the only punishment that Henry had inflicted on these men after his accession.

they intended seizing the king and his sons in the New Year celebrations at Windsor and then arranging for Richard's release. By some means, perhaps through the treachery of Rutland, Henry learned of the scheme. Hurriedly returning to London, he summoned a force from the midlands and closed the ports. The rebels in the meantime had retreated westwards along the Thames valley, proclaiming Richard as king as they did so. In Gloucestershire their followers melted away, and at Cirencester on 8 January Salisbury was rounded on by the townsmen and lynched. Despenser managed to escape to Bristol, but was seized and murdered there on the 15th. Huntingdon, who had apparently lingered in the south-east, was seized at Pleshy in Essex and beheaded.[99]

By the second week of January the rising was all but over. Henry had scored a near effortless triumph over his opponents. The rebel leaders had been poorly organized and drew on little support in the country. All the same, their disloyalty brought home to Henry the vulnerability of his regime so long as Richard lived. The matter of the former king's future was considered by the council on or around 8 February. The minute made of the meeting was strangely portentous: if Richard was alive, it said, he should be kept in safe-keeping; but, if he were dead, he should be shown openly to the people, so that they would be aware of the fact.[100] The implication of the minute, if scarcely spelled out, was clear: Richard was to be disposed of. Whether or not a direct order to this effect was sent to Pontefract there is no way of knowing. But certainly in mid- to late February Richard met his end. Usk gave the date of his death as the last day of the month; the consensus of the other writers was a fortnight earlier.[101] The chroniclers speculated wildly regarding the manner and cause of his death.[102] Generally, the line taken by writers unsympathetic to Henry was that the cause was foul play. According to one account, that of the *Traison et Mort*, the former king was set upon and hacked to death by a group of henchmen led by a knight called Sir Piers Exton.[103] The *Traison*'s story circulated widely, and it ultimately found its way into Shakespeare; but Sir Piers Exton is a figure otherwise unknown to history, and the story must be dismissed as an invention.[104] According to a parallel, but more believable

---

[99] The fullest account of the rising of the earls is still that of J.H. Wylie, *History of England under Henry IV* (4 vols, London, 1884–98), i, 91–111; but see also J.L. Kirby, *Henry IV of England* (London, 1970), 87–90, and D. Crook, 'Central England and the Revolt of the Earls', *HR*, lxiv (1991), 403–10.

[100] *PPC*, i, 107.

[101] *Chrons. Revolution*, 229, 241.

[102] For discussion of the sources, see T. Amyot, 'An Inquiry concerning the Death of Richard II', *Archaeologia*, xx (1824), 424–42; P.W. Dillon, 'Remarks on the Manner of Death of King Richard II', ibid., xxviii (1840), 75–95.

[103] *Chrons. Revolution*, 233–4.

[104] No marks of violence were found on Richard's body when it was exhumed in the nineteenth century: A.P. Stanley, 'On an Examination of the Tombs of Richard

tradition, the former king was starved to death by his gaolers. This was the version of events given by the Whalley Abbey chronicler and, later, by John Hardyng;[105] and in 1405 it was espoused by Archbishop Scrope in the manifesto for his rebellion.[106] Among the writers of Lancastrian persuasion an entirely different explanation found favour. This was that Richard had died of a combination of grief and voluntary abstinence. Walsingham's version was that Richard became so depressed by the failure of the earls' rising that he denied himself food: as a result, the orifice leading to his stomach contracted and when he wanted to eat he could not.[107] According to the simpler version of the *Eulogium* writer, he simply became so sad that he refused all food.[108] Various other writers veered uneasily between the two theories. The Monk of Evesham commented that he had heard that the king had refused all food: but then went on to say that others maintained, with some truth, that he had been starved.[109] Usk, in a Delphic pronouncement, managed to combine the two versions in a single statement. Richard, he wrote, 'grieved ever more sorely and mourned even to death, which came to him most miserably on the last day of February, as he lay in chains in Pontefract castle, tormented by Sir [Thomas] Swynford with starving fare'.[110] Usk, like the other commentators on the subject, was driven to inconsistency or speculation because of the lack of clear evidence for the king's fate. Oddly, the one contemporary who was willing to admit his ignorance was Froissart. For once forswearing invention, he said merely that 'of the manner of Richard's death I know nothing'.[111]

The government reacted swiftly to receipt of the news from Pontefract. On 17 February a payment of £80 was made to one William Pampilion esquire to go to the town 'to transport the body of Richard, former king of England . . . to London'.[112] The journey southwards was slow. There were lengthy stops in the major towns to allow the body to be put on display. Walsingham – or, at least, someone to whom Walsingham had spoken – saw the body at St Albans. 'That part of the king's body' was shown, the chronicler wrote, 'by which he could be

---

II and Henry III in Westminster Abbey', *Archaeologia*, xlv (1880), 309–27. The name 'Exton' is possibly a corruption of 'Bukton': Peter Bukton was constable of Knaresborough (*Kirkstall Abbey Chronicles*, 82; *Works of Geoffrey Chaucer*, 539, 864).

[105] *Chrons. Revolution*, 51; *Chronicle of John Hardyng*, ed. H. Ellis (London, 1812), 357.

[106] Wylie, *History of England under Henry IV*, i, 112.

[107] Ibid., 229.

[108] *Eulogium*, 387. See also Gower's *Cronica Tripertita*, *Major Latin Works of John Gower*, 324–5.

[109] HVR, 166; *Chrons. Revolution*, 241.

[110] *Chrons. Revolution*, 243.

[111] Froissart, ii, 708.

[112] *PPC*, 107; E403/564, 17 Feb., 6 April.

recognized, namely from the base of his forehead down to his throat'.[113] As a clerk in King's Bench wrote in 1413, Richard's body was 'seen as dead by thousands upon thousands in the city of London and elsewhere in the realm'.[114] The policy of putting the body on display was almost certainly dictated by Henry himself. An anonymous English chronicler wrote that Henry was anxious that everyone should know that the body was Richard's 'and no one else's'.[115] The king's belief was presumably that the more widely his predecessor's demise was acknowledged, the less likely disaffected elements would be to seek his restoration. In a limited sense the king was right. Among the politically aware – the nobility and gentry – there were few apart from the Percys who seriously supposed that Richard was still alive – or had returned from the dead. Among the lower orders, however, the position was different. Not only did stories of the risen Richard stubbornly persist; well into the new reign an obscure impostor, Thomas Ward of Trumpington, managed to pass himself off as the real Richard in exile in Scotland.

A number of reasons can be offered for the pervasiveness of the myth of Richard's survival. At one level, the myth was a natural enough expression of the tradition of loyalist opposition – of the belief, in this case, that Richard's continued lordship could legitimize the opposition to his successor. Deeper down, however, the myth had its origins in the view that the usurpation had unbalanced the world: that the traditional order had been upset and that the only hope of restoring it lay in the rule of a just king. Henry's policy of constantly having his predecessor's body put on display could never address this underlying source of anxiety: only the legitimacy that he so conspicuously lacked could allay it. Henry may never have been as badly tormented by Richard's ghost as Macbeth had been by Banquo's; but all the same, the appearances of the ghost were a constant reminder of the doubtful legitimacy of his regime.[116]

Richard's coffin, when it arrived in London, was taken almost immediately to St Paul's.[117] The solemn journey through the capital was made on a hearse draped in black cloth and adorned with the arms of St

---

[113] *Annales*, 331.

[114] *Select Cases in the Court of King's Bench under Richard II, Henry IV and Henry V*, ed. G.O. Sayles (Selden Society, lxxxviii, 1971), 212.

[115] *An English Chronicle*, ed. Davies, 21.

[116] P. McNiven, 'Rebellion, Sedition and the Legend of Richard II's Survival in the Reigns of Henry IV and Henry V', *BJRL*, lxxvi (1994), 93–117; P. Morgan, 'Henry IV and the Shadow of Richard II', *Crown, Government and People in the Fifteenth Century*, ed. R.E. Archer (Stroud, 1995), 1–31; P. Strohm, 'The Trouble with Richard: The Reburial of Richard II and Lancastrian Symbolic Strategy', *Speculum*, lxxi (1996), 87–111.

[117] *Chronicle of John Hardyng*, ed. Ellis, 357.

George and St Edward.[118] On Saturday, 6 March a requiem mass was celebrated in the cathedral which Henry himself attended. The royal almoner distributed 25 marks to 'various religious priests' to say a thousand masses for the king's soul, while a confessor doled out pennies to the poor.[119] On the following day a second mass was celebrated at which the nobility and the London citizenry paid their respects.[120] At the end of these ceremonies the body was taken to the Dominican friary at King's Langley, where it was laid to rest. The body arrived at the house in the dead of night, and the ceremony of interment took place on the following morning. It was a simple affair, devoid of pomp, and the only dignitaries in attendance were the bishop of Lichfield, Richard's former confessor, and the abbots of Waltham and St Albans.[121] As Adam of Usk wryly observed, 'how many thousand marks [Richard] had spent on burial places of vainglory among the kings at Westminster! But Fortune ordered it otherwise.'[122]

Richard's body remained in its grave at King's Langley for the duration of Henry IV's life. But on Henry V's accession it was exhumed and reburied in its intended resting place at Westminster. Henry V's initiative probably originated in two motives: his desire to atone for his father's usurpation and his need to silence the rumours that Richard was still alive. The ceremony of reinterment was a grandiose if sombre one. A special hearse was commissioned and fixed up with lights for the service, and the banners used only a few months previously for Henry IV's funeral were borrowed for the occasion from Canterbury. Richard's body was stripped of its leaden lap and laid in a new elm coffin. A large congregation of bishops, abbots, lords and knights followed the procession to the abbey, and 100 marks were distributed as largesse along the route. The service of reinterment was attended by Henry himself. Subsequently the king made detailed arrangements for Richard's future commemoration. He ordered that four large tapers were to burn continually at the tomb; at the same time a dirge and a requiem mass were to be sung and 6s 8d to be given to the poor each week, along with £20 in pennies at each yearly anniversary.[123] Richard himself had made elaborate arrangements for his funeral in the will which he had dictated in April 1399, before his departure for Ireland.[124]

[118] Creton, 221n.

[119] E403/564, 20 March.

[120] Annales, 331.

[121] Ibid. The bishop of Lichfield was John Burghill, himself a Dominican: see above, 320. Waltham was, of course, a house of royal foundation.

[122] Usk, 205.

[123] For the reinterment, see J.H. Wylie and W.T. Waugh, The Reign of Henry V (3 vols, Cambridge, 1914–29), i, 207–11. Cf. Shakespeare, Henry V, Act IV, scene i, 291–301.

[124] Foed., viii, 75–6.

A generation later Henry V, his second cousin, ensured that his wishes were honoured in the spirit if not in the letter.

The tomb in Westminster Abbey, which the king had commissioned on his wife's death, was Richard's last resting place. Even here, however, his remains were not left in peace. On numerous occasions over the centuries the bones were disturbed by hands being inserted through openings made in the panelling on the sides. In 1766, according to Gerrard Andrewes, later dean of Canterbury, a Westminster schoolboy helped himself to Richard's lower jawbone. In 1871, when the tomb was opened and an inspection carried out, the remains, though well preserved, were in disarray. Anne's skeleton was nearly gone. Richard's was fairly complete, except for the lower jaw, clavicle, scapula and some ribs, but throughout the tomb there was evidence of disturbance and a variety of foreign objects had been introduced.[125] These objects were all gathered and examined. It was evident that some of them had been pushed in at various times through the panelling; but one or two others, notably a pair of plumber's shears, had probably been left at the reinterment in 1413. On Dean Stanley's initiative, the artefacts were assembled in a box and placed separately, and the bones of Richard and his queen arranged as nearly as possible in their proper position. At the same time, at the suggestion of Queen Victoria, who had earlier visited the tomb, replacement bronze cushions were made for the two effigies, the originals having at some stage been lost.

Richard's choice of a resting place in the Confessor's chapel at Westminster sprang from his concern to emphasize his place in the dynastic succession. His tomb was the last in a series in the chapel. In the bays to the east and the north were the tombs of his predecessors – Edward III, Edward I and Henry III; while in the feretory in the centre were the remains of his patron, St Edward the Confessor. There was an irony in the king's abiding preoccupation with lineage, for Richard was the last in his family's direct line. On his death the Angevin or 'Plantagenet' family became extinct: his successor, Henry of Lancaster, was the head of a junior branch of the family; and sixty years later, when a senior line represented by the duke of York took its place, descent was claimed through the female line. Richard's deposition thus marked a turning point in the history of the English medieval monarchy. For the first time since 1199 the hereditary principle had been broken. A dangerous new element of instability had been introduced into politics. In Tudor

[125] Stanley, 'On an Examination of the Tombs of Richard II and Henry III', 309–27. The openings which had appeared were in the spaces formerly occupied by shields. Anne's skeleton suffered worse than her husband's because it was nearer to the openings.

historical writing the many ills that were to afflict the realm in the
fifteenth century were attributed to this one dramatic event.[126] So how
had the deposition come about? How had a ruler seemingly so strong
been overthrown with such ease?

The deposition of Richard II shared a number of characteristics with
that of Edward II three-quarters of a century earlier. On both occasions
the king had been removed at the very summit of his power: Richard
after his triumph over the former Appellants, and Edward after his
crushing of the Contrariants.[127] On both occasions there was a striking
lack of support for the threatened ruler from the local and national
elites – the majority of the nobility and gentry either remaining neutral
or siding with the invader. On both occasions deposition (or enforced
abdication) had been carried out with the consent of an assembly of
estates, whether or not that assembly was called a parliament. On both
occasions the fallen king was to be the object of moves to secure his
release and restoration: in Richard's case by his former courtiers, in
Edward's by Thomas Dunheved and his friends. And on both occasions
the fallen king was done to death when his successor decided that it was
no longer convenient to keep him alive.

These analogies all point to an underlying similarity in the circumstances attending the two depositions. Richard and Edward were both,
in a sense, the victims of their massive accumulation of power. In
Edward's case, the process of accumulation had begun with the royalist
victory over the Contrariants at Boroughbridge in 1322. Lancaster and
the other Contrariant lords had been defeated and either imprisoned
or executed; their lands had been taken into royal custody; county
society was reshaped, and the internal expression of dissent suppressed.
Richard's establishment of an ascendancy was more gradual, but in the
end no less complete. Again the critics or opponents of the crown were
arrested and proscribed; again there was a massive redistribution of
lands, and again the internal expression of dissent was suppressed. As a
result of their broadly similar treatment of their opponents, the two
kings had been able to establish themselves in unparalleled positions of
strength; and, in so doing, they were also able to make themselves
extremely wealthy.[128] Neither king, provided he managed his resources
carefully, had any reason to summon a parliament or great council for

---

[126] See above, 1–2.

[127] The Contrariants were the rebel lords – the earl of Lancaster and his allies –
who had opposed Edward in 1322. The similarities between the circumstances of
Edward's and Richard's depositions were first touched on by Stubbs (W. Stubbs, *The
Constitutional History of England* (3 vols, Oxford, 1875–8), ii, 508–9).

[128] At the end of his reign Edward II had an unspent hoard at the exchequer of
nearly £62,000: N.M. Fryde, *The Tyranny and Fall of Edward II* (Cambridge, 1979),
105.

years to come. Deposition was in a sense a consequence of this build-up of power. Neither Richard nor Edward could be made accountable, or be brought under control, in the usual ways – by parliamentary enactment, the imposition of a council or the drawing up of a document like the Ordinances. The only solution to the king's unsatisfactory rule was to seek his replacement by someone better.

A broad similarity is also to be noted in the two kings' management of their respective nobilities. Both kings, at least in their final years, narrowed their distribution of patronage to a small group of lords. The beneficiaries of Edward II's favour were his two allies, the elder and the younger Despenser, and those close to them, the earl of Arundel, Lord Beaumont and a few others. Richard's favour was restricted to the so-called 'duketti' and the earls of Worcester, Wiltshire and Gloucester at court, and to the Cheshiremen and the more substantial king's knights outside it. In both reigns, and particularly in Richard's, this narrowing in the bestowal of favour followed a period when it had been given more widely. In Richard's reign, in the seven or eight years between 1389 and 1397 the greater part of the nobility had been included in the distribution of patronage, and the king's position had been correspondingly strengthened.[129] When this broader pattern of distribution was replaced by a narrower one, the gains of the earlier policy were imperilled. The king's power base became circumscribed; an insufficient number of magnates and gentry had an interest in the king's survival, and when a challenge to him was mounted he was toppled. After each reign, it is true, there was a revanchist backlash; and the backlash in 1400 was substantial. But on both occasions it failed. The deposed king, whether it was Richard or Edward, had sufficient support in the country to cause annoyance to his successor, but insufficient to bring about his total removal.

While it is obvious that there were factors in common to both fourteenth-century depositions, it is equally clear that there were differences. One of the most important relates to the state of the regimes' preparedness. In 1399 Richard was taken completely by surprise by Bolingbroke's arrival at Ravenspur: the king was in Ireland when his adversary landed and was without even the means to return. Three-quarters of a century earlier Edward and the Despensers had been far better equipped for the coming challenge: the ports had been placed under surveillance, the royal castles fortified, and the levies arrayed in the shires.[130] The explanation for the contrast is clear. Edward and his favourites knew perfectly well how unpopular their regime was, whereas

---

[129] For Richard's use of patronage in this period, see Mott, 'Richard II's Relations with the Magnates', 106–57.
[130] Fryde, *Tyranny and Fall of Edward II*, 183–5.

Richard did not. By the mid-1320s, in the wake of Boroughbridge, there was ample evidence of popular opposition in the shires: former Contrariants were attacking royal castles; malcontents like Ewer were fomenting rebellion; and assaults were being launched on the king's justices.[131] In the years of Richard's 'tyranny' there was far less evidence of popular unease. The only open challenge to the regime appears to have been the Bampton uprising of 1398; other expressions of dissent were minor. Richard, lulled by the apparent calm of his realm, became complacent and, supposing his position stronger than it was, went off to Ireland. His decision to go to Ireland has been identified as the single most serious error that he made in that fateful year. According to C.M. Barron, it deprived the realm of effective royal leadership at just the time when it was most needed.[132] It is certainly true that in similar circumstances in the 1320s the Despensers had insisted that Edward stay in England: in 1324, when the French king had demanded his presence in Paris to perform homage, they had sent his son in his place. But it is open to question whether the king's presence or absence was the determining factor in his fate. The fact that Edward was present in England in 1326 had little or no effect on events: his regime still collapsed in a few weeks. If a king was confronted by an external challenge, what he needed above all was the support of the political class; and Edward and Richard, for their different reasons, both lacked this. Given the widespread popular dislike felt for Richard in 1399, he would still have had difficulty retaining his throne even if he had been present to meet his adversary.[133]

Beyond the contrast in degrees of preparedness, there is a further difference to be noticed between the two depositions. In Edward's reign the four and a half years of tyranny had been marked by a ruthless campaign of land-grabbing and extortion by the king's favourites: wealthy heiresses had been browbeaten into signing away their lands, and lesser figures – freeholders and minor gentry – had been arbitrarily disseised with the aid of the family's estate officials. During Richard's tyranny, there appears to have been no counterpart to this campaign of self-aggrandizement. Chroniclers and poets alike complained of the courtiers' avarice,[134] but the complaints were a literary topos. In the wake of Richard's downfall there was no avalanche of petitions against the courtiers as there had been after Edward's – despite the opportunity to complain being extended in the October parliament.[135] This is not to deny that Richard's courtiers were highly unpopular: the treatment

---

[131] Ibid., 149–64.

[132] Barron, 'The Deposition of Richard II', 137–8.

[133] For evidence of the king's unpopularity see above, 388–90.

[134] For example, *Brut*, 358; *Mum and the Sothsegger*, 4–23.

[135] The majority of the petitions in *RP*, ii, 378–418, relate to the misdeeds of the

meted out to the rebels at Cirencester shows that they were. But the main source of their unpopularity was their association with an unjust king rather than their own misbehaviour. Very few of the courtiers had a record of violence and disorder. One of the minority who did was the king's councillor, Sir William Bagot. Bagot had been involved in acts of thuggery and corruption in Warwickshire for over a decade. In 1387 it was alleged that during his term of office as sheriff four years previously he had extorted money from innocent defendants, maintained a variety of evildoers and on one occasion committed a murder. Five years later he became embroiled in a bitter dispute with the mayor and burgesses of Coventry, in the course of which it was said that he had laid siege to the town and provoked an uprising there. Twelve months after that he was involved in a disturbance at Warwick assizes during which a retainer of the earl of Warwick was assaulted and badly injured.[136] Bagot, the younger son of a Staffordshire knight, was a newcomer to Warwickshire society and probably rode roughshod over local interests in order to establish himself there. One or two other knightly retainers of the king are known to have acted high-handedly. Sir Nicholas Sharnsfield, Richard's standard bearer in the early 1390s, was accused of disseising one John Horn and his wife of the manor of Woolwich; and his master of the horse, Sir John Russell, was involved in a bitter struggle for power in his native Worcestershire.[137] In the wake of the king's downfall, furthermore, a handful of complaints were made about the lawless behaviour of members of the Cheshire retinue.[138] But, somewhat remarkably, no evidence survives that a 'reign of terror' was perpetrated by any of the major courtiers. It would be wrong to suggest that the countryside was entirely peaceful in these years: Richard's divisive rule since 1397 had engendered faction and strife. But those who enjoyed his favour, it seems, acted with greater restraint than their equivalents three-quarters of a century earlier.

The implication of this evidence from the shires is that the revolution

Despensers and their hangers-on. The only complaints against Richard's men, by contrast, are the few noted below. Walsingham reports a general denunciation, in the judgment against the courtiers, of the latters' extortions and oppressions of the common people, and of the misdeeds of their dependants (*Annales*, 319).

[136] SC8/138/6875; KB27/541 Rex m.26; KB9/176 m.12 *et seq.*; *Rolls of the Warwickshire and Coventry Sessions of the Peace 1377–1397*, ed. E.G. Kimball (Dugdale Society, xvi, 1939), 76–7. It is also worth noting Bagot's involvement in the long-running litigation between John Catesby and Lewis and Alice Gardian over the manor of Ladbroke. Catesby alleged, probably rightly, that Bagot was the Gardians' maintainer: Post, 'Courts, Councils and Arbitrators', 297–8, 320. For Bagot's career more generally, see *House of Commons*, ii, 99–103.

[137] SC8/115/5729; *House of Commons*, iv, 248–51.

[138] KB9/179 m.1; KB9/184/1 m.9; *RP*, iii, 439, 440–1; Morgan, *War and Society in Medieval Cheshire*, 200.

of 1399 was brought about by one factor above all: the failings and
misdeeds of Richard himself. No one else was responsible. Edward II, it
could be argued, had been driven from power less on his own account
than that of his favourites. The same could hardly be said of Richard.
Richard was the sole author of his misfortune. At the time of his
downfall, he enjoyed an unparalleled ascendancy over his realm: he
determined the direction of policy, and made all the decisions that
mattered. Unlike Edward II, he was not the victim of manipulation by
over-mighty councillors or courtiers. It was Richard himself who had
raised the crown to such dizzy heights of power and fame; and it was
Richard himself who created the conditions in which, 'like glist'ring
Phaethon', he was brought down.

Chapter 17

RICHARD: KING AND MAN

The death of a king usually gave the chroniclers the opportunity to look back over and reflect on a reign. Edward III's death had prompted the writing of lengthy obituaries, the majority of them favourable. Richard's death in 1400 generated relatively little comment. Only a small number of formal obituaries were written.[1] Possibly the chroniclers found it painful to look back over such an unhappy, faction-ridden reign; and perhaps one or two of them felt inhibited by the accession of a usurping king. Certainly there was little inclination to analyse.

The chroniclers, however, did not allow the opportunity to moralize slip by. Richard was in their eyes a ruler whose hubris had been the cause of his nemesis. So naturally some comment on the mutability of human affairs was in order. Froissart made the point briefly but with precision: 'Consider,' he said, 'all you dukes, prelates, earls and lords how changeable are the fortunes of the world.'[2] Adam of Usk, writing at greater length, drew on the image of the wheel of fortune. Richard, he wrote, had been 'as fair as Absalom, as wealthy as Solomon . . . and had built as magnificently as Belus; yet, like Chosroes, king of Persia, who was delivered into the hands of Heraclius, he fell in the midst of glory, as Fortune turned her wheel.'[3]

Only a handful of writers addressed in any detail the nature and causes of Richard's decline and fall. In general their observations were unoriginal. A common complaint was that the king had been led adrift by youthful counsel. The Kirkstall writer reported the opinion of 'learned men' that he had spurned the advice of 'the dukes and the wiser heads' in favour of reliance on 'younger lords and others who were inexperienced in weighty decisions, rather in the manner of Edward of Caernarfon'.[4] Adam of Usk voiced similar views, drawing on the biblical analogy with King Rehoboam. Richard, he said, could be likened to Rehoboam, son of Solomon, who lost the kingdom of Israel

---

[1] The fullest and most informative is the Monk of Evesham's (*Chrons. Revolution*, 241–2). There is no obituary in Walsingham.

[2] Froissart, ii, 708.

[3] Usk, 202–3. In a similar vein: *Eulogium*, 384.

[4] *Kirkstall Abbey Chronicles*, 83; cf. *Mum and the Sothsegger*, ed. Day and Steele, 6.

because he followed the advice of younger men.[5] A couple of chroniclers also complained about the harshness of Richard's rule. Kirkstall
commented on his treatment of the nobility: Richard, he said, had
caused the deaths of the duke of Gloucester and the earl of Arundel,
and had exiled the dukes of Hereford and Norfolk and the archbishop
of Canterbury: so it was hardly surprising that these men had plotted his
downfall.[6] The Evesham writer condemned the fiscal burden of his rule.
'He imposed crushing tenths and taxes almost continuously through
the reign . . . ; yet when, under pretext of defeating the enemy, he had
acquired this enormous wealth, he spent it all on his foolish wantonness.'[7] John Gower, a friend of Chaucer and a prolific writer of social
and political criticism, also condemned Richard's financial exactions.
In *O Deus Immense,* a poem of advice to the king, he warned against
avarice and urged him not to plunder his subjects' gold.[8] A commenta-
tor outside England, the French chronicler royal at St Denis, added his
voice to these writers' condemnation of Richard's exactions from his
people.[9]

Occasionally, critical reference was made to Richard's disregard for
the law. The fifteenth-century author of a prose version of the *Secreta
Secretorum,* drawing on the lessons of Richard's reign to illustrate arguments of a general nature about government, said that no ruler who put
God's law below his own could ever be held in honour; a wise king
should love God and enforce his laws, and his words should be in
accord with his deeds.[10] The author of *Richard the Redeless,* addressing
Richard more in sorrow than in anger, spoke in similar terms. The king,
he said, should uphold the law and imprison evildoers, and not
waste his money on dancing and wine; for, if he continued to treat the
law with levity, assuredly he would come to an unhappy end.[11] In these
two writers' opinion, Richard's kingship constituted a paradigm of
misrule.

These judgments owe something to the fact that they were made after
1399, when Richard's reputation was systematically blackened. However, there is evidence that public opinion was turning against the king
well before his downfall. Gower's major poems became steadily more
critical of the king in the course of the 1390s. Gower's early work had
been relatively sympathetic to Richard. In the first version of the *Vox*

---

[5] Usk, 190. For the story of Rehoboam, see 1 Kings 12
[6] *Kirkstall Abbey Chronicles,* 83.
[7] *Chrons. Revolution,* 242.
[8] *Complete Works of John Gower,* iv, 362–4.
[9] *CRSD,* ii, 670–1.
[10] *Three Prose Versions of the Secreta Secretorum,* ed. R. Steele (EETS, extra series, lxxiv,
1898), 136–7.
[11] *Mum and the Sothsegger,* 20–1.

Clamantis, written before 1381, the poet had grieved at the decay of the realm, but held Richard himself free of blame. In an epistle in Book 6 he addressed the monarch in terms of affection and hope and implicitly blamed misgovernment on the lords and council.[12] By the time he revised the *Vox*, in about 1386, his attitude had changed. Richard was criticized for following youthful counsel and for failing to impose self-discipline; and in a new epistle Gower warned the king that 'his royal majesty would be venerated only so long as he ruled honourably'.[13] Gower's growing disenchantment with Richard can also be traced in another of his works, the *Confessio Amantis*. In the *Confessio*'s original prologue Gower had said that he had written the poem at Richard's suggestion; in 1391, however, that prologue was rewritten to include a dedication to Henry of Derby. In the original version Gower had included a concluding tribute to Richard; in a revision made roughly a year later that tribute was excised and a prayer for the state of the realm put in its place.[14] In poems written after 1399, notably the *Cronica Tripertita*, Gower continued his criticism of the king.[15] But in these later works, written in old age, he did not say anything that he had not said years before. The crucial shift in his opinion had occurred while Richard was alive.

The onset of disillusion, so evident in Gower's work, is mirrored in the writings of Thomas Walsingham. Walsingham's earliest narrative of the reign was written in or shortly before 1388. In this largely factual account his commentary on events was sparing. In 1394, however, Walsingham made a number of revisions which struck a more critical note. Richard's dismissal of Richard, Lord Scrope from the chancellorship in 1382, which had earlier been passed over without comment, was now made the occasion for criticism of the king's wilfulness and predilection for favourites. In further revisions to the chronicle made between 1397 and 1399 more sweeping criticisms were introduced. Walsingham suggested that Robert de Vere had resorted to black magic to gain ascendancy over Richard, and by skilful glossing of the narrative he implied that the relationship between Richard and de Vere was a homosexual one. Moreover, a novel emphasis was now placed on Richard's lack of consistency and want of application. In short, every opportunity was

---

[12] *Complete Works of John Gower*, 245–6; *Major Latin Works of John Gower*, 232–3.

[13] *Complete Works of John Gower*, 246; *Major Latin Works of John Gower*, 232. For the nature and date of Gower's revisions to the *Vox*, see Fisher, *John Gower*, 102, 112–14.

[14] *Complete Works of John Gower*, ii, 2; iii, 468–75; Fisher, *John Gower*, 117–18. For the background to the deletion of the dedication to Richard, see G.B. Stow, 'Richard II in John Gower's *Confessio Amantis*: Some Historical Perspectives', *Medievalia*, xvi (1993), 3–31.

[15] *Complete Works of John Gower*, iv, 314–43; *Major Latin Works of John Gower*, 290–326.

seized to blacken Richard and to place an unfavourable interpretation on his actions.[16]

Richard's accession to the throne in the summer of 1377 had been greeted with enormous goodwill. People had had high expectations of the new king. But in the course of his reign those early hopes evaporated. So what went wrong? The process of disillusion appears to have set in at the beginning of the 1380s. An underlying cause lay in the government's failure to regain the initiative in the long-drawn-out war with the French. Since the expiry of the truce in 1377 a series of expeditions had been mounted against either the French or their Castilian allies. None of these had yielded any significant advantage. Gradually England's continental allies, sensing their partner's weakening commitment, fell by the wayside. In 1381 the duke of Brittany made an accord with the French, and four years later the Ghentois surrendered to the duke of Burgundy. Criticism of the government mounted: ministers were accused of incompetence, and Richard himself was called on to offer a more vigorous lead. Allied to the unease over the conduct of foreign policy was a growing concern about the realm's internal governance. There was criticism of Richard's tendency to neglect the counsel of the magnates for that of untried younger lords like de Vere, and suspicions were voiced that money granted for the war was disappearing into the pockets of corrupt courtiers. After the realm had been threatened with invasion in two successive summers in the mid-1380s, anger boiled over in parliament. Chancellor de la Pole was dismissed and impeached and a commission of government appointed to hold office for twelve months. Richard's failure to co-operate with the commission paved the way for the Appellants' takeover in the following year.

After Richard's recovery of power in 1389, and his promise in the Marcolf chamber of better government in future, there was an improvement in his relations with his subjects. But before long disillusionment set in once more. In the early 1390s Richard's style of government became increasingly assertive. A novel emphasis was placed on the powers of the prerogative and on the subject's obligation to obey. Richard reacted heavy-handedly to challenges to his will. In 1392 he confiscated the liberties of the city of London when the Londoners refused to give him a loan. Five years later he demanded the submission of the commons after Haxey had presumed to criticize the household. Simultaneously with his reassertion of the prerogative the king began to fashion a grander and more exalted style of monarchy. The court became larger and more rigidly defined. In a break with earlier practice, a royal affinity was built up among the gentry class in the country.

[16] Stow, 'Richard II in Thomas Walsingham's Chronicles', 68–102.

The growing assertiveness of Richard's government was reflected in the expenditure of the household, which rose from £13,000 in 1390 to £35,000 nine years later.[17] In 1389, when he had dismissed the Appellant ministers, Richard had promised an easing of the burden of taxation on his subjects. So far from easing, however, that burden had stayed virtually unchanged. Four and a half subsidies were granted by parliament between 1390 and 1398. To his subjects it appeared that Richard was indulging personal pleasures at public expense.

Richard's aim in the 1390s had been to establish a new political consensus in England. For the previous century or more England had been organized essentially as a 'war state'. The king and the political community had joined forces in the waging of external war. Together they had exploited the fiscal and other resources of the realm to pay for their endeavours. In Edward III's reign war had strengthened the crown and profited the military elite. But once the successes became fewer, as they did in the 1370s, the strains in the polity began to show. Recruitment to royal armies became more difficult, and there was criticism of the continuing bloodshed.[18] The Appellants' unsuccessful initiatives in 1388 highlighted the difficulty of renewing and intensifying the war. Richard's decision after 1389 to seek peace with the French represented a way of easing the pressures. But the policy gave rise to as many problems as it solved. War had had the beneficial effect of stimulating loyalty to the king. Once its unifying quality was removed, it was not clear how a similar sense of loyalty could be created. Richard's solution was to place a novel emphasis on the prerogative. The crown itself was to be the focus of the emotions that had earlier gone into war. This, of course, was a policy with a greater appeal to the king than to his subjects. For the latter, an emphasis on the prerogative meant little more than demands for obedience and the imposition of taxes. The real need was for a broader and more appealing vision in which subjects as well as ruler could share. But temperamentally Richard was incapable of providing this. He had little or no feel for the aspirations of his subjects. He expected their homage and allegiance; he did not realize that, in addition to these, he needed their affection. More than anything, it was because of his failure to win their affection that in 1399 they abandoned him. As the author of *Richard the Redeless* succinctly put it, allegiance without affection is nothing worth.[19]

Richard's attempt to establish a new political consensus was thus ultimately unsuccessful. But does it follow from this that the policies he pursued never stood any hope of success? Would he have been toppled

---

[17] Given-Wilson, *Royal Household and the King's Affinity*, 270–1.
[18] See above, 206–7.
[19] *Mum and the Sothsegger*, 4.

even if he had not made an enemy of Bolingbroke? Questions like this are never easily resolved, but in each case there are grounds for supposing that the answer might be no. In his governance of England Richard anticipated a number of the initiatives that were later to serve the Yorkists and early Tudors well. The most striking of these was the formation of a 'bastard feudal' affinity. Richard's affinity was effectively the first of its kind in England to be raised by a king. Earlier kings had surrounded themselves with a corps of household retainers – that is, with men who took a fee from, and served, the king; but generally these men's employments had been military. Richard's affinity was innovatory to the extent that its function was largely political: the knights and esquires who composed it were valued for their service in providing an informal network of communication between crown and locality. Richard's affinity was unpopular and was quickly dissolved in 1399, but later royal affinities were based on it. Henry IV appears to have built up and used the Lancastrian affinity much as Richard had used his: in other words, to strengthen his grip on parts of the country where royal authority was weak. Sixty years later Richard's example was more directly followed when Edward IV reconstructed the royal affinity after his return from exile in Flanders. Edward, like Richard, recruited men directly into the royal household, and in particular into the chamber; Edward, like Richard, also attracted men's service indirectly by working through courtier magnates whose retainers, in function, were scarcely distinguishable from his own. In the years after Bosworth Henry VII and Henry VIII continued with Edward's policy; indeed, they took it further. Whereas Edward IV had limited the scale of his retaining in the interests of economy, the richer Tudors set virtually no limit, and by Henry VIII's reign the number of gentlemen attached to the household was twice or three times earlier levels. With the massive expansion of numbers went another initiative of Ricardian origin, the distribution of badges. Richard had contented himself with using two main badges – the white hart and the sunburst. Under the Tudors the number of badges multiplied. There were the Tudor rose, the Beaufort portcullis, the red rose of Lancaster and the various emblems of Catherine of Aragon, such as the pomegranate.[20] The Tudors' employment of symbolism and labelling was a natural successor to and extension of Richard's policy. Where Richard had led, his successors were to follow.

There were more general ways in which Richard's practice of government anticipated that of the Yorkists and early Tudors. In the latter part of the 1390s the whole business of royal government was characterized by a brisk, not to say a ruthless, efficiency which foreshadows that of

---

[20] Starkey, 'The Age of the Household', 268–73.

Richard's later fifteenth-century successors. The council, for example, was fashioned into a powerful and dependable instrument for executing the royal will. Increasingly the place of the largely non-partisan figures of earlier years was taken by a small, tightly knit group of men totally committed to Richard's view of government. Bushy, Bagot, Russell and Green, the leading members of the group, were in every sense the political ancestors of Henry VII's Empson and Dudley; and Bushy and Green, indeed, were to meet with the same grisly fate as Empson and Dudley. The intolerance of dissent which Richard's ministers showed also anticipates that of later rulers. In the 1460s Edward IV was to use the constable's court, under his ally Sir John Tiptoft, to silence or eliminate his opponents. Seventy years earlier Richard II had used the court of chivalry, under Aumerle, and the council to like effect.[21] Similarities are also to be observed between Richard's methods of controlling his subjects and those of his Tudor successors. Richard had secured obedience by resort to collective oaths, forced loans and blank charters; Henry VII was to do the same by means of bonds, recognizances and acts of attainder. Certainly, in Richard's reign the instruments of autocracy were less highly developed than they were to be later. But the king's aim was essentially the same: the creation of a stronger, loftier and more effective monarchy that could sustain its position under challenge.[22]

Richard's political legacy could thus hardly be considered sterile. In other hands, and at other times, the techniques that he pioneered were to prove the lifeline of the English monarchy. The question then arises of why those techniques served Richard himself so badly. Part of the answer lies in the fact that the political conditions of the early sixteenth century worked in the Tudors' favour. By the early 1500s the age of near-continuous war with France was over. Kings were no longer as dependent on the military support of the nobility as they had been. Disciplining errant lords became easier. There was even a readiness on the nobility's part to consider a civil, as opposed to a chivalric, definition of noble values. A second difference is that by the sixteenth century the position of the crown had become stronger. As a result of the long blood-letting many of the old regional lineages had been removed – the Nevilles from Yorkshire, the Mowbrays from Norfolk and the Hastingses from the midlands. The crown stood almost alone as a focus of allegiance and political authority. Henry and his successors

---

[21] In 1398 Richard empowered Aumerle, as constable, to hear cases involving the king's person – presumably slander and disparagement – and to deal with them in the court of chivalry: *CPR 1396–9, 505.* For Richard's use of the council to suppress dissent, see above, 388, 390.

[22] C.M. Barron, 'The Art of Kingship. Richard II, 1377–1399', *HT*, xxxv (June, 1985), 30–7.

faced few if any serious rivals in the competition for retainers and hangers-on.

This was a situation far removed from that in which Richard had found himself a century earlier. In the fourteenth century the power of the territorial nobility was still entrenched. Magnates exercised informal rule over the shires through the agency of retainers whom the crown, at their suggestion, appointed to local office. The essence of successful kingship lay in the delicate task of managing the nobility and harnessing their power and influence to the crown. If kings risked challenging the magnates' interests they invariably came off the worse, as the fate of Edward II showed. The point has often been made that medieval government had something of the character of a joint-stock enterprise in which king and nobility both had stakes. The observation is no less true for being repeated. A key requirement for the successful exercise of kingship was good relations with the principal power-brokers at court and in local society.

The nature of the late fourteenth-century polity, in other words, made it difficult for Richard to achieve the ends that he was seeking. But there was a second reason for his failure. At the heart of his political thinking lay a deep and ineradicable inconsistency. Richard's aim was the establishment of 'peace' –peace in the sense of a strong and united realm: a people at one in their acceptance of the king's rule.[23] But the means by which Richard hoped to secure peace were productive merely of faction and discord. By the time that Richard fell, society in the localities was being torn apart by in-fighting. County or regional elites that had once been harmonious were faction-ridden and divided, and political differences which in the past had been largely contained were beginning to spill over into fighting. The outbreak of this discord was to play a major role in bringing about Richard's downfall.

The nature of the interactions of the divisions at national and local level can nowhere better be illustrated than in the case of Gloucestershire. In political terms Gloucestershire was a 'single faction' society: the social and political life of the county was dominated by the presence of a single resident baronial family – the Berkeleys of Berkeley castle. The head of the Berkeleys, the fourth Thomas, Lord Berkeley (d. 1417), brokered the flow of royal patronage and favour to the local gentry, and the family's power was reflected in the presence of many of its retainers in the leading offices.[24] In the later years of Richard's reign, however, the Berkeleys' ascendancy was challenged by the rise to royal favour of another lord with interests in the county: Thomas, Lord

[23] See above, 387.
[24] For Gloucestershire politics in this period, see Saul, *Knights and Esquires*, in particular chs III and IV.

Despenser, who held the honor of Tewkesbury. Despenser was a close ally of Richard's, and at the end of the parliament of September 1397 was made earl of Gloucester. In the wake of Despenser's sudden rise, Berkeley and his followers found themselves rapidly pushed to the political sidelines. The leading office-holders appointed for the county in 1397 were Despenser, and not Berkeley, clients, and Lord Berkeley himself found it increasingly difficult to uphold the interests of his men.[25] By early 1398 the growth of factionalism in the county was spilling over into violence. Shortly before Easter 1398 a series of attacks was made on the property of Sir Andrew Hake of Winterborne, a newcomer to the county and a man with curial connections. Hake had risen to prominence by marrying Blanche, Lady Bradeston, a Gloucestershire widow favoured at court, and his presence in the county was resented.[26] Around Easter 1398 a group of malefactors led by Richard Panter and John Crok of Betsley gathered at Winterborne, ransacked Hake's property and drove off his tenants.[27] The malefactors almost certainly acted with Berkeley's tacit approval if not on his instructions. The nature of Berkeley's feelings about the state of affairs in Gloucestershire became apparent in the following year, when he welcomed Henry of Lancaster to his castle and brokered the deal with York. The governance of Richard and his cronies no longer commanded his confidence. In the new reign it was Hake's turn to feel the chill of official disfavour. Although the knight did not himself suffer in the revolution, his prospects were uncertain. In January 1400 he threw in his lot with the conspirators and, though pardoned, he spent the rest of his life in obscurity.[28]

The pattern of events in Gloucestershire was replicated elsewhere in England. A little to the north, in Warwickshire, there was upheaval

---

[25] Ibid., 80, 113, 124; Hanna, 'Sir Thomas Berkeley and his Patronage', 888–92.

[26] Hake, who was a Scot, had fought in Arundel's naval expeditions of 1387 and 1388 (C76/71 m.7; C76/72 m.14). He was drawn into the courtier circle by his marriage in around 1394 to Blanche, widow of Sir Edmund de Bradeston of Winterborne. Blanche's connections with the court went back to the early years of the reign. In 1379 Richard had granted her and her first husband 40 marks yearly 'with an annuity of £80 from the issues of Oxfordshire' (*CPR 1377–81*, 317). In 1396 he awarded her a life grant of the manor of Dymock (Gloucs.) without render (*CPR 1391–6*, 660). She herself gave the king, as a present, a gilt mirror with an image of Our Lady (E101/411/9).

[27] SC8/212/10568; SC8/221/11045.

[28] For his rebellion and pardon, see A.L. Brown, 'The Reign of Henry IV: the Establishment of the Lancastrian Regime', *Fifteenth Century England, 1399–1509*, ed. S.B. Chrimes, C.D. Ross, R.A. Griffiths (Manchester, 1972), 4, 25. His only subsequent appearance is in 1413, when Henry V had him arrested on suspicion of conspiring with the Scots and Thomas Ward of Trumpington, the pseudo-Richard: E. Powell, *Kingship, Law and Society. Criminal Justice in the Reign of Henry V* (Oxford, 1989), 137.

following the arrest of the Beauchamp earl of Warwick in 1397. Warwickshire was a county that had been under Beauchamp rule for nearly
as long as Gloucestershire had been under the rule of the Berkeleys;
and with the sudden removal of the family's power, the normal rhythms
of local life were disrupted. The man to whom Richard granted the bulk
of the comital estates was an outsider, his nephew Thomas Holand,
duke of Surrey. Surrey, when he entered into possession of his Warwick
lordship, symbolically planted the white hart over the castle gateway;[29]
but he had difficulty establishing much of a presence in the county.[30] It
is doubtful if more than a handful of local men were willing to enter his
service and the signs are that the majority of his officials were outsiders.[31] The weakness of Surrey's position became apparent in July
1399. As soon as the news of Bolingbroke's landing was received in the
county, probably on the 4th, a group of Beauchamp partisans took over
and occupied the castle.[32] Little or no resistance was offered. In the eyes
of the local gentry Holand was a 'foreigner': an outsider. His presence
in the county was resented and was removed as summarily as it had been
imposed.[33]

Roughly midway between the tensions generated at court and locally
in the shires was the discord brought about by Richard's heavy reliance
on the Cheshiremen. Richard's infatuation with the Cheshiremen is
one of the striking idiosyncrasies of the final years of his rule. It appears
to have had its origins in his feelings of personal insecurity. At the
beginning of the 1390s, when he had embarked on the policy of
retaining, Richard had drawn recruits from almost every corner of the

[29] Post, 'Courts, Councils and Arbitrators', 323.

[30] Few of the Beauchamps' retainers abandoned their service; and one who can be
shown to have done so – Thomas Throckmorton – entered the earl of Gloucester's
service and not Surrey's (*House of Commons*, iv, 610). One cause of the duke's
weakness was that he appears not to have spent much time at Warwick. Whenever
mention is made of him in John Catesby's account of his dispute with the Gardians
over Ladbroke, he is either at Northampton or London (Post, 'Courts, Councils
and Arbitrators', 321–2).

[31] It is by no means clear who the duke's principal lieutenants were in Warwickshire, but it may be significant that when Catesby sought the duke's assistance in the
Ladbroke manor dispute he approached his steward, Nicholas Gascoigne, who was
almost certainly a member of the Yorkshire family of that name (ibid., 321–2). The
Holands had extensive estates in Yorkshire and may have drawn the core of their
retinue from that county.

[32] Mott, 'Richard II and the Crisis of 1397', 176. The raid was led by Robert
Hugford, one of the Beauchamps' leading retainers: Mott, 'Richard II's Relations
with the Magnates', 73.

[33] Evidence of continued loyalty to the Beauchamps is found in a petition to the
earl, probably of *c.*1400, from one John Mountford in which Mountford said that
he had served the earl for more than twenty years and had loyally supported him 'in
all his travails around this time' (Mott, 'Richard II's Relations with the Magnates',
264).

land. After the coup against the Appellants, however, he fell back on a much narrower power base and concentrated on recruiting in the north-west. In a limited sense his shift of focus was successful: he provided himself with a body of dependants who were to prove utterly trustworthy and loyal. But the price that he paid for his success was that of alienating potential supporters elsewhere in England. Writers like Walsingham complained of the arrogance and indiscipline of the Cheshiremen, while the people of neighbouring counties like Staffordshire and Shropshire inveighed against incursions by the Cheshiremen which they were powerless to resist. Richard's infatuation with Cheshire ultimately worked to his disadvantage. It won him the affection of a small community of subjects who stood by him to the end, but it weakened his hold on the affections of his subjects more generally.

The tensions generated by Richard's meddling with the local and provincial power structures bear witness to the inconsistency that lay at the heart of his rule. On the one hand, he proclaimed that he was establishing 'peace': peace in the sense of unity. On the other hand, by his manipulative governance he sowed discord and division. It is doubtful if Richard himself was aware of any contradiction in his actions. His own view was that his policies strengthened and exalted the crown: it was the Appellants who had fomented division; and by removing them he had restored 'peace'. In the eyes of his subjects, however, the contradiction was clear. The image that he presented was of a remote, almost a godlike, ruler, but the reality, as they experienced it, was one of extreme 'intimacy'. Through the actions of his retainers, Richard interfered more in their daily affairs than any previous king. The tension in these images between 'distance' and 'intimacy' was never properly resolved. Richard the godlike was the king who allowed his Cheshire archers to call him 'Dycun' and whom his favourites referred to as a 'foster parent'.[34] As the author of the *Secreta Secretorum* pointed out,

---

[34] Clarke, *Fourteenth Century Studies*, 98; *Annales*, 307. Walsingham reports Lord Cobham as saying in 1399 that Richard's favourites boasted 'We, foster-children, to King Richard, etc.' ('Nous, nurres a le Rey Richard, etc.'). The contrast between 'distance' and 'intimacy' is neatly captured by Shakespeare in *The First Part of King Henry IV*. Henry recalls his predecessor's kingly style to his errant son:

> The skipping King, he ambled up and down,
> With shallow jesters, and rash bavin wits,
> Soon kindled and soon burnt, carded his state,
> Mingled his royalty with cap'ring fools,
> Had his great name profaned with their scorns,
> And gave his countenance against his name
> To laugh at gibing boys.
>
> (Act III, scene ii, 60–6)

Richard's words and deeds were at odds.[35] The king was inconstant: he promised one thing but delivered another.

The contrast between image and reality in Richard's kingship is a major theme of Shakespeare's play about the king. Richard in Shakespeare's portrayal is a man who is two things at once: thoroughly kingly in appearance and manner and yet utterly deficient as a ruler. His deficiencies are clearly demonstrated in Acts I and II. In these acts the king is shown disseising Bolingbroke, contemptuously ignoring the advice of his dying uncle and delivering himself to the advice of foolish young sycophants. In Acts III–V he pays the terrible price for his mistakes. His supporters desert him and he forfeits possession of the crown to his cousin and rival. The audience is never in any doubt as to his fate: from the moment of his return to Wales it is obvious that his reign is over. Yet, as the substance of power slips from his grasp, he is invested by Shakespeare with a grandeur previously lacking, and eloquent speeches are put into his mouth about the divinity of the kingly office. Kantorowicz saw in the play a commentary on the theory of the king's 'two bodies'. Richard, he argued, is both king and man in the first two acts; gradually, however, he is divested of his dual nature to the point where, at the end, only the human aspect of his persona is left.[36] There is much to be said for Kantorowicz's reading of the play, but it is possible that he exaggerated the distinction between king and man. In the later fourteenth century, and in particular in Richard's reign, a gradual shift took place in the human setting of kingship. In the early medieval period it had been usual to emphasize the sanctity inherent in the kingly office. In the fourteenth century, by contrast, far more was made of the personal and outward marks of autocracy. Richard, for example, projected an image of his rule through the medium of his patron saints, the arms of St Edward the Confessor and devices like the sunburst and the white hart. As a result, it became more difficult than before to distinguish the man from his kingly persona: king and man became virtually one. The effect of the shift was to highlight the importance of personality in determining the character of a king's governance. So what impression can we form of Richard the man? And how far can a picture of his personality be built up from the sources?

A first impression of Richard the man can be formed from the observations of the chroniclers.[37] One or two of the main chronicle writers, notably the Monk of Westminster, had observed the king at

---

[35] *Three Prose Versions of the Secreta Secretorum*, 137.

[36] E.H. Kantorowicz, *The King's Two Bodies. A Study in Medieval Political Theology* (Princeton, 1957), ch. 2.

[37] G.B. Stow, 'Chronicles versus Records: the Character of Richard II', *Documenting the Past. Essays in Medieval History Presented to G.P. Cuttino*, ed. J.S. Hamilton and P. Bradley (Woodbridge, 1989), 155–76.

close quarters; the Monk, indeed, may even have met him. The general impression conveyed by the writers is hardly favourable. The Westminster monk offers a more balanced view than some, but even in his work there are criticisms. In the early part of the chronicle the Monk shows the king to have been impetuous and quick-tempered, but later he has him gaining in maturity and self-control. He recognized the better side of the king's nature: he even commented on one occasion on the king's 'kindly nature' and in 1388 praised him for his defence of the abbey's liberties.[38] But for all his sympathy he recognized Richard's faults. He said that the king lusted for glory, followed the advice of evil counsellors, did not keep his promises to the lords, and kept 'superabundant' retainers.[39] The Monk's critical note is echoed in the work of another contemporary, the Monk of Evesham. This author begins with a rare physical description of the king. He says that Richard was fair-haired, of pale complexion, with a rounded, feminine face, which was sometimes flushed; and he adds the interesting detail that he was abrupt and stammering in speech. He then launches into a devastating assault on his character. He says that Richard's behaviour was capricious and that he rejected the advice of his elders; he was 'prodigious with gifts', extravagant in dress and faint-hearted in war; towards his servants he was imperious; and he often spent 'half the night up carousing with his friends and indulging himself in other unmentionable ways'.[40]

An unsympathetic assessment of the king is also found in the work of Thomas Walsingham. Walsingham never offered a general description of Richard, but his views are evident from the passing comments he made on his behaviour: Richard, he says, was too sympathetic to foreigners, followed the counsel of young lords, lacked martial prowess and burdened his subjects with impositions and bonds.[41] There are further insights into Richard's character in the work of other chroniclers. Froissart became increasingly critical of Richard with the onset of tyranny, but he also recalled the courtesy that he showed when receiving him at Eltham in 1395.[42] Adam of Usk, who met him in 1399, was just as unsympathetic as the others and criticized the king's tyranny; but even he was moved by his sorrowful demeanour in the Tower in 1399.[43]

---

[38] *WC*, 502, 326.

[39] Ibid., 138, 114, 206, 166. For discussions of the Monk's attitude to the king, see Miss Harvey's introduction to *WC*, lxxiii, and Gransden, *Historical Writing in England, II*, 182, 184.

[40] *HVR*, 166–7; *Chrons. Revolution*, 241; G.B. Stow, 'The *Vita Ricardi* as a Source for the Reign of Richard II', *Vale of Evesham Historical Society Research Papers*, iv (1973), 63–75.

[41] *HA*, ii, 97, 119, 149, 152, 103; *Annales*, 199–200.

[42] Froissart, ii, 571, 577. For Froissart's attitude, see G.B. Stow, 'Richard II in Jean Froissart's *Chroniques*', *JMH*, xi (1985), 333–45.

[43] Usk, 30, 182; Gransden, *Historical Writing in England, II*, 181–4.

Taken as a whole, the chroniclers' comments provide a valuable series of snapshots of Richard the man: still-lifes, as it were, which illuminate his changing moods and behaviour. On the other hand, they scarcely provide a rounded view of his character. A couple of centuries earlier Henry II had been brilliantly brought to life in the writings of Walter Map and Gerald of Wales. Walter and Gerald were insiders – men with easy access to the court who knew the king well. The fourteenth-century chroniclers did not enjoy their predecessors' advantage: they were outsiders and wrote from a distance. Valuable though their testimony is, by itself it is inadequate. We need to look at other sources to fill out our picture of the king.

An impression, however vague, of the king's outlook and cultural tastes can be gained from the main series of record sources – the wardrobe books, exchequer issue rolls and chancery enrolments. Richard emerges from these as a man of catholic taste. His mind ranged across a variety of interests: from religious and dynastic concerns through geomancy and astrology to hunting and hawking. Many of his interests had their origin in his powerful historical sense. He had an abiding fascination with the coronation regalia: in March 1390 he replaced a missing slipper of St Edmund which had fallen off at his coronation.[44] He was deeply conscious of his lineage: he was devoted to the cult of St Edward the Confessor and keenly promoted that of his great-grandfather Edward II (plate 25).[45] He seems to have had a taste for antiquarian pursuits. He took a particular delight in his discovery of the holy oil of St Thomas in the Tower in 1399; and ten years earlier he had insisted on seeing some 'old sterlings' which had been unearthed at St Hilda's chapel at Whitby.[46] His antiquarian tastes fed into, and informed, his piety. He was a keen relic collector and made several additions to the royal collection: in 1398 he acquired a tooth of St John the Baptist from one John Glazier, to whom he granted a pension of 4d a day.[47] He showed a special interest in the cults of the pre-Conquest English saints: at various times he visited the shrines of St Edmund, St Erkenwald, St Chad and St Winifred.[48] His deeply instinctive piety was reinforced by his orthodoxy. He took a leading role in the suppression

---

[44] *WC*, 414–16. William Sudbury's treatise on the regalia, incorporated in the *Speculum Historiale*, was dedicated to the king: *Ricardi de Cirencestria Speculum Historiale de Gestis Regum Angliae*, ed. J.E.B. Mayor (2 vols, Rolls series, 1863–9).

[45] See above, 311–13, 323. Further evidence of his consciousness of lineage is found in his order of May 1398 for the repair of Henry I's tomb at Reading Abbey: *CPR 1396–9*, 346.

[46] Sandquist, 'The Holy Oil of St Thomas of Canterbury', 330–44; *CPR 1385–9*, 162. Walsingham considered him 'a curious investigator of the relics of his ancestors': *HA*, ii, 239.

[47] *CPR 1396–9*, 329.

[48] See above, 310–11.

of heresy: on the epitaph that he commissioned for his tomb he prided himself on 'suppressing the heretics and scattering their friends'. Exceptionally among English rulers, he was vigorous in sponsoring the conversion of unbelievers: on two occasions he was present when Jews were received into the faith in the chapel of his manor at King's Langley.[49]

However, if his piety was of the dogmatic sort, he was also willing to reflect. He enjoyed listening to sermons, was assiduous in the observance of saints' days and took an informed interest in matters ecclesiological.[50] He was deeply conscious of the religious dimension to his kingly office and developed a fondness for images of himself in semi-divine pose. Simultaneously with his religious interests, he developed an awareness of the legal and ideological dimensions of his office. It seems that he was familiar with the arguments of the civil lawyers and may have dipped into their work himself. The ideas of Giles of Rome appealed to him. But he should not be seen as a kingly *sage* in the mould of Charles V of France. He is unlikely to have been widely read in academic treatises. Such evidence as there is suggests that his preferred reading was found in the lyrics and romances beloved of the higher nobility; reading, in other words, was for him mainly a recreational pursuit. Like other kings of the time, he showed an enthusiasm for physical activities. His favourite sport was probably the chase. He regularly hunted each summer, and in 1386 spent £25 on an elaborate gilt hunting knife and horn.[51] He took a keen interest in horseflesh: in 1382 he sent four envoys to Prague to improve his stud from the Luxemburg stables.[52] He also had a penchant for hawking. He took a considerable pride in his collection of falcons: according to the issue rolls, in 1399 the huge sum of £78 was spent on 'falcons . . . purchased for the king's use'.[53]

In many respects Richard's outlook and cultural tastes were firmly traditional: Edward I had been addicted to hunting and falconry and Edward III had been an avid collector of relics. But there is evidence that the king had an interest in the newer, more refined preoccupations of the late fourteenth-century royalty and aristocracy. He had a liking for fine clothes: *haute couture* became for him a medium for visual display. He was interested in *haute cuisine* too: the recipe book known as *The Forme of Cury* was compiled by his master cook at his behest.[54] He displayed a personal fastidiousness lacking in his predecessors: he

---

[49] E403/527, 14 Dec. 1389; *Issues of the Exchequer*, 250.
[50] See above, 322, 232–3.
[51] *Issues of the Exchequer*, 231.
[52] Mathew, *Court of Richard II*, 22.
[53] *Issues of the Exchequer*, 268.
[54] *The Forme of Cury*.

was almost certainly the first king to use a handkerchief and he had bath-houses installed at Eltham and Sheen.[55] There is evidence of the interest that he took in the fashionable science of astrology. In 1391 he commissioned a book of geomancy, of which two copies survive, and he had at least a couple of quadrants in his possession.[56] The fact that in 1399 his clerk Richard Maudelyn was accused of dabbling in the magical arts suggests that a fascination with astrology was widespread in his circle.[57]

Evidence of the level of Richard's contemporary awareness is also afforded by his intense preoccupation with his self-image. In the second half of the fourteenth century, especially in the decade or two before his accession, rulers in continental Europe began developing an interest in individualized, naturalistic representations of themselves. The Emperor Charles IV is known to have commissioned a portrait of himself while at Feltre in Italy in 1354, and John II of France and his sons commissioned a series of panel portraits in the 1360s and later.[58] Richard shared his contemporaries' enthusiasm for the genre. He was highly conscious of his image and more likenesses survive of him than of any English ruler before Henry VIII.[59] The images are all to a certain extent icon-like and 'official': this is a natural consequence of the king's desire to project an image of himself as a demi-god. But they also show considerable realism, for Renaissance notions of portraiture were being absorbed in England at this time. Before the late fourteenth century, likenesses of rulers had been highly stylized. Richard is the first of his line of whose appearance we can be reasonably certain.

The finest and possibly the most haunting of the surviving portraits is the image by the coppersmiths Nicholas Broker and Godfrey Prest for the king's tomb in Westminster Abbey. According to the surviving contract, the effigy was made according to a 'patron' – a pattern or design that already existed.[60] It can be assumed, then, that it had been inspected by the king and had his approval. Richard was depicted with striking, but slightly feminine, features (plate 20). He has unusually high cheekbones and a long, straight nose ending in flared nostrils. The eyes are large and heavy-lidded. On either side of the chin appear

[55] See above, 332.

[56] See above, 324–5.

[57] Carey, *Courting Disaster*, 94–5. Carey says that it was Richard who handed Maudeleyn over to parliament for examination; in fact, it was Henry: *Annales*, 301.

[58] Meiss, *French Painting in the Time of Jean de Berry*, 75.

[59] In addition to those discussed below, there were others now lost. In 1393, at the king's command, statues of the king and queen were placed above the gate to London Bridge: Barron, 'The Quarrel of Richard II with London', 195–6. For more detailed discussion see S. Whittingham, 'The Chronology of the Portraits of Richard II', *Burlington Magazine*, cxiii (1971), 12–21.

[60] *Age of Chivalry*, no. 446.

the tufts of a goatee beard, while a small moustache droops over the extremities of the lips. The hair is short and relatively wavy, and around the temples is held in place by a circlet. Many of the characteristics found in this likeness appear in other portraits. The much-restored Westminster Abbey portrait of c.1395 shows the same youthful-looking but slightly feminine features (plate 21).[61] Richard is again shown with a long nose, large eyelids and a short goatee beard. Broadly similar characteristics appear in a series of portraits in the historiated initials of manuscripts. A particularly fine example is the Shrewsbury borough charter of 1389. Richard in this instance is shown enthroned, leaning forwards and looking slightly to his right. He has the familiar long nose and large eyelids, but this time his hair is much longer (plate 15). Almost identical to the Shrewsbury portrait is one in the Book of Statutes in St John's College, Cambridge (plate 12). Richard's hair is again very long and his face has the same elongated features. Portraits of inferior quality showing the same characteristics are found in the Ipswich borough charter and Roger Dymock's treatise against the Lollards (plate 10). The portrait which is the exception in the series is the one in the Wilton Diptych. In the Diptych, contrary to usual practice, Richard is shown clean-shaven. There can be little doubt that Richard was sporting a beard by the time that the painting was commissioned: indeed, he had probably had one since about 1386. Possibly, then, the Diptych's is an idealized likeness. It was by no means uncommon for rulers to be represented younger than they were. In miniatures painted in the 1590s Queen Elizabeth was habitually shown as if she were thirty years younger. An alternative explanation is that the painter of the Diptych was mindful of Richard's forthcoming marriage to the six-year-old Isabella of France. The king could have been given his boyish looks to gloss over the age difference that separated him from his bride-to-be.[62] Whatever the explanation, one thing at least is certain: it is not realistic. By the middle or later 1390s Richard, while undeniably younger-looking than his years, was a fully grown adult: bearded and probably mustachioed. A more accurate record of his appearance is given by the tomb effigy and the better executed of the illuminations.

The impression of the king's elegant, but slightly feminine, appearance is reinforced by the descriptions of the chroniclers. All those who commented on his appearance were agreed on what they call his 'beauty'. Gower, writing near the beginning of the reign, described him

---

[61] For a full discussion of the painting, see Hepburn, *Portraits of the Later Plantagenets*, ch. 1.

[62] Gordon, *Making and Meaning*, 24, suggests that the intention was to show Richard as he looked at his coronation. The technical evidence cited to support this is not convincing; nor is it apparent what the object of so doing could have been.

as 'the most beautiful of kings' and 'the flower of boys'.[63] Maidstone, fifteen years later, said that he was 'as handsome as Paris' and 'as gracious as Absalom'.[64] Usk in an obituary notice said that he was 'as beautiful as Absalon'.[65] Archbishop Arundel, no admirer of his, described him as a 'beautiful' man, though also the falsest one.[66] Even to the ardently pro-Lancastrian Lydgate, writing in the 1430s, he was 'a man of grete beaute'.[67]

The emphasis constantly placed in these passages on Richard's 'beauty' gives the impression that people considered him slightly epicene. The Evesham writer commented on his 'rounded, feminine face' and his faint-heartedness in foreign war.[68] Possibly the reason for this is that the chroniclers were measuring him against the manliness of his father, who in his prime had been an exceptionally vigorous man. Whether or not this is so, Richard was no weakling. Physically, he was an impressive man. He was tall: when his tomb was opened in 1871, his skeleton was found to be six feet long.[69] He was also vigorous and active. Like his predecessors, he was fond of the chase: every summer he spent five or six weeks at his lodges tracking down game.[70] There is evidence that he could ride well. Walsingham says that in 1383 he made the journey from Daventry to London by riding 'all night, by relays, without stopping'.[71] It seems that he was undaunted by the prospect of heading an army. He led three major expeditions in the British Isles: the Scottish expedition of 1385 and the two expeditions to Ireland in the 1390s; and, as the Irish expeditions show, he could easily survive the rigours of the camp. On the other hand, he rarely participated in tourneying and jousting. He staged a number of large-scale tournaments in the course of his reign – the most important of these being the tournaments at Smithfield in 1386 and October 1390 and an event that Froissart says was less well attended at Windsor in 1399.[72] Richard appreciated the

---

[63] Complete Works of John Gower, iv, 265–6

[64] Political Poems and Songs, i, 283, 285.

[65] Usk, 43, 202.

[66] Eulogium, iii, 382.

[67] The Minor Poems of John Lydgate, ed. H.N. MacCracken (EETS, old series, cxcii, 1934), 721.

[68] HVR, 166; Chrons. Revolution, 241.

[69] Stanley, 'On an Examination of the Tombs of Richard II and Henry III', 323.

[70] His summer itineraries tended to be built around stays at hunting lodges such as Woodstock, Easthampstead and Henley-on-the-Heath: see Appendix. The Westminster chronicler commented on his fondness for the chase: WC, 342. It is a comment on his taste that between 1387 and 1390 he spent £450 on improving the hunting lodges of the New Forest: HKW, ii, 986.

[71] HA, ii, 103.

[72] E101/401/16 m.2; WC, 450; Froissart, ii, 477–81, 681.

lustre that patronage of tournaments shed on his monarchy,[73] but, except at the Smithfield event of 1390, he does not appear to have participated in them himself.[74] This was hardly because of any lack of skill: as an accomplished horseman he could easily have acquitted himself creditably. A more plausible reason is that he was concerned to maintain his 'distance'. Tourneying with his subjects would have required him to come down to their level; and that would hardly have accorded with his exalted image of himself. Like Henry VII later, he preferred to be 'a princely and gentle spectator'.[75]

Richard's preoccupation with 'distance' highlights the overall similarity between his kingly style and that of his fellow rulers in Europe. In many European states at this time princes were seeking to 'distance' themselves from their subjects. The stimulus to their action was provided by the growing prosperity of the lower orders: as people grew richer and traditional distinctions were eroded, rulers needed to reassert their pre-eminence by exalting or 'distancing' themselves. Richard was intellectually attracted to the notion of 'distance', but there was probably also something in it that appealed to his temperament. Richard found it difficult to establish relations of any warmth with people outside a small, select circle. He lacked his grandfather's easy charm and affability, and his relations with the higher nobility were often strained. There are signs that he was by nature introspective: in the haunting portrait in Westminster Abbey he comes across as a lonely, even a bitter, man. The origins of his difficulties – and of his brittleness more generally – are probably to be found in his upbringing. His elder brother Edward of Angoulême had died when he was four and he had spent the greater part of his youth as an only child.[76] Even when he was an adolescent there were relatively few companions in his nursery. The

---

[73] J.L. Gillespie, 'Richard II's Knights: Chivalry and Patronage', *JMH*, xiii (1987), 143–59; J.R.V. Barker, *The Tournament in England 1100–1400* (Woodbridge, 1986), 69.

[74] It is not certain that he participated at Smithfield. The Westminster writer says that he did and, moreover, that he took the honours on the first day (*WC*, 450). But Froissart, in a full account, gives no such report (Froissart, ii, 477–81). Barker implies that he participated in the earlier Smithfield event of March 1386, quoting expenditure on armour for the occasion (E101/401/15 m.2, *rectius* E101/401/16 m.2). Again, however, the silence of the chroniclers is telling: Froissart does not mention the event, and the Westminster writer says simply that 'there was jousting at Smithfield' (*WC*, 164). It is possible that the armour was for the king's use in a formal procession of the kind staged four years later (see above, 342).

[75] The words of Sir Francis Bacon, cited in D. Starkey, 'Intimacy and Innovation: the Rise of the Privy Chamber, 1485–1547', *The English Court from the Wars of the Roses to the Civil War*, ed. D. Starkey (London, 1987), 77.

[76] Richard cherished the memory of his deceased elder brother: in 1391 he had a tomb made for him at King's Langley (E403/533, 27 April).

receiver's account of 1377 records only the presence of Henry of Derby and John Arundel; and with the former at least his relations were unhappy.[77] His experience of isolation was reinforced by the fact that for years he saw relatively little of the court. His father had resided during his years of illness chiefly at his manors of Berkhamstead and Kennington, and it was at these properties rather than at Windsor or Westminster that his son was brought up. Yet at the same time as enduring this companionless existence Richard was treated with deference and respect by his inferiors; and from 1376 he was accorded the honour due to an heir apparent. The effects of his upbringing are likely to have given him a powerful sense of his uniqueness while leaving him inexperienced in the handling of relations with the great men of the realm. The problems that Richard was later to encounter in dealing with the nobility may have owed a great deal to the experience of his lonely boyhood.

Though in many ways cold and remote, Richard was not without a capacity for friendship. From the days of his youth he had always cherished the company of a select group of male friends. His deep affection for Robert de Vere in the 1380s is well known. In the 1390s he appears to have been on intimate terms with a number of the senior clerks in his service. The Evesham writer says that the bishops of Worcester and Carlisle were prominent among his boon companions in 1398.[78] His friendships with other men were almost certainly close and intense; but it is possible that they were also fickle. His friendship with Thomas Mowbray, for example, in the early 1380s did not last. In the 1390s, as he moved from adolescence to adulthood, there are signs that he took a greater delight in female company. Contemporaries commented on the number of ladies who thronged his court.[79] It is noticeable that from 1396 the courtier ladies benefited more than before from his patronage. A particular favourite appears to have been Blanche, Lady Poynings. In 1397 Richard presented her with a precious ring, and in the following year he granted her £40 'of his gift'.[80] It is hard to know what degree of affection lay behind Richard's favour to Lady Poynings and her like. The presence of women was a common characteristic of late fourteenth-century courts, and the gifts were

---

[77] E101/398/8. Robert de Vere may have been a youthful associate; but de Vere was brought up, as a royal ward, in the king's household, not the prince's (Tout, *Chapters*, iii, 406).

[78] *HVR*, 165.

[79] *RP*, iii, 339.

[80] E403/556, 22 Oct.; E403/561, 30 Nov. Blanche, Lady Poynings, was the widow of Thomas, Lord Poynings, who died in 1375. She had probably joined the court circle as a result of her marriage, in around 1377, to Sir John Worth, steward of the lands of the princess of Wales (*CP*, x, 662). In 1388 she had been expelled from court by the Appellants (*WC*, 230).

possibly no more than token marks of favour. If evidence is to be sought of Richard's attraction to, and delight in the company of, the opposite sex, it would probably be better to focus on the success of his first marriage. His relationship with his queen, Anne of Bohemia, was one of the most companionate at this level of society in England in the middle ages. Richard and his bride had been brought together by the imperatives of international diplomacy, but the tie between them developed into one of deep mutual attachment. More than any other English medieval royal marriage, the marriage to Anne bore witness to the theologians' claim that affective love could develop within an arranged match.

It is unfortunate that Queen Anne is a figure who leaves a blurred impression on the pages of history. Her arrival in England aroused little interest in the chroniclers. To the Westminster writer she was only 'this tiny scrap of humanity'.[81] Twelve years later, when she died, the tributes paid were no more than conventional. Walsingham described her blandly as generous with alms and a friend of the poor.[82] Unlike some earlier royal consorts she appears to have taken little part in politics. Her interventions were for the most part confined to acts of intercession. In 1388 she pleaded with the Appellants for the lives of Sir Simon Burley and the justices.[83] Four years later she begged her husband to show forgiveness to the Londoners who had offended him by refusing a loan.[84] It was conventional in the later middle ages for the king's consort to be cast in the role of an intercessor.[85] Appropriately, the only surviving manuscript illumination of Anne shows her in this capacity: in a beautifully decorated initial of the Shrewsbury borough charter she kneels before her husband in the act of receiving the charter from his hands (plate 15).[86] Very likely Anne was content with the limited role that convention found for her: it does not appear that she was an ambitious woman. But there are signs that intellectually she was capable of aspiring to higher things. She could read in three languages – German, Latin and Czech.[87] It seems that she was a patron of new religious cults. In 1382 she sought permission from Urban VI for the

---

[81] WC, 24.

[82] Annales, 168.

[83] WC, 330; KC, 502.

[84] WC, 502. In 1384 she had interceded for the radical London leader, John of Northampton (ibid., 92).

[85] P. Strohm, 'Queens as Intercessors', Hochon's Arrow. The Social Imagination of Fourteenth-Century Texts (Princeton, 1992), 95–119.

[86] Shrewsbury Museum, MS 1.24. Whether or not Anne was instrumental in securing the charter is not known. It is worth noticing that Anne's hair is shown plaited.

[87] A. Hudson, 'Lollardy: the English Heresy?', Studies in Church History, xviii (1982), repr. in her Lollards and their Books (London, 1985), 155.

feast of her patron, St Anne, to be celebrated 'more solemnly' in England.[88] There are reports from early in the next century that she attempted to read the Bible in the English vernacular: according to a Lollard tract written between 1401 and 1407, Archbishop Arundel praised her at her funeral 'for notwithstanding her foreign birth, having in English all the four gospels together' with vernacular glosses on them.[89] There are problems in interpreting this account, which may well be embroidered. But it is possible that she should be seen as a patron of the *devotio moderna* in England.

From the beginning of the 1390s there is evidence that Anne was earning the respect of the English political elite. Around this time Sir John Clanvow included a compliment 'to the queen at Woodstock' in his *Boke of Cupid*, a work composed for the St Valentine's Day festivities of the court.[90] In 1392 the archbishop of Canterbury and the abbot of Bury, contesting the right to exercise the franchise of return of writs in a hundred in Suffolk, agreed to let Anne's bailiffs temporarily execute writs on their behalf.[91] On the epitaph composed for her tomb Richard chose to honour his wife for her skill in settling disputes.[92] Had she lived she might have emerged as a figure of considerable political stature. But in 1394, while still only in her twenties, she was struck down, possibly by the plague. Richard was distraught at her loss. According to the Evesham writer, for a year he would not enter any chamber that she had been in, and he ordered the manor of Sheen, where she had died, to be destroyed.[93] Richard and his queen had been married for just over twelve years and their relationship had been close. Unusually for a royal couple they had travelled together on all major itineraries.[94] In 1382 and 1383 Richard had taken her on two lengthy itineraries of his realm to introduce her to his subjects. On the rare occasions when they were separated they kept in touch by letter.[95] There is no record on either side of infidelities. Yet strangely (and it was noted by contemporaries)[96] the marriage was childless. C.M. Barron has suggested that the couple could have sought chastity within marriage: Richard was devoted to the

---

[88] *HVR*, 134; and see above, 324.

[89] M. Deanesley, *The Lollard Bible and other Medieval Biblical Versions* (Cambridge, 1920), 278–81. For discussion of the date and authorship of the tract, see Hudson, *Lollards and their Books*, 67–84.

[90] *Works of Sir John Clanvow*, 9–10, 14.

[91] BL, Cotton MS Tiberius B XI, fo.90ʳ.

[92] 'Jurgia sedavit': *Royal Commission on Historical Monuments. Westminster Abbey*, 31.

[93] *HVR*, 134.

[94] This is evident from PSO1/20; C81/1354/15; *CPR 1381–5*, 311; *CPR 1391–6*, 208, 422. Walsingham says Richard rarely if ever allowed her to leave his side (*HA*, ii, 119).

[95] BL, Cotton MS Tiberius B XI, fo.90ʳ.

[96] *HVR*, 134.

cult of St Edward the Confessor, and a model for their lives could have been provided by the Confessor's chaste liaison with Edith, Earl Godwin's daughter.[97] The suggestion certainly makes sense in the context of the king's piety. But what counts against it is Richard's need for a male heir. Richard had a powerful sense of lineage, and would have wanted his line to continue; if he and Anne were capable of siring an heir, they would surely have done so. The most likely explanation for the couple's childlessness is that either she was barren or he infertile.[98]

Richard's relationship with his second wife Isabella was very different.[99] Isabella was only six when she was handed over to Richard in 1396 at Ardres; and she was only nine when he was deposed. The age difference meant that the relationship between them could never, in the short term at least, be that of a husband and wife; rather it approximated to that of father and daughter.[100] Richard appears to have treated the young Isabella as the child that he never had. He indulged her various whims and fancies, and at Christmas and other festivals he showered her with presents.[101] On one occasion, when the bishop of Durham gave him a present of a whistle inlaid with precious stones, he immediately handed it over to her.[102] Isabella's standing in England was closely related to the fortunes of the Anglo-French *entente* of which she was the personification, and as Anglo-French relations worsened, as they were doing by 1398, she and her entourage became the object of criticism. Complaints were made about the size, and possibly too the activities, of Isabella's attendants, and a dozen or more ladies were sent home to France.[103] Richard's own attitude to his bride appears to have been unaffected by these problems. In the will that he made in 1399 he

---

[97] C.M. Barron, 'Richard II: Image and Reality', *Making and Meaning. The Wilton Diptych* (London, 1993), 15. J.M. Bowers offers support for the suggestion in the context of a discussion of the virginity of the Pearl Maiden in '*Pearl*: Chaste Marriage: Fashion and Texts at the Court of Richard II', *Pacific Coast Philology*, xxx (1995), 15–26.

[98] It is possible, as Binski has recently suggested, that Richard's devotion to the Confessor could have grown in response to his childlessness (Binski, *Westminster Abbey*, 220 n.176). On the other hand, there are grounds for believing that the foundations of that devotion were as much political as personal. The source of the Confessor's attraction to Richard was that he legitimized the king's leanings to 'peace': see above, 312.

[99] For Isabella, see Mirot, 'Isabelle de France'.

[100] It may have been for this reason that the king looked for a substitute for the marriage tie in his relationship with his patron, St Edward the Confessor. From roughly late 1394 he began to impale the royal arms with the mythical arms of the Confessor: impaling expressed the relationship of a husband to a wife.

[101] E403/555, 16 May; E403/556, 4 Dec., 26 Dec.

[102] E101/411/9, m.14.

[103] See above, 407.

bequeathed to her the jewels that she had brought with her from France.[104] Had he lived, it is possible that a companionate liaison would have developed with Isabella similar to that which had linked him to Anne.

Richard's generosity to his wives affords the clearest indication of his capacity for warmth – and there is ample evidence of that quality finding expression in other ways. On occasion the hardships of his servants aroused his compassion. In December 1384 he gave no less than £200 to one of his esquires, John Rose, to assist him with his marriage.[105] In 1396, when he was leaving Dartford for London, he gave 10d to a couple of his esquires who had to be left behind because of illness.[106] For a ruler so signally lacking in the martial spirit he was surprisingly concerned for the well-being of retired veterans. In December 1397 he gave 20 marks to 'diverse gentlefolk' who had fought in the wars, to maintain them in their estate.[107] The issue rolls record a host of other small or smallish gestures of kindness. In 1388, for example, he discharged the debts of the prisoners in Newgate gaol 'out of respect for God and the festival of Easter'.[108] And a decade later he granted no less than 1,000 marks to his esquire John Windsor for his long service.[109] Alongside this evidence, however, has to be set that of his cruelty, vindictiveness and lack of feeling. Proof of these failings is afforded by his treatment of the former Appellant lords in 1397. The earl of Arundel, a senior and well connected lord, was sent to his death after a mockery of a trial in parliament, while Thomas of Woodstock, his own uncle, was done to death in the sordid surroundings of a Calais hostel. The king's vindictiveness is well attested by his treatment of the former Appellants' kinsmen and allies: not only did he bring charges in parliament against the Appellants' lesser allies like Cobham and Plessington; he even visited punishment on their retainers and dependants by cancelling all the corrodies, fees and annuities which they had granted.[110] Parallel with this streak of vindictiveness went a distrust of,

[104] *Foed.*, viii, 77.

[105] E403/505, 12 Dec.

[106] E101/403/10, fo.37ʳ. Is it significant that he considered marriage more deserving of his bounty than infirmity?

[107] E403/556, 4 Dec.

[108] E403/519, 10 April.

[109] E403/555, 23 July. One further instance of royal kindness from the rolls of King's Bench: in 1397 a thief was caught red-handed in Westminster Hall and sentenced to be hanged but Richard, passing by, ordered stay of execution and shortly afterwards pardoned him: G.O. Sayles, 'King Richard II of England: A Fresh Look', *Transactions of the American Philosophical Society*, cxv (1971), repr. in his *Scripta Diversa* (London, 1982), 277–83.

[110] Ross, 'Forfeiture for Treason', 574. Some of the former Appellants' retainers

even a contempt for, his subjects which showed itself in the regime of bonds and oaths which he laid upon them in 1398. Richard was seemingly incapable of understanding the moods and aspirations of his subjects. And they, reciprocating his lack of faith in them, abandoned their own faith in him.

Richard can easily emerge from the evidence as a bundle of contradictions – on the one hand, a kindly, generous, considerate, and thoughtful man, and on the other, a tyrant: cruel, arrogant and capricious. Is there any way in which, a coherent picture can be formed of Richard's character and personality?

The most plausible way of reconciling the opposites is to see Richard's personality as essentially narcissistic. Narcissism describes a condition in which only the person himself – his own body, his own needs and feelings – are experienced as fully real: everybody and everything else lacks reality or interest. Generally a narcissistic person achieves a sense of security in his own subjective conviction of his perfection, rather than through being related to others. He needs to hold on to his narcissistic self-image – for, without it, his sense of worth and identity is lost. Commonly, if his narcissism is wounded by criticism or humiliation, he reacts with intense anger, whether or not he shows it or is even aware of it. The intensity of this aggressive reaction is evident from the fact that hardly ever will such a person forgive anyone who has wounded his narcissism. Very often he feels a burning desire for vengeance which would be less intense if it had been his body or property that had been attacked.[111]

Narcissistic tendencies are commonly found in rulers with a powerful sense of their providential mission. Richard displayed signs of such a sense in the final two years of his reign when he arrested his former enemies and reasserted the prerogative. The highly public way in which he achieved his ends owed much to the narcissist's craving for recognition and outward success. It seems likely that the cruelty which he visited upon his enemies among the former Appellants had its origins in so-called 'narcissist aggression'. In the assault which they had launched on the prerogative ten years earlier the Appellants had shattered Richard's narcissistic self-image. In the manner characteristic of his type he now exacted a terrible revenge on them.

Narcissistic tendencies are noticeable in some general aspects of Richard's behaviour. The most obvious of these is his appetite for self-worship. Richard had a deeply nurtured sense of his uniqueness. He

were arrested in autumn 1397: *CPR 1396–9*, 242. For discussion, see Mott, 'Richard II's Relations with the Magnates', 287–97.

[111] E. Fromm, *The Anatomy of Human Destructiveness* (London, 1974), 201–2.

had an exceptionally exalted view of the royal office; and, more particularly, he totally identified himself with that office. He took a deep
interest in matters of style and self-image: no English king before Henry
VIII devoted so much attention to the portrayal of himself. His ego fed
on the attentions of others. The chroniclers testify to the delight that he
took in rituals and public ceremonies in which he occupied a central
position. Crown wearings appealed to him because they made him the
object of deference and attention. He constantly accorded his own
needs and preoccupations a higher importance than those of others.
The system of bonds and oaths which he fashioned in his final years and
which so alienated his subjects was driven entirely by his obsession with
security.

Equally indicative of Richard's narcissism is his gradual detachment
from the real – the external – world. By the final years of his reign there
can be little doubt that Richard's grasp on reality was becoming weaker.
From the end of the Westminster parliament of autumn 1397 he was
largely cut off from his subjects. At court he surrounded himself with
self-seekers and sycophants. On his itineraries he was always attended by
his company of Cheshire archers. His major policy decisions became
strangely myopic. When he set sail for Ireland in 1399 he fatally under-
estimated the scale of the threat posed by Bolingbroke in Paris. He
affected a far greater fondness for the trappings than the substance of
power. In a way common to narcissistic personalities he was fascinated
by the symbolism and imagery of power. Many of the major artistic
works of his later years are richly decorated with the symbols and
devices that he used. In the Wilton Diptych his mantle is decorated with
the white hart and the French king's collar of the broom pods. On his
tomb effigy his robes of state are powdered with the white hart, the
broom pod and other kingly emblems such as the sunburst and
tree-stock, while his wife's effigy has the Bohemian ostrich and her
personal emblem of rosemary.[112] Many of the innumerable plates,
hanaps, dishes and altar vessels in his collection were treated with these
devices and with the royal arms quartered with those of St Edward.[113] In
the later fourteenth century it became increasingly common to have
buildings or objects decorated with such devices, for they could display
ownership at an instant. Richard doubtless valued them for this reason;
but he also appears to have invested them with a life – and a reality – of
their own.

Another sign of the king's narcissism was his taste for self-
dramatization. A tendency to engage in self-dramatizing behaviour has

---

[112] J.G. Nichols, 'Observations on the Heraldic Devices on the Effigies of Richard
II and his Queen in Westminster Abbey', *Archaeologia*, xxix (1842), 32–59; *Royal
Commission on Historical Monuments. Westminster Abbey*, 31.

[113] E101/411/9; *Ancient Kalendars and Inventories of the Exchequer*, iii, 309–61.

been a characteristic of modern leaders of narcissistic type. The most obvious examples are Hitler and, to a lesser degree, Churchill. Richard exhibited the tendency from his earliest adolescence. At the meeting with the rebels at Smithfield in 1381, when Tyler was struck down, he immediately rode forward, proclaimed himself the rebels' leader and led them from the field.[114] On later occasions he used theatricality to project an image of power. At Coventry in September 1398, when he cancelled the tournament between Hereford and Norfolk, he did so at a time and in a way calculated to emphasize his command over people and events. At other times his sense of theatre could take a macabre turn. In November 1395, when he attended the reburial of Robert de Vere's body at Earl's Colne, he ordered the coffin to be opened so that he could touch his friend's fingers and gaze on his face one last time.[115] A couple of weeks earlier, as Abbot Colchester was to recall, at Bishop Waltham's obsequies in Westminster Abbey he was so deeply moved by the sight of his friend's body that he promised to give a vestment in his memory embroidered with the tree of Jesse.[116] Richard's fascination with bodies was apt to combine with his finely honed sense of the theatrical possibilities of burial. Several times in his later years he intervened to secure for a servant or friend reburial in grander or more dignified surroundings. One of the first to be honoured in this way was Bishop Waltham. Waltham had requested burial in his cathedral church at Salisbury, but Richard, ignoring his wishes, sent Sir William Scrope to the city to claim the body for burial in the Confessor's chapel at Westminster. The dean and chapter of Salisbury being in no position to refuse, the body was handed over and Richard himself, as we have seen, attended the obsequies (plate 18).[117] Only three months earlier Richard had intervened in the case of the celebrated condottiere Sir John Hawkwood. Hawkwood had died in 1394 in his adoptive city of Florence and had been buried there; Richard, however, wrote to the Florentine authorities and secured the return of his body to England.[118] In the following year Richard intervened twice more. In August, when he was passing through Canterbury, he learned that Archbishop Courtenay, who had died in the previous month, had requested burial in the collegiate church at Maidstone. Overriding his wishes, Richard

---

[114] To highlight Richard's sense of drama on this occasion is not to deny the element of advance planning which went into the occasion: see above, 71.

[115] *Annales*, 184–5. De Vere's body had been brought back from Louvain, where he had died.

[116] WAM 5262A.

[117] SC8/141/7050; *HA*, ii, 218. For fuller discussion of this episode, see Saul, 'Richard II and Westminster Abbey'.

[118] J. Temple-Leader and G. Marcotti, *Sir John Hawkwood (L'Acuto)* (London, 1889), 293–4.

insisted that he be buried in the choir of Canterbury Cathedral.[119] Three months later Richard acted in similar fashion when his chamber knight Sir John Golafre died. Golafre had requested burial at the Grey Friars' church at Oxford, but as he lay dying he received a request from the king, to which he acceded, to allow his body to go to Westminster.[120] In a few of these cases – those of Waltham and Golafre – there was an obvious enough justification for Richard's intervention. From 1388 Richard was promoting Westminster Abbey as a mausoleum for royal servants in much the same way that the French kings were promoting St Denis, and Waltham and Golafre were servants whom he thought deserving of interment in its surroundings. But there is no easy explanation for his interference in the cases of Hawkwood or Courtenay. Richard, in the last resort, was interested in reburial for its own sake. It afforded him a uniquely theatrical way of displaying his power over his subjects: indeed, of proclaiming his control over their destinies even in death.

The undoubted extravagance of Richard's behaviour in his later years has led a number of historians to suggest that he became mentally unbalanced. The first scholar to advance this theory appears to have been Bishop Stubbs in the 1870s. Commenting on Richard's behaviour after his second marriage, Stubbs said that 'Richard's policy as well as his character seems to have changed'; and this may have been because 'the sight of continental royalty wrought in him a craving for absolute power . . . or because his mind, already unsettled, was losing its balance altogether'.[121] Seventy years later Anthony Steel offered a fuller development of the thesis in his *Richard II*. Steel, writing under the influence of Freud, argued that Richard was a victim of a clinical neurosis. He found the origin of the king's problems in his youth. The young Richard, he believed, although not a coward, 'was very probably a physical weakling'. As a result it was impossible for him to become a great knight in the mould of his father. Despite this handicap he was determined to be a powerful monarch who would exercise the prerogatives of his office to the full. All his life he was tortured by the problem of reconciling his ambitions to physical reality: a problem which he could solve only by rejecting the chivalrous ethic of the age. Very likely, Steel believed, there was no other course for him than the lonely, autocratic one that he followed. But the strain on him took its toll. The loss of Anne deprived him of whatever sense of security he had. From

[119] Dahmus, *William Courtenay*, 228–9; C. Wilson, 'The Medieval Monuments', *A History of Canterbury Cathedral*, ed. P. Collinson, N. Ramsay, M. Sparks (Oxford, 1995), 472–3.

[120] Saul, 'The Fragments of the Golafre Brass', 24.

[121] Stubbs, *Constitutional History of England*, ii, 490. I am grateful to Professor G.B. Stow for drawing this passage to my attention.

1394 onwards he became 'progressively more unbalanced, reckless and impatient'. Eventually 'the slightest hint of opposition was enough to arouse tortured memories of the Appellant regime and pathological suspicions of a plot. . . . Not only the preservation but an extreme, almost an insane, interpretation of the regality' became his main, and ultimately his fatal, obsession.[122]

Steel's interpretation of Richard found a measure of support in the work of May McKisack. McKisack argued that the change which occurred in Richard's behaviour from 1397 suggested 'a sudden loss of control, the onset of a mental malaise'. She did not identify the cause of that malaise; nor did she speculate on the possible effects on Richard of the loss of Anne. But she judged that, if the king were still sane by 1397, 'it was the sanity of a man who pulls his own house about his ears'. The case for deposing him, she concluded, looked stronger than the case for deposing his great-grandfather, Edward II. The latter had simply been foolish and weak; 'but Richard had become dangerous, perhaps dangerously mad'.[123]

The suggestion that Richard suffered from a form of insanity was rightly criticized by V.H. Galbraith.[124] Galbraith pointed out that the theory, in the form presented by Steel, rested on two convenient but separate assumptions – the first, that Richard began life a physical weakling, and the second that he died a schizophrenic. Neither of these is sustainable. The first, indeed, is inherently implausible. Richard is known to have been of full height. We have seen that when his tomb was opened, his skeleton was found to have measured nearly six feet.[125] The signs are that he was physically strong. If he chose not to take part in jousting, it was by deliberate choice, not as a result of physical incapacity. The suggestion that he was schizophrenic is equally unconvincing. Richard may have acted strangely from 1397, but it is doubtful if he was suffering from a split personality. His behaviour did not exhibit any of the usual symptoms of schizophrenia. At no time is there any indication that he lost self-control.[126] His conduct towards the end was of a

---

[122] Steel, *Richard II*, 41–2, 203–4. For discussion of Steel's views, see J.M. Theilmann, 'Stubbs, Shakespeare and Recent Historians of Richard II', *Albion*, viii (1976), 116–17.

[123] McKisack, *The Fourteenth Century*.

[124] V.H. Galbraith, 'A New Life of Richard II', *History*, xxvi (1942), 223–39, repr. in his *Kings and Chroniclers. Essays in English Medieval History* (London, 1982). Galbraith is supported by Taylor, 'Richard II's Views on Kingship', 200.

[125] See above, 452.

[126] It was once supposed that Richard threw a fit while interrogating the Carmelite friar at Salisbury in April 1384 (for the affair of the Carmelite friar, see above, 131–2). But this interpretation has now been shown to rest on an editor's error of transcription: L.C. Hector, 'An Alleged Hysterical Outburst of Richard II', *EHR*, lxviii (1953), 62–5.

piece with what went before: throughout, there were the same craving for attention and fondness for extravagant gestures. Undoubtedly there was something highly individual in his conduct; but that individuality is not to be identified with the symptoms of madness. We return to the point that Richard's personality is best seen as narcissistic. He experienced acute difficulty in relating to the external world. Only his own needs and his own feelings seemed real to him; everything else was perceived more or less intellectually and lacked colour and weight. The result of this distortion was that he showed severe defects of judgement and lacked a normal capacity for objective thought.

When Steel pictured Richard as a 'neurotic', he saw him essentially as a creature of passion. He denied him the ability to make rational or considered choices. As Galbraith pointed out, Steel's Richard was in many senses a victim of his personality – 'more sinned against than sinning'.[127] Because he was not in possession of his faculties, he was not responsible for his actions; and because he was not responsible for his actions, he could not be blamed for them. However, once the case for Richard's insanity is rejected, he can no longer be excused moral responsibility. It is true that by 1397 his behaviour was hardly of the kind that would generally be considered 'normal'. Nevertheless he always retained the capacity to choose. He could discriminate between different courses of action; and he could weigh the consequences of what he decided. In forming a view of Richard's career, it should not be supposed that we are studying the working out of a neurosis. Rather, we are looking at the interplay normal in the human condition between a man and his world: in this case, at a king's attempts to fashion a new style of monarchy in England and at these attempts' failure under the weight of their internal contradictions.

In the epitaph that he commissioned for his tomb in Westminster Abbey Richard pictured himself as an entirely different kind of king from his predecessors. Edward III's epitaph had stressed that king's martial qualities; Richard's, on the other hand, stressed his wisdom and prudence:

> Prudent and elegant;
> Richard, by oath, the second, overtaken by fate;
> lies here, portrayed and under marble;
> he was true in speech and full of reason;
> noble in body, and judicious in mind like Homer. . . .

The picture conveyed by the epitaph was that of an English Solomon: a ruler who, under the guidance of reason, governed in the best interests

---

[127] Galbraith, 'A New Life of Richard II', 226.

of his people. The model for the king's chosen self-image was probably Charles V of France, of whose kingly style he would have learned from the reports of Simon Burley, Michael de la Pole and others. Charles had pictured himself as a royal 'sage' – a scholar king who sought the lessons of wisdom and applied them to the business of government. Charles, who was scholarly by temperament, looked convincing in his chosen role. It is doubtful if the same could be said of Richard. Richard, it seems, was a man of no more than average intelligence and limited application. He lacked the inclination and temperament of a scholar, and he had none of Charles V's natural love of learning. Between the theory and practice of his kingship there was a yawning and, almost certainly to observers, obvious gulf. Richard aspired to be an English Solomon; but in reality he was an English Rehoboam. It was not wisdom and prudence that were the characteristics of his rule; it was chastisement and tyranny. In the final years of his reign his subjects chafed under the vexations that he laid on them. The immediate cause of his fall was his treatment of Bolingbroke. But given the nature of his programme, and the contradictions within it, it was probably inevitable that he would be overthrown sooner or later. The only matters to be settled were the timing and the circumstances of his fall.

In Shakespeare's version of his final months, Richard is shown reacting to his fall with a mixture of anger and resignation. In Act V, set in the cell at Pontefract, he is in reflective mood:

> Thus play I in one person many people,
> And none contented. Sometimes am I king,
> Then treasons make me wish myself a beggar,
> And so I am. Then crushing penury
> Persuades me I was better when a king;
> Then am I king'd again, and by and by
> Think that I am unking'd by Bolingbroke,
> And straight am nothing. But whate'er I be,
> Nor I, nor any man that but man is,
> With nothing shall be pleas'd, till he be eas'd
> With being nothing.
> (Act V, scene v, 31–41)

At an earlier point (Act IV, scene i), during his 'trial' in parliament, Richard's mood had been characterized less by resignation than by a consciousness of his suffering. Richard was aware of the scale of his loss, and of the consequences of his fall. In resigning his crown, he had given everything away; even his anointed 'characters' were gone:

> With mine own tears I wash away my balm,
> With mine own hands I give away my crown,
> With mine own tongue deny my sacred state,
> With mine own breath release all duteous oaths;
> All pomp and majesty I do forswear;
> My manors, rents, revenues I forgo;
> My acts, decrees, and statutes I deny.
>
> (Act IV, scene i, 207–13)

The fallen king, humiliated and degraded, no longer had anything to live for. All that he could reign over, he said, was his griefs:

> But still my griefs are mine.
> You may my glories and my state depose,
> But not my griefs; still am I king of those.
>
> (Act IV, scene i, 191–3)

Richard uncrowned had become a nobody. Without the panoply of state, without the power and prerogatives of office, all that was left to him of his kingship was the memory of it. Yet paradoxically he still thought of himself as a king. As a ruler he had been utterly deficient in the qualities of rulership most required of him; and the result had been the loss of his throne. Yet when freed from the burden of power he could not shake off the burden of majesty; it was as if the man and his office had become fused.

Shakespeare saw in this the very essence of Richard's tragedy: that Richard, though unkinged, was still kingly. This powerful insight, the fruit of Shakespeare's fascination with Richard, affords a clue to the many difficulties that he experienced as a ruler. To a greater degree than his predecessors, Richard had allowed the exercise of power to become fused in his mind with his own sense of being. He saw attacks on his kingship as attacks on his own personality. He could not separate the questioning of policy from criticism of him personally. In a medieval monarchy it was never easy for any ruler to make the mental separation of person from office; and in the late middle ages, as the distinction between the two became blurred, so the task became more difficult.[128] A few kings managed after a fashion to cope with the dilemma – Edward III, for example. But Richard utterly failed: the narcissistic streak in his personality stood in his way. Shakespeare, better than anyone, appreciated the dilemma because his reading of the king's character was so acute. All the most vital aspects of Richard's being – his intense self-regard, his craving for attention, his taste for the theatrical,

---

[128] See above, 446.

his appetite for grandeur and at the same time his greatest weakness, his inner emptiness – find a place in his reading. Shakespeare offered the insights of a dramatist and not a historian. But his characterization of the king and his understanding of what mattered to him probably bring us closer to the historical figure than many a work of history. It is true, of course, as has been pointed out, that Shakespeare distorted the historical record to suit his dramatic purpose: he unduly compressed events; and he invented entire scenes, such as Richard's appearance in parliament. But his achievement was to capture the essence of his subject. Perhaps the actor in Shakespeare responded to the actor in Richard. Certainly in the theatre of medieval monarchy there was no keener actor than Richard. His tragedy was that he mistook the illusion of the stage for the reality of the world around him.

APPENDIX

RICHARD II'S ITINERARY, 1377–99

This itinerary is compiled from a variety of sources – wardrobe or household accounts, instruments under the signet or privy seal, charter witness lists, chronicle narratives, account rolls of lords with whom the king stayed and records of council meetings at which the king's presence was noted. These sources are of unequal value. The most useful for the first half of the reign are letters warranted by the signet. The signet, the smallest of the three seals, was used by the king to authenticate his personal correspondence. Since its custodian, the secretary, generally travelled with the king, it affords a highly accurate guide to his itinerary. Letters under the two other seals – the great and the privy seal – are generally less reliable. Letters under the great seal for much of the time are place-dated at Westminster – giving the impression that the king was there, when it is evident from other sources that he was not. By convention letters under the great seal bore the place and date of the originating warrant, which from October 1386 was generally the privy seal; and since the privy seal had by this stage 'gone out of court' and settled at Westminster, letters under the great seal bore the place-date Westminster too. In the early to mid-1390s there are periods when batches of letters were place-dated elsewhere – commonly at locations in the north. The explanation for this is to be found in the movements of the chancellor, Thomas Arundel, archbishop of York. Each summer, when Arundel went north to his diocese, he authorized the dispatch of certain minor classes of business by informal warrant; and it is these which bear the northern place-date.

For several periods of the reign the evidence of the place-date clauses can be checked against that of a different, but highly useful, source, the series of wardrobe accounts. More or less complete runs of wardrobe accounts survive for the years 1383–5, 1389–90, 1392–4 and 1395–6. What the wardrobe accounts offer is a guide to the movements of the king's household. But the qualification needs to be made that the movements of the household may not invariably correspond to those of the king. On a provincial itinerary the household might settle at a property of some size – say, a palace or a castle – while the king stayed at a hunting lodge nearby; but at least it can be assumed that the king and his household were in roughly the same neighbourhood.

In addition to the record sources, the chronicle narratives preserve a certain amount of information relating to the king's movements. The most valuable of these – at least for the middle years of the reign – is that of the Monk of Westminster. The monk, writing at Westminster Abbey, assists in the resolution of a major difficulty in the way of constructing an adequate itinerary – establishing just when the king actually was at Westminster: for, as we have seen, the dating clauses on the great seal enrolments afford no guide to this. If the king paid a visit to Westminster Abbey, or if he held court at the palace, the monk often says so. The monk and one or two of the other chroniclers also give information about the king's movements around the realm. For example, both the monk and Thomas Walsingham give details of Richard's visit to East Anglia and the north in 1383; Knighton records visits to the midlands. Sometimes the writers also say where the main festivals were kept. In the following itinerary the king is only given a location when his presence in a place is firmly attested. Otherwise, a gap is left in the run of dates.

1377 JUNE 22–6 Kennington. JULY 4–9 Kennington. 16 Westminster. 20–8 Kennington. AUGUST 6–10 Windsor. 12 Henley-on-the-Heath. 20 Berkhampstead. SEPTEMBER 1 Windsor. 5–10 King's Langley. 15–18 London. OCTOBER 12 Westminster. 26–8 Sheen. 30 Hatton-by-Hounslow. NOVEMBER 1 Sheen. DECEMBER 28–30 Windsor.

1378 APRIL 3 Sheen. 22–3 Windsor. MAY 20–2 Worldham. JUNE 14 Kennington. JULY 6–7 Beckley. AUGUST 12 Rockingham. 29 Oakham. SEPTEMBER 13–16 Windsor. OCTOBER 20-mid-NOVEMBER Gloucester and Tewkesbury. 28 Westminster. DECEMBER 26 Windsor.

1379 JANUARY 6 Windsor. 26–FEBRUARY 28 Sheen. MARCH 7 Westminster. APRIL 9–11 Eltham. MAY 20 Sheen. AUGUST 6 Leicester. OCTOBER 20 Windsor. NOVEMBER 2 Windsor. DECEMBER 1 Westminster.

1380 JANUARY 16 Westminster. MARCH 23–6 Eltham. JUNE 7 Westminster. 13 Pleshy. JULY 5 Hadleigh. SEPTEMBER 17 Moor End. OCTOBER 5–6 Nottingham. 18 Oakham. NOVEMBER 2 Oakham. 5 Moulton. 8 Northampton. 27 Moor End. DECEMBER 8–10 Moulton. 28 Woodstock.

1381 JANUARY 10–21 King's Langley. FEBRUARY 1 Westminster. 13 Sheen. 16 Westminster. JUNE 2 Henley-on-the Heath. 10 Windsor. 11–22 Tower of London and Westminster. 22–3 Waltham Forest. 24 London. 27–30 Havering. JULY 2 Colchester. 6–7 Chelmsford. 7 Havering. 8–10 London. 12 Barnet. 13–20 St Albans. 22–3 Berkhampstead. 24–7 King's Langley. 28–9 Henley-on-the-Heath. AUGUST 1–4 Easthampstead. 5–11 Reading. 13 Easthampstead. 14 Reading. 15–20 Sheen. 22–5 Eltham. 26–30 Leeds. SEPTEMBER 3–4 Otford. 5 Eltham. 6–9 Sheen. 15 Sheen. 20 Westminster. OCTOBER 6–10 Berkhampstead. NOVEMBER 3 Westminster. 20 Kennington. 30 Westminster. DECEMBER 1 Kennington.

1382 January 2 Windsor. 10 Westminster. 18–23 Westminster. FEBRUARY 23 Kennington. MARCH 3–5 Windsor. APRIL 11 Eltham. 23–4 Windsor. MAY 2 Easthampstead. 6–8 Westminster. JUNE 8–9 Eltham. JULY 9 Eltham. 20 Easthampstead. AUGUST 3–16 Woodstock. 18 Beckley. 28 Devizes. SEPTEMBER 9–23 Bristol. OCTOBER 6 Westminster. 12 Eltham. NOVEMER 1 Eltham. 13 Fulham. 16 Eltham. 19 Rochester. 20 Canterbury. DECEMBER 25 Westminster.

1383 JANUARY 6 Windsor. FEBRUARY 2 Windsor. 9 Havering. 15 Sheen. MARCH 12–16 Eltham. APRIL 6 Eltham. 20 Sheen. 24 Windsor. MAY 7 Sheen. 8–10 Easthampstead. 20–1 King's Langley. 28 Babraham. JUNE 2–9 Bury St Edmunds. 14 Norwich. 18 Great Yarmouth. Late JUNE-early JULY Ely. JULY 17 Drayton. 21 Fotheringhay. 23 Huntingdon. 24–8 Stamford. AUGUST 2–7 Nottingham. 11–12 Hull. 25–6 Bishopthorpe. Mid-SEPTEMBER Daventry. OCTOBER 5–7 Sheen. 18 Eltham. NOVEMBER 1–14 Eltham. 15–DECEMBER 21 Sheen. 22–31 Eltham.

1384 JANUARY 1–16 Eltham. 20–1 Dartford. 22 Ospringe. 23 Canterbury. 24–6 Dover. 27 Ospringe. 30 Eltham. FEBRUARY 2–3 Eltham. 6 London. 9–22 Havering. 23–7 Sheen. 28 Eltham. MARCH 7 Westminster. 10–31 King's Langley. APRIL 4–15 Berkhampstead. 22–3 Windsor. 24 Easthampstead. 27 Basing. 28 Andover. 29 Salisbury. MAY 2–31 Clarendon. JUNE 2 Cranborne. 3 Wimborne. 4–9 Corfe. 10 Wimborne. 11 Canford. 13–15 Wimborne. 16–17 Breamore. 19 Hatheburgh. 20 Southampton. 22 Brockenhurst. 25 Beaulieu. 28–9 Southampton. 30–JULY 1 Southwick. 2–3 Chichester. 6–7 Arundel. 8 Knapp. 10–11 Worth. 13–14 Westminster. 18–21 Eltham. 27–AUGUST 3 Windsor. 5–8 Henley-on-the-Heath. 15–17 Easthampstead. 18–20 Reading. 21–3 Odiham. 25 Selborne. 28 Sheen. 31–SEPTEMBER 6 Westminster. 13–23 Havering. 24–6 Windsor. 30–OCTOBER 10 Sheen. 13–14 Westminster. 15 Eltham. 19–20 Rochester. 22 Canterbury. 24–5 Rochester. 26 Dartford. 28–NOVEMBER 8 Eltham. 15 Sheen. 22–30 Westminster. DECEMBER 6–20 Sheen. 28 Windsor.

1385 JANUARY 1–FEBRUARY 3 Windsor. 5–9 Sheen. 11–14 Westminster. 19–26 Sheen. 27–MARCH 6 Eltham. 7–11 Westminster. 12–APRIL 10 Eltham. 12–23 Sheen. 25 Windsor. 26–MAY 3 Easthampstead. 4 Reading. 8 Easthampstead. 12 Sheen. 13 Windsor. 14 Easthampstead. 15 Reading. 16–17 Easthampstead. 19–31 Henley-on-the-Heath. JUNE 2 Easthampstead. 3–5 Reading. 10–12 Westminster. 14–19 Eltham. 20–2 Westminster. 24–6 Sheen. 30 King's Langley. JULY 1 Berkhampstead. 4 Burley-on-the-Hill. 7 Leicester. 9–10 Nottingham. 14 Pontefract. 16 York. 22–3 Bishopthorpe. 26 Durham. 29–30 Newcastle-upon-Tyne. 31 Morpeth. AUGUST 6 Hoselaw. 11 Newbattle. 12 Edinburgh. 20 Newcastle-upon-Tyne. 21 Durham. 24 Bishopthorpe. 25–8 Nottingham. 29 Leicester. SEPTEMBER 1–8 Westminster. 9–14 Sheen. 16–17 Westminster. 19 Sheen. 21–4 Windsor. 25 Easthampstead. 26–OCTOBER 18 Windsor. 23 Westminster. 26–31 Eltham. NOVEMBER 5–10 Westminster. 12–13 Sheen. 14–15 Westminster. 19–20 Sheen. 21–DECEMBER 3 Westminster. 4–17 Sheen. 19–21 Westminster. 22 Sheen. 23–31 Eltham.

1386 JANUARY 1–7 Eltham. 8–18 Westminster. 19–26 Sheen. 28–FEBRUARY 15 Windsor. 17 Westminster. 20 Sheen. 21–6 Windsor. 27–8 Easthampstead. MARCH 5–9 Westminster. 10–16 Sheen. 17–22 Westminster. 24–6 Sheen. 28-APRIL 30 Eltham. MAY 5–6 Sheen. 9 Windsor. 10–11 King's Langley. 13 Windsor. 14–18 Easthampstead. 20 Henley-on-the-Heath. 21–6 Easthampstead. 27–JUNE 14 Henley-on-the-Heath. 16 Chichester. 18 Midhurst. 20 Henley-on-the-Heath. 22–3 Easthampstead. 24 Henley-on-the-Heath. 26–7 Reading. 28–3 JULY Marlborough. 7–11 Devizes. 12–13 Bath. 16–25 Bristol. 26–8 Thornbury. 30 Berkeley. AUGUST 1–2 Gloucester. 7–11 Oxford. 12–15 Shipton-under-Wychwood. 17–25 Woodstock. 29 Beckley. 30–1 Notley. SEPTEMBER 1–4 Windsor. 8–15 Westminster. 17–19 Sheen. 21 Westminster. 23–30 Sheen. OCTOBER 2–4 Westminster. 5–6 Windsor. 7–18 Westminster/Eltham. NOVEMBER 25 Sheen. DECEMBER 4 Windsor. 23–8 Windsor.

1387 JANUARY 6 Windsor. 19–21 Windsor. 22 Easthampstead. 29 Sheen. FEBRUARY 9 Westminster. 15 Beaumanoir. 21–6 Nottingham. MARCH 17 Nottingham. 25 Royston near Barnsley. 27 Lincoln. APRIL 3–8 Nottingham. 23 Windsor. 27–9 Easthampstead. MAY 8–13 Reading. 22 Woodstock. JUNE 10–13 Coventry. 14–16 Banbury. 26–7 Drayton Basset. 29–30 Lichfield. JULY 3 Stafford. 4 Stone. c.7 Heighley. 12–16 Chester. 26 Malpas. 28 Blakemere. AUGUST 1–5 Shrewsbury. 6 Acton Burnell. 8–13 Worcester. 14 Alvechurch. 20 Groby. 25–9 Nottingham. SEPTEMBER 2–8 Clipstone. 9–11 Nottingham. 16–17 Leicester. 20–OCTOBER 15 Woodstock. 30 Windsor. NOVEMBER 2 Windsor. 9 Sheen. 10 Westminster. 21 Sheen. DECEMBER 1–3 Windsor. 16–17 Windsor. 30 London.

1388 JANUARY 1 Westminster. 18 Eltham. 31 Eltham. FEBRUARY 3–13 Westminster. 18 Westminster/Kennington. 22 Westminster. 23 Kennington. MARCH 26–7 Eltham. APRIL 1 Eltham. 15 Westminster. 18 Kennington. MAY 31 Westminster/Kennington. JUNE 7 Sheen. 15 Kennington. 26–30 Windsor. JULY 22–7 Oxford. 28 Beckley. 29–AUGUST 4 Oxford. 18–21 Abington-by-Northampton. SEPTEMBER 9–OCTOBER 16 Cambridge. 31–NOVEMBER 2 King's Langley. 14 Westminster. 22 Sheen. 29–DECEMBER 7 Windsor. 9 Salisbury. 14 Sherborne. 19 Windsor. 24–9 Eltham.

1389 JANUARY 6–7 Eltham. 20 Westminster. FEBRUARY 1 Westminster. 9–14 Sheen. 25–6 Windsor. MARCH 4–5 Windsor. 7–9 King's Langley. APRIL 5–20 King's Langley. 27 Windsor. MAY 3 Westminster. 31 Kennington. JUNE 5–8 Henley-on-the-Heath. 24 Windsor. JULY 1 Westminster. 3 Sheen. 11 Windsor. AUGUST 9 Westminster. 10 Eltham. 15 Sheen. 19–20 Windsor. SEPTEMBER 4 Brockenhurst. 12–15 Clarendon. 26 Windsor. OCTOBER 3 Sheen. 9–10 Eltham. 15 Westminster/Kennington. 24 Eltham. NOVEMBER 2–15 Havering. 17–28 Sheen. DECEMBER 2–11 Reading. 18–19 Osney. 20–31 Woodstock.

1390 JANUARY 7 Osney. 8 Abingdon. 10 Wallingford. 12 Windsor. 15–16 Sheen. 17–FEBRUARY 27 Kennington. MARCH 3–20 Sheen. 21–APRIL 14 Eltham. 17–24 Sheen. 30–MAY 8 Kennington. 14–22 Sheen. 26–9 Kennington. 31–JUNE 12 Easthampstead. 14 Notley. 19–24 Woodstock. 29 Cirencester. 30 Faringdon. JULY 1 Marlborough. 2–11 Devizes/Gloucester. 12–13 Marlborough. 14 Faringdon. 17–20 Woodstock. 21 Brackley. 22 Daventry. 23 Coventry. 24–8 Leicester. 29 Loughborough. 30 Nottingham. AUGUST 2 Oakham. 12 Milton Basset. 16

Clifton Campville. 21 Towcester. 23 Buckingham. 25–30 Windsor.
SEPTEMBER 14 Easthampstead. OCTOBER 10–14 London/Kennington.
15 Windsor. 18–31 Easthampstead. NOVEMBER 20 Westminster.
DECEMBER 24–31 Eltham.

1391 JANUARY 1–5 Eltham. FEBRUARY 11 Gloucester. MARCH 11–12
Bristol. 22–9 Bristol. APRIL 12–13 Reading. 23–4 Windsor. MAY 2 West-
minster. 21 Henley-on-the-Heath. AUGUST 2–4 Windsor. 15–16 Eltham.
20–4 Canterbury. SEPTEMBER 5 Leeds. 13–20 Eltham. 27–OCTOBER 5
Windsor. NOVEMBER 1 Sheen. 11 Westminster. DECEMBER 10–15
Sheen. 24–7 King's Langley.

1392 JANUARY 5–6 King's Langley. FEBRUARY 2 Sheen. 12–16 Westminster. 25–6 Eltham. MARCH 5–10 Leeds. 14 Ospringe. c.16 Canterbury.
25–26 Leeds. APRIL 6–7 Eltham. 14–15 Eltham. 27–9 Windsor. MAY 5
Easthampstead. 9 Windsor. 19–31 Stamford. JUNE 2–4 Rockingham. 5–15
York. 16–JULY 9 Nottingham. 11 Northampton. 16-AUGUST 7 Windsor.
20 Kennington. 21–2 London. 24 Sheen. SEPTEMBER 5–20 Woodstock.
22–7 Oxford. 29–OCTOBER 6 Woodstock. 7 Thame. 8 High Wycombe. 9
Windsor. 10 Sheen. 11 Westminster. 12–NOVEMBER 3 Sheen. 4 Ruislip.
5–DECEMBER 9 King's Langley. 10 Denham. 11–16 Windsor. 17–22
Sheen. 23–31 Eltham.

1393 JANUARY 1–6 Eltham. 7–9 Sheen. 10 Windsor. 11–12 Denham.
13–14 King's Langley. 15 Windsor. 16 Easthampstead. 17 Farnham. 18–19
Bishops Sutton. 20–FEBRUARY 11 Winchester. 12 Farnham. 13–19
Windsor. 20–MARCH 27 Sheen. 28-APRIL 20 Eltham. 21 Sheen. 22–3
Windsor. 24-MAY 12 Sheen. 13–18 Easthampstead. 19 Sheen. 20 Eltham.
21 Rochester. 22 Ospringe. 23–1 JUNE Canterbury. 2 Ospringe. 3
Rochester. 4 Eltham. 6–10 Sheen. 11 Kennington. 12 London. 13–21
Sheen. 22–5 Windsor. 26-JULY 11 Easthampstead. 12–20 Henley-on-the-
Heath. 21–2 Farnham. 23 Alton. 24–5 Winchester. 26–7 Romsey. 28
Downton. 29 Cranborne. 30 Wimborne. 31–AUGUST 9 Corfe. 11
Cranborne. 12 Downton. 14–18 Salisbury. 19 Downton. 21–SEPTEMBER
14 Beaulieu. 15 Southampton. 16 Winchester. 17 Bishops Sutton. 18
Farnham. 19-OCTOBER 13 Windsor. 14–NOVEMBER 16 Sheen. 17–
DECEMBER 22 King's Langley. 23–31 Westminster.

1394 JANUARY 1–6 Westminster. 7–26 Sheen. 27 Westminster. 28–
MARCH 15 Sheen. 20–1 St Albans. 22–APRIL 10 King's Langley. 11–30
Windsor. MAY 1–8 Sheen. 9–20 Windsor. 21-JULY 29 Sheen. 30 Wands-
worth. 31 Southwark. AUGUST 1 London. 2–10 Westminster. 11
Uxbridge. 12 Thame. 13 Oxford. 14–15 Witney. 16 Northleach/
Cirencester. 17–19 Gloucester. 20 Newent. 21–4 Ross-on-Wye. 25–
SEPTEMBER 4 Hereford. 6 Newport. 8 Cardiff. 10 Coity. 11 Margam. 13
Kidwelly. 14 Carmarthen. 15 Llawhaden. 18–19 St David's. 24–8
Haverfordwest. 29–30 Milford Haven. OCTOBER 2 Waterford. 22
Jerpoint. 26 Leighlin. 29 Laneroc. NOVEMBER 6–DECEMBER 31
Dublin.

1395 JANUARY 1–18 Dublin. 19–20 Drogheda. FEBRUARY 4 Dublin. MARCH 1 Dublin. 5–21 Drogheda. 24 Dublin. 28 Connell. 29 Castledermot. 30 Carlow. APRIL 3–7 Kilkenny. 16 Kilkenny. 20–8 Waterford. MAY 1 Waterford. 15–17 Salisbury. 20 Winchester. 28 Westminster. JUNE 23 Rochester. 24 Leeds. JULY 7–18 Leeds. 20–6 Eltham. 27 Dartford. 28–9 Leeds. AUGUST 15–17 Eltham. 24–6 Windsor. SEPTEMBER 9–OCTOBER 16 Windsor. 27–NOVEMBER 2 Woodstock. 4 Oxford. 5–*c.*20 Abingdon. 22 Earl's Colne. 26–DECEMBER 22 Abingdon. 23–4 King's Langley. 25–31 King's Langley/Kennington.

1396 JANUARY 1–7 King's Langley. 9 Thame. 10–16 Woodstock. 17 Burford. 18 Northleach. 19 Gloucester. 20–1 Tewkesbury. 22–4 Worcester. 25 Warwick. 26 Coventry. 27 Nuneaton. 28 Leicester. 29–MARCH 15 Nottingham. 16 Clipstone. 18–19 Blyth. 20 Doncaster. 21 Pontefract. 22 Tadcaster. 23–APRIL 5 York. 6 Doncaster. 7 Worksop. 8–9 Nottingham. 10 Leicester. 11 Market Harborough. 12 Northampton. 13 Newport Pagnell. 14 Dunstable. 15 King's Langley. MAY 1–18 Easthampstead. 19–JUNE 1 Henley-on-the-Heath. 2–5 Windsor. 6–8 Westminster. 9–28 Havering. 29–JULY 2 Westminster. 3–16 Eltham. 17 Kingston upon Thames. 18–23 Windsor. 24–6 Westminster. 27–8 Eltham. 29 Leeds. 31–AUGUST 1 Rochester. 2 Ospringe. 3–4 Canterbury. 5–6 Dover. 7–22 Calais. 23 Dover. 24 Canterbury. 25 Rochester. 26–7 Eltham. 28 Kingston-on-Thames. 29–SEPTEMBER 20 Windsor. 22 Dartford. 23 Rochester. 24 Ospringe. 25 Canterbury. 26–7 Dover. 28–OCTOBER 26 Calais. 28–30 Ardres. 31–NOVEMBER 7 Calais. 12 Saltwood. 18–20 Rochester. 23 Kennington. DECEMBER 29–30 Eltham.

1397 JANUARY 2 Eltham. 7 Westminster. 23 Westminster. FEBRUARY 6 Westminster. 14 Westminster. 27–8 Westminster. MARCH 18–28 Westminster. APRIL 12–25 Eltham. MAY 7–8 Windsor. 27 Westminster. JUNE 1–20 Westminster. JULY 10–11 Westminster/Pleshy. 14–17 Windsor. 20–3 Westminster. AUGUST 5 Nottingham. 14 Lutterworth. 17–22 Woodstock. SEPTEMBER 9 Westminster. 15 Kingston upon Thames. 17–27 Westminster. OCTOBER 22 Westminster. 31–NOVEMBER 1 Woodstock. 11–12 Abingdon. 15–21 Woodstock. 23–6 Banbury. DECEMBER 15 Woodstock. 22 Banbury. 25–31 Coventry.

1398 JANUARY 1–7 Coventry. 17 Lichfield. 18–23 Great Haywood. 25 Lilleshall. 26–FEBRUARY 7 Shrewsbury. 8 Lichfield. 9–11 Clifton Campville. 12 Coventry. 23 Oswestry. 28–MARCH 3 Worcester. 4 Hanley Castle. 6 Gloucester. 7 Evesham. 8 Winchcombe. 9–14 Gloucester. 17–23 Bristol/Bath. 27–8 Reading. APRIL 1–4 Westminster. 22–9 Windsor. MAY 9 Westminster. 24–7 Lichfield. JUNE 14 Stafford. 22–6 Lichfield. 28–JULY 8 Nottingham. 12 Tutbury. 26 Leicester. AUGUST 2 Shrewsbury. 14 Macclesfield. SEPTEMBER 1 Newcastle under Lyme. 8 Lichfield. 14–18 Coventry. 20–3 Leicester. 24–5 Northampton. OCTOBER 3 Windsor. 9 Westminster. 10 Brentford. NOVEMBER 21 Lambeth. DECEMBER 6 Windsor. 16 Coventry. 25 Lichfield.

1399 JANUARY 7–16 Coventry. 19 Wolverhampton. 24 Shrawardine. FEBRUARY 10 Chester. 20 Newcastle under Lyme. 21 Great Haywood. MARCH 9–10 King's Langley. 16–18 London/Westminster. Early APRIL Canterbury. 16 Westminster. 23–5 Windsor. 30–MAY 2 Oxford. 4 Burford. 5 Gloucester. 8 Cardiff. 9 Cowbridge. 11 Margam. 14 Carmarthen. 15–26 Haverfordwest. 27 Milford Haven. JUNE 1 Waterford. JULY 1 Dublin. *c.*16 Waterford. *c.*24 Milford Haven. 29 Whitland. 31 Carmarthen. AUGUST 12–15 Conway. 16 Flint/Chester. 16–20 Chester. 21 Nantwich. 22–3 Stafford. 24–5 Lichfield. 26 Coventry. 27 Daventry. 29 Northampton. 30 Dunstable. 31 St Albans. SEPTEMBER 1–late October Tower of London.

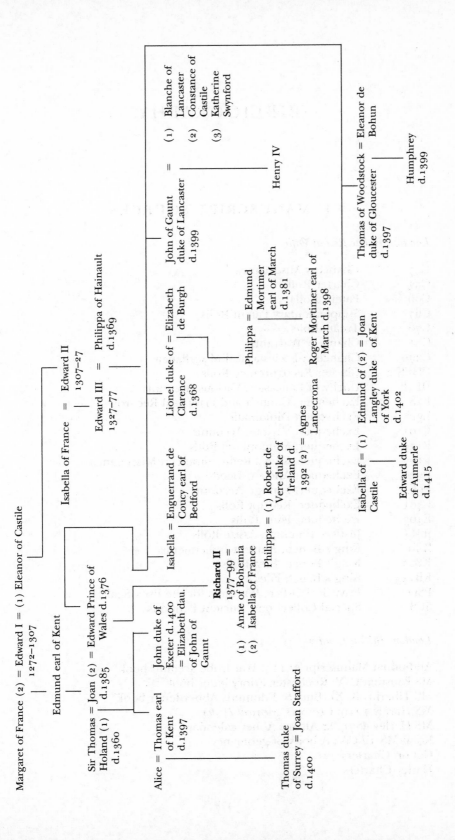

BIBLIOGRAPHY

I. MANUSCRIPT SOURCES

London, Public Record Office

C47	Chancery Miscellanea
C53	Charter Rolls
C66	Patent Rolls
C67	Supplementary Patent Rolls
C76	Treaty Rolls
C81	Chancery Warrants
C270	Chancery: Ecclesiastical Miscellanea
CHES 2	Chester Recognizance Rolls
DL28	Duchy of Lancaster, Various Accounts
E28	Exchequer, Council and Privy Seal Records
E30	Exchequer: Diplomatic
E101	Exchequer, Various Accounts
E159	Exchequer, Memoranda Rolls
E163	Exchequer, King's Remembrancer: Miscellanea
E326	Exchequer, Ancient Deeds
E364	Exchequer, Foreign Accounts
E401	Exchequer, Receipt Rolls
E403	Exchequer, Issue Rolls
Just.I	Justices Itinerant, Assize Rolls
KB9	King's Bench, Ancient Indictments
KB27	King's Bench, Plea Rolls
KB145	King's Bench Files
PSO 1	Privy Seal Office, Warrants for the Privy Seal
SC8	Special Collections, Ancient Petitions

London, British Library

Additional Manuscript 35115: Wardrobe account book
MS Faustina C. V: Rochester Priory letter book
MS Tiberius B. XI: Bury St Edmunds Abbey letter book
MS Harley 1319: Creton's *Metrical History*
MS Harley 3775: St Albans Abbey calendar
Royal MS 12 C.V: A book of geomancy
Cotton Charters
Harley Charters

London, Lambeth Palace Library
Reg. Arundel, i: Register of Archbishop Arundel

London, Westminster Abbey
Muniment nos 5262A, 6221, 6226, 9473–4, 19637–51, 19870–82, 22517–32
Book 1: Liber Niger

Cambridge, St John's College
MS A 7: A book of statutes

Cambridge, Trinity Hall
MS 17: Dymock's treatise against the Lollards

Cambridge, University Library
Ely Diocesan Records D5/7a: Household account of Bishop Arundel

Canterbury Cathedral Library
FA1: Canterbury city accounts
DCC Feretrar 1: Feretrar's account

Cornwall Record Office, Truro
AR37/41/1: Expenses of Sir John Dinham's journey to London

Edinburgh University Library
MS 183: Royal letter book

Lichfield, Joint Record Office
D30/2/1/1: Dean and Chapter Acts Book 1

Oxford, Bodleian Library
MS 581: Book of geomancy

Shrewsbury Museum
MS 1.24: Borough Charter

Winchester College
Muniment 1: Household account of Bishop Wykeham

Worcester Cathedral Library
Liber Albus

York Minster
Dean and Chapter chamberlains' accounts E1/9

II. PRINTED SOURCES

The Ancient Kalendars and Inventories of the Treasury of His Majesty's Exchequer, ed. F. Palgrave (3 vols, London, 1836).

'The Anglo-French Negotiations at Bruges, 1374–1377', ed. E. Perroy (*Camden Miscellany*, xix, Camden Society 3rd series, lxxx, 1952).

Anglo-Norman Letters and Petitions, ed. M.D. Legge (Anglo-Norman Text Society, iii, 1941).

Annales Monasterii Sancti Albani a Johanne Amundesham, ed. H.T. Riley (2 vols, Rolls series, 1870–1).

Annales Ricardi Secundi et Henrici Quarti, in J. de Trokelowe *et* Anon., *Chronica et Annales*, ed. H.T. Riley (Rolls series, 1866).

The Anonimalle Chronicle 1333–81, ed. V.H. Galbraith (Manchester, 1927).

The Brut, or The Chronicles of England, ii, ed. F.W.D. Brie (EETS, original series, cxxxvi, 1908).

Calendar of Charter Rolls 1341–1417 (London, 1916).

Calendar of Close Rolls 1377–1399 (6 vols, London, 1914–27).

Calendar of Fine Rolls 1377–1399 (3 vols, London, 1926–9).

Calendar of Letter Books of the City of London . . . Letter Book H, ed. R.R. Sharpe (London, 1907).

Calendar of Papal Registers, iv, 1362–1404 (London, 1902).

Calendar of Papal Registers, v, 1396–1404 (London, 1904).

Calendar of Patent Rolls 1377–1399 (6 vols, London, 1895–1909).

Calendar of Select Plea and Memoranda Rolls of the City of London, 1381–1412, ed. A.H. Thomas (Cambridge, 1932).

Cartulaire de l'Eglise collegiale Saint-Seurin de Bordeaux, ed. J.A. Brutails (Bordeaux, 1897).

Chaucer Life Records, ed. M.M. Crow and C.C. Olson (Oxford, 1966).

Chronicle of John Hardyng, ed. H. Ellis (London, 1812).

Chronicle of Louth Park Abbey, ed. E. Venables (Lincolnshire Record Society, i, 1889).

Chronicles of London, ed. C.L. Kingsford (Oxford, 1905).

Chronicles of the Revolution, 1397–1400, ed. C. Given-Wilson (Manchester, 1993).

Chronicon Adae de Usk, ed. E.M. Thompson (London, 1904).

Chronicon Anglie 1328–1388, ed. E.M. Thompson (Rolls series, 1874).

Chronique de la traison et mort de Richart II, ed. B. Williams (London, 1846).

Chronique du Religieux de Saint-Denys, ed. M. Bellaguet (6 vols, Paris, 1839–52).

Chroniques de J. Froissart, ed. S. Luce *et al.* (Société de l'Histoire de France, 14 vols, Paris, 1869–).

The Complete Works of John Gower, ed. G.C. Macaulay (Oxford, 4 vols, 1899–1902).

A Descriptive Catalogue of the Manuscripts in the Library of St John's College, Cambridge, ed. M.R. James (Cambridge, 1913).

Diplomatic Correspondence of Richard II, ed. E. Perroy (Camden Society, 3rd series, xlviii, 1933).

An English Chronicle of the Reigns of Richard II, Henry IV, Henry V and Henry VI, ed. J.S. Davies (Camden Society, 1856).

English Historical Documents IV: 1327–1485, ed. A.R. Myers (London, 1969).
Eulogium Historiarum sive Temporis, ed. F.S. Haydon (3 vols, Rolls series, 1858–63), iii.
FAVENT, T., *Historia sive Narracio Mirabilis Parliamenti*, ed. M. McKisack (Camden Society, 3rd series, xxxvii, 1926).
Feet of Fines for the County of Somerset, 21 Edward III to 20 Richard II, ed. E. Green (Somerset Record Society, xvii, 1902).
Feudal Aids (5 vols, London, 1899–1920).
The Forme of Cury, ed. J. Nichols (London, 1780).
Four English Political Tracts of the Later Middle Ages, ed. J.-P. Genet (Camden Society, 4th series, xviii, 1977).
FROISSART, J., *Chronicles*, ed. T. Johnes (2 vols, London, 1862).
——, *Oeuvres*, ed. Kervyn de Lettenhove (Brussels, 26 vols, 1867–77).
GOWER, J., *Confessio Amantis*, ed. R.A. Peck (Toronto, 1980).
Historia et Cartularium Monasterii Sancti Petri Gloucestriae, ed. W.H. Hart (3 vols, Rolls series, 1863–7).
Historia Vitae et Regni Ricardi Secundi, ed. G.B. Stow (Philadelphia, 1977).
Historians of the Church of York, ed. J. Raine (3 vols, Rolls series, 1879–94).
Inventories of Christ Church, Canterbury, ed. J. Wickham Legg and W. St John Hope (London, 1902).
Issues of the Exchequer, Henry III–Henry VI, ed. F. Devon (London, 1847).
John of Gaunt's Register, 1372–1376, ed. S. Armitage-Smith, 2 vols (Camden Society, 3rd series, xx–xxi, 1911).
John of Gaunt's Register, 1379–1383, ed. E.C. Lodge and R. Somerville (2 vols, Camden Society, 3rd series, lvi–lvii, 1937).
The Kirkstall Abbey Chronicles, ed. J. Taylor (Thoresby Society, xlii, 1952).
Knighton's Chronicle 1337–1396, ed. G.H. Martin (Oxford, 1995).
Life of the Black Prince by the Herald of Sir John Chandos, ed. M.K. Pope and E.C. Lodge (Oxford, 1910).
Literae Cantuarienses, ed. J.B. Sheppard (3 vols, Rolls series, 1887–9).
Lives of Edward the Confessor, ed. H.R. Luard (Rolls series, 1858).
The Major Latin Works of John Gower, ed. E.W. Stockton (Seattle, 1962).
A Metrical History of the Deposition of Richard II attributed to Jean Creton, ed. J. Webb, *Archaeologia*, xx (1814).
MÉZIÈRES, P. de, *Letter to King Richard II*, ed. G.W. Coopland (Liverpool, 1975).
The Minor Poems of John Lydgate, ed. H.N. MacCracken (EETS, old series, cxcii, 1934).
Mum and the Sothsegger, ed. M. Day and R. Steele (EETS, cxcix, 1936).
Oxfordshire Sessions of the Peace in the Reign of Richard II, ed. E.G. Kimball (Oxfordshire Record Society, liii, 1983).
The Peasants' Revolt of 1381, ed. R.B. Dobson (London, 2nd edn, 1983).
Political Poems and Songs Relating to English History, ed. T. Wright (2 vols, Rolls series, 1859–61).
Proceedings and Ordinances of the Privy Council of England, ed. N.H. Nicolas (7 vols, London, 1834–7).
Recueil des Actes de Jean IV, Duc de Bretagne, I, 1357–1382, ed. M. Jones (Institut Armoricain de Recherches Economiques et Humaines, xxviii, 1980).

Reports from the Lords Committees Touching the Dignity of the Peerage (5 vols, London, 1820–9).

Ricardi de Cirencestria Speculum Historiale de Gestis Regum Angliae, ed. J.E.B. Mayor (2 vols, Rolls series, 1863–9).

Rogeri Dymmok liber contra XII errores et hereses Lollardorum, ed. H.S. Cronin (London, 1922).

Rolls of the Warwickshire and Coventry Sessions of the Peace 1377–1397, ed. E.G. Kimball (Dugdale Society, xvi, 1939).

Rotuli Parliamentorum (6 vols, London, 1767–77).

Rotuli Scotiae (2 vols, London, 1814–19).

Rotulorum Patentium et Clausorum Cancellarie Hibernie Calendarium, ed. E. Tresham (Irish Record Commission, 1828).

RYMER, T., *Foedera, Conventiones, Litterae etc.*, ed. G. Holmes (20 vols, London, 1704–35).

Select Cases in the Court of King's Bench under Richard II, Henry IV and Henry V, ed. G.O. Sayles (Selden Society, lxxxviii, 1971).

Select Documents of English Constitutional History, 1307–1485, ed. S.B. Chrimes and A.L. Brown (London, 1961).

Somers Tracts, ed. W. Scott (2nd edn, London, 1809).

Statutes of the Realm (11 vols, London, 1810–28).

Testamenta Vetusta, ed. N.H. Nicolas (2 vols, London, 1826).

Three Prose Versions of the Secreta Secretorum, ed. R. Steele (EETS, extra series, lxxiv, 1898).

The Treaty of Bayonne (1388), ed. J. Palmer and B. Powell (Exeter, 1988).

WALSINGHAM, T., *Historia Anglicana*, ed. H.T. Riley (2 vols, Rolls series, 1863–4).

The Westminster Chronicle 1381–1394, ed. L.C. Hector and B.F. Harvey (Oxford, 1982).

William Thorne's Chronicle of St Augustine's Abbey, Canterbury, ed. A.H. Davis (Oxford, 1934).

The Works of Geoffrey Chaucer, ed. F.N. Robinson (London, 2nd edn, 1957).

The Works of Sir John Clanvow, ed. V.J. Scattergood (Cambridge, 1975).

York City Chamberlains' Account Rolls 1396–1500, ed. R. B. Dobson (Surtees Society, cxcii, 1978–9).

III. SECONDARY SOURCES

The Age of Chivalry. Art in Plantagenet England, 1200–1400, ed. J. Alexander and P. Binski (London, 1987).

AMYOT, T., 'An Inquiry concerning the Death of Richard II', *Archaeologia*, xx (1824).

ASTON, M., *Thomas Arundel* (Oxford, 1967).

——, 'The Impeachment of Bishop Despenser', *BIHR*, xxxviii (1965).

——, 'Lollardy and Sedition, 1381–1431', *P&P*, xvii (1960), repr. in *Peasants, Knights and Heretics*, ed. R.H. Hilton (Cambridge, 1973).

——, 'Richard II and the Wars of the Roses', *The Reign of Richard II. Essays in Honour of May McKisack*, ed. F.R.H. Du Boulay and C.M. Barron (London, 1971).

ATKINSON, R.L., 'Richard II and the Death of the Duke of Gloucester', *EHR*, xxxviii (1923).

BALDWIN, J.F., *The King's Council in England during the Middle Ages* (Oxford, 1913).

BALDWIN, J.W., 'The Capetian Court at Work under Philip Augustus', *The Medieval Court in Europe*, ed. E. Haymes (Munich, 1986).

BARBER, R., *Edward, Prince of Wales and Aquitaine* (London, 1978).

BARKER, J.R.V., *The Tournament in England 1100–1400* (Woodbridge, 1986).

BARRON, C.M., 'The Art of Kingship. Richard II, 1377–1399', *HT*, xxxv (June 1985).

——, 'The Deposition of Richard II', *Politics and Crisis in Fourteenth Century England*, ed. J. Taylor and W. Childs (Gloucester, 1990).

——, 'The Parish Fraternities of Medieval London', *The Church in Pre-Reformation Society*, ed. C.M. Barron and C. Harper-Bill (Woodbridge, 1985).

——, 'The Quarrel of Richard II with London, 1392–7', *The Reign of Richard II. Essays in Honour of May McKisack*, ed. F.R.H. Du Boulay and C.M. Barron (London, 1971).

——, *Revolt in London: 11th to 15th June 1381* (London, 1981).

——, 'Richard II. Image and Reality', *Making and Meaning. The Wilton Diptych* (London, 1993).

——, 'The Tyranny of Richard II', *BIHR*, xli (1968).

BELLAMY, J.G., 'The Northern Rebellions of the Later Years of Richard II', *BJRL*, xlvii (1964–5).

BENNETT, M.J., *Community, Class and Careerism. Cheshire and Lancashire Society in the Age of Sir Gawain and the Green Knight* (Cambridge, 1983).

——, 'The Court of Richard II and the Promotion of Literature', *Chaucer's England. Literature in Historical Context*, ed. B. Hanawalt (Minneapolis, 1992).

——, '*Sir Gawain and the Green Knight* and the Literary Achievement of the North-West Midlands: the Historical Background', *JMH*, v (1979).

——, 'Richard II and the Wider Realm', *Richard II. Power and Prerogative*, ed. A. Goodman (Oxford, 1997).

BIGGS, D., ' "A Wrong whom Conscience and Kindred bid me to right": A Reassessment of Edmund of Langley, Duke of York, and the Usurpation of Henry IV', *Albion*, xxvi (1994).

BINSKI, P., *Westminster Abbey and the Plantagenets. Kingship and the Representation of Power 1200–1400* (New Haven and London, 1995).

BIRD, R., *The Turbulent London of Richard II* (London, 1949).

BIRD, W.H.B., 'The Peasant Rising of 1381: the King's Itinerary', *EHR*, xxxi (1916).

BORENIUS, T., and TRISTRAM, E.W., *English Medieval Painting* (Florence, 1927, repr. New York, 1976).

BOULTON, D'A. J.D., *The Knights of the Crown. The Monarchical Orders of Knighthood in Later Medieval Europe 1325–1520* (Woodbridge, 1987).

BOWERS, J.M., 'Chaste Marriage: Fashion and Texts at the Court of Richard II', *Pacific Coast Philology*, xxx (1995).

——, '*Pearl* in its Royal Setting: Ricardian Poetry Revisited', *Studies in the Age of Chaucer*, ed. L.J. Kiser (New Chaucer Society, xvii, Columbus, Ohio, 1995).

BREWER, D.S., *Chaucer* (London, 3rd edn, 1973).

BRIDBURY, A.R., 'The Black Death', *EcHR*, 2nd series, xxvi (1973).

BROOKS, N., 'The Organization and Achievement of the Peasants of Kent and Essex in 1381', *Studies in Medieval History Presented to R.H.C. Davis*, ed. H. Mayr-Harting and R.I. Moore (London, 1985).

BROWN, A.L., 'The Latin Letters in *MS. All Souls College 182*', *EHR*, lxxxvii (1972).

——, 'The Reign of Henry IV: the Establishment of the Lancastrian Regime', *Fifteenth Century England, 1399–1509*, ed. S.B. Chrimes, C.D. Ross, R.A. Griffiths (Manchester, 1972).

BURROW, J.A., *Ricardian Poetry: Chaucer, Gower, Langland and the Gawain Poet* (London, 1971).

Cambridge Economic History of Europe, ii, ed. M.M. Postan and E. Miller (2nd edn, Cambridge, 1987).

CAMPBELL, M., 'Gold, Silver and Precious Stones', *English Medieval Industries*, ed. J. Blair and N. Ramsay (London, 1991).

CAREY, H., *Courting Disaster. Astrology at the English Court and University in the Later Middle Ages* (London, 1992).

CARPENTER, D.A., 'King, Magnates and Society: the Personal Rule of Henry III, 1234–1258', *Speculum*, lx (1985).

CASPARY, G.E., 'The Deposition of Richard II and the Canon Law', *Proceedings of the Second International Congress of Medieval Canon Law* (Boston, 1965).

CATTO, J.I., 'An Alleged Great Council of 1374', *EHR*, lxxxii (1967).

——, 'Religion and the English Nobility in the Later Fourteenth Century', *History and Imagination. Essays in Honour of H.R. Trevor-Roper*, ed. H. Lloyd-Jones, V. Pearl , B. Worden (London, 1981).

——, 'Sir William Beauchamp between Chivalry and Lollardy', *The Ideals and Practice of Medieval Knighthood*, iii, ed. C. Harper-Bill and R. Harvey (Woodbridge, 1990).

——, 'Wyclif and Wycliffism at Oxford, 1356–1430', *The History of the University of Oxford, II. Late Medieval Oxford*, ed. J.I. Catto and T.A.R. Evans (Oxford, 1992).

CAZELLES, R., *Société politique, noblesse et couronne sous Jean le Bon et Charles V* (Geneva, 1982).

CHAMBERS, E.K., *William Shakespeare. A Study of the Facts and Problems* (2 vols, Oxford, 1930).

CHERRY, J., 'Late Fourteenth-century Jewellery: the Inventory of November 1399', *Burlington Magazine*, cxxx (1988).

CHERRY, M., 'The Courtenay Earls of Devon: the Formation and Disintegration of a Late Medieval Aristocratic Affinity', *Southern History*, i (1979).

CHRIMES, S.B., *An Introduction to the Administrative History of Medieval England* (Oxford, 1952).

——, 'Richard II's Questions to the Judges, 1387', *Law Quarterly Review*, lxxii (1956).

CLARKE, M.V., 'Forfeitures and Treason in 1388', *TRHS*, 4th series, xiv

(1932), repr. in her *Fourteenth Century Studies*, ed. L.S. Sutherland and M. McKisack (Oxford, 1937, repr. 1968).

——, 'The Wilton Diptych', *Burlington Magazine*, lxxiii (1931), repr. ibid.

CLARKE, M.V., and GALBRAITH, V.H., 'The Deposition of Richard II', *BJRL*, xiv (1930), repr. ibid.

CLEMENTI, D., 'Richard II's Ninth Question to the Judges, 1387', *EHR*, lxxxvi (1971).

COBBAN, A.B., *The King's Hall within the University of Cambridge in the Later Middle Ages* (Cambridge, 1969).

The Complete Peerage, ed. G.E. Cokayne *et al.* (12 vols in 13, London, 1910–57).

COSGROVE, A., 'England and Ireland, 1399–1447', *A New History of Ireland, II. Medieval Ireland, 1169–1534*, ed. A. Cosgrove (Oxford, 1987).

COULBORN, A.P.R., 'The Economic and Social Preliminaries of the Crusade of 1383', *BIHR*, x (1932–3).

The Court of Richard II and the Artistic World of the Wilton Diptych, ed. L. Monnas and C.M. Barron (London, 1996).

CROOK, D., 'Central England and the Revolt of the Earls', *HR*, lxiv (1991).

——, 'Derbyshire and the English Rising of 1381', *HR*, lx (1987).

CROWDER, C.M.D., 'Peace and Justice around 1400: a Sketch', *Aspects of Late Medieval Government and Society*, ed. J.G. Rowe (Toronto, 1986).

CURTIS, E., *Richard II in Ireland, 1394–5, and Submissions of the Irish Chiefs* (Oxford, 1927).

——, 'Unpublished Letters from Richard II in Ireland', *Proceedings of the Royal Irish Academy*, xxxvii (1927).

DAHMUS, J., *William Courtenay, Archbishop of Canterbury, 1381–1396* (Philadelphia, 1966).

DAVIES, R.G., 'Alexander Neville, Archbishop of York, 1374–1388', *YAJ*, xlvii (1975).

——, 'The Episcopate and the Political Crisis in England of 1386–1388', *Speculum*, li (1976).

——, 'Richard II and the Church in the Years of "Tyranny"', *JMH*, i (1975).

——, 'Some Notes from the Register of Henry de Wakefield, Bishop of Worcester, on the Political Crisis of 1386–1388', *EHR*, lxxxvi (1971).

DAVIES, R.R., 'Richard II and the Principality of Chester', *The Reign of Richard II. Essays in Honour of May McKisack*, ed. F.R.H. Du Boulay and C.M. Barron (London, 1971).

DEANESLEY, M., *The Lollard Bible and other Medieval Biblical Versions* (Cambridge, 1920).

DELACHENAL, R., *Histoire de Charles V* (5 vols, Paris, 1909–31).

DICKENS, A.G., 'Monarchy and Cultural Revival', *The Courts of Europe. Politics, Patronage and Royalty, 1400–1800*, ed. A.G. Dickens (London, 1977).

Dictionary of National Biography (63 vols, London, 1885–1900).

DILLER, G.T., 'Froissart: Patrons and Texts', *Froissart: Historian*, ed. J.J.N. Palmer (Woodbridge, 1981).

DILLON, P.W., 'Remarks on the Manner of Death of King Richard II', *Archaeologia*, xxviii (1840).

DOBSON, R.B., 'Beverley in Conflict: Archbishop Alexander Neville and the Minster Clergy, 1381–8', *Medieval Art and Architecture in the East*

Riding of Yorkshire, ed. C. Wilson (British Archaeological Association, ix, 1989).

——, 'The Church of Durham and the Scottish Borders, 1378–1388', *War and Border Societies in the Middle Ages*, ed. A. Tuck and A. Goodman (London, 1992).

DU BOULAY, F.R.H., *Germany in the Later Middle Ages* (London, 1983).

DUGDALE, W., *Monasticon Anglicanum* (6 vols, London, 1846).

DUNBABIN, J., 'Government', *The Cambridge History of Medieval Political Thought, c.350–c.1450*, ed. J.H. Burns (Cambridge, 1988).

DVOŘÁKOVÁ, V. and others, *Gothic Mural Painting in Bohemia and Moravia, 1300–1378* (Oxford, 1964).

DYER, C., 'The Social and Economic Background to the Rural Revolt of 1381', *The English Rising of 1381*, ed. R.H. Hilton and T.H. Aston (Cambridge, 1984).

EBERLE, P.J., 'The Politics of Courtly Style at the Court of Richard II', *The Spirit of the Court. Selected Proceedings of the Fourth Congress of the International Courtly Literature Society*, ed. G.S. Burgess and R.A. Taylor (Woodbridge, 1985).

EDWARDS, J.G., 'The Parliamentary Committee of 1398', *EHR*, xl (1925), repr. in *Historical Studies of the English Parliament*, I, ed. E.B. Fryde and E. Miller (Cambridge, 1970).

ELTON, G.R., 'Tudor Government: the Points of Contact. III. The Court', *TRHS*, 5th series, xxvi (1976).

EMBREE, D., ' "Richard the Redeless" and "Mum and the Sothsegger": A Case of Mistaken Identity', *Notes and Queries*, ccxx (1975).

EMDEN, A.B., *A Biographical Register of the University of Cambridge to 1500* (Cambridge, 1963).

——, *A Biographical Register of the University of Oxford to A.D. 1500* (3 vols, Oxford, 1957–9).

EMERY, A., *Dartington Hall* (Oxford, 1970).

The English Court from the Wars of the Roses to the Civil War, ed. D. Starkey (London, 1987).

FAITH, R., 'The "Great Rumour" of 1377 and Peasant Ideology', *The English Rising of 1381*, ed. R.H. Hilton and T.H. Aston (Cambridge, 1984).

FARMER, D., *The Oxford Dictionary of Saints* (Oxford, 2nd edn, 1987).

FERRIS, S., 'Chaucer, Richard II, Henry IV and 13 October', *Chaucer and Middle English Studies in Honour of Rossell Hope Robbins*, ed. B. Rowland (London, 1974).

FISHER, J.H., *John Gower. Moral Philosopher and Friend of Chaucer* (London, 1965).

FOWLER, K., *The King's Lieutenant. Henry of Grosmont, First Duke of Lancaster 1310–1361* (London, 1969).

FRAME, R., 'English Officials and Irish Chiefs in the Fourteenth Century', *EHR*, xc (1975).

——, ' "Les Engleys Nees en Irlaunde": The English Political Identity in Medieval Ireland', *TRHS*, 6th series, iii (1993).

Froissart: Historian, ed. J.J.N. Palmer (Woodbridge, 1981).

FROMM, E., *The Anatomy of Human Destructiveness* (London, 1974).

FRYDE, E.B., *The Great Revolt of 1381* (London, 1981).

FRYDE, N.M., *The Tyranny and Fall of Edward II* (Cambridge, 1979).

GALBRAITH, V.H., 'A New Life of Richard II', *History*, xxvi (1942), repr. in his *Kings and Chroniclers. Essays in English Medieval History* (London, 1982).

——, 'Thoughts about the Peasants' Revolt', *The Reign of Richard II. Essays in Honour of May McKisack*, ed. F.R.H. Du Boulay and C.M. Barron (London, 1971).

GILLESPIE, J.L., 'Dover Castle: Key to Richard II's Kingdom?' *Arch. Cant.*, cv (1988).

——, 'Ladies of the Fraternity of St George and of the Society of the Garter', *Albion*, xvii (1985).

——, 'Richard II's Archers of the Crown', *JBS*, xviii (1979).

——, 'Richard II's Cheshire Archers', *Transactions of the Historic Society of Lancashire and Cheshire*, cxxv (1974).

——, 'Richard II's Knights: Chivalry and Patronage', *JMH*, xiii (1987).

——, 'Thomas Mortimer and Thomas Molineux: Radcot Bridge and the Appeal of 1397', *Albion*, vii (1975).

GILLINGHAM, J., 'Crisis or Continuity? The Structure of Royal Authority in England 1369–1422', *Das Spätmittelalterliche Königtum im Europäischen Vergleich*, ed. R. Schneider (Sigmaringen, 1987).

GIROUARD, M., 'Wardour Old Castle', *Country Life*, 14 February 1991.

GIVEN-WILSON, C., 'Adam Usk, the Monk of Evesham and the Parliament of 1397–8', *HR*, lxvi (1993).

——, 'The King and the Gentry in Fourteenth-Century England', *TRHS*, 5th series, xxxvii (1987).

——, 'The Manner of King Richard's Renunciation: a "Lancastrian Narrative"?', *EHR*, cviii (1993).

——, 'Richard II and his Grandfather's Will', *EHR*, xciii (1978).

——, 'Richard II, Edward II, and the Lancastrian Inheritance', *EHR*, cix (1994).

——, 'Royal Charter Witness Lists, 1327–1399', *Medieval Prosopography*, xii, ii (1991).

——, *The Royal Household and the King's Affinity. Service, Politics and Finance in England 1360–1413* (New Haven and London, 1986).

GOODMAN, A., *John of Gaunt. The Exercise of Princely Power in Fourteenth-Century Europe* (London, 1992).

——, 'John of Gaunt', *England in the Fourteenth Century*, ed. W.M. Ormrod (Woodbridge, 1986).

——, 'John of Gaunt, Portugal's Kingmaker', *HT*, xxxvi (June 1986).

——, *The Loyal Conspiracy. The Lords Appellant under Richard II* (London, 1971).

GORDON, D., 'A New Discovery in the Wilton Diptych', *Burlington Magazine*, cxxxiv (1992).

——, *Making and Meaning. The Wilton Diptych* (London, 1993).

GRANSDEN, A., *Historical Writing in England, II, c.1307 to the Early Sixteenth Century* (London, 1982).

GRANT, A., 'The Otterburn War from the Scottish Point of View', *War and Border Societies in the Middle Ages*, ed. A. Tuck and A. Goodman (London, 1992).

GREEN, R.F., 'King Richard II's Books Revisited', *The Library*, xxxi (1976).
——, *Poets and Princepleasers. Literature and the English Court in the Late Middle Ages* (Toronto, 1980).
GRIFFITHS, R.A., 'The Crown and the Royal Family in Later Medieval England', *Kings and Nobles in the Later Middle Ages*, ed. R.A. Griffiths and J. Sherborne (Gloucester, 1986).
——, 'Gentlemen and Rebels in Later Medieval Cardiganshire', *Ceredigion*, v (1964–7).
——, 'The King's Court during the Wars of the Roses', *Patronage, Princes and the Nobility. The Court at the Beginning of the Modern Age*, ed. R.G. Asch and A.M. Birke (Oxford, 1991).
HAINES, R.M., ' "Our master mariner, our sovereign lord": a Contemporary Preacher's View of Henry V', *Medieval Studies*, xxxviii (1976).
HANNA, R., 'Sir Thomas Berkeley and his Patronage', *Speculum*, lxiv (1989).
HANSEN, H.M., 'The Peasants' Revolt of 1381 and the Chronicles', *JMH*, vi (1980).
HARRISS, G.L., *King, Parliament and Public Finance in Medieval England to 1369* (Oxford, 1975).
——, 'Thomas Cromwell's "New Principle" of Taxation', *EHR*, xciii (1978).
——, 'War and the Emergence of the English Parliament', *JMH*, ii (1976).
HARVEY, B.F., 'Draft Letters Patent of Manumission and Pardon for the Men of Somerset in 1381', *EHR*, lxxx (1965).
HARVEY, J.H., *English Medieval Architects. A Biographical Dictionary down to 1550* (Gloucester, 2nd edn, 1984).
——, 'Richard II and York', *The Reign of Richard II. Essays in Honour of May McKisack*, ed. F.R.H. Du Boulay and C.M. Barron (London, 1971).
——, 'The Wilton Diptych – A Re-examination', *Archaeologia*, xcviii (1961).
HEATH, P., *Church and Realm, 1272–1461* (London, 1988).
HECTOR, L.C., 'An Alleged Hysterical Outburst of Richard II', *EHR*, lxviii (1953).
HENNEMAN, J.B., 'The Military Class and the French Monarchy in the Late Middle Ages', *American Historical Review*, lxxxiii (1978).
HEPBURN, F., *Portraits of the Later Plantagenets* (Woodbridge, 1986).
HERBERT, W., *The History of the Twelve Great Livery Companies* (2 vols, London, 1836–7).
HILL, J.W.F., *Medieval Lincoln* (Cambridge, 1948).
HILTON, R.H., *Bond Men Made Free. Medieval Peasant Movements and the English Rising of 1381* (London, 1973).
——, *The Decline of Serfdom in Medieval England* (London, 1969).
——, 'Freedom and Villeinage in England', *P&P*, xxxi (1965), repr. *Peasants, Knights and Heretics*, ed. R.H. Hilton (Cambridge, 1973).
——, 'Peasant Movements in England before 1381', *Essays in Economic History*, ii, ed. E.M. Carns-Wilson (London, 1962).
The History of Parliament. The House of Commons 1386–1421, ed. J.S. Roskell, L. Clark, C. Rawcliffe (4 vols, Stroud, 1992)
History of the King's Works, ed. R.A. Brown, H.M. Colvin, A.J. Taylor (3 vols, London, 1963).
HOLMES, G., *The Estates of the Higher Nobility in Fourteenth Century England* (Cambridge, 1957).

——, *The Good Parliament* (Oxford, 1975).

HOLT, R., 'Thomas of Woodstock and Events at Gloucester in 1381', *BIHR*, lviii (1985).

HORROX, R., 'Caterpillars of the Commonwealth? Courtiers in Late Medieval England', *Rulers and Ruled in Late Medieval England. Essays Presented to Gerald Harriss*, ed. R.E. Archer and S. Walker (London, 1995).

The Household of Edward IV, ed. A.R. Myers (Manchester, 1959).

HOUSLEY, N., 'The Bishop of Norwich's Crusade, May 1383', *HT*, xxxiii (May 1983).

HOWGRAVE-GRAHAM, R.P., 'The Earlier Royal Funeral Effigies', *Archaeologia*, xcviii (1969).

HUDSON, A., 'Lollardy: the English Heresy?', *Studies in Church History*, xviii (1982), repr. in her *Lollards and their Books* (London, 1985).

HUGHES, J., *Pastors and Visionaries. Religion and Secular Life in Late Medieval Yorkshire* (Woodbridge, 1988).

The Hundred Years War, ed. K. Fowler (London, 1971).

HUTCHISON, H.F., 'Shakespeare and Richard II', *HT*, xi (April 1961).

ILG, U., 'Ein wiederentdecktes Inventar der Goldschmiedearbeiten Richards II von England und seine Bedeutung für die Ikonographie des Wiltondiptychons', *Pantheon*, lii (1994).

ILLINGWORTH, W., 'Copy of a Libel against Archbishop Neville, temp. Richard II', *Archaeologia*, xvi (1812).

JARRETT, B., *The Emperor Charles IV* (London, 1935).

JOHNSON, L.S., 'Inverse Counsel: Contexts for the *Melibee*', *Studies in Philology*, lxxxvii (1990).

JOHNSTON, D.B., 'The Draft Indenture of Thomas, Duke of Gloucester, as Lieutenant of Ireland, 1391', *Journal of the Society of Archivists*, vii (1983).

——, 'The Interim Years: Richard II and Ireland, 1395–1399', *England and Ireland in the Late Middle Ages: Essays in Honour of Jocelyn Otway-Ruthven*, ed. J.F. Lydon (Dublin, 1981).

——, 'Richard II and the Submissions of Gaelic Ireland', *Irish Historical Studies*, xii (1980).

——, 'Richard II's Departure from Ireland, July 1399', *EHR*, xcviii (1983).

JONES, M., *Ducal Brittany 1364–1399* (Oxford, 1970).

——, 'The Ransom of Jean de Bretagne, Count of Penthièvre: an Aspect of English Foreign Policy, 1386–8', *BIHR*, xlv (1972).

JONES, R.H., *The Royal Policy of Richard II: Absolutism in the Later Middle Ages* (Oxford, 1968).

KANTOROWICZ, E.H., *The King's Two Bodies. A Study in Medieval Political Theology* (Princeton, 1957).

KEEN, M., *England in the Later Middle Ages* (London, 1973).

——, 'Wyclif, the Bible and Transubstantiation', *Wyclif in his Times*, ed. A. Kenny (Oxford, 1986).

KENNY, A., 'The Realism of the *De Universalibus*', *Wyclif in his Times*, ed. A. Kenny (Oxford, 1986).

KIPLING, G., 'Richard II's "Sumptuous Pageants" and the Idea of the Civic Triumph', *Pageantry in the Shakespearean Theatre*, ed. D.M. Bergeron (Athens, Georgia, 1986).

KIRBY, J.L., *Henry IV of England* (London, 1970).

KNOWLES, D., *The Religious Orders in England* (3 vols, Cambridge, 1948–59).

KRIEHN, G., 'Studies in the Sources of the Social Revolt in 1381', *American Historical Review*, vii (1901–2).

LAIDLAW, J.C., 'Christine de Pizan, the Earl of Salisbury and Henry IV', *French Studies*, xxxvi (1982).

LEACH, A.F., 'A Clerical Strike at Beverley Minster in the Fourteenth Century', *Archaeologia*, lv (1896).

LEHOUX, F., *Jean de France, Duc de Berri* (3 vols, Paris, 1966–8).

LEWIS, N.B., 'The "Continual Council" in the Early Years of Richard II, 1377–80', *EHR*, xli (1926).

——, 'The Feudal Summons of 1385', *EHR*, c (1985).

——, 'The Last Medieval Summons of the English Feudal Levy, 13 June 1385', *EHR*, lxxiii (1958).

LINDENBAUM, S., 'The Smithfield Tournament of 1390', *Journal of Medieval and Renaissance Studies*, xx (1990).

LOOMIS, R.S., 'The Library of Richard II', *Studies in Language, Literature and Culture of the Middle Ages and Later*, ed. E.B. Atwood and A.A. Hill (Austin, Texas, 1969).

LYDON, J.F., 'Richard II's Expeditions to Ireland', *Journal of the Royal Society of Antiquaries of Ireland*, xciii (1963).

——, 'The Impact of the Bruce Invasion, 1315–27', *A New History of Ireland, II. Medieval Ireland, 1169–1534*, ed. A. Cosgrove (Oxford, 1987).

MCFARLANE, K.B., *John Wycliffe and the Beginnings of English Nonconformity* (London, 1952).

——, *Lancastrian Kings and Lollard Knights* (Oxford, 1972).

MCHARDY, A., 'The Effects of War on the Church: the Case of the Alien Priories in the Fourteenth Century', *England and her Neighbours 1066–1453*, ed. M. Jones and M. Vale (London, 1989).

MCKISACK, M., *The Fourteenth Century 1307–1399* (Oxford, 1959).

MCNIVEN, P., *Heresy and Politics in the Reign of Henry IV. The Burning of John Badby* (Woodbridge, 1987).

——, 'Rebellion, Sedition and the Legend of Richard II's Survival in the Reigns of Henry IV and Henry V', *BJRL*, lxxvi (1994).

MARKS, R., *Stained Glass in England during the Middle Ages* (London, 1993).

The Master of the Game, ed. W.A. and F. Baillie-Grohman (London, 1904).

MATHEW, G., *The Court of Richard II* (London, 1968).

MAXWELL-LYTE, H.C., *Historical Notes on the Great Seal of England* (London, 1926).

MAY, T., 'The Cobham Family in the Administration of England, 1200–1400', *Arch. Cant.*, lxxxii (1967).

MEISS, M., *French Painting in the Time of Jean de Berry. The Late XIV Century and the Patronage of the Duke* (2 vols, London, 1967).

MEYER, P., 'L'Entrevue d'Ardres', *Annuaire-Bulletin de la Société de l'Histoire de France*, xviii (1881).

MILNER, J.D., 'Sir Simon Felbrigg, KG: the Lancastrian Revolution and Personal Fortune', *Norfolk Archaeology*, xxxvii, i (1978).

MIROT, L., 'Isabelle de France, reine d'Angleterre', *Revue d'histoire diplomatique*, xviii (1904) and xix (1905).

——, 'Une Tentative d'invasion en Angleterre pendant la guerre de Cent Ans, 1385–6', *Revue des études historiques*, lxxxi (1915).

MORANVILLÉ, H., 'Conférences entre la France et l'Angleterre (1388–1393)', *Bibliothèque de l'École des Chartes*, l (1889).

MORGAN, D.A.L., 'The House of Policy: the Political Role of the Late Plantagenet Household', *The English Court from the Wars of the Roses to the Civil War*, ed. D. Starkey (London, 1987).

MORGAN, P., 'Henry IV and the Shadow of Richard II', *Crown, Government and People in the Fifteenth Century*, ed. R. Archer (Stroud, 1995).

——, *War and Society in Medieval Cheshire, 1277–1403* (Manchester: Chetham Society, 3rd series, xxxiv, 1987).

MOTT, R.A.K., 'Richard II and the Crisis of July 1397', *Church and Chronicle in the Middle Ages: Essays presented to John Taylor*, ed. I. Wood and G.A. Loud (London, 1991).

——, 'A Study in the Distribution of Patronage, 1389–99', *Proceedings of the Leeds Philosophical and Literary Society*, xv (1974).

MYERS, A.R., 'The Wealth of Sir Richard Lyons', *Essays in Medieval History Presented to Bertie Wilkinson*, ed. T.A. Sandquist and M.R. Powicke (Toronto, 1969).

MYRES, J.N.L., 'The Campaign of Radcot Bridge in December 1387', *EHR*, xlii (1927).

A New History of Ireland, II. Medieval Ireland, 1169–1534, ed. A. Cosgrove (Oxford, 1987).

NICHOLS, J.G., 'Observations on the Heraldic Devices on the Effigies of Richard II and his Queen in Westminster Abbey', *Archaeologia*, xxix (1842).

OMAN, C., *The Great Revolt of 1381* (Oxford, 2nd edn, 1969).

ORME, N., *From Childhood to Chivalry. The Education of the English Kings and Aristocracy, 1066–1530* (London, 1984).

ORMROD, W.M., 'The Origins of the *Sub Pena* Writ', *HR*, lxi (1988).

——, 'The Peasants' Revolt and the Government of England', *JBS*, xxix (1990).

——, 'The Personal Religion of Edward III', *Speculum*, lxiv (1989).

——, *The Reign of Edward III. Crown and Political Society in England 1327–1377* (New Haven and London, 1990).

OTWAY-RUTHVEN, A.J., *A History of Medieval Ireland* (London, 1968).

PALMER, C.F.R., 'The King's Confessors', *The Antiquary*, xxii (1890).

PALMER, J.J.N., 'The Anglo-French Peace Negotiations, 1390–1396', *TRHS*, 5th series, xvi (1966).

——, 'Articles for a Final Peace between England and France, 16 June 1393', *BIHR*, xxxix (1966).

——, 'The Authorship, Date and Historical Value of the French Chronicles on the Lancastrian Revolution: I and II', *BJRL*, lxi (1978–9).

——, 'The Background to Richard II's Marriage to Isabel of France (1396)', *BIHR*, xliv (1971).

——, 'England and the Great Western Schism, 1388–1399', *EHR*, lxxxiii (1968).

——, *England, France and Christendom, 1377–99* (London, 1972).

——, 'English Foreign Policy, 1388–1399', *The Reign of Richard II. Essays in*

Honour of May McKisack, ed. F.R.H. Du Boulay and C.M. Barron (London, 1971).

——, 'The Impeachment of Michael de la Pole in 1386', *BIHR*, xlii (1969).

——, 'The Last Summons of the Feudal Army in England, 1385', *EHR*, lxxxiii (1968).

——, 'The Parliament of 1385 and the Constitutional Crisis of 1386', *Speculum*, xlvi (1971).

——, 'The War Aims of the Protagonists and the Negotiations for Peace', *The Hundred Years War*, ed. K. Fowler (London, 1971).

PALMER, J.J.N. and WELLS, A.P., 'Ecclesiastical Reform and the Politics of the Hundred Years War during the Pontificate of Urban V (1362–70)', *War, Literature and Politics in the Late Middle Ages*, ed. C.T. Allmand (Liverpool, 1976).

PATTERSON, L., 'Court Politics and the Invention of Literature: the Case of Sir John Clanvowe', *Culture and History, 1350–1600. Essays in English Communities, Identities and Writing*, ed. D. Aers (Detroit, 1992).

PAYLING, S., *Political Society in Lancastrian England. The Greater Gentry of Nottinghamshire* (Oxford, 1991).

PEARSALL, D., 'The Alliterative Revival: Origins and Social Backgrounds', *Middle English Alliterative Poetry and its Literary Background*, ed. D. Lawton (Cambridge, 1982).

——, *The Life of Geoffrey Chaucer* (Oxford, 1992).

——, 'The *Troilus* Frontispiece and Chaucer's Audience', *Yearbook of English Studies*, vii (1977).

PERKINS, J., *Westminster Abbey. Its Worship and Ornaments* (Alcuin Club, xxxiv, 1930).

PERROY, E., *L'Angleterre et le grand Schisme d'Occident* (Paris, 1933).

——, 'Gras profits et rancons pendant la guerre de cent ans; l'affaire du comte de Denia', *Mélanges d'histoire du moyen âge dédiés à la mémoire de Louis Halphen* (Paris, 1951), repr. in his *Études d'histoire médiévale* (Paris, 1979).

PETIT-DUTAILLIS, C., 'Causes and General Characteristics of the Rising of 1381', C. Petit-Dutaillis and G. Lefebvre, *Studies and Notes Supplementary to Stubbs' Constitutional History*, ii (Manchester, 1915).

PFAFF, R.W., *New Liturgical Feasts in Late Medieval England* (Oxford, 1970).

PHILPOTTS, C.J., 'John of Gaunt and English Policy towards France, 1389–1395', *JMH*, xvi (1990).

PLUCKNETT, T.F.T., 'State Trials under Richard II', *TRHS*, 5th series, ii (1952).

Politics and Crisis in Fourteenth Century England, ed. J. Taylor and W. Childs (Gloucester, 1990).

POLLARD, A.F., 'The Authorship and Value of the *Anonimalle Chronicle*', *EHR*, liii (1938).

POST, J.B., 'Courts, Councils and Arbitrators in the Ladbroke Manor Dispute', *Medieval Legal Records Edited in Memory of C.A.F. Meekings*, ed. R.F. Hunnisett and J.B. Post (London, 1978).

——, 'The Obsequies of John of Gaunt', *Guildhall Studies in London History*, v (1981).

POWELL, E., *The Rising in East Anglia* (Cambridge, 1896).

POWELL, E., *Kingship, Law and Society. Criminal Justice in the Reign of Henry V* (Oxford, 1989).

POWELL, J.E. and WALLIS, K., *The House of Lords in the Middle Ages* (London, 1968).

PRESTWICH, M., 'An Estimate by the Commons of Royal Revenue in England under Richard II', *PH*, iii (1984).

——, *The Three Edwards. War and State in England, 1272–1377* (London, 1980).

PRINCE, A.E., 'A Letter of Edward the Black Prince Describing the Battle of Najera in 1367', *EHR*, xli (1926).

PUGH, R.B., and SAUNDERS, A.D., *Old Wardour Castle* (London, 2nd edn, 1991).

QUICKE, F., *Les Pays-Bas à la veille de la période bourguignonne, 1356–1384* (Brussels, 1947).

RACKHAM, R.B., 'The Nave of Westminster', *Proceedings of the British Academy*, iv (1909–10).

RAMSAY, J.H., *The Genesis of Lancaster 1307–1399* (2 vols, Oxford, 1913).

The Regal Image of Richard II and the Wilton Diptych, ed. D. Gordon, L. Monnas, C. Elam (London, 1998).

The Reign of Richard II. Essays in Honour of May McKisack, ed. F.R.H. Du Boulay and C.M. Barron (London, 1971).

Richard II. Power and Prerogative, ed. A. Goodman (Oxford, 1998).

RICHARDSON, H.G., 'Heresy and the Lay Power under Richard II', *EHR*, li (1936).

RICHARDSON, H.G., and SAYLES, G.O., 'Irish Revenue, 1278–1384', *Proceedings of the Royal Irish Academy*, lxii (1962).

RICHMOND, C.F., 'The War at Sea', *The Hundred Years War*, ed. K. Fowler (London, 1971).

RICKERT, E., 'Richard II's Books', *The Library*, 4th series, xiii (1933).

RITCHIE, N., 'Labour Conditions in Essex in the Reign of Richard II', *Essays in Economic History*, ii, ed. E.M. Carus-Wilson (London, 1962).

ROBSON, J.A., *Wyclif and the Oxford Schools* (Cambridge, 1961).

ROGERS, A., 'Parliamentary Appeals of Treason in the Reign of Richard II', *American Journal of Legal History*, viii (1964).

ROGERS, N.J., 'The Old Proctor's Book: A Cambridge Manuscript of *c*.1390', *England in the Fourteenth Century*, ed. W.M. Ormrod (Woodbridge, 1986).

ROSKELL, J.S., *The Commons and their Speakers in English Parliaments, 1376–1523* (Manchester, 1965).

——, *The Impeachment of Michael de la Pole, Earl of Suffolk, in 1386* (Manchester, 1984).

——, *Parliament and Politics in Late Medieval England* (3 vols, London, 1981–3).

——, 'Sir John Bussy of Hougham', *Parliament and Politics in Late Medieval England* (3 vols, London, 1981–3), ii.

——, 'Sir John Cheyne of Beckford', *Parliament and Politics in Late Medieval England* (3 vols, London, 1981–3), ii.

——, 'Sir William Sturmy', *Parliament and Politics in Late Medieval England* (3 vols, London, 1981–3), iii.

ROSS, C.D., 'Forfeiture for Treason in the Reign of Richard II', *EHR*, lxxi (1956).

Royal Commission on Historical Monuments. Westminster Abbey (London, 1924).

RUSSELL, J.G., *The Field of Cloth of Gold* (London, 1969).

RUSSELL, P.E., *The English Intervention in Spain and Portugal in the Time of Edward III and Richard II* (Oxford, 1955).

ST JOHN HOPE, W.H., 'The King's Coronation Ornaments', *The Ancestor*, i (1902).

SANDERLIN, S., 'Chaucer and Ricardian Politics', *Chaucer Review*, xxii (1987).

SANDQUIST, T.A., 'The Holy Oil of St Thomas of Canterbury', *Essays in Medieval History Presented to Bertie Wilkinson*, ed. T.A. Sandquist and M.R. Powicke (Toronto, 1969).

SAUL, N.E., 'Chaucer and Gentility', *Chaucer's England. Literature in Historical Context*, ed. B. Hanawalt (Minneapolis, 1992).

——, 'The Commons and the Abolition of Badges', *PH*, ix (1990).

——, 'The Fragments of the Golafre Brass in Westminster Abbey', *Transactions of the Monumental Brass Society*, xv, i (1992).

——, *Knights and Esquires. The Gloucestershire Gentry in the Fourteenth Century* (Oxford, 1981).

——, 'Richard II and Westminster Abbey', *The Cloister and the World. Essays in Medieval History in Honour of Barbara Harvey*, ed. W.J. Blair and B. Golding (Oxford, 1996).

——, 'Richard II and the Vocabulary of Kingship', *EHR*, cx (1995).

——, *Scenes from Provincial Life. Knightly Families in Sussex 1280–1400* (Oxford, 1986).

SAYLES, G.O., 'The Deposition of Richard II: Three Lancastrian Narratives', *BIHR*, liv (1981).

——, 'King Richard II of England: a Fresh Look', *Transactions of the American Philosophical Society*, cxv (1971), repr. in his *Scripta Diversa* (London, 1982).

——, 'Richard II in 1381 and 1399', *EHR*, xciv (1979).

SCAGLIONE, A., *Knights at Court* (Berkeley, 1991).

SCARISBRICK, J.J., *Henry VIII* (London, 1968).

SCASE, W., 'St Anne and the Education of the Virgin: Literary and Artistic Traditions and their Implications', *England in the Fourteenth Century*, ed. N. Rogers (Stamford, 1993).

SCATTERGOOD, V.J., 'Chaucer and the French War: *Sir Thopaz* and *Melibee*', *Court and Poet*, ed. G.S. Burgess (Liverpool, 1981).

——, 'Literary Culture at the Court of Richard II', *English Court Culture in the Later Middle Ages*, ed. V.J. Scattergood and J.W. Sherborne (London, 1983).

The Scrope and Grosvenor Controversy, ed. N.H. Nicolas (2 vols, London, 1832).

SEARLE, E., and BURGHART R., 'The Defence of England and the Peasants' Revolt', *Viator*, iii (1972).

The Sermons of Thomas Brinton, Bishop of Rochester (1373–1389), i, ed. M.A. Devlin (Camden Society, 3rd series, lxxxv, 1954).

SHAKESPEARE, W., *King Richard II*, ed. J. Dover Wilson (Cambridge, 1939).
——, *King Richard II*, ed. P. Ure (London, 5th edn, 1961).
——, *The First Part of King Henry IV*, ed. A.R. Humphreys (London, 5th edn, 1966).
SHERBORNE, J., 'Charles VI and Richard II', *Froissart: Historian*, ed. J.J.N. Palmer (Woodbridge, 1981), repr. in his *War, Politics and Culture in Fourteenth-Century England*, ed. A. Tuck (London, 1994).
——, 'The Cost of English Warfare with France in the Later Fourteenth Century', *BIHR*, i (1977), repr. ibid.
——, 'The Defence of the Realm and the Impeachment of Michael de la Pole in 1386', *Politics and Crisis in Fourteenth Century England*, ed. J. Taylor and W. Childs (Gloucester, 1990), repr. ibid.
——, 'The English Navy: Shipping and Manpower, 1369–89', *P&P*, xxxvii (1967), repr. ibid.
——, 'Perjury and the Lancastrian Revolution of 1399', *WHR*, xiv (1988), repr. ibid.
——, 'Richard II's Return to Wales, July 1399', *WHR*, vii (1975), repr. ibid.
SHERMAN, C.R., *The Portraits of Charles V of France (1338–1380)* (New York, 1969).
SIMMS, K., 'The Norman Invasion and the Gaelic Recovery', *The Oxford Illustrated History of Ireland*, ed. R.F. Foster (Oxford, 1989).
SIMPSON, A., *The Connections between English and Bohemian Painting during the Second Half of the Fourteenth Century* (New York, 1984).
SMITH, J.B., and PUGH, T.B., 'The Lordship of Gower and Kilvey', *Glamorgan County History, III: The Middle Ages*, ed. T.B. Pugh (Cardiff, 1971).
SPARVEL BAYLY, J.A. 'Essex in Insurrection, 1381', *Transactions of the Essex Archaeological Society*, new series, i (1878).
STAMP, A.E., 'Richard II and the Death of the Duke of Gloucester', *EHR*, xxxviii (1923).
STANLEY, A.P., 'On an Examination of the Tombs of Richard II and Henry III in Westminster Abbey', *Archaeologia*, xlv (1880).
STARKEY, D., 'The Age of the Household: Politics, Society and the Arts, c.1350–c.1550', *The Later Middle Ages*, ed. S. Medcalf (London, 1981).
——, 'Intimacy and Innovation: the Rise of the Privy Chamber, 1485–1547', *The English Court from the Wars of the Roses to the Civil War*, ed. D. Starkey (London, 1987).
STEEL, A., *Richard II* (Cambridge, 1941).
——, *The Receipt of the Exchequer, 1377–1485* (Cambridge, 1954).
——, 'The Sheriffs of Cambridgeshire and Huntingdonshire in the Reign of Richard II', *Proceedings of the Cambridgeshire Antiquarian Society*, xxxvi (1934–5).
STOREY, R.L., 'Liveries and Commissions of the Peace, 1388–90', *The Reign of Richard II. Essays in Honour of May McKisack*, ed. F.R.H. Du Boulay and C.M. Barron (London, 1971).
——, 'The Wardens of the Marches of England towards Scotland, 1377–1489', *EHR*, lxxii (1957).
STOW, G.B., 'Chronicles versus Records: the Character of Richard II', *Documenting the Past: Essays in Medieval History Presented to G.P. Cuttino*, ed. J.S. Hamilton and P. Bradley (Woodbridge, 1989).

——, 'Richard II and the Invention of the Pocket Handkerchief', *Albion*, xxvii (1995).

——, 'Richard II in Jean Froissart's *Chroniques*', *JMH*, xi (1985).

——, 'Richard II in John Gower's *Confessio Amantis*: Some Historical Perspectives', *Medievalia*, xvi (1993).

——, 'Richard II in Thomas Walsingham's Chronicles', *Speculum*, lix (1984).

——, 'The *Vita Ricardi* as a Source for the Reign of Richard II', *Vale of Evesham Historical Society Research Papers*, iv (1973).

STOW, J., *A Survey of London*, ed. C.L. Kingsford (Oxford, 1908).

STROHM, P., 'Queens as Intercessors', *Hochon's Arrow. The Social Imagination of Fourteenth-Century Texts* (Princeton, 1992).

——, *Social Chaucer* (Cambridge, Mass., 1989).

——, 'The Trouble with Richard: The Reburial of Richard II and Lancastrian Symbolic Strategy', *Speculum*, lxxi (1996).

STUBBS, W., *The Constitutional History of England* (3 vols, Oxford, 1875–8).

SUGGETT, H., 'A Letter Describing Richard II's Reconciliation with the City of London, 1392', *EHR*, lxii (1947).

TAIT, J., review of A. Steel, *Richard II*, in *EHR*, lvii (1942).

——, 'Did Richard II Murder the Duke of Gloucester?', *Historical Essays by Members of the Owens College, Manchester*, ed. T.F. Tout and J. Tait (Manchester, 1902).

TAYLOR, J., *English Historical Literature in the Fourteenth Century* (Oxford, 1987).

——, 'Richard II's Views on Kingship', *Proceedings of the Leeds Philosophical and Literary Society*, xiv (1971).

TEMPLE-LEADER, J., and MARCOTTI, G., *Sir John Hawkwood (L'Acuto)* (London, 1889).

THEILMANN, J.M., 'Stubbs, Shakespeare and Recent Historians of Richard II', *Albion*, viii (1976).

THOMSON, S.H., 'Learning at the Court of Charles IV', *Speculum*, xxv (1950).

THOROLD ROGERS, J.E., *A History of Agriculture and Prices in England* (7 vols, Oxford, 1866–1902).

TILLYARD, E.M.W., *Shakespeare's History Plays* (London, 1946).

TOUT, T.F., *Chapters in the Administrative History of Medieval England* (6 vols, Manchester, 1920–33).

TUCK, A., 'Anglo-Irish Relations, 1382–1393', *Proceedings of the Royal Irish Academy*, lxix (1970).

——, 'The Cambridge Parliament, 1388', *EHR*, lxxxiv (1969).

——, 'Carthusian Monks and Lollard Knights: Religious Attitude at the Court of Richard II', *Studies in the Age of Chaucer, Proceedings, 1, 1984: Reconstructing Chaucer*, ed. P. Strohm and T.J. Heffernan (New Chaucer Society, Knoxville, Tennessee, 1986).

——, *Crown and Nobility, 1272–1461* (London, 1985).

——, 'Nobles, Commons and the Great Revolt of 1381', *The English Rising of 1381*, ed. R.H. Hilton and T.H. Aston (Cambridge, 1984).

——, 'Richard II and the Border Magnates', *Northern History*, iii (1968).

——, *Richard II and the English Nobility* (London, 1973).

——, 'Richard II and the House of Luxemburg', *Richard II. Power and Prerogative*, ed. A. Goodman (Oxford, 1997).

——, 'Richard II and the Hundred Years War', *Politics and Crisis in Fourteenth Century England*, ed. J. Taylor and W. Childs (Gloucester, 1990).

——, 'Richard II's System of Patronage', *The Reign of Richard II. Essays in Honour of May McKisack*, ed. F.R.H. Du Boulay and C.M. Barron (London, 1971).

TUDOR-CRAIG, P., 'The Medieval Monuments and Chantry Chapels', C. Wilson, R. Gem, P. Tudor-Craig, J. Physick, *Westminster Abbey* (London, 1986).

VALE, M., *The Angevin Legacy and the Hundred Years War, 1250–1340* (Oxford, 1990).

VAUGHAN, R., *Philip the Bold. The Formation of the Burgundian State* (London, 1962).

Victoria History of the County of Stafford, xiv, ed. M.W. Greenslade (London, 1990).

Victoria History of the County of Warwick, ii, ed. W. Page (London, 1904).

WALKER, S.K., 'Letters to the Dukes of Lancaster in 1381 and 1399', *EHR*, cvi (1991).

——, 'Richard II's Views on Kingship', *Rulers and Ruled in Late Medieval England. Essays Presented to Gerald Harriss*, ed. R.E. Archer and S. Walker (London, 1995).

——, 'Sir Richard Abberbury (*c.*1330–1399) and his Kinsmen: the Rise and Fall of a Gentry Family', *Nottingham Medieval Studies*, xxxiv (1990).

——, *The Lancastrian Affinity 1361–1399* (Oxford, 1990).

——, 'Yorkshire Justices of the Peace, 1389–1413', *EHR*, cviii (1993).

WALLON, H., *Richard II* (2 vols, Paris, 1864).

War and Border Societies in the Middle Ages, ed. A. Tuck and A. Goodman (London, 1992).

WARREN, W.L., 'A Re-appraisal of Simon Sudbury, Bishop of London (1361–1375) and Archbishop of Canterbury (1375–1381)', *JEH*, x (1959).

WATHEY, A., *Music in the Royal and Noble Households in Late Medieval England* (New York and London, 1989).

WEBSTER, B., 'The Community of Kent in the Reign of Richard II', *Archaeologia Cantiana*, xcix (1984).

WEEVER, J., *Ancient Funerall Monuments* (London, 1631).

WESTLAKE, H.F., *Westminster Abbey* (2 vols, London, 1923).

WHITTINGHAM, S., 'The Chronology of the Portraits of Richard II', *Burlington Magazine*, cxiii (1971).

WILKINS, N., 'Music and Poetry at Court: England and France in the Late Middle Ages', *English Court Culture in the Later Middle Ages*, ed. V.J. Scattergood and J.W. Sherborne (London, 1983).

WILKINSON, B., 'The Peasants' Revolt of 1381', *Speculum*, xv (1940).

WILSON, C., 'The Gothic Abbey Church', C. Wilson, R. Gem, P. Tudor-Craig, J. Physick, *Westminster Abbey* (London, 1986).

——, 'The Medieval Monuments', *A History of Canterbury Cathedral*, ed. P. Collinson, N. Ramsay, M. Sparks (Oxford, 1995).

WOOD, M., *Donnington Castle* (London, 1964).

WOODMAN, F., *The Architectural History of Canterbury Cathedral* (London, 1981).

WORKMAN, H.B., *John Wyclif* (2 vols, Oxford, 1926).

WRIGHT, H.G., 'The Protestation of Richard II in the Tower in September, 1399', *BJRL*, xxiii (1943).

WROTTESLEY, G., 'A History of the Bagot Family', *Staffordshire Historical Collections*, new series, xi (1908).

WYLIE, J.H., *History of England under Henry IV* (4 vols, London, 1884–98).

WYLIE, J.H., and WAUGH, W.T., *The Reign of Henry V* (3 vols, Cambridge, 1914–29).

UNPUBLISHED THESES

ALEXANDER, A.F., 'The War with France in 1377' (University of London Ph.D. thesis, 1934).

ARCHER, R.E., 'The Mowbrays, Earls of Nottingham and Dukes of Norfolk to 1432' (University of Oxford D.Phil. thesis, 1984).

BUTLER, L.H., 'Robert Braybrooke, Bishop of London (1381–1404), and his Kinsmen' (University of Oxford D.Phil. thesis, 1952).

CHERRY, M., 'The Crown and the Political Community in Devonshire, 1377–1461' (University of Wales Ph.D. thesis, 1981).

ECHERD, A.R., 'Canonization and Politics in Late Medieval England: the Cult of Thomas of Lancaster' (University of Chapel Hill, NC, Ph.D. thesis, 1983).

JOHNSTON, D.B., 'Richard II and Ireland, 1395–9' (Trinity College, Dublin Ph.D. thesis, 1976).

MOTT, R.A.K., 'Richard II's Relations with the Magnates, 1396–9' (University of Leeds Ph.D. thesis, 1971).

PRESCOTT, A.J., 'Judicial Records of the Rising of 1381' (University of London Ph.D. thesis, 1984).

SINCLAIR, A.F.J., 'The Beauchamp Earls of Warwick in the Later Middle Ages' (University of London Ph.D. thesis, 1987).

SMITH, C.R., 'Richard Maidstone, *Concordia facta inter regem Riccardum II et Civitatem Londonie*' (Princeton University Ph.D. thesis, 1972).

STANSFIELD, M.M.N., 'The Holand Family, Dukes of Exeter, Earls of Kent and Huntingdon, 1352–1475' (University of Oxford D.Phil. thesis, 1987).

VALE, B., 'The Scropes of Bolton and Masham, *c.*1300–*c.*1450. A Study of a Northern Noble Family' (University of York D.Phil. thesis, 1987).

WARNER, M.W., 'The Montagu Earls of Salisbury, *c.*1300–1428: A Study in Warfare, Politics and Political Culture' (University of London Ph.D. thesis, 1991).

INDEX